HIMMLER

HIMMLER

Reichsführer-SS

Peter Padfield

Henry Holt and Company ▪ New York

Library of Congress Cataloging-in-Publication Data
Padfield, Peter.
Himmler : Peter Padfield—1st American ed.
p.   cm.
Includes bibliographical references and index.
ISBN 0-8050-1476-4
1. Himmler, Heinrich, 1900-1945. 2. National socialists—
Biography. 3. Germany—Politics and government—1933-1945.
I. Title.
DD247.H46P33   1991
943.086'092—dc20
[B]   90-20609
                                        CIP

Henry Holt books are available at special discounts
for bulk purchases for sales promotions, premiums,
fund-raising, or educational use. Special editions
or book excerpts can also be created to specification.
For details contact:
Special Sales Director, Henry Holt and Company, Inc.,
115 West 18th Street, New York, New York 10011.

First published in hardcover by Macmillan London Limited in 1990.

First American Edition—1991

Printed in the United States of America
Recognizing the importance of preserving
the written word, Henry Holt and Company, Inc.,
by policy, prints all of its first editions
on acid-free paper.

1   3   5   7   9   10   8   6   4   2

To the memory of Hans and Sophie Scholl,
and the 'White Rose' of
the University of Munich

whoever today still doubts the real existence of demonic powers has widely misunderstood the metaphysical background to this war. Behind the concrete, behind material perceptions, behind all factual, logical considerations stands the irrational, i.e. the battle against the demon, against the emissaries of the Anti-Christ. . . .

(from a leaflet of the White Rose, Munich, February 1943)

Contents

Acknowledgements

First I must thank Bradley Smith, the authority on Himmler's early life, for offering to 'fill up a suitcase' of his photocopies and transcripts of Himmler's early letters and diaries and bring them to London with him from America. In the event, bleary-eyed from deciphering too many German scripts, I declined his offer, only asking for and receiving selected letters and diary pages. However, the gesture and the response to my request for specific documents were so open and generous that Bradley Smith has to head the list of those I thank. And I should add that my account of Himmler's early life is based on his work.

It is apparent from the suitcase episode that I have not read everything I could have read; I have not read a tenth or perhaps a hundredth of what I might have read. Had I read all the primary and secondary material this book would never have been written. A balance had to be struck and I believe I have spent more than sufficient time peering into Himmler's mind through his diaries, letters, decrees and file notes. I do not believe that another five years of the same would have altered the picture substantially. Ultimately one reaches the unknowable, and that is where I arrived. Nevertheless there is ample scope for others to fill in details and areas of his life I have barely touched.

Of those, apart from Bradley Smith, who have laid foundations for this biography I should like to acknowledge my great debt to Josef Ackermann, whose penetrating study of Himmler's mind, *Heinrich Himmler als Ideologe*, was invaluable, also to the works of Jochen von Lang, Helmut Heiber, Heinz Höhne, Martin Broszat and Gerald Reitlinger, listed below and/or in the Bibliography and Reference sections.

I owe a great debt to Michael Tregenza, whose biography of Christian Wirth will appear shortly, for the great generosity with which he has shared his hard-won research on the death camps in Poland and the time he has spent answering my queries and providing photocopies of source material from his extensive archive.

I did not interview anyone who knew Himmler personally. The few whom I thought might contribute because they had been exceptionally close to him in a working relationship would neither see me nor answer my letters. This is not as serious as it might appear, as I found when researching for *Dönitz* that too much time has elapsed since the Nazi era, too many evasions and downright lies have circulated and passed into common currency, and as a consequence it has become impossible to separate fact from fiction in any recollections of participants unless they are supported by the documentary record.

This applies of course to published memoirs. Several of the sources I have used are suspect, the memoirs of Himmler's masseur, Felix Kersten, and the recollections of his adjutant, Karl Wolff, as prime examples. Yet these two were probably closer to Himmler than anyone and to disregard their observations would be as silly as to take everything they wrote on trust. Before citing them I have applied the simple test of asking whether on this or that point they had reason to lie. In any case I have always indicated the source and if necessary the doubts. So far as Felix Kersten is concerned, there is much independent corroboration that the topics he records having discussed with Himmler were indeed on Himmler's mind on the day or in the period he gives; it comes both from records of Himmler's talks with officials and from his table talk which, like Hitler's, was thought worthy of recording for posterity. I have less difficulty in believing Felix Kersten than some historians; conversely I have far more difficulty in believing Karl Wolff.

Of those who have helped in different ways I should like to thank Professor Yehuda Bauer of the University of Jerusalem for his analysis of the diaries of Himmler's daughter, Gudrun, which I was unable to see. He considered them 'basically unenlightening . . . what is interesting is what is *not* there.' He considers that they do not help to clarify Himmler's relationship with his wife Marga during the time he had a second family with his mistress 'Häschen' Potthast.

I owe much to the help of Mrs Wichmann and all at the Wiener Library, London, who guided me through the Himmler collections, helped with translations of German colloquialisms, answered queries and made many vital suggestions about books to consult. And I should like to express my great thanks to Martin Goldenberg for his help in deciphering several of the more difficult handwritten letters. Similarly I owe much to Philip Reed of the Imperial War Museum for his great help with the Himmler material there and also the Nuremberg and Doctors' Trials transcripts. My brother Tim made photocopies of letters to and from Himmler, and Himmler's speeches on microfilm at the National Archives Washington – see References; my son Guy added immeasurably to those parts of the book which touch on philosophy by virtue of his knowledge of Sanskrit and the Indian texts which so attracted Himmler.

I should like to thank Volker Berghahn, lately of Warwick University, as ever immensely helpful in loaning vital books, who also read parts of the draft touching on economic matters and made valuable suggestions. Harald Lohl loaned me many books and other material from his library, and Kristina Behnke, formerly secretary to the late and sadly missed Frank Lynder, helped with photocopies of material difficult to find in this country. I should also like to thank President Chaim Herzog of Israel and Niall MacDermot, Secretary-General of the International Commission of Jurists, who wrote detailed accounts of Himmler's last hours, Dan van der Vat, who pointed me in the right direction at the beginning, Stanislaw

Rutkowski, who described wartime Warsaw from personal recollection, Lord Douglas-Hamilton, Martin Gilbert and many others who replied to my requests for information or material.

I thank Mrs Lucy Butler, Robert Byron's sister, for permission to quote extracts from her brother's diary which appeared in the *Spectator*; the editor of *Germania Judaica, Bulletin der Kölner Bibliothek zur Geschichte des deutschen Judentum*, for permission to quote from George Hallgarten's recollections of Himmler as a schoolboy. And I am grateful to the following publishers and authors for permission to quote extracts from their works: Oldenbourg Verlag, Munich, for H. Heiber, *Reichsfuhrer! Briefe an und von Himmler*, M. Broszat (ed.), *Kommandant in Auschwitz*, A. Krebs, *Tendenzen und Gestalten der NSDAP, Erinnerungen*, R. Diels, *Lucifer ante Portas*, Diogenes Verlag, Zurich, for A. Andersch, *Der Vater eines Mörders*; Droste Verlag, Düsseldorf, for K. Moczarski, *Gespräche mit dem Henker*; Dr Heinz Boberach for his illuminating multi-volume compilation, *Meldungen aus dem Reich*; Century-Hutchinson for F. Kersten, *The Kersten Memoirs*, R. Hewins, *Count Folke Bernadotte*, J. Heygate, *These Germans*; John Murray for P. Leigh Fermor's marvellous travel memories, *A Time of Gifts*; Weidenfeld & Nicolson for H.R. Trevor-Roper (ed.), *The Bormann Letters*, H. Kamen, *The Spanish Inquisition*; Chatto & Windus/The Hogarth Press for H. Guntrip, *Schizoid Phenomena: Object Relations and the Self*; Methuen for S.H. Roberts, *The House That Jack Built*; Geoffrey Bles for B. Fromm, *Blood and Banquets*; Constable for G. Lean, *Frank Buchman: A Life*; Routledge & Kegan Paul for R.G. Overy, *Göring: The Iron Man*; André Deutsch for W. Schellenberg, *The Schellenberg Memoirs*; Secker & Warburg for H.R. Trevor-Roper (ed.), *The Goebbels Diaries*; The Bodley Head for J. von Lang and C. Sibyll (eds), *Eichmann Interrogated*; Collins for M. Gilbert, *The Holocaust*; Harper & Row, NY, for F.W. Winterbotham, *The Nazi Connection*; F.A. Herbig Verlagsbuchhandlung, Munich, for J. von Lang, *Der Adjutant: Karl Wolff, der Mann zwischen Hitler und Himmler*; Macmillan for H.R. Trevor-Roper, *The European Witch Craze of the Sixteenth and Seventeenth Centuries*, R.J. Lifton, *The Nazi Doctors*, W. Strik-Strikfeldt, *Against Stalin and Hitler*, and Lord James Douglas-Hamilton for permission to quote from his excellent *Motive for a Mission*.

Finally I should like to thank Adam Sisman of Macmillan for support and encouragement over the long haul this has been, Peter James for his imaginative professionalism in editing and bringing to my notice connections I had missed, my bank manager at the National Westminster for once again keeping his nerve, and my wife, Jane, who kept hers and provided invaluable back-up and help with research.

But I must not omit you, reader. The book can only be completed with your active engagement. What manner of man Himmler was, you must judge. Whether his life has anything to tell *us* is for you to say. For my part, I have attempted to tell the story straight and use words precisely. No doubt I have slipped up here and there or allowed emotion to cloud the text, but I believe you will not find the words 'brutish', 'brutal' or 'inhuman' used to describe the utterly nauseating things Himmler and his subordinates did to those for whom they deliberately coined the word *Untermenschen*.

Part One

FORMATION

1

Background

We waited in the church, gazing at rich marble pillars and white statues and gilt stucco curlicues rising behind the altar to the concave oval ceiling painted with men and angels against a swirling blue heaven. The style and sumptuousness were as much a surprise as the overflowing size of the congregation.

This was in the village of Wies, not far from Füssen in the Bavarian Alps, where the Himmler family had vacationed in the early years of the century. They must surely have come here for they were compulsive church visitors and – we learned afterwards – this church is famous not only as a place of pilgrimage, but as a masterpiece of German rococo.

I thought of young Heinrich Himmler as the choirboys entered in procession. They wore white robes and had serious eyes. Heinrich had been a serious boy and a believer. 'Mag es gehen, wie es will, Gott werde ich immer lieben . . .', he had written in his diary as a young man of nineteen – 'Come what may, I shall always love God, pray to Him and adhere to the Catholic Church and defend it, even if I should be expelled from it.'[1]

Of course he had found another faith very soon inimical to the Church and had expelled himself, then attacked with all the force he dared, declaiming against priests as the greatest cancer a people could have. Yet like Robespierre, another serious, rather puritanical revolutionary who lived by an inner vision, Himmler always believed in God. It was the institution of the Church he, like Robespierre, sought to destroy because it stood for the existing order and old values incompatible with the new era. In the autumn of 1944, as the sands of the new era and the thousand-year Reich were running away, he recognised his mistake; the Church was stronger than the Party. He wondered whether it still had room for him and, ordering the release of a group of priests from his concentration camps, he mused whether, if he were dead, they would pray for his soul.[2]

Himmler's bones lie in an unmarked spot beneath the dust of the north German plain and here, on this Sunday in Wies, to all outward appearances it was as if he had never lived.

Were these the *Herrenvolk*, the master race? Darkish hair was predominant, or grey, and broad heads and thick, stocky figures; remarkably few

were representative of that long-headed and blond, blue-eyed 'Nordic' race
which had so captivated Heinrich Himmler's imagination, and the thought
passed, not for the first time, how could he, a Bavarian, neither long-headed
nor fair, growing up among Bavarians with such distinctly square skulls, have
devoted his life to the theory of the Nordic superman?

Robespierre had believed in the perfectibility of man. He and the
'physiocrats' who laid the path for the French revolution were as blind
as Himmler to the living, erring, real men and women about them; they
had believed in their inner vision of 'man' with a conviction that denied
observation or experience, history or literature, the teachings of every
major religion or indeed self-knowledge; they had believed with an inner
certainty that justified the Terror. But in their case, too, the Church had
proved stronger.

By the time we left, we had guessed why the church was so packed;
we had chanced on a Sunday when the preacher – and it was an enormous surprise when he announced himself – was the Greek Orthodox
Archbishop of Jerusalem, Dr Lutfi Laham. 'But no,' said a man we
asked on the way out, of rather more Nordic complexion than most we
had seen, and he shook his head seriously. 'That was not the reason at
all. It is just the same every Sunday'. And this was confirmed later by
others.

Climbing back into our car among scores of Mercedes and coaches, we
imagined these devout people in their traditional attire about to transform
themselves into the aggressive drivers who had hounded us mercilessly on
every Bavarian road.

The sun was hot, the air fresh and cool, tasting a little of snow from
the mountain peaks, invigorating as the streams that tinkled on every
hand. The lake sparkled; beyond it ash, elm, sycamore, beech, spruce
climbed a slope where a castle had stood centuries ago. An elderly
couple walked by, he in knee-length *Hosen* and stockings and stout
boots, digging the point of an alpenstock into the path as they nodded a
greeting.

'Grüss Gott.'

In following the Himmler family to the streets in which they lived,
the churches in which they worshipped, the resorts they had chosen
for their long vacations and so to a lake near Schloss Hohenburg a
few kilometres from the alpine village of Lenggries, we had been led
to the most ravishing places, each more idyllic than the last. And so
it was to prove throughout, prompting the inevitable conclusion that it
could not have been physical environment that caused young Heinrich
to turn out as he did. Whether natural or man-made, the surroundings
in which he grew could hardly have been more delightful or conducive,
one would have thought, to quiet manners, reflection and philosophy. If
environment made the man one would have expected a Rousseau or an

Albert Schweitzer to have been produced from these places, not a mass murderer.

He had been to this lake as a boy; we knew that from his diary entries for 1910: '15 July. Morning in the garden. In the afternoon over the Mühlbach to the park. Here we ran into three bears. We were very frightened'.[3] It was not a park now, but evidently it had been one earlier in the century when Schloss Hohenburg had belonged to the Grand Duke of Luxemburg. As we walked on we came to a division in the track and a signpost, one arm inscribed 'Sonnenweg Hohenburg', the other 'Hohenburg-Mühlbach'. We started up the incline.

These tranquil regions also bred hallucination. Three centuries before the Nazi terror began in Bavaria another extreme form of persecution flourished in the alpine hinterlands, spreading to the plains and throughout Germany and indeed Europe. In one decade in the 1620s the Bishop of Würzburg caused 900 witches to be burned, and it has been estimated that in the whole of Germany during the seventeenth century as many as 100,000 witches were sent to the stake – a trifle compared with the mass murders instigated by Himmler, although hardly a trifle to the individuals concerned.

In his masterly enquiry into the subject Hugh Trevor-Roper points out that as a phenomenon involving whole societies the witch craze was associated particularly with highlands, the Alps and the Pyrenees and their foothills.[4] He ascribes this to social forces, specifically the feudal society of the plain clashing with the individualism of the mountains. In the struggle to assimilate the mountain peoples the Catholic Church (as the religious arm of feudalism) manufactured out of pagan customs and superstitions found in the mountains the 'heresy' of witchcraft, using it ruthlessly in the campaign to enforce orthodoxy, and so successfully that the Church hierarchy convinced themselves of its truth. It gained a momentum of its own; the existence of witches came to be accepted by the greatest thinkers of the day. They were Satan's agents on earth. Anointing themselves by night with the fat of murdered infants, they slipped out of their homes through keyholes or chimneys, mounted broomsticks or airborne goats and flew to meeting places, sabbats, there to worship their master and take part in promiscuous sexual and gastronomic orgies. This system, built up as Trevor-Roper puts it 'from the mental rubbish of peasant credulity and feminine hysteria' – and no doubt from the sexual hallucinations of the Dominican friars, the most active inquisitors – was created entirely by the Church. Yet the pressure came from the people. The Dominicans, moving among the people, were responding to popular pressure to find a scapegoat for social frustration.

> If the Dominicans, by their constant propaganda, created a hatred of witches, they created it in a favourable context. Without that context their success is inexplicable. . . . From the very beginning it was they who detected the social

pressure. It was they who mobilised it, they also supplied the mythology without which it could never have become a European movement.[5]

Moving forward three centuries, it was the representatives of the Nazi Party, young Himmler included, moving among the people in these regions and responding to social frustration, who propagated the demonology of the Jew, and later the *Untermensch*, or 'subhuman'. Like the witch, the Jew and the *Untermensch* served both as scapegoats for the ills of society and as means of spreading orthodoxy, the Nazi orthodoxy of the pure blood of the *Herrenvolk*. As with the demonology of witchcraft, the formulation of Jew and *Untermensch* owed much to projections of sexual fantasy and hysteria from the subconscious: as Trevor-Roper points out in his study of the witch craze, there has always been a psychological connection between persecuting orthodoxy and sexual prurience – 'The springs of sanctimony and sadism are not far apart.'[6] To judge by his diary entries, the young Heinrich was an astonishing prig. The Nazis did not have to invent their image of the Jew. The Dominicans among others had done much of the groundwork, particularly in Spain, where their efforts culminated in the institution of the Spanish Inquisition. There are many similarities between the persecution of the Jews in Imperial Spain and in Nazi Germany: in both cases they were better assimilated into the life of the host nation than in any other European country of the time. In Aragon and Castile in the twelfth and thirteenth centuries Jews established themselves in commerce, science and the professions, held key positions as ministers, royal counsellors, financiers and tax gatherers, virtually monopolised the medical profession and practised all trades, forming by far the largest part of the middle class between the arms-bearing nobles and the peasants.[7] This was similar to the position they occupied in Germany before the Nazis took power: sciences, the arts, the professions, especially the medical profession, held a far higher proportion of Jews than their numbers in the German population warranted, and they were popularly believed to hold most of the strings of finance and commerce. In both cases intermarriage with Christians provided an entrée into the nobility, whose usually impoverished estates benefited from the wealth they brought; this 'tainting' of the blood assumed crucial significance.

There were sporadic cases of anti-Jewish legislation in thirteenth-century Spain, seldom properly enforced, and anti-Jewish riots which, as in all pogroms, had more to do with robbery and the cancellation of debts due to Jewish moneylenders than to spiritual matters. The Church, however, particularly the Dominican Order, focused popular resentments by creating a stereotype of the iniquitous Jew, as of the witch, and by preaching that God's wrath would descend on the land that harboured him. God's wrath descended rather frequently in fulfilment of the prophecy, and the persecution acquired its own momentum and inevitably its fanatics. One was the Dominican friar Hernando Martinez, whose incitement of the people to 'rise up and destroy this accursed race, these enemies of God, these crucifiers of the Saviour' set off in 1391 large-scale massacres, accompanied by sacking and pillaging, which cost the lives of some 50,000 Jews.

Early in the next century the Church inspired drastic racial legislation. Jews and Moors – the other alien race in the Spanish peninsula – were required to wear distinguishing badges, were excluded from official posts, were deprived of the rights to bear arms, to possess titles or to hire Christians to work for them, were banned from medicine, surgery, chemistry and numerous trades, and were not allowed to mix with or even talk to Christians. Judarias or 'ghettos' were to be walled around. These laws dramatically increased the numbers of Jews accepting Christian baptism, who were known as 'Conversos'; but while publicly professing the Christian faith most Conversos adhered to Judaism and continued to practise its rites in secret.

To their anathemas against the Jewish race, the Church added denunciations of Judaising Conversos, and it was in response to this perceived threat to the faith that in 1478 the joint monarchs, Ferdinand and Isabella, introduced the Inquisition to Spain. The man said to have persuaded Queen Isabella of the necessity for this step was the Dominican friar of Seville, Alonso de Hojeda; the first inquisitors were Dominicans, the first Inquisitor-General the Dominican friar from Segovia, Tomas de Torquemada. It was Torquemada who in a famous scene in 1492 finally persuaded the joint monarchy to expel from Spain all Jews who would not accept Christian baptism. When Jewish leaders pleading against expulsion offered the monarchs 30,000 ducats Torquemada stormed into the audience, shouted that Judas Iscariot had betrayed the Lord for thirty pieces of silver and, raising his crucifix, dashed it to the table, crying, 'Take Him then, and barter Him for 30,000 pieces of silver!' A painting of this encounter, said to have sealed the fate of the Jews, won a prize at the Berlin Exposition in 1891.[8]

If one asks what were the pressures that led to this final solution of the Jewish problem in Spain, one is led to the issue of *limpieza de sangre*, purity of the blood. For the 'problem' itself had existed for centuries: the alien practising his uncanny rites had been singled out for reprisal in periods of tension and disaster, had been robbed of his wealth by forced levies and by violence, had been stereotyped as begotten of a race which had not merely killed the Lord but regularly celebrated the occasion by abducting Christian children for ritual crucifixion, a race which had been responsible for the Black Death, was made up of poisoners, traitors, homosexuals – the learned indictments are as psychologically revealing as the abominations ascribed to witches. Yet the Jews had survived. Moreover they had been indispensable and not only psychologically: nobles, whose occupation was fighting, were not permitted to engage in commerce, usury or trade; by providing these services and the money necessary for fighting the wars of reconquest and unification Jews had made an essential, *the* essential contribution. Now they were to be rooted out from the land.

It is surely not coincidence that this happened in the year that the recently united kingdoms of Aragon and Castile drove the Moors from Granada to return the whole Iberian peninsula to Christianity and financed the voyage of Christopher Columbus westward to the Indies. This was a young nation state in a period of dynamic imperial expansion, led by a military caste as certain of the Faith as it was proud of its noble lineage. Yet the lineage was seriously compromised. Over the centuries all the nobles families, including that from which Ferdinand himself was descended, had been infiltrated with Jewish blood by marriage. This was the threat, not merely to the Faith but to the ideals and exclusivity, hence the status and power, of the aristocracy, that demanded the ultimate solution. Already, before the Inquisition, *limpieza de sangre* was demanded for a number of official and university posts; the movement gained momentum after the Inquisition began its operations until it became impossible to take an official post, enter a military or religious order or a learned profession or even gain a university degree without proving pure blood stretching back several generations. The Inquisition, set up to protect the Faith from heresy, became the organ for ensuring racial purity.[9] It is interesting that Torquemada and his successor as Inquisitor-General were of Converso origin, that is of Jewish descent, as were countless others prominent in hounding the race from the peninsula.

The Inquisition soon gathered to itself jurisdiction over all moral and intellectual deviations. It became the agent of censorship of books and ideas which did not conform to the prevailing orthodoxies, the hammer of immorality, of clergy who lapsed from celibacy, of homosexuality, the 'unspeakable crime', and, of course, of witchcraft.

Its most effective weapon was the terror inspired by secrecy. When a man fell into its clutches, he disappeared from the sight of the world, his friends and his family; he was not shown the depositions that had been made against him, nor confronted with his accusers; the witnesses were examined in secret; his confession was extracted in the secrecy of the torture chamber. Long afterwards he appeared again in public as a penitent or 'abandoned to the secular arm'; in both cases his wealth and property were seized by the Church.

'Abandonment to the secular arm' is an example of the use of formal procedure, legality and euphemism as chilling as anything conceived in the Third Reich. The Church of God could not be a party to killing, hence it cast out the heretic, abandoned him to the secular authorities and besought them earnestly not to shed his blood or put him in the danger of death. The papal bull *ad extirpanda* on the other hand required the secular authorities to put him to death within a term of not more than five days on pain of excommunication and themselves being prosecuted as heretics. Of course the heretic was burned as a public spectacle.

As with witchcraft, it would be wrong to think that the persecution and terror were imposed on a reluctant people. Historians of the

Inquisition point out that it rested on popular support. Thus Henry Kamen:

> The fear of denunciation, the weight of suspicion and hostility was something created in the community itself by its whole-hearted support of the anti-semitic campaign. . . . The records of the Inquisition are full of instances when neighbours denounced neighbours, friends denounced friends, and members of the same family denounced each other. . . . The equanimity with which Spaniards accepted violation of their personal thoughts and consciences brings one back with a start to the twentieth century. . . . [10]

Torquemada's lay brothers of the Order of St Dominic, the Militia Christi, remind one of Himmler's black order of the SS. The lay brothers came from every profession, called perhaps by devotion or public duty, perhaps by immunity from taxes or from prosecution in the courts. An elite, they were the eyes and ears of the Holy Office, forming a secret police of hitherto unparalleled efficiency. When Torquemada went abroad they formed an escort of 150, mounted and on foot, dressed in black with the white cross of St Dominic on doublet and cloak.

Torquemada has not been accused of insincerity, nor the Friar Hernando Martinez who instigated the 1391 massacres of the Jews, nor indeed the members of the black Order of the Militia Christi who inveighed against Jews and secret Judaisers at every market place and street corner. If fervour, if fanaticism are guides, these men believed in what they did. If Torquemada's life is a guide, he despised earthly wealth and show as much as he preached against it and against the Jews who, in his eyes, had no interest but the acquisition of wealth. He was an ascetic; he slept on a plank, as a celibate, ate no meat, made no personal use of the riches he extracted from Conversos, declined the archbishopric of Seville when it was offered. He lived for the glory of God, believing in exclusive salvation for the followers of the Lord.

Had someone accused him and his black familiars of mass murder he would not have understood, nor would the 'Old Christians' who supported him, both nobles and peasants, whose honour lay in their Faith and in their pure blood.

We visited Dachau on a grey day. Wind swept across the flat land north of Munich spattering flurries of rain against the windows of the car, nurturing imagination. Inevitably the site of the concentration camp, preserved as a memorial, could not match the visions the name conjured. The square, squat watchtowers along the perimeter wall looked menacing, but inside the impression was of well-ordered space. Of thirty-four long accommodation huts which had been arranged in a double row either side of the main road through the centre of the camp only one stood, and that a reconstruction; the rest were marked by their concrete foundations and a number. The road, lined with poplars planted by the prisoners and running past the vast area of the *Appellplatz*, where roll-call or interminable punishment parades had been held, was surfaced with clean, loose granite chippings which crunched crisply underfoot. The single-storey utility block (*Wirtschaftsgebäude*) which ran the length of the *Appellplatz* opposite the huts was white. Behind it the equally long, low *Lagerarrest* or *Bunker*, comprising small cells down either side of a central passage, where things were done to prisoners which even the SS did not talk about, retained its secrets. In the *Bunker* yard where executions had taken place against the wall, and seven posts had stood, each with four hooks to suspend men by their bound wrists, arms behind their backs, their feet swinging above the ground, the only sounds were made by the wind and by visitors' voices and footsteps on the granite chips. Impossible to freeze agony in time, or cries in space.

Yet the attempt has to be made. The wife of a man who died in a concentration camp said recently, 'A generation has grown up, two generations who cannot imagine the evil that can come from hatred, intolerance and – power, when it has got into the wrong hands.'

The museum housed in the former utility block comes closest to capturing what Dachau represented. Yet even here among photographs and documents blown up several times larger than life and explicit captions one remains an onlooker trying to comprehend, failing inevitably, listening for obscenities and jeering laughter and blows as SS guards bully new arrivals naked through the showers – once here in this block. There is not the faintest echo, and no chill. The floor shines; well-presented photographs cover the walls and screens arranged to guide one logically through the story of the Nazi revolution and what it led to here. Visitors stare a moment and pass on.

We come face to face with the camp's founder, the Reichsführer-SS, Heinrich Himmler, looking out mildly from a large portrait photograph, to all appearances a well-meaning, probably short-sighted clerk or minor official.

Immediately after the war a survivor of the camp, Maximilian Reich, described an inspection Himmler made of the prisoners drawn up on the *Appellplatz* just outside. It was in April 1938, but the impression remained sharp. Himmler had stopped before him; Reich looked him in the eye. 'I once saw a buzzard holding a mouse in his claws. He did not kill the poor beast at once, apparently enjoying its distress, its heart pounding with fear. I recognised the eyes of this buzzard again behind the spectacles of the Reichsführer-SS.'[11] Not a hint of this comes through the photograph. It is easier to imagine this man comforting a destitute old lady as he described it in a diary entry when he was twenty-one.

24 November: . . . Visit to Frau Kernburger. The poor old woman. This is true misery. She is almost too weak from hunger and exhaustion to walk. . . . People

are as hard and pitiless as they can be. . . . I fetched rolls for her and added a small cake which I put down without her noticing.[12]

To explore the riddle Himmler represents, to try and match the entries of those of his surviving youthful diaries which indicate an often compassionate, always idealistic, prudish youngster with the heartless monster known to history, one is driven to psychology. Psychologists have no hesitation in diagnosing a schizoid condition – a description frequently advanced to explain the psyche of mass murderers. In the extreme form of this condition the sufferer withdraws into a hidden, inner world, observing the outside world as if from a distance without feelings or involvement. However, this lack of involvement can be masked very effectively by the creation of what one authority, Dr Harry Guntrip, defines as 'a kind of mechanised, robot personality',[13] another, R.D. Laing, as a 'false self'.[14] Guntrip defines this operational personality or 'ego of everyday living' as 'more a system than a person, a trained and disciplined instrument for "doing the right and necessary thing" without any real feeling entering in'.[15] Similarly Laing describes it as acting out a series of impersonations; there can be no real feeling since people are being perceived and dealt with not by the 'true self' but by this partly dissociated 'false-self-system'.[16]

It is a beguiling explanation for a mass murderer's apparent indifference to the fate of his victims. They are not real flesh and blood, but mere figments of his 'false-self-system' being disposed of by that unreal, unemotional system, not by his true self. In a scientific age it is a comfort since it offers 'explanation' – in language that can be mistaken as scientific – and the inference that 'normal' people do not become mass murderers. As a schizoid Himmler becomes both comprehensible and different, outside the 'normal' run of humanity.

What then of Himmler's aides and enthusiastic abettors, Reinhard Heydrich, Karl Wolff, Adolf Eichmann, the death camp Kommandants, the camp doctors, the whole bureaucracy that made genocide possible and the web of Party and SS chiefs who supported and took an active part in the programme? Were they all schizoid personalities? If so the term appears to lose its distinct meaning. Possibly they and Himmler were all too normal human beings.

Nonetheless, clinical experience gained from the study of cases labelled 'schizoid' or 'schizophrenic' cannot simply be disregarded by the true seeker after what may have been happening inside Himmler's mind since it offers startling parallels to his behaviour. There is little agreement on the causes of these conditions. In the Freudian tradition to which both Guntrip and Laing belong, the condition is produced very early in life from the infant's relations, particularly with its mother. Recent research, however, has suggested hereditary factors affecting the transmission of messages between the brain cells, or brain damage before, during or after birth causing a similar malfunction. At the Institute of Psychiatry in London it is believed that there are degrees of genetic disposition to schizophrenia: 'where it is strong the illness starts of its own accord. Where it is weak some environmental "insult" is needed to trigger it, such as stress over exam work and family relationships.'[17] Research at the Maudsley Hospital, London, indicates that families which are critical and make demands on the sufferer are three times as likely to trigger a relapse as are calmer families.[18]

Freudian explanations grow increasingly unfashionable, yet the models put forward are useful; it is not necessary to accept the mechanics – Freudians naturally devise solutions in terms of their own training and belief – but the observations on which the explanations are based are surely valid. In the well-argued and comprehensible, most seductive interpretation proposed by Dr Harry Guntrip in *Schizoid Phenomena*, the premise is that the first psychic drive of an infant is towards an object, namely the mother's breast. The successful achievement of this aim, soon widened to the mother herself, is defined as good 'object-relations', its frustration as bad 'object-relations'. The gratification and pleasure derived from good object-relations are not desired in themselves but point the way to the goal – as Guntrip expresses it, 'we seek persons not pleasures.'[19] It is as a result of success in the continuing drive for 'objects' during the individual's growth that he develops a healthy ego and acquires the capacity to love and maintain loving relationships; conversely frustration in this basic psychic drive will inhibit his ego development and hence his capacity to maintain relationships.

The theory is that the earlier in life such frustration occurs the deeper the effect. If in the early months of an infant's life his mother refuses her breast, is impatient with him, punishes him, is absent when he wants her or is merely aloof and unresponsive, the infant ego withdraws into an inner psychic world, internalising her as a 'bad object' and seeking to control and possess her in his inner world as he has failed to do in the outer or real world. Thus a pattern of desire and withdrawal is established, what Guntrip calls the 'in and out programme' of the typical schizoid. As he grows the child may withdraw from other desired objects such as father, siblings, schoolfellows who reject him, into this inner world he has created; there they become fused with the original bad object of the breast–mother, provoking similar attempts at mastery and control which never succeed but lead to internal frustration, anger, profound anxiety and guilt.

In an attempt to cope with the situation the ego, according to the theory, splits three ways, that is it functions in three differentiated modes. Two of these, labelled 'libidinal' and 'anti-libidinal' modes, operate in the internal psychic world; the libidinal ego, excited by the internalised bad object, feels its always unsatisfied desires in angry and sadistic ways, while the anti-libidinal ego, identifying with the rejecting aspects of the bad object, persecutes the weak and already suffering libidinal ego – inducing sado-masochistic dreams and fantasies.

Meanwhile there is the real world outside. This is dealt with by the ego in its third mode, the ego of everyday living – sometimes called the 'central' ego – still striving for objects. However, the objects it perceives are only idealised versions of the internalised bad objects projected outwards on to the everyday world; it makes mistakes therefore and cannot achieve good object-relations. Put the other way, emotions generated in the subconscious inner world distort the vision of outer reality. This happens with everyone to an extent – indeed the sceptic would argue that our entire knowledge of the world is an inner construction. It still remains observable that those labelled schizoid reveal an eccentric view of what is termed outer reality and tend to deal with it in an impersonal, mechanical way because, according to the theory, their ego, split and unable to develop properly, remains in its infantile state. Typically they withdraw into detachment and apathy, which lead to breakdown if allowed to go too far. Typically they erect defences to prevent this: obsessive routine, performance of duty, affectation of superiority and intellectualising or moralising are common ways of keeping the real world of relationships at a safe distance: so too is the erection of 'a façade of compulsive sociability, incessant talking and hectic activity'.[20]

All these symptoms can be deduced from Heinrich Himmler's early diaries, notes and letters. As a student of twenty-one in Munich he constantly berates himself for talking too much: '1 December: . . . I'm a wretched prattler, can never hold my tongue, inconsiderate and immature, when will I take myself thoroughly in hand?'[21] The diaries display an obsession with trivia and time, to the extent of noting how many minutes he is late for a train; and he recorded on most letters received, however inconsequent, the date and time they arrived; he also kept a record of every book he read with brief comments on the contents and usually the date he read it. The moralising and intellectualising, dealing with ideas rather than actual people and situations, that were key features of his years of power are copiously represented in both book-list comments and diaries. For instance, as a nineteen-year-old student:

11 November: For whom I work, at present I do not know. I work because it is my duty, because I find my peace in work, and I work for my ideal of German womanhood with whom, some day, I will live my life in the east and fight my battles as a German far from beautiful Germany.[22]

The undertones of self-pity are consistent with an ego cruelly divided against itself and it is surely significant that he finds 'peace' or escape from the pressures of the outer world 'in work'. The idealisation of 'womanhood' is typical of many entries. He dealt in stereotypes rather than real people, debated sex and morals with himself and others and laid down rules of conduct as an escape from real relationships with girls or perhaps as a result of the unsatisfying relationships he experienced. As the authority on his early life, Professor Bradley Smith, has pointed out: 'The tone of his descriptions clearly indicates that, even though he wanted warm relations with people, his fears and self doubts forced him to erect strong, defensive walls.'[23]

This might be a description of the schizoid 'in and out programme', rushing into relationships and at once withdrawing to his inner world. If hints of his stratagems for escape – in work, in hectic social activity, incessant talking, in obsession with minutiae and time, in moralising and dealing with people as ideas – are abundant in his diaries, so too are echoes of an inner conflict. There are references to pains in his stomach, so often a symptom of psychic stress, and almost certainly so in his case since he suffered them every day during his years in power and could be relieved only by his masseur. There are also frequent references to dissatisfaction with himself and to inner struggles.

The struggle to retain rigid control is something which recurs frequently in the diaries. At the age of twenty-two, after a party where couples lay close together and he had to exert all his powers to curb himself, he noted:

> It is the hot, unconscious longing of the whole individual for the satisfaction of a terribly powerful natural drive. That is why it is also so dangerous for the man and involves so much responsibility. One could do as one wills with the helpless girls, and yet one has enough to do to struggle with one's self. I am so sorry for the girls.[24]

This entry becomes more significant when taken alongside speeches he made during his years of power accusing Jews and *Untermenschen* of seeking to exterminate the German race. In both cases the complete reversal of roles is striking. He is attributing his own desires to the object of his desire: here his sexual desire for the 'helpless girls' which must be suppressed; in the east in 1941 a sadistic urge to exterminate which must be rationalised. The expulsion of prohibited images from the self to the outer world is a common defence of personality known as 'projection'. It is described by Guntrip:

> When an individual is inwardly menaced by an involuntary schizoid flight from reality he will fight to preserve his ego by taking refuge in internal bad object fantasies of a persecutory or accusatory kind. Then unwittingly projecting them on to outer reality, he maintains touch with the world by feeling that people are either plotting his ruin or criticising or blaming him. . . .[25]

This is perhaps the most crucial insight into Himmler's subconscious that psychology can provide. Obviously the mechanical features of the model, the bad object, the anti-libidinal ego and the rest, have no more reality than quarks in atomic theory; yet like quarks they have been put into the model to account for observed behaviour; in that sense they must be regarded as representative of powerful forces. If schizoid tendencies can be deduced from Himmler's early diaries – and if they appear to be supported by his later career – it may be assumed that he was indeed tortured by inner frustration, anger and guilt, and persecuted by a cruel 'anti-libidinal ego' which caused him sado-masochistic dreams and fantasies, and that in order to obtain relief he was tempted constantly to project these feelings on to the external world.

It is not necessary to move from Dachau to obtain confirmation. There are photographs in the museum here of medical experiments conducted on live, conscious inmates into the effect of high-altitude falls and resuscitation after freezing, experiments which he patronised enthusiastically and personally witnessed; the most useless of these, in terms of practical results, were carried out at his suggestion.

The psychological explanation also allows one to make sense of what otherwise appears inexplicable, the numerous diary entries from his earlier years indicating compassion – his grief at the pitiful state of old Frau Kernburger was one example. On another occasion he described seeing an 'unyielding and stiff-necked' father refusing to allow his daughter private dancing lessons: 'The poor little girl wept tears. I truly pitied her. But she had no idea how pretty she was in tears.'[26] Here, as with Frau Kernburger, what appears to be compassion is, according to the theory, 'identification' with the other person, projecting on to her his own feelings of anxiety and self-pity.[27]

That cruelty and compassion are closely related was known centuries before the birth of modern psychology. Buddhism teaches that the practice of friendliness should precede compassion in order to purify the heart of ill-will, manifest and latent.[28] Both cruelty and compassion imply sensitivity to the sufferings of others: the cruel derive pleasure, the compassionate pain, yet these feelings too are closely allied in sado-masochism. Standing in Dachau museum before the portrait photograph of the mild, shortsighted, clerkish man wearing an unlikely-looking peaked cap with the insignia of the death's head on the band, one is face to face with physical proof of the link between pity and self-pity, suffering and sadism.

A case described by Dr Guntrip may have something to tell us about this man.

> The patient, a man in his forties, had a most unhappy early home-life, and was a badly depressed child. He grew to despise himself as a 'cry-baby' and 'a little worm'. He repressed this tearful little boy and built up a rigidly controlled, capable, unemotional, and aloof central ego to deal with the outer world. But he suffered from recurring bouts of depression and his emotional inner world was expressed in violent sado-masochistic fantasies and dreams.[29]

It was a relief to return to the highlands, to swim deliciously in lakes, surrounded by forested slopes, sunlight glistening from peaks of the Alps beyond, cutting the blue sky, and to reflect on these Germans, so ruthless behind the wheels of Mercedes, so meticulous in preserving the natural peace of these regions. There were no motor boats to foul the crystal water, no hideous sounds from radios, no litter on the grass banks nor beneath the bushes where silver-washed fritillaries settled, nor along the paths marked through the scented woods.

We travelled on and reached Füssen, where the Himmler family had vacationed when Heinrich was under a year old and again when he was nearly six. From the walls of the path rising to the Hohen Schloss which dominates the town we heard a carillon of bells from the tall, painted tower of what was originally a Benedictine foundation, then a princely seat, now the Rathaus. It was early evening; the resonances of the bass reverberated over the baroque courtyard and the steep-pitched roofs, twisting around the medieval streets, as it must have rung on summer evenings in the Himmlers' ears.

In a bookshop in the Altstadt next day I asked for a book I had been unable to obtain in German libraries at home. It was by the novelist Alfred Andersch, entitled *Der Vater eines Mörders – The Father of a Murderer*. They did not have a copy, but would order one. Two days later it arrived, *Der Vater eines Mörders*, not a novel but an *Erzählung*, a narration of the author's brief but illuminating, not to say incandescent acquaintance with Heinrich Himmler's father. I could not wait to open the covers; the pages smelled fresh as only new books can.

'Die Griechisch-Stunde sollte gerade beginnen . . .'[30]

A Greek lesson was about to commence. It was eleven o'clock on a sunny May morning in 1928. The author, Alfred Andersch, translated into the third person as Franz Kien for reasons of artistic licence and greater objectivity, sat at his desk in a classroom in the Wittelsbacher Gymnasium, Munich, idly waiting for the teacher, Kandlbinder, to begin. Unexpectedly Professor Himmler, the headmaster, entered. A corpulent man, he wore a light-grey suit with the jacket unbuttoned, exposing a white shirt rounded over his paunch, and an immaculately knotted blue tie. His hair was smooth and white, his face surprisingly unlined for someone of sixty-three, and lightly flushed. As the boys stood, his blue eyes inspected them benevolently from behind spectacles with a thin, gold frame: 'the gold and blue together gave something of a twinkling, lively appearance. . . .[31]' But Franz Kien had the immediate impression that Himmler, despite managing to give an amiable appearance, was not harmless.

So it proved. Himmler took over the lesson, which became progressively more alarming. Kien was called to the blackboard and taken through a short translation word by word in a bullying, belittling manner, Himmler bestowing no recognition for correct answers, only mocking, '*Donnerwetter! An achievement!*'

As he returned to his place afterwards Kien had a feeling that his ordeal was not over. Himmler paced back and forth in silence, apparently pondering, then turned to the teacher, Kandlbinder, and asked him, in view of Kien's poor showing, what he proposed.

'Coaching,' Kandlbinder replied.

'Coaching is expensive.' Himmler made a dism[...] cannot pay. He cannot even meet the school fee[...] exemption from fees at his father's request.'

Kien felt his cheeks flame. 'The cur!' he thoug[...] announce publicly that my father cannot meet the [...] fees . . . the swine . . . to stand before the class [...] we have become poor. . . .'[32]

'We have granted Kien exemption from fees [...] request, although the decision was not justified. Exemption from fees may only be granted to outstanding pupils. But I believed for the son of an officer with high decorations for bravery, who probably through no fault of his own has fallen on hard times – I believed I could make an exception for such a boy. And how has he rewarded the school and his poor father?'

Himmler answered his own question with a recital of Franz Kien's low grades in maths and Latin. 'It would not do, it simply would not do,' he said as he went on pacing, 'to let him sit around for another year so that he could get a low grade in Greek.' He stopped to look at Kien again. 'Your brother, Karl, is another. How he reached the *Untersekunda* is a mystery.'

Abruptly he changed his threatening tone. 'How are things really with your father?'

'The sanctimonious *Lump!*' Kien thought. 'Bad,' he replied sullenly. 'He has been ill for a long time.'

'Oh, I'm sorry to hear that. Because it will not please him to learn that his sons are not suitable for education at a high school.'

Thus, the author, Alfred Andersch, recollected his own and his brother's simultaneous dismissal from Himmler's school. Making every allowance for the possible effects on memory of such an obviously traumatic experience, the account reveals 'the old Himmler' in a monstrous light.

In a postscript Andersch speculated whether such a father necessarily produced such a son as Heinrich Himmler by understandable psychological laws, or whether both father and son were the products of a milieu and a political situation or, conversely, the victims of an unavoidable fate. He confessed to having no answer – indeed had he known the answers he would not have written the book.

There is another question raised by his account. If father and son were both so exceptionally unpleasant, might hereditary factors be a simple and sufficient explanation, certain genes or evil combinations passed down, perhaps missing the other brothers – but we hardly know enough about them – producing a disposition to bully the helpless and enjoy their suffering? For it appears that both men exhibited these traits in marked degree, yet on the face of it they had very different childhoods and presumably different psychic stresses.

It must be doubted if anything is so simple. The Himmlers, father and exhibit their loathsome characteristics in isolation. For me the prising sentence in Andersch's book came near the end. After the lesson during which he had been humiliated before the class for his her's poverty, Franz Kien walked home alone, joined by none of his fellow pupils. Perhaps I read more into this line than the author intended or than was there; perhaps friends had already expressed their sympathy and their abhorrence of the sadistic exhibition. Nonetheless, Andersch's account is far from the only example in German literature of a sadistically bullying master accepted by staff and pupils – the type was a familiar and apparently acceptable face of school. And in the case of the son, Heinrich Himmler, it is a fact which cannot be disputed since it rests on the evidence of a thousand documents that he was aided in his historic exhibition of sadism not simply by silence but by the active support of thousands, indeed millions. We are looking at the characteristics not of an isolated man, nor of a monster, but of a man who came to embody the miasmas rising from a nation, a man who was the focus of a national disaster as natural as an earthquake or an epidemic disease.

As Henry Kamen wrote of the Spanish Inquisition, 'the weight of suspicion and hostility was something created in the community itself by its whole-hearted support of the anti-semitic campaign . . .';[33] as Hugh Trevor-Roper wrote of the witch craze, 'Great massacres may be commanded by tyrants but they are imposed by peoples. Without general social support, the organs of isolation and expulsion cannot even be created.'[34] Himmler, as indeed Hitler, was more victim than creator of the natural disaster that engulfed Germany and the world. It is no more helpful to speculate on his genes and his psychology in isolation than it would be to analyse the fused constituents of a boulder hurled from the mouth of a volcano to find out why it demolished a house. A man is not what he does so much as what he is allowed to do; otherwise what would each of us not do to change the world and our lives?

It is not right or just to blame the German nation alone for creating and supporting Himmler and all he personified – not that 'blame' is the word one would use in describing the causes of an earthquake. Germany was at that time stress-centre of a world system that has always caused upheavals releasing the foulest stenches: the system is material progress, an uneven process that naturally sets up stresses. In this case a major fault-line ran through Germany, but none of the allied powers who constituted the exterior pressure could look back on a blameless past: not Russia, where Stalin had accounted for more millions in purges and forced starvation of peasants than stand to Himmler's account; not America, a great deal of whose wealth was built on the exploitation of slaves and land taken from the natives; not Great Britain, whose world empire had been founded on the barter, transportation and exploitation of African negroes, and whose colonisers had decimated indigenous peoples; nor France, whose trading and colonial history was only less successful. The Nazis indeed saw the world with a childlike vision as it was, and human beings as they were. With childlike lack of sophistication they only wanted to be the greatest humans, the master race. They did not invent the system, nor the human strengths and weaknesses which made it what it was. They were the *halbgebildeten*, drunk, as is the way with the half-educated, with the half-truth.

2

Youth

On his father's side, Himmler stemmed from a family of peasants and artisans from Ansbach in northern Bavaria. An initial climb from peasant to the lower regions of the middle class was made by Heinrich's grandfather Konrad, illegitimate son of one Johann Hettinger and Johanna Himmler who raised him. Konrad left home at eighteen to become a soldier; at thirty-five he joined the police force in Munich, transferring ten years later to the Bavarian police, and finally at the age of fifty-three, having risen to sergeant, he obtained a post in the district administration of Lindau in the Bavarian Alps. Here he married Agatha Kiene, twenty-nine-year-old daughter of a watchmaker from the neighbouring town of Bregenz, and three years later their only child, Gebhard – Heinrich's father – was born. Konrad Himmler died when Gebhard was seven.

The boy now continued the ascent up the class ladder by way of a *Gymnasium* education and Munich University, where he read philosophy, then philology, the study of the classical languages. No doubt his widowed mother was very ambitious for him, no doubt she lavished all her love on her only son; probably she spoiled him, or perhaps she was wise enough not to. At all events he emerged from the university in 1894 a member of the educated middle class, with the credentials to rise further in the social scale and with a powerful desire to do so.

There is ample testimony to this. A fellow pupil of Heinrich Himmler's prior to the first war, the historian George Hallgarten, has recorded that Professor Himmler was known in Munich as 'laughably pushing and fawning towards the upper classes'.[1] And in the 1920s Alfred Andersch's father described him as a 'careerist. . . . Every Sunday he goes to High Mass in the Michaelis Church in the Kaufingerstrasse. There you can see them all together, those who want to belong to the cream of Munich.'[2] Something of the pedantic correctness of manner with which he pursued his goal comes out from an anecdote of Hallgarten's: his own father, clad in bathing costume, chanced on Professor Himmler naked under a shower at the baths in Munich. Himmler at once seized a small towel, held it in front of him with both hands and formally presented himself with a deep bow. 'That could only happen in Germany,' Hallgarten senior – born an American – laughed afterwards. 'There the man stood, as God had made him, and he introduced himself to me with all his titles.'[3]

The German empire was a confederation of states. While the Prussian Hohenzollerns provided the Emperor, or Kaiser, and Prussia exercised effective power through the constitution devised for this purpose by Bismarck, each state retained its own traditional ruling house. Bavaria, largest counterweight to Prussia in the south, was a kingdom ruled by the house of Wittelsbach. The Wittelsbachs were monarchs in more than a constitutional sense: Bavarian society was set in a pre-industrial mould, all the more firmly fixed by separatist tendencies running across the grain of Prussian domination and pan-German nationalism, and hardened by the threat from those deviant forms of life and thought which had emerged from the overcast of the great industrial cities and were represented spectacularly in the Bohemian quarter of the Bavarian capital, Munich. The house of Wittelsbach was apex and focus of Bavarian nationalism and of the essentially pre-industrial social order. Gebhard Himmler was naturally attracted by its glamour. After leaving university he obtained a post with Prince Arnulf of Bavaria as tutor to his son, Heinrich. At the same time he began his career as a classics teacher in a Munich *Gymnasium*. That he combined the two posts successfully is attested by the firm ties he established with Prince Arnulf's family.

Three years later he married Anna, daughter of a tradesman named Heyder. Her parents were dead, and she evidently brought some money with her – as Gebhard's mother had done at her marriage. Thus the profits of trade came through the female side to make life more comfortable for the assiduous Himmler males. Comfortable is a useful word to describe the home Gebhard and Anna Himmler made in a second-floor flat in the Hildegardstrasse in the centre of Munich; another word would be bourgeois, for both embodied the bourgeois virtues of solidity, diligence, respectability, respect for the established order and the established Catholic Church; another word no doubt would be *gemütlich*, for we are speaking of Bavaria and snug sociability over cream cakes and hot chocolate or beer steins and men and women of often ample proportions.

Their first child, a boy, was born the following summer, 1898, and named Gebhard; Heinrich was the second son, born two years later on 7 October 1900. It is typical of Professor Himmler's pedantry that he reported the baby Heinrich's precise weight and dimensions in a letter he wrote to his one-time charge, Prince Heinrich of Bavaria, who agreed to be godfather.[4] It is also typical of the interest he took in both sons. However hard a taskmaster he became, it is evident that in the early years he lavished as much attention and affection on the young boys as his work allowed. When Heinrich went down with an acute lung infection at just over two years old, his father's anxiety lest it prove to be tuberculosis was huge. On the doctor's advice the family was packed off to a mountain village where the air was pure, while Gebhard remained at home, visiting them as frequently as he could. Much the same happened when the elder boy, Gebhard (junior), suffered from repeated chest infections the following year. So far as can be judged from family letters and their father's own notes on the boys' progress and sayings, Gebhard and Heinrich were surrounded in their early years by the loving care of both parents and a maid-cum-children's nurse, Thilda. It is possible indeed that in this atmosphere Heinrich as the younger, and frequently ill, was over-indulged – certainly this is the impression given by some of his letters when he first left home.

Some two months after Heinrich's fifth birthday a third son was born; christened Ernst, he was the last of the Himmler children. By this time the family was living in a third-floor flat in Amalienstrasse, an elegant street of neo-classical façades running immediately behind the University, and the elder boy, Gebhard, had begun school.

Next summer the family spent the long vacation near Füssen and the two elder boys – Heinrich now coming up to six – were no doubt walked up to the Hohen Schloss, and taken out to see the fairy-tale castle of Neuschwanstein, built of white limestone against a Wagnerian gorge by Ludwig II – ancestor of Heinrich's godfather – and the less immediately spectacular but equally impressive Hohenschwangau Castle nearby. If their activities on other vacations are a guide they must also have walked through the lush grass and flowers of the meadows there, swum in the lakes where Wittelsbach swans drifted and dragonflies darted over the crystal water, and visited the different examples of rococo churches in the vicinity, including no doubt the Wieskirche.

On their return to Munich, Heinrich was started at the cathedral school which his brother already attended. Here he experienced all the usual childish illnesses and a recurrence of the old lung infection; in all he missed so much school that Professor Himmler hired a tutor to coach him. Much the same had happened in Gebhard's first school year and from now on both boys had to contend not only with their work in class, but with rigid supervision from their father at home. Both obtained excellent results.[5]

Some idea of their home life can be gathered from what Willi Frischauer, Heinrich Himmler's first biographer, gleaned from an interview with his brother Gebhard in the early 1950s. Their flat was crowded with antique chests, mirrors, paintings and *objets* which the boys had to treat with care. One room apparently was 'set aside and turned into a shrine devoted to the memory of the family's ancestors. It soon came to include souvenirs and gifts from relatives and the more important friends.'[6] Professor Himmler collected stamps, coins and writings on Germanic history, all of which he catalogued meticulously in a filing system. According to Frischauer he also dabbled in the fashionable hobby of archaeology; probably the *Ahnenzimmer*, or ancestors' room, contained artefacts from German prehistory as well as family treasures.

In this respect an anecdote recounted by Alfred Andersch is interesting; it concerned a lecture Professor Himmler gave a young cub of the nobility named von Greiff who had cheeked him in class. The Himmlers, he told the lad, were a much older family than the Greiffs; 'we can prove our origin from the ancient *Stadtpatriziat* [town patriciate] of Oberhein. There is a house of Himmler in Basle and one in Mainz. That in Basle bears the date 1297!'[7] Besides revealing the caste-consciousness of Bavarian society, a fact confirmed in Hallgarten's memories of his schooldays with Himmler,[8] the story indicates a lack of self-confidence in 'the old Himmler' which impelled him to promote his peasant forebears in this way.

In the evenings after dinner in the Himmler home, while their mother sewed in a corner, Professor Himmler would read to the boys from books on German history taken from his large and ever-growing library. According to Frischauer, by the time he was ten young Heinrich could recite the names and dates of all the famous battles, and when he entered senior school he rivalled his teachers in knowledge of Germany's martial past.[9]

The boys were also regaled with stories about their grandfather when a soldier. Professor Himmler, who had known him so little, idolised him and wove tales of adventure 'in a rhythmic, studied language' around exploits he must have learned of chiefly from his mother. The hero of these adventures, Konrad Himmler, had entered the 1st Royal Bavarian Regiment as a private, and served subsequently as a soldier of fortune abroad. It was of this later time, especially campaigns in which he had fought in Greece, that Professor Himmler liked to speak.[10]

Both boys had piano lessons at home but, while Gebhard learned to play well, Heinrich had no talent. He persevered or was made to persevere, and it was many years before he eventually gave up, defeated. Gebhard showed Frischauer the piano in his own rooms after the war. He also showed him an ivory statue of Christ on the cross to which the boys had said their prayers before going to bed.

The next glimpses of family life appear in the diary which Heinrich began at his father's instigation in July 1910 immediately after he completed his primary education. Professor Himmler wrote the first entry himself to set the standard. It was the day they left for their vacation; the times of departure and arrival at their destination, Lenggries, were followed by the briefest description of the house they had taken ('very pretty') and their afternoon's activity ('we drank coffee at the coffee house').[11] Heinrich's entries were little more illuminating, hardly surprising since he was not quite ten, but they leave the impression that the family did most things together, that Heinrich loved his parents – thus for 22 July: '13th wedding anniversary of my dear parents'. It also indicates the schoolmasterly interest Himmler took in his sons; he corrected or added to Heinrich's diary entries and imposed a routine of half a day's school work every day for the two weeks before the start of the autumn term.

In September Heinrich entered the Royal Wilhelm Gymnasium, again following two years behind his older brother. Here we obtain a sharp glimpse of him through the recollections of his fellow pupil, George Hallgarten.

For some time after the second war Hallgarten had no idea that the boy he had known before the first war and the notorious Reichsführer-SS were one and the same. In 1949, while reminiscing with a former classmate, he happened to say how dreadful it must have been for *their* Himmler to have had such a bandit as a brother. 'Brother?' the other said, surprised. 'Do you really not know that our Himmler was the notorious one?' Hallgarten could not believe it. The contrast between the Himmler they had known and the fearful figure of later years was too great: it was simply impossible. Yet it was so. He tried to make some sense of how it could have happened. The boy he recalled was:

> of scarcely average size, but downright podgy [*plump*], with an uncommonly milk-white complexion, fairly short hair, and already wearing gold-rimmed glasses on his rather sharp nose; not infrequently he showed a half-embarrassed, half-sardonic smile either to excuse his short-sightedness or to stress a certain superiority.[12]

The description ties in exactly with what one might expect from Heinrich's love of cakes and (as he termed them) 'goodies', manifest in his later diaries, and with the hours of deskwork his father forced him to put in at home. He was known as a *Star*, the Bavarian expression for a youngster highly thought of by teachers, who failed in manly things – a swot.

He was hopeless at gymnastics, the chief, indeed the only school-sponsored sport, and the gym instructor, Carl Haggenmüller, was a source of terror to him. Hallgarten describes one session of torture Heinrich had to endure: he was supposed to be performing knee circles around the horizontal bar – something he could never do – and had failed to complete the forward turn. He was hanging with his left knee bent over the bar when Haggenmüller took the gold-rimmed glasses from his nose, entrusting them to the assistant instructor, seized the other thick leg and swung it up and down mercilessly until the boy was practically blue in the face. 'Finally helped by Haggenmüller up to a knee-sitting position on the bar, the later Reichsführer-SS, totally finished, looked down at the hooting class with a strange expression of mixed anger and disdain in his short-sighted eyes.'[13]

Such scenes were fairly frequent; it is not necessary to be a psychiatrist to imagine the effect they had on the boy. If in addition he was accustomed to being mollycoddled at home by his mother and nurse on account of his weak constitution and had heavy academic demands made on him by a stern father one can well imagine that he may have retreated into an inner world.

German society was aggressively masculine. The tone was set by the Prussian military which had unified and now ruled the empire. The ideal was the warrior-hero of spartan simplicity, uncorrupted by materialism, tempered against 'womanly' weakness. The attitudes and manners of the officer caste, supposed to embody this ideal, had permeated every stratum to such an extent that to be a civilian was scarcely to be a man, to be sensitive was to be soft. In such a society more than most, Himmler must have despised himself for his short sight, awkward, unathletic body, constitutional weakness and physical ineptitude, perhaps even have despised his father for being a civilian or one or other of his parents for handing him down his hateful qualities; and the periods of torture at Haggenmüller's hands must have driven these feelings of inferiority deep; perhaps it is here on the horizontal bar in the Wilhelm Gymnasium and in the contrast between his own physique and the intensely male demands of German society that one should seek the determining explanations of his psyche.

One anecdote recounted by Hallgarten may be significant: 'Haggenmüller, after putting Himmler through an overlong session of knee-bends, asked him what he wanted to be. Close to tears, Himmler got out, "Naval officer."'[14] At this time the Navy was being expanded rapidly and officer recruits were being canvassed from the educated middle classes, who as non-nobles, had little chance of entering the officer corps of the Army. The young Heinrich Himmler, whose short sight alone ruled him out for the Navy, was it seems already fantasising about an officer's career.

Whatever was happening in his inner world as a schoolboy, Heinrich Himmler coped well with the outer world – with the exception of the gym apparatus and Herr Haggenmüller. He was a hard worker, in all respects a model pupil who earned the favour of all the masters and invariably obtained a grade one in every subject. According to the recollections of former classmates Hallgarten spoke to in 1950, he was not top of his class, but always second.[15]

As a *Star* he was not exactly popular; nevertheless, he was respected by the other boys for his brains or his application and did not lack friends. Hallgarten counted himself among them. He recalls Himmler coming frequently into the garden of his house by the River Isar flanked by two classmates, 'the largest in the form, Franz Müller, son of a major-general, and the smallest, Fritz Esslinger'; there they used to sit by the river, surrounded by shrubs, eating sandwiches and drinking strong cocoa or chocolate, which Himmler loved.

Each summer holiday the Himmler family vacationed as they had since the earliest days in Bavaria, usually in the Alps – or in 1913 in Austria – and Heinrich recorded the details in his diary. He was still sparing of descriptions and feelings. There is of course a psychological explanation for this: according to one analysis it reveals a 'repressed character who experienced only weak and limited feelings . . . a schizoid personality who was systematic, rigid, controlled and restricted in emotional expression'. His later diaries, however, show at times turbulent emotion.[16] Surely these early entries were flat and unemotional because they were written as an exercise for his father, who inspected and corrected them. Probably he was doing what his father expected of him, as at school he did what his teachers expected; he was a supreme conformist, and the adolescent diaries probably tell us more about the father than the son. He had after all written the first entry – their times of departure and arrival at the village of Lenggries, with nothing of the charm of the place or its magnificent Alpine setting. 'Kennst du den Ort so herrlich schön . . . ?' runs the song of Lenggries; 'Know'st thou the place so marv'lous fair, with its hills, its mountains there . . . ?' Hallgarten described Heinrich Himmler's bespectacled face as *biedermännischen* – philistine, uninspired. That exactly describes his adolescent diaries; it also describes the father who inspected and corrected and first set the banal tone in Lenggries.

Perhaps the real question posed by Heinrich Himmler's adolescent diaries concerns his feelings for his mother; when he wrote 'my dear mother', was he doing it from duty rather than affection like the typical schizoid personality, or did he really love her? '17 July 1912: at 10.20 dear mummy and we three boys left for Lindau. After a four-hour trip we reached the splendid Bodensee whose beauty and size captivated us.'[17]

In 1913 Professor Himmler obtained the post of *Konrektor* or Deputy Head of the *Gymnasium* in Landshut, a town on the Isar just over forty miles north-eastwards from Munich. There the whole family moved, taking up residence in the principal street, the Altstadt, at the end away from the river where it narrowed into the road to Munich. Originally the town gate stood there. One tower still stands opposite where the Himmlers lived, and from it the old wall leads up a rise which in summer is bright with hairbells, gentian, dandelions and all the flowers of limestone provenance to a double-moated castle, Burg Trausnitz.

From the early middle ages, when the castle and town walls were begun by Ludwig der Kelheimer, Landshut served as administrative seat of the Wittelsbach dukes. The mediaeval splendour can be sensed in the Altstadt, a wide and handsome street showing all variety of steep, curved, stepped or pointed gables above which the tower of the principal church of St Martin soars. Walking into the town from their house the Himmlers would pass a statue of a knight in armour, hands resting on broadsword – 'Ludwig der Reiche, Duke of Bavaria'. They could hardly have moved to a place more suitable for keeping alight their interests in archaeology and the 'Germanic past'.

The boys moved schools, Gebhard and Heinrich to attend their father's *Gymnasium*. One of Heinrich's Munich schoolfellows named Falk Zipperer also moved to Landshut about this time and no doubt the two were thrown together as new boys in an established class. Professor Himmler encouraged the friendship, for Zipperer's stepfather was a man of influence, President of the regional government of Lower Bavaria. At all events Heinrich and Falk became close companions and kept in touch later in life.

Next summer, 1914, the Himmlers holidayed at Tittmoning, a walled town with a double moat and narrow gateway at either end of a broad main street or square, not unlike Landshut in feeling, with a castle on a rise above the main town. Just to the east the river marking the Austrian border ran through flat, wooded land.

It was in Titmoning on 29 July that Heinrich entered in his diary, 'Gebhard's birthday. *Beginning of war between Austria and Serbia.* Excursion to the Waginger See. . . .' On 1 August he noted German mobilisation, on the 2nd the German declaration of war on Russia, on the 3rd the attacks by France and Russia on the German borders, and on the 5th: '*England has declared war.*'[18] The next day the family returned to Landshut.

For a boy of almost fourteen brought up by his father on tales of knightly wars in a nation that had been schooled for years in the Prussian brand of nationalism by the semi-official press, by the patriotic associations (the Colonial Navy-, Defence- and Pan-German-Leagues), by popular novelists, by military soothsayers, by university professors – 'the Kaiser's Intellectual Brigade of Guards' – by schoolmasters, even by pastors from the pulpits, this was naturally an exciting time. His diary entries took colour with snippets of war news and patriotic sentiment; his imagination was engaged.

On Sunday, 23 August, for instance, after recording the usual family attendance at St Martin's church, and meeting lots of people, then playing with his young brother Ernst in the garden, he noted:

> Victory of the German Crown Prince north of Metz. Prince Heinrich wrote to Daddy. . . . The Germans in Gent. Played piano. Bavarian troops were very brave in the rough battle. Especially our 16th . . . . The whole city is bedecked with flags. The French and Belgians scarcely thought they would be chopped up so fast.[19]

The following Sunday a train full of wounded soldiers came in to Landshut station and his father and mother went to help distribute food and drink: 'The whole station was full of curious Landshuters who were crude and almost violent as the *severely* wounded Frenchmen (who are surely worse off than our wounded in that they are prisoners) were given water [and] bread.'[20]

Towards the end of the following month, as German successes continued, he wrote:

> Now it's going along famously. I'm pleased about these victories, the more so because the French and especially the English are angry about them and the anger is not exactly insignificant. Falk [Zipperer] and I would like best of all to be fighting it out with them. Just look how the German Michael and his loyal ally Austria are not afraid even before a world of enemies. . . . An English cavalry brigade has been thrashed (I'm glad! Hurrah!).[21]

He must have learned by this time that his short sight made him ineligible for the Navy. There is no mention of the service in his diaries, but war fever and the greater opportunities now for the educated middle class to become Army officers turned his head in that direction. It became his

burning ambition and he confided to his diary several times how he longed
to be at the front. He also expressed his disgust at the 'silly old women,
and *kleinen Leute* (lower-middle classes)' in Landshut who disliked the war
and spread fearful rumours when the papers reported German reverses.
'Whenever there is talk of our troops retreating they wet themselves,'
he noted.[22] It can probably be assumed that both the longing to be out
at the front and the contemptuous attitude to the faint-hearted were the
common talk of his schoolfellows. It is interesting that the accusation of
chicken-heartedness was visited on the social inferiors of these sons of the
haute bourgeoisie.

However, one is tempted to read other meanings into his entries, for
it may be that the images of war and French and Belgians being 'chopped
up fast', British cavalry being 'thrashed', which gripped his imagination and
caused his diary to break out from the straitjacket of time and place, were
ripples from submerged sadistic fantasies caused by a divided and cruelly
persecuting ego. Such a theory is lent support by verses he was writing five
years later – after the end of the war – concerned with similar imagery.
One, cautioning the French to watch out 'for there will be no pardon for
you', continues in literal translation which sounds rather better than the
original:

> Our bullets will whistle and whizz
> And spread terror and dread among you
> As we ravage so frightfully there.[23]

As a poet he was the supreme *Biedermann*. For a young man educated
in the classics and humanities and nineteen years old when he wrote the
poem he appears remarkably immature.

He started a collection of newspaper cuttings about the war and
related subjects, joined the Jugendwehr (Youth Defence), which was
drilled and instructed in military subjects as a preparation for the Army,
played with toy soldiers and started a daily regime of dumbbell exercises
to strengthen his muscles. Otherwise his life went on much as before: his
father continued to impose a strict regime of homework and coached him
in languages; he persevered at the piano, attended to collections like his
father's, of stamps, coins, postcards, pressed flowers, stones and relics from
the middle ages, and now newspaper cuttings, visited church regularly with
the family and went with them on social visits to numerous relations and
friends; he also suffered colds and 'flu rather frequently, and in February
and July 1915 noted stomach trouble.

In the spring of 1915 he was evidently much smitten by the daughter
of a family who visited them, Luisa Hager. She promised to write to him
and, when he received a card from her the day after the family left, he
noted being 'very very' pleased.[24]

As summer came round again the Himmlers went on holiday, this time to Burghausen, near Tittmoning, and as usual hiked, made boat trips on lakes, swam and visited churches; indeed, they visited more churches than usual, keeping a vow made to God when Gebhard had been seriously ill about the time of the move to Landshut; they had been unable to fulfil it the previous year because of the outbreak of war. Heinrich recorded the details in his cataloguing style, numbering off each swim he took; on 16 August he 'swam for the fifteenth and last time'.[25]

The following year Gebhard left school to begin an officers' training course, and in spring 1917 Falk Zipperer also left for officer training with the 2nd Bavarian Infantry – no doubt through the influence of his stepfather. This increased Heinrich's longing to join up. His father wanted him to complete his education first and take his *Abitur*, the final exams which would qualify him for higher education, but Heinrich pestered him and eventually he gave way – perhaps to show that he, too, could exert influence in the right quarters. Heinrich's godfather had died of wounds the previous year, but Professor Himmler wrote to the Chamberlain in Princess Arnulf's household; the Chamberlain obliged by writing to the commanding officer of the 1st Bavarian Infantry, and also sent Heinrich 1000 Marks as a gift on behalf of his late godfather to enable him to pay his way into this elite regiment. It was already oversubscribed with applicants, however, and Heinrich's application was rejected.

Now, it seems, Professor Himmler was really stung into proving his influence although it may be he was simply frightened that unless his son began officer training he could be conscripted into the ranks when he reached the age of seventeen. He made a list of every Bavarian regiment, the town in which it was based and the people of influence he knew there, and began applying to them. As Heinrich returned to school again in September, the first rejections came in and, evidently giving way to panic lest he be drafted, he applied for auxiliary war work. On 6 October, one day before his seventeenth birthday, he left school to begin at the Kriegsfürsorgebüro (War Welfare Office) which provided for war widows and orphans and the disabled. Soon afterwards it was announced that *Gymnasium* pupils were not liable to call-up and he returned to school for the last few weeks of the autumn term.

In the Christmas holidays a letter of acceptance arrived out of the blue from the 11th Bavarian Infantry Regiment. He was to report to their training camp at Regensburg on 1 January as a *Fahnenjunker*, or officer trainee. Proud and delighted, he wrote to tell his friends and relations that he was now a soldier.

Not surprisingly for a youth who had never been away from his parents he suffered terribly from homesickness during his first weeks at the camp. Since the initial training was very physical, this was perhaps increased by the sort of scenes he had suffered at Haggenmüller's hands in the Munich gymnasium. None of his fellow cadets has published an account, so this is speculation. All that is known is that in his first month, January 1918, he wrote home twenty-three times, and despite receiving about a dozen replies complained that he had to wait 'a painfully long time' for them.[26] Besides these complaints and requests for letters, he asked for food to supplement the meagre and unappetising official rations and for money to enable him to eat out. Probably he was no different from his fellow cadets in this respect, but the sarcastic or peremptory tone of the requests suggests a pampered youth who expected his mother to provide; she did.

In his first week he fell for a story that he was to be sent straight out to the front and begged his father to write for help to a relative of theirs in the regiment, Lieutenant Ludwig Zahler. Otherwise his hopes of becoming an officer would be at an end. His father obliged and Zahler, whom he came to know well afterwards, was able to assure him there was no danger of being posted before he had completed his training.[27]

After the first month, he was allowed home at weekends, and between February and June he took these short leave passes at least three weeks in every four.[28] He brought his bicycle back to camp and after the day's work made trips to visit relations or family friends in the vicinity or went sightseeing or to the opera. The impression left by the letters in which he described these activities to his parents is that he was lonely and unhappy and often unwell. That he so frequently sought sympathy instead of trying to reassure his parents – as might be expected of a young man genuinely concerned for them – again suggests he had been over-indulged and spoiled at least by the women in the household.

On the course itself there is little doubt he strove to be a model soldier and win the approval of the instructors as at school he had striven to win the approval of the masters. There is nothing to suggest he was not equally successful. The training had been shortened considerably because of the demands of war and by the middle of October he was drilling new recruits while expecting a posting to the front. The tone of his letters home suggests he was genuinely anxious for practical experience to qualify him for a commission.[29]

It was not to be. The German fronts collapsed; mutiny spread from the ships of the High Seas Fleet to the naval ports, from thence to industrial centres throughout the country, and revolutionary leaders, inflamed by communist propaganda, set up workers' or soldiers' councils. With the nation in the grip of anarchy and the civilian population half starved, the princely houses began to topple, the Wittelsbachs first of all; finally the Kaiser abdicated, the imperial administration collapsed and on 11 November a hastily formed government headed by the Social Democratic Party bowed to the peace terms of the western allies. The officer recruits were sent home.

Stories that *Fahnenjunker* would be able to complete their time at a war school and so obtain commissions raised Heinrich's hopes of becoming an officer despite the collapse and he hurried back to Regensburg to be on the spot. Here he had his first taste of active politics. Regensburg was a centre of the counter-revolutionary movement in Bavaria, and in November the Bayerische Volkspartei (BVP) was founded there to rally the loyalist, conservative forces of the middle class and the mass of the peasants, particularly the Catholics, against the communist and anarchist groups. Heinrich attended Party meetings and began to show that conspiratorial compulsion to be 'in the know' that was to distinguish him later. He wrote home advising his parents to buy up all the coal and food they could, told his father he must join the BVP, it was the only hope, and added in shorthand, which his father had taught him: 'Now only for you. I don't know how it is in Landshut. Don't let mother go out alone at night. Not without protection. Be careful in your letters. You can't be sure.'[30] The following day he wrote again telling his parents not to worry about him: 'I am as crafty as a fox.'[31]

However revealing this sentence is with hindsight, he was as unaware of his natural aptitudes as might be anyone of his age and conformist character brought up on the ideal of the warrior-hero; he only wanted to be an officer. When the regiment returned from the front in mid-December and he learned that the war school was a chimera, that all *Fahnenjunker* of his year were to be discharged, it was probably the most disappointing moment of his life. He returned to Landshut just before Christmas, a year almost to the day since he had received the letter of acceptance into the 11th Bavarian Infantry. Unlike Gebhard, who had won battlefield promotion to ensign (*Fähnrich*) and later received the Iron Cross, 1st class, he had seen no fighting. He had not been commissioned. He was merely *Fahnenjunker* a.D. (retired).

Early next year, 1919, he returned to school, not to the normal upper forms of the *Gymnasium* he had missed, but to a special course designed for those who had left school early to serve their country: two years were telescoped into two terms. Meanwhile, outside, the character of the future Germany was being formed in revolution.

The Third Reich is often represented, particularly in Germany, as a radical departure from the normal line of Prusso-German history; it is sometimes represented as the consummation of that history. Unquestionably it was both. It was born in revolution against the established order, but like all revolutions led to the establishment of the same order in more extreme form under a new ruling class.

The other great revolutions of modern times demonstrate this characteristic. France, distinguished under the *ancien régime* by centralisation of power, became more centralised and more bureaucratic under the Republic; whereas the American colonies, distinguished by state assemblies which were the most nearly democratic bodies in the civilised world and by a population whose lack of concern for rank astonished European observers, became more democratic after its revolt from the British Crown, its people more socially mobile. In the Russian revolution, Tsarist centralisation and oppression of the peasantry were succeeded by a more powerful Marxist–Leninist centralisation and the physical liquidation of the peasantry under Stalin.

'Nations as well as men', de Tocqueville observed, 'almost always betray the most prominent features of their future destiny in their earliest years.'[32] The distinguishing feature of Prussia had always been its Army, the distinguishing feature of the Prussian Army its discipline. In the eighteenth century Prussia was described not as a state supporting an army but as an army supporting a state. As soldiers existed to serve an army in obedience without question, so Prussians existed to serve the state. The more that materialist or plainly subversive attitudes were spread with the growth of industry, the more the Prussian ruling class, feeling threatened, exaggerated their state-centred warrior code.

Its expression changed with the changing intellectual world of the nineteenth century. Darwin had the most striking effect. 'The struggle for existence' and 'the survival of the fittest' had obvious resonances in a soldier state. Darwin's cousin, Francis Galton, helped to focus them by applying the principles of selection to human society. Arguing that medicine and civilisation acted against natural selection by protecting the unfit and eroding the pressure to adapt, he proposed that human breeding be guided to favour the better stock. He called his proposals Eugenics.

Nietzsche raised Galton's pseudo-science into moral (or super-moral) philosophy. Assuming that traditional ideas of God were myths and Christian morality a set of myths designed by the weak to protect themselves against the strong, a 'slave morality' that tamed, weakened, emasculated the vigorous natural impulses of man, he maintained that nothing was true, hence everything was permitted – a theory of relativity in values that naturally followed the removal of any fixed points of reference such as God or morality. He destroyed the logic of the argument – not that he valued logic or reason – by assuming that the theory of evolution was true and that, while the laws of morality were a tissue of inventions, the laws of heredity were also true. Thus he defined truth – and in the most unsubtle, unscientific and materialistic manner. However, it permitted him to insert, in place of God, man as evolved into Superman. Put another way, if there was no God – and evidently there was not – there was no will of God, only man's will.

Schopenhauer had previously identified will as the reality behind all appearances – not individual will, that was an illusion, but a vast universal will which permeated all creation. Man's will was a fraction of this cosmic will, part of the oneness of the universe. Nietzsche defined the universal will – which in Schopenhauer had no end or purpose – in a Darwinistic sense as the will to power: 'This world is the will to power – and nothing else.'[33] He defined the Superman who must necessarily result from the will to power when everything is permitted as the antithesis of the masses, whom he called the 'bungled and botched'. The Superman conquered and ruled the masses as he conquered and ruled himself, the world, even destiny, to become master of the world.

It is no coincidence that Nietzsche's hero was Bonaparte. His Superman is little more than the idealisation or fantasy of the warrior-hero and Supermachiavelli combined, employing violence and cunning, cruelty and crime, although there was no conventional 'crime' in Nietzsche's system – only the will to power.

Nietzsche went mad in 1888. He was, of course, mad all the time; his writings were inspired revelations from the deepest subconscious levels of his own psyche which mirrored the culture that produced him. Since that culture was about to burst forth on the world stage they were also extraordinary books of prophecy touched with genius. That he was not a Prussian Junker, but the bourgeois son of a Protestant pastor, or that others from other cultures expressed similar views are beside the point. He was expressing in extreme, grotesque form the masculine, martial code that inspired Bismarck in the Prussian wars of unification, and by stirring in the new 'laws' of evolutionary biology justified intellectually the compulsions of a warrior caste. Had his visions not corresponded to those of his countrymen he would not have spawned so many in his own image; as it was his language entered the German vocabulary, and men who might never have read his books spoke with his tongue, that is to say with those phrases which sank into the national consciousness because they had emerged from it.

Some of the most pernicious of these concerned breeding to produce a race of Supermen. Nietzsche proposed choosing the best racial specimens for breeding, but prohibiting the reproduction of the unfit, sterilising criminals and annihilating misfits. Such a programme of 'race hygiene' was espoused towards the end of the century by Alfred Ploetz, who prefaced his book *The Fitness of Our Race*[34] with a quotation from Nietzsche, 'Upward leads our way from the Species into the Superspecies'.[35] Ploetz followed Galton and his English successors in seeing disease as a positive selecting out of the unfit, hence like them he perceived a fundamental contradiction between modern medicine and the health of the race. Since the race stood higher in his order of things than the individual, he proposed that the health of the individual be subordinated to race hygiene. In 1904 he founded the Society for Race Hygiene which sought to publicise practical ways in which this principle could be realised; they included new marriage laws and a new concept of sexual morality which would encourage the most fit to propagate the greatest number of children. Combined with the sterilisation of the *Minderwertigen*, or inferior specimens, this would breed in the best, select out the worst and so improve the racial gene pool. The highest race was assumed to be the white race, the highest branch the Aryan. Aryans were to be bred like stallions into a Superspecies.

Such state-centred biological views were only Nietzschean in the sense that Nietzsche gave them their most memorable expression. Actually they permeated German military, political, intellectual, economic and even artistic life. They were enshrined in a new German view of history. As expounded by Heinrich von Treitschke around the turn of the century at the University of Berlin to overflow audiences, including military, diplomatic and commercial men as well as students, civilisation evolved in the struggle between nations. War was the dynamic of history by which the fittest nations imposed their culture on the less fit. In this inexorable process the individual had to forget himself: 'He must realise how insignificant his life is compared with the whole . . . how little his life counts beside the glory of the state. . . .'[36]

To take an even-handed approach and recognise that there were Anglophile historians and Manchester-school economists in Germany, Nietzschean philosophers, racists, Social Darwinian imperialists and eugenic biologists in England and America, or to take a contrary approach and suggest that the state- and race-centred trend of German thought was anti-democratic and therefore encouraged the totalitarian evil of the Third Reich, is in both cases to miss the point. To put it another way, it would be surprising if a nation with Germany's embattled history and geographical position in the centre of a continually warring continent either could or would have evolved a philosophy which would have had much meaning for the Anglo-Saxon nations, England and America, whose geographical positions, hence historical and economic experience, were so entirely different. Nor could their philosophers have much meaning for Germany. The ruling philosophy of a nation is transmitted from the compulsions of its dominant groups to its intellectual propagandists by some mysterious osmosis; it has always been so. To suggest that Germany in the twentieth century could or should have been liberal and democratic – soft and effeminate to the German view – is as misleading as it would be to suggest that the Anglo-Saxon nations could have become authoritarian and militarist. Particular ideas that command national acceptance arise from particular conditions that compel it.

In Germany around the turn of the century the particular conditions were a Prussian warrior caste that had succeeded in unifying and imposing its will and its code on the German empire, but which was threatened on the one hand by the wealth and aspirations of a new class of merchant industrialists and on the other hand by socialist militance among newly industrialised workers. In international affairs it felt squeezed between the growing industrial might of the United States, the potential of Russia and the naval and colonial power of Great Britain and France. Bertrand Russell summarised Nietzsche's philosophy in the words of King Lear:

> I will do such things –
> What they are yet I know not – but they shall be
> The terrors of the earth.[37]

Russell went on to suggest that it never occurred to Nietzsche that the lust for power with which he endowed his Superman was itself an outcome of fear. 'Those who do not fear their neighbours see no necessity to tyrannise over them.' This insight extends of course to the Prussian ruling class whom Nietzsche was idealising. The more they were threatened by internal and external developments the more they felt the need to propagate the world-view or martial justification worked up by the intellectual brigade and so unify the Germans spiritually and prepare them for their destiny, to carry their higher culture to the world by war. This was done consciously and of course by state direction, and so successfully that by the outbreak of the first war it had spread throughout every level of society. It was inevitable therefore that those who sought to rescue Germany after defeat and revolution should have been stamped with this *Weltanschauung*, inevitable in the nature of revolution that they should exaggerate it further.

The chief vehicles in the early stages were the Germanenorden, a secret society formed in Berlin in 1912 which had established throughout Germany lodges modelled on masonic lodges, and its offshoot the Thule Society. This was supported by the Navy but was camouflaged as a literary circle for the study of German history and customs. It took its name from the ancient Ultima Thule, supposedly birthplace of the Germanic race, and members had to prove racial purity for at least three generations. Its motto was 'Remember that you are German! Keep your blood pure!'[38] It was rabidly anti-semitic and anti-communist and was devoted to preserving the purity of the German race. Its ultimate aim was to unify Europe under the leadership of a greater Germanic Reich. Its symbol was the swastika.

The Bavarian network of the Thule was directed from rented rooms in the Hotel Vier Jahreszeiten. The membership was not large but it was distinguished: the nobility, the judiciary, higher academics, leading industrialists and police officers were represented, to the virtual exclusion of the lower-middle classes or workers. It conducted open nationalistic propaganda through its own newspaper, the Munich *Völkischer Beobachter*. More important was its clandestine work; it set up a secret intelligence service which infiltrated communist groups, maintained arms depots hidden from the eyes of the allied control commission overseeing German disarmament, supplied volunteers for the semi-official bands of freebooting ex-soldiers and sailors known as Freikorps which put down communist risings with the utmost savagery, supported murder gangs and maintained its own Freikorps Oberland. And, to win workers to its nationalist, racial (*völkisch*) cause the society promoted a German Workers Party fronted by a genuine working man, Anton Drexler. It was this party which Adolf Hitler joined while working as a political agent for a regular Army captain named Ernst Röhm; later the name was changed to the German National Socialist Workers Party (NSDAP), in the shortened form Nazi Party.

Meanwhile the colony of intellectuals which had flourished in Munich since long before the war, devoting themselves to the Bohemian life and savaging the established order and established morality by every satirical means, had formed a Union of Revolutionary Bavarian Internationalists. It is significant that the most radical leaders of this group of communists and anarchists were Jews. They were joined in early 1919 by three Jewish emissaries from the Bolshevik government of Russia – Lewien, Levine-Niessen and Axelrod – and in April they ousted the elected government of Bavaria and set up a Soviet (*Räte*) republic in the city.

The central government in Berlin sent a force of Regular Army units under General von Oven to quash them. As local volunteer formations prepared to join von Oven Heinrich Himmler was due to start the second term of his crash course in Landshut. Despite this and despite his father's objections he joined the Freikorps Landshut and the Reserve Company of the Oberland where he became aide to the commanding officer. However, the company remained in reserve while von Oven quickly overcame the 'Red' Army and marched into Munich. Once again Heinrich was cheated of the active service he craved.

One of the final acts of the Munich revolutionaries was to execute a number of hostages against the wall of the Luitpold Gymnasium in the city; among these were seven members of the Thule Society, four of them nobles. It is against this background that Heinrich Himmler's views were formed. Anti-semitism had been a principal feature of the middle-class *völkisch* movement in and around Munich since the latter half of the nineteenth century when capital in the shape of big industry, department store and property speculators had begun forcing artisans, small shopkeepers and farmers out of business. The Jews had been identified with capital; thus an article in the Munich paper *Deutsches Volksblatt* in 1895 had concluded, 'If we do not solve the Jewish question, we shall not solve the social question either.'[39] Now Jews had led the communist take-over of Munich and the subsequent reign of terror.

Despite his service with the Oberland Himmler completed his course successfully; in the prevailing conditions it is probable that allowances were made. Up to this point he had expected that the Oberland would be incorporated into the Regular Army and hoped that he would be taken up with it; this is known from a letter he wrote to his former regiment on 17 June asking for his papers to be forwarded. Instead the government ordered the brigade's disbandment; with it his last hope of an Army commission disappeared. He had to decide on some other career.

He turned to agriculture. No direct evidence has been found to explain this choice. A family- and school-friend of the Himmler brothers named Karl Gebhardt, later Professor of Medicine and chief of the SS hospital at Hohenlychen, stated at Nuremberg that it was Himmler's father who chose Heinrich's career for him in order to remove him from politics,[40] by which he must have meant the swashbuckling nationalist, *völkisch*, ultra-right politics of the Freikorps Oberland and the Thule Society.

It is known that Heinrich quarrelled violently with his father over his politics a few years later, but it seems more likely that at this stage, in the wake of his great disappointment at once again missing an Army commission, it was he who chose farming for himself, impelled by the romantic, anti-urban, 'back to the land' ideals which formed the strongest threads in his mature philosophy.

Such views were in common circulation. In 1923 a society called the Artamen was formed to embody them. But the founder, Dr Willibald Hentschell, had coined the word *Artamen* before the war; it was formed from two old middle-German words – *Art*, agriculture, and *Manen*, men – and expressed an attitude which saw cities as sinks of decadence and the land as the real source of strength of a people.

Hentschell was an exponent of race hygiene and in 1906 had founded the Mittgart Society, whose aim was to renew the Germanic race. The Artamen Society aimed to do this by reversing the flow of people from the land to the cities and directing it eastwards as a *Volk* movement of settlers.[41]

That Himmler was already thinking along these lines is suggested by a diary entry he made on 11 November that year, 1919, thus only a few months after he made his choice of career. The entry has been quoted in the opening chapter; it is significant enough to cite the concluding phrases again: '. . . I work for my ideal of German womanhood with whom, some day, I will live my life in the east and fight my battles as a German far from beautiful Germany.' It was in pursuance of this romantic vision, we must assume, that he aimed to do a year's practical work on a farm, then enter the Technical High School in Munich to study agronomy. The family was about to move from Landshut northwards to Ingolstadt at this time as Professor Himmler had been appointed *Rektor* or head of the *Gymnasium* there and he had found a farm just outside Ingolstadt whose owner agreed to take Heinrich on. He began on 1 August.

It was harvest time; the work was hard and it must have been especially so for Himmler after the desk-work at school. He started at four in the morning with the horses, and after a short coffee-break at 5.30 the real work began in the fields, sheaving wheat or rye, or loading straw on wagons, continuing until six in the evening with a short break for beer and sandwiches in the early afternoon. Little wonder that on his first Sunday mornings he fell asleep in church.

He made time to write letters home. Like his letters from the training camp in Regensburg, they contained requests for food, especially 'goodies'. His mother obliged and, worried lest the work overtax his strength, kept asking him how much he had to do and if he was keeping healthy – another indication of his weak constitution as a boy and of her protective attitude. Professor Himmler also expressed concern.

At the beginning of September, a bare month after he had started, he collapsed with fever and diarrhoea and was sent to hospital where a paratyphus infection was diagnosed. He remained there for the next three weeks, reading much and detailing every book with the date he read it, and usually with brief comments on the content in a small notebook he started for the purpose. Over the next fifteen years two further notebooks were added in which altogether 270 books were listed. His comments and little passages of self-revelation in those of his diaries which have survived provide a probably unique glimpse of emergent fanaticism – not how or why, but precisely when.

At the beginning, as a youth of nineteen in hospital in Ingolstadt, he was not a fanatic. He was a devout Catholic, a believer and regular churchgoer, a nationalist patriot with an admiration for the soldierly virtues and a disappointed longing to be an officer. He was *völkisch* in that he believed in the Germanic race, but he was no more anti-semitic than was normal for his class and time; no doubt the Jewish leadership of the *Räte* Republik had fuelled perceptions of Jews as a threat, but he had probably not met many – they were separated into the 'C' classes at schools – and it is evident from later diary entries that he did not hate them as persons. His father was not an anti-semite, according to Andersch's father, and had no objection to meeting them socially.[42]

For the rest, Heinrich was a romantic idealist brought up on a romantic vision of German history and virtue – as indeed British or American or French youths of his age would have been brought up on nonsensical versions of their own country's past. A simple but important example of the Germanic distortion was neglect of the economic facts of war. Two of the great heroes of more recent German history, Frederick the Great and Bismarck, had been deprived of their purses: in the former case the English gold which supported Prussia's wars, in the latter case the Jewish financier who prepared the way for the triumphs of German unification. The disappearance of this Jew, Bleichröder, from German history and biography until quite recently is a telling indication of the extent to which historians both reflect and perpetuate the prejudices of their age and society. So Heinrich Himmler, raised on a misty, Wagnerian picture of the past, and more immersed in it than most because of his father's collections, wished to return to the roots of that past, which he evidently saw in the simple life close to the soil still to be won for Germanism in the east.

His reading in hospital consisted for the most part of novels and a few German classics, probably brought by his father from his library, and the futuristic adventures of Jules Verne, evidently his favourite author at this period. Hitler also read Jules Verne avidly.

Despite recovering from his illness his general condition did not satisfy the doctors and on 24 September he was sent to the family doctor in Munich, Dr Quenstedt: 'At 3.00 p.m. to Dr Grunstädt [sic]. Dilation of the heart not significant, but [must] break off for a year and study.'[43] Professor Bradley Smith discounts Dr Quenstedt's diagnosis of an enlarged heart caused by over-exertion, since although a common diagnosis at the time it finds no acceptance today. It is impossible to say what was really wrong with Heinrich, but in view of his later stomach cramps at times of stress and the fact that as he recorded he had already had 'an unpleasant last conversation' with his foreman, for what reasons are not known, it may be that his condition was psychosomatic, and that he was not happy at the farm. In any case, since he was ordered to convalesce, take only light exercise, avoid becoming nervous – surely a significant instruction – and restrict himself to only moderate social activity, it was decided that he should defer the practical year and do at least a year of his Technical High School course first. He enrolled in October.

Now began a year in Munich living in a rented room in the Amalienstrasse, not far from the flat he had lived in as a boy with his parents. Both his brother Gebhard and his cousin Ludwig Zahler, formerly in the 11th Bavarian Infantry, were students in Munich, and the three of them had meals at the home of a widow, Frau Loritz, who took in students professionally. She had two daughter, Kaethe and Maja, and a boy, Willi; her home provided Heinrich with a family environment, where he enjoyed companionship, impromptu musical evenings, discussions about art and books, and long, intimate talks about the things which have always concerned students. It would be wrong to say he was content; it is evident from his diary entries, especially during the first months, that he was in inner turmoil. Part of this was because he fell for Maja, who was already Ludwig's (Lu's) girlfriend. After a long discussion with her about religion early in their acquaintanceship he recorded in his diary that he had now found a sister. He convinced himself first that Lu did not understand her, 'his golden girl',[44] and within a few days that Lu had a bad character. He felt sorry for them both and sank into deep depression:

> What a miserable creature is man. . . . The heart is turbulent until it rests in the [ground?]. Oh God! How powerless we are; we cannot help [others?]. I can only be a friend to my friends, do my duty, work, struggle with myself and never lose control over myself.[45]

The next day he recorded that he never allowed his gloomy thoughts and emotional struggles to show to others.

It was not long before Lu transferred his attentions to Kaethe, leaving Maja without a boyfriend. Heinrich wanted desperately to fill that place. 'After the meal music was made. Maja and I sat there hand in hand and I believe understood one another. May God look graciously on this!'[46]

It is interesting that after leaving the Loritzes and returning to his own room, where he found a visiting card left by his old friend, Falk Zipperer, he worked on a Russian language course he had started. It is surely not stretching speculation too far to assume that he believed he had now found the 'ideal of German womanhood' with whom he dreamed of farming in the (Russian) east and fighting his battles 'as a German far from beautiful Germany'.

The following day, 18 November, he attended morning lectures:

> Then home. Read. At 12 to eat. After meal wrote Russian. . . . From 2–8
> lect. Then to dinner. At 9 Maja came. We sat together, later even [using
> the familiar] *Du* and chattering. I am certainly not calm. Thoughts and worries
> chase themselves in my head. It is an exhausting situation. . . .[47]

The next evening, the 19th, was a big occasion for him as it saw
his initiation into the student fraternity, Apollo. His diary entry gives no
account of the ritual, but it appears a far less rowdy, drunken ceremony
than is often described:

> Then to the *Kneipe* [inn where the fraternity met]. Was then admitted; am
> happy and proud to be in a student Association. At the *Ex-Kneipe* I sat at the
> Praesidium table. I set up two tankards of beer and spoke some words of thanks
> etc. The President said in prophetic spirit he thought I had not spoken from this
> position for the last time. Am curious to know whether he was right. . . .[48]

Brotherhoods such as the Apollo, each with its own *Gasthaus* or
beer-cellar, distinctive coloured cap and ribbons and duelling matches
against rival fraternities, were the focus of student social life; they were
at the same time initiation into manhood. The duelling was not so much
a test of skill as an ordeal to be withstood without flinching, the sewing
up afterwards a trial of *Selbstbeherrschung* – iron self-mastery. Beer was
drunk in the same spirit at the *Kneipen* until it leaked from every flushed
pore while songs of 'knights and giants, of chivalry and wine and honour'
were roared out.[49] Heinrich Himmler, with his weak constitution, was
granted a beer dispensation; he tried to make up for this failure with
songs and recitations – as he did on this occasion at his initiation with a
piece called 'The Hour of the Lion'.[50] It is evident he remained sober, for
after returning to his room at eleven that night he sat down to study.

Much as he longed to win Maja it became apparent that she did
not look at him in anything more than a friendly or sisterly light. His
reaction seems to have been to escape into fantasies of martyrdom on the
battlefield:

> I am once again in a frightful state of inner struggle; if only I had dangers to
> endure now, could put my life at risk, fight, it would be a real pleasure. O man
> with his inclinations, his indefinable longing, his heart in a turmoil of struggle,
> is a miserable creature. And yet I am proud to fight this fight, I do not intend
> to be defeated.[51]

He seems to have touched the bottom on 8 December: 'Today inside
myself I have cut loose from everyone and now depend on myself alone.

If I don't find a girl whose character suits mine and who loves me, I'll go to Russia alone.'[52]

The previous object of his infatuation, Luise Hager, was living in Munich at this time and he had seen her but found her changed; he did not understand her, nor she him. He put it down to her 'complete and utter' immaturity.[53] Probably she, too, rejected him for it appears that he had no successful relationships with girls during his time as a student, nor indeed for years afterwards. This was not through lack of desire nor lack of opportunity; he was either quite unattractive to girls or too critical of their failings, or too repressed to give himself, always exercising *Selbstbeherrschung* or, as he expressed it in his diary, 'curbing himself with an iron bit'.[54] The psychological explanation would be that he exhibited the schizoid characteristic of being attracted to a person but immediately withdrawing into his inner world, internalising him or her as a 'bad object', the typical 'in and out' programme. Whatever explanations are chosen, the fact remains that he failed in an area that was quite as important to his self-esteem as knee-circles in the gym had been once, and it follows that it reinforced feelings of inferiority. It seems probable that in attempting to flee from despair he 'projected' his tortured inner psyche on to the outer world, in the first place on to his older brother Gebhard; he began to criticise and show him, in Professor Bradley Smith's words, 'veiled condescension'.[55]

He also continued to indulge dreams of military glory. The country was still in turmoil. Neither the right, the former ruling strata – nobles, officer corps of both Army and Navy, judiciary, upper civil servants, leaders of commerce and industry – nor the extreme left of communist leaders and industrial workers accepted the Republic, which had been born in defeat and revolution. The right were monarchists almost to a man and looked forward to a restoration, the left wanted the establishment of a Soviet-style dictatorship of the proletariat. For both, democracy was outside their experience, beyond their comprehension, a messy system of eternal compromise. They liked the Social Democratic government of the Republic even less. For the moment, though, the conservative monarchists were prepared to co-operate with the socialists to maintain order. Communist risings still boiled up from one end of the Republic to the other and both regular Army and volunteer Freikorps units were used by the government to put them down as they had been at the time of the Munich *Räte* Republik. As with other civil wars, no mercy was shown on either side. Several of the Freikorps leaders established fearsome reputations and large bodies of men became conditioned to street violence of the most extreme kind.

The Freikorps movement has been described as the 'vanguard of Nazism'. A recent analysis of the writings of Freikorps members by Klaus Thewelweit, entitled *Male Fantasies*, provides insights into the psyche of these men which suggest that they formed not only the physical cadre of Nazi stormtroops, but the very spirit or soul of the Party, which acted out their subconscious desires when it came to power. The parallels between the 'male fantasies' culled by Thewelweit and entries in Himmler's diaries are remarkable, again suggesting that it is not so much his individual psyche that is interesting as an explanation of his career – except that it evidently impelled him towards these soldiers of fortune – as the background spirit of time and place into which as a natural conformer he merged himself. Practically all the love objects claimed by Freikorps man are to be found in Himmler's diaries and letters and are later repeated again and again in his speeches; they include the Fatherland, the soil of the homeland, the German people, the Germanic blood community, the uniform, comrades, superiors, subordinates, weapons and fighting. Thewelweit concludes from his study: 'In other words these men claim to "love" the very things that *protect* them against real love-object relations.'[56]

Women were generally excluded from Freikorps man's real feelings and were stereotyped in three categories: those who had been left behind at home; the idealised, chaste noblewoman set on an unreachable or 'sisterly' pedestal; finally aggressively sexual 'Red Women', the class enemy, always imagined as whores. Freikorps man delighted in killing these latter, in Thewelweit's analysis in order to annihilate the threat posed by their sexuality and render the world safe and masculine again. Thewelweit interprets the Nazi rallies as mass expressions of the subjugation of the female element within Freikorps man and the triumph of the hard exterior over the soft, embarrassingly fluid interior.[57]

This is no place to detail or discuss the theory; the fact remains that these three Freikorps categories of women and bitter efforts to resist the threat of female sexuality can be discerned many times in Himmler's diaries and letters during these student days in Munich.

In early November 1919 he, Gebhard and Lu had joined the 14th Alarm Company of the Protection Brigade in the city, an official Army reserve which undertook weekend training and could be called out at short notice when trouble threatened. They had no doubt that it would; although the *Räte* Republik had been overthrown, communist unrest was liable to flare up at any time in the industrial suburbs. Heinrich recorded that he looked forward to the struggle when he would 'wear the King's uniform again'[58] – assuming that the fight when it came would be for a restoration of the monarchy.

At the beginning of December he recorded: 'Today I have my uniform on once again. It is as always quite my favourite dress.'[59]

Term ended a few days before Christmas and he went home to Ingolstadt. His diary entry for that day, 21 December, is rather typical in its mixture of either trivial or unexpanded detail with the occasional short flash of genuine feeling:

At 8.00 to the church, then with both my large trunks to the station, bought ticket. The trunks checked in as passenger baggage. The train goes at 12.30. Went to the Loritzes. Lt Rentel and I annoyed Maja in a conversation about man and woman. At 11.30 ate. Then to the railway. During the journey slept and read newspapers. At 5.00 arrived in Ingolstadt. At home drank chocolate. It is just lovely to be home again, one can be a child again and let oneself go a bit.[60]

He and Gebhard did a lot together at home over the holiday, decorating the Christmas tree, shopping for presents, looking for books with their father in his library; on Christmas Eve they set the dinner table and lit the candles on the tree before their parents and young 'Ernsti', then just fourteen years old, were allowed in for the ritual of handing out presents. 'Es war schön, wunderschön, der heilige Abend.'[61] They had bought their mother 'a beautiful jardinière', their father a book; Heinrich received chiefly books. He gave Gebhard a book of guitar music he had chosen, as he records, with deliberation. ' "Now, farewell my beloved homeland".' He noted, 'It will be played in four years' time.'[62] He and Gebhard then helped their mother with the meal as the cook had gone home. Afterwards Gebhard played the piano and they sang to the guitar, finally drinking punch before setting out for the midnight service. In church they stood before the choir: 'The festive Matins moved me powerfully; the Church makes an impression on people through its magnificent ritual, God through the humble, good child.'[63]

These are surely not the expressions of a young man without feelings, or with mechanical, robot feelings. Reading that entry for Christmas Eve, one gains an impression of a comfortably off, close-knit family enjoying themselves in a most civilised way, and of the author of the diary as profoundly affected by the story of the Christ-child and the solemn emotions aroused in church.

The family was in church again a few hours later on Christmas morning, then they – or Heinrich alone, it is not clear – paid a call on a blind, ill academic named Lang. Afterwards a 'magnificent lunch', and then Heinrich read, practised the guitar, walked a little, wrote Russian – thus his choice of a present for Gebhard, 'Now, farewell my beloved homeland' – and in the evening danced, 'somewhat testing'; he had started dancing lessons the previous term in Munich.

The next day they were in church again in the morning, afterwards visiting two people in hospital; again he spent the afternoon 'reading etc.'. From his book list, it appears he was reading Albert Daiber's *Elf Jahre Freimaurer* (*Eleven Years a Freemason*), for he noted starting it on this day, 26 December. It was perhaps one of his Christmas presents. He was no newcomer to the subject of masonry; it was one of the current conspiracy theories which helped to explain Germany's defeat. It is probable he had discussed the theme with family and fellow students. Certainly he had read one volume on the subject while recovering from his illness in September or October. His comments when he finished this latest one four days later, on 30 December, suggest he considered himself something of an expert: 'A book that brings out nothing particularly new about freemasonry and merely represents it as awfully harmless. I might question which side it was written from.'[64]

Evidently he accepted the hostile view of masonry as typified by the book he had read while convalescing, Friedrich Wichtl's *Weltfreimauerei, Weltrevolution, Weltrepublik* (*World Freemasonry, World Revolution, World Republic*). This was one of a legion of polemics appearing from German publishers linking Jews, masons and Roman Catholics usually in worldwide plots to bring about war, topple monarchies, subvert peoples and generally inherit the earth, usually for democracy. They read like the products of diseased imaginations. Yet set in the historical context of the witch craze and the Inquisitions occurring at times of social distress they do not seem unduly surprising. The nation was rent by internal strife and had been subject to humiliation at the peace treaty of Versailles, signed that June: the Army, formerly the greatest in the world, was so restricted by its terms as to be incapable of defending even one of its borders; the fleet, built at such expense to challenge the Royal Navy, had been scuttled in captivity, and new tonnage was equally restricted; the country was prohibited from building military aircraft, aircraft carriers or submarines; factories, dockyards and arsenals were subject to inspection by an allied control commission to ensure that the Germans were abiding by the treaty limits; huge war reparations were being argued over; and the Germans were being asked to acknowledge guilt for initiating the war. After the heady years of the Kaiserreich when Germans had been led to believe they were on the march towards world power, the shock and its manifestations are understandable. Those who had the highest responsibility for this state of affairs, the small Prussian ruling circle who had tipped the world into war in 1914 largely to preserve their own power position within the Reich, also perhaps because they had come to believe their own propaganda, fostered the paranoia by editing and falsifying the official record. Young men like Heinrich Himmler who needed an emotional focus for idealism were naturally prey to the feelings generated. Heinrich's comment on Friedrich Wichtl's poisonous tract, which Professor Bradley Smith believes may have been inserted at a later date since it is cramped into the space, ran: 'A book that explains all and tells us against whom, in the first instance, we have to fight.'[65]

Heinrich's reading on that afternoon, 26 December, was interrupted by the whole family going out to a Christmas celebration at a Catholic club. While listening to a priest giving a sermon, he found himself torn 'as never before' by an inner struggle over his belief. He had noted the beginning of doubts before leaving Munich. The question of duelling was the catalyst; he wanted desperately to prove himself, as he wanted to prove himself on the battlefield, yet duelling was against Church doctrine. On 15 December he had noted: 'I believe I am coming into collision with my religion. Come what may, I shall always love God, pray to Him and adhere to the Catholic Church and defend it, even if I should be expelled from it.'[66]

Now, on the day after Christmas, this conflict kept rising to the surface of his mind: 'In the evening I prayed. I had of course already practically subdued it [conflict]. God will help me further with all my doubts.'[67]

On 3 February 1920 the allies requested the surrender of 895 Germans for trial as 'war criminals'; the names ranged from the Kaiser and his military and civilian entourage, admirals and generals to U-boat commanders and junior officers. Although the service chiefs formed a united front, refusing to surrender themselves or their subordinates, the episode heated the potent brew of humiliation and belligerence supped in monarchist circles, and increased their scorn for the socialist government which had signed the peace. In the tense atmosphere, rumours of plots quickened across the country, including stories of an allied plot to kidnap those they wanted to stand trial. Heinrich, back in Munich with his ear close to the ground, warned his parents by letter of the imminence of a bloody struggle with the Bolsheviks.[68] The monarchists struck first: the coup was fronted by a Prussian official named Wolfgang Kapp, and was carried through by naval Freikorps with the tacit support of the naval High Command and the Army, who stood by as the paramilitary units marched on Berlin in the early hours of 13 March. The government fled.

The Kapp putsch was an emotional exercise, ill prepared and not thought through. The central government re-established itself in Stuttgart and called for a general strike. Already there had been repeats of the mutinies of 1918 in the naval ports; officers were arrested and several ships, taken over by their petty officers and crews, hoisted the red flag. Industrial workers throughout the country responded to the strike call and, as transport and factories stopped, communist groups seized their opportunity. Violence erupted. Kapp had no idea how to get the country back to work and on 17 March, four days after taking over, he resigned. Power passed back to the legitimate government, but such was the state of anarchy, especially in the Ruhr, that they felt compelled to call on the Army leadership to restore order. The Army, which had hoped to see the end of the Republic, now felt compelled to defend it against rampant Bolshevism, so a truce of stalemate was reached. The monarchists had discovered they could not count on the support of the people; the people, in the shape of the socialist government, had found once again that they needed the support of the monarchist armed forces. The naval Freikorps, which had turned them out of office a few days earlier, were soon marching into the Ruhr on their behalf.

Meanwhile in Munich a less spectacular coup had been entirely successful. The driving force had been the leader of the Einwohnerwehren or Residents' Defence Forces, volunteer loyalist groups in which students were strongly represented. The Army commander and the police president had lent their support and the elected Social Democratic government had been forced to resign; a rightist government was put in under Gustav von Kahr, who enjoyed the confidence of the loyalist paramilitary formations.

The 14th Alarm Company of the Protection Brigade was called out during the emergency and Gebhard and Heinrich, unquestionably in a state of high excitement, patrolled the streets in armoured cars. Heinrich wrote a short note to his parents, sending them 'his most loving greetings'; he explained he was forgoing his Easter vacation and staying in Munich because it was his 'absolutely sacred duty'.[69]

Shortly after this the allies, seeing auxiliary units like the Protection Brigade as a device to get around the numerical limitations imposed on the Army – as they were – forced their disbandment. Heinrich then joined the Einwohnerwehr. He was already a member of a war veterans' league, the Reichs Kriegsteilnahmer Verband, and he now joined another, thinly disguised as a rifle club, the Schutzengesellschaft Freiweg. In addition he spent much time with his fraternity at *Kneipen* and other social activities and training for his real initiation by duel. It is evident he had resolved his religious doubts in favour of his earnest desire to prove himself a sound fellow.

Despite leading a full social and loyalist–political life, he remained tormented by inner doubts and struggles. The most serious of these concerned his unsatisfied longing for the ideal girl, and for sex. He discussed women and sex with his companions, sometimes – as he recorded in his diary – in 'thoroughly dirty' (*recht dreckig*) fashion, and tried to glean what he could from books. Here he was ill served, on the one hand by the idealistic picture of women and marriage painted in many novels of the time, on the other hand by pious tracts urging chastity for men before marriage.

Since he had grown up without a sister or close girl friend and seemed unable to form relationships with girls, it is not surprising that his view of them remained romantic. He described it in a diary entry the following year: a woman was a trinity of 'dear child' who needed to be protected and if necessary punished by her man, 'faithful, understanding comrade' fighting life's battles alongside him, and 'goddess' of purity to be worshipped for her moral inspiration; she was also a dangerously carnal temptress.[70] These are precisely the categories Thewelweit discovered hidden in the imagination of Freikorps man. Where Heinrich Himmler differed from his less idealistic fellows was in transferring this vision to everyday; thus he imposed on himself sexual abstinence and continued the search for his ideal soul-mate for the east.

Another topic of conversation with his fellow students was the Jewish question. Since he read two books about it at this time it is possible to gain an idea of his attitude. The first, read in little over a week in mid-April 1920 – suggesting interest at least – was Arthur Dinter's *Die Sünde wider das Blut* (*The Sin Against the Blood*). This has been characterised as 'a distasteful mixture of pornography and pseudo-Theosophy'.[71] He commented that it was a 'terrifyingly plain' introduction to the Jewish question, disposing one to investigate the documents on which it was based. His immediate conclusions, however, were that the author was 'somewhat blindly enraged in his hatred of Jews', and the book was a 'tendentious novel with anti-semitic themes'.[72]

A little later he read a novel called *Ultimo* in which one of the leading figures was an unscrupulous Jewish banker; his comment was that it 'characterised the Jews very well'.[73] It can be stated with confidence, therefore, that in early summer 1920, nearing the end of his second decade, he was quite prepared to believe in the usual stereotype of the Jew, but equally prepared to disbelieve the more bizarre perversions attributed to the race. More interesting, perhaps, in view of his later convictions, he was prepared to try and evaluate the evidence. In short, he was not a fanatic. This critical faculty is evident in some of his comments on other books, for instance 'one-sidedly Catholic point of view' after reading a monograph on Goethe and Schiller,[74] 'too one-sidedly Christian' after reading a Spanish travel book.[75] Of course these may have been symptoms of his growing doubts about the Church.

By this time it can be seen that most of the ideas characterising his later view of the world were present in his mind – the stereotype of the Jew, the link between world Jewry and world masonry and their plans to subjugate the world, the necessity for a movement back to the soil whence the race derived its vigour, the beckoning spaces of eastern Europe where this could be accomplished, the *völkisch* myth of the purity of the race, the ideal of womanhood, the necessity for stern self-discipline, hatred of Bolshevism, fascination with the myths of Germanic history, loyalty to the Germanic peoples as a whole rather than his particular province; he was, for instance, disillusioned with the Bayerische Volkspartei for showing separatist tendencies. Since the Party was closely tied to the Catholic Church this helped to increase his religious doubts. Yet there was nothing immoderate either in the views – which were the normal stuff of the society around him – nor in his comments; he appears to have been a genuine seeker after truth. Even the black moods recorded in his diary are not unusual for young men of his age facing the demands of adulthood.

It is to a book he read in the last week of October that year that one should look for indications of something different in his make-up that could have caused a fundamental change and set those views in stone. The book was *Brand*, a verse drama by Ibsen intended for reading rather than acting. It made a profound impression on him at this time and he re-read it exactly a year later in an attempt to renew the inspiration he had derived from it. Evidently it spoke to something deep inside him.

The hero of the drama, Brand, was a priest of uncompromising character. Early in Act One we learn something of his boyhood from a former schoolfellow; he used to keep to himself and never played with the others. Brand replied that it was true:

> all of you down south seemed
> made of some other stuff than I,
> who was born by the water
> in the shadow of a barren precipice.[76]

Here, perhaps, was the first identification. In a diary entry in 1922 Himmler contrasted two types of people, 'the melancholic, stern, among which I include myself', and the easy-going, hot-blooded sort who followed their desires without too much thought or sense of responsibility;[77] Austrians and Rhinelanders – 'southerners' – fell into the second group.

However that may be, there can be no doubt that Heinrich identified with the adult Brand, the priest. Brand's message was that of Kierkegaard, the prophet of existentialism: the revolt against rationality and moderation. Like Nietzsche, Brand despised the merciful and loving God of his generation. Humanity and love were words used to cover weakness and cowardice. He preached the Old Testament God, whose love was not weak or mild, but 'hard even unto the terror of death'. He demanded the leap of faith and the will to follow wherever it led without compromise.

> When the will has won in strife like this
> then comes the time for love. . . .
> But here, in a slack and slothful age,
> the best love is hate! (*in horror*)
> Hate! Hate![78]

He declared war on everything the rational and well-meaning stood for; it was by will alone that man could transform himself. From his followers he demanded life without compromise, 'all or nothing'. Having preached this message to his flock Brand is forced through the course of the play to follow it himself, thereby losing first his beloved son, then his loving and dutiful wife and at the end all his followers when finally he makes it clear that their way to Canaan can only be through the desert of sacrifice, and they must die to conquer.[79]

It is not clear how much Himmler knew of Kierkegaard and his concepts of the 'Absolute paradox', the necessity for a leap beyond rationality or of contact with the Almighty through *Angst* – fear and dread – all of which resound throughout the play. Probably he knew little or nothing; pure philosophy does not figure in his reading list. But how much he knew or understood is largely irrelevant. The play plumbs the depths of pessimism; he responded. That surely is the point.

He wrote in his booklist: 'It is in relation to morality and the training of the will one of the best and most perfect dramas I know. It is the *book of the will* and morality and life without compromise.'[80]

The importance of this comment lies not so much in showing that he tried to make these ideals his own – although he did – as in the revelation that Brand's cold view of the meaning of life and his call for total self-abnegation keyed in with his own psyche. A young man of twenty brought up in materially most comfortable circumstances and on the threshold of his career, he responded to the ultimate pessimism of the play. He desired self-mortification and sacrifice to an all-consuming God of wrath.

He re-read the play in November 1921 and noted, 'I will make his [Brand's] uncompromising directness [*Geradheit*] my pattern.'[81]

To suggest from this that Himmler modelled his life on the philosophy of Kierkegaard as revealed by Ibsen through *Brand* would be as misleading as to suggest that Hitler derived his *Weltanschauung* from Schopenhauer and Nietzsche or that Robespierre followed the doctrines of the 'Physiocrats', or Torquemada the holy writ. These things may in part be true; more significantly, these men took from contemporary thinking what they needed to satisfy their subconscious drives. It can be demonstrated in Himmler's case from his numerous diary entries recording inner struggle, despair and determination to exercise iron self-control and sexual abstinence long before he read *Brand*. That merely served to reinforce him in the path his psyche had to take him.

His circumstances at the time he made the comment give added point to this. He had begun his deferred practical year on a farm far removed from the *Angst* of student life in Munich. The farm was at Fridolfing in rolling countryside adjacent to the Austrian border just south of Tittmoning. He had gone there in September, and could not have found more congenial conditions. He liked the farmer, Herr Rehrl, to whom he had been introduced by Frau Loritz; he found him kind and extremely well informed and was able to talk to him man to man about everything from farming to the state of the world and of course Germany. He went walking, shooting and fishing with him, joined the group in which he sang and also a local history group; he took his meals, which he described as 'excellent and abundant', with him and his wife, and was treated just as a member of the family, accompanying them to the social events of the country calendar. They were careful not to tire him because of his weak heart. Frau Rehrl did his washing, a maid cleaned his room. He could not have found a pleasanter way of learning the practicalities of his intended career, and to judge by his letters home was very fit. Yet he remained internally tormented, hence Brand's message pierced him. There are clear indications that in relationships with family and friends he was acting on Brand's pattern: he hurt his elder brother deeply by criticising him for being too easy-going, careless and ready to adjust himself to circumstances. That he himself was not prepared to compromise with the age is made clear by a letter from Ludwig Zahler, whom he saw while visiting Munich that November. 'Dear pessimist [*Schwarzseher*],' Zahler began, 'you urgently

need some cheering up; being alone so much is turning you bitter, I fear.'
Evidently the bitterness was directed at the condition of Germany and
people's present attitudes, for Zahler went on:

> you must know that in the darkest hour a great light penetrates the gloom –
> love and friendship shining the brighter the worse things are. I urge you to look
> towards the light always and do not accept the difficulties and the darkness. I
> am sure it would make things easier for you. In this world there are no ideal
> states, so why seek them?
>
>   The Fatherland has been going to wrack and ruin since 1914, and indeed
> the sooner it comes the sooner it will be over – sad, crying out to heaven, but
> it cannot be altered. The future will tell us what we have to do; more than ever
> we live for the moment and no amount of looking back or forward offers any
> explanation or guide, only a wall of impenetrable darkness. To act at the right
> moment, to recognise the opportunity, that is the spirit of the times. . . . [82]

Unfortunately, he went on, for many this merely meant taking advantage
of others. Everyone in the great city was buying presents and filling their
stomachs without thought for the great things of life.

Zahler himself had become engaged to Kaethe Loritz. Heinrich saw
her while he was in Munich and they had a bitter argument; what it was
about is not clear, but after returning to the farm he tried to make it up
in writing, and sent her a book as a gift. She was moved, and replied that
everything had been made good by his letter, which revealed the depth of
his goodness and insight; she would treasure it for ever. She went on, in
much the tone her fiancé had used, urging him not to set himself too high
a standard:

> Look, Heini, when you sometimes follow your emotions, you feel that you
> are giving in and are weak. Do not forget that these silent hours bring strength,
> more power perhaps than anything else can give you. I am well aware that there
> are limits here, naturally it must not lead to eternal day-dreaming, yet there is
> no danger of that with you. Therefore, Heini, don't pull too hard on the reins,
> so that you do not lose thereby the finest things life has to bestow.

She signed herself 'your little sister'.[83]

He had plenty of time to himself that winter and, besides working for
the exams he would face when he returned to Munich, he did a great deal
of general reading, copying out passages which appealed to him. Professor
Bradley Smith has noted that 'examples of unsung heroes unappreciated by
their peers show up frequently' among these, as do caustic references to
'the ignorance and stupidity of the rabble'.[84] However, Heinrich also made
a collection of local songs and proverbs, and noted peasant customs. In the
early summer of 1921, he started on a correspondence course to improve
his memory and brain power.

*

His farm year ended in August 1921. After a short additional practical in a farm machinery company in Ingolstadt, he returned to Munich in November to complete the final year of his course.

There he fell into his old round of activities immediately, practising fencing for the duel he hoped for, attending fraternity *Kneipen* and dances, renewing acquaintance with paramilitary or school fellows, making social calls on family friends and relatives and his old nurse, Thilde, whose cooking he loved; on his first visit she plied him with 'dumpling soup, filet of veal, potato salad and noodles with beer, and then apple pie, then coffee and cake', and afterwards gave him more cake, 'goodies' and an apple to take home. 'I was up to my old form of talking a great deal about everything,' he recorded.[85]

He appeared very conscious of his incontinent tongue throughout this term.

13 November 1921: I told a lot of jokes, talked much and jeered a lot. Oh why can't I stop it!
18 November 1921: It will be a long time before I have the distinguished sureness of manner I desire. When will I lose the habit of talking a lot?
1 December 1921: I'm a wretched prattler, can never hold my tongue, inconsiderate and immature, when will I take myself thoroughly in hand?[86]

He was dissatisfied, too, about his constancy of purpose, particularly in the efforts he was making to improve his mind. On 7 December he noted that he must start a daily regime of work and training for he was 'still lacking so frightfully much'. He was unable to keep to it, not surprising in view of his multifarious social and fraternity activities. At the end of the following month he was in deeper despair.

What kind of a wretched creature man surely is. I am a phrasifier and loudmouth [*Spruchmacher und Schwätzer*] without energy, succeeding in nothing. . . . They [Gebhard and his friends] think of me as a gay fellow who is amusing and takes care of everything. Heini will see to it all right.[87]

Here is another aspect of his character which shows through very clearly in his later life: his compulsion to take part, to be in the know and to be responsible, to manage and fix things, to politick and intrigue and ingratiate himself by doing favours and passing on information. This was his way of being someone. He found opportunity in fraternity affairs, passing on gossip, organising factions in the frequent rivalries and quarrels, officiating at duels, helping drunken members home, visiting others in hospital. He was also active in the affairs of the student organisation, Allgemeiner Studenten Ausschuss or ASTA. Analysing his diary entries, Peter Loewenberg suggests that during this year probably the most frequent was 'Akten studiert', meaning that he was working on the ASTA files.[88] Although the Einwohnerwehr had been disbanded now, due to pressure from the central government in

Berlin, he kept in touch with loyalist activities through the officers' association of his regiment and the veterans' Rifle Club, Freiweg. There is an intriguing diary entry for 5 July 1922 in which he records that he approached the head of the Freiweg to volunteer for 'special missions', another for 26 January in which he describes meeting Captain Röhm at a club gathering in a Munich beer cellar. Röhm was 'pessimistic about Bolshevism'. The way in which the entry is written suggests that Heinrich might already have been acquainted with him.[89]

As in his earlier student year, his intense activity and the knowing, talkative front he showed the world concealed deep insecurity. Hard as he tried at the fraternity, he failed to gain a nomination in the election for officers that February and suspected people of talking behind his back.[90] Hard as he tried to master Russian, and now Spanish – in case he might have to emigrate to South America to farm – he lacked consistency, and frittered his time away in idle gossip; yearn as he did to find his ideal life partner, his relationships with girls remained wooden.

This was demonstrated in February at Fasching, the carnival period when Munich let its hair down and aspired to its title of Paris on the Isar. He dressed up as Abdul Hamid for a fancy-dress party at the Loritzes, and with Lu Zahler, costumed as Ben Akiba, performed a sketch, 'Oriental Life', which, he recorded, went down very well. Later they did a snake-charming act, and then told fortunes. After the party he walked home with Lu, discussing the temptations a man was subject to at such times. As he recorded it in his diary:

> We discussed the danger of such things. I have experienced it, one lay so closely together, by couples, body to body, hot human being by human being, one catches on fire and has to summon all one's rational faculties. The girls are then so far gone they no longer know what they are doing. It is the hot, unconscious longing of the whole individual for the satisfaction of a frightfully powerful natural drive. That is why it is also so dangerous for the man and involves such responsibility. One could do as one wants with the helpless girls, yet one has enough to do to struggle with oneself. I am indeed sorry for the girls.[91]

What appears striking in this entry is not just the 'projection' of his own feelings on to the 'helpless girls', but the impersonal generalisations in which he is thinking; this of course would be the keynote of his years in power.

At an earlier dance, he did enter an account of an individual, his dancing partner Fräulein von Bück, who was a stranger to him: 'a nice girl with very sensible opinions, very patriotic, no bluestocking and apparently rather profound'.[92] Looked at closely even this appears impersonal. He seems chiefly concerned with her opinions; they were evidently as strongly loyalist as his own, she was therefore 'nice' and 'no bluestocking'. 'Rather profound' was a stock expression he often applied to girls. Afterwards he accompanied her home. 'She did not take my arm which, in a way, I appreciated. Rather tired and in a nasty mood home. A few exercises, to bed.'[93]

One of the longest descriptions of a girl in his diary came that summer. He and a companion went to the Reichsadler, a classy bar with a large Jewish clientele. A dancer his companion knew, named Inge Barco, came up to them. He noted afterwards:

> She is a quiet girl, simple, not vain or toffee-nosed [*hochnäsig*], places some value on good manners. No one would know she was a dancer. She is Viennese, but a Jewess, has however absolutely nothing of the Jew in her manner, at least so far as one can judge. At first I made several remarks about Jews, I ruled her out as one. However, she does have the Austrian way of talking and behaving, joking harmlessly and good-naturedly without ever being offensive. She is no longer innocent as she freely admits. But she has given her body only from love. She is madly in love with a student, Kurt Wetterstein, and is absolutely loyal to him. Things are bad for her at home, but she sends money nevertheless. In a word, a girl who deserves admiration, notwithstanding the conceits of bourgeois opinion.[94]

Perhaps this account, so different from his usual stock descriptive phrases, belies the impression of impersonality. Evidently she made an individual impact on him. Yet the description is clinical in its categories: she was a dancer yet had an idea of manners and was not vain, a Jewess yet did not show any signs of Jewishness, an Austrian and, yes, she behaved as Austrians are supposed to behave. Finally he admired her for her loyalty to her parents and to her lover. Was she a real person, or an abstraction – a specimen for his files on which he could pass judgement? One is straining through opaque layers of time; one cannot be certain what feelings prompted him to write this or omit that or what his companion may have said to him about her. The only certainties are that he wrote this description of a Jewess in July 1922 and twenty years later was responsible for the murders of countless categories like her. Was the dancer Inge Barco a generalisation like the 'helpless girls' at Fasching parties for whom he felt such pity?

There is no doubt that the thought of her giving her body titillated him. Whether girls were innocent or could be 'had' was a theme of his diary entries, as were discussions about sex. A few weeks previously he had told a doctor's wife he met that he had never courted a girl. She had teased him, giving rise to his thoughts on the two types of men already noted in relation to *Brand*: 'the melancholic, stern, among which I include myself', and the gay, easy-going type 'who kiss and copulate without thought merely because it is human and fun'.[95]

The combination of Jewishness and sex would have given him an added frisson, for the subject of Jews was one that cropped up with some frequency in his discussions, if not with the same regularity as sex. Recently he had read another of the poisonous tracts emanating from one of the anti-semitic publishing houses called *Judas Schuldbuch* (*Judas Guiltbook*), a compilation of the usual accusations with the usual sexual innuendoes and concern for the dangers of mixed breeding. The message had been reinforced by Houston Stewart Chamberlain's pamphlet *Rasse und Nation* (*Race and Nation*), which he had read afterwards and on which he commented: 'A truth, of which one is convinced: it is objective and not hate-filled anti-semitism. Therefore it is all the more effective. This atrocious Jewry.'[96] The Englishman Chamberlain enjoyed tremendous vogue in Germany, because the message of all his writings was that for 1500 years the Germanic race had been the unique creative force of European civilisation.

'How stupid we pure Aryans are,' Himmler noted in his diary after a late-night walk with Ludwig Zahler, who had read *Judas Schuldbuch* the previous year and discussed it with him then; and cryptically he added, 'and thank God that we are so stupid.'[97] His diary description of meeting the dancer Inge Barco is preceded by an account of a demonstration of democratic students and the Republican Reichsbund against the 'black–white–red' – thus nationalist – terror at the Munich universities; he did not go to the meeting himself, but described one of the student organisers as a *Judenlaus*, Jewish louse. And it is significant that his first remarks to the dancer concerned Jews.

There is, of course, nothing unusual or abnormal in the fact that he showed concern about sex – particularly as he had chosen the path of abstinence – nothing unusual in his view of the Jews and the danger they constituted to pure-blooded Germans. Indeed, given his youth and inexperience and the company he kept and the evil mood of the nationalists and officers, to whose ranks he still aspired, it would have been scarcely conceivable for him to have had any other views.

They were the old pan-German, biological–racist views grown more extreme in the forcing-house of Bavarian politics. The traditions of separatism, Catholicism and loyalty to the Wittelsbach monarchy had always led Bavarians to distrust Berlin. Now, humiliated by defeat and disgusted with the Republican central government, large sections of the Bavarian monarchists and people were pulling away from central control more strongly than ever. The leader of the Bayerische Volkspartei, convinced that Prussia and central Germany must eventually fall to Bolshevism, had plans for the creation of a Catholic bloc of the southern states and union with Austria. In consequence Bavaria had become a haven for enemies of the Republic, members of the extreme nationalist Freikorps prominent among them. Since these men believed in the greater Germanic Reich, there was a fundamental split between them and the Bavarian loyalists. Nevertheless they preserved unity against the threat from Bolshevism. Thus the Nazi Party, conceived by the extreme pan-German Thule Society and nursed jointly by the Bavarian Army district staff officer Ernst Röhm and the Munich Police President Ernst Poehner to be the popular expression of pan-Germanism and physical hammer of the left, was prepared to work with the old guard of Bavarian separatists against the 'swine- and government-Jews' in Berlin;[98] the Bavarian government was prepared to accommodate it and shelter the nationalist terror squads. Meanwhile Marxist bands from the industrial quarters of the city were as physical as the ex-Freikorps men Röhm had injected into the Nazi Party, and quite as determined that the future lay with international communism.

Anti-semitism rose from this social ferment as it had from similar conditions in the past. In this case the process can be closely observed. It was fuelled by inflation, which had been growing steadily since the end of the war, probably as much a result of government and industrial resistance to the allied demands for reparations as of the financial deficits of the war years. In the past year the Mark had fallen from 75 to over 400 to the dollar, and the rate was increasing. While industrialists and financiers were able to take advantage, discounting huge bills at the Reichsbank and repaying them in depreciated currency, small men were ruined and the savings of the middle classes wiped out.

So countless individual failures and resentments were added to the national feeling of humiliation. Extremist writers and orators played on this, raising as a scapegoat the old bogey of the Bavarian *völkisch* and south German and Austrian nationalist movements – the Jew. The most successful of the orators was, of course, Adolf Hitler, the man whom Röhm had chosen and befriended and helped to the leadership of the Nazi Party. It is through Hitler that the process can be followed minutely. For Hitler's power came from his ability to sense the fears and hopes of his audiences and give them back in heightened form. This talent has been described by nearly all who have written of him from personal experience. Otto Strasser, for instance, believed that Hitler had the powers of a medium.[99]

Himmler had not yet met Hitler, but he moved in the circles that backed him. Moreover he had experienced so many defeats to his psyche in his own life. He was also affected by the inflation, particularly in his relations with his family. His father, as a salaried man with savings, was hard hit, the more so as he had three boys going through school or higher education. Heinrich was constantly asking him for money, and Professor Himmler was constantly seeking to control Heinrich's expenditure and to ensure that he worked rather than spent his time on student fraternity affairs or socialising. The two also disagreed politically since Heinrich did not approve of the separatist trend of the Bayerische Volkspartei, which his father supported. They quarrelled bitterly.

It seems that this unhappiness and uncertainty made Heinrich vulnerable to the anti-semitic myths, for by the summer of 1922 he had succumbed. Two years earlier, he had described *Die Sünde wider das Blut* as 'tendentious', its author blinded by his hatred of Jews, and he had felt inclined to investigate the sources. The sources were provided in *Judas Schuldbuch* and he was satisfied they were a 'marvellous collection'. Chamberlain's

pamphlet had moved him to execrate 'This atrocious Jewry'. He was able
to admire the Jewish dancer's qualities of loyalty yet when in June a terror
squad murdered the Jewish Foreign Minister, Walther Rathenau, he noted
in his diary that he was glad for he was convinced that, 'whatever he did,
he did not do for Germany.'[100] Evidently he thought Rathenau had been
working for the international Jewish–Marxist conspiracy. Discussing the
murder at his lodgings two days later, he found his views in a minority:
'O blind people,' he pronounced.[101] He had some inside knowledge of
the affair for when some of the perpetrators were captured a few days
later, he noted, 'Organisation "C". Dreadful if everything should become
known.'[102]

The following week he approached the chief of the Freiweg to
volunteer for special missions; whether this had anything to do with the
Rathenau affair, whether he wanted to join one of the murder groups like
'C' (Consul), is not revealed, but from his frequently expressed longing to
serve and hazard his life it would have been in character. In any case there
is no doubt that he had been radicalised and politicised. He even seems to
have been rethinking his future, for that May he applied for admission to
the political science course at the university. He was granted an exemption
from fees, but Professor Himmler felt unable to support him, so much was
the inflation biting.

One of his few satisfactions that summer was securing at last the duel
he had been trying to arrange for months. An Englishman, John Heygate,
witnessed a student duel at Heidelberg at about this date. 'Heaven forbid,
I couldn't do it!' he thought as he watched the breast-padded figures with
wire face-masks hitting at each other in prescribed bouts to the shouts of
the umpire. 'I shouldn't be strong enough in the arm! Or brave enough.
Or such a fool.'[103] The duellists stood their ground on a floor, spread with
sawdust which became spotted with blood, and hit and suffered hits with
the long, slender duelling sabres, without flinching or moving a foot.

> The doctor staunched and examined the gashes. And then with the blood
> already beginning to trickle down into the poor young man's eyes again, he
> had to go on. . . . You could *hear* him being hit. And every time he was hit
> – a few seconds afterwards, and the inevitable line of pin-points forming into
> a continuous gash on cheek or forehead. It was the most cold-blooded thing I
> ever saw.[104]

In his duel Himmler felt he performed well; he noted afterwards in his
diary: 'I certainly did not get agitated. Stood very well and fought technically beautifully. My opponent was Herr Renner, Alemanians [fraternity],
he struck honest blows.'[105]

Himmler was disabled in the thirteenth of fifty scheduled bouts. Then
came the stern test when the duellists were led away by their seconds to
be stitched up. Heygate described a military doctor at Heidelberg passing

a heavy needle to and fro as if stitching canvas while the student maintained perfect composure without a blink or a twitch, let alone a sound to betray pain.

Himmler had taken five cuts, for which he received five stitches and a ligature: 'I really did not flinch once,' he noted. 'Distl held my head in old comradeship.' The head was buzzing as he returned to his room and after talking over the duel with his brother Gebhard and Ludwig Zahler, who came for tea, he went to bed early; 'did not sleep especially well because the dressing was always pulling.'[106] It was a small price to pay. He had proved himself.

That summer he passed his exams and left the Technical High School with a diploma in agriculture. In August an offer of a job reached him via one of his former masters at the Munich *Gymnasium*, as assistant in an agricultural fertiliser company, Stickstoff-Land GmbH of Schleissheim, a Munich suburb. It was far from the farm management post he wanted, but in the difficult conditions of the time it offered a chance of supporting himself and not having to rely on his father and account to him for every penny – at least it seems reasonable to conclude these were the considerations that prompted him to accept. He started a fortnight later at the beginning of September.

3

Revolutionary

Little is known of Himmler's time with Stickstoff-Land. From a letter he wrote nineteen years later it seems that he was employed as a technical *Assistent* concerned with the preparation of reports showing that farmers could increase their yield by using large quantities of the company's fertiliser.[1] Although there can be little doubt that he worked conscientiously, for that was his nature and it is proved by his record, it is certain that nitrogen-calcium fertilisers claimed less of his real interest than nationalist politics. The country was heading for internal chaos. Inflation dominated. The rate mounted by the week, swathing hardship, misery, ruin, even suicide through wider sections of the middle classes. His father had been appointed *Rektor* of the Wittelsbach Gymnasium, Munich, a position of high status and salary, yet his mother worried about such a basic foodstuff as flour, and told Heinrich in one letter in November 1922 on no account to buy more than half a kilo; they did not have the money.[2]

Early in the new year, 1923, the campaign of resistance to reparations led to French and Belgian troops occupying the Ruhr. Berlin responded by ordering 'passive resistance', paying for the thousands put out of work in the resulting strikes, shut-downs and sabotage in this prime industrial region by printing money. The rate of inflation took off. In six months the Mark, which had been quoted at 9 to the US dollar at the end of the war, fell from 18,000 to over 350,000 to the dollar. It continued falling by the day, by the hour until it was worth less than the paper used to print it; piles of notes were weighed and measured for height rather than counted; in November a glass of beer cost one billion Marks. Long before then barter had largely replaced the money economy in the countryside while town dwellers suffered hunger, even starvation.

A few financiers, large businesses and smart operators profited; the only others to do so were radical politicians, mob orators and paramilitary leaders of both left and right; the ranks of their followers were swollen by thousands of normally apolitical people, embittered by personal ruin and the general feeling of breakdown and hopelessness. The Nazi Party, whose growth had been modest until then, began to count its members and sympathisers in tens of thousands; its paramilitary arm, the Sturmabteilung or SA, numbered some 10,000.[3] Other nationalist formations grew at the same pace. In the industrial areas communist-inspired strikes and street violence increased.

Himmler was one of many who did not limit their paramilitary activities to a single unit. He joined several, but attached himself in particular to Captain Ernst Röhm in the Reichsflagge, and when this organisation split, he followed Röhm into the Reichskriegsflagge. Röhm was, of course, one of the key figures in the nationalist movement. He was channelling secret Army funds via two ostensibly private companies into the groups he supported, which included the Nazi Party and its fighting arm, the SA, now led by the first-war air ace, Hermann Göring. In August 1923 Himmler joined the Nazi Party; his membership number was 42,404.[4]

This did not go down well with his father. Hitler was a demagogue of still seedy appearance – despite having an entrée into polite society through Göring and a few wealthy supporters. His speeches were cries of hate, focusing the resentments of his chiefly *kleinen Leute*, lower-middle-class supporters against the 'November criminals', those 'traitors to their state' who had signed the ignominious peace treaty 'and should be hanged for it', and against 'the Jew who is ruining our country'.[5] The SA street-fighters were rowdy tavern brawlers. Above all, there was the old divergence between the Bavarian People's Party, which Professor Himmler supported, still pulling away from Berlin and the Reich, and the pan-German nationalism Heinrich had always espoused, which Röhm, Hitler and the Nazis represented in extreme form.

Heinrich's commitment to extreme politics was fully matched, as ever, by his puritanical personal code; they were two sides of the same psychic drive. This was demonstrated that spring. The previous year his brother Gebhard had become engaged to a cousin of theirs called Paula Stölzle from Weilheim, some twenty-five miles south-west of Munich. Considering Professor Himmler's correct attitudes, it had been a surprisingly unconventional engagement; Gebhard had not asked Paula's father; he had simply written to announce the betrothal as an accomplished fact, enclosing an enthusiastic note from his own parents. Now, however, he suspected Paula of unfaithfulness with a teacher called Rieger and he asked Heinrich to see her and sort matters out, on the face of it an extraordinary request to a third party, but an indication of the trust and respect in which he held his younger brother, confirming Heinrich's earlier, despondent diary entry, 'They think of me as a gay fellow who is amusing and takes care of everything. Heini will see to it. . . .'[6]

He took up the task earnestly; it is reasonable to conclude that he enjoyed it for from this time on he appears to have taken the decisions in the engagement. He went to see Paula, extracted a pledge of future fidelity from her and confirmed it in writing; the draft survives, revealing truly extraordinary pomposity together with extreme pessimism about the future.

'I assume you have long expected this my letter and have feared it,' the draft begins, 'above all because such a difficult affair . . . is not to be settled without something new, good will, tears and kisses.' He would like to believe, he went on, that she accepted this, yet that was not sufficient. A man had to have certainty from his bride that even if he were absent for years and she did not see him or even hear anything from him for a long time – 'which in the coming imminent war years can only too easily be the case' – she would not be untrue to him with a single word or glance, kiss, touch or thought: 'and the more lively [*lebhaften*], frivolously [*leichtsinniger*], ardently [*feuriger*] the inclination, the more controlled [*gebundigter*], severe [*strenger*] and iron [*eisener*] must the good in this woman suppress the bad'.[7]

Surely there could be no more psychologically revealing statement: the adjectives hammer home the message; the 'southern' part – the feminine side within himself perhaps – the natural carnal desires, the bad, must be subdued by the 'northern' – the Prussian male armour.

'You had a test which you could have and *had to* withstand,' he went on, but 'disgracefully' did not withstand. Her fiancé had also withstood the test poorly, but in another way because he was too good and had too little knowledge of people and women. He meant presumably that Gebhard had been too trusting during their separation.

> If your union is to be a fortunate one for you both and the health of *das Volk*, which must be built on healthy, moral families, you must curb yourself with barbaric severity. Because you are not strict and hard enough with yourself and only control yourself to a small degree, and your future husband, as I have already said, is too good for you and possesses too little knowledge of people and will not learn it because it cannot be learned in this age, someone else has to do it. Because you both turned to me and drew me in to this affair, I feel bound to do it myself.

Whether or not the precise wording was sent to Paula is not important; as a draft it shows the young Himmler's naked feelings unmodified by subsequent gloss. It gives a startling insight; for here, fully formed, is the self-righteous voice of the later Reichsführer-SS. It is also of course the voice of Brand demanding life without compromise, 'all or nothing' from 'this blind, stumbling generation'.

He must have sent a letter very like this for Gebhard admitted to Paula that his brother had gone too far. For her part, she took some ten weeks to answer the letter, then wrote expressing her gratitude for being led back to reconciliation with her 'beloved Gebhard' by Heinrich's words. This seems like irony, yet by the end of her letter she appears to have worked herself into a feeling of real appreciation and she concluded by saying she would be grateful for the rest of her days for his harsh words, which had restored her to her senses. 'With heartfelt greetings, and thanking you once more, Yours, Paula.'[8] But perhaps this was also ironic, perhaps dictated by a desire to keep on the right side of Heinrich for the sake of her engagement to Gebhard.

It was far from being the end of the affair. Early the next year, 1924,

Heinrich found out or believed he had found out that she had broken her pledge to him while staying in Munich. Without informing Gebhard, he began working on his parents to have the engagement ended; family honour demanded it. When he had convinced them, he put it to Gebhard, who also allowed himself to be convinced. It seems that Paula probably heard Heinrich's arguments through the wall of an adjacent room while staying with them. At any rate she was fully prepared when Gebhard wrote to her. She replied that the engagement had to be broken off, but 'not because of anyone else'. She went on:

> The unexampled coldness with which you reproached me was the outcome of all that I had experienced with you, and the last blow to my firm resolve was the long discussion which you and Heinrich had at night, which I had to listen to without wanting to, from the adjoining room. There was a good reason for me saying not a word to you about my intentions – I wanted to talk with my parents first.
>
> I must say to you openly, dear Gebhard, that my earlier great respect and esteem for your character has unfortunately suffered severe damage, which I shall never be able to get over. By your completely helpless attitude to me more than once and the way you put up with Heinrich's tutelage and suffered him to come between us. Moreover it was incomprehensible to me and often bitterly wounded my feelings how, for instance, your two-years-younger brother imagined he had to educate me on your behalf according to his experience of life and his best methods. You will recall that you yourself could not find his letter to me wholly proper.[9]

She went on to refuse to accept the word 'relationship' in the case of Rieger. In any case she had considered that matter closed after Gebhard had forgiven her, and she rejected 'insinuations' that she had been unfaithful while staying in Munich recently. Finally she asked that they might part without resentment: 'I will my life long hold you in fond memory.'

Paula's father sent Gebhard a dignified and most civilised letter. Had he, Max Stölzle, known Gebhard as well when the two became engaged as he did now, he would have refused to accede to it: he would have said, 'Give yourselves time! . . . First become acquainted!' He went on to reprove Gebhard for making insinuations; if he knew any facts about Paula's unfaithfulness he should come out with them; otherwise he should refrain from besmirching a girl's name.[10]

This exchange of letters was accompanied by the return of betrothal presents, but it did not end the affair, at least in Heinrich's eyes. He viewed Paula's father as 'very sly and nimble', and suspecting that he and Paula were spreading nasty stories about the Himmlers, engaged a private detective to report on Paula and her family so that, should it become necessary, he would have ammunition to protect the Himmler reputation. His attitude can only be described as obsessive. It is shown clearly in an extraordinary letter he wrote to a mutual friend, Hugo Höfl, that May.

Hugo and Friedl Höfl had asked Gebhard to look out for a car for them in the Munich car dealers' showrooms. Gebhard was doing so after work each evening, when Friedl sent a postcard to Frau Himmler saying they were desperate for a car and asking why none of her sons could stir themselves. She mentioned that Paula was staying with them. Heinrich at once jumped to the conclusion that Paula had been agitating against him and Gebhard; he could think of no other explanation for the accusatory tone of the card. Once again, he had no business in the affair since on his own admission he understood nothing about cars. He plunged in nonetheless, writing a long and pedantic letter to Hugo – 'since there is no sense in replying factually to a furious and subjective woman' – itemising under points one, two, three the dates of each letter from the Höfls requesting a car and Gebhard's efforts to find one for them in the short time between leaving work in the evening and the showrooms closing. Having established that his brother could not have done more than he had, he came to the real point at issue, Paula's incitement of Friedl against the Himmlers – of which, of course, he had not a shred of proof.

The style of the card of 20.5.24 to my mother, which we received in the morning of 22.5.24, is decidedly insulting and therefore rather uncalled-for. Even the beginning 'In my necessity' I find at least extremely inappropriate. To speak of a *necessity* today because one has received no answer in the matter of a car is at the least exaggerated. Apparently Friedl does not know what necessity means!

Then to write, 'if none of your sons can stir themselves'. I hope that you and Friedl are convinced that I am, not from conventional grounds – which I do not recognise – but from inner conviction thankful to you for your affectionate hospitality and for the friendliness which you have shown me formerly. I also believe you remember that I said to you you could count on me at any time even if it should come to a *real* emergency. I believe I can also say that I have always attended to even small wishes of yours as if for myself.

If, therefore, Friedl distrusted Gebhard, despite it being entirely unjustified, she could certainly have turned to me in the knowledge that I do not allow matters to hang fire.

The card, however, I could not understand, despite everything, except as a sad confirmation of what I had already foreseen on my first visit to you, and as I said several times to Friedl, 'Look, if Paula comes, do not stir things up!' Paula has come, and Friedl has to all appearance promptly started stirring. And now be so good as to give Paula Stölzle the following message:

1) She should be very careful about making mischief against any one of us even in the softest, most insidious way while she is with you or anywhere else. I am a totally good-natured person and treat everyone in a handsome way; I can however become altogether different if anyone forces me to it, and will then not stop on grounds of false compassion until the adversary concerned has been socially and morally deleted from the ranks of society. If she has stirred things up – and *I* certainly assume that even if she denies it – I warn her for the first time.[11]

Under '2)' he gave a further warning that if she incited people against the Himmlers again she would not be able to prevent being publicly branded herself. 'And now,' he finished, 'the matter has been elucidated and I hope concluded all round.' He had written thus, he said, because he was always for 'openness'.

Apart once again from the incredible pomposity, it is interesting that he declined to recognise 'conventional grounds' for expressing thanks for the Höfls' hospitality and in the same spirit rejected 'false compassion'. The whole diatribe is put into stark relief by two ironic lines Gebhard added at the end of his own letter to Hugo Höfl listing cars he had examined: 'Friedl seems from her card today to have become somewhat "auto-infatuated", a disease against which cold compresses and showers are much to be recommended.'[12]

Gebhard seems to have been a normal, extremely good-natured young man; his comments on each of the cars he had inspected for the Höfls – Rovers, Opel sports, a Koco-Kleinauto and others – indicate the care he had taken on their behalf. But again he appears to have been weak in allowing himself to be dominated by his younger brother's moralising attitudes. As for Heinrich Himmler, the whole affair from beginning to end demonstrates that, whatever the rights and wrongs on either side, he already possessed all those qualities of priggish self-assurance and vindictiveness which formed the cornerstones of his later career. He had no need to change; he had only to wait for his niche in life to catch up with him. Of course, he had no idea of this.

He was unemployed at the time. Why he left Stickstoff-Land is not clear; his first biographer, Frischauer, stated that the deteriorating economic situation forced Stickstoff to lay people off and Himmler, presumably because he was one of the last in, was one of the first out. Professor Bradley Smith, on the other hand, suggests that Himmler himself made the decision to leave because he had once again sensed a possibility of a military career. That had been in September the previous year, 1923, twelve months after he had started with the firm.

Political extremism had brought the country to the verge of civil war; in particular a communist take-over had threatened Bavaria's northern neighbour, Thuringia. While Bavarian Army detachments were moved up towards the Thuringian border, volunteer replacement units had been formed from right-wing paramilitary groups and Himmler had applied to join one of these, Kompanie Werner of the 1st Battalion 19th Infantry; he had been accepted on 15 September – this tends to support Bradley Smith's interpretation that he left Stickstoff voluntarily.

Meanwhile the Berlin government, threatened with revolutions in the Ruhr, the Rhineland, Saxony, Thuringia and Hamburg, and with potential nationalist and separatist revolts in Bavaria, had been attempting a cure at the seat of infection by negotiating with the former allied powers to lift the occupation of the Ruhr; in the event they were forced to climb down. On 25 September the end of 'passive resistance' was announced, and two days later Germany resumed shipments of reparation goods. For the nationalist leaders in Bavaria this was another demonstration of cowardice and treachery by the Republic. Hitler was able to brand the settlement as capitulation to the enemies of Germany. He had been appointed leader of a Kampfbund, or Fighting Association, formed from the Bavarian pan-German and nationalist paramilitary groups. These were all either Thule Society offshoots like the Freikorps Oberland, the Nazi Party, its SA formations and the Wiking Bund – which was funded and armed in secret by the Navy – or like Reichsflagge led by a Thule Society member, Ernst Röhm, who was of course siphoning off Army funds and small arms for the cause.

Following Hitler's appointment as political chief of the Kampfbund, Röhm had resigned his Army commission. Hitler was agitating for the overthrow of the Republican government, and Röhm had had practical experience earlier in the year that the Army High Command in Berlin, while supporting the general aims of the nationalists, had no more intention of allowing a putsch from the right than one from the left. The Commander-in-Chief, von Seeckt, knew that either would lead to the disintegration of the country in civil war. Röhm, however, felt a critical situation had been reached and was prepared to stake everything on Hitler. If Himmler's diaries for this period were available they would perhaps reveal how much his decision to join the Nazis in August had been connected with Röhm's views. Röhm was absent from Munich during the summer, but his resignation, announced on 26 September, would not have been a sudden decision.

The situation in Bavaria was extraordinarily complex. The right was divided broadly into the Thule-supported, pan-German Kampfbund under Hitler and Röhm, who wanted to march on Berlin and topple the Republic, and the Bavarian People's Party, which wanted above all to restore the Wittelsbach dynasty to Bavaria. The government in Munich was generally of this persuasion, but was further divided between those who wanted a more autonomous Bavaria within a German federation and those who flirted with the idea of leaving Berlin and Protestant north Germany to their own devices and forming a Catholic south German union. All sections of the right were, however, united in their opposition to the Republic – and of course to the communists – yet the strongest single power factor in the rightist camp was the Army, which was commanded from Berlin; and von Seeckt, as stated, was determined to preserve the constitution from attack by either left or right.

It is unnecessary to follow the political gyrations which Hitler, the Bavarian government and the Bavarian Army chief, von Lossow, danced around each other during the next month. Heinrich Himmler had no important part to play; it is doubtful if he had even met Hitler at this stage. The waltz ended in the Bürgerbräukeller, Munich, on the night of 8–9 November 1923. The leader of the Bavarian government, von Kahr, had called a mass meeting. It was evidently important, for nationalist leaders from all parts of Germany mixed with the Bavarian right in the packed hall. Hitler was there by the door, looking somewhat ridiculous in an ill-cut morning coat. He was convinced, or pretended to be convinced, that von Kahr was about to announce Bavarian independence. In any case he had decided to force the issue with a pre-emptive bid for a march on Berlin – in effect capturing the Bavarian separatists for his own revolutionary purpose. He had deployed the SA outside the hall and at a prearranged time soon after von Kahr began talking Göring burst in with twenty-five armed, steel-helmeted men of Hitler's guard (named the Stosstrupp Hitler), set up a maxim gun at the entrance, and forced a passage for Hitler through the packed audience to the front. There Hitler, in the words of one witness, looking like a waiter, jumped on a chair, fired a pistol shot through the ceiling and shouted, 'The national revolution has begun! The hall is occupied by 600 heavily armed men. No one may leave.'

Röhm, meanwhile, was leading his unit, now named Reichskriegsflagge, towards the War Ministry buildings in the centre of Munich. Both Gebhard and Heinrich Himmler were with him, and Heinrich was bearing the banner, an imperial German ensign. This suggests he had drawn himself to Röhm's attention by his dedication and reliability. The intention was to occupy the Ministry, but Röhm could not gain access and had to be content with throwing a barbed-wire and machine-gun barricade around the building. The police were soon on the scene and the Reichskriegsflagge cordon was itself surrounded. Röhm could do nothing but wait for relief from Hitler and thousands of Kampfbund members who had been ordered to converge on Munich through the night.

Hitler for his part, having sprung his surprise in the Bürgerbräukeller, had called Field Marshal Erich Ludendorff to the scene. Ludendorff, victor of the battle of Tannenberg and virtual dictator of Germany during the last part of the war, enjoyed immense prestige in nationalist circles. He supported Hitler and the Kampfbund and, although he had not been told of the putsch, he immediately threw in his lot with the 'national revolution' and convinced von Kahr, the Army chief von Lossow, and the chief of the Bavarian police von Seisser that they should do so too. The agreement of these three was probably tactical; when Hitler was called away from the hall, they took the opportunity to disappear. The key figure was von Lossow. Whether or not his pledged support for Ludendorff and Hitler had been genuine, he was called to order directly he returned to his headquarters. His adjutant had left the hall before him and alerted Berlin. Now von Seeckt made it clear that if von Lossow did not act to suppress the putsch, he would do so himself. Von Lossow had no option but to use the Bavarian Army divisions against the putschists; von Kahr and von Seisser had little option but to throw their weight behind the Army, especially as the Wittelsbach heir, the Crown Prince Ruprecht, made his opposition to the 'rebels' – Hitler, Röhm and Ludendorff – quite clear. He reminded the Bavarian officers of their oath to his dynasty. From this point Hitler's opportunistic and ill-prepared putsch was doomed.

The London *Times* correspondent found him obviously overwrought and 'dead tired' together with Ludendorff and a few others in a small upstairs room of the Bürgerbräukeller the following morning: 'He scarcely seemed to fill the part – this little man in an old waterproof coat with a revolver at his hip, unshaven and with disordered hair, and so hoarse that he could scarcely speak. . . .'[13]

In a desperate attempt to retrieve the situation by persuading the Army to change sides, Hitler and Ludendorff led a mass rally towards the War Office building where Röhm was sealed off. Kampfbund units had been converging on the Bürgerbräukeller during the night and they formed an immense column headed by Stosstrupp Hitler, SA and Oberland. Pushing through the first police cordons and threatening to shoot Jews and social-ists taken hostage, they were almost at their destination, approaching the Odeonsplatz through a narrow lane, when their way was barred by State Police with loaded carbines raised; beyond the police were Army units. What happened next is open to several interpretations. They tried to force their way through; there were volleys of shots; Hitler was pulled to the ground as his chief bodyguard threw himself on top of him. Göring and others were wounded; one of the Stosstrupp and a dozen Oberland men were killed; so were several of the police. Ludendorff and his adjutant marched on alone and unscathed and were arrested, while behind them the column, leaderless, broke in confusion. Hitler made his escape in a car, the wounded Göring into a nearby house. So the 'national revolution' ended ingloriously, yet the events of that morning, 9 November, and the martyrs who fell and the place they fell outside the Feldherrnhalle in the Residenzstrasse, were to become enshrined in Nazi mythology.

Heinrich Himmler's part with the Reichskriegsflagge outside the War Office was captured in photographs and in a fragment of a letter sent to him some months later by a girl named Mariele Rauschmayer, a friend of the family. She was no fanatic but a well-educated young woman who saw clearly the vicious elements sheltering among the nationalists. It is a measure of the desperation felt by all classes that in the letter in which she enclosed her unfinished memorial of that day she explained it as an expression of gratitude for the attempted putsch: 'I should like to thank you and your people for the one beautiful hour in the morning of 9 Nov.'[14] She stressed that it was a modest note written in the excitement of that day: 'but do not be proud, Heinrich, it praises you so much; it was only by chance that you were the one I knew best. When you can laugh about it, then throw it away, it is then of no more value, do you understand that I want to thank you all?'

The note itself was breathless with emotion:

Troops of the Reichskriegsflagge in front of the War Ministry, Heinrich Himmler at their head carrying the flag; one could see how secure the flag felt in his hands and how proud he was of it. I go up to him, incapable of speaking a word, but ringing in my ears is:

> Be proud I carry the flag
> Have no cares I carry the flag
> Love me I carry the flag.[15]

Röhm surrendered after a brief exchange of fire which killed two of his men. He was arrested and his followers disarmed, then allowed to disperse. Martial law was declared. The Nazi Party, the SA, indeed the whole Kampfbund were dissolved, and the Nazi newspaper, the *Völkischer Beobachter*, was banned. To all appearances it was the end of Hitler and his Party. It was certainly the end of Heinrich Himmler's resurrected dream of an Army career, for Kompanie Werner was also dissolved. He was now without a job and without a legitimate vehicle for the political cause which had become more important to him than a job. This is clear from a letter written to Gebhard by a former schoolfellow the following summer. 'I am very sorry that Heiner is now high and dry [*im Trockenen sitzen*]. The misfortune is precisely that he has no occupation and that only because he has placed all his thoughts and actions in the service of the great affair, and indeed completely.'[16] The 'great affair' was of course the *völkisch* or racial–nationalist movement and the fight against the ideological enemy which Himmler described in a letter to a Schleissheim colleague in January 1924, two months after the failed beer-hall putsch: 'this hydra of the black and red International of Jewry and Papacy [*Ultramontanismus*], of free-masons and Jesuits, of the business spirit and cowardly bourgeoisie . . .'.[17]

It is plain that he had by now severed most of his ties with what might be called the rational or pragmatic world and was living in a ferment of revolutionary idealism. He was indeed acting out his dreams in a cloak-and-dagger way, organising letter drops to keep his former Reichskriegsflagge members in touch with one another and their leaders in prison. As he wrote in the same letter, 'we have a duty to each other and to the [*völkisch*] movement to hold ourselves in readiness for the struggle.'

Besides this, he continued, he was studying French conversation two hours a week at the Berlitz school – why French now is not clear, unless France was more clearly identified with the enemy after the reparations humiliation and he was perhaps hoping for an undercover role. He could not have been expecting to farm in France. For the rest, he was still attempting to improve his mind:

otherwise I read and study the whole day, as much as I have time: for example H. St. Chamberlain, 'Richard Wagner', a marvellous book, Bav[arian] stories, Klopstock, 'Oden' (which I learn by heart), Häckel, 'Welträtsel'; Hitler's speeches; political pamphlets, agricultural matters, sheepbreeding, O my God, how we could talk. . . .

Houston Stewart Chamberlain was, of course, the prophet of racial Germanism. Himmler's comments on his life of Richard Wagner in his book-list are more respectful than enthusiastic: in fact he described it as hard going.[18] Friedrich Klopstock was an early-nineteenth-century poet whom he found inspiring: 'the man was a German.'[19] His book-list comments on Ernst Häckel's *Die Welträtsel* (*The World Riddle*) are more interesting. The first half of the book, a summary of current doctrine in natural science, he approved; the second half, concerned with 'the denial of a personal God' by 'unproven slanderings collected from everywhere', struck him as 'actually loathsome';[20] and he found it laughable that Häckel should write of something as 'finally proved' – an indication that he had not completely lost touch with reality.

Himmler was still attending church. This is known from surviving fragments of his diary from February 1924; the entry for the 17th reads: '11.30 in the cathedral, beautiful sermon on "Why did God create the world?"'[21] From this it appears that Christian concepts of the creation had at least as much interest for him as current scientific myths. In January, he had read Ernest Renan's *Das Leben Jesu* (*The Life of Jesus*), which had confirmed him in the view that 'Christianity was and is the most outstanding protest of the Aryans against Jewry, of good against evil.'[22] This paradox was made possible by the belief, propagated by Houston Stewart Chamberlain and other mythologists of Aryanism, that Jesus had not been a Jew but the illegitimate son of a Roman centurion. *Das Leben Jesu* reinforced Himmler's belief, despite the author's contrary views, that 'Jesus was no Jew.' No doubt this was necessary for his continued attendance at Christian services.

The speeches of Hitler mentioned in the letter were in von Koerber's *Adolf Hitler, sein Leben und seine Reden* (*His Life and Speeches*); Himmler commented: 'He is in truth a great man and above all genuine and pure. His speeches are marvellous specimens of Germandom and Aryanism.'[23]

His other reading in 1923 and 1924 was similarly biased towards racialist and religious themes. Professor Bradley Smith has identified thirty-seven of the eighty-one books he listed reading between August 1922 – the end of his time as a student – and July 1924 as being either *völkisch* or anti-semitic in content or causing him to write anti-semitic comments.[24] His comments taken as a whole reveal that he was obsessed on the one hand with the Artamen idea of the original virtuous, pure Aryan German living on the land, and on the other hand with the worldwide conspiracy of Jews, Jesuits and freemasons who had undermined this idyllic past state by interbreeding with the Aryans and introducing capitalism, materialism, hence modern decadence, and Bolshevism to his unfortunate nation.

Most revealing of all is a polemic work by Hans Günther, *Ritter, Tod und Teufel* (*The Knight, Death and the Devil*), which he read at the end of February 1924 inside a week. It was a pure Nietzschean extract in praise of ruthless heroes, creative in destruction, strong in hate, with the will to victory whatever it cost in extermination of lesser breeds. Such heroes could be produced only from the Nordic stem of the Aryan race.

The physical attributes of this 'most talented and beautiful' Nordic race were described in great detail from slim, broad-shouldered, narrow-hipped men to the more softly contoured, charmingly slender women: 'with man harder chiselled features, with woman tender features, with both shining skin flushed with blood, blond hair, clear, conquering eyes, with both the perfect movements of a perfect body – a royal species among men!'[25]

All this was fantastic enough – although it can probably be matched between the lines of popular Anglo-Saxon idolators of the period, Dornford Yates, Jeffery Farnol and the rest. What makes it ludicrous was that it was published and imbibed in Munich, where the Nordic ideal must have been as rare as an Anglophile. Here is a young Englishman, Patrick Leigh Fermor, ten years later attempting to describe the 'transformation that beer, in collusion with almost non-stop eating', could wreak on human beings as observed in Munich:

> The trunks of these feasting burghers were as wide as casks. The spread of their buttocks over the oak benches was not far short of a yard. They branched at the loins into thighs as thick as the torsos of ten-year-olds and arms on the same scale strained like bolsters at the confining serge. Chin and chest formed a single column, and each close-packed nape was creased with its three deceptive smiles.[26]

This was the real world outside. Röhm was not quite so gross, nor Göring, yet, and Hitler was always an exception, but Leigh Fermor came closer to Munich man, as represented in the Nazi Party and SA, than Hans Günther.

Experience had taught Günther that all the good things of Nordic man would be abused by *Minderrassigen* (inferior races) and *Fremden* (foreigners). He advocated bringing in 'Nordic racial legislation' to guard against this. One had to carry a strong hate within one to temper the soul, and recognise that the Nordic race represented the aristocracy among men. Himmler's comment was: 'A book that expresses in wise, considered [*überlegten*] words and sentences what I have felt and thought since I [first] thought.'[27]

One of his favourite authors at this period was another Nordic populariser, Werner Jansen. After reading his *Das Buch Liebe* that autumn, he commented: 'The glorious hymn to the Nordic woman. This is the ideal picture which we Germans dream of in youth and as men are prepared to die for, and in which one always believes despite so often being deceived.'[28] The *Niebelungenlied*, which his father had read to them in boyhood, he read and found 'of deathless, eternal beauty in language, depth and Germanness'.[29] There are many other examples of his complete identification with the Nordic heroic legend – this, so far as is known, before he had met Rosenberg or Darré, the Nazi popularisers of the Aryan myth, who were supposed to have been his great influences.

The ideological enemy was treated with similar hyperbole. After reading Theodor Fritsch's *Handbuch der Judenfrage* (*Handbook of the Jewish Question*) in the autumn of 1923 – the twenty-eighth edition of the book which had been published in Hamburg only four years previously – he noted, 'even an initiate shudders when he reads all this with understanding. If only some of those who will never be convinced could have it placed before their eyes.'[30] The same author's *Der falsche Gott* (*The False God*), which he read just after the failed putsch at the beginning of December 1923, reinforced his view of 'this frightful [Jewish–capitalist] scourge of God and danger which will throttle us!'[31] Similarly his views about the danger represented by Jesuits were confirmed by *Die Jesuiten*, which he was reading at the time of the putsch, and Alfred Miller's *Ultramontanes Schuldbuch* (*Ultramontane Guiltbook*) read in the spring of 1924:

> A new frightful insight into the workshop of the enemy. Bitterness seizes one when one reads all this. What have we done to these people that we should not live. And now with a vengeance. We want to be German and will always fight for this against every enemy. What kind of enemies of belief and of the Christian religion of love are these people indeed.[32]

At the same time he was reading *Der Bolschewismus von Moses bis Lenin* (*Bolshevism from Moses to Lenin*), a collection of dialogues between Dietrich Eckart and Hitler. Eckart had been Hitler's first intellectual mentor and enthusiastic supporter from a higher social background. A dropped-out law student before the first war, he had turned to writing, generally about Nordic and mystical themes, and had enjoyed great success. He was a member of the Thule Society and had started his own *völkisch*, anti-semitic newspaper, *Auf gut Deutsch*, in Munich in December 1918. Recognising Hitler's genius in street politics early he had taken it upon himself to groom him as the charismatic non-establishment leader he thought Germany needed. The dialogues on Bolshevism which he edited and published in 1924 made a tremendous impression on Himmler, opening his eyes to historic perspectives 'which one had not seen hitherto. I want everyone to read this collection.'[33]

So the links in the international conspiracy against the Aryan race latched together in Himmler's mind: Jews – Bolsheviks – freemasons – Jesuits. His other reading consisted of memoirs of great Germans, including three of the key figures of the German bid for world power, Kaiser Wilhelm II, Admiral Tirpitz and Ludendorff, and a biography of the key Foreign Minister, von Bülow. All these books were flawed by biased editing and even falsification of facts, complete refusal to acknowledge even a particle of blame for the world catastrophe, refusal to learn anything and a vengeful spirit against the former allies, which could not have failed to reinforce Himmler's hatred of the powers that had forced the Treaty of Versailles on his country and no doubt his convictions that Germany had been defeated not by arms but by the 'hydra of the Black & Red International'.

The narrow range of his reading is striking. Up to the spring and summer of 1924 he listed just over 200 books. Only a handful of these came from outside his own culture. In the early days there had been the science-fiction adventures of Jules Verne; later he read two of Alexander Dumas' adventures, two novels by Émile Zola, two of Dostoievsky's lesser-known works and Homer's *Odyssey* in German translation. Apart from these the only foreign authors he had read were Ibsen, Gobineau and Houston Stewart Chamberlain – all of whom were pillars of what might be called the Nietzschean Aryan *Weltanschauung* he had adopted – and Oscar Wilde, who was of course not. Wilde was the only representative of the Anglo-Saxon liberal culture that he had read – so far as his book-list shows – and it was an unfortunate choice. *Der Priester und der Mesnerknabe* (*The Priest and the Acolyte*) was, as he noted, 'An idealisation of homosexual man'. He was shocked and it put him in a 'frightful mood'.[34]

Four other books he read at this time are interesting: *Der Spiritismus* (*Spiritualism*), which allowed him 'for the first time really to believe in spiritualism';[35] Professor Friedrich zu Bosen's *Der zweite Gesicht* (*Second Sight*), which he read at the end of November 1923 a few weeks after the failed putsch and which also impressed him with its clear, scientific account of psychic phenomena, 'astrology, hypnotism, spiritualism, telepathy etc.'.[36] Then, while staying in the home of a *völkisch* colleague in February 1924 he found two books of a type he did not usually come across and devoured them both in a day: *Ein Sadist in Priesterock* (*A Sadist in Priest's Clothing*), banned on publication, and *Das Lustwäldchen* (*The Pleasuregrove*), an illustrated collection of erotic verse; he found this the 'poetry of decay'.[37]

By early 1924 the leaders of the outlawed Nazi Party and paramilitary units not in prison had begun re-forming their membership in *völkisch* political parties and attempting to unite them in a *Völkischer Sozialer Block* to fight elections for the state parliament, the Landtag, in the spring. Himmler involved himself in the election campaign as a speaker in country districts. He was an experienced motorcyclist; he had acquired a machine when he started his practical farming year in 1920, probably because his father hoped that this would reduce travelling expenses. The mobility this conferred on him together with his burning conviction must have made him a useful worker for the cause. Whether he was a good speaker is not apparent. It is clear from his earlier diary extracts that he was a fluent talker and his later speeches show that he developed an unforced, natural even somewhat ironic style which allowed him to go on at great length, probably without boring his listeners. A few of his diary pages from February 1924 survive and on the last one, 25 February, he recorded speaking to the farm people

at Rohr for one and a half hours, 'I think quite well.' To hold the attention
of a meeting for this length of time suggests that already he was no mean
orator. There is no doubt that he was working on their grievances, for the
topics listed for his previous days' speeches were the Jewish question, the
enslavement of workers by stock-exchange capitalism, the labour question,
wages and food hoarding. Moreover, he noted that at the end of his speech
a buyer for a Jewish hop dealer came into the village and was, he believed,
given some hostile treatment afterwards (*zwischen die Finger nahmen*). At
the end of such meetings he and the other speakers circulated among the
crowd giving individual enlightenment. 'Bitterly hard and thorny is this
service to the *Volk*, this deluded often badly treated suspicious *Volk* which
is filled with dread [*Angst*] of war [and] death.'[38] Thus, just as in the middle
ages the Dominicans had moved among the people of the foothills of the
Alps and Pyrenees mobilising social frustrations by supplying the mythology of the witch in intellectual dressing, Himmler and the other *völkisch*
propagandists, having drunk at the poisoned wells of the pan-German
publishers, moved through the peasant communities of Bavaria harnessing
the simple *Angst* they found by propagating the demonology of the Jew –
and, if Himmler is any guide, with dreadful sincerity.

This speaking tour was in the area north of Munich between Landshut
and Regensburg. The previous week he had been to visit Röhm in
Stadelheim prison, taking him a copy of the *Grossdeutscher Zeitung* –
the banned *Völkischer Beobachter* under a new name – and some oranges.
They talked for twenty minutes. 'We had an excellent conversation and
spoke rather unreservedly,' he recorded in his diary. 'He still has his good
sense of humour and is always the good Capt. Röhm.'[39] This was eleven
days before the trial of Röhm, Hitler and the other leading putschists was
due to begin. Obviously Himmler was very much at the centre of events,
although in a subordinate role.

He was living with his parents in Munich now that he was unemployed,
and it was not an easy time. The currency had been stabilised with a new
gold so-called Renten Mark equivalent to 1000 million of the old paper
Marks. Consequently the financial pressure was no longer acute. Instead
there was the pressure caused by his fanatical attachment to the pan-German
movement, his resulting scorn for the Bavarian People's Party to which his
father and most of his social circle adhered. No doubt the difference was
sharpened by the excitements of the election campaign. His parents also
disapproved of his placing unpaid political activity before gaining a secure
job. In fact, during February he was corresponding with a Turkish former
student he had met at the Technical High School to see if he could find him
a position as a farm manager in Turkey; likewise with the Soviet Embassy
to see if there were prospects in the Ukraine. Since he did not speak
Turkish, had apparently dropped his Russian studies and was trying French
conversation instead, it is questionable how serious these enquiries were.

What is not in doubt is that, at the time he was apparently thinking of emigration, he was preparing his *völkisch* speeches for the rural propaganda tour and probably writing articles. He wrote one which was published in a rural paper and it is unlikely it was the only one.

He was still enjoying deep discussions on all his favourite themes whenever he met a sympathetic partner. Thus on the speaking tour, the day after reading the tale of the sadistic priest and *The Pleasure Grove*, he had a 'marvellous' talk with a friend:

> Belief in God, religion, religious doubts (immaculate conception etc.), confession, views on duelling – blood, sexual intercourse, man and woman – (he would like to confess but cannot believe in some dogma: therefore impossible, he was very keen on it, however, because [he] held it cowardly if one fetched in the pastor at life's end). That is a highly proper standpoint.[40]

The following week the trial started that was to turn Hitler, hitherto scarcely known outside Bavaria, into a national, even an international, figure for a few weeks. He, Ludendorff, Röhm and the Munich police chief Pöhner, together with five others involved in the putsch, were charged with high treason. As the three principal witnesses, von Kahr, von Lossow and von Seisser, had as much to hide as the men in the dock, and as the Bavarian Minister of Justice, Dr Franz Gürtner, was sympathetic to their goals, as indeed was the whole judiciary, the 'trial' was 'little more than a grandstand play to appease Berlin'.[41] Hitler took the leading role and played it for all he was worth and in terms that his audience would understand. His ambition, he said in an impassioned closing speech, had always been to become the destroyer of Marxism: 'I shall achieve this task.' Of the young men who fell outside the Feldherrnhalle, 'it will be said one day, "These, too, died for the liberation of the Fatherland."'[42] And of the Army, the Reichswehr, he said he was glad they had not fired, only the police. 'The Reichswehr stands as untarnished as before. One day the hour will come when the Reichswehr will stand at our side, officers and men.'[43]

Sentence was pronounced on 1 April: Hitler, Pöhner and two of the paramilitary leaders were given the minimum sentence of five years' fortress detention and a fine of 200 Marks (£10); they were, however, to be released on their own recognizances after six months. Röhm and the others except for Ludendorff were given fifteen months and a fine of 100 Marks, but were to be released at once on their own recognizances. Ludendorff was acquitted. The correspondent of *The Times* of London reported, 'Munich is chuckling over the verdict, which is regarded as an excellent joke for All Fools Day.'[44]

Probably Himmler was among the crowds thronging outside the court cheering as Hitler appeared at a window smiling and bowing his acknowledgement. 'The trial has at any rate proved', *The Times* correspondent continued, 'that to plot against the constitution of the Reich is not considered a serious crime in Bavaria.'

Fortress detention was a very much lighter sentence than prison; the only real hardship was loss of liberty. Otherwise Hitler and his friends passed a pleasant even luxurious existence in the old castle of Landsberg and, free from the stress of active politics, Hitler started dictating his memoirs, published the following year as *Mein Kampf* (*My Struggle*). One of his closest disciples, Rudolf Hess, took over as his secretary after returning from hiding in Austria and being sentenced to a short term for his part in helping to plan the putsch.

Hess was the son of a prosperous German merchant in Egypt; he had volunteered for the Army in 1914 and served through the war in the 16th Bavarian Infantry – the same regiment as Hitler – ending as a lieutenant. After the war he had entered Munich University as a student of economics and had come under the influence of Professor Karl Haushofer, an Army general, who was pioneering a new discipline, 'geopolitics', or political geography. As a military man and pan-German disciple of Heinrich von Treitschke and Houston Stewart Chamberlain, Haushofer endowed his subject with the current nationalist preoccupations dressed up in biological imagery. Through Haushofer, Hess was able to help Hitler put an academic gloss on the political arguments of *Mein Kampf*.

Hitler differed from Haushofer in at least two fundamentals: for Haushofer the biological element was the state, for Hitler it was the race, and since he considered Jews a bacillus undermining racial purity, anti-semitism was as fundamental to Hitler's outlook as anti-(Jewish-inspired) Bolshevism. Haushofer was not a racist in that sense; he had married into a Jewish merchant family. The other chief point of difference was in the direction Germany should move. Haushofer proposed expansion into south-east Europe in co-operation with Russia, while regaining colonial territory outside Europe in competition with Great Britain. Hitler considered that the greatest mistake of the pre-war German statesmen had been to antagonise Great Britain by challenging her naval and colonial hegemony. He advocated an agreement with Great Britain to leave her a free hand overseas while Germany had a free hand on the continent to push Russia back and colonise eastern Europe. He did not realise how consistently this policy had been tried by the Kaiser's Chancellor, Bethmann-Hollweg, before the first war, nor how it had always foundered on the simple fact that British interests demanded, had always demanded, a balance of power in Europe, for a single bloc once formed would naturally challenge her overseas dominance whatever promises had been made. This was and had always been a fundamental axiom of British policy because it was such a basic prop of British vital interests: Hitler was mistaken in thinking he could get around it.

Mein Kampf presented his goals, which never changed; his means of attaining them may have been opportunistic but his motivation and the aims of his policy remained the same virtually to the end. They were to be gleaned by those who had the time and endurance to plough through the indigestible prose. Few had; even the eager Heinrich Himmler apparently took some eighteen months. He eventually concluded that the book presented an 'uncanny abundance of truths' but the first chapter about Hitler's youth 'contained many weaknesses'.[45]

Hitler's oratory at the trial as reported in the press throughout Germany had more impact on events. It is credited with swinging many traditional conservative, Catholic and liberal voters to the *völkisch* camp in both the Bavarian and national elections that spring. At all events the urban lower-middle classes, who had lost their savings, shops, businesses and livelihoods during the inflation, and the peasantry rallied to the cause; in the Bavarian elections the *Völkisch Sozialer Block* became the second largest party with 17 per cent of the vote. In the country as a whole the former Nazis and *völkisch* groups of the north and Bavaria who had allied to form the National Socialist Freiheitsbewegung (Freedom Movement), gained thirty-two seats in the Reichstag with some 6 per cent of the votes cast.

One of the organisers of this grouping who was elected to the Bavarian Landtag was shortly to become a decisive force in Himmler's life. This was the former Nazi Party and SA leader for Lower Bavaria, Gregor Strasser. Like Hitler and Hess, he had served at the front throughout the war, in his case in the 1st Bavarian Foot Artillery; he had been commissioned from the ranks and ended as a lieutenant of the reserve with numerous decorations and the Iron Cross 1st and 2nd class.

He had entered the war with vague socialist leanings inspired intellectually by his father, a lower-rank Bavarian official, and emotionally by a personal grudge; he had wanted to become a doctor but had had to settle for becoming a chemist as his father's salary did not allow him to study medicine. His war experiences had reinforced his dissatisfaction. The comradeship of the trenches, which he remembered as the best part of his life, suggested to him that society could be ordered on similar lines where performance instead of class or privilege determined a man's position and status. He defined his goal as a true socialist community, viewing both 'so-called democracy' and Marxism as schemes by which international Jewish financiers undermined the economic independence of nations.[46]

Little as he probably realised it himself, his ideas were conditioned more by pan-German *völkisch* propaganda than by his war experience or home background. He was a simple, even a naive, emotional man, strong in his national pride, straightforward, fearless, enthusiastic, a hard worker and natural leader and organiser. He was not a thinker; his 'socialism' never advanced beyond received slogans and nostalgia for the equality and humanity of the trenches translated somehow into ordinary life.

In 1919 Strasser had served as a company leader in von Epp's Freikorps helping to liberate Munich from the red government. Then after passing his final exams he had become a chemist's assistant, still taking an active part in paramilitary and ex-servicemen's groups. In 1920 he had married and in the following year established his own chemist shop in Landshut. It is not clear how he acquired the capital for this at a time when inflation was high – although it was by no means as bad as it was to become. Nor is it clear exactly when he joined the Nazi Party; it was probably in the autumn of 1922. He was appointed SA leader of Lower Bavaria in the spring of 1923, and proved himself an outstanding organiser. While taking no part in the actual putsch of 8 November he had brought his contingent to Munich that night and guarded a bridge over the Isar, remaining there until told of the collapse of the attempt in the late afternoon. Characteristically he had then marched his men to the main railway station singing patriotic songs and entrained back to Landshut. Afterwards he had been active in uniting the *völkisch* groups to fight the 1924 elections, until arrested in February for attempting to recruit for the banned Nazi Party. Sent to join Hitler's smoking circle in the fortress of Landsberg, he had been released on his election to the Landtag.

Strasser now combined his duties as a Landtag deputy with leadership of his former SA and Nazi groups in Lower Bavaria – serving under the banner of the National Socialist Freiheitsbewegung since the ban on the Party. He also travelled extensively throughout Germany to liaise with other *völkisch* groups and speak at their meetings. Consequently he needed an assistant to look after his office, and in June he started looking for a full-time secretary. He chose Himmler. Probably he had met him already for the Himmlers were of course well known in Landshut, and Heinrich's *völkisch* activities had taken him into Strasser's region. Possibly Himmler was recommended by Röhm. In any event Strasser could not have made a better choice. Himmler not only shared his own passionate convictions, enjoyed immersing himself in paperwork and bringing order to files, as he had at the student organisation, but he had learned to type after a fashion on a machine the family used at home, and he had his motorbike which enabled him to visit the remoter branches of the district.

It seems he told no one when he took up the post, but simply vanished from Munich. He had been out of work nine months and something of his prickly mood and his parents' despair comes through the lines of the letter Mariele Rauschmayer wrote to him at this time enclosing her note about the putsch of 8/9 November:

> At your mother's request I asked my acquaintances in Wolfegg whether, perhaps, by any chance there was anything (in the way of a post) open for you. Unfortunately I received only negative replies. At best there are only departmental positions in the central administration of both self-managed estates. . . . For these Herr H. is naturally too young, moreover he has as yet no practical experience.
>   . . . I gladly write, only ask you to detail what it is exactly that you are looking for. In any case Herr Dr Kuchtner will think of you, that is of me, if he hears anything. Do not be childish, Heinrich, and get annoyed that I, a ridiculous 'Also-*völkisch*', take you under my wings! In

the view of Herr Dr Kuchtner it is a great advantage to be one of my protégés. . . .

Or have you found something in the meantime? I would be glad of that because I know what it means to seek so long and not to find. People have no idea what a loss it is for them to do without Heinrich Himmler! When that becomes known sometime, my dear, then look out! . . . but one thing I have wished: that you do not think so lightly of going abroad where the same chains exactly are not to be shaken off so easily.

She ended, after sending greetings from his family:

To you yourself – if *I* may say that – an optimistic *Heil!* that is meant naturally for Germany and you, that you are again almost in work.

In good friendship! (even if you are at times a trifle annoyed with me!).

Maria R.[47]

It appears from this letter that joining Strasser may have been as much an act of desperation as a positive affirmation of his *völkisch* ideals. At the least it indicates that he had suffered months of indecision, and could have taken a post abroad if one had been offered; yet that too was probably an idealistic dream given his lack of practical experience.

The following month Ludwig Zahler called on his parents. They either could not or would not tell him what 'Heini' was doing, only that he was staying in Landshut in a room over the Chemist Hintermaier – actually Strasser's shop. Zahler sent him a card there to wish him well on his name day 'in the sincere hope that you too will soon find a permanent position'. He added, 'I would be pleased to hear from you, you "run-away".'[48]

It seems probable, therefore, that the move marked a complete break with his parents. Alfred Andersch was told by his father, a Ludendorff supporter, thus well informed about the *völkisch* movement, that the young Himmler had quarrelled with 'the old Himmler' and the two were 'deadly enemies'.[49]

Himmler's first biographer, Frischauer, states – possibly from what he was told by Gebhard after the war – that Heinrich's salary while working for Strasser was 120 Marks, or approximately £6, a month. Professor Bradley Smith states that it did not exceed 150 Marks a month. This was scarcely a living wage and he was forced to borrow. One of those who lent him money in his first months in Landshut was his old schoolfriend, Falk Zipperer, now working for a film company in Munich. In August Falk wrote to say that he was hard-pressed himself, and would be grateful for a return of the loan until the end of the month, when he would again have some cash. He added, 'Perhaps you will write to me when you have a moment for yourself, which to be sure is never the case. . . .'[50]

Himmler visited Munich over the first weekend in September but missed Falk, who was in the hills. Falk wrote to him on his return, regretting that Heini had not told him he was coming to the city, there was such a lot he had to tell him: he had become engaged the previous month. He went on:

> Now, dear Heini, about the wretched money! It is very painful for me to have to talk about it! I don't need it for myself, but I'm pressed from another side to pay Mk 50, and it would be of great help if I could have that soon. It would be easier for me eventually to advance it to you again after a couple of weeks. Naturally I don't know your present financial circumstances. If it is impossible for you, don't worry, it will just have to be. I would be content even with Mk 20. Therefore, no offence meant and I remain until we meet again soon, which I look forward to very much, my old friend, with many cordial greetings,
>   Your loyal Falk[51]

The few photographs of Himmler in these early days show him with a lean and hungry look, very different from the rather plump features of his days of power. Undoubtedly he was working exhausting hours for very little but he was tasting a certain fulfilment. As he wrote in August, he enjoyed running the organisational work on his own. Yet the strength of his commitment made him prey to the old black moods that others could not see what was so plain to him. He was frankly pessimistic about the chances of the seeds they were sowing bearing fruit, at least in the near future. He told one correspondent that August that he was working for the long term. Nonetheless – and here the old familiar tones of self-pity and extraordinary sententiousness surfaced – 'we few do this hard work undeterred, out of boundless love for the Fatherland . . . a selfless service to a grand idea and a grand cause.'[52]

The depths of his periods of despair may be gleaned between the lines of one letter to him that August from Mariele Rauschmayer. She was replying to a letter of his:

> There is one thing I never want to read again: Germany betrayed you? No, Heinrich, you yourselves are Germany and you liberate yourselves. We are Germany and we cannot live like this. The others? A rabble, Heinrich, but not Germany; philistines who are all alike, but not Germany. And on that 9 Nov. those who stood before the War Ministry did not betray you – or us. . . .[53]

The whole of her long letter was concerned with the cause to which Himmler had dedicated himself. She tried to point out why she could not commit herself wholeheartedly:

> I have always had the feeling, and partly still have today, that I am more *völkisch* than these people. Now you laugh, Heinrich, I see you exactly; your condescending laugh about my delusion! But steady, *mein Herr*, how many of you really know what Germandom is in the fullest sense? for

example *Ritter, Tod und Teufel, Buch Treue*, etc. You are quite right: *to be* is the essential thing. But how many are? With how many does the *völkisch* 'to be' consist only in anti-semitism? Or opposition to the Bavarian People's Party?[54]

She admired Ludendorff, whom she had heard speaking for the first time the previous year, but was repelled by Esser and Streicher and she warned him how little there was that could be trusted without reserve: 'For me, what your *völkisch* Party urges is indeed right and I adhere to you; but *self* and *we* I cannot say. Yours is a battlegroup which wants to drain a bog, and swamp-devils and bog-witches are such a repulsive riff-raff I want to have nothing to do with them.'[55] She turned to the question of the 'noble German woman', answering something he must have said in his letter:

> If I am asked what is to be done, I say: take a preserving jar and preserve the best girls that you find in Germany, so that they remain pure German women – so that the men, who today have no time for them, will know one day where they can find their women. There will not be many because the struggle for existence is much more difficult for a woman today than for a man. . . . certainly it will be difficult to discover the right ones. . . .[56]

She assured him that German women were aware they would be championed, and they strove – if not always successfully – to be worthy; 'that too is often a struggle.'

Evidently Himmler's dreams in that direction had not changed. Equally he was not alone in his views. The whole letter is interesting for the light it sheds on the mood among young and educated people who had been exposed to the Nordic myth by the spate of books like *Ritter, Tod und Teufel* and *Buch Treue*, which Mariele mentioned. She remained basically balanced, however, and prescient in her warning about the diabolical creatures in the swamps of *völkisch* politics, but of course her message of moderation could have no meaning for him.

Meanwhile further grounds for his pessimism about the future of the movement became evident. The government under Stresemann sanctioned the Dawes Plan whereby an international credit of 800 million Marks was opened at the Reichsbank secured by mortgages on the German railways and certain industries, and an international commission sat in Berlin to supervise these industries and oversee the German budgets and reparations payments. While this seemed to support Strasser's bitter denunciations of international stock-exchange capitalism controlling the country, it did wonders for the economy and soon removed the crisis conditions in which the extreme parties of both left and right thrived. At the same time, with Hitler in prison and several leaders contending, the *völkisch* groups split into rival factions. It needed a large effort of faith to see much hope for the cause. Himmler had that faith; like Brand, he saw the road to Canaan

leading through the desert of self-sacrifice. He needed the desert, and the
will to cross it.

Strasser's brother Otto later wrote an account of Gregor talking
about his 'new adjutant'. In view of Otto's unpleasant experiences with
the Nazi Party there is every reason to expect bias in his reminiscences
– he is certainly wildly out for dates – but this description of Himmler by
his brother rings true:

> 'A remarkable fellow. Comes from a strong Catholic family, but does not
> want to know anything about the Church. Looks like a half-starved shrew. But
> keen I tell you, incredibly keen. He has . . . a motorbike. He is under way the
> whole day – from one farm to another – from one village to the next. Since I've
> had him our weapons have really been put into shape. I tell you, he's a perfect
> arms-NCO. He visits all the secret depots.'[57]

If Otto Strasser's recollection is correct, Himmler had made his break
with the Church before he took up the post, therefore at some date between
17 February, when he recorded hearing a beautiful sermon in Munich
cathedral, and July 1924; perhaps it coincided with his break with his
family. On the other hand his enthusiastic comments on such Nietzschean,
anti-Christian views as were contained in Günther's *Ritter, Tod und Teufel*
or the argument of Miller's *Ultramontanes Schuldbuch*, both in March,
suggest that the break with the Church came first, perhaps helping his break
with his father.

However that may be, Gregor, in Otto Strasser's account, asked
himself why his new factotum took his job so seriously. He had put it
down to the fact that Himmler suffered dreadfully from having missed
active service. 'Now he surely wants to make up for the deficiency with
redoubled zeal.'[58] This agrees with Himmler's diary entries on the theme
of war service.

In October 1924 the Reichstag was dissolved and a new election
campaign began. Himmler again went on speaking tours round the rural
communities in his district. There are no records of his speeches for this
period and no diaries, but a speech and an article from 1926 survive.
Since both are concerned with Jewish exploitation and the enslavement of
workers by capitalism, both of which he recorded attacking in the earlier
election campaign of 1924, it can be assumed that his main themes did not
vary. No doubt he also spoke of replacing the Jewish 'spirit of money' with
an idealised version of the old Germanic self-supporting communities, for
unsigned, typewritten drafts of an essay on these lines from about this
date or 1925 have been found among his papers.[59] And, of course, such
ideas accorded with his chief's woolly portrayal of 'national' as opposed to
international socialism: thus Gregor Strasser in a speech in 1925: 'We want in
place of an exploitive capitalist economic system a real socialism, maintained
not by a soulless Jewish–materialist outlook, but by the believing, sacrificial

and unselfish old Germanic community sentiment, community purpose and community feeling.'[60] What this meant in a modern, industrialised society and how it was to be brought about was not seriously addressed.

Himmler developed the theme of leading the people back to the soil in the context of race hygiene. At the beginning of October when the election campaign began he was reading both Jansen's *Das Buch Liebe*, which he characterised as the 'glorious hymn to the Nordic woman . . . the ideal picture which we Germans dream of in youth and as men are prepared to die for . . .',[61] and a volume put out by the pan-German Schutz-und Trutzbund called *Eine Unbewusste Blutschande* (*An Unconscious Blood-disgrace*). This he thought a 'marvellous volume . . . a pioneerwork', and significantly 'especially the last part, how it is possible to improve the race again'.[62] Earlier he had been reading a handbook on animal breeding.

The elections, held on 7 December, proved a disaster for the *völkisch* movement. The vote dropped by over a half to less than a million, and only fourteen of the thirty-two Reichstag seats won in the spring were retained. One of these went to Gregor Strasser.

With the movement reduced to the fringe of politics and divided internally, the Bavarian authorities released Hitler. He should already have been released on 1 October when his six months expired but he had been held on account of his association with Röhm, then building a nationwide paramilitary organisation called the Frontbann. After his release Hitler was considered so harmless because of the poor showing in the polls that the ban on the Nazi Party was lifted – either that or his supporters in the Bavarian hierarchy believed the Nazis were still necessary as hammers of socialists (SPD) and communists (KPD). Both of these were mass parties which shared the greater part of the industrial workers' vote between them, so this is a more likely explanation.

Now Hitler was free the power struggles in the movement were brought to a head. Hitler had no use for alliances. He was fascinated by Mussolini's fascism in Italy and wanted a similar monolithic party with himself as leader. In any case his egocentricity dictated it. One of the keys to uniting all the fragmented groupings under his own leadership was Gregor Strasser. He was the most effective political speaker, had much influence and carried respect among the north German groups he had been cultivating, and he and Heinrich Himmler had constructed a model organisation in their district, or *Gau* – the old Germanic word used by the Party. Hitler met Strasser privately in mid-February 1925, and Strasser agreed to support him, making the distinction that he came as a colleague (*Mitarbeiter*), not a follower (*Gefolgsmann*). This would not have been possible had Strasser stayed in Munich, but it was also agreed that Strasser, who was moving to Berlin to take his seat in the Reichstag, should be free to organise the northern districts of the re-formed Party. With this crucial agreement in his pocket, Hitler staged a mass rally of all factions at the scene of his recent disaster, the Burgerbräukeller. One of his fund-raisers, Kurt Ludecke, likened the mood he conjured there by his oratory to a revivalist meeting: 'Women wept, the crowd pressed from the rear . . . men who had been bitter enemies mounted the platform and shook hands. . . .'[63]

So the factions were united behind him – for the moment at least – apparently through his medium-like powers of mass suggestion. Otto Strasser rated him one of the greatest speakers of the century. His audiences were, of course, self-selected. The very fact that they belonged to an extreme organisation meant they had certain emotional needs. Undoubtedly one of these was for strong leadership. Hitler responded. With more balanced individuals Hitler did not have such success in these early days.

The National Socialist Freiheitsbewegung under which the original Nazi groups had sheltered during the ban on the Party had been dissolved earlier that month. Now most simply came back again under the Nazi banner, retaining their *Gau* and group leaders and their organisation. Thus Heinrich Himmler became once again a member of the Nazi Party, this time with an official post as Deputy Gauleiter (*Gau* leader) of Lower Bavaria.[64] It gave him considerable importance for with the Gauleiter, Strasser, spending most of his time organising the northern *Gaue*, much of the rest of his time in the Reichstag, Himmler was *de facto* chief in the district – one of the most important for the movement: Ludecke described Lower Bavaria as 'really the kernel of the new Hitler party, the nucleus of the second epoch of the Hitler movement'.[65] Moreover, his proximity to the Party centre in Munich together with his contact with his chief, Strasser, and through him with the north and central German Nazis, Josef Goebbels, Karl Kaufmann, Erich Koch and many others who were to become leading Party figures, placed him in a strategically central position which gave every scope to his natural compulsions to be 'in the know' and to mediate and intrigue between factions. Although he is usually written off as a rather unimportant petty official at this stage, he was impressing a large number of useful allies with his intelligence, organising ability and fanatic zeal. He was, at last, someone. Bradley Smith concludes that it was through his commitment to the Party that Himmler became adult: 'It was his role as a professional Party worker which allowed him to overcome his problems of identity and become a man. An adult Heinrich Himmler separate from the Party and its ideology never existed. Himmler *was* Nazism.'[66]

If this is accepted it cuts out the problem of how someone apparently intelligent and educated could believe, disseminate and act out the nonsense at the core of the movement, how a youth with a soft heart for enemy prisoners of war in Landshut and young girls and old women in distress could become an ice-cold murderer: for his beliefs were not intellectual, but emotional, indeed a part of him.

The extent to which they had become a part of him is shown in a letter he wrote to Kurt Ludecke in 1925, asking his opinion on a project which, he said, he had had in mind for some time. This was to 'publish the names of all Jews, as well as of Christian friends of the Jews living in Lower Bavaria'. He asked for Ludecke's opinion on account of his 'great experience in the Jewish question' and knowledge of 'the anti-semitic fight in the whole world'.[67]

Ludecke showed the letter to Gregor Strasser, suggesting jokingly that he take Himmler with him to Berlin to make a list of the Jews there. According to his account, Strasser laughed. 'That's just like him. He sees in every creature who doesn't "think" Nazi a Jew or a Jew serf, a Jesuit or a freemason. He's devoted to me and I use him as a secretary. He's very ambitious, but I won't take him along – he's no world-beater, you know.'[68]

In the winter of 1926, Himmler met his ideal woman. It was in a Bavarian resort, Bad Reichenhall or, according to Otto Strasser, Berchtesgaden. He was apparently seeking shelter in a hotel lobby and showered her with melting snow as he swept his hat off after nearly colliding with her. Her name was Margaret, 'Marga' for short. His brother Gebhard told Himmler's second biographer, Fraenkel, that her hair was the outstanding attraction.[69] It was blonde, and her eyes were blue. Undoubtedly she impressed him as truly Aryan, although there was a width to her face and frame more suited to Wagnerian opera than to the ideal of Nordic womanhood expressed in *Ritter, Tod und Teufel.*

He was also attracted to her mind; how much she consciously matched her views to his enthusiasm can only be guessed. She was thirty-four, thus eight years the older, daughter of a German landowner in Goncerzewo, Poland/West Prussia, a qualified nurse, and now, after a brief marriage which had ended in divorce, she ran a clinic she had opened with her father's money in Berlin. Apparently she distrusted conventional medicine; she was more interested in homeopathy, hypnosis, the old herbal remedies of the country. Despite having set herself up in Berlin, a sink of decadence according to his ideas, she apparently shared all his views of the good life on the land, so much so that she was prepared to sell her clinic and buy a smallholding to work with him. She was a managing woman. Probably after realising how much she had impressed him, she managed the courtship, much of which was by post. He, the most strictly pedantic, prudish young man, was her 'wicked darling'. According to Otto Strasser, she seduced him. It is generally agreed that she was the first woman with whom he had sexual relations. 'And high time!' Otto said when Himmler told him in 1927 in Berlin.[70]

Himmler had little to offer her. His salary when they eventually married in July 1928 had been increased to 200 Marks a month, but was still barely enough to support one. His prospects were dim. The Party was in the wilderness and there was no sign of any promised land. Still she wanted him and he obviously wanted her.

He was working at Party headquarters in Munich by then. He had transferred from Landshut in September 1926 after Gregor Strasser was appointed head of propaganda – or in the inflated Party style Reich Propaganda Leader. Strasser had suggested to Hitler that propaganda needed more central co-ordination, but since he saw his role as travelling the country making speeches the co-ordination was left to his assistant, Himmler, who was appointed Deputy Propaganda Leader. So it was that the land he and Marga bought from the proceeds of the Berlin clinic was outside Munich in the eastern suburb of Waldtrudering. There was a small farmhouse, and they started in business by buying some fifty hens and planting herbs. Their idea was to supplement his salary with profits from the sale of eggs and produce. Whether they made much is doubtful; money problems crop up in the surviving letters from those days. What is not in doubt is that after building the henhouse, Himmler virtually left the running of the farm to her.

In coming to Munich he had not dropped his *Gau* responsibilities. He remained Deputy Gauleiter of Lower Bavaria, only transferring his office to the city. His propaganda duties were in addition to this. They involved organising speakers, arranging their itinerary and protection from the 'red' opposition, distributing posters and leaflets and going on speaking tours himself. One of the most brilliant of the young orators, Dr Josef Goebbels, noted in his diary on 30 October 1926: 'Zwickau. Himmler, gossip, slept.'[71] Earlier that year he had met Himmler in Landshut and recorded his impression: 'a good fellow and very intelligent; I like him.'[72]

Later, during his years of power, Himmler liked to yarn about this 'time of struggle'. One of his stories thought worthy of immortality and typed for the file by his secretary concerned a Gauleiter Stier, who used to put him up when he spoke in the Halle area.

Stier drank a lot. If in the morning he was plastered he used to go on the rampage and shoot up street-lights with a pistol. There was a strict prohibition in the Party on carrying arms in those days. The local gendarme was well disposed, but said he couldn't tolerate this for long. Stier was not an ornament of the Party.[73]

Another Gauleiter he stayed with on a tour to northern Germany was a former sailor named Viereck, whose wife worked as a milliner to support him while he looked after the *Gau*. For his evening meal at the Vierecks Himmler was given a *Leberwurst*, which was off. Whether he realised this and like Julius Caesar ate it out of politeness is not revealed by the file notes of the tale. In any case it gave him a bad stomach and he was still suffering the next evening when he rose to address the scheduled meeting. He had not been speaking for long before the hall and audience began to swim before his eyes. Summoning all his powers he steadied himself, broke off the speech and returned to his seat – as he put it when telling the story, he did not want to offer the communists the spectacle of him falling full length from the podium.[74]

Such were the uneducated men from humble backgrounds who formed the overwhelming majority of the Party membership in these days and filled most of the *Gau* leadership positions.

Himmler's altogether different background, superior education, wide reading in the 'literature' and ability with words gave him great social advantages over these Party workers which must have been useful compensation for his insecure, self-persecuting ego. One Party member, Albert Krebs, later purged because of his independent views, said that he affected 'ostentatiously crude and lower-class' manners;[75] most accounts stress his pedantic, schoolmasterly style; no doubt he adapted himself to his surroundings. Nevertheless, it seems probable that it was not only Party ideology keying in with his own need for a cause, but also his own social facility vis-à-vis the Party membership that enabled him to feel 'someone' at last, and caused him to identify so completely with the Party.

As for the content of his speeches, it never varied much. An article he wrote in April 1926 for Strasser's paper, the National Socialist *Briefe*, edited by Josef Goebbels, gives the flavour. It was about the bleak future facing working farmers. Behind their desperate situation was the Jewish vulture, slowly but systematically depressing the price of land. When it had been reduced to 'junk prices' it would be bought up by stock-exchange capital:

> When the catastrophe comes and a substantial portion of German land is in Jewish hands, not a single stalk of grain will grow on it. Then, without the protection of German agriculture, we will be entirely at the mercy of money-market foodstuffs. These will not then be supplied at the present undercut prices, but food prices will be driven up to exorbitant levels. It is evident that no other trade is so useful [to the Jew] as foodstuffs since without nourishment people cannot manage.[76]

Strasser's biographer, Peter Stachura, credits Himmler with 'devising the saturation method of propaganda in selected areas over short periods of time, which soon became a hallmark of NSDAP [Nazi] activity.'[77]

On top of his propaganda and *Gau* duties, Himmler was Gauführer for Bavaria of the Artamen Society,[78] official Party liaison (*Verbindungsmann*) with that movement and assistant editor of the local *völkisch* journal, the *Kurier für Niederbayern*. As if this were not sufficient, he was also made deputy leader of the recently founded Schutzstaffel, or SS.

The SS had emerged in the confused conditions of early 1925, just after Hitler was released from the fortress of Landsberg. The SA was then banned in most states and had gone underground, camouflaged in gymnastic and sporting clubs, for the most part incorporated in Röhm's Frontbann. Hitler had asked Röhm to bring this organisation back into the Party, but had demanded submission of the paramilitary to the political leadership – for one reason because he had become convinced after the failure of the various putsches that power could be obtained only through the ballot box. Under these conditions Röhm had refused. Since it was essential to have strong-arm men to defend Party meetings against 'red' attack, Hitler had entrusted to the leader of his personal guard, his chauffeur/bodyguard Julius Schreck – who drew the same salary as Himmler, 200 Marks a month – the task of setting up similar protection squads, or *Schutzstaffeln* in each district. They were to consist of eight to ten picked men aged from twenty-three to twenty-five, of powerful physique, healthy, not habitual drunkards or bad characters, and resident for at least five years in their area. From the beginning they were seen and regarded themselves as an elite.[79]

As uniform they were supposed to wear the usual brown shirt, with a black tie, black-bordered swastika armband and black Austrian ski cap with a silver death's-head badge, as had been worn by Hitler's original Stabswache, or headquarters guard, in early 1923; the emblem had been taken over by the larger Stosstrupp (Shock-troop) Hitler which had taken part in the beer-hall putsch. In fact the death's head had been used even earlier as the company emblem of an SA troop raised by Kurt Ludecke; then it had been placed in the centre of the swastika on the armband. Whatever the psychological connotations of the death's head and the colour black, which remained the distinguishing marks of the SS, and which could hardly be improved as expressions of the mood and direction of the Party itself, the skull motif was rationalised as an expression of duty unto death.

As Deputy Gauleiter of Lower Bavaria, Himmler organised and led the SS unit in his district; his personal SS number was 168. He and his men took part in the second Party rally at Weimar on 4 July 1926, during which Hitler conferred a signal honour on a new leader or Reichsführer of the SS, Joseph Berchtold, by presenting him with the so-called 'Blood-banner', the flag carried to the Feldherrnhalle during the abortive beer-hall putsch of November 1923. Himmler wrote to a Party colleague afterwards that the Party Day had been 'as you could gather from the press a marvellous demonstration'.[80]

The same letter reveals that he still had money problems: 'Unfortunately it only occurred to me today . . . that I borrowed M20 from you on the journey. I am transferring it directly to you from our Postcheque account. Please forgive my neglect, and apart from that accept my thanks for the "help in need" you have rendered many times. . . .' He ended the letter in the hearty, fulsome style he used to colleagues and acquaintances: 'With my most civil greetings to your esteemed Frau-mother and Frau-wife and loyal German greetings, I am always your devoted Heinrich Himmler. To the Herr-son an extra greeting!'[81]

The following year, 1927, Berchtold was succeeded as Reichsführer-SS by his deputy, Erhard Heiden, and in the autumn Himmler was made Heiden's deputy. He had been working at Party headquarters for twelve months by this time and Hitler had had opportunity to observe his organising ability, zeal and fanatic conviction. When they first met is not known, nor any details of their relationship at this period, but Hitler had an infallible nose for men who would follow him blindly, and it must be assumed from Himmler's later awe-struck devotion to 'the greatest brain of all time' that he acquired his admiration and reverence during these early days in Munich. For those prepared to drop all critical faculties, either because, like Himmler, they needed to believe, or like the majority because they came from strata unused to reasoned debate, Hitler could exert a powerful fascination. His close circle of intimates who had been with him from the beginning regarded him, in Ludecke's words, 'as not only a genius, but an inspired prophet. They hung on his every word, hardly interrupting, even with a question.'[82] In this group Hitler alone talked. Several educated men also fell under the spell: Eckart, Hess, 'Putzi' Hanfstaengl, a Harvard graduate who was a partner in a Munich art-publishing house, Ludecke himself.

Some of the most striking testimony to his appeal in these early days comes from the diary of a highly educated, highly articulate young man, Dr Paul Josef Goebbels. The son of a Rhineland factory foreman, his intelligence had won him Catholic scholarships to several universities. He may have been affected by rising educationally way above his background. He had certainly been affected by failing as an aspiring novelist, playwright, then newspaper reporter. He also suffered psychologically from being extremely small and having a club foot which had kept him out of the war. For whatever reasons, he was consumed inwardly by anger. With this background and temperament he had been a natural convert to the 'socialist' wing of the *völkisch* movement, and had been taken on by the Strasser brothers when Gregor moved to north Germany and started publishing *völkisch* newspapers, apparently with the proceeds of the sale of the chemist's shop in Landshut. Goebbels became editor of the *Briefe* and Gregor's secretary, while his undoubted talents as an orator soon made him much in demand as a speaker at Party meetings. In many ways he was Himmler's counterpart in the north. He was paid the same salary of 200 Marks.

He broke with the Strassers in early 1926. The occasion was Hitler's move to assert his personal leadership over what he felt to be an independent bloc of northern and western Gauleiters organised by Strasser. Hitler's method was, as always, to override rational debate with the emotion he knew he could generate at a mass meeting. The chosen venue was Bamberg in northern Bavaria, and he organised the occasion with care. His own supporters were present *en masse*, and cars decorated with swastika banners were provided to ferry the northern delegates from the railway station to the hall. Goebbels accompanied Gregor Strasser to the meeting, and according to Otto Strasser it was the sight of the cars and the power and luxury they represented that decided the little doctor to renege on Gregor and throw in his lot with the Führer. Otto was not a reliable witness on other aspects of the conference, but undoubtedly Goebbels did choose the occasion to desert his chief.

The Bamberg conference ended for the moment any bid Strasser might
have been making for the leadership. It appears from Goebbels' own diary
entry that the Strassers' cynicism about his motives was correct: 'Certainly
one of the greatest disappointments of my life. I no longer have complete
faith in Hitler.'[83] However, he heard Hitler speaking two months later
and was won back. Hitler also captivated him as a person: 'He squeezed my
hand. Like an old friend. And these large blue eyes! Like stars! He is
glad to see me. I am supremely happy. . . .'[84]

Such was the mesmeric effect of the leader on those who needed a
cause to serve. After the Party Day in Weimar in July 1926, Goebbels
recorded the effect of Hitler's speech in religious terms: 'Deep and
mystical. Almost like a Gospel. One shudders as one skirts the abyss
of life with him. . . .'[85] Can it be doubted that Himmler, who had
the same tormented core as the little doctor and the same unsatisfied
spiritual hunger, also fell under the spell at this time and believed, as
Goebbels believed, that Adolf Hitler had been sent by Divine Providence
to be the saviour of Germany? For his part, Hitler had found the ideal
executive. Gregor Strasser's patronising remarks about Himmler rest on
the testimony of Otto Strasser and Kurt Ludecke, neither of whom were
impartial. On the other hand Röhm had evidently found him a valuable
aide. Recently Alfred Andersch has described his father's admiration
for 'the young Himmler' whom he probably knew through an ex-officers'
association, the Deutschvölkischen Offizierbund which Heinrich belonged
to until June 1926. Andersch senior regarded him as 'outstanding, a
Hitler-follower, but not one-sided' since he also associated with other
nationalist organisations. Of the young men he knew Himmler seemed to
him 'the most intelligent and reliable, calm but of iron determination',
indeed he would have liked to have had him in his company in the
trenches. As a final accolade, in contrast to old Professor Himmler, he
said, 'the young Himmler would never sit at the same table with Jews,
Jesuits or freemasons.'[86]

One of the qualities that made him useful to the Party at that
time of faction when all groups infiltrated and spied on all others
was his natural bent for nosing out information and for intrigue. A
letter from an official of the Deutschvölkischen Offizierbund at the
time he resigned in June 1926 accused him of plotting on behalf of
the Nazis to undermine the local group.[87] However that may be, the
tasks of the early SS, in addition to providing protection at meetings,
included selling subscriptions and advertising space for the Party paper,
Völkischer Beobachter, and gathering information on the intentions of
hostile or rival nationalist organisations. This intelligence function was
important for Himmler in his other hat at propaganda since, of course,
most of the propaganda was directed against internal enemies; Jews, communists, freemasons, Jesuits and social democrats. According to Frischauer,
Himmler's room at Party headquarters was crammed with newspaper files

and shelves stacked high with correspondence. Undoubtedly many of the files contained cuttings from 'hostile' papers and journals and information on these organisations and their leaders. In view of his later predilection for card indexes, it would be surprising if he had not meticulously cross-indexed the information.

Combining as he did the organisation of Party propaganda, which depended so much on timely intelligence, and the leadership of the SS in one of the most important *Gaue*, Himmler was already at the centre of SS activities when he was appointed deputy Reichsführer in September 1927. His minute attention to detail and discipline were felt immediately. On 17 September SS Order No. 1 promulgated strict regulations for uniform, behaviour, training sessions and intelligence duties. In place of the variegated *Lederhosen* or coloured sports gear which the men were wont to wear on duty, black breeches, brown shirts, black ties, black leather accoutrements were made mandatory with the black cap. Each *Staffel* was to be paraded in military order before meetings and inspected; the men were to produce their Party membership book, SS pass and SS songbook, and any arms were to be confiscated. Hitler's path of legality was to be followed to the letter.

Each *Staffel* was to attend the first local group meeting of the month in the course of which no SS man was to smoke nor leave the hall during the speeches nor take part in any discussion. SS leaders were never to involve themselves in areas which did not concern them. This included the political leadership and the SA, again incorporated as the mass paramilitary arm of the movement under another ex-Army captain, Pfeffer von Salomon. The watchword was: 'The SS keeps apart from all quarrels.'[88]

Each *Staffel* was to hold two drill and singing sessions each month and, if there were no official duties in the month, they were to arrange a meeting with a neighbouring *Staffel* or carry out a propaganda march: 'The SS man should be the most ardent propagandist for the movement. . . . the SS [should] appear in public as indistinguishable from an active service formation.'[89]

The intelligence duties laid down are particularly interesting, both as foreshadowing the system of universal snooping which Himmler was to introduce throughout the Reich, and as an indication of the extent to which the SS was from the beginning a security organ for the Führer against rival factions within the Nazi Party and the SA. Thus SS leaders were instructed to report 'in urgent cases immediately' if they believed that anything was not in order in the political leadership or SA spheres, also to report any SA men who dressed even partly in SS uniform.

The 'enemy' intelligence duties were laid down thus:

The SS leader, and each SS man through him, reports all striking [*auffallenden*] news of the opponents, especially strong activity of the Reichsbanner [the social democratic organisation], the KPD [Communist Party], especially prominent leaders and the like; all freemasons and outstanding Jewish leaders known with certainty to the SS; all special events in political or other areas . . . which could be of interest to us.[90]

According to Otto Strasser, Himmler's models at this time were Napoleon's chief of police, Fouché, and the head of Stalin's secret police, Dzerzhinsky. He apparently read books about these two and 'his eyes shone' when he described to Otto their 'ruses and successes'.[91] His reading list provides little confirmation. He did read several books on modern Russia between the end of 1925 and spring 1926, and among them one on Stalin's secret police, the Cheka. He did not approve of this, however, since the author, Georg Popoff, failed to use the word 'Jew' despite the Cheka being, in Himmler's opinion, 'almost entirely Jewish'.[92] He was confirmed in this opinion when he read Katharina Haug-Haough's *Hinter den Kulissen des Bolschewismus* (*Bolshevism Behind the Scenes*). He commented, 'The Jews [behind Bolshevism] have unleashed the animal [in man] and crime.'[93]

Whether or not Himmler read or knew much about Fouché, according to Otto Strasser he wrote a memorandum on the need for a Cheka-style secret police to monitor Party members and the SA, and convinced Hitler that the SS should perform the function, assuring him that they would be his most loyal guards: 'They will be blindly devoted to you and continue the tradition of the Stosstrupp Hitler of 9 November 1923.'[94] The story certainly accords with Himmler's zealous pushfulness and with the needs of the Party at that time when the SA leaders were boisterous condottieri and even their leader von Salomon gibed at acknowledging political leadership. Certainly SS Order No. 1 confirms that internal surveillance was an important function of the SS from the beginning of Himmler's time as Deputy Reichsführer.

A book-list comment he made in early 1925 shows that he also had a clear idea from the very beginning of the kind of elite formation he wanted the SS to become. The book was Franz Haiser's *Freimaurer und Gegenmaurer im Kampf um die Weltherrschaft* (*Freemasons and Antimasons in Battle for World Mastery*). He noted, 'Kshatriya-caste, that is what we must be. That is the salvation.'[95] The Kshatriyas were the noble warrior caste of the Aryans who conquered and ruled India some 1700 years before Christ.

Bringing forward his earlier book-list comments on racial purity, the evil effects of interbreeding with inferior races, the possibility of breeding out racial impurities, and his views on the international Jewish conspiracy to subvert the world, together with his Artamen idyll of colonising eastern Europe with pure Germans, it can be seen that all the features which were to distinguish the SS in its years of power were present in Himmler's imagination before he took over as Deputy Reichsführer: the SS was to be at once a secret police and a warrior elite, an instrument of internal conformity and a breeding ground for the purification of the race, the hammer of Jews, masons, Slavs, communism and democracy, and the agency for settling the east with Nordic farmers. It was to herald the Germanic millennium.

It was a romantic view with fearful consistency. Its realisation – if such a thing were possible – implied war on a grand scale. But this was consistent with the current Nietzschean, biological reading of history: as Hitler forever pointed out, life *was* struggle; only the fittest survived. To be as fit as the dedicated communists threatening Germany from within and from the east, Germans had to be indoctrinated with an equally uncompromising creed. The SS was to be the instrument.

Himmler was obsessed with the vision. Consequently he failed to comprehend the scale of the sacrifices, particularly the moral sacrifices, which would become necessary. One of the last books on his reading list in 1926 was Franz Helbing and Max Bauer's *Die Tortur* (*Torture*). He noted: 'A frightful [*grausames*] book about the animal in man as it appears, even officially, in every century of history. One notices the book is in parts friendly to Jews. . . .'[96] It seems from this comment that he not only failed to foresee the necessary future if his dreams were to be realised but completely failed in self-perception.

Two other books on his reading list are interesting, for they show that he had not been cut off completely from alternatives to the Nietzschean *Weltanschauung*. At the end of 1924 he had read two of Hermann Hesse's novels, *Damian* and *Siddhartha*. Probably they appealed to him because they told of young men searching for the truth – the quest on which he himself had set out so earnestly. Moreover Hermann Hesse's truth was essentially Buddhist – Siddhartha indeed may be read as an allegory of the Buddha and there is a sense in which the fatalism of Buddhist philosophy keyed in with his own austere dedication to will and duty whatever the cost. The Ferryman in the story, one of the Buddha's traditional guises, teaches the hero Siddhartha the value of detaching oneself from passion, doing what is right and allowing things to take their course; they will in any case. 'I can see you are suffering,' he says when Siddhartha loses his son, 'suffering pain over which one should laugh, over which you will soon laugh yourself.' Siddhartha feels only emptiness. 'He felt something die in his heart; he saw no more happiness, no goal.'[97] How many times had Himmler experienced similar breaks within? How many times had he practised detachment? How many times in the future would it be necessary for him to detach himself from the suffering over which he had to preside in the course of doing what was right as events took their ordained path?

At the end of the book Hesse depicts a mystical vision in which Siddhartha's great friend sees the unity of all life through all ages, fish, animals, men, hunters and hunted, victors and victims, lovers and avengers: 'Each one was mortal, a passionate, painful example of all that is transitory. Yet none of them died, they only changed, were always reborn, continually had a new face; only time stood between one face and another. . . .'[98]

It is clear from Himmler's letters and conversations that he accepted what he termed the Indo-Germanic peoples' belief in rebirth, as well as the Hindu doctrine of Karma, and it is known that later he kept a notebook of favourite quotations he had copied from the Hindu *Vedas* and *Bhagavad-Gita*. Undoubtedly his interest sprang from his belief in the Aryan ancestry of the Germanic race rather than the novels of Hermann Hesse. Yet the fact that his interest extended to belief in certain doctrines indicates the selectivity of his mind. Hesse's ultimate message about the unity of the cosmos and the importance of loving the world, not despising it, was censored out by his convictions in the other direction. Hermann Hesse's books were banned after Hitler took power.

Photographs of Himmler at this 'time of struggle' show him usually with a militarily stiff posture that appears forced, sloping shoulders, short arms, wide hips and a pinched, pale face dominated by round spectacles giving him a prim, clerkish look. A neat moustache, tight, pursed lips and poor chin do nothing to diminish this impression. His hair, shaved at back and sides, was dark – so dark his clean-shaven chin was described as blueish; his eyebrows were very darkly defined and of somewhat quizzical aspect, his short-sighted, steel-blue eyes glittered behind the thick lenses. One can imagine the supercilious schoolboy described by Hallgarten better than the martial dreamer revealed by the young man's diaries. He appears a thin, incongruous figure among the bulky ex-Freikorps soldiers of fortune and tavern brawlers of the Party. Yet he had qualities of perseverance and that unsatisfied hungry core which the photographs cannot show, and which had nothing to do with his beliefs; or as Siddhartha says of the Buddha, 'his deeds and life are more important to me than his opinions.' Moreover Hitler had detected in him that capacity for absolute belief and blind loyalty that goes with the inner need for a cause to lose oneself in and a star to follow.

On 17 January 1928, SS Order No. 4 stated that all practical duties of the SS would be arrranged by Pg. (Party-comrade) Himmler; all orders would be signed by Heiden or Himmler. As it had been in his student days, so now: 'Der Heini macht es schon,' 'Heini will see to it.' On 20 January 1929, he succeeded Heiden as Reichsführer-SS.[99]

Under normal conditions this would not have been a historic nor even an important event to anyone but Heinrich Himmler and his wife Marga, already suffering his absences due to long hours of work and travel. The Party was still on the fringe of German politics. The SS was a force of under 300 men scattered in some seventy-five *Staffeln*, many of which existed only on paper; moreover they were subordinate to the SA. But conditions were not normal. The nation was about to be fired-up to a point at which its mood began to harmonise with the extreme convictions of the Party – a groundswell of financial support built largely of frustration was about to lift the Hitler movement on a dizzy ride to power.

Himmler could scarcely have guessed at the speed with which events were about to unfold as he set about the task of building up the strength of his command, and devising selection procedures to produce the racial elite he wanted. Albert Krebs, Gauleiter of Hamburg, found himself closeted with him on a six-hour railway journey at this time, travelling north to inspect and set up new SS units in his area. In an often-quoted passage of his memoirs, Krebs wrote that he had never heard so much political nonsense in such concentrated form as the 'stupid and fundamentally empty claptrap' he was served up by the new Reichsführer.[100] The judgement need not be taken at face value. It was written after the war when many others who had been closer to Himmler than Krebs also discovered how bizarre were the views they had once supported enthusiastically. Nevertheless, his account of Himmler's preoccupations is undoubtedly true:

> What concerned him were the 'secret' conditions. Did the former Kapitanleutnant X really have a Jewish or half-Jewish wife? How did SA-leader Conn come by his remarkable name? Was it perhaps a camouflage for Cohn? What bank had Gauleiter Lohse [of Schleswig-Holstein] worked for? Could he thereby have fallen into Jewish dependence?[101]

Krebs admitted that the 'Wise Men of Zion', world freemasonry and the Jesuit conspiracy belonged to the intellectual arsenal of his Party, but suggested that for most Nazi leaders these were propaganda subterfuges rather than convictions: 'For Himmler, on the contrary, I had to assume, after this conversation, that he lived among these conceptions, that they represented his world, in face of which the real, practical world with its problems and tasks fell into the background.'[102] Himmler's correspondence over the next fifteen years proves beyond any possible doubt that Krebs was right about his world. What is not certain is Krebs' contention that this was a different world to that in which other convinced Nazis lived.

The outside world obtruded that summer when Marga bore Himmler a daughter; she was named Gudrun, supposedly after the heroine of Werner Jansen's *Das Buch Liebe*. Much as he was devoted to her, his family life continued to suffer from the fanatical demands he made on himself in the cause of the Party. To judge by her resigned letters, Marga spent most of her time alone at their small home in Waltrudering with her infant daughter and one maid. 'Only today I was thinking how we could celebrate your birthday,' she wrote in one undated letter when he was on one of his frequent journeys, 'My love, let's go to some exhibition together. We've never done that.'[103]

4

Reichsführer-SS

There were indications through 1929 that the Party was emerging from the wilderness. Hitler purchased a palace on the Briennerstrasse, Munich, for Party headquarters, and began remodelling it to the most lavish plans while taking up residence in a nine-roomed flat in the equally grand Prinzregentenstrasse. Since his release from the fortress of Landsberg he had not lacked patrons to guarantee his personal spending, but this signified patronage of a different order, the outward, soon to become most visible sign of large-scale financial support. It came from a powerful section of heavy industry, chiefly from Fritz Thyssen, chairman of the United Steelworks, encouraged and strongly supported by Emil Kirdorf, the biggest name in Ruhr coal.

These were, so far as is known, the first representatives of big business actively to back Hitler. Naturally they did so to manipulate him for their own purposes. Kirdorf was a pan-German who had supported the most extreme annexationist aims of the war; in internal politics he was opposed to democracy and the workers' movement even in moderate guise, and wanted to overturn the social and union policies employers had been forced to concede during the revolutionary turmoil and subsequent social democratic rule. His attitudes had a sound economic basis. The workers' movement had overplayed its hand: wages and welfare provisions had outstripped productivity in the labour-intensive heavy industries which he and Thyssen represented, squeezing profits and discouraging investment.[1] The position had been exacerbated by changes in the structure of the economy brought about by the new light industries and sharpened by a drastic decline in demand for steel products, particularly armaments and ships, both practically forbidden to Germany by the Versailles Treaty; added to this, Germany had been excluded from former overseas markets by the victorious allies, who evidently intended to keep her out by so restricting her naval and merchant naval strength. As if this were not sufficient, the threat of nationalisation by the socialists in power hung over this whole sector of the economy. It is easy to understand how Kirdorf, Thyssen and their fellows in the Ruhr and Upper Silesia felt that they could do business with the National Socialists, easy to see how Hitler, wooing industrial support, could tailor his message to suit them. According to Otto Strasser, he made a compact with Kirdorf in the summer of 1929: in return for 'lots of money'[2] the industrialists could dictate Party policy; the millions spent on the new Party headquarters show that some agreement on these lines was concluded.

At about the same time Hitler was coming to an agreement with the leader of the Deutschnational Party, Alfred Hugenberg. He was another particularly virulent specimen of pan-Germanism – as described by one Berlin hostess, a veritable caricature 'with his military haircut, full-spreading moustache, small eyes hidden in rolls of fat' – who represented both owners of heavy industry and the Prussian Junker landholding interest. The Junkers were a power group which also felt threatened by democracy and the changing structure of the economy, and their impoverished even bankrupt estates in the east were worked in traditional labour-intensive ways and like heavy industry had the threat of nationalisation hanging over them. In addition they were suffering a drastic fall in agricultural prices which threatened ruin.

The immediate cause of the Hitler–Hugenberg agreement was a plan for the final settlement of German war reparations drawn up that summer by an allied committee under the chairmanship of the American banker, Owen Young. The Young Plan provided for the removal of allied controls on the German economy, the winding-up of the allied control commission policing German disarmament and the withdrawal of troops still occupying the Rhineland, and called for payment of reparations at a slightly reduced annual rate of just over 2000 million Marks for the next fifty-nine years. It was a goad to nationalists of every description. Hugenberg formed a national committee to fight reparations and the 'lie' of German war guilt on which they rested, and asked Hitler to join. The Deutschnational leader was a newspaper tycoon with a nationwide chain of papers and journals, but his committee was representative of the upper 'reactionary' strata, and he needed a voice to speak to the people. Hitler demanded funds and complete freedom to conduct his campaign in his own way.

In the autumn the trade and agricultural depression turned into a worldwide economic slump. In October the New York stock exchange crashed. The chiefly American Dawes Plan loans which had generated prosperity over the last few years ceased or were called in, adding to the downward spiral; bankruptcies, suicides and unemployment climbed as steeply as they had in the time of the great inflation, and once again Nazi Party speakers had bitter personal failures and resentments to play on as they campaigned against 'the enslavement of the German people' by the Young Plan. With the funds made available by Hugenberg and nation-wide coverage in his newspapers Hitler and the National Socialists became household names throughout the country. The campaign failed to prevent legislation to fulfil reparations, but even this was turned to propaganda advantage; the government which had signed the Young Plan was added to the list of traitors and enemies of the people alongside the original 'Novemberlings' who had signed the Versailles Treaty, and the Jews and

Marxists and stock-exchange capitalists seeking to enslave the nation. As unemployment mounted through 1930, going above the three-million mark in September, more and more Germans, particularly among the young, sucked in this message of hate. At Reichstag elections called that month, nearly six and a half million voted for the National Socialists, carrying them in one bound from an insignificant fringe group less than a quarter the size of the Communist Party to the second-largest national party with 107 seats. One of the seats was allotted to Heinrich Himmler.

On their way to the first session of the new Parliament, a group of Nazi deputies uniformed in brown celebrated by smashing department-store windows down the Leipzigerstrasse; 'by some odd chance,' a Jewish journalist noted in her diary, 'the casually aimed projectiles hit only non-Aryan targets.'[3] It was broad daylight; no one saw them doing it; no one was arrested. Inside the chamber, they snapped to the Hitler salute and shouted the Party slogan in chorus, 'Deutschland erwache!' – 'Germany awake!'

At Party headquarters in Munich a new mood was in the air. The *Machtergreifung*, or seizure of power, was talked of now not as a mirage in the distance, but as a tangible event to plan for. One of Himmler's close colleagues, Karl von Eberstein, who travelled the country recruiting for the SA and SS, told a young naval lieutenant he knew, named Reinhard Heydrich, that the *Machtergreifung* was close; the world economic crisis had driven the petty bourgeoisie into the arms of the Party.[4]

It would be as true to say that the traditional conservative power groupings who had never accepted defeat in the war or the humiliating terms of the Versailles Treaty or the Republican democratic form of government – which they viewed as another form of defeat inflicted by the allied powers in consort with the Marxist traitors at home, who had stabbed the armed services in the back – were reaping the harvest from the seeds originally planted by the Navy through the Thule Society, and the Army through Captain Röhm, nourished by the Freikorps and the pan-German publishing houses and the secret funds of both armed services. They had achieved a party of the people, whose leader was dedicated to their own vengeful aims both externally and internally.

The Party marched obediently behind its leader. Even Gregor Strasser had toned down and soon lost his 'socialist' rhetoric altogether. He beat the nationalist drum with increased fervour, vowing vengeance on all external and internal enemies: when the Party gained power there would no longer be Marxist or even democratic politicians. 'Those who owe allegiance to any International . . . will be strung up . . . and if we have to walk up to the knees in blood for Germany's sake, so be it.'[5] He let Jews off rather more lightly, merely demanding their exclusion from German life.[6] It is possible, even probable, that his change of course was only tactical, for he remained in close touch with his younger brother, Otto, who broke away from the Party in the summer of 1930 rather than betray his socialist convictions.

Otto has left an account of his last meeting with Hitler when he tackled him on his betrayal of the movement to capitalism. Hitler argued that in industry as everywhere the struggle for existence prevailed. Capitalist factory owners had worked their way to the top by virtue of their superior fitness to rule – an argument he had used to persuade the industrialists he was on their side. Otto very reasonably replied that selection for capitalism was by money, the very worst criterion for a heroic people, and he suggested that the ideals of service to the community implied by a socialist system would result in a wholly different kind of selection. He went on to argue for a closed economic system working only to supply the needs of the nation, entirely independent of the world system.

'That is the most wicked dilettantism,' Hitler replied.

> We are dependent on the import of all important raw materials, and no less dependent on the export of industrial products. . . . our task is to take in hand a great organisation of the whole world so that each country produces what is most suitable to it; it is for the white race, the Nordic race, to carry through this gigantic plan. Believe me, all National Socialism would be worth nothing if it were limited only to Germany, and did not seal for one to two thousand years the mastery of the superior-value race over the whole world. . . . We must provide this leadership in common with the Anglo-Saxons.[7]

Otto said he was appalled at such a goal, which matched the aims of world finance, and Gregor, who was also present, backed him up; he was also of the opinion that economic autarchy was the goal, and involvement in the world economy had to be limited to the bare minimum.[8]

If Otto recorded this discussion accurately, it shows that at this date, 22 May 1930, both Strasser brothers were arguing for economic arrangements which came to be associated with the leaders of the giant IG Farben chemicals trust and other representatives of the new light industries. During the years of prosperity champions of 'US-style mass-production, mass-consumption capitalism' harnessed to the world market, they were now beginning to think in terms of an independent German-led European bloc. By March 1931 Carl Duisberg of IG Farben was speaking of 'a closed economic bloc from Bordeaux to Sofia'.[9] Hitler, on the other hand, was arguing on the lines of heavy industrialists like Thyssen who also looked to German hegemony in Europe, but in co-operation with US capital.

Probably Gregor Strasser was already IG Farben's man inside the Nazi leadership. Kirdorf had his men; one was the Führer himself, another a former bank clerk named Josef Terboven, whom Kirdorf had inserted as early as 1927 and who was now Gauleiter of Essen in the heartland of heavy industry. It is unlikely that the immensely powerful new chemical, automobile and light industrial grouping had not taken similar steps as the world crisis forced them to reappraise policy, and it became evident that the Nazis were making headway with substantial backing from rival groups.

In any case after the September election success all major interest groups joined the struggle to influence Nazi policy through their own candidates in the leadership and there is no question that IG Farben and the light industrialists put their money on Strasser as the heavy industrialists put theirs on Hitler and Göring.

With this backing on the one hand and the deepening recession and increasing unemployment on the other, the Party grew at a furious pace, and increasingly drew members from the higher social classes. The reasons which prompted some of these people to throw in their lot with a party which had been the preserve of *kleinen Leute*, freebooting ex-soldiers, extremists and recently the unemployed are outlined in an interesting circular which Prince Eulenburg-Hertefeld sent to his peers in February 1931. He had, he said, been a member of the Deutschnational Party since its inception. It was no easy matter for him to part from it, but if they did not want Bolshevism there was no choice but to join '*the* Party' which today was supported by the masses and 'despite many socialist ideas' stood at the opposite pole to Marxism and Bolshevism.

His positive reasons were as important:

> Men with leadership qualities must decide to enter the NSDAP and work in it. There must be many, not only individuals, so that after the *Machtergreifung* they are available for the leading positions. He who thinks of making himself available only *afterwards* will in the best case be a second-class citizen, after the Italian pattern, and will not be allotted leadership tasks.
>
> The deciding factor should not be egotism or opportunism, but above all the desire and the will to place his capacities – especially his leadership qualities – in the service of those whom we can hope will be successful in destroying Marxism.[10]

There could have been no plainer statement of intent. The Nazi Party represented that 'patriotic' consensus which the Prussian leadership had sought to build before the first war to preserve its power position against strong socialist and separatist trends within the Reich. It had failed until it played the ultimate patriotic card of European war. Now the stakes were even higher. In the face of more dangerous economic and revolutionary pressures than in 1912 to 1914 it was necessary to establish a leadership position within '*the* Party' seen as about to seize power from the increasingly demoralised and undermined democratic politicians.

So the real struggle within Germany moved inside the Nazi Party even before the *Machtergreifung*. The nobility and its extension, the officer corps of the Army, and the owners of the older heavy industries had their own differences but were united in their fear of the social and economic forces threatening their position – not simply the communists and social democrats, but the thrusting new industrialists like Carl Duisberg of IG Farben, who saw the need for modernisation of the whole social, industrial and agricultural fabric of the nation. As brokers and mediators between the economic interest-groups the big banks had the major role since they performed the functions that in America, Great Britain and France were performed by money markets and stock exchanges; they were both the largest shareholders and providers of capital for big business and the agents for amalgamations and cartels between concerns. Hence at the same time as the Party was becoming politically and socially acceptable it was the focus for intrigue between the highest hereditary, industrial and capital interests – and not only national interests since foreign, chiefly US capital was tied in directly with big German banks and with the German economy.

Thus in scarcely over a year since Heinrich Himmler had been appointed Reichsführer-SS the Party was catapulted into the stress centre of German and world finance and politics. Exactly when he realised this or when he realised that his conception of the SS as the elite of the Party was about to be fulfilled is impossible to say, but the greater the intra-Party rivalries forced by these pressures, the more the SS came to play the key role as the loyal, unquestioning praetorian guard of the Führer and the more Heinrich Himmler himself became the key figure.

'The SS will be an Order sworn to the Führer,' he had told Otto Strasser soon after his appointment in 1929. 'For him I could do anything. Believe me, if Hitler were to say I should shoot my mother, I would do it and be proud of his confidence.' 'Heinrich, I shudder at you,' Otto replied. It became a catchphrase with which he used to greet Himmler. 'He always took it with a laugh, indeed he was flattered.'[11]

At that time Himmler was trying to recruit Otto as leader of the northern district of the SS, centred on Berlin. It is an indication of his methods that the carrot he dangled was the chance of vengeance on Goebbels, now Gauleiter of Berlin, whom he knew Otto hated. 'That Goebbels will be green and blue with rage. You would naturally be subordinate only to me, no one could interfere with you in any way. You could finally take your revenge on Goebbels.'[12] But Otto declined.

Eventually Himmler selected another man with a grudge. This was Kurt Daluege, a war veteran, former Freikorps member and founder of the Berlin SA – in which he had distinguished himself as a street- and tavern-fighter – who was displaced as group leader in Berlin by Walter Stennes, deputy leader of the SA under Pfeffer von Salomon. Under Daluege the SS passed its first major test of loyalty when Stennes struck against Hitler's leadership shortly before the September 1930 elections. How much this was inspired by the industrial–financial groupings opposed to the direction the Party had taken, how much by other groupings attempting to splinter the Nazi movement is difficult to estimate. The ostensible cause of the revolt was a demand that the SA be allocated more of the Reichstag seats the Party was expected to win in the election, and generally have more political influence. Daluege's troop held firm behind the Munich leadership.

Hitler flew to Berlin and patched up the politically damaging split, at least for the time being, but he dismissed Pfeffer von Salomon, took over the supreme leadership of the SA himself and persuaded Röhm back to the fold as his SA Chief of Staff. Himmler, who assisted in the wooing of his former mentor, then in South America, was given the task of increasing the strength of the SS to some 10 per cent of the SA – a continually moving target since the SA was expanding at a tremendous rate and reached 60,000 that winter. Himmler insisted on high standards in selection. As he told a meeting of his officers, known as SS-Führers, on 8 December that year, 'the greatest caution must be exercised in enrolment for we want only the best human material. . . . Adolf Hitler has allowed himself to be caught once and that must not happen a second time. . . . Hitler therefore needs a troop on which he can rely.'[13] Röhm repeated the message to the Munich and Upper Bavarian SS gathered in the Burgerbräukeller in March 1931; as SA-Chief of Staff, he was Himmler's immediate superior. He enjoined them to loyalty, sense of duty and discipline to the Führer, and concluded his address with a pledge that the SS would support Hitler until the goal was reached.[14]

Meanwhile the rumblings in the Berlin SA had been continuing. SS informers kept Daluege and Munich headquarters fully apprised. Hitler also used SS men in a plot to lure Stennes into another, more far-reaching revolt against his leadership on 1 April 1931. He and Röhm then used the revolt to destroy Stennes and weed out his adherents from the SA leadership of the northern and eastern *Gaue*. Afterwards Hitler let it be known that he owed his victory over the dissidents solely to the vigilance of the SS, and he sent Daluege a letter in which he used the phrase, 'SS-Mann, Deine Ehre heisst Treue'[15] – 'SS man, your honour signifies loyalty.' This was, of course, precisely Himmler's idea; probably he suggested it to Hitler, for the whole episode of the 'Stennes putsch' has the smell of 'divide and rule' and deliberate myth-making to foster rivalry and alarm. In any case, it became the slogan of the SS and was inscribed on the SS belt buckles – 'SS-Mann, Deine Ehre heisst Treue'.

In June Himmler addressed a convention of the northern SS-Führers at Daluege's Berlin headquarters strategically placed on the corner of Lützowstrasse and Potsdamerstrasse opposite SA headquarters. It was the main speech of the day and was delivered in the benign, schoolmasterly manner his officials knew so well. His light Bavarian accent and a simple vocabulary, seasoned with colloquialisms, helped to establish rapport with his audience. There were no histrionics, no rhetorical tricks, simply calm reasonableness. He demonstrated points with analogies culled from his eclectic stock of historical and racial lore, following whatever rambling and repetitive paths these led. It was a trait that became more marked in later speeches; consciously or unconsciously he seemed to show off his knowledge as much to establish superiority, or merely to indulge himself, as to convince. He was the father who knew more than his children. He also demanded. The way he demanded hardness and self-abnegation – especially in his later speeches – and the meandering, repetitive way he spoke seem all of a piece with the chaotic thoughts entered in his adolescent diaries. There is every reason to suppose, however, that he held his listeners, no doubt because he made self-evident in vivid rather than profound ways what they already felt and believed. He was the supreme interpreter and legitimiser of their task.

In this case his theme was 'the purpose and goal of the SS'. The Corps was to be developed through the selection of specially singled-out men into the guard of the nation. The SA was the line, the SS the guard, which in times of crisis would be deployed as the last reserve of the Führer – and he listed examples from history from the ancient Greeks to Napoleon and Frederick the Great.

In early times, he went on, the men of the Guard had always been selected for size. For the SS it was to be race: 'for us, standing sublime above all doubt, it is the blood carrier, who can make history; the Nordic race is decisive not only for Germany, but for the whole world.'

> Should we succeed in establishing this Nordic race again from and around Germany and inducing them to become farmers, and from this seedbed producing a race of 200 million, then the world will belong to us. Should Bolshevism win, it will signify the extermination [*Austilgen*] of the Nordic race . . . devastation, the end of the world. . . . We are called, therefore, to create a basis on which the next generation can make history.[16]

This vision seems to be a development, at least in numerical terms, of his long-held views on the settlement of the east with German farmers, and of the SS as a racial elite. It sounds very like the 'gigantic plan' Hitler had outlined to Otto Strasser in May 1930. At the same time the far-reaching goal was less immediate than it was soon to become. The idea of merely creating a springboard for the *next* generation was restrained by comparison with later speeches.

Coming to methods of selection for the elite guard, he stressed that the primary requirement was racial: candidates had to be at least 1.7 metres (five feet nine inches) – or if they came from Schleswig-Holstein 1.76 metres. Himmler himself was 1.75 metres. With young men appearance (*Äusseren*) counted above all.

> A typical Slav-face would scarcely be taken in to the SS by an SS-Führer, because he [the Slav] would very soon notice that he had no community of blood [*Blutsgemeinschaft*] with his comrades of more Nordic origin. The photographs which have to accompany the application form serve the purpose of allowing the faces of the candidates to be seen at headquarters [the Reichsleitung in Munich]. . . . in general we want only good fellows, not louts [*nur Kerle und keine Scheisskerle*]. . . .[17]

By this date the SS was a nationwide organisation, 10,000 strong, but Himmler still attended to the detailed administration himself. He

virtually was the SS-Reichsleitung, running the desks described in a police
report earlier that year as 1a, business, 1c, security, and 1d, finance, while
a Freiherr von Thüngen ran 1b, recruiting, under his direction. In order to
standardise and administer racial selection, he added an independent Race
Office which came into life officially on 1 January 1932. As its chief he
appointed Hitler's agricultural expert, Walter Darré, whose views on race,
human breeding and the value of peasant stock were as extreme as his own.
Two books had established Darré's name in this field: *Das Bauerntum als
Lebensquell der nordischen Rasse* (*The Farming Community as Life-source
of the Nordic Race*), 1928, and *Neuadel aus Blut und Boden* (*New Nobility
from Blood and Soil*), 1930.

There is no doubt that Darré and Himmler had had many talks about their
common obsession for Darré had been an honorary SS-Standartenführer –
the highest rank at that time – for some while. Darré was the older of the two
by five years and by far the more experienced. Born in the Argentine, he had
been to school in Germany and for his final two years in England at King's
College School, Wimbledon. He had volunteered for the war, been commissioned as a reserve officer and afterwards studied agriculture, passing
out as a *Diplomlandwirt* in 1923, a year after Himmler. He had, however,
spent the next five years employed on land administration. His views were
in one sense mumbo-jumbo, a mystical fusion of race and the springs of life
in the ground. In another sense he was a practical land economist with
sound views on the necessity for modernising German agriculture. One
great Junker landowner who saw this clearly at that time was Graf von
Arnim. He replied to Prince Eulenburg's February 1931 circular – quoted
previously – that while Hitler's own views might be flawless, his agricultural
adviser Darré had extraordinarily uncomfortable ideas which constituted 'a
slap in the face of the nobility'.[18] A member of his family working on Hitler's
staff had mentioned the same doubts about Darré to him – an interesting
remark showing that Prince Eulenburg was by no means ahead of his time
when he suggested that the leading families should enter and take the lead
in the new Party; many were in already and spreading word of its policies
through their social connections.

One such was Himmler's Chief of Staff, the Erbprinz zu Waldeck
und Pyrmont. The Prince, four years older than Himmler, had followed
the military career statutory for his class and had been badly wounded
during the war; afterwards he too had studied agriculture. He had joined
the Party in November 1929, soon after Hitler's alliance with Hugenberg,
and Himmler had taken him over the following year. It must have been a
boost to Himmler's self-esteem, now growing – as will be seen – as fast
as his responsibilities. Yet behind it there remained the self-doubt of his
schooldays and adolescence, and the sense of failure at having missed the
initiation at the front which had formed his Führer, Strasser, Darré, his
Chief of Staff and most of the old guard of the Party.

During 1931, before the new Race Office came into being, he and

Darré thrashed out the principles of racial selection. Since the object was not merely the establishment of an elite guard, but the provision of a seedbed of pure Nordic stock to spread through and reinvigorate the whole German nation, it was axiomatic that SS wives had to pass the same selection procedures as the men. Accordingly on 31 December 1931, the day before the new office started functioning, Himmler promulgated an 'Engagement and Marriage Decree'.

1. The SS is an association of German men of Nordic determination selected on special criteria.
2. In conformity with the National Socialist *Weltanschauung* and recognising that the future of our people depends on the selection and retention of racially and hereditarily sound good blood, I establish with effect from 1 January 1932 the 'marriage consent' for all unmarried members of the SS.
3. The goal striven for is the hereditarily sound, valuable extended family [*Sippe*] of German, Nordically determined type.
4. Marriage consent will be granted and denied solely and exclusively on the criteria of race and hereditary health.
5. Every SS man who intends to marry has to apply for this purpose to the Reichsführer-SS for the marriage consent.
6. SS members who marry despite having been denied the marriage consent will be dismissed from the SS; they will be given the option of resigning.
7. The appropriate processing of marriage requests is the task of the Race Office of the SS.
8. The Race Office of the SS manages the 'Clanbook of the SS' [*Sippenbuch der SS*], in which the families of SS members will be entered after the granting of the marriage consent or approval of the request for registration.
9. The Reichsführer-SS, the head of the Race Office and the specialists of this office are bound to secrecy on their word of honour.
10. The SS is clear that with this order it has taken a step of great significance. Derision, scorn and misunderstanding do not affect us; the future belongs to us.
    Heinrich Himmler[19]

Marriage consent was nothing new in the German armed services. Up to 1918 every officer in the Army and Navy had needed the Kaiser's consent to marry; the criteria demanded of Kaiserlichen brides-to-be were social and financial, to try and ensure that they would not bring the officer corps into disrepute and that the couple would be able to live to the standard befitting an officer's family. The SS marriage-consent investigations were considerably more thorough since they were designed as the realisation of the positive ideals of the race-hygiene or eugenics theories to which Himmler and Darré and indeed the Party as a whole subscribed. Therefore girls had to provide medical testimony to their own and their family's physical and mental health, and undergo a medical examination, measurement and scrutiny of their features to ensure that they conformed to certain 'Nordic' requirements.

The negative side of the programme was the elimination of blood admixtures from Jewish, Slavish, Mongolian, eastern or negro forebears. Hence both SS men and their wives-to-be had to provide genealogical details to prove the purity of their descent back five generations if possible. These names – sixty-three when their own was included – were entered on their personal 'Ancestor Table'. The eventual goal was that all SS officers and their wives should prove pure Aryan origin back to 1750, SS men back to 1800.

The decree illustrates the sense of power Himmler had acquired by this date which, augmenting his ingrained self-righteousness, could produce such a grandiose vision of his own importance and the importance of the task before him. This was not the view within the SS. The Nordic myth had gripped a large part of the nation, certainly that part which sought entry to the elite guard, and those who could prove their blameless ancestry were naturally proud of it. The marriage decree merely enlisted or pandered to their belief and codified their pride.

One of the best illustrations of this comes from the record of the remarkable exchanges between SS-Gruppenführer Jürgen Stroop and a Polish resistance fighter, Kazimierz Moczarski, when both were imprisoned in the same cell after the war, both under sentence of death. In these uniquely intimate conditions Moczarski was able to gain insights into Stroop's psyche which would have been impossible under normal interrogation, and his book *Gespräche mit dem Henker* (*Talks with the Executioner*) provides probably the most detailed and accurate portrait of a certain, probably prevalent type of SS officer in existence.

Stroop was the living embodiment of Nordic racial belief. His ideal was a tall, slim man with a long skull and narrow forehead, blond hair, blue eyes, a light skin-colour and no body hair, not even under the armpits or in the genital area. Although he himself conformed to a large extent to this description he was not satisfied. 'My forehead is too broad,' he confided one day. 'One of my forebears must have married a woman who was not completely Nordic.'[20] Moczarski realised that Stroop had his hair cut very short at the sides of his head to try and give a narrower appearance to his brow. He also noticed many small punctures on Stroop's chest, where he had removed hairs.

Despite the disastrous outcome of the war, Stroop remained unconditionally loyal to both his Führer and his Reichsführer-SS, expressing his devotion by referring to them always as 'Adolf Hitler' and 'Heinrich Himmler', never by surname or first name alone. He regarded Himmler as a master-mind in the racial field, and repeatedly told Moczarski that he (Heinrich Himmler) was one of the best judges of race. 'In addition to exact knowledge, he had creative imagination and the questing mind of a scientific researcher.'[21] Moczarski came to the conclusion that Stroop's rapid advance through the SS ranks was due not solely to obedience, but to the fact that he and his Reichsführer were twins in ideology.

It is interesting that Himmler, whose physique, colouring and facial features were about as far from the Nordic ideal as was possible, like Stroop had his hair shaved at the sides and back of his head, leaving a dark, round island at the top. But no amount of shearing, nor the high-peaked black cap he wore, could disguise the fact that his face was more wide and oval than long and narrow.

While Himmler's long-term goal was to provide the racial elite and pattern for the coming Nordic supremacy, his more immediate task was to guard the Führer and the Party both from their external enemies and from the increasingly serious internal threats as the financial power groupings focused their rivalries inside the Party. The key here was intelligence. He was his own intelligence chief, attempting in conjunction with his manifold other duties to evaluate, file and cross-index the reports coming in from his district 1c – intelligence – officers. Obviously he needed to find a man who could devote his whole time to the task and build up an active espionage and counter-espionage service.

Both the Party and the SA had their own services, and Röhm revived the compromised SA intelligence service that summer, 1931, by appointing a new chief, Graf Karl Leon Du Moulin Eckart, a lawyer from a landowning family. His task was to create a net of SA agents to report principally on the Army and rival paramilitary groups and most importantly to hunt out agents from other groups within the SA. Although the SS was in organisational terms a part of the SA, Himmler obviously could not rely on Du Moulin since the SA was itself the greatest potential threat to Hitler's leadership, indeed to the whole political organisation of the Party. It was a mass paramilitary movement now 100,000 strong with a mercenary and revolutionary tradition. Like 'the mob' throughout history it was unstable and vulnerable to the blandishments of the highest bidder, now emerging as IG Farben and the new industrialists.

For the head of his new secret service, Himmler chose a recently discharged naval lieutenant, von Eberstein's protégé, Reinhard Heydrich. In retrospect this can be seen as the most potent appointment he made in his career. It is of course impossible to say that Nazi, German and world history would have followed a different course without the Himmler–Heydrich axis at the hinge of events, but it is hard to imagine that it could have been quite the same. Himmler was Hitler's man within the Party; Heydrich became Himmler's, therefore also Hitler's man. All deployed different but complementary talents, all shared an obsessive ruthlessness in pursuit of their goals which none of the other groups and combinations either understood – until it was too late – or matched.

Heydrich was four years younger than Himmler, thus twenty-seven in the summer of 1931. He was the son of a musician, opera singer and composer named Bruno Heydrich, an entirely self-made man whose father had been an impecunious carpenter. He had died when Bruno was twelve and his mother had then married a mechanic named Gustav Süss – a fact which came to play an important part in the Heydrichs' life since, although this Süss was not a Jew, Süss was a Jewish name. Despite his humble circumstances, Bruno's musical talent was fostered by scholarships; he became a heroic tenor in Wagnerian opera, but never reaching the first flight turned to composition, again failing to achieve the outstanding success he craved. However, he gained social acceptance when he married the daughter of his teacher, the director of the Royal Conservatory of Music in Dresden. Soon afterwards he founded his own music conservatory in Halle, and it was there that Reinhard Heydrich was born; he was preceded by a sister, Maria, and followed by a brother, Heinz.

Bruno Heydrich was a passionate Wagnerian, not only in his musical style, but in his outlook; Reinhard was named after the hero of his first opera, *Amen*, a tragic figure in the mould of Siegfried. One of the Conservatory's first financial backers, who became a friend of the family and godfather to the infant Reinhard, was Major Freiherr von Eberstein, also a Wagner enthusiast. A basic theme of Richard Wagner's philosophy was, of course, absolute scorn for Jews. Unfortunately Bruno was in appearance and manner just what many of the good citizens of Halle took to be Jewish – even von Eberstein's son Karl described him as looking 'really Jewish'[22] – moreover he was fond of mimicking an 'Isidor', as Jews were known, and when it was discovered that he sent a monthly money order of 300 Marks to a Frau Ernestine Süss in Meissen – actually his mother – there could be no doubt. He was spoken of as the '*Jud* Süss'; Reinhard and his brother Heinz were taunted at school with 'Isi! Isi!' Then in 1916, when the two boys were attending the *Realgymnasium*, an encyclopaedia of music had appeared in which the entry for Bruno ran, 'Bruno Heydrich (really Süss) . . .'.[23] Bruno managed to have this expunged from subsequent editions, but the whole affair and the continuing rumours, which were never silenced, wounded him deeply, and obviously had their effect on the whole family.

It is said that Reinhard, an introspective lad who was at a vulnerable age at this time, was particularly disturbed and despite his father's denials wondered if this dark, rather comical, pushing figure did perhaps have Jewish origins, and became confused and resentful.[24] Apparently he later told one of his 'crew' comrades – his own year group of entrants to the Navy – that, because his father was called a Jew, he himself had become especially active in anti-semitic circles and it was soon said, 'The old Heydrich cannot be a Jew if his Reinhard is such a rampant anti-semite.'[25]

Karl von Eberstein told Heydrich's biographer, Schlomo Aronson, that as a schoolboy Reinhard had been 'extremely *völkisch*', had joined several *völkisch* groups and had developed into an 'absolute race fanatic',[26] and Heydrich himself stated in a questionnaire in 1937 that he had belonged to the Deutschvölkischer Schutz- und Trutzbund during 1920–2, his last two years at the *Gymnasium*.[27]

This Schutz- und Trutzbund, whose publishing arm had brought out several of the volumes on Heinrich Himmler's reading list, was an extreme nationalist and pan-German organisation with aims exactly corresponding to those of the Thule Society which had spawned the National Socialist Party; its symbols were a blue cornflower and a swastika, its motto 'Wir sind die Herren der Welt!' – 'We are the masters of the world!' – and saw its task as awakening the German people to the nature and extent of the danger threatening them from Jews and other non-German elements, in particular from 'the influence of Jewish and foreign thought and feeling'.

In the revolutionary times immediately following defeat in the first war, the young Heydrich had joined the Freikorps of General Maercker, which carried out a 'cleansing action' against communists attempting to set up a Soviet republic in Halle. He was too young for active service, but served as a messenger. Afterwards he had joined the Freikorps Halle, and had been active as a street-fighter against the 'reds' and anarchists – according to von Eberstein, to the detriment of his studies. During this time the inflation and disturbances brought his father's Conservatory to the verge of bankruptcy.

It can be seen that during his formative years he came under just the same sort of influences as Himmler in Munich. It can also be argued that just as Himmler had a deep complex about his inadequacy in physical pursuits as a boy, Heydrich had an equally deep complex caused by confusion over his origins, hence his identity as a German. By all accounts he was an arrogant young man whose prime trait was competitiveness.

He had entered the Navy as an officer cadet in 1922, a gangling youth over six feet tall, with very light blond hair, striking light-blue eyes set rather close and a beak of a nose dominating his long and equine face. He had a high voice and a bleating laugh, on account of which he was called the *Ziege* – nanny-goat. Another of his nicknames was the '*blonde* Siegfried'; this was a play on his doubtful origins, stories of which had followed him into the service, and his anti-semitic convictions. Little else can be said of him with certainty because of the tissue of invention woven around him after the war by officers concerned to distance the service from the crimes of the Third Reich. Probably, as was asserted, he had no real friends among his crew comrades. Probably they did feel he was 'different'; for one thing he took a violin with him and, as might be expected from the circumstances of his upbringing, was an excellent musician. Yet there is no documentary evidence of his time in the Navy.

There can be no doubt that one of the decisive influences in his career was the executive officer of the training cruiser *Berlin*, in which he completed his time as a cadet. This was Kapitänleutnant Wilhelm Canaris, already a legend in the service. He had made his name as an intelligence officer in von Spee's cruiser squadron early in the war, subsequently as chief of a network of agents in Spain reporting on allied shipping movements. After the war, he had been initiated into political intrigue when the communist 'Spartacist' leaders Karl Liebknecht and Rosa Luxemburg carried the workers' revolution to Berlin. He was a staff officer liaising between the naval Freikorps and the Guards division which put down the uprising in the capital. He may well have been implicated in the subsequent murders of Liebknecht and Luxemburg and was certainly the key figure in preventing the perpetrators, naval officers from the Freikorps, from being brought to justice. Before their trial by court martial he coached them in a fabricated story to confuse the identity of the actual murderers and entirely conceal the name of the Guards commander, Captain Pabst, who had ordered the assassinations. He even staged rehearsals in which some of the accused took the parts of judge and prosecuting counsel.

His machinations paid off. The chosen scapegoat among the accused was sentenced to two years and four months in prison for allowing Rosa Luxemburg to be shot while in his charge and subsequently disposing of the body by throwing it into a canal. The others were acquitted. Canaris then sprang the sentenced officer from prison with forged papers and spirited him out of the country.

If one considers the result of this trial in Berlin's Landgericht 1 (Higher District Court 1), and the sentences passed on Hitler and the beer-hall putschists in Munich, and earlier trials at the German Supreme Court in Leipzig of 'war criminals' nominated by the victorious allies – for instance the U-boat officers found guilty of murdering defenceless survivors of a hospital ship they had torpedoed, and sentenced to four years' imprisonment, actually serving six months – it can be seen that the German legal system was in the hands of men serving not justice but the 'nationalist', anti-communist, anti-democratic, anti-Versailles cause, long before the National Socialists came to power.

The naval officer corps was permeated with this same spirit, and Canaris, who had a natural bent for intrigue and a fascination with intelligence work, was its most active agent in the political sphere. He was a leading figure in the secret rearmament to circumvent the Versailles Treaty ban, using contacts from his secret service time in Spain to have boats built to German design in Spanish yards. He had been intimately involved in the Naval Brigade support of the Kapp putsch in 1920. Subsequently on the staff of Baltic naval command at Kiel, he had organised the illegal sales of arms and equipment abroad to help found and fund the extreme right Organisation Consul from naval Freikorps officers. This was the secret society which had provided squads to assassinate the Jewish Foreign Minister, Rathenau, and Finance Minister, Erzberger, during Himmler's final year as a student in Munich. Himmler's knowledge of this – as proved by his diary entries after Rathenau's murder[28] – is not surprising since these same Freikorps naval officers had been especially active in Bavaria; they had indeed been co-founders and trainers with Röhm of the SA. Whether Canaris and Hitler had met at this time is a matter of speculation, but in the summer of 1923 prior to the beer-hall putsch Organisation Consul had been liaising with the other nationalist organs in Bavaria. It was at this time that Canaris was posted to the cruiser *Berlin* where Heydrich was a cadet.

They formed an immediate attachment, perhaps because both he and Heydrich were different from the normal run of naval officers moulded during their training into rather extreme imitations of Prussian Army officers. Canaris' forebears were Italian; he possessed a Latin subtlety and ambiguity quite foreign to the Prussian soldierly propensity for regularity and order. He was a lonely man. Heydrich was also a lonely individual and his upbringing in the Conservatory at Halle had probably given him more cultural points of contact with the 'Levantine', as Canaris was known, than most officers had. However it came about, the relationship between the executive officer and the music-loving cadet soon became that of fond master and devoted disciple; Heydrich was taken into the Canaris family circle and played second violin at musical evenings arranged by Canaris' wife Erika. Meanwhile he became fired by Canaris' tales of spying and intrigue, and acquired an enthusiasm for the techniques of intelligence work which led him later to specialise as a wireless officer – since Canaris convinced him of the decisive importance of communications. Later he served as intelligence officer on the staff of the naval station, Kiel.

It was here in the late spring of 1931 that something happened which caused him to leave the service. The legend was fostered, particularly after the war, that he was dismissed because he broke with a girl he had been courting to become engaged to another. He did become engaged in December 1930, but even the exaggerated code of honour of the naval officer corps did not preclude changes of mind in the choice of a wife. The story was so absurd that it was elaborated by officers claiming to have sat on the Court of Honour. It was not so much his behaviour to the jilted (and so far undiscovered) girl that caused his dismissal, as his arrogant manner towards the Court. Given the respect for rank inculcated into naval officers from their first day as a cadet, and Heydrich's known overweening ambition, this story is even more absurd. His own statement in his SS personal file is: 'At the end of April 1931 I was dismissed on grounds unconnected with duty on the decision of the Reich President against the decision of my superiors.'[29] In early August 1931 a Frau Dr Lehmann, who knew him through mutual acquaintances, met him by chance in the restaurant car of an express train. It seemed to her that he had been through a hard time. He explained that he had been dismissed from the Navy because of his sympathy for the Hitler movement;

however, he said he was much happier standing beside the Führer than he would be in the Navy.[30] Later an *Encyclopaedia of the Third Reich* stated that he had been dismissed from the Navy on 'political grounds'.

There are problems about this version, however, since if sympathy with the Nazi Party had been a crime the Commander-in-Chief of the Navy, Admiral Raeder, should have been dismissed, together with the greater part of the officer corps, including Canaris. The Navy had particular reasons for being pro-Nazi; it was the junior service, a veritable parvenu in historical terms, which felt its aims and indeed its reason for existence unappreciated by republican politicians or even the Army; it had humiliating corps memories of the mutinies which had started the collapse of the home front in 1918, and of further mutinies at the time of the Kapp putsch when serving officers had been arrested and maltreated by 'red' petty officers and men; and it remained particularly vulnerable to communist subversion and cell-building techniques in the two chief naval ports. Feeling so insecure and threatened on every side, it is not surprising that the Navy responded enthusiastically to the anti-Versailles Treaty, anti-communist, pro-nationalist slogans of the Nazi Party. The feeling was particularly strong among younger officers and the association of retired naval officers, but it permeated all ranks, and Raeder himself was in touch with Hitler via the retired Admiral von Levetzow.

There is little doubt that the Kiel naval station, intelligence and counter-intelligence section, still had active links with the Nazis, no doubt at all that Heydrich himself was kept up to date on Party affairs by his boyhood friend, now SA-Oberführer Karl von Eberstein, who was a close colleague of Himmler. There seem therefore to be only two possibilities to account for his departure from the Navy. Either he transgressed the rule that serving officers did not attend political meetings – his new fiancée, Lina von Osten, was an enthusiastic Hitler supporter and he may perhaps have been foolish enough to attend a meeting with her. Alternatively his dismissal may have been a cover operation by Raeder to insert a naval officer into the intelligence apparatus of the Nazi Party just as large industrial concerns arranged for the 'dismissal' of men whom they wished to insert into the Nazi organisation to represent their interests – just as the great Junker landowners already had their men in leading positions in '*the* Party'. The fact that Heydrich apparently received two years' severance or transitional salary at 200 Marks a month tends to support this latter theory.[31]

On 31 May 1931, as his latest biographer, Edouard Calic, points out, the day after his discharge from the Navy became legally binding, Heydrich joined the Nazi Party in Hamburg. It seems probable from an account given to Calic after the war by a Hamburg communist that he organised an assault troop on military lines equipped with vehicles which made lightning strikes on social democrat and communist meetings in the industrial quarter of Hamburg that summer, waded in with staves, and as rapidly made off before the police arrived.[32]

Von Eberstein, meanwhile, arranged an appointment for him with Heinrich Himmler. According to post-war legend Himmler cancelled the meeting because he had a cold, but Heydrich, pressed by his fiancée, went nonetheless and saw him at his house in Waldtrudering. It is more likely that the meeting was at Waldtrudering because Himmler wanted to keep a potential secret service chief out of the way of Du Moulin's snoopers at Party headquarters. Again according to the legend, Himmler thought he had an intelligence officer before him, whereas he actually had a wireless specialist; in fact, von Eberstein must have told him that Heydrich had been an intelligence officer at Kiel for three years, and had been initiated into the game by the Navy's legendary expert in the field. Himmler gave him twenty minutes to write an account of how he would organise an SS intelligence service. As impressed by the result as by Heydrich's 'Nordic' appearance, he appointed him to the post.

Heydrich fell short of the strict Nordic ideal; his hips were too wide. Himmler's later adjutant, Karl Wolff, described them as 'womanly and unGermanic'.[33] There was also a Mongolian cast to his eyes which caused Himmler when annoyed to rebuke him with descent from the hordes of Genghis Khan. It was an apt comment. Even his photographs convey an impression of cruelty; the long, asymmetric face, thick lips and slightly inclined, icy grey–blue eyes suggest something both infinitely calculating and diabolic. One of his later colleagues, Werner Best, characterised him as 'the most demoniacal personality in the National Socialist leadership'.[34] Himmler could not have made a better choice. How large a part chance played is arguable, but there is no doubt that had Heydrich not proved ideal and, moreover, like Jürgen Stroop, an ideological twin, he would have been moved aside quickly, as many of Himmler's early appointees were.

Heydrich started his duties in August at the new Party headquarters in the former Palace. It was now called the Brown House. Nothing could have been further removed from the offices that had served the leadership before. The rich façade was adorned by huge swastika flags from staffs. Inside, through great bronze doors guarded by two SS men, it was a world of undisguised opulence. The lobby was faced with marble; a tablet on one wall recorded the names of the thirteen who had fallen outside the Feldherrnhalle; standards of the different SA regiments lined another wall; the third, so visitors were told, was to be used to record all those National Socialists 'murdered' in the street and meeting-hall battles against their political opponents.

Beyond was the great hall, the stucco walls incised with countless swastikas. A grand staircase swept up to Hitler's and Hess's apartments and the grandiloquently named and furnished Senators' Chamber, a huge room designed to accommodate the elect of the new rulers after the *Machtergreifung*. There were sixty-one red leather armchairs, deep-pile carpets woven with swastika motifs, marble and mosaic work adorning the walls on which plaques commemorated the stages of the NSDAP from its founding. In Hitler's great study nearby and throughout the building it was the same; rich woods, costly materials, intricate craftsmanship and heavy draperies breathed unlimited money, mocking the title German Workers' Party. One astonished early visitor recorded his impression of the building as Hitler's Court, from where he intended to rule Germany.

Despite the millions spent on the rebuilding and office equipment, including banks of card indexes recording the details of Party members, Heydrich had to share an office and a typewriter with another SS officer, so the story goes. It may be true, since this was only a temporary position under cover of the title SS-PI-Dienst (Press and Information). In the New Year he moved out of the Brown House altogether to set up what came to be known as the Sicherheitsdienst, or SD, in his own flat in Munich. This was after he had married Lina von Osten. As a wedding present, Himmler stepped him up to SS-Sturmbannführer – equivalent to major – a more rapid advance than he could possibly have achieved in the Navy.

His responsibilities were also far wider than he could have hoped for in the service: at his SD *Zentrale* (Control), he supervised a team expanding Himmler's card indexes recording the names and details of the political and ideological enemies of the Party under the different categories, 'Jews', 'Free-masons', 'Political Catholics', 'Communists', 'Social Democratic leaders', 'Bourgeois conservatives', 'Nobility hostile to National Socialism', processed information coming in from the 1c departments of the SS areas (*Abschnitte*) and regimental (*Standarte*) organisations, instructed their 1c officers in the enemies' methods of infiltration, and set up a central department to root out spies within; he also travelled the country recruiting officials, academics and industrialists as unpaid SS agents. He had an exaggerated respect for the English system by which, as he imagined, all members of the upper classes were honorary secret agents. His fascination with the English secret service later extended to signing himself 'C' in green ink after the style of Admiral Sir Mansfield Cumming, founder of MI6. In addition he conducted extortion campaigns against industrialists to pay for SS expansion. A simple and effective method was to abuse the target concern or personalities in Party papers until they paid the sums demanded. Jewish businesses and newspaper proprietors were natural victims; among the list of 'subscribing members' of SS-Abschnitt-1 in the spring of 1932 the names Goldschmitt, Levi, Rosenzvet, Rosenberg, Hirschmann appear.[35] Social democratic or liberal supporters were also targeted and since the judiciary was 'nationalist' the victims seldom had recourse to the courts. Martin Bormann was using similar methods for the Party treasury. The gangster state within the state had emerged.

Heydrich's work was not simply security and blackmail. It was positively directed towards the *Machtergreifung*. The card indexes were used to draw up lists of the most dangerous enemies, differentiating between those who would be put away for good after the assumption of power by execution or arrest, and those who could be frightened off. The creation of a network of unpaid and invisible V-men – confidential agents – in every branch of public life was to ensure a flow of information about the defensive counter-moves of the government against the Party, and when the time came a smooth take-over of power. There was a contingency plan for a forcible strike against the state, in which the V-men in the police, service transport detachments, railways and government departments played a crucial role. According to Calic's information from SA officers after the war, this envisaged creating the illusion of a communist uprising by blowing up or setting fire to selected targets throughout the country. Again according to Calic Heydrich set up a special training school for sabotage in Braunschweig.[36] For this eventuality, as for Hitler's preferred solution of a 'legal' take-over of power, control of the police forces was vital, and a great deal of Heydrich's effort went into winning over police officials. One who was to play a vital role after the take-over was Arthur Nebe, a leading criminologist in charge of the robberies division in the Berlin Police Praesidium; he became a 'subscribing member' of the SS in 1931, and in 1932 formed a National Socialist associa-tion among his fellow criminologists while acting undercover as a V-man to the Berlin SS leader, Daluege.

The importance Heydrich and his Sicherheitsdienst achieved inside six months is indicated by a summary list of addresses and telephone numbers of Munich Party leaders to be called in the event of an 'Alarm etc.'. The list is dated March 1932, and contains thirty-five names in all; of these fourteen underlined members were to be called first; Hitler, Röhm, Reiner and Graf Du Moulin head this select group, after which the list continues in alphabetical order with ten further names underlined, Heinrich Himmler, Wasserburgerlandstrasse 109, Waldtrudering (telephone 029309) and Erbprinz zu Waldeck, Parsevalstrasse 19, among them; Reinhard Heydrich, also underlined, Lochhausen 55, appears out of alphabetical order, suggesting that his name had been inserted later.[37] That Himmler, his adjutant and his secret service chief were in this select group is testi-mony to the importance of the SS by this date and lends weight to the idea that Heydrich's SD had an important role in the master plans for the *Machtergreifung*. His extraordinarily rapid rise in the hierarchy also suggests that he was picked out of the Navy deliberately to deploy his service intelligence and explosives training in the service of the Party.

The struggle for control of the 'national' tide in Germany was now in full swing. All major power groupings were agreed that the time had come finally to topple democracy, eradicate once and for all the danger of Marxism, solve the industrial and unemployment problems of the nation in traditional authoritarian ways, and harness the national power so created to achieve European and eventually world hegemony. In revolutionary crisis the state was proving true to its origins in the Prussian soldier state. This applied to the bankers and big businessmen financing the revolution.

German capitalism had always shown state-centred traits. By contrast with

America, which had taken over from Great Britain as linchpin of the world economic order and chief exporter of capital to developing countries after the first war, German capital had always been concentrated in development of the national economy and promoting exports. Traditionally it had been managed by the state for these purposes through tariffs, subsidies, regulation and legislation. American capitalism on the other hand had always been market-oriented, serving the customer rather than national interests. Competition had been preserved, choice maximised and prices minimised by outlawing the price-fixing rings known as cartels and syndicates. German industry was positively encouraged to form cartels and syndicates both by the big banks and by state legislation; competition was thus restricted and prices kept artificially high by basing them on the costs of the least efficient members of the cartel to the obvious detriment of the consumer.

Paternalistic welfare provisions failed to prevent the rift between managers and industrial workers who, as in all industrial nations, felt their living standards, their very humanity crushed beneath the giant concentrations of capital growing up and benefiting the few very rich. Authoritarian attitudes in management and organisation natural to the ethos of a soldier state exacerbated this feeling. While American capitalism managed the inevitable conflicts by, in effect, buying off the workers with mass-production consumerism and the promise, indeed the realisation, of individual self-improvement, German workers became proletarianised, radicalised and ripe for Marxism. The 'pre-revolutionary' situation thus created early in the century was one of the prime causes for the Prussian leadership's unleashing of the first war.

Now, as world depression bit deep, the contrasts between the two systems became exaggerated. While in America workers grew more organised, trade unions gained a position of real power and competition was strengthened by an increasing volume of anti-cartel, anti-trust, anti-syndicate legislation, the reverse happened in Germany, capital and big business combining in ever greater mergers, and cartels seeking – and soon to achieve – the suppression of the workers' movement, while increasingly working for 'national' goals defined by the state. This worked to the inevitable economic and political disadvantage of the citizens as consumers. Even those leaders of the newer, light industries of the second industrial revolution like the giant IG Farben concern who had flirted with mass production and mass consumption during the years of prosperity induced by American loans swung back into line. Thus in both systems it was as if the depression showed up the individuals apparently in control as mere puppets dancing to wires in the hands of their forefathers – the Teutonic knights and the Founding Fathers. Professor Volker Berghahn has concluded from his analysis of this growing divergence: 'If one looks at the Second World War from an economic perspective, it seems that this giant conflict was about which of the two "models" of capitalist organisation would apply to Europe and elsewhere.'[38]

The Nazi Party, as the only 'national', anti-socialist mass movement, was the vehicle chosen to realise the aims of big business. Himmler's SS, as the most reliable Party formation which had by now attracted a relatively large proportion of nobles and the upper-middle class into its officer corps, largely bypassing the original *kleinen Leute*, was supported by a large number of industrialists apart from those whose contributions were extorted by protection or blackmail. Thus, although it was kept on a tight financial string by the Party treasurer and his nominal chief, Röhm, Himmler was able to expand the SS at a tremendous rate through 1932. Between April and June numbers leaped from 25,000 to over 40,000 officers and men organised in forty regimental groups covering the whole country.[39]

It is impossible to know which of the major industrial groupings backed the SS at this date since company archives have not been studied, or in most cases opened for inspection. Also V-men were well camouflaged, and the banks mediated between interest-groups to harmonise their divergent aims. Judging by the agricultural views of both Himmler and his Race Office chief, Darré, and their desire to create in place of the old nobility a new racial elite, IG Farben and the light industrialists opposed to the costly protection of the great Junker landholders and aiming to promote capital-intensive farming should have been natural bedfellows. Yet the big-business liaison man with whom Himmler seems to have been associated most closely was Wilhelm Keppler, generally assumed to have been a representative of heavy industry. Himmler introduced Keppler to Hitler, and the 'Circle' of business advisers whom Keppler founded for the Führer in May 1932 later became the Freundeskreis RFSS – Circle of Friends of the Reichsführer-SS – and contributed huge sums annually to the SS.

According to the Marxist historian Kurt Gossweiler, Keppler was actually a cleverly hidden V-man for IG Farben, and the power behind him was the Cologne banker Kurt von Schröder. It was Schröder who harmonised the very divergent aims of IG Farben – directed against both traditional agriculture and heavy industry – with the Hugenberg or pan-German wing of heavy industry which Keppler seemed to represent. They were able to come together since they shared the common aim of building German hegemony in Europe in a closed economic bloc independent of American capital and the world market. This policy was threatened by the Thyssen group of heavy industrialists who wished to co-operate with American capital to build European hegemony – or, as Gossweiler puts it, wanted 'a firm union of German with American imperialism and war against the Soviet Union in alliance with the U.S.A.'.[40] The most influential exponent of this group was the former president of the Reichsbank, Dr Hjalmar Schacht, who was known as 'the American'. He had come out publicly in favour of the Nazis very early; his wife was in the habit of adorning herself with swastika brooches in rubies and diamonds.

The divergent interests of the great financial and power groupings were worked out in tortuous manoeuvres throughout 1932 and the first weeks of 1933. Gregor Strasser, Röhm and the SA were the most visible exponents of the IG Farben line within the Party and Strasser and Röhm formed an axis with the former Army intelligence chief, von Schleicher, who emerged as chief political power-broker. A man of great vivacity and personal charm who had a wider vision of the national interest than the traditional Prussian, he attempted to bring the moderate wing of the trade union movement into his alliance with Strasser. He was opposed by the Prussian power elite of Junkers and Army, and the owners of the labour-intensive heavy industries who wanted to break the unions altogether. They backed Hitler and Göring. Thus the Party faced a dangerous split, and Heinrich Himmler and the SS, and especially perhaps Heydrich and his secret intelligence and security office, became the vital elements of Party unity. Whether Himmler was, as Gossweiler asserts, IG Farben's second line of defence – that is, an exponent of the 'middle way' negotiated by Kurt von Schröder between the light industrialists and the pan-German group of heavy industrialists – to be called on if the first-line Strasser–Röhm partnership failed, he was above all loyal to Hitler. It is at this personal and personality level that Marxist analysis by class and interest-groupings probably breaks down.

Outside the Party, the power struggle manifested itself in quick changes of government. During the resulting election campaigns it was the task of the SA and the SS to heighten alarm about the Bolshevik danger by inciting supporters of the communist and social democratic formations to bloody street battles. Heydrich organised the sharpest of these provocations in Hamburg's industrial suburb of Altona on Sunday, 17 July 1932. SA and SS formations were bussed in, and marched behind bands, standards and banners with an escort of police. When fired on from rooftops and windows, they returned fire. The demonstration left some nineteen dead and the wounded ran into hundreds. In the whole of that July, thirty-eight Nazis joined the list of martyrs for commemoration in the Brown House; the communists lost thirty. The tactics succeeded in further radicalising politics so that both extreme parties gained at the expense of the middle. The Nazis gained most and, in Reichstag elections at the end of the month, emerged as by far the largest party with 13.75 million votes and 230 seats against the social democrats' 8 million and the communists' 5.25 million.

Still there was no overall majority for a government of either the right or the left, and the political confrontation between the power groupings inside the exclusive Herren Klub in Berlin and the industrialists' and bankers' villas and inside the Nazi Party continued. On the streets Brownshirt mayhem and murder rampaged. Von Papen, the adaptable political representative of both capital and landed elites, headed a 'presidential' Cabinet which governed without a majority, much as Prussian cabinets appointed by the Kaiser before the war. Hitler was offered a post as Vice-Chancellor, with Strasser as Commissioner for Prussia; he refused, demanding the Chancellorship as his due as leader of the largest party. The President, von Hindenburg, who took an instant aversion to the 'Austrian', refused to entrust power to him and his murderous revolutionary band. Von Schleicher, now Minister of War and self-appointed Cabinet-maker, stepped up his attempts to separate Strasser and his adherents from Hitler. Meanwhile the Nazi tide in the country began to turn back. In elections called by von Papen in November the Party vote went down by 2 million and they lost thirty-four seats – although still remaining the largest party in the House.

The situation now appeared more of a stalemate than before. Von Schleicher took over as Chancellor, hoping to be able to manufacture a majority based on the 'Strasser' wing of the Nazis and the moderate trade unions. The plan was flawed: Strasser had no cohesive group behind him, and neither he nor the unions would be tolerated by the Junker landowners or those industrialists whose aim was to suppress the workers' movement, not bring it into partnership. These same industrialists stopped the flow of funds to the Nazi Party because they feared that Strasser and radical and anti-capital elements like Gottfried Feder had Hitler's ear and might do just this. As a result, and because of huge election expenses laid out in expectation of being able to pay them back with the proceeds of power, the Party faced bankruptcy. Moreover the decline in the polls, matched by a falling-off in Party membership, a serious decline in morale and disaffection in the SA at being denied the power they expected threatened Hitler's bargaining position.

It was now that the banker Kurt von Schröder emerged as the decisive mediator and with him Heinrich Himmler and Wilhelm Keppler, organiser of Hitler's Freundeskreis of industrial leaders. The first meeting between these three, with the deputy Party leader, Hess, also present, was on 11 November, less than a week after the election. It is significant that it was at about this time that Strasser coined the remark, 'It seems to me that Hitler is completely in the hands of his Himmler and *Anhimmlers* [fans].'[41] He meant chiefly Göring, Goebbels and Röhm, whom he characterised as respectively 'a brutal egotist', 'a lame devil' and 'a filthy creature'.[42] Letters proving Röhm a homosexual had been published during the July election campaign. Strasser was also very disturbed about Hitler's close connection with heavy industry and the great landowners.

While von Schröder tried to negotiate a middle way acceptable to all capital and landed interests, Party propaganda focused on another election campaign; this was for the *Land*, or regional government, of Lippe, an agricultural area whose distressed farmers and labourers could be expected to give the Party the sort of success it badly needed after the November decline. All the Party leaders campaigned there, and the local SA and SS formations were instructed to unleash terror on the streets. Leading the SS troop in the regional capital, the lovely old town of Detmold, was a recent recruit not yet out of his probationary year named Joseph Stroop and it was here in the savage bludgeoning of the 'enemy' and the sacking, looting and burning of their files and offices that Stroop first came under the eye of his Reichsführer. Stroop enjoyed his work, which he termed *action directe*, and Himmler liked what he saw. From then on Stroop's career was made; his promotions followed in rapid succession.

In the event a certain success was scored in Lippe although scarcely justifying the saturation propaganda and brutal tactics: the Party recorded a 5 per cent increase in votes above the November figures.

Of infinitely greater importance for the *Machtergreifung* was the suborning of the President of the Republic, von Hindenburg. 'The old gentleman', as von Hindenburg was known to his intimates, was an imposing figure, six feet five inches tall with cropped, iron-grey hair, a granite expression and the deepest voice one surprised listener had ever heard in a human being. He might have been the living embodiment of Prussia, and inhabited a Prussian aura of heavy, dark furniture, dark tapestries and pictures of war. Yet he was eighty-five years old and tiring, and in one respect at least failed to measure up to the image of spartan simplicity demanded by the warrior ethic: he had been party to a considerable tax evasion. His bankrupt family estate at Neudeck had been presented to him recently by the nation, but to avoid inheritance tax the deeds had been made out to his son Oskar. Moreover the subsidy known as the *Osthilfe* established to support East Prussian agriculture had become a scandalously abused source of income for the Junker families, for whom he was both figurehead and representative. On both counts he and those he represented were open to political pressure.

Heydrich's SD gathered material evidence of the scandals in the *Osthilfe* for use in putting pressure particularly on von Hindenburg's son Oskar, as stiff and morose a caricature as the President himself, who in consort with State Secretary Meissner virtually controlled the old man. Hitler's strategy was on the one hand to threaten Oskar personally and the Junkers as a class with exposure, on the other hand to bribe him with Army rank and additional land for his estate. By this means he was to be persuaded to overcome his father's refusal to appoint Hitler as Chancellor. At the same time Heydrich was working on the next stage: once Hitler was Chancellor and before a general election could dent his legitimacy a pretext had to be manufactured that would persuade the old President to grant him emergency powers to rule without the Reichstag. This pretext was to be a communist uprising to topple the Nazi–Nationalist government. Since it was clear that the communists had been ordered by Moscow to do nothing of the sort, but to allow the economic crisis which had destroyed so many successive governments to destroy the expected Nazi government and since the social democrats had the same strategy, it was necessary to fake the uprising, and find dupes to be presented as the perpetrators. This was Heydrich's major task. How much he or Himmler contributed to the conception of this strategy is, of course, impossible to say: it was little more than an extension of the political campaigns by which the Party had grown, and was as fundamental to Hitler's and Goebbels' thought patterns as the use of terror. In practical planning and execution, however, the task was entrusted to Heydrich; this was what Himmler had selected him for.[43]

Meanwhile von Schröder's negotiations led to a decisive meeting between Hitler and von Papen. It took place on 4 January 1933 at von Schröder's Cologne villa. Hitler's escort consisted of the three who had met the banker soon after the election defeat in November – Hess, Keppler and Himmler. Minutes of the resulting discussion recorded agreement in four main areas. The first was a strengthening of the fight against Bolshevism. 'In his answer Hitler gave an assurance that communists, social democrats and Jews would be removed from leading positions in Germany, and it was necessary to recreate order in public life.'[44]

The next subject was the reconstruction of industry; it was agreed that employers' associations should be formed in which all concerns would be united and would have greater influence than heretofore – in short, national cartels. Third, the business cycle would be stimulated through state contracts:

> Hitler promised to increase the armed forces from 100,000 to 300,000 men, to take in hand the construction of Autobahns, to make credit available to state and local authorities for highway construction, and government credits available for the aircraft and automobile industries and their ancillaries.

This was clearly a programme to suit the new industries, and in view of the first point of agreement it foresaw the expropriation of Jewish by 'Aryan' concerns.

Finally Hitler agreed to work for 'the abolition of the Versailles Treaty and the restoration of a militarily strong, economically independent Germany . . .'. Von Papen then assured him that his appointment as Chancellor would follow in the next few days, and it was agreed that both he and Hugenberg would have a place in Hitler's Cabinet.[45]

If Hitler and the Nazi Party as a mass movement were conceived in the pan-German Thule Society and nursed by the Army and Navy combined, this programme reveals that finally they were brought to the altar of power by high finance and industry, in particular by the owners of the new light industries of the second industrial revolution, supported by the banks, in particular the giant Deutsche Bank to which von Schröder's Cologne Bank was affiliated. Emil Georg von Stauss of the Deutsche Bank was prominent in the group of investors von Schröder formed after this key meeting to underwrite Nazi Party debts.[46] And among the numerous large firms and combines in which the Deutsche Bank was both investor and participator in management through its representatives on the governing boards – something which could not have happened legally in the American model of capitalism – were IG Farben, the electrical combine Siemens & Halske, UGF Rayon, BMW (Bavarian Motor Works), Daimler Benz and the world's largest building combine Philip Holzmann. On 17 January Goebbels, who had been in despair about the weight of debt threatening to sink the Party, noted in his diary, 'the financial situation has improved suddenly.'[47]

Now only one obstacle stood in the way – the President himself. Apparently Hitler removed this on 22 January in private conversation with Oskar von Hindenburg. Afterwards Oskar was 'extremely silent', according to President von Hindenburg's State Secretary, Meissner, who accompanied him to the meeting: 'the only remark he made was that it could not be helped – the Nazis had to be taken into the government.'[48] Meissner was not a disinterested witness; he too had influence with 'the old gentleman'. In this shadow world of Sicilian 'protection' no one's word can be accepted as anything more than an attempt to confuse or hide the truth.

Himmler and his secret service chief remained out of the way in Munich during these final preparations for power, one can imagine with what sense of heightening excitement and feverish self-importance, alternating with anxiety lest at the last moment von Schleicher, Strasser, von Papen or even Röhm should somehow cheat them of the prize. Whichever of the two was the real mastermind behind the plot against the constitution, the Berlin branch of the SD, led by Hans von Kobelinski, played a major role, as did Heydrich's younger brother Heinz; he was a journalist in the capital, thus well placed to leak disinformation on instructions from Munich.

On 27 January Himmler detached Heydrich as SS-Standartenführer for special duties and sent him to Berlin. It is probable he travelled the same day since everything had been building up to this and he must have been prepared. In the capital Heydrich went to earth, wearing civilian clothes and living with his wife Lina in a flat on the corner of Eichenallee, while secretly supervising a group of specially trained saboteurs in preparations for the real take-over of power after the legal formalities about to take place.[49]

On 28 January von Schleicher resigned. Two days later von Papen's promise to Hitler at Kurt von Schröder's villa was fulfilled: von Hindenburg asked him to form a government. By this time Himmler was also in Berlin. At lunch six years later to the day, 30 January 1939, he reminisced about sitting in the Kaiserhof Hotel, Hitler's headquarters while in the capital, waiting with Röhm and the other Party leaders for the Führer to return as Chancellor. In the afternoon, he and some others attended a festival called 'Green Week', where they 'felt themselves reasonably secure against being followed'.[50] Perhaps this relates to the fear that von Schleicher was instigating a march on Berlin by the Potsdam garrison to prevent the formation of the Hitler–von Papen government. Hitler apparently feared this: the SA and SS in the capital were on full alert and the Nazi supporters in the high command of the Army, General von Blomberg and his Chief of Staff, Colonel von Reichenau, had been called to Berlin to steady the old President and take over the reins of the service directly Hitler was appointed Chancellor.

Yet the rumours of an Army plot were as likely to have been caused by the deliberate disinformation coming from Himmler's own SD; it is possible that both he and Hitler in retrospect enjoyed indulging exaggerated ideas of the dangers they faced on that momentous day when the fate of Germany and Europe, indeed the world, fell like a ripe plum into their anxious palms. Or perhaps they liked to justify the revenge they took on von Schleicher the following year.

In the evening the SA and SS staged a gigantic and obviously well-prepared torch-light parade to celebrate the 'victory'. The Jewish socialite and newspaper columnist Bella Fromm watched in agitation:

> In the flickering light of a sea of torches they paraded – from the west to the Knie – through the Tiergarten to the Wilhelmstrasse. An endless sea of brown. An ominous night. A night of deadly menace, a nightmare in the living reality of 20,000 blazing torches.
>
> Hindenburg stood with Meissner at his special window on the first floor to the left. I don't know whether it was my imagination or not, but as the brown and black masses thudded past, his face, like cast bronze, seemed bewildered and somewhat startled.[51]

Himmler, living his dreams, had the same impression. Six years later he recalled it for his lunch guests. 'I can see it as if it were today, Hindenburg – the great, massive form standing there looking down at the march-past of the SA and SS as if he still couldn't fully grasp it.'[52] Then he retold the old jest that had gone the rounds at the time: von Hindenburg to Meissner, 'Tell me, Meissner, where have all these Russian prisoners come from?' It was a reference to the old man's victory at Tannenberg. Doubtless it drew the same knowing laughs as it had in that heady time of the first taste of power.

A few days later at the annual ball of the old nobility, Bella Fromm heard how the trick had been worked: apparently von Papen had called on von Hindenburg and given him a highly coloured account of an imminent Army revolt and a plot to assassinate von Schleicher. He – and no doubt Meissner and Oskar – had panicked the old man into the decision. Judging by Himmler's and Heydrich's later coups against the Army, it is quite likely that the SD furnished proofs of some kind to assist von Papen in this plot; it is even possible they convinced him too. At the ball many of the nobles confessed to Bella that they supported the new masters of the Reich. She noted, 'More than one mask was dropped for good.'[53]

No more apt analogy has been coined for those who put Hitler into power than Alan Bullock's: he likened this improbable combination of pre-industrial nobles, soldiers and hard men of finance and business to the innocent young lady of Riga who went for a ride on a tiger. They deceived themselves; they had taken the majority in Hitler's Cabinet, and occupied the important posts: von Papen, Vice-Chancellor, was also Reichskommissar for Prussia, as ever the most powerful single state: Hugenberg held the key strategic ministries of Economics and Agriculture; Seldte, leader of the nationalist troop, Stahlhelm, the Ministry of Labour; von Krosigk, Finance; von Blomberg, War; von Neurath, Foreign Affairs; the Nazi Party had only three representatives, Hitler as Chancellor, Frick as Minister of the Interior, and Göring as Prussian Minister of the Interior – in theory subordinate to von Papen. That Hitler, who commanded the largest political party in the country, should have agreed to a minority in the Cabinet and such relatively unimportant posts might perhaps have warned the realists; yet they believed they had brought him to power and held the whip hand. Undoubtedly he played up to this idea; he did not have to act the gauche 'Corporal': for all his training in society he remained horribly ill at ease. It was not difficult for him to lull his allies into an entirely false sense of security.

Himmler also hid his real goals beneath a ruse of weakness; perhaps it was a natural cloak since he was such a prim and clerkish figure beside the heroes of the movement; perhaps it was a learned response that had become instinctive. But now, as Hitler seemed to grant all power to the representatives of the power-elites seated in his Cabinet, while secretly plotting to undermine them, Himmler, apparently prepared to forgo the fruits of power, retired modestly to Munich, leaving the capital and the final storming of the Republic to Göring and the SA leaders. Had these flamboyants been able to glimpse the iron behind his pince-nez, they would not have felt easy. As it was, Heydrich appeared the more immediately dangerous.

Göring, as Prussian Minister of the Interior, immediately set about bringing the Prussian police into line; he appointed the Berlin SS group leader, Daluege, as Chief of Police, hived off the police Political Department 1A into a separate Geheime Staatspolizei (Secret State Police) or Gestapo, under his own man, Rudolf Diels, and purged those suspected of leftish or liberal tendencies. To enforce the national and socialist concept of order on the streets, he incorporated SA and SS units as auxiliary police, and made it plain to the whole force that he expected firearms to be used against the communist 'enemy'. 'I cannot act against the red mob with policemen who have to fear disciplinary proceedings when they do their duty,' he told assembled police officials on 20 February. 'The responsibility must be clarified. It does not lie with the petty officials on the streets – I must hammer it into your heads, the responsibility lies with me alone. You must understand, if you shoot, I have shot. If a dead man lies there, I have shot him even if I am sitting in the Ministry, because that is my responsibility alone.'[54]

This was in preparation for the final reckoning with the internal enemy. The plans were fully prepared; they were an exercise in the highest cynicism, designed not so much to cloak the take-over of dictatorial powers with legitimacy as to work through rather than against the existing system, with rather than in opposition to the bureaucracy, for Hitler and Goebbels, who were probably the chief authors of the plan, knew the vasselage of German officialdom to rules and the least word from higher authority. Everything was geared to yet another election for the Reichstag. Hitler had ensured this by putting impossible demands to the Centre Party, which might otherwise have come to an arrangement and enabled the new government to form a majority.

In parallel with the public campaign, which included the usual provocations to street violence by both extremes, Heydrich's preparations for a giant and ultimate provocation went ahead in concert with Göring. Heydrich was in direct contact with Himmler in Munich at this time and with his SD chief in Berlin, SS-Sturmführer Hans von Kobelinski, through a secret telephone link.[55]

Shortly after his unequivocal explanation of the 'shooting decree', Göring instructed Diels to put through the next stage of the operation: on 24 February, communist headquarters in Berlin was surrounded by flying-squad cars and motorcycles and all side streets cordoned off while Diels' men searched the complex of buildings for compromising material. Nothing sensational was found, but that evening Göring issued a press release intimating that plans for a nationwide communist uprising had been discovered. Simultaneously the SD began inspiring rumours to the same effect. No doubt Heydrich's brother Heinz used his contacts in the newspaper world. On 26 February the morning papers carried stories of a society soirée held by the 'Court Astrologer', Hanussen, and reported him as prophesying in a trance, 'I see a blood-curdling crime committed by the communists. I see blazing flames. I see a terrible firebrand that lights up the world.'[56]

Such was the unsubtle build-up to the plot. The following evening the correspondent of *The Times* of London, by chance approaching the Reichstag shortly after nine, saw the central dome blazing furiously. Only a few firemen and police had arrived as yet, and he was able to make his way in. He found the central chamber 'a mass of flames reaching high up into the dome', and was told by police officers that the fire had broken out simultaneously in four or five different places, including the cellars. A man had been arrested inside; it seemed he was a Dutch communist.[57]

Diels was with one of his colleagues in a coffee house in Unter den Linden when he was startled by the cry that the Reichstag was burning. Hurrying there, he must have arrived somewhat after *The Times* man as he had to climb over fire brigade hoses to make his way in. He was taken to where the Dutch incendiarist was held, a pale exhausted youth still breathing heavily from his exertions, but with a wild, triumphant glow in his eyes. Interrogating him, Diels came to the conclusion that he was 'a crackpot'.[58] Later Hitler's adjutant summoned Diels to the still-burning central chamber of the Reichstag. It must have been some time later since, according to *The Times*, Hitler did not arrive until 10.20. There on a balcony above the circular hall Diels found Hitler, Goebbels, Göring and entourage. Göring stepped up to him immediately. 'This is the beginning of the communist uprising – they will now let loose the attack. There is no time to lose—'

He was interrupted by Hitler screaming in an apparently uncontrollable frenzy, 'Now there will be no mercy! Whoever stands in our way will be cut down! The German *Volk* will have no sympathy with lenience. Every communist official will be shot where he is found. The communist deputies must be hanged this night. Everything connected with the communists is to be settled – no more indulgence will be shown the social democrats or the Reichsbanner.'[59] Hitler was, of course, supreme at histrionics because he believed in the parts he played.

Göring ordered Diels to place all police authorities on the highest alert and to instruct them to arrest all communist officials according to a long-prepared list. It is difficult to believe that all police authorities were not already on the highest alert. His last words, apparently, were, 'No communist and no social democrat should escape us.'

The chief players in the drama, and probably Diels as well since he was Göring's confidant and secret police chief, were aware that the Reichstag fire had been started by an SS team from Munich, calling themselves *Staatsräuber* – state hijackers – led by Heydrich. Some time before the act they had gathered in the Reichstag President's official residence – Göring was Reichstag President. On the evening of the 27th they made their way with incendiary materials along an underground passage leading from the residence to the cellars beneath the Reichstag, emerged, started fires and then departed again through the same underground passage. The Dutch communist youth, Marinus van der Lubbe, previously recruited by Nazi agents who had infiltrated his group, was left to be caught red-handed at the scene, and he was later tried and executed without being allowed to communicate with his family.

Obvious as it appeared to most informed observers that the Reichstag fire had been started by the Nazis themselves – even the method of access by the underground passage formed a topic of conversation the following day, 28 February[60] – the pretext of an imminent communist uprising allowed Hitler to persuade von Hindenburg to sign a decree 'for the Protection of the People and State' which suspended all guarantees of civil liberty or freedom of expression in the constitution, and gave the central government full powers in the federal states. This allowed all those listed communists and social democrats rounded up in their beds in the early morning following the fire – indicating the attention to detail of the planning – to be held in 'protective custody' – *Schutzhaft* – without trial for as long as the authorities decided to keep them. Diels put their number at about 4000 throughout the Reich. Over the next weeks some 20,000 more, chiefly rank-and-file communists, were arrested by groups of SA and SS auxiliary police on the rampage for revolutionary action and revenge.

The captives were thrown into makeshift prisons or *wild* concentration camps extemporised from whatever derelict spaces or empty buildings were available, and there starved, tortured, even killed.

In tens of thousands of cases, however, 'reds' simply went over to the winning side. Patrick Leigh Fermor, travelling through the Rhineland later that year, was put up for the night by a young factory worker who had done this. Leigh Fermor found the man's room 'a shrine of Hitleriana. The walls were covered with Nazi flags, photographs, posters, slogans and emblems.' Yet the year before, the young man told him, it had all been red flags, hammers and sickles, pictures of Stalin and Lenin. 'You should have seen me! Street fights! We used to beat the hell out of the Nazis and they beat the hell out of us. . . . Then suddenly, when Hitler came into power, I understood it was all nonsense and lies. I realised Adolf was the man for me.'[61] All his workmates had changed over too.

The communist 'danger' apparently revealed by the Reichstag fire served also as one of the main planks of Nazi propaganda in the final few days of the election campaign. Allied with it was a pledge to restore order with the most ruthless methods. Thus Göring, with characteristic bombast, promised to 'destroy and exterminate [*vernichten und auszurotten*], nothing else'. It was an accurate forecast. The scare and the promises served to increase support for the Party by some 5.5 million to 17.75 million, still only 44 per cent of the total votes cast, although with the addition of 3 million votes for Hugenberg's nationalist party the government gained a simple majority of seats in the Reichstag. This was not sufficient to force through the constitutional change Hitler had promised his supporters. Since, however, the communist and several social democrat deputies were held in *Schutzhaft* and unable to take their seats, and sufficient others were demoralised by threats and intimidation by the SA, the government found more than the necessary two-thirds majority for an Enabling Law allowing them to govern without further parliamentary restraint. So the German experiment in democracy was buried, to the satisfaction of the traditional power groupings, and with sufficient outward semblance of legality to ensure the loyalty of the bureaucrats, whose higher ranks were in any case in sympathy with Nazi–nationalist aims. Now more than ever the struggle between interest-groups had to be carried on within the Party; there was no other forum.

Heydrich seems to have tried to distance himself from his involvement in the essential preliminaries to the final seizure of power – the Reichstag fire and the resulting emergency decree – for he concocted a message to Göring's Police Chief, SS-Gruppenführer Kurt Daluege, on the notepaper of the Berlin Hotel Savoy and dated 5 March: he had tried in vain to contact him (Daluege) by phone since Thursday, he wrote. Thursday was 2 March. The implication was that this was the date he had arrived in the capital, thus after the Reichstag fire. Since it is inconceivable that Daluege would have been 'out' to Himmler's secret service chief on special duty in Berlin at such a momentous time, and since receipt of the message in Daluege's office is date-stamped 15 March, ten days after it was supposedly written, this is an obvious subterfuge. It is more indicative of his role that he was promoted on 21 March to SS-Oberführer, while his immediate subordinate in the Berlin SD, Kobelinski, received promotion at the end of February.[62]

Meanwhile Heydrich had returned to Munich to assist in the seizure of power in Bavaria, where the state government under the Minister-President Held was reverting to its monarchist and separatist traditions. On 9 March the Nazi Gauleiter of Bavaria, Adolf Wagner, and Ernst Röhm supported by massed SA formations presented Held with a demand that the Nazi sympathiser, General Ritter von Epp, be appointed Generalstaatskommissar, or plenipotentiary in Bavaria for the central government. Held refused, but the emergency decree arising from the Reichstag fire allowed Berlin to intervene directly. A telegram had already been prepared announcing von Epp's appointment, and this was sent to Munich. Held did not receive it, whereupon Heydrich, according to his widow's recollections, took an SS troop to the telegraph office and, pistol in hand, demanded the telegram and delivered it to the state Chancellery.

That same evening von Epp appointed Nazis to the important posts in the Bavarian administration. Wagner became Minister of the Interior, Hans Frank Minister of Justice, Heinrich Himmler Police President, Heydrich his chief of Department VI – the Political Police. These appointments, which must have been agreed in advance, indicate that Himmler and Heydrich had already staked their claim to control of the police by their creation of the intelligence service, SD, and the efficiency they had achieved in surveillance and infiltration. Evidently Röhm, Himmler's immediate superior and chief of the real power behind the Munich take-over, the revolutionary army of the SA, was impressed with his former aide's zeal in this field. Evidently, too, he did not regard him as a rival despite the fact that one of the chief aims of the SS security service was to counter the power of the SA and the threat it posed to the Führer and the political leadership. They were on *Du* terms, and Röhm evidently looked on him, as his old comrade of the *Reichskriegsflagge*, as a loyal, trustworthy, painstakingly energetic subordinate. In the dangerous cross-currents within the movement loyalty was the quality he must have looked for above all others. It was the quality Himmler took the greatest pains to communicate – loyalty upwards to his chiefs and downwards to his officers and men.

Röhm was by temperament an easy-going 'southerner', a swashbuckling soldier of fortune, now riding high on success, and like Strasser he failed to recognise the tortured psyche behind the pince-nez. So Himmler slipped quietly in to the Munich Police Praesidium, and Heydrich moved in with him. For the moment it appeared they were well away from the levers of real power in Berlin, where Göring was in control and glorying in the role which he had cast for himself, *Der Eiserne* – 'The Iron One'. 'He is certainly no *Eiserner*,' Göring's sister told Diels. 'He is as soft as a woman.'[63] This was an oversimplification, but by comparison with the iron in Himmler it was true.

Heydrich had files on the Munich police officials, and there is little doubt that several, like the specialist from the communist department in the Political Police, Heinrich Müller, had been approached beforehand. In any case the police departments, as in Berlin, were rapidly brought into line to work dutifully, and remarkably long hours, for the new masters. Meanwhile communists, social democratic leaders, even monarchists and conservatives of the Bavaria People's Party, opposition journalists, Jewish businessmen and other enemies on Heydrich's card indexes were rounded up from lists already prepared before the take-over, and thrown into prisons in all the main towns in Bavaria and, when these were full, into *wild* concentration camps such as had been established in Prussia.

One of these *wild* camps was extemporised by the local SS troop in a derelict munitions factory at Dachau on the northern outskirts of Munich. It was here that Himmler decided to found the first official concentration camp. It was opened on 22 March. In a press release, he explained it would have a capacity of 5000:

> Here the entire communist and – so far as is necessary – Reichsbanner and Marxist officials who endanger the security of the state will be concentrated because it is not possible in the long run to hold individual communist officials in prison without overburdening the state machinery, and on the other hand it is equally impossible to allow these officials their freedom again.[64]

Night of the Long Knives

According to his brother, Gebhard, Himmler had tried to disguise his satisfaction at becoming Police President, shaking his head when he was offered congratulations by saying how sad he felt that his new duties would bring him into contact only with the lowest species of humanity when all his thoughts and hopes were for the elite of the race.[1] He made similar remarks later in his most sententious vein; yet whether he was conscious of it or not – and probably he was not – it cannot be doubted that his new powers provided him with extraordinary fulfilment, allowing him to take revenge on the world and boost his battered ego at the expense of those he categorised as the enemy. This certainly applied to his concentration camp at Dachau.

The Kommandants he appointed and the regimes they instituted under his direction make this clear. First was SS-Obersturmführer Hilmar Wäckerle. In early June his partiality for murder under the guise of punishment for offences listed in a savage penal code was brought to the attention of the Bavarian Minister of Justice, Hans Frank. There was a tacit agreement between Frank and Himmler that, while criminal cases were dealt with by the Justice Department, 'political' cases were exclusively Himmler's concern, and bypassed the normal courts. Dachau was used only for 'political' prisoners at this time and Frank would not have involved himself with the murders in the camp had they not been pressed on him by those members of the Bavarian government and judiciary who had not yet adjusted to the new concept of 'revolutionary justice'. Among these was the titular head of the administration, von Epp, now known as the Statthalter. He was already attempting to wrest control of *Schutzhaft* from Himmler, to reduce the numbers held by having them restricted to 'leading anti-national oriented persons', and to forbid their physical maltreatment.[2] Since he was working through the Minister of the Interior, Wagner, who supported Himmler's aims and methods, he was getting nowhere. However, Himmler evidently felt sufficiently threatened by the pressure for a murder enquiry to bend to it and dismiss Wäckerle. He obtained his revenge by appointing as his successor the equally brutal Theodor Eicke.

Eicke had volunteered for the Army as a youngster of seventeen before the war, served through the war in the Paymaster's department, and afterwards tried to make a career in the police; he had been dismissed from several forces for being 'reactionary', but eventually secured a position in the security service of IG Farben, satisfying his aggression by joining the SA and later the SS. His activism eventually led him to fall foul of the police and he fled across the border to the Tyrol, there taking charge of a camp for other SS men on the run. Then, returning home after the seizure of power, he became involved in SA and SS action against the local *Gau* leadership, and was thrown into *Schutzhaft*, from whence he was consigned by an old Party rival to a mental institution. Himmler earned his lasting gratitude by rescuing him. On the same day, 26 June, he appointed him Kommandant of Dachau.

When he took over, the camp was little changed from the original *wild* institution, the guards a heterogeneous collection of Bavarian police and SS men sent there by officers who did not want them. Eicke asked Himmler for a permanent troop subordinate only to himself. This was granted, and before long he had created a specialist SS-Wachverband – guard unit – which he described later to Himmler as 'an outstanding selection of men showing a splendid corps spirit . . . [whose] ideals were loyalty, bravery and duty-fulfilment',[3] the traditional German virtues. Many of the later concentration camp Kommandants learned their business in this unit at Dachau, among them Rudolf Höss of Auschwitz. In his memoirs Höss explained the kernel of Eicke's method: it was to convince his men by repeated lectures, admonitions and orders that the inmates were dangerous enemies of the state. 'Through his continual influence in this direction, he generated a hate, an antipathy, against the prisoners which is inconceivable to those outside.'[4] Eicke stressed that any compassion for an enemy of the state was unworthy of an SS man. There was no place for weaklings, who would do well to withdraw as soon as possible to a monastery. He needed only hard, resolute men, who obeyed orders regardless. 'You stand as matchless soldiers even in peacetime day and night against the enemy, against the enemy behind the wire!'[5]

What Höss rationalised as hate for the enemies of the state might be better described as a sense of power and contempt for the inmates fostered in the guards by the camp system. Sadists had licence and delighted in their ability to cause suffering, especially if their victims pleaded for mercy.[6] As Höss noted, 'they were continually in search of new methods of mental and physical torture.'[7] The others were led to it by admonition and example, by the need to prove hardness, after a while by indifference. All had been indoctrinated in their value as the racial elite from the moment they entered the SS. The shaven-headed inmates of the camps were forced by fear of the consequences to show them exaggerated marks of respect, to allow themselves to be made objects of sport, to work like beasts of burden. Long-term prisoners became gaunt and weak from hunger, often racked by diseases related to malnutrition and the constant stress of camp life, arbitrary maltreatment, and the worse stress, as Höss observed, of not knowing when, if ever, they would be released – 'that was the most punishing [stress] that lamed even the firmest will.'[8] Inevitably the guards, whom Höss himself admitted were generally of limited outlook, regarded them as lesser, inferior creatures. That indeed was the aim of the system, to break down and dehumanise the 'enemies' within. They were numbers, not names, referred to as 'pigs' or 'filth' and worse. Jews, when they were brought in, were *Dreckjuden*, 'filth- or trash-Jews'. Obscenity and ridicule provided the everyday, one-way traffic.

Himmler was not sole originator of concentration camps or of the degrading treatment of inmates. Throughout the large conurbations of Germany similar barbarities were being perpetrated by the new rulers, who, tasting power, were releasing their resentments at their former lives and circumstances, and expressing those hates built up by the constant propaganda that had led them to predominance in the SA or SS in the first place. Diels, who saw too much of them in Prussia, tried in his memoirs to describe the predominant type that can be seen in so many photographs of the period: 'the bulky, bloated forms with that special development of the upper neck, the roundish faces, the uninspired eyes, the heavy unathletic walk, and thick, pipe-like boots growing out of brown breeches, in sum the very opposite of the racial ideals of Nordic man they lauded and demanded.'[9] They were loud and absolutely certain of their opinions, petty images of their Führer: 'the thought never came to them that they could err, or that contradiction could lead to clarity. There was, therefore, no possibility of discussion with them . . . and whoever contradicted was the "enemy".'[10]

Where Himmler differed from most of the other men with pipe boots in this wild phase of the Nazi revolution was in the single-minded way he systematised the terror and the skill with which he gathered all the strings into his own hands. While in Prussia local SA and SS groups continued to run their own prisons, camps and torture chambers outside state control, and Diels, according to his memoirs, learned of some only from reports in the foreign press, Himmler and Heydrich first managed to have all *Schutzhaft* committals in Bavaria registered and sanctioned by the Political Police, then gradually made the Political Police sole executive organ for *Schutzhaft* with a department inside Dachau – and other camps later – nominally responsible to the camp Kommandant but actually reporting to Heydrich's Political Police in Munich.

By establishing this triangle – Political Police (later Gestapo) – concentration camp – SS – Himmler gained complete control of the system of terror for and in the state of Bavaria. At the same time, by dividing the power within the system he ensured that his own overall command could not be challenged: Heydrich could determine who was taken into *Schutzhaft* and when or if they should be released, but he had no say in their treatment inside Dachau. Eicke and his successors had absolute control over the inmates, but had no say over who they should be or the length of their sentence.

Undoubtedly Himmler was supported by his immediate superiors, the

Interior Minister, Wagner, and the SA Chief of Staff, Röhm; obviously the Justice Minister, Hans Frank, was content to allow him jurisdiction in political affairs. Nevertheless considerable political skills must have been necessary to achieve such a position so quickly in a situation so tense with change and replete with loud, ambitious characters. In fact he had to give up the Munich Police Praesidium to one of these, SA-Obergruppenführer August Schneidhuber, in April; instead he became Political Police Commander of Bavaria – retaining the central Political Police authority in Munich. Evidently he compromised skilfully, and unlike those who were simply grasping for position and power, his goals were quite clear, and they matched Hitler's goals. His energy and attention to detail were those of a still young man, thirty-three, and a zealot. His enemies were indexed on Heydrich's cards – and Heydrich was even younger than he, only twenty-nine. Besides all this he undoubtedly knew how to ingratiate himself and play rivals off against one another.

However it was done, Himmler knew with the rational side of his brain exactly what he was doing. This is demonstrated by the 'action' of 26 June, by coincidence the day that Eicke received his appointment as Kommandant of Dachau. Communist and social democratic leaders had been the first victims of the round-ups immediately after the seizure of power. Trade union leaders had been next in early May; their arrest and the occupation of their offices and seizure of assets had been co-ordinated nationwide by Robert Ley, later chief of the state association Arbeitsfront, allegedly formed to look after the interests of the workers. It is an indication of Nazi priorities and of the nature of Hitler's industrial aims and backers that this suppression of the trade unions came so soon after the *Machtergreifung*. Those considered most dangerous and intractable – or in Himmler's description, *unverbesserlich*, incorrigible – from these former classes of enemy had been retained in Dachau when those committed from the action of 26 June began to come in. They were leaders of the Bavarian People's Party – which of course Himmler's father and most of his circle had supported – at first mostly Reichstag and Landtag deputies, then other officials, some 2000 in all. Most were not held for much longer than a week, some only five days, then they were released. It was a warning, not only to the 'conservative reactionaries', monarchists and separatists among them, but to all their acquaintances in all strata of society in the towns and villages of Bavaria. They were not allowed to speak of what they had seen or suffered inside, but their silence and evident *Angst* enhanced the sense of undefined, therefore limitless terror which it was Himmler's and Heydrich's purpose to propagate. Whether the idea was taken from the Spanish Inquisition whose methods it so resembled or from the example of the Russian secret police, whether it sprang from Himmler's own zealotry, it was a deliberate policy designed to suppress by fear all actual or potential opposition or even criticism of the regime.[11] Dachau was not simply a cage for the *unverbesserlich*; it was a standing threat to every citizen who might think of stepping out of line. The other political parties hurriedly dissolved themselves, and on 14 July a law was published whereby the NSDAP was named as the only political party in Germany; anyone organising another or forming a new party would be punished by penal servitude or prison.

After the parties the next action was against the Catholic Church. Here, however, Himmler and Heydrich had to move more carefully, so strongly was Catholicism embedded in the region, and indeed throughout areas of Germany; moreover Hitler was negotiating a concordat with the Vatican. For the moment they admitted defeat, but it was precisely because of the strength of the opposition and the danger it represented to the new ideology that the retreat could only be tactical. After the priests it was the turn of the Jews. On 19 July it was announced that all Jewish organisations apart from synagogues and purely charitable institutions were to be disbanded and their assets confiscated. Jews were not taken into *Schutzhaft* as a racial group, although individual Jews were already inside Dachau as political opponents.

So the political and ideological enemies were isolated and picked off separately. But the speed and success with which the terror system had been created, the arbitrary powers Himmler had accumulated, and the terrible rumours emerging from Dachau caused unease and revulsion, not least within the Bavarian government, bureaucracy and sections of the judiciary. The old soldier, von Epp, led the opposition but failed to break the shield of Wagner's protection until that autumn when another series of deaths in Dachau provided fresh ammunition. Neither Wagner nor Hans Frank was able to contain the pressure that boiled up for an enquiry, and on 5 December it was decreed at a ministerial meeting that the Public Prosecutor should institute judicial proceedings 'instantly and with all energy' to clarify the circumstances surrounding the deaths in the camp. In this situation, so similar to that in June when he had dismissed Wäckerle, Himmler turned for help to Röhm.

Exactly what arguments he used are not known since he went in to see his chief alone. He had already told Hans Frank that to allow an enquiry would constitute a victory for the enemies of the revolution and its chief vehicles the SA and SS. He presumably followed the same line with Röhm. When he emerged, he called in his liaison man with the Ministry of Justice, the lawyer Dr Walther Stepp, and Röhm gave Stepp a message to take back to Hans Frank:

> The camp Dachau is a camp for *Schutzhaft* prisoners arrested on political grounds. The events in question are of a political nature and must under all circumstances be decided by the political authorities. They appear to me extremely unsuitable for settlement through the legal authorities. That is my opinion as Chief of Staff and as Reichsminister with an interest in the Reich not being damaged by the events in question. . . . Tomorrow I will discuss the affair with the Führer and request a decision.[12]

In the meantime, he instructed Himmler not to allow the legal authorities into Dachau, nor to allow the camp staff to co-operate with them. Three days later Hitler's decision was made known: the proceedings were to be dropped. This ended the last official resistance to revolutionary justice in Bavaria. It had taken nine months from the day von Epp set up the new government in Munich for all illusions about the nature of National Socialism to be quashed. The same day the Justice Department dropped another case involving the death of a Dachau inmate shot by a guard.[13]

Himmler looked on Dachau as he looked on the SS, as an instrument for achieving his goals; in retrospect both can be seen as extensions of his will and psyche. The camp was run from the first on military lines. As in the Army everything was subject to minutely detailed regulations – how a guard was to be saluted, how each bunk was to be left in the morning with the straw palliasse completely level and the blue-and-white chequers on the sheets forming perfect parallels with the sides and ends of the rectangle. It was distinguished from an Army camp by the minimal rations, deliberate dehumanising of the inmates by abuse, humiliation, blows, a brutal code of punishment and long hours of work permitting no time or energy for recreation.

The plans of the first accommodation units which superseded the derelict factory buildings show long timber huts of a design which remained basically unchanged during the life of the camp and of the others spawned later in its image. Each of these first huts, or 'blocks', was divided into five rooms, each sleeping fifty-four persons in a wooden bunk structure with two rows of nine bunks, heads abutting, in three tiers or levels – a most efficient use of space that became standard. At the end of each of these bunk structures were three tables for eating, and between the two rooms at each end of the block was a washroom with communal sink and six lavatory cubicles; these are shown with doors, but they soon lost these and the partitions between. The total of twelve lavatory bowls was completely inadequate for the 270 inmates of the block, especially since little time was allowed between reveille and morning rollcall and much of that was taken in tidying the room and bunks until they were in immaculate order. As a result of this and because of the many inmates suffering dysentery and other diseases caused by diet and conditions, 'the morning scramble in the washhouse was', according to a survivors' history of the camp, 'indescribable'.[14] This was part of the deliberate attempt to break down the prisoners' personality.

At rollcall each room of fifty-four men paraded as a platoon, the five platoons of each block forming a company with a prisoner called a Feldwebel – sergeant – responsible for discipline and routine. After numbers had been checked work parties were detached under guard. One reason why Himmler had established the camp at Dachau was to provide labour to build an SS base there within convenient distance of the city, but this could not be started for some years. In the meantime the inmates were worked like slaves from six in the morning to six at night clearing the derelict buildings, remaking their own camp and on other tasks for the SS. Undoubtedly Himmler regarded this not just as an appropriate punishment for those whose aim was to poison and destroy Germany, but as a living example of the natural order whereby inferior specimens worked for the superior-value species. He expressed the idea in many later speeches. The main gates bore the lettering in wrought iron: 'ARBEIT MACHT FREI' – 'Work liberates'. Conceived by Eicke or one of his stamp this would have been a brutal joke; with Himmler it was not even an irony. The same went for the slogan he had painted later along the pitched roof of the long utility building built by the prisoners facing the huts across the *Appelplatz*: 'There is one way to freedom. Its milestones are: obedience, zeal, honesty, order, cleanliness, temperance, truth, sense of sacrifice and love for the Fatherland.'[15]

Himmler believed in this moral code, yet of course there is no virtue under compulsion, and all these ideas save 'honesty' and 'truth' and 'love for the Fatherland' were enforced by brutal disciplinary regulations: sabotage or causing any material damage in the camp or at work outside carried the death penalty; so did attacking a guard, refusing to obey an order, refusing to work, inciting others to these acts, or shouting or complaining. Talking politics for subversive ends, making provocative remarks, forming cliques, loitering with intent, transmitting news from the camp or trying to make contact with the outside were among other offences listed as punishable by hanging. Lesser crimes, among them 'making unfavourable remarks in letters or other communications about National Socialist leaders, the state or the government', making 'ironical or jeering remarks to a member of the SS' or intentionally omitting to salute as laid down were punishable by cell detention on a diet of water and bread, preceded and followed by twenty-five strokes with the whip.[16]

Höss described the first beatings he saw. The *Wachtruppe* was paraded around four sides of an open square in the middle of which was the *Bock*, a slatted structure like a gym horse. The victims were brought in with all usual shouted military formalities, after which the first one bent over the *Bock*. Two guards seized his head and arms, holding him down as two others took turn and turn about administering the strokes with bull-whips. He took it without a sound, but the second victim started shrieking with the first blow and struggling to shake himself free, and continued to make a dreadful noise until the last stroke. Höss found himself going hot and cold and trembling as he was forced to watch from the front rank; it affected him far more than the first execution he witnessed.[17] Former inmates have given more graphic descriptions of these savage beatings and of victims with bleeding buttocks being taken to the sick block and unable to move for several days afterwards.[18]

The penal code satisfied Himmler's obsession with regulations and the guards' need for rules, but neither Eicke nor those he indoctrinated felt themselves bound by its provisions. Punishments became arbitrary. As it was put in a survivors' history, any inmate 'could be locked in the punishment cell, struck, starved, tortured, killed for a variety of reasons whose seriousness was decided by the SS'.[19] After December there was not even the hope of recourse to outside authority; the camp was a sealed world, the Kommandant the only law. So Eicke transformed Dachau into a model institution which Himmler loved to show off to guests he wished to impress, certain that the demonstration block, *Appelplatz*, workshops and kitchens would be spotlessly clean and orderly, the inmates would march obediently to work or inspection parade, sing SS songs word-perfectly and reveal no hint of what was practised inside except by the expression in their eyes, and their haggard faces and subdued bearing – which was as it should be for enemies of the state.

Himmler's goals were not confined to Bavaria. His aim was to unify the separate regional Political Police forces and so impose his system of 'Political Police – concentration camps – SS' throughout the Reich. His eventual aim was to unify all police – 'political', 'criminal', 'order', and the green Schutz-Polizei – and incorporate them into the SS as a national internal 'protection' force. According to a high official in the SD, Dr Werner Best, this idea was fully developed in his mind by 1933.[20] As already mentioned, Otto Strasser suggests that Himmler had prepared a memorandum on these lines for Hitler during his earliest days as Reichsführer-SS.[21]

He started to realise the idea that autumn, taking over, one by one, different Political Police forces. Precisely how it was done is not clear. It happened over some three months between October 1933 and January 1934, by which time he was Political Police Commander in every *Land* except Prussia. In several cases the way was opened by SS officers who had obtained leading positions in the police: Best for example was Police Commissioner in Hessen, SS-Sturmbannführer Streckenbach chief of the newly formed Political Police in Hamburg. Elsewhere Heydrich's network of V-men could provide inside information for use in the manoeuvres for power. Himmler also had an ally in the Reich Interior Minister, Dr Frick, who had the similar goal of unifying all police forces of the Reich – under his own Ministry. He must also have had Hitler's ultimate backing, although no documentary evidence has surfaced to indicate a Führer decree. Judging by events in Bavaria, he had the support of his '*Duz*-friend', Röhm too. This is understandable for Röhm needed friends himself at this time when SA excesses were conjuring powerful enemies. It is interesting that in September, just before Himmler began the series of police take-overs, Röhm issued an order valid for SA, SS and Stahlhelm – which he had incorporated into the SA – that in service matters the Reichsführer-SS was to be addressed as 'Mein Reichsführer!'[22]

In the separate negotiations with regional authorities leading up to his appointments, Himmler showed his political flair, using existing rivalries to further his suit, always prepared to make concessions to gain the main point in view. He and Heydrich were objects of deep unease throughout the Reich – the 'black *Diaskuren*' (heavenly twins), as Diels referred to them, not simply on account of the black SS uniforms. On the other hand the reputation for efficiency of the 'Political Police – concentration camp' system in Bavaria, and Dachau's notoriety, worked to Himmler's advantage; so did the success he had achieved in recruiting a high proportion of nobles and young lawyers into the SS, giving it a conventionally as well as racially elite status.

This other face of the SS, reassuringly reasonable, intelligent but realistic, socially ultra-acceptable, was epitomised by Himmler's new adjutant, Karl Wolff. Like Heydrich he conformed closely to the Aryan ideal, six feet tall, blond hair, blue eyes with a high enough forehead to give his face the required length. He was six months older than Himmler, and had the advantage of having served a year at the front where he had won promotion and the Iron Cross 1st and 2nd class for bravery and zeal. His father had been a director of the district court in Darmstadt, thus a member of the haute bourgeoisie, and Wolff had attended the most socially acceptable *Gymnasium* in the city. His war service had been with the exclusive Hessian Guard–Infantry Regiment 115 led by the Grand Duke of Hessen-Darmstadt in person. Demobilised after the war, Wolff had taken a variety of bank and commercial jobs, married into a good family and gravitated to Munich as the nationalist mood boiled up just before Hitler's putsch. There in 1924, at a time when Himmler was despairing and unemployed, Wolff's agreeable personality had won him a post in a branch of a Hamburg advertising company and he performed so well that he was soon head of the branch. Within a year he had formed his own advertising firm, and it was only when this ran into trouble in the economic crises of 1931 that he had taken himself to the Brown House and signed an enrolment form for the SS:

> I undertake to commit myself to the idea of Adolf Hitler, to maintain strictest Party discipline and to carry out the orders of the Reichsführer of the Schutzstaffeln and the Party leadership conscientiously.
>
> I am German, of Aryan descent, belong to no freemasons' lodge and no secret society and promise to support the movement with all my powers.[23]

The form passed up the chain of officials in the Reichsführung, arriving on Himmler's desk some three weeks later, where the photograph attached was scrutinised through the pince-nez for non-Aryan blemishes in the features – Himmler claimed that all photographs were so examined – and sent out, approved, the same day.

Such was the man with the bearing of a soldier, the easy manners of an assured background, a naturally agreeable, persuasive personality – and with a National Socialist *Weltanschauung* soon grafted on to his nationalist outlook by the SS officer school – who, less than two years later, Himmler chose for his closest aide. It has been said that Himmler wanted to woo the Army at the time, and picked Wolff for the purpose, but Wolff was an asset in any company Himmler wished to impress, and did as well with the 'Friends' Circle' of bankers and industrialists who donated to SS funds as with the officers of the Reichswehr or *Land* or Reich officials, or indeed SS or SA officers with proposals or quarrels. He was both reasonable persuader and emollient, and attempted to shield his chief as much as he could from the consequences of the immense responsibilities he was taking on. Heydrich was the fearful face of the Reichsführer-SS, Wolff his 'public relations' face. Himmler used both for his take-over of the regional Political Police. At the same time, by creating a rivalry between these two very different but most capable men, he sharpened their zeal and attachment to him, and safeguarded his own power position.

The picture of the unsoldierly, bespectacled Himmler, 'to outward appearance a grotesque caricature of his own laws, norms and ideals',[24] flanked by two such specimens of Aryan manhood and evidently compelling their devotion is something which has intrigued all commentators. And it was not only these two; there were a host of other blond, Nordic men from every background who looked up to him. Stroop was one.

His zeal and ruthlessness under Himmler's eye had won him rapid promotion to SS-Hauptsturmführer – captain's rank – and he paraded that autumn for the Nuremberg Party rally with a new, tailored uniform, 'the collar of black material, aluminium-edged', as he described it to his cell-mate Moczarski, after the war, 'on the left two brilliant mirror-wires and three four-cornered starlets, on the right a silver shoulder strap'.[25] His mirror-black boots were new too; unfortunately he had ordered them too late to attend a fitting and, returning to his home town afterwards with painful heels, he struck the shoemaker in the mouth. 'The delivery of uncomfortable boots for a parade is sabotage,' he explained to Moczarski.

He had taken to changing his underclothes every day, and taking a bath every day 'like a gentleman'.

'And did you use perfume every day?' Moczarski asked him.

Stroop nodded. 'After a bath one always uses eau-de-Cologne.'[26]

Himmler influenced and compelled the respect of at least the majority of his diverse corps not simply by virtue of his position – although of course he could not have done it without his position – but also by what has been described as 'old-fashioned patriarchal charm' and the 'artless honesty of a pedagogue'.[27] That, in truth, is what he tried to be, father and teacher to his men. His obvious concern for them, unsparing work and attention to detail, his mastery of a *Weltanschauung* which challenged, flattered and promised them the earth, his closeness to the already legendary figure of the Führer, Adolf Hitler, his loyalty and stress on the other old Germanic virtues of their forefathers, his whole uncompromising, uncomplicated message evidently compelled, and overcame those physical and physiognomic disadvantages which appear so striking to the unattached observer seeing him on photographs or film.

It was a triumph of will, and those closest to him knew how much it cost in nervous stress. At times when Wolff saw him at his desk as if concentrating on the files always awaiting him, his elbows on the desk-top, his short, plump fingers clasped around his head with its round plate of dark hair sitting on the crown, he realised his chief was in pain. At first, apparently, Himmler admitted the extent of the pain only to his brother Gebhard, who relayed what he had said to his first biographer, Frischauer, after the war: 'the pressure of thoughts, the power of concentration made his head feel like a ball of fire'; it was as if every nerve inside his skull were leading a separate existence and trying to torment him.[28] He also suffered from the stomach cramps he had noted in early diaries.

While a large part of the influence Himmler exerted was due to his style of leadership as earnest father–counsellor – a part he could play to perfection because it was him, or one side of him – he also drew power from his own father-figure, the Führer, and radiated that. But undoubtedly a part of his hold over his men resulted from the other dark, vindictive side of his nature, which he showed to those breaking his rules or simply making mistakes. Some years later his chauffeur, while driving an otherwise empty car, had the misfortune to be involved in an accident with a motorcyclist at a crossing; neither man was injured seriously, but Himmler had the chauffeur thrown into a cell without a hearing and had him kept there without being able to communicate with his wife or even to let her know where he was for six weeks. Then he was released, broken and trembling, sworn to silence, and dismissed from Himmler's service.[29]

SS-Standartenführer Hans von Kobelinski, head of the Berlin SD, was let off more lightly after a transgression in early 1934. He let slip secrets to a girl, compounded the mistake by accusing a subordinate of lying and when he was sent on leave pending a disciplinary enquiry threatened, 'according to the unanimous statements of four witnesses', that he intended giving Himmler and Heydrich a piece of his mind. He was degraded to the ranks as an ordinary SS man. Communicating this decision to him, Himmler wrote, 'I have not seen fit to institute a severer punishment in view of your long membership of the SS.'[30] It would be truer to say that since the former SD chief was privy to the events leading to the *Machtergreifung* and the Reichstag fire, and much else including current undermining operations within the Prussian police, Himmler had to retain him in the SS or have him quietly eliminated; the only other option was an indefinite period of *Schutzhaft* in Dachau. Von Kobelinski was probably fortunate. Heydrich perhaps interceded for him.

In part Himmler's effectiveness as a leader stemmed from his still extraordinary idealism. This remained his most obvious trait. Thus at the same time as he was operating with guile in the practical political business of extending his power over the Reich, he was living in the Teutonic fantasy he had built for himself as a youth. This helped to focus his will; it also served to complete his disguise. Heydrich was regarded as the more dangerous of the *Diaskuren*. Heydrich's biographers have generally perpetuated the idea, but a comparison of his subsequent career with Himmler's, and of their very different ends, suggests the contrary. Heydrich was obviously demoniacal and played the part; Himmler, lurking in the shadows, ever-watchful, ever voracious with an appetite that could never be sated, seems in retrospect by far the more lethal predator. Heydrich lived exclusively in the 'real' world of the National Socialist revolution; Himmler lived in the same world and simultaneously in his own world. Both were equally valid for him, and obviously they were complementary, but it was the fantasy or eccentricity that struck most 'realists' who knew him, and this surely diverted their attention from the fact that he was on their plane as well, circling as warily as they were circling their rivals.

'Never forget,' Himmler liked to tell his SS-Führers, 'we are a knightly Order.' That autumn, 1933, while he travelled the Reich with Wolff gobbling up new Political Police departments and inducting the officials in his methods, he was on the look-out for a castle that would serve as the seat of his Order. In November he found Wewelsburg, once stronghold of the bishops of Paderborn, now derelict and neglected on a hill overlooking the Westphalian plain and the River Alme. Just to the east was the Teutoburger forest where in AD 9 Hermann the Cherusker, having succeeded in uniting the Germanic tribes of Westphalia and Hesse, defeated the Roman army of occupation under its brutal commander Varus. The historical associations were important to Himmler. He leased Wewelsburg for a nominal rent and began planning its conversion into an SS school. Perhaps that is what he intended; more probably it was a cover to turn away ridicule and preserve secrecy, for as the plans developed the castle became – in his eyes – what Camelot had been to King Arthur and the Knights of the Round Table, Monsalvat to Perceval and the Knights of the Holy Grail, a mystical seat hidden from the gaze of the uninitiated, the towered sanctum of the higher orders of SS chivalry.

'Never forget,' he told a gathering of SS-Führers little over a year later, 'we are a knightly Order, from which one cannot withdraw, to which one is recruited by blood and within which one remains with body and soul so long as one lives on this earth.'[31]

Already it seems he had succeeded in creating something of this spirit. When, at the end of December 1933, he sent SS-Oberführer Richard Hildebrandt a silver SS *Totenkopf* – death's head – ring, Hildebrandt wrote thanking him for something which, making all allowance for the flattery due to his commanding officer, evidently represented more than a mere gift. It was, as he expressed it, 'a proud and binding avowal of everlasting and joyous struggle for a pure Germanic Deutschland'.[32]

Himmler's personal life – so much as his continuous activity allowed one – had changed very obviously, and his appearance with it. The gaunt cheeks of the years of struggle were plumped out and he had developed a double chin under the inadequate bone structure; this became especially evident when he laughed. His mirror must have been a standing reproach.

He had sold the house and chicken farm at Waldtrudering and moved into a flat of spacious rooms close to Hitler's apartment in the Princeregenten-strasse. He had also bought a large villa called Lindenfycht at Gmund on the Tegernsee, a lake south-east of Munich enclosed by mountains, whose resorts and summer houses were favoured by the Party powerful, indeed it was known as the Lago di Bonzi – the lake of the bosses. Marga established herself there with little Gudrun, whom they called 'Puppi', now four, and a boy they had adopted; the forty-year-old Marga was unable to have another child herself.

It is evident from her letters that her *Lieber Guter*, her dear treasure, was prevented by pressure of travel and work from spending much time at home – not that this was anything new in their marriage – and when he did come back for flying weekends his files accompanied him. His new status was an obvious source of pride to her and she no longer had the financial hardships of their first years together, yet it is probable she felt, as before, lonely and excluded. For she would not have needed extraordinary perception to realise that his work meant more to him than their relationship, that he was more at home in his office or parading at the head of his Order, showing off his *weltanschauliche* erudition, exchanging Party truisms or singing from the SS song book at the all-male gatherings of the collective than he was with her. Yet she still tried. To all outward appearance they remained a devoted couple. She continued to manage that part of his life which she was allowed to enter, and it is evident from Gudrun's later diaries that strains in the relationship were not obvious to the children. To Gudrun he was always a warm and loving father.

It is not clear what his salary was now. Wolff received 450 Marks a month, sufficient for a very reasonable standard of living, and it must be assumed that Himmler allowed himself a great deal more. However, in keeping with the puritan ethic he preached, he gave the impression that he lived simply, managed on very little and was scrupulously honest, not even charging personal travel or hotel bills to his expense account. Undoubtedly, by comparison with Göring and other Party dignitaries, his style was unpretentious and abstemious. Yet he lived well, and whether or not he was scrupulous over his personal expenses is irrelevant when viewed against the giant system of corruption the SS represented, and the huge misappropriations of funds he connived at for those he wished to favour. The legend of incorruptibility he sought to foster was a supreme – perhaps unconscious – hypocrisy.

He was reconciled with his family by this time. His father had retired in 1930 full of honour with the title of *Geheimrat* – literally privy councillor – and both he and Frau Himmler were now intensely proud of their son's importance despite what he had done to the Bavarian People's Party, indeed every party, despite his renunciation of the Catholic Church and so many of the values Professor Himmler had spent his life upholding before his pupils. The relationship had changed; now it was Heinrich who was able to do things for them. He was also able to look after his brother Gebhard, taking him into the SS, where he reached the rank of Standartenführer on his staff.

By the end of January 1934 only the Prussian Political Police, the Gestapo, remained outside Himmler's grasp. Göring was determined to keep it so; it was the key to his real power in Prussia. In co-operation with his telephone-tapping service, the Forschungsamt, it was also the key to the maintenance of his position in face of dangerous rivalries within the Party and the influential groupings which had helped the Party to power.

Among the things Göring learned from his telephone tapping were that his nephew called him 'Hermann the Terrible' or 'Lohengrin'; Himmler's friend, Gauleiter Kube, called him the 'Thick Fellow'; Röhm and the Berlin SA leader, the ex-waiter named Karl Ernst, referred to him as a reactionary swine and called his present love, the actress 'Emmy' Sonnemann, his 'slut'. But what Göring learned of the seditious plans of his rivals, in particular of Röhm, is as little known as the true extent of such plans.

Two things, however, can be said with certainty: the SA, now a huge, heterogeneous and generally discontented army of 4 million, threatened the hereditary leadership of the Army, the Junker landowners, the bureaucracy and the heavy industrialists with a continuation of the revolution – or, as they termed it, 'the second revolution' – to complete the *Machtergreifung* by toppling these 'reactionary' groupings, whose creature they believed Göring to be; as indeed he was. The other certainty is that everything Göring learned was immediately made available to Himmler and Heydrich. They had infiltrated the highest levels of the Gestapo, and both key departments, the so-called Bewegungs (Movements) department, dealing with communists and all the other enemies within, and Landesverrat und Spionage (High Treason and Espionage), were headed by their agents, Arthur Nebe and Günther Patchowsky respectively. Göring's Gestapo chief, Diels, knew of Nebe's orientation, but was unaware of Patchowsky's. In addition there was an acknowledged line through SS-Brigadeführer Henze to a liaison department named 'SS-Kommando-Gestapa', located in Columbia Haus, Columbia Strasse, where SS-Group East had a jail notorious even beside the hellish grottoes of the SA. Diels himself had taken out insurance in the form of an honorary SS rank.

Exactly when Göring realised he was not going to be able to keep Himmler and Heydrich out of the Gestapo is not clear. He was still trying hard to do so in December 1933, still fighting against Frick's plans for a unified Reich police force. He had already moved the Gestapa (Gestapo offices) physically from the Berlin Police Praesidium into a palatial building, formerly an art school, on Prinz Albrecht Strasse close by his own residence. On 30 November he removed it administratively from the Prussian Interior Ministry, over which he presided, to subordinate it and its district out-stations, known as *Stapostellen*, directly to himself in his capacity as Prussian Minister–President – a post he had taken over from von Papen in April. Then in January 1934, Frick gained Hitler's support for a law transferring the sovereign rights of the *Länder* (regions) to the Reich. It was a great victory, in theory depriving Göring of the Prussian police. It must have been evident to Göring by then that the Führer wished Himmler to preside over a unified Reich Political Police. The shock was terrible. Diels described how recognition that Hitler could remove the basis of his power with a decree – that without Hitler he was nothing – literally laid him low, and he took to his bed.[33] 'I have done it all wrong,' he confided, 'all wrong! How could I have wanted to strengthen Prussia when Hitler wanted the Reich. Yet I cannot hand over the police. Never! Otherwise I am simply a bogy, a Minister-President without a territory . . .'

It was in these circumstances that Göring decided he would have to seek an accommodation with Himmler; but he also needed SS support in the struggle with those dangerous enemies in the SA leadership who regarded him as a friend and supporter of the reactionaries. In any case he began negotiations some time in February and they were concluded by mid-March, when he summoned Diels and told him he was dismissed; he had decided to entrust the Prussian police to Himmler. 'I remain chief,' he added.[34] This was the compromise which Himmler, with his usual flexibility, had agreed to in order to gain his end, entry into the Prussian citadel.

There was a curious hiccup that same night. Diels had already seen the early editions of the next morning's papers announcing Himmler's appointment when he was summoned to Göring again, and told that Hitler wished him to remain at his post. 'Stay, Diels, the Führer wishes it.' When Diels raised objections, Göring promised to have the early newspapers seized; when he still demurred he was commanded to report to the Führer the following morning. According to Diels' account Hitler began the interview by declaiming against Röhm and his cronies, but said he had no desire to see Göring bring in Himmler to help him sort out the mess, and pressed Diels to remain, promising him full powers and offering him the post of Minister of Police. Diels, knowing that his life was forfeit if he continued to act as a buffer against Himmler's ambitions to take over the Gestapo, pleaded ill-health and was eventually allowed to retire. Still enjoying Göring's patronage he was appointed head of the regional government in Cologne.[35]

There are several possible explanations for Hitler's last-minute intervention. It might appear an example of the way he habitually tried to balance power so that no single individual or organisation grew mighty enough to challenge his own leadership. Yet he cannot have wished for a permanent separation of the vital Political Police functions between Göring in Prussia and Himmler elsewhere. Or Röhm, hearing of Himmler's appointment, may have become alarmed at the potential of the new alliance evidently directed against him and sought Hitler's intervention. If, as seems very likely, Hitler had already decided to act against the SA leadership, his support for Diels as a block to Himmler may be seen as part of a larger charade to lull Röhm into a false sense of security. On the other hand Heydrich's biographer, Schlomo Aronson, suggests that, if Hitler had already decided to act against Röhm, he may have wished to preserve Diels because of his experience in Berlin and his knowledge of the relationships between SA, Party, bureaucracy and Army.

Certainly Diels had been in the forefront of the fight against SA excesses in the capital. He had closed down their *wild* concentration camps, presented Hitler with thick dossiers on brutalities and sadism in their city torture chambers, on homosexual rings centring on Röhm and other SA leaders, and on their corruption of Hitler Youth members. One presentation in mid-December 1933 had caused Hitler unusual agitation.

Turning to Göring, he had said, 'This whole camarilla around Chief of Staff Röhm is corrupt through and through. The SA is the pacemaker in all this filth [in the Hitler Youth movement]. You should look into it more thoroughly – that would interest me!'[36]

The hint had been dropped. Göring managed to maintain his composure, but his excitement surfaced directly as they left the audience and he instructed Diels to go to work immediately. Diels said it would cost him his head, and he (Göring) would be unable to protect him. Nevertheless he went to work, amassed another bulky dossier on SA outrages and took it to Hitler's mountain retreat at Obersalzberg in mid-January 1934. Ushered in to the presence, he found Hitler in conversation with Göring; they were discussing treason and the 'great traitors' who were influencing lesser men in the Party and SA to revolt. He learned – so he wrote in his guarded memoirs, although he must already have known very well – that General von Schleicher and Gregor Strasser were conspiring with Röhm and the SA leadership to topple the regime, and that Hitler wished these enemies of the state to be cleared out before they could make their bid for power. 'It is incomprehensible', Hitler said, 'that Strasser and Schleicher, these arch-traitors, have survived to this day.'[37]

When they left the great hall with its view of glistening peaks and snow-encrusted firs down the slopes outside the eyrie, Göring turned to Diels with mixed gruffness and joviality, 'You understand what the Führer wants?' Diels returned his gaze. 'These three must disappear,' Göring said, 'and very soon. They are downright traitors, I can assure you of that.'

Diels asked whether a court could not be convened to try them.

'The Führer's order means more than a court. The most important is

Strasser. He can commit suicide – he is a chemist after all. I hold you responsible with your head that no one learns anything of the affair.' He spoke urgently and forcefully – in Diels' description, a chained dog that had just been unleashed.[38]

It was then that Diels saw the worm in the apple. For such an intelligent man it had taken a long time. But reading between the lines of his alternately revealing and deliberately misleading memoirs, and his descriptions of being offered the post of Reich Police President by both Göring and Hitler, it is apparent that he knew he was in an impossible position between the barons of the SA and the SS, and that the police forces of the state, infiltrated from top to bottom and commanded by SA or SS leaders, were of little use to him. He declined to put his head on the block and was content, wisely, to transfer to the quieter life of the provinces. Thus he survived the war.

Göring had no option but to call in the Reichsführer-SS to his aid. According to Karl Wolff, Hitler had told Göring the police had to be unified 'if we want to get rid of Röhm'.[39] So it was that on 19 April 1934 Himmler entered the building whose cellars were to become a synonym for dread, No. 8 Prinz Albrecht Strasse. He brought Heydrich with him, and Wolff, installed them in offices adjacent to his own, and began unceremoniously to replace Diels' officials chiefly with men from his own Bavarian police or the SS. On 25 April the chief of Diels' Press Office, Lützow, came back from lunch to find his desk had been broken into, and the chief of the former legal department, Volk, sharing his office since his own had been commandeered for Heydrich, found his files strewn on the floor. Infuriated, Lützow went to Himmler's and Heydrich's lobby to tackle them:

The ante-room was like an army camp, black [SS] uniforms everywhere, between them girls with hair in tight coils, all speaking in Bavarian dialect. I did not succeed in seeing either of the two governors. I only received a reply from Himmler via his adjutant, Wolff, that I should remain in the building with all the higher officials.[40]

The core of the new Gestapa which took shape before the end of the month was Hauptabteilung (Main Department) II, devoted to the surveillance and suppression of internal enemies of the state. Heydrich took personal charge of it, relying on two professional police officials from Munich for the detailed work of the desks. The more significant of these, who was to become almost the living embodiment of the Gestapo, was Heinrich Müller, the expert on communism in the Munich Political Police who had thrown in his lot with Heydrich on the take-over of power in Bavaria. He was an archetypal middle-rank official: of limited imagination, non-political, non-ideological, his only fanaticism lay in an inner drive to perfection in his profession and in his duty to the state – which in his mind were one. That the state happened to be Hitler's Third Reich was a matter of circumstance, although he perhaps felt some emotional identity since he disliked educated people of the higher bureaucracy. A smallish man with piercing eyes and thin lips, he was an able organiser, utterly ruthless, a man who lived for his work. Heydrich could have found no more suitable instrument.

Müller was placed in charge of II 1A – communism, Marxism and all affiliated organisations, trade unions and subversion (in sum the most ideologically and practically dangerous enemies of the regime); II 1C – reactionaries, opposition, Austrian affairs; II 1D – *Schutzhaft* and concentration camps; and II 1H – surveillance of the National Socialist Party and its affiliated organisations. The pattern seems clear: Heydrich was using his most trusted expert to establish a corner of the triangle, 'Political Police – SS – concentration camps', which had proved successful in Bavaria. As in Bavaria, Müller's jurisdiction extended no further than the political offices which were established inside the gates of the concentration camps. His department judged who were the enemies of the state, committed them to *Schutzhaft* or ordered their release if it was deemed appropriate, but inside the camps the Kommandant had sole power. Later that summer Himmler completed the triangle by appointing Eicke Inspector of Concentration Camps with the task of bringing all camps in the Reich into line with the system in Dachau. By creating this triangle inside which the state could not penetrate, in which he alone had jurisdiction, Himmler threw down an open, contemptuous challenge to his erstwhile allies, Göring and Frick, and to the whole state bureaucracy. By then he was strong enough to do so.

It is an indication of Heydrich's practical sense of priorities that the enemies highest on Himmler's ideological list, the agents of the international conspiracy of Jews, Catholics and freemasons working behind the scenes to subvert and destroy Germany, were relegated to II 1B under Müller's colleague, Flesch, and the desk on Jews and freemasons was staffed by only three men. However, this was also a reflection of the immediately urgent matter which had enabled Himmler and Heydrich to ally with Göring in the first place and take over the Gestapa – officially as his subordinates. It was the completion of Hitler's *Machtergreifung* and, as with the earlier 'legal' stages of the process, it was accomplished by deception and disinformation prepared by Heydrich's SD, followed by sudden radical action, this time marked by blood. It became known as 'The Night of the Long Knives'.

On its most obvious level the affair concerned Röhm's ambition to take over the Defence Ministry and turn the Reichswehr into a revolutionary People's Army incorporating SA rank and file. Naturally the traditional Army leadership was concerned to prevent this. The other conservative landowning and heavy industrial groupings who had nursed Hitler to power were equally apprehensive of the SA, whose slogans were becoming scarcely distinguishable from those of the Marxist and leftist groups from which so many of the new Brownshirts had come. Hitler had been as good as his word in suppressing communists, socialists and trade unions, but the SA was filling the vacuum as an anti-capital, anti-landholding, anti-bourgeois, anti-tradition mass movement, and Hitler appeared unwilling or powerless to curb it. Goebbels at the Propaganda Ministry actively incited it. The excesses of SA street rowdies continued: no business manager could feel free from the threat of extortion; no ordinary citizen could pass by an SA collecting box without having to dip one hand in his pocket and raise the other in the Hitler salute; no social event was sacrosanct.

It is probable that Hitler had decided to act against Röhm some months before, as Diels was led to believe, and was simply using the SA threat as a lever to put pressure on the Army leadership. The old President von Hindenburg was failing fast and was not expected to outlive the summer. The conservative groupings hoped to restore the monarchy in his place as focus for the nation, Commander-in-Chief of the armed forces and counterbalance to the further spread of the Nazi revolution. Naturally Hitler had no intention of sharing power with a hereditary monarch or helping to support the 'reactionaries" pretensions to their old status. He intended to take over as head of state himself, and it is generally thought that by mid-April he had come to an agreement with the leadership of the armed services guaranteeing this. The outward and visible signs were the adoption that February of the swastika eagle as an element of the uniforms and ensigns of the armed forces, although it is said that the alliance was not finally sealed until 12 April aboard the *Deutschland*, when Hitler, the Minister of Defence, General von Blomberg – long an enthusiastic Nazi supporter – and the Commanders-in-Chief of Army and Navy, General von Fritsch and Admiral Raeder, went aboard the armoured cruiser to watch manoeuvres.

Göring had already approached von Fritsch in February to warn him of Röhm's ambitions and urge Army support for action against the SA. It is interesting that one of the arguments he used was that he was being forced to place a dismissed officer who hated the officer corps – Heydrich – at the head of the Gestapo. 'How is that possible?' von Fritsch had asked. 'The Führer has decided it,' the great man replied.[41] Behind the scenes Heydrich was using his SD network to alarm the Army and swing them to Hitler's support by fabricating and spreading rumours about a planned SA putsch. That he held a grudge against the officer class is suggested by a remark he is said to have made when outlining the scheme to his agents: 'High time we made the gentlemen with uniforms and monocles toe the line.'[42] When, a few days after the alleged pact aboard the cruiser *Deutschland*, Heydrich and Himmler officially took over the Gestapo, one of the first things he told his imported section chiefs was that the 'swine in the SA' were hatching a plot against the Führer, as a result of which it was necessary, for the time being, 'to dance with the generals'. Specifically he advised them of reports about an SA scheme to support the existing (monarchist) plans of the reactionaries by inspiring a foreign incident before the death of the President, and taking advantage of the resulting tensions.[43]

The desks Heydrich allotted Heinrich Müller may be seen in the light of these plots and counterplots: II 1C – reactionaries, opposition, Austrian affairs; II 1H – surveillance of the National Socialist Party and its organisations; II 1D – *Schutzhaft*; II 1A – communism, trade unions, subversion. Austrian affairs were included since, in conjunction with his plans for a radical solution to the internal strains in the Reich, Hitler planned an action by Austrian Nazis to demonstrate to their countryfolk that he was the leader for them too. To discover why trade unions were also included it is necessary to probe the industrial–financial backing for the SA. Here the waters are as muddied as elsewhere. Nevertheless the Marxist historian Gossweiler has produced a credible hypothesis. He suggests that the situation in the spring of 1934 was identical to that in January 1933 before Hitler became Chancellor: the same power groupings with the same opposing aims were locked in struggle inside the Party.

In this view Röhm was the representative of IG Farben and the dynamic section of modern industry, termed by Gossweiler the electro-chemical section. As noted, this was tied in with the Deutsche Bank, sought a closed European economic bloc and opposed the distortions in the economy caused by excessive state intervention for rearmament and protection of the Junker landowners. Gossweiler asserts that IG Farben supported Röhm and the SA directly and indirectly through key men in government who ensured massive state funding. These men were Dr Schmitt, to whom Hitler had given Hugenberg's Ministry of Economics, Darré, who had been given Hugenberg's Ministry of Agriculture, and two ministers without portfolio, Hess and lately Röhm himself. With such powerful advocacy, the SA received 3 million Marks monthly for salaries, uniforms and arms purchases, and with direct subventions from the electrochemical industry – and extortion – was enabled to grow at a prodigious rate through 1933. This alarmed the landowning and 'pan-German' heavy industrial supporters of the deposed Hugenberg – linked to the Deutsche Bank and seeking a closed European economic bloc – as well as the 'American' heavy industrial grouping represented by Thyssen and Schacht, whose links went through the Dresdner Bank to US capital. The armed-services leadership naturally supported this combined opposition to the IG Farben–SA axis, since they feared Röhm's ambitions and were tied by family to the Junkers and by rearmament to the heavy industrialists. Göring was chief representative of these conservative groupings inside the Party.

Von Schleicher and Strasser enter this picture as Röhm's allies, von Schleicher still seeking to unite the 'Strasser wing' of the Party with the moderate wing of the trade union movement at the expense of the traditional conservative elites. His plans, so far as they can be discerned through the fog of Heydrich's fabrications, included retaining Hitler as Chancellor – but as a figurehead only – taking von Papen's place as Vice-Chancellor himself, giving Gregor Strasser the Economics Ministry, Röhm the Defence Ministry, the former social democratic Chancellor, Brüning, the Foreign Ministry, and installing the exiled Kaiser's fourth son, Prince August Wilhelm, 'Auwi', who had been strutting in society in a brown SA uniform since before the *Machtergreifung* – as Regent. According to Gossweiler, Gregor Strasser was actively involved and was also in contact with his brother Otto, who was conducting a clandestine propaganda campaign against the Hitler regime from Vienna.

Gregor certainly seems to have made his bed with the capitalists against whom he had once railed so angrily. He was a director of a chemical–pharmaceutical subsidiary of IG Farben called Schering-Kahlbaum, and chairman of the prestigious German Pharmacology Industry Association. Nevertheless, his recent biographer, Peter Stachura, believes he was faithfully keeping a written promise to Hitler that he would renounce politics, shunning his former political associates and doing everything possible to deny Party rumours of his collusion with von Schleicher and Röhm.[44] Göring's biographer, Richard Overy, goes further and states that both Strasser and von Schleicher were politically inactive.[45] If this is the case the rumours were deliberate fabrications spread by Heydrich's SD agents in furtherance of the plot against Röhm. Wherever the truth lies, there is no doubt that the interests of light industry conflicted with those of the heavy industrial and conservative groupings, and both von Schleicher and Strasser, however active or inactive, were potential political allies of Röhm and the IG Farben–light industrial grouping. And even if Strasser were originally doing his best to keep away from politics, Hitler pulled him back in that spring.

In Gossweiler's analysis, Himmler was still IG Farben's second or 'compromise' choice to be called in once it became evident that the first-line assault group, Röhm–Schleicher–Strasser, could not prevail. In January 1933 Himmler and Keppler had appeared at the decisive meeting when the banker Kurt von Schröder mediated a middle way with Hitler and von Papen reflecting the interests of both IG Farben and the opposing capital and landed groups. Now again Himmler and Keppler – who had been appointed Hitler's official adviser on all economic questions – represented the IG Farben–electrochemical group's 'middle way' and the Deutsche Bank's safeguard against the Göring–Thyssen–Schacht – thus Dresdner Bank–US capital – axis gaining the upper hand. In this picture Himmler's alliance with Göring was a temporary compromise with the opposition, allowing more than a suspicion that he was prepared to move either way when the showdown came – against Röhm and the SA, or against Göring and the Reichswehr – as indeed Hitler might have done. Thus Himmler instructed Heydrich to gather a dossier of Gestapo excesses under Diels and Göring as well as a dossier on SA excesses under Röhm and the SA leaders.[46]

The suggestion that there were hidden wirepullers behind the 'long knives' of the SS is supported by Himmler's known contacts with industry. At the 1933 Party rally his adjutant Karl Wolff looked after Hitler's circle of friends, which was soon to become Der Freundeskreis des Reichsführer–SS and donate huge sums to the SS.[47] Keppler was perhaps the instigator of this group of businessmen and bankers, but von Schröder was its leading spirit; it was his Cologne Bank that held the Freundeskreis donations in a special account 'S'.[48] For the Party rally in the autumn of 1934 just after the bloody resolution of the crisis, the members of the Freundeskreis were invited to Nuremberg and put up at the Grand Hotel as 'guests of the Reichsführer-SS'. The charming Wolff played host again as he continued to do in succeeding years. Those present included Keppler and Fritz Kranefuss, another of Himmler's personal adjutants, who was soon to displace Keppler in the management of the Freundeskreis. Both great banking groups were represented – besides von Schröder there were von Halt of the Deutsche Bank, Meyer of the Dresdner Bank, Reinhardt of the Commerzbank and possibly Olscher of the Kreditbank. Heavy industry was represented by, among others, Steinbrinck of the Flick steel consortium, dynamic light industry by Bingel of the giant electrical combine, Siemens. Bütefisch of IG Farben and Walz of the chemical concern, Bosch, were probably there; there is no doubt about their attendance in later years.[49]

The circumstantial evidence for Himmler's role as a mediator between the financial–industrial groupings is strong but not conclusive. Undoubtedly Keppler and von Schröder and the great industrialists like Carl Siemens who are known to have donated hugely to SS funds as early as 1933[50] intended to influence him in their desired direction. There is equally no doubt that he was prepared to act against anyone or any group irrespective of patronage or ties of association. However, it is doubtful if he had much, if any, say in which group was to be struck down. That decision was surely made by Hitler.

Hitler is often represented as wavering between the SA and the Army. Finally, it is said, he was tricked into acting against Röhm by false evidence of an SA putsch concocted by Göring, Himmler and Heydrich. Certainly the evidence of an immediate putsch seems to have been fabricated, and it is probable that he did leave his options open for as long as he could. Yet it would have been out of character for Göring or Himmler to have taken it upon himself to deceive the Führer for his own ends; both were devoted disciples who owed their position to him. Himmler had created his elite troop as the 'guard of the nation' which, he had told his SS-Führers in June 1931, 'in times of crisis would be deployed as the last reserve of the Führer'.[51] On the other hand it would have been absolutely in character for Hitler to have inspired a campaign of deception which led his old comrade Röhm to believe that he would decide in his favour when the time was ripe – and how could Röhm have believed anything else after their long and close revolutionary association? By encouraging him and the condottieri around him to show their hand, so driving the Army and 'reactionaries' into his own camp, Hitler was able to disarm, literally, his erstwhile colleague, then when he least expected it, strike him down with the SS. These were the tactics he had employed against Stennes, when Himmler received the accolade, 'SS-Mann, Deine Ehre heisst Treue'. He was to employ a similarly brilliant deception before attacking Russia in 1941. All the signs point to him as the author of deception, Göring, Himmler and Heydrich as his chief executives.

The question of why he decided for the Army and the heavy industrialists and Junker landholders against the representatives of his own revolutionary army and the more dynamic younger industries and technologies who were equally prepared to support his drive to the east – on the face of it an eccentric decision – may have turned on the advice Keppler was giving him from the circle of friends, who in turn were linked to the world banking centres of New York, London and Paris. On the other hand it may have been a simple calculation of the strength of forces. It may have derived from both. What is not in doubt is his long-term objective. This was to drive back the boundaries of Bolshevism and create a single European economic bloc under German hegemony from the Atlantic to the Urals; that was the first stage. All the power groups were united with him on this goal. It may be that his precondition for the drive eastwards – a neutral England for a one-front war – decided the issue. Röhm and von Schleicher were advocates of military alliance with France, as indeed were IG Farben and much of the electrochemical grouping who favoured co-operation with French capital and industry to achieve their aims in the east.[52] But France was turning to closer collaboration with Russia, and Hitler and the leaders of the armed forces were preparing for war against a Franco-Russian coalition while bending all efforts to an alliance or at least an agreement on spheres of influence with England.

A British intelligence agent, Group Captain Winterbotham, has described an interview he had with Hitler that February. Hitler explained to him that there should be only three major powers in the world, the British empire, the Americas and the future German empire, which would include all Europe and the lands to the east. 'All we ask', he went on, 'is that Britain should be content to look after her empire and not interfere with Germany's plans of expansion.' He had then treated Winterbotham to an extraordinary tirade against communism.

> Colour suffused his face; the back of his neck, I could see, went red; his eyes started to bulge even further; he stood up and, as if he was an entirely different personality, he started to yell in a high-pitched staccato voice. . . . He ranted and raved against the Communists. . . .[53]

When at length he sat down again he smiled, giving Winterbotham the impression that 'somewhere carefully tucked away this little Austrian had got a sense of humour'. Accounts of his early days leave no doubt this was so.

Later that February Winterbotham was granted an even more extraordinary interview; it was with von Reichenau, the staff officer chiefly concerned with planning the drive against Russia. To Winterbotham's astonishment, von Reichenau began telling him in almost perfect English exactly how he planned to invade Russia with three tank spearheads advancing about 200 miles a day, beginning in spring after the melting of the snows and completed before winter froze the ground. Speed and surprise were to be the elements of victory. Air strike forces would prepare the way for the columns, and supplies would be brought up by air; special aerodrome units would follow the tanks, together with motorised infantry to mop up the enemy left cut off and disoriented on the flanks. It was the first time Winterbotham had heard the word *Blitzkrieg*. When the detailed and enthusiastic briefing was over, von Reichenau said he hoped it would convince the people in London of Nazi intentions.[54]

That April, about the time Himmler took over the Gestapo, the England expert, von Ribbentrop, was appointed special commissioner for disarmament with the brief of winning support in London for an increase of 300,000 men in the Reichswehr in return for a reduction in the paramilitary SA of 700,000–800,000 men. Meanwhile the naval staff under Raeder planned a construction programme to bring the service up to one-third of the Royal Navy's tonnage in the three larger classes of vessel. This was above the Versailles limitation, but the ratio was chosen carefully as one that would not alarm the British. Hitler planned to formalise it in a bilateral treaty, and such was the gullibility – not to use a stronger word – of the British naval staff and the Foreign Secretary, Sir John Simon, that he succeeded in the following year, 1935.[55] In fact there was much sympathy for Hitler's anti-communist stance in British governing circles, reflected in the Nazi sympathies of the editor of *The Times*, of the press lord, Rothermere, and of the Governor of the Bank of England, to name but a few.

It is clear that Hitler was following the programme laid out ten years before in *Mein Kampf* – aiming to avoid the Kaiser's mistaken naval policy which he believed had forced England into the hostile camp, instead offering her a free hand on the oceans if she would allow Germany a free hand in Europe. This implied German domination of France, and it may be that it was Röhm's flirtation with the French that doomed him. There was also the consideration of the massive rearmament programme Hitler was committed to in defiance of Versailles. This involved both the older heavy industries and the newer automobile, aircraft and oil industries and depended to a large extent on imported raw materials, hence foreign exchange. Here Thyssen, Schacht and other exponents of the world market and links to US and British capital evidently won the argument. Alternatively, as Gossweiler asserts, the Deutsche Bank was forced to capitulate to US capital since Germany was weak and isolated and a US financial blockade would have caused a crisis sufficient to bring down the regime.[56] In either case it seems Röhm was sacrificed to international capital, a suggestion which is supported by the

fact that in the wake of the action against him 'the American', Schacht, was
appointed Economics Minister in place of the representative of IG Farben
and the modern light industrial groupings, Dr Schmitt.

Such were the grand-strategical, political, economic and even tactical
considerations that shaped Hitler's final choice of allies. All had at their
core the ideological crusade against Bolshevism and the material drive for
Lebensraum in the east as the first stage of a German climb to world mastery.
Those hesitations and periods of sick anxiety which have been ascribed to
Hitler before the decision – which Göring and Himmler allegedly had to
overcome – were human doubts before the magnitude of the treachery
intended, and marks of his peculiarly hysterical nature.

The detailed preparations for the strike probably began in February;
that is when Himmler started negotiating with Göring for the Gestapo.
About this time or early March the SA leadership noticed a decided change
in the attitude of the SS leadership: an internal SA report of 22 March noted
relations with the 'entire SS leadership significantly improved'. It added that
complaints about SS arrogance were now limited to lower positions.[57] Röhm
was conferring normally with Hitler. On 6 March he reported to him on a
meeting with the French Ambassador, François-Poncet, and both he and
von Schleicher met François-Poncet quite openly at the Dahlem, Berlin,
home of the financier Regendanz later that month. In April Hitler opened
talks with Gregor Strasser, initially through Hess, about Strasser entering
the Cabinet.

Towards the end of April Himmler went to see Röhm at his headquarters, taking Wolff with him. According to Wolff he implored Röhm
to dissociate himself from his evil companions, whose prodigal life, alco-
holic excesses, vandalism and homosexual cliques were bringing the whole
movement into disrepute. 'Chief of Staff,' he said with moist eyes, 'do not
inflict me with the burden of having to get my people to act against you.'
As always with Röhm he used the familiar *Du*. Röhm, also with tears in
his eyes by the end of the interview, thanked his old comrade for speaking
out so openly.[58]

Wolff told this story word-perfectly at several interrogations after the
war. It is not necessary to disbelieve it all. Himmler's moral homilies were
notorious. It is highly improbable that he threatened his chief with direct
action though. If he warned him of what was being said of the depravities
of several of the highest SA officers it was doubtless to assure him of his
own personal loyalty 'as soldier and friend' – his words when conveying to
him birthday greetings from the SS only five months before: 'it was and is
our greatest pride, ever to belong to your loyalest following.'[59] No doubt
he used this occasion in April to lull Röhm into a feeling of security and
absolute confidence in the SS, leaving himself free to strike against him or –
should the plan be changed – against his enemy, Göring. Count Helldorff, a
Berlin SA leader who survived the purge, regarded Himmler as 'the greatest
actor of his time'.[60] Wolff was, with reason, among the greatest distorters of

truth after the war. What was actually discussed at the April meeting will never be known. All that can be said, perhaps, is that little over a month later Röhm invited a number of higher SS officers to a northern cruise to begin in August.[61]

By May Himmler and Heydrich were working on a detailed list of people to be eliminated in the action. It was known with usual sententiousness as the 'Reich List of Unwanted Persons', and it came to include many more non-SA than SA. Göring and another who had joined the cabal, the Propaganda Minister Josef Goebbels, contributed names, and there is no doubt Himmler added people whom Hitler wished to have disappear or whose survival thus far caused the Führer astonishment. Several were to be silenced for their knowledge of embarrassing secrets – among them the Reichstag arsonists – several for their political, religious or ideological opposition, some for personal reasons. Diels alleged that his name was on the list – until Göring struck it off at the last moment – because of Heydrich's malevolence. It might as easily have been Himmler's malevolence. During that same month, May, Schacht had a private meeting with the Governor of the Bank of England, his personal friend and business associate Montagu Norman. Among Norman's 'fundamental dislikes', his biographer has recorded, were 'the French, Roman Catholics, Jews'.[62]

On 4 June Röhm had a discussion with Hitler lasting five hours, and there is no doubt from the course of subsequent events that he left convinced he could rely on his Führer, and that affairs would be settled in his favour against 'the gentlemen with uniforms and monocles' when Hitler had stabilised the foreign political situation – he was probably told this would be in September. Three days later Röhm published the fact that he was going on sick leave together with a recommendation to SA leaders to begin organising their own leave. A limited number of officers and men should take it in June, 'for the majority July will be a period of complete relaxation in which they can recover their strength.'[63] Summer leave was normal for the SA; the only unusual things about this announcement were that it was made public, and that it carried a sting indicative of the extent of the crisis:

> If the enemies of the SA delude themselves with the hope that the SA will not report back for duty after their leave, or only report back in part, we should leave them in their hopeful expectations. They will receive a fitting answer at the time and in the form which appears necessary. The SA is and will remain Germany's destiny.[64]

On 11 June Schacht and Montagu Norman had another 'secret conclave' at Badenweiler in the Black Forest. According to the German opposition in exile Schacht assured his friend that there would be no 'second revolution' in Germany; on the contrary the SA would be reduced.[65] On 17 June von Papen, still clinging to the form if not the substance of power as Vice-Chancellor, made a speech before von Hindenburg, generals and students at the University of Marburg which thoroughly expressed conservative and Roman Catholic revulsion against the SA. No nation could afford a permanent revolution from below. Those who toyed with such ideas should not deceive themselves about how easily a second wave could be followed by a third; 'he who threatens the guillotine is the first to come under the knife.' The speech was aimed not only at Röhm, but at the social and nationalisation programme of the SA's political and economic backers: 'Have we experienced an anti-Marxist revolution in order to put through a Marxist programme?'[66] It was also directed against the Nazi Party's progress towards a monopoly of power, and called in veiled terms for a restoration of the monarchy. The extent of von Papen's own power was made plain by Goebbels, who banned reporting of the speech.

Goebbels' action was at least in part caused by the need to convince Röhm and his backers that they had Hitler's support against 'the *Reaktion*'. Hitler's negotiations with Gregor Strasser had the same purpose and were concluded about this time. On 20 June Otto Strasser heard from his brother that he had reached provisional agreement with Hitler that he (Gregor) would enter the Cabinet in September; Göring would be removed. Three days later Gregor's Golden Party badge was returned to him. Meanwhile on 19 June Himmler had told those SS officers who had received Röhm's invitation to a northern cruise more than two weeks before that they were not to accept. Two days later, on 21 June, Hitler visited von Hindenburg – who had retired, sick, to his country estate – to assure him that the agreement he had made with von Blomberg to act against the SA would be fulfilled within the next days. Exactly what was said will never be known.

By this time Himmler was in personal contact with Colonel von Reichenau about details of SS–Reichswehr co-operation in the coming action. It had been agreed that the SS would carry out the strike, the Army generally remaining in the background, but providing the necessary arms, transport, barrack accommodation, and support in emergency. In order to keep the preparations and the Army state of alert hidden from the SA, the area commanders of the Reichswehr were to be told of the possibility of an SA putsch either imminent or in the autumn. The general staff officer Major Heinrici noted the briefing instructions:

> Commanders to be instructed, however, only to say that there are rumours the SA or the communists could attack. . . . Check guard on barracks, ammunition, weapons. Where guard insufficient, in case of necessity call in SS. These are on our side. (Troops as such should be held in action-readiness and not divided into guard duties.) Prussian police in state of alert. SS and police will turn to us (if they cannot master the situation themselves). Weapons to be given to the SS if they require them. Later they must be returned. . . . SA to be disarmed. . . . all these things should be concealed as much as possible from the outside. There are only individual *desperados*, not the majority of the SA. Basically avoid annoying the SA. . . .[67]

On 25 June, as the Army was placed on a state of alert, all leave cancelled and the troops confined to barracks, Himmler summoned his SS and SD area (*Abschnitte*) commanders to a conference in Berlin. He briefed them on the expected SA putsch, convincing them of its reality, and outlined plans for co-operation with the Reichswehr and the regional political and uniformed police in a pre-emptive strike to seize Röhm, key SA leaders and other enemies of the state involved with them. No doubt he also gave them a homily on the need for hardness in carrying out their duty for the Führer – for they would be striking against colleagues and even friends – and reminded them of their status as the 'guard of the nation'. Each was handed sealed orders to be opened only on receipt of a code word. Until then absolute secrecy was to be maintained. No one was to be informed beforehand except for *Standarte* (regimental) commanders in Silesia, the centre of the revolt.[68]

There seems little doubt that the SA in Silesia, far from planning revolt, was the first to react to the Army alert. Long before Himmler's SS leaders left Berlin on the 27th, the Army commander in Silesia, von Kleist, was receiving 'a flood of reports and information which gave a picture of feverish preparations on the part of the SA'. The information came from the troops themselves, members of the SA, former *Stahlhelm* men, and local SS and government authorities. Tension built up to such an extent that on the 28th von Kleist called SA-Obergruppenführer Heines in to warn him that he knew of his preparations. Heines replied that he knew all about Reichswehr preparations and had put his own men on the alert because he thought they were directed against him. He gave von Kleist his 'word as an officer and as an SA leader that he had not planned or prepared any surprise attack on the Army'.[69] Later that evening he rang von Kleist to tell him he had learned that the Army throughout the Reich was on the alert against an SA putsch. Von Kleist immediately flew to Berlin to tell the Commander-in-Chief, von Fritsch, of his opinion that the Army and the SA were being incited against each other by Himmler. Von Fritsch called in von Reichenau, who replied laconically, 'That may be true, but it's too late now.'[70]

This suggests that von Reichenau, von Blomberg's former Chief of Staff and like him a convinced supporter of Hitler, and on *Du* terms with Himmler, had been the driving force behind the Army High Command's support for the action, using Heydrich's falsified evidence to convince von Fritsch of the reality of the threat. It may be significant that von Reichenau had married into the Silesian nobility and counted among his close circle Himmler's commander in Silesia, Udo von Woyrsch. Von Woyrsch had been involved in the successful plot to infiltrate Dr Patchowsky into Diels' counter-espionage division as an SD informer. That the SA in Silesia were on the alert so early suggests deliberate incitement in order to provide substance for the allegations of a planned putsch.

However that may be, by the night of the 28th/29th it was, as von

Reichenau said, 'too late'. The plan was in motion. Hitler and Göring had been in Essen that day, heartland of heavy industry, as witnesses at the wedding of Gauleiter Josef Terboven – the former unemployed bank clerk whom Emil Kirdorf had inserted into the Party. The previous day Göring had installed Diels as President of the regional government in Cologne and before leaving he had warned Diels, 'Look out for yourself in the next few days.'[71] While in Essen, Hitler and Göring visited the Krupp works, where they had a meeting with the head of the concern, Gustav Krupp von Bohlen und Halbach.

That evening Hitler phoned Röhm, who was resting at the Hotel Hanselbauer in the Tegernsee resort of Bad Wiesee, and directed him to convene a conference of the SA leadership at Wiesee on the 30th at midday; he himself would attend. No doubt he had arranged something of the sort with Röhm at their last long meeting. The call served the double purpose of gathering the SA chiefs in one out-of-the-way spot, and reassuring Röhm that, despite the rumours flying about, their mutual compact was safe. No doubt Röhm expected the discussion to centre on the radical change of government in his favour promised for the autumn. That this was the general expectation in SA circles is suggested by a statement made after the purge by an SA staff officer, Dr Kloeppel.

> If, as we believed, the Führer, directly he had achieved the stabilisation of the foreign political position he was striving for, gave the order for the SA to advance and simultaneously for SA leaders to occupy the leading positions in the Reichswehr, *Länder* police and administration (the so-called 'second revolution') then with one blow all was lost for the *Reaktion*; all was lost especially for heavy industry and the large landowners, who indeed we fancied were in league with Minister-President Göring and the Reichswehr; these circles then had to reckon with the socialistic tendencies of National Socialism coming to realisation since the formerly constricting foreign political considerations had been removed. . . .[72]

On 29 June, Friday, Hitler made a scheduled inspection of the labour service camp at Lünen, thence to his favourite Hotel Dreesen in the Rhine resort of Bad Godesberg near Bonn. Tense and withdrawn, he waited for the telephone call that would signal the next move. Göring had returned to Berlin. The police and the SS had been placed on a state of alert, and that afternoon, the 29th, Göring summoned police and Interior Ministry officials who were to form his headquarters staff for the action to take up temporary residence in his palace on the Leipzigerstrasse. Himmler ordered Karl Wolff there that evening with toothbrush, shaving gear and a change of shirt for a stay of a couple of days. Meanwhile Sepp Dietrich, commander of the Bavarian elite SS troop, the Leibstandarte Adolf Hitler, which had been transferred to Berlin in February, sent eighteen of his crack shots to Gestapo headquarters, Prinz Albrecht Strasse. Heydrich briefed them on the imminent SA putsch, then instructed them individually who their targets were to be.

The code words went out that evening. The police threw a cordon around the Leipzigerstrasse Palace, deploying Reichswehr machine guns from the roofs, allegedly because of a threat to Göring's life. Two companies of the Leibstandarte entrained for the little station of Kaufering, near Landsberg in south Bavaria, there to join units of Eicke's Dachau guards and drive out to Bad Wiesee in personnel carriers provided by the Army. Meanwhile the Silesian SA commander, Heines, had flown in to Munich and alerted his Bavarian colleagues to the imminence of an SS–Reichswehr putsch against them. The Munich SA was called out and staged noisy rallies on the Oberwiesenfeld while the Police President and chief of Munich and Upper Bavarian SA, August Schneidhuber, went to see the Gauleiter, Adolf Wagner. Wagner was an ally of Himmler as he had been earlier; at any rate he attempted to reassure Schneidhuber. The SA demonstrations were called off and the men dispersed, although Schneidhuber remained at his post at the Ministry of the Interior. Heines, meanwhile, had driven out to Bad Wiesee to rouse Röhm to the threat hanging over them. That he failed completely is a measure of Röhm's trust in Hitler, and Heydrich's success in misleading SA intelligence and causing divisions in their ranks. This was probably facilitated by the homosexual cliques into which the SA leadership was divided. Röhm retired to bed apparently oblivious of his fate. Heines took a fair-haired SA youth up to his bedroom.

At the Hotel Dreesen, Hitler had received a telephone call apparently about the SA disturbances in Munich. With his SS escort and entourage including Goebbels and SA-Obergruppenführer Viktor Lutze – who had been drawn into the plot by the prospect of taking over Röhm's position – not that Lutze admitted that even to himself – he was driven to Bonn and across the Rhine to the airport where two Junkers Ju-52 stood ready. By then it was Saturday morning, 30 June. He took off at 2.00 a.m., landing at Munich in the dawn light. The story has been told often of how he drove from the airfield into Munich to have Schneidhuber arrested and collect a squad of detectives, thence out along the early-morning roads stirring with farm carts and labourers going to work, to surprise Röhm and Heines and the other SA leaders in their beds at the Hanselbauer, and how Röhm exclaimed sleepily 'Heil, mein Führer!' as Hitler strode in, pistol in hand to tell him he was under arrest.

The scene in Berlin where Göring and Himmler directed operations from Göring's study has not received so much attention. Wolff, who was there for three days, by his own account on the telephone the whole time, remembered almost nothing. Much of his phoning was to Gestapo headquarters where Heydrich directed SS action-groups in the arrest and murder of SA leaders and the other state enemies named on the *Reichsliste* of unwanted persons. Otherwise Wolff was relaying questions about listed individuals for decision to his chief or Göring: 'with almost every name . . . it was a question of life and death.' However, 'with over 7000 telephone conversations in seventy-two hours one is so busy one cannot exactly recall any more.'[73]

An official of the Prussian Interior Ministry, Hans-Bernd Gisevius, who accompanied Daluege to the Leipzigerstrasse Palace that morning, has left vivid descriptions of the scene, and the 'evil atmosphere of hate, nervousness, tension, above all of blood and more blood'[74] which met him there. Adjutants and police officers and officials stood in groups in the great hall, their faces and their hushed, earnest words imprinted with knowledge of chilling events. Messengers ran through carrying self-important envelopes to the 'execution committee' in Göring's study. Liveried servants moved among the groups with plates of sandwiches.

Through the half-open door into the study Gisevius could see Göring, his under-secretary Koerner, Himmler and Heydrich, who had evidently emerged from his post at Prinz Albrecht Strasse. He could not hear what was being said, only occasional exclamations, raucous laughter and shouts.

> They do not appear to be in bad spirits. Göring exudes an air of cheerful complacency. He struts to and fro, an unforgettable picture: with his flowing head of hair, his white tunic, his grey–blue military trousers, his white boots with their tops reaching over his fat knees. . . .
>
> Things suddenly begin to get very noisy in there. Police Major Jakobi rushes out of the room in great haste with his helmet on and the chinstrap under his red face. Göring's hoarse voice booms out after him, 'Shoot them down. Take a whole company . . . shoot them down . . . shoot . . . just shoot them down . . . shoot!'[75]

Outside the heavily protected building, as in Munich and Breslau in Silesia, police cars and SS squads in lorries careered through the streets to seize listed persons or in a few important cases kill them. General von Schleicher was shot in his study, and his wife, who came running in, was murdered with him. Von Reichenau's predecessor at the Ministry of Defence, General von Bredow, who was suspected of having written an account of the machinations leading to Hitler's appointment as Chancellor, published by the opposition in exile, was also shot. Erich Klausener, former head of the police department in the Prussian Ministry of the Interior, and the President of the politico-religious pressure group Catholic Action, was murdered in his office; a transparent attempt was made to fake suicide. Two of von Papen's principal aides, one his press officer and principal author of the Marburg speech, were shot at work.

Gregor Strasser was at lunch at home when five Gestapo officials called and insisted he accompany them to his office, which they needed to search. Instead he found an SS detachment waiting there. He was taken to Gestapo headquarters and locked in a cell to await 'interrogation'. According to an account given to his brother Otto later, Gregor was quite calm but resigned to his fate when he was taken down to cell number 16. About 4.30 that afternoon, he was lying on the cot when two senior SS officers, one of them believed to be Heydrich himself, and two corporals approached the cell. One of them shot at him through the sliding window. Wounded, he attempted to remove himself from the line of fire, whereupon they entered and gave him the *coup de grâce*. Gisevius gives a crueller description of Heydrich allowing him to bleed to death in the cell.

The top SA leaders rounded up in Munich and Wiesee were taken to Stadelheim prison and executed by SS firing squads, except for Röhm. Apparently Hitler could not bring himself to have his old comrade shot. Those arrested later in Berlin were taken to Gestapo headquarters or direct to the Lichterfelde barracks of the Leibstandarte for execution by firing squad. In Breslau, where von Woyrsch supervised the action, several SS officers got out of hand and settled personal grudges or went on the rampage against Jews.[76] Elsewhere it seems local SS commanders confined themselves to routine arrests of SA leaders, and in several cases kept them rather than sending them to an uncertain fate in Berlin. Only in Silesia was there any organised resistance, and that was brief.

Somehow, despite the considerable SS–Army–police preparations, the obviously tense situation and all the rumours and alarms, the SA leadership had been caught literally asleep. It was a masterpiece of deception by Hitler and Himmler. Equally Heydrich must have played a key role with the SD, for not only Röhm but the SA staff as a whole must have been led to believe that SS–Army negotiations were a ruse, and when the moment came the SS would be found side by side with their old comrades.

Hitler arrived back at Tempelhof aerodrome, Berlin, against a blood-red sunset late that evening. Göring, Himmler, Frick, Daluege and a posse of police officials were waiting to greet him. Gisevius described the scene as Hitler emerged from the plane and shook hands with each in turn, the monotonous click of the heels of leather boots the only sound in the silence. The Führer wore a brown leather jacket over his brown shirt and black tie, brown breeches and high black leather boots – 'all dark tones in the darkness'. His white, unshaven face appeared 'gaunt and puffed out at the same time',[77] and his eyes stared out without expression from under the locks of hair pasted down over his forehead.

How many people were liquidated between 30 June and 4.00 a.m. on 2 July, when Hitler called off the killings, can never be precisely established. Hitler admitted to 76; the real number is probably nearer 200 or 250.[78] Bodies were found in fields and woods for weeks afterwards and files of petitions from relatives of the missing remained active for months. What seems certain is that less than half were SA officers.

Röhm did not escape. It is said that Göring and Himmler convinced Hitler that the purge would be senseless without the head of the leader of the revolt, but this must have been clear to Hitler himself on calm reflection. Next day, Sunday, 1 July, Eicke was instructed to offer the SA Chief of Staff the honourable option of taking his own life. Accompanied by two aides Eicke entered the cell where Röhm was held and gave him a Browning loaded with one bullet. Röhm asked to speak to Hitler. Eicke replied that he had ten minutes in which to shoot himself, then he and his escort retired. They waited; hearing no report they returned in the stipulated time. Röhm faced them with bared chest. One of the aides shot him in the throat; he was given the *coup de grâce* on the floor after he collapsed with 'Mein Führer!' on his lips.

So the hereditary nobility preserved its status and its landed estates and offices, striking down the revolution without openly bloodying its hands – unless those many of its representatives in the SS like Obergruppenführer von Woyrsch and Gruppenführer Prinz zu Waldeck und Pyrmont, Himmler's former adjutant, who was active in the Stadelheim executions, were noticed. The action was ascribed to a dispute within the Nazi Party; the executions and murders had been carried out by the SS.

Von Reichenau was jubilant at the success of the plot: he wired in less than perfect English to the head of armed services counter-intelligence – Abwehr – a naval captain Patzig who had undoubtedly liaised with Heydrich, 'All catched!' Von Hindenburg was delighted and sent Hitler a telegram congratulating him on his 'decided action' and 'courageous personal performance' in 'nipping all high treasonable intrigues in the bud'. He had 'saved the German people from a grave danger'.[79] Von Blomberg was pleased to explain to the officer corps the extent of the intrigue which had linked von Schleicher, Strasser, Röhm and von Bredow with French money and French hopes for a civil war in Germany. Hitler had acted for the people against these perverse, anti-social forces. Von Blomberg demanded that the Wehrmacht (armed forces) for its part show Hitler its loyalty. When von Hindenburg died on 2 August it did so by supporting Hitler's claim to succeed as Reichspresident. The same day the officers took their loyal oath to him as Führer of the German Reich and people, and Commander-in-Chief of the armed forces.

The more discerning among the generals like von Fritsch and Beck perhaps saw the quagmire into which they had been drawn. In moral terms, they had compromised their most sacred honour by acting as accessories to murder – including the murder of three of their own, General and Frau von Schleicher and General von Bredow. In practical terms they had surrendered the high ground 'above politics' – although they had never truly held it. In the process they had simply exchanged the immediate threat from the SA for the threat from Himmler's more disciplined and goal-oriented black guard. That von Fritsch recognised this is suggested by Wolff's description of him at the champagne (*Sekt*) celebration to which Göring invited those who had taken part in the action shortly after it ended. For all his social adroitness, Wolff found the General unapproachable. The sight of all the black uniforms at the reception evidently affected his nerves; 'his face twitched nervously, the *Sekt* glass shook in his hand with the first drink.'[80]

Wolff was promoted from Standartenführer to Oberführer by Hitler decree on 4 July. Heydrich was two ranks above him, having been stepped up to Gruppenführer on the day of the action itself, a dizzy climb by both these young men. The leader of the murder commando that had disposed of Klausener, then seized the Berlin SA leader Ernst and conveyed him to his rendezvous with a firing squad at Lichterfelde barracks, received promotion on 3 July. In all, between 1 and 6 July, 142 SS officers received a step up the promotion ladder.[81]

Himmler received the first part of his reward on 20 July when Hitler raised the SS to an independent arm of the Party, no longer subordinate to the SA Chief of Staff – now Viktor Lutze. The second part was formalised in a top-secret memorandum signed by the Minister of Defence, General von Blomberg, and sent to the service chiefs, the Reichsminister of the Interior and the Reichsführer-SS on 24 September that year – about the time Röhm had been led to expect his own assumption of von Blomberg's office: it established the formation of a so-called Verfügungstruppe to be trained on military lines.

For *special inner-political tasks*, which can be assigned to the SS by the Führer . . . a) The SS will form an armed standing Verfügungstruppe of the strength of *3 SS regiments and one intelligence department*. . . . The SS-Verfügungstruppe will be subordinated to the Reichsführer of the SS. *There will be no organisational connection with the armed forces in peacetime*. . . . b) In cases of necessity up to 25,000 men of the SS can be mobilised for the use of the Political Police. Their arming will follow mobilisation for police service and be for the duration only. . . .

4) *In case of war* it is agreed: a) Members of the SS will be placed at the disposal of the armed forces in conformity with the call-up law [*Wehrgesetz*]. Up to 25,000 men can be held back for the strengthening of the Political Police. b) The SS-Verfügungstruppe (No. 3a) will be placed at the disposal of the armed forces . . . [and] *will in peace be prepared for its war tasks to the instructions of the Reich Defence Minister*. . . .

11) For the preparation of their military employment in case of war (No. 4) the SS-Verfügungstruppe will be subordinate to the Reich Defence Minister. . . .[82]

The document illustrates Himmler's negotiating technique. He has his foot in the door of an armed SS formation trained as a military unit. This is sufficient; the future will bring opportunities to force the door wider. For the moment he is prepared to concede the carefully phrased limitations on numbers and independence by which von Blomberg seeks to preserve the Army's status as sole arms-bearer of the nation. The armed SS troop is envisaged as taking over the Army's responsibility for internal order, leaving the Wehrmacht free to engage external enemies. And it is interesting to see that the idea of augmenting the Political Police with SS men to keep order behind the lines in occupied territory in war – the drive eastwards which von Reichenau had outlined to Group Captain Winterbotham that February – was already established: '4) *In case of war* . . . Up to 25,000 men can be held back for the strengthening of the Political Police. . . .'

Von Blomberg had tried to limit Röhm's ambitions with the same kind of signed agreement. Perhaps he deluded himself that Himmler really was the reasonable, if somewhat besotted, unambitious official devoted only to Führer and Fatherland that he seemed. Probably he believed he could rely on Hitler's word. Certainly he believed in rearmament, smashing the Versailles Treaty and the coming war of expansion in the east. Perhaps these things, which Hitler promised, enabled him to blank out any qualms he might have felt about first calling in SS assassins to do the Army's work, then institutionalising a standing body of armed SS. Or perhaps by setting limits to this body he sought to damp down the alarm the Army leadership began to feel about SS power and ambition in the wake of the Röhm purge. Perhaps there was a deeper psychological reason for his blindness. Gisevius' colleague, Arthur Nebe, expressed it after watching Hitler return from Munich in the evening of 30 June: 'Depend on it, it is precisely this Hitler going on his way over heaps of bodies, whom they [the generals] have yearned for in their deepest heart of hearts.'[83]

Whether von Blomberg felt himself forced into the alliance with Himmler, or whether his belief in Hitler committed him, it cannot be doubted that with each compromise to the black guard he not only increased Himmler's standing but further undermined the moral standing of the officer caste in whose interests he believed he was acting. Finally it was the moral confusion and collapse which were to prove fatal.

As for Himmler, he had proved loyal to his Führer once again. In doing so he not only acted against his first chief, Gregor Strasser, and his early friend and mentor, 'the good captain Röhm', but had woven an intricate plot of deception around them first. The man who had superseded him as Police President of Munich, August Schneidhuber, was also liquidated, and Diels would have been had Göring not intervened and warned him; he had taken to the mountains until the hunt was called off. Himmler spoke to his Gestapo officials in October:

> For us as Secret State Police and as members of the SS, 30 June was not – as several believe – a day of victory or a day of triumph, but it was the hardest day that can be visited on a soldier in his lifetime. To have to shoot one's own comrades, with whom one has stood side by side for eight or ten years in the struggle for an ideal, and who had then failed, is the bitterest thing which can happen to a man.[84]

The great significance of 30 June, he went on, was to prove internally and externally that Hitler's state would not be overcome. It was proof that the Führer could lay the heads of all who were disloyal or not decent at their feet. It was further proof of the absolute reliability, loyalty and sense of duty 'in the truest sense' of the Secret State Police.

> For everyone who knows the Jews, freemasons and Catholics, it was obvious that these forces – who in the final analysis caused even 30 June in so much as they sent numerous individuals into the SA and the entourage of the former

Chief of Staff and drove him to catastrophe – these forces were very much annoyed at the rout on 30 June. Because 30 June signified no more and no less than the detonation of the National Socialist state from within, blowing it up with its own people. There would have been chaos, and it would have given a foreign enemy the possibility of marching into Germany with the excuse that order had to be created in Germany.

It had been clear to him, he told them, that as a result of 30 June they would be beset for months by the sharpest hostility of all enemies of the state, obviously including the opposition in exile and the whole foreign press. There had been countless articles all tending in the same direction 'representing us, the Secret State Police, as an unscrupulous, cold and insensitive Cheka, for whom nothing remains concealed' – an unfeeling instrument without heart or character. 'That the Jews and our other enemies would not proceed against us with direct attacks must have been clear to each of you – even those who have no knowledge of them. The attack of the Jews and all secret enemies occurs, as it has for centuries, via seeds of discord, via lies, calumny, via shameless intrigue.'

This was the way in which he rationalised the deceits he had played on his old comrades. Or perhaps the crisis drove him even deeper into the ideological fantasy he inhabited, which distinguished him from the more obviously ruthless, practical and ambitious men surrounding him. Whatever the hidden springs of his personality or his rationalisations, his real nature was surely expressed in his acts. On 7 July, Gregor Strasser's widow Else received an urn containing ashes and inscribed: 'Gregor Strasser, born 30.5.92 in Geisenfeld, died 30.6.34 Gestapo, Berlin'. She was warned to make no public show or acknowledgement of her husband's death; officially he had committed suicide.[85] The ashes of other Party comrades were returned to their families in pasteboard cartons.[86]

6

Chief of the German Police

The murders of 30 June 1934 marked the emergence of Himmler as power broker of the Third Reich. The factors behind Hitler's choice of Himmler over Röhm seem clear, but underlying these reasons of state and underlying the position Himmler had achieved before 30 June, which allowed him to take action against his nominal chief, was the personal factor. Hitler knew Himmler was devoted to him. Röhm was too, but in an independent, frequently critical way. With his sure nose for men who would submerge personal judgement and serve as pure extensions of his own will, Hitler had chosen Himmler, 'der treue Heinrich', as the guardian of his Reich. In this sense the Night of the Long Knives, the 'German St Bartholomew's night', was prepared long before during the time Himmler worked at Party headquarters in Munich. When on 30 June Hitler turned him loose, he knew he could do so in perfect confidence.

'Now, after 2000 years, fate has given us once again a chance, once again a possibility, and sent us this leader, Adolf Hitler,' Himmler told a convention of SS-Führers gathered in Breslau in January 1935,

who has raised this Germany once again, and in these his years, this his era is attempting – not to conjure up a last bloom from the age of the Caesars, a last imperial epoch, which would allow Germany in the course of a few centuries of dictatorship and world mastery to expire completely – but he has allotted himself another task. He has set us the goal for our generation to be a new beginning – he wants to return us to the source of the blood, to root us again in the soil – he seeks again for strength from sources which have been buried for 2000 years. And already he has in fact established the beginning of a new thousands of years of German future and German history.[1]

Copying his idol, Himmler travelled the new Reich in an open, heavily armoured Maybach tourer, spreading the message to his district commands. The faithful Wolff, who accompanied him, had to listen to endless variations on his standard themes: the German race as the elite of mankind, the SS as the elite of the German race, carriers of the pure blood, guardians of the ideals of National Socialism – a sworn Order, fighting the good fight against freemasonry, the Church, world Jewry, Marxism and democracy in defence of the old Germanic virtues of loyalty, honour, integrity, frugality.[2]

And I know as well as each one of you know, as hundreds of thousands of well-meaning people in Germany know, that 1935 must be the year of the purification of the movement and the state. In particular there is a whole mass of people, and they still exist today, who from 1933 onwards – from the moment of the intoxication of power and the intoxication of swelling to prominence – on the one hand forgot where they had risen from, what sacrifices it had all cost, and on the other hand believed that by external brilliance, by disorderly and undisciplined behaviour they could make up for that which they lacked in inner value and innate ability for the creative tasks of the times.[3]

Often on these tours Himmler and Wolff were accompanied by their wives. They were an oddly assorted group, in the front the dark-browed blue-chinned Himmler with his wide, blonde Marga, in the back Wolff, paragon of Nordic manhood, with Frieda Wolff, an attractive brunette. There are photographs of them having sandwiches and coffee by the open car at the roadside – like photographs of Hitler and entourage. What strains are concealed behind these glimpses? The most frequent descriptions of Himmler by those closest to him are of the archetypal German pedagogue: 'He was like a schoolmaster who graded the lessons of his pupils with a finnicky exactitude, and for each answer would have liked to enter a mark in the class-book.'[4] Marga remained the archetypal matron, a managing woman who appeared to Heydrich's wife Lina able to twist Himmler round her little finger. After the war Lina Heydrich characterised her as narrow-minded and humourless, and, since her husband's sudden elevation, endlessly concerned about protocol. 'Size 50 knickers, that's all there was to her,'[5] she concluded scornfully. Frieda Wolff, by contrast, was lively and attractive, and both she and Wolff had a worldly poise and sophistication utterly lacking in their superiors in the front seats. Yet Wolff was ruled by his prospects as right-hand man of his chief and had to mould himself to him. Already he was living way beyond his SS salary with a large villa he rented in the exclusive Berlin suburb of Dahlem, and he had his sights on a plot of land on the shores of the Tegernsee to build a country home – an ambition he realised over the next few years solely on the strength of his position, and of Himmler's support, for he could not begin to pay for the splendid villa with foreshore and the boat houses he erected. In the same way Frieda needed to get along with Marga.

And what repressed sexual tensions were concealed from the lens? Was Frieda aware that her husband had taken a mistress, the young Gräfin (Countess) von Bernstorff? She had an entry in the Gotha handbook – through her husband, an old man – and moved in Berlin society. Moreover, and perhaps more to the point, she possessed the external characteristics of Nordic blood which Frieda herself, with her brown hair and eyes, conspicuously lacked. Probably Marga did not suspect her own 'Lieber Guter' of infidelity – although she was to have cause to before long – but it may be that a taste for whipped cream and an increasing amplitude marked by observers were signs of dissatisfaction with her marriage. No one will ever know. Only the pictures of this mixed group of 'the blood' journeying to inspire the faithful remain to tantalise.

Himmler himself was living out his youthful fantasy during these middle years of the thirties of the century and his own age by extending the SS into all his areas of enthusiasm. In December 1935 he founded Lebensborn e.V. – literally the Fount of Life Society – to care particularly for unmarried mothers of good blood made pregnant by SS or police officers and men, and to allow them to have their children in private. These were then placed with SS families who wanted to adopt a child, or efforts were made to induce the father to shoulder his responsibilities and marry the girl. It was an attempt to prevent recourse to abortion, then frequent, and the consequent loss to the nation of 'valuable' racial stock. Stories spread later that Lebensborn maternity homes were little more than stud farms, where SS officers could meet suitable pure-blooded girls to propagate for the Reich or, as the word went, to 'present the Führer with a child'.

After the war Jürgen Stroop spoke to Moczarski of his Lebensborn liaisons outside marriage. They had the thrill of a hotel adventure or a secret affair with a secretary.

'Did your wife know you were in Lebensborn?'

'She never learned.'[6]

Others to take advantage of the confidential facilities of the maternity homes were ladies of the upper classes wishing to avoid abortions. Himmler was not averse to either of these usages: he was greedy for 'valuable' blood wherever it came from but to judge by files of letters addressed to him by grateful Lebensborn mothers, the homes served their original intended purpose quite as much.[7] The care provided was good and they were also used by SS wives to have 'legitimate' offspring.

Lebensborn was placed under the SS Race and Settlement Main Office – RuSHA – administered by its Families (or Clans) Department – Sippenamt – which was responsible for the genealogical side of SS entry and marriage investigations. It was thus well placed to conduct similar investigations into the mothers-to-be who applied to Lebensborn. Both they and the fathers-to-be, if not already SS men, were investigated. Only if they measured up to the racial standards demanded in the SS were the girls admitted. The first home was opened at Steinhöring, not far from Munich, in 1936. At the same time the Sippenamt began setting up family welfare offices at *Standarte*, or regimental, level, primarily to care for SS widows and orphans, but they also acted as liaison offices between Lebensborn and the fathers or prospective adopters of the children.

Himmler was chairman of the board of Lebensborn and took personal, detailed interest in every aspect of its affairs down to diet and confinement periods, the decoration of the wards or runic logos for the letterheading. Early in 1938 he had the society removed from the control of the Sippenamt and placed under his own personal office run by Wolff. And undoubtedly he was behind the method of financing whereby contributions were deducted from the salaries of SS officers and men according to rank and the number of children they had. The deduction tables were compiled in the light of his premises that an SS man should not be encouraged to marry too young – below the age of twenty-six – and that every SS family should have at least four children. Thus men under twenty-six and men with four children in general contributed nothing; in the higher ranks and over the age of forty-one – why this age should have been chosen is not clear – men with four children did have a small amount deducted. As examples of the contributions, a bachelor of captain's rank (Hauptsturmführer) aged twenty-seven had 1 per cent of his total salary deducted; this rose to 4 per cent by age thirty-four. By this age a Brigadeführer had 5.75 per cent, and an Obergruppenführer (full general) 6.75 per cent, of his salary deducted for Lebensborn. The deduction for a thirty-four-year-old married captain with no children was 3 per cent, with one child 2 per cent, two children 1.25 per cent and three children 0.4 per cent. However, a thirty-four-year-old general with three children contributed 3.25 per cent.[8]

Himmler saw Lebensborn primarily as a contribution to the genetic selection for the *Herrenvolk* – the master race – the opposite, positive pole of the sterilisation laws ordering the forced sterilisation of the psychically ill and physically deformed, including blind and deaf – which had been enacted six months after the Party came to power – and the plans in preparation to drive out Jews and other *minderwertigen* – 'inferior' – peoples.

Himmler explained to a gathering of Hitler Youth in May 1936 that the sterilisation laws would guard against genetic selection of negative qualities:

> however, in my opinion, a much greater selection process called forth by National Socialism will take place and make itself felt. The German people, especially German youth, have learned once again to value people racially – they have turned away once again from the Christian theory, from the Christian teaching which ruled Germany for more than a thousand years and caused the racial decay of the German *Volk*, and almost caused its racial death – they have learned once again to look at bodily forms and according to the value or non-value of this our God-given body and our God-given blood to summon it for our race. . . .[9]

One could see it, he continued, in marriage nowadays and more plainly in the dance hall. In the past it had been the girl of little racial value who found dancing partners while the racially valuable girl was always the wallflower: 'It is quite clear that those sections of our *Volk* with not so valuable blood always mature earlier than our own intrinsic type. They are sexually always more engaging and compliant than our type and for that reason were often or in very many cases married. Now comes the change. I believe we have an era before us in which the Nordic girl will marry and the other remain sitting.'

Racial selection was not, it seemed, a matter of fair hair and blue eyes

only. No doubt it was necessary for him it should not be so. For, going on
to explain to the youngsters the procedure for eighteen-year-olds applying
to enter the SS, he made the final selection sound almost arbitrary: having
provided personal medical certificates and a certificate of hereditary health
and an ancestor table – for the current year, 1936, it needed to go back only
to 1850, for 1937 it would be 1750 and inside three years it would be taken
back to the ultimate datum point 1650 – having supplied these proofs the
applicant came to the last hurdle, the Race Commission:

> In animal breeding one has known it for a long time. If anyone wants to buy a
> horse he will sensibly take himself for advice to someone who is a horse expert
> – also when the pedigrees of two or three or four horses are equally valuable and
> whose blood is likewise equally valuable. Then it is well, despite this, to ask the
> expert which of these four animals he would take, merely by using his eyes and
> his feelings and experience. Often he will not be able to say, 'I take this one here
> for this or that exactly logically definable reason,' because that will be judged
> afterwards – how the creature behaves [*geht*], how it reacts to challenges, how
> it sees and how it moves. These are all manifestations which are unmeasurable
> and imponderable – despite which each individual manifestation is an expression
> of its personal value. That is recognised by everyone in animal breeding.

A thousand years of Christian education, he went on, had caused this
lesson to be lost so far as human breeding was concerned. The body
was regarded as sinful; the shape of the body in a bathing costume was
a sin. No doubt this drew some appreciative laughs. 'Why so?' he asked
rhetorically:

> Because the body and because each movement of the hand or foot, the
> stride, the gait or tramp, because all that represents a value, because it is
> not inconsequential like the ear, and because it is not inconsequential like
> the structure of the skeleton, and because, as every old soldier knows, it
> is not inconsequential like a man's eyes. They can be blue and despite
> that we will not take the man with blue eyes. You see, if you look at
> him, speak with him, that his eyes flicker or his eyes, locked in deepest
> introspection, weak-willed, declare to you: I am not willing to endure the
> battle of life – despite the fact that according to scientific classification he is
> racially immaculate.

Bearing was another important factor, he went on; the ones which
they wanted displayed in every attitude soldierly bearing combined with
the carriage of a free *Herrenmensch*. Such were the imponderable, unmeas-
urable manifestations which one had to know, which were infinitely more
important than psychological tests – since of course the Jew was craftier
at tests than a farmer from Schleswig-Holstein. It was his conviction that
psychological testing produced in many cases a completely negative selection. 'For us,' he said, concluding this part of his explanation, 'the racial
examination by the Race Commission is decisive.'

So far as an examination of Himmler's own character is concerned, there are two phrases of special interest in this talk – the first already quoted in the section about imponderables – 'because, *as every old soldier knows . . .*'. Afterwards there came the more revealing: 'We, *who took part in the war* and come from that generation . . . have *as soldiers, as front-fighters . . .*'.

Marriage, children and racial purity, the positive side of his self-imposed task with the SS, occupied such a large part of his speeches in the mid-thirties – and indeed throughout his life – that it is legitimate to conclude that the theme was a sublimation of the sexuality which had been driven deep by his own failures and abstinence in adolescence. Probably, too, he found the ideas popular with his audiences. Here he is in November 1936, on the eve of the annual remembrance of the beer-hall putsch, sharing his concerns in fatherly manner with the highest levels of the SS leadership:[10]

Look here, our men frequently complain, 'God, where can we get to know decent women, decent girls whom we can marry? We should dearly like to marry!'

Those [girls] who gad about at balls and in society one does not marry. Perhaps one likes to make friends with them. That is a perception we must bring home to our men – that not every dance-hour love has to be married. I see in our marriage requests that our men frequently marry in a complete misunderstanding of what marriage means. With the requests I often ask myself, 'My God, must that one of all people marry an SS man' – this chit of misfortune and this twisted, in some cases impossible shape who might marry a small eastern Jew, a small Mongolian – for that such a girl would be good. In by far the greater number of instances, these concern radiant, good-looking men.

One must not, he went on, immediately marry a girl met at a ball who appeared typically Germanic or Nordic; they should bring that home to their men in a suitable way. There was a huge residue of bourgeois Christian notions remaining in this area. For instance, a man might be going out with a girl for three or four months, only to find out suddenly that she had a brother or an uncle in a lunatic asylum. Because of the length of the courtship the man might feel himself almost bound to her.

No, *meine Herren*, that will be enquired into in the most pleasant manner *beforehand*. He can manage that if he is not completely stupid. He simply talks with the girl about her family and, without being tactless, allows her to tell him details about them. One can speak about it all openly and, in the most tactful way, can talk about one's own family and even of our [SS] aspirations. Then one will soon prick up one's ears if the girl says, my father shot himself, an aunt was in a mental institution, a cousin is in a lunatic asylum and so on. Then the man has to say completely on his own responsibility, 'Hands off!' In such cases one does not get engaged and does not go out for three months with a girl.

For an unmarried man – I should like to stress this equally – it is no disgrace if he has a friendship with a girl. He must, however, be fully aware from the start: 'I shall not marry you because I cannot be responsible for that.' How he reconciles that is his own affair: each is master and judge before his own conscience. The

SS man may never act without decency, on the contrary he must say openly: 'I am sorry, I cannot marry you, because there have been too many major diseases in your family.'

He continued with clear indications of the hubris which had overtaken him – marked in earlier decrees and speeches – that the marriage-request procedure was necessary because he was 'not able to make good in three years the false and stupid views of three centuries'.

He asked the listening Gruppenführers not to promulgate all this openly, but to convey it to their officers and men individually so that gradually the idea became accepted – although, human nature being what it was, he saw it as a never-ending task which would occupy 'the tenth or twentieth Reichsführer after me'. It is evident that he saw himself as founder of an Order which would last as long as the German millennium ushered in by the Führer, Adolf Hitler.

His enthusiasm for German pre-history whose ideals were to form the basis of the new era was catered for by two societies he formed about the same time as Lebensborn: the Research and Teaching Foundation, Ancestral Heritage – Ahnenerbe for short – and the Society for the Promotion and Care of German Cultural Monuments. He had already acquired a publishing house, Nordland-Verlag, to spread his ideas to the general public. The SS itself was served by a weekly propaganda newspaper *Das Schwarze Korps – The Black Corps –* whose first issue came out in March 1935. He also had a porcelain factory, named Allach, to manufacture 'Germanic' cult objects to replace Christian symbols. Thus a heavy-looking 'Yule-tide candleholder' – *Julleuchter* – apparently copied from 'an old specimen handed down from the early past of our *Volk*'[11] was sent to all SS families as a replacement for the Christmas symbols to which they adhered obstinately – and continued to adhere. Similar 'Life candleholders' – *Lebenleuchter* – were sent to SS mothers on the birth of their first child.

Plans for the systematic creation of a cultural framework to replace Christianity, referred to as the 'development of the Germanic heritage', were worked out between Himmler's personal staff under Wolff and academics in early 1937. A key draft obviously expressing Himmler's ideas stated that now 'in the age of the final showdown with Christianity' it was one of the missions of the SS to provide the German people with 'the proper ideological [*weltanschaulichen*] foundations' within which to conduct and frame their lives.[12] This project resulted early the following year in the opening of the Deutschrechtliche Institute at the University of Bonn under Professor Karl Eckhardt.

Himmler paid lip-service to pure research, but each of these cultural and historical associations controlled by his personal office was dedicated to the service of his fixed ideological goals. Had they not been they would not have survived. A controversy over a cosmic theory called the *Welteislehre*, or 'world ice doctrine', illustrates this. The *Welteislehre* proposed that all events in the cosmos resulted from an eternal struggle between the heat of the sun and quantities of ice in space. This Manichaean argument of opposing forces locked in never-ending conflict fitted in with the 'Darwinian' doctrine of the 'struggle for existence' which Hitler had made his own – and Himmler too. Hence it had been adopted as part of the 'Nordic' *Weltanschauung*. It was nonsense. This was pointed out by astronomers. One strong criticism labelling the doctrine regrettable for Germany's scientific prestige was sent to Himmler from the German Ministry of Education and Science. He reacted angrily, demanding that the Ministry reject 'this priggish line of high-school professors'. He himself stood for free research in every form, 'therefore also for free research into the *Welteislehre*'. He intended to support this free research warmly: 'and find myself here in the best company, since the Führer and Chancellor of the German Reich, Adolf Hitler, has also been a convinced adherent for a long time of this despised doctrine. . . .'[13]

Ahnenerbe experts were marshalled to refute the attacks, and an enormous correspondence was raised, during the course of which Himmler found by accident, and to his astonishment, that an official on his own staff named Polte not only was opposed to the *Welteislehre* but had been requesting expert opinions from the Ministry of Education and Science and forwarding them up to him. He had Polte sent on immediate leave and stripped him of uniform and badges, writing to Heydrich about the man's 'total lack of objectivity'; the whole affair, he continued, was 'absolutely unprecedented'.[14]

He ran the cultural and research institutes with donations solicited by Wolff from the Freundeskreis of industrial backers. Most resources were concentrated in Ahnenerbe, which mounted costly expeditions to search for or restore sites supposed to be old Germanic settlements or shrines or burial grounds, but true to his administrative principle of never concentrating power in one authority, he kept the other research organs separate. Cultural Monuments was concerned very largely with the construction of the Castle of Wewelsburg as the seat of the SS Order, the Deutschrechtliche Institute with research into Germanic pre-history and history, to produce a historical library which would refute current teaching that their ancestors had been 'cultureless barbarians'.[15]

The new moral philosophy based on the supposed beliefs of the old Indo-Germanic tribes, to which the Institute's researches were primarily directed, had been formulated already by Alfred Rosenberg, the 'Party Pope'. So, too, had the form for two principal ceremonies adapted from pagan rites to replace Christian festivals – those of the summer and winter solstices. An English visitor attended a summer solstice festival as Rosenberg's guest in 1936: a circle of Hitler Youths with fair hair chanted consciously pagan litanies in preparation for the moment at midday when the sun reached its zenith. As it hung overhead there was silence, 'then a

paean of praise rang out for the Aryan god.'[16] In this field Himmler started
as Rosenberg's disciple, but he was becoming his rival.

He shared his thoughts about the new rites with his Gruppenführers
in November 1936.[17] His father had died of cancer the previous month,
and had been buried in a Roman Catholic ceremony which he himself had
attended very publicly barely a week before he spoke. There is no doubt he
was still under the influence of the turmoil of emotions he had experienced.
'I should like to say some things about all the festivals, all the celebrations
in human life, in our life, whose Christian forms and style we cannot accept
inwardly, which we can no longer be a party to, and for which, in so and
so many cases, we have not yet found a new form.' All his measures thus
far, he went on, had been concerned with the future of the SS, not with
the past. But it must be obvious to them all that those things which old
people held sacred should not be torn from them.

> I myself, in my personal case, have acted in that way. My father was
> – according to the tradition of our family – a convinced Christian, in his
> case a convinced Catholic. He knew my views precisely. However, we did
> not speak on the religious issue – with the exception of discussions over the
> political perniciousness and corrupting effects of the Christian Church, on which
> we were both at one. I never touched on his convictions and he did not touch
> on mine.

That, he believed, was how they had to proceed with old people who
did not come over to their way of thinking of their own accord. He had
always shown sympathy to anyone who said to him, 'in consideration of
my parents, I must baptise my child.'

> Please! *Jawohl!* One cannot change people of seventy. There is no point in
> upsetting the peace of mind of people of sixty or seventy. Destiny does not
> require that, nor our own ancestors of the earliest times – who merely want us
> to do it better in the future. And each of you knows that for us, the younger
> generation, the period in our youth until we saw our way clear was a period of
> much inner difficulty, inner rejection and struggle.

He had commissioned Professor Diebitsch – an SS-Sturmbannführer – to
take up the question of funeral ceremonies within the RuSHA (Race and
Settlement Head Office), and would be bringing out schemes some time
in the near future, 'corresponding to the clan beliefs, corresponding to the
family beliefs, corresponding to the honouring of ancestors, the honouring
of parents and our forefathers'. For everything in life needed to be given
a customary form which would take root.

He itemised existing Party festivals: 9 November, the beer-hall putsch,
which they would celebrate the following day; harvest thanksgiving, which
suited the old custom; 1 May, of which the same was true; and the Nazi Party
Day in September. Then there was 20 April, the Führer's birthday. 'This is

already today one of the greatest festive days, and I should like to predict that in future centuries it will be, perhaps, the greatest day of celebration of probably half or the entire world.'

Now there were the two solstice festivals of the deepest significance. Dealing with the summer solstice, the celebration of life, he made the long detour into SS marriage and the necessity for finding out about the girl's family already quoted. Returning at length to the festival, he told his audience that in the days of their forefathers the period between the spring festival and the summer solstice had been a time when the youth of each village, each *Gau*, engaged in contests for the selection of the fittest. They were tested intellectually in the wisdom of their forefathers, and physically in games and races, both girls and boys. 'Then it was usual for the youth of each year group to dance and skip with one another to the solstice festival. There marriages were sealed.' There, too, the recognition of the whole village or *Gau* was bestowed on those who had proved themselves the most capable in the preceding contests. 'I propose that the sporting contests of the SS, which we will hold every year, always take place between Easter and the summer solstice. Then at the summer solstice the prize-giving will take place. . . .'

The winter solstice, the Yule, was the time when one remembered one's ancestors and the past, and when the individual reflected that without his ancestors, without honouring them he was nothing.

> Why do I stress that? Because I – I have already said it – know accurately that we will be unconquerable and imperishable as a *Volk*, truly deathless as an Aryan–Nordic race, if we hold firm to the law of blood selection and if we, living in honour of our ancestors, know the eternal cycle of all being and all happening and other lives in this world. A *Volk* that honours its ancestors will always have children; only those *Völker* who know no ancestors are childless.

The solstice celebrations would be improved year by year, he promised. The summer celebrations next year would include prize-giving for the first time, the Hitler Youth would perform their part better, and the girls of the sister organisation would give a better rendering of the solstice dance. He stressed, however, that he would set the tempo of the advance. There was the danger of those outside the SS finding the new rites amusing. It was no jesting matter. He showed a similar sensitivity to outside opinion when he turned to birth and marriage ceremonies. These should be private affairs, not held in public, nor even in SS regimental halls or the like, only in the family circle. He himself had not yet attended an SS marriage ceremony which had not taken place in the family circle. 'If the pair are not [afterwards] going to be married in church, the ring will be given in the family celebration, and indeed with the phrase I have established for this: "I wish you not only the old wish, that your life may be without beginning and end, but I wish that your clan [*Sippe*] may be without beginning and end.'

The idea of the individual as a link in the eternal chain of the extended family stretching back into the past and forward into the future was another of the leitmotifs of his speeches.

He had arranged that bridal couples would each receive silver beakers, one for the man, one for the woman, as a gift from the SS. Turning to birth ceremonies, he said that when he himself was the child's sponsor – the equivalent of godfather in a Christian ceremony – he gave a small silver tankard, from which the child could drink when it grew up, also a silver spoon. There was a beautiful old custom, he went on, that one gave the child a large blue 'life-riband' (*Lebensband*) of lovely blue silk that accompanied the child and the adult throughout life. These were all things they would adopt gradually, for – in reference presumably to the weight of Christian tradition that had to be overcome – it was a path that could only be taken slowly. They could say, however, that in the last three years they had come a very long way.

It is impossible to say how many of Himmler's senior officers took his notions as seriously as, for instance, Stroop, how many were prepared to go along with them for the sake of their rank and elite status, or to identify the points where his ambitions did dovetail in precisely with their own ideas of themselves as guardians of the Germanic virtues, members of the master race, future conquerors. All that can be said is that those who labelled him a crank did so after the lost war. At the time he was considered a persuasive speaker. Professor Gebhardt, who knew him and his family intimately over a long period, stated that his good point – and the point that at the same time led him to disaster – was his belief in everything he said at the moment he said it, and the fact that everyone believed what he was saying.[18] Stephen Roberts, an academic from Australia who visited Germany at this time and published his impressions in 1937, wrote of him: 'No man looks less like his job than this police dictator of Germany and I am convinced that no one I met in Germany is more normal. Many people behind the scenes believe that he is the man who will ultimately succeed Hitler.'[19]

Wolff, of course, had to believe in his chief's vision. On 4 January 1937, two months after Himmler's homily to the Gruppenführers, he had the new birth or name-giving ceremony performed for his own son, then practically a year old. It took place at the new house he had had built at Rottach-Egern on the Tegernsee. Himmler was chief sponsor; the other sponsors were Heydrich, the Professor Diebitsch who had been set the task of drafting the form of the new ceremonies, and Diebitsch's partner in this work, an Austrian who called himself Weisthor and had won his way into Himmler's confidence by claiming descent from the *Sippe* of Hermann the Cherusker, the legendary Germanic hero who had defeated the Roman Varus just to the east of where Wewelsburg now stood.

Weisthor, who also claimed he had supernatural contact with the ancient Germans, was either a fraud or insane, yet he impressed Himmler with his

'Germanic' mysticism to such an extent that he was advanced rapidly to Brigadeführer-SS, and it was he who officiated in the naming ceremony. He waited with the blue 'life-riband' as Wolff reported the birth of the child formally to Himmler, and Himmler replied formally that it would be entered in the birth book and the *Sippenbuch* of the SS. Wolff then handed the child to its mother and Weisthor came forward to wrap the blue riband around it. 'The blue band of loyalty', he pronounced, 'extends itself throughout your life. Who is German and feels German must be loyal! Birth and marriage, life and death are united in the imagery of this blue band!' And turning to the parents, 'And now may this your child be at one with my innermost wish that he become a real German boy and upright German man.'[20]

Weisthor took the silver (birth) tankard, which presumably Himmler had given the child, and announced, 'The source of all life is *Got*.' The word was given only one 't' in the transcription, allegedly the old Germanic spelling, but it was chiefly useful, probably, to distinguish the SS God from the conventional Christian *Gott*. 'From *Got* your knowledge, your tasks, your life-purpose and all life's perceptions flow. Each drink from this tankard be witness to the fact that you are *Got*-united.'

Weisthor then took the birth spoon and gave it to the mother; it was to bear witness to her love for the infant. Then he took the birth ring. 'This ring, the *Sippen*-ring SS of the Wolff family, you, child, should wear in days to come when you have proved yourself a youth of the SS and proved your *Sippe*-value. And now, I give you, according to the wishes of your parents and on behalf of the SS, the names Thorisman-Heinrich-Karl-Reinhard.' Thorisman came from the ancient Nordic god of the skies, maker of thunder and lightning and protector of the rest of the gods; the other three forenames, of course, came from the triumvirate Himmler, Wolff, Heydrich, although the child was known at first as Karl-Heinz – a linking of Wolff's and Himmler's first names.

Weisthor brought the ceremony to a conclusion by charging the parents and sponsors to bring up the child with a 'genuine, brave, German heart according to the will of *Got*'.

The brevity and simplicity of the ceremony accorded with Himmler's distaste for ostentatious display, his belief in the ancient frugalities; the stress on *Got* expressed his belief in a Creator or first cause. This idea was as fixed as his others and he repeated it frequently in public and private. 'It is the worst misunderstanding of our whole manner of life if anyone should believe that we could dare to tackle the tasks given us by the Führer and devolving on us from our own laws,' he told an audience of farmers and agricultural workers in November 1935,

if we did not believe in a Lord God [*Herrgott*] from the deepest inner conviction, and did not reject all atheists as arrogant, presumptuous and foolish people unsuitable for us. Be assured one cannot be incorporated between ancestors and children in an – according to human ideas – eternal past and the – for human calculation so long as this star earth exists – eternal future of our people if one does not believe in deepest humility in a godly ruler and a God-given order for men.[21]

The same year he edited a propaganda booklet called *The Schutzstaffel as Anti-Bolshevik Battle Organisation*, compiled from his speeches, which was published by the Party press in Munich. Under the heading 'The God-given Order' he wrote:

all that there was and is on this earth was created by God and animated by God. Foolish, malicious and brainless people have created the fable, the fairytale that our forefathers worshipped gods and trees. No, they were convinced, according to age-old knowledge and age-old teaching, of the God-given [*göttlichen*] order of this whole earth, the entire plant- and animal-world.[22]

From the conventional spelling of *Gott* in this booklet and in renderings of his speeches before 1937 it appears that the formulation *Got* emanated from Professor Diebitsch or Brigadeführer Weisthor during their collaboration on the new ceremonies. Apparently Himmler and Wolff in their own conversations referred to the Deity as the *Uralten* – literally the original or ancient one – allegedly another old Germanic form for God.

A card had already been opened for Karl-Heinz – now Thorisman – Wolff in Himmler's personal 'gift' card-index cabinet. Here, with his habitual attention to detail, he kept a green card for everyone to whom he gave presents, a red card for everyone who gave presents to him. The cards were headed by the person's name and rank, and if married the spouse's name, number of children, address, date of birth, notes on current employment and often the form of address he (Himmler) used, *Sie* or *Du*, and his style of greeting. For Ley, leader of the German Labour Front, it was 'Lieber Parteigenossen' – 'Dear Party comrade'; for Göring, 'Mein lieber Parteigenossen'; for intimates it might be 'liebe' or 'liebste' – 'dearest'. However, the main space on the card was reserved for dates and brief descriptions of the present sent – or received – the reason, such as 'birthday', and a brief remark, for instance if he had not been thanked for the present.[23]

At the same time as he found fulfilment in the positive aspects of his task, he was making steady progress with the negative side – overcoming the ideological enemies of Germany.

'You may be in no doubt', he told a gathering of his officers in Breslau in January 1935,

we are joined in battle with the oldest enemy our *Volk* has had for centuries – with Jews, freemasons and Jesuits. We did not seek this battle. It is there, it must be there, as it has always been there in history as Germany, after bleeding to death, rose from the ground and regrouped its forces. It is there according to historical law.[24]

His views on this 'many-headed hydra', as he had described it in his earlier diary, are encapsulated in his 1935–6 propaganda booklet about the SS as an anti-Bolshevik battle organisation. Here, those who in his youthful reading and book-list notes had been *minderrassigen* – racially inferior – had become *Untermenschen* – sub-humans. It appears to be the first time he used this concept.

> One talks of Bolshevism a lot today and most are of opinion that this Bolshevism is a phenomenon which has only appeared in our present, modern era. Many even believe that this Bolshevism, this battle of the *Untermenschen* organised and conducted by Jews, is completely new in world history and has become a problem for the first time.
>
> We hold it right to state in this respect that so long as there have been men on this earth, the struggle between men and *Untermenschen* has been the rule, that this battle against peoples conducted by Jews has belonged, so far as we can look back, to the natural course of life on our planet. One can calmly reach the conviction that this struggle of life and death is quite as much a law of nature as man's struggle against some epidemic, as the struggle of the plague bacillus against the healthy body.[25]

One is reminded of Professor Gebhardt's statement that Himmler believed everything he said at the moment he said it. If this is the case the imagery of the Jew as a plague bacillus can have led him to only one conclusion. It was a conclusion shared by his leader; probably, like so much else, he took it from his leader.

To support the statement that Jewish Bolshevism was of ancient root, the booklet cited the biblical story of the Jewish rising in Persia at the time of King Ahasuerus – celebrated still as the feast of Purim – during which the Jews had slaughtered the leading men of this ancient Aryan race. That was always the way with Bolshevism. They cut down the leaders and enslaved the rest of the population – another revealing statement in view of the policy the SS was to adopt in the east. Afterwards the Jews had robbed the Persians of their racial value by interbreeding, and within a historically brief period nothing was left of this high Aryan culture but the knowledge that 'once there had been such a *Volk*.'[26]

The other mortal enemies of Germany were, of course, the Church and the freemasons. Here the mediaeval witch trials and the French revolution were called in as historical examples: 'The French revolution and its reign of terror was purely and simply a revolution of the Order of freemasons, this outstanding Jewish organisation.' It had resulted in the 'slaughter of the blond and blue-eyed, the best sons of France'. Freemasons had not only owned up to it all, but had gloried in their victory and their act for freeing mankind.[27] From thence the text passed to the Russian revolution prepared by the Jew, Kerensky. So the story was brought up to date.

The next section dealt with 'Our *Volk*', its ancient culture, its reverence for the Creator and His order, extending even to legal rights for animals since they were a part of creation, reverence for ancestors, and the bravery and strength testified to by the Romans who had not been able to subdue the German tribes. Despite all, German leaders had failed to create a state and over the past 2000 years the history of this *Volk* 'endowed with all the intellectual and physical talents' had been the saddest one could conceive. Why? Because their enemies in whatever guise had worked against them continually with sober calculation of the realities of the political struggle, advancing step by step, 'and despite their worse quality and despite their inferior blood and despite their low culture they have always been victorious over us.'[28]

The last war had shown that the Germans had still not learned the lessons of their history. Now, however, fate had sent them the Führer who embodied in his person a complete understanding of historical forces and of the blood of the German *Volk*, and he had taken them into his school. So Himmler arrived at 'The Schutzstaffel' which 'within the framework of the movement [Hitler had founded] had received from the Führer the special task of preserving the inner security of the Reich'.[29]

The first principles for the SS, the booklet continued, had been and remained 'recognition of the value of the blood'. Selection 'concentrated on the choice of those who came closest to the desired physical image of the Nordically determined man. Outward signs such as size and racially suitable appearance played a role.' However, the more experience was gained in selection the more accurate it would become; their successors in a hundred years or so would require much more from individuals than was required today.

The second principles were 'will to freedom' and 'battle spirit' – *Kampfgeist* – the third, 'loyalty' and 'honour', which were inseparable one from the other, as expressed in the phrase bestowed on the SS by the Führer: 'Meine Ehre heisst Treue.' Whoever violated loyalty excluded himself from their society. 'Because loyalty is an affair of the heart, never of the understanding.'

The fourth principle was 'obedience'. Here Himmler seems to have borrowed from a paradox of St Paul's:

> Unconditional and highest freedom of will comes from obedience, from service to our *Weltanschauung*, [obedience] which is prepared to render each and every sacrifice to pride, to external honour and to all that which is dear to us personally; obedience which never once falters but unconditionally follows every order which comes from the Führer or legally from superiors. . . .[30]

This is a key passage in terms of Himmler's relation to Hitler. He is according him the status which St Paul accorded God. If it is a true reflection of his belief, it shows that he needed to surrender himself totally, and had merely substituted Hitler and the National Socialist *Weltanschauung* for his youthful faith in Christ and the Catholic religion. It is also a key paragraph for understanding the SS and its place in the spectrum of Prusso-German history and Prussian soldierly values.

The booklet went on to describe the marriage laws of the SS and their purpose in ensuring the continuance of good blood in the eternal *Sippe*, reiterated the SS belief in God and the rejection of atheists, then turned to 'The Security Service and Secret State Police':

> I know there are many people in Germany who feel ill if they see this black uniform; we understand this and do not expect to be loved by over-many people. All those who have Germany at heart will and should respect us, all those who in some way or at some time have a bad conscience in respect to the Führer and the nation should fear us. For these people we have constructed an organisation called the Security Service [*Sicherheitsdienst*] and in the same way we as SS appoint men for duty in the Secret State Police [Gestapo]. . . .[31]

The booklet ended with a passage encapsulating Himmler's mystical sense of mission:

> So we have taken our place and march according to unalterable laws as a National Socialist order of Nordically determined men and as a sworn community of their *Sippen* along the way to a distant future, and wish and believe we may not only be the grandsons who fought the fight better, but in addition, later, the ancestors of the generations necessary for the eternal life of our *Volk*.[32]

What distinguished Himmler from Rosenberg, Darré and other mystics of the blood was the flair he brought to the practical and political tasks of realising his vision. Hitler's support was a necessary condition, but not the sole one. However loyal, Himmler would not have prevailed against his many rivals in the 'struggle for survival' that Hitler fostered among his paladins had he not proved himself the 'fittest' by creating a superb instrument in the SS. Part of the secret, revealed in this propaganda booklet and all his speeches, was the simplicity, indeed the naivety of his vision, hence its concentrated power. This was probably due more to his emotional compulsion to extremes and his need to surrender to a cause than to a stunted intellect. He had always wanted to conform and a large part of his secret was that his doctrine and his goals conformed with ascendant German feelings and aspirations. Like his Führer he was as much expression as creator of his following. The industrialists in the Circle of Friends supported him for the immediate benefits but also because his goal of order within a European bloc dominated by the *Herrenvolk* suited their economic aims. The *Herr Professoren* and *Herr Doktoren* flocked to his service because of the material benefits of swimming with the tide, but also because like Candide's German tutor, Pangloss, who taught the metaphysico-theologo-cosmolo-nigology – in English, tomfool-ogy – they were attracted by the cosmic system he provided, within which most of them, like Pangloss, could prove 'admirably that there can be no effect without a cause . . .'.[33] The sons of the nobility liked to swim with the tide, too, but they were equally attracted by the lure of fighting and conquering for the Fatherland, and of course they were flattered with the knowledge that they belonged to the racial elite. Those, like Stroop and the farmers and peasants' sons whom Himmler recruited in numbers – 'I am myself by descent, blood and nature a farmer', he said to them – whose formal education had been short, were attracted by a position and importance they could not otherwise achieve, and simply swallowed his simple proscriptions. Himmler led these men because he called to some of their deepest needs. He persuaded them they were the vanguard of the new Germany. Group Captain Winterbotham observed in the summer of 1936 that the young of the new Germany especially 'gloried in a new-found purpose, in the promised fulfilment of a dream of a great German empire'.[34]

Himmler also provided the young with glamour, the psychic glamour of a secret Order sworn to a creed running counter to the rules of bourgeois Christian society, whose symbol was the death's head, and the more obvious glamour of the uniform, black from peaked cap with a silver death's-head badge to glistening boots – black tie, black tunic, black belt, black leather pistol holsters, black breeches, black leather buttons on the brown shirt (changed to white at the end of 1937). For guard duty the SS men wore white gloves, an inspired touch.

They were chiefly visible to the public as immaculate, robot figures guarding the Chancellery and other public and Party buildings, or forming cordons for the Party great when they moved among the people, or riding on the running boards of Mercedes speeding through the streets with Party prominents or their guests while other vehicles pulled in obediently to the sides. They carried out each of their protection drills with the precision to be expected of an elite guard, but with an additional zip and urgency peculiarly a mark of the SS.

Hitler had his own escort commando from the SS, Leibstandarte Adolf Hitler. When he visited a Munich tea house or a hotel in Berlin or Bad Godesberg, the first sign the guests had was the sight of his black guard forming two parallel ranks, back to back through the entrance lobby, leaving a corridor of space between. The Führer walked down this corridor, after which the lines dissolved into a circle of black at tables around the one reserved for him. Later, when he made a sign that he was ready to go, the guards rose and re-formed the human corridor with lightning speed.[35] Winterbotham had an intimate glimpse of this technique when he accompanied Hess to a sports display of Hitler Youth, finding himself walking between a 'living, impenetrable wall of six-foot-tall, black-uniformed, white-gloved, steel-helmeted giants standing shoulder to shoulder'.[36]

Besides the uniformed guard Hitler was protected by police officials of the Reichssicherheitsdienst (RSD) – Reich Security Service – another part of Himmler's empire, under SS-Gruppenführer Hans Rattenhuber. Some forty officials of Bureau 1 formed permanent teams responsible for the Führer's security at his permanent residence in Berlin, Munich and the Obersalzberg, and on his frequent journeys. Hitler made it a principle to be unpredictable in his movements, frequently changing his destination or method of travel at the last moment, sometimes apparently by the toss of a coin. But the routes Hitler was to take on his triumphal motorcades were secured beforehand by thorough investigation of all the owners, tenants and janitors of buildings lining the route, and holding them responsible for reporting any strangers and newcomers. In addition janitors, hotel doormen and other functionaries were employed on a permanent basis as snoopers for the Security Service to report anything untoward within their 'block' of buildings. Later Himmler went further and directed all regional SS leaders to have security officials in the towns in their area 'form a friendly relationship' with all tenants and janitors in blocks lining routes which the Führer might use in future.[37]

The diary of the society columnist Bella Fromm provides a vignette of Himmler's personal security precautions: in July 1937 she was waiting for friends to join her outside a small Berlin cinema showing *Broadway Melody*, when she became aware of two uniformed SS men; one was noting the number of her car, the other taking a quick photograph of her. When her friends arrived it seemed to reassure the two that her searching glances had had no sinister intent. But, curious about their presence, she did not go in at once, and shortly saw the arrival of Himmler – as she put it, 'complete with his dirty-blonde, insipid, fat wife and grim bodyguard'. Marga had grown wider since she had last seen her. She commented, no doubt from the gossip she heard from Party confidants, 'the pleasures of the table are apparently about all the pleasures she gets, since Himmler keeps her at home.'[38] A visit to a cinema showing a glossily decadent foreign film does not fit the image Himmler liked to project; Marga probably induced him to go.

Himmler's practical achievement in creating an elite guard as an extension of his goals was matched by his political achievement in gathering the power to do exactly as he wished with all those opposing his goals. The triangle, 'Political Police – concentration camps – SS', which he had established in Bavaria, he now established throughout the Reich. Nominally he remained subordinate to Göring, but in practice Eicke, as Inspector of Concentration Camps, ran this part of his empire without regard to administrative or legal restraints from outside. The same kind of complaints about deaths and brutalities in the camps which had assailed Himmler in Bavaria – addressed to him now by the Reich Minister of Justice, Dr Gürtner – were met with the same obfuscations, denials or in the last resort appeals to the Führer, who invariably came down on his side. Against this refusal to listen to argument or be bound by any customary or legal restraints, the Prussian and state bureaucracy found themselves powerless, and they gave up.

Himmler was now master of a state within the state. Those suspected of
hostility to or deviance from the Party line were committed to the camps
by his Secret State Police. Inside they came under the savage disciplinary
and punishment code Eicke had drawn up for Dachau, administered by the
individual camp Kommandants and their trained guard units, now known
as 'Death's-Head Formations' – SS-Totenkopfverbände – who formed an
integral part of the sworn community of the SS. Victims had no recourse
to legal or outside agencies of any kind; once caught they were lost to the
outside world until the Secret State Police decided they might be released.

'Whether our actions run counter to an article [of the law] is of
absolutely no consequence to me,' Himmler told a gathering of legal officials
in October 1936. 'In fulfilling my task I do basically what I can answer for
to my conscience in my work for Führer and *Volk* and what conforms to a
healthy person's understanding. Whether others moaned about laws being
broken in these months and years in which it was a matter of life or death
for the German *Volk* was totally immaterial.' Naturally, he went on, it was
said abroad and in the foreign press that the state was in a lawless condition.
'In truth, through our work, we have laid the foundations of a new system
of laws, the right to life of the German *Volk*.'[39]

As an example of the ineffectualness of the state administration in this
area, the Reich Minister of the Interior, Dr Frick, did not set foot inside
a concentration camp until the summer of 1938. This was no oversight on
Himmler's part. Party leaders, Gauleiters, SS and SA generals, bankers and
industrial leaders from the Freundeskreis, and others whom Himmler wished
to impress, were taken on conducted tours of the camps from the earliest
days. Karl Lindemann of Norddeutscher Lloyd described one of these: first
he and his colleagues were shown through the Allach porcelain factory at
Dachau, then they watched field exercises by one of the SS regiments
quartered at the barracks there; finally they entered the forbidden portals
of the concentration camp through the gates with the wrought-iron legend
'ARBEIT MACHT FREI'. There Himmler took over as their guide. A squad
of prisoners was paraded so that the visitors could see some 'typical
criminal physiognomies'; Emil Helfferich of the Hamburg-Amerika Line
commented afterwards that he had seen 'no happy face' among them.[40]
Himmler then performed his customary act for visitors, picking out one
prisoner at a time from the ranks and asking the reason for his detention.
Anyone who lied, Höss wrote in his memoirs, had his memory refreshed
from the card index, after which Himmler awarded Sunday punishment
work.[41] Himmler explained to his guests that all the prisoners were criminals
or anti-socials who would be brought back into the community of the *Volk*
by their training here.

Sachsenhausen was the camp chosen for Dr Frick's first visit in 1938
in company with a number of regional government presidents and police
chiefs. Once again Himmler conducted the party. According to Höss, at
that time adjutant at Sachsenhausen, he was in the best of moods. He

was showered with questions by his guests and answered them all 'calmly and good-humouredly, often however sarcastically'. Uncomfortable topics such as the total numbers of inmates in camps in the Reich, which he had decreed should be kept secret, he sidestepped, 'but very amiably'. According to Höss, Frick and the other guests were visibly impressed.[42] Sachsenhausen was a model camp. Like all camps it was kept in a state of immaculate order and cleanliness, while the inmates knew better than to complain about conditions.

Frick can hardly have been as satisfied as Höss assumed. The question of unrecorded deaths in the camps still plagued his department, and earlier that summer the perennial question of camp executions disguised as 'shot while attempting escape' had flared up in exchanges between the Justice Minister, Dr Gürtner, and Himmler. The correspondence catches the air of injured innocence Himmler pretended or perhaps genuinely felt: he had been plagued by Gürtner for years. His address was severely formal:

16.5.1938

Sehr geehrter Herr Minister!

For some two months you have been telling me that in your view too many people in the concentration camps have been shot while attempting escape. Despite the fact that I personally was not of your opinion . . . I instructed Eicke to impress on the Totenkopfverbänden, who do guard duty in the concentration camps, that they should only shoot in the most extreme necessity.

The outcome has shocked me!

The day before yesterday I was in camp Buchenwald and was shown the body of a worthy twenty-four-year-old SS man whose skull had been smashed by two criminals with shovels. Both the criminals escaped.

I have taken a fresh look at the inmates of the camps and am deeply saddened by the thought that because of too great a leniency, which is always the case if curbs are placed on the service instructions regarding shooting while attempting escape, one of my decent men has had to lose his life.

I may tell you that I have lifted my order only to shoot in the most extreme necessity, and the old order is in force again, by which strictly in accordance with the service instructions shooting is employed after calling three times or in the case of violent attack without a warning call.

Two further criminals, who patently knew of the break-out attempt, were shot in flight – after the SS man had been killed – in the camp on their way home at a distance of fifty or sixty metres. I am employing all means in the search to apprehend the real murderers.

I can tell you now that I shall request the Führer, when the Court has pronounced the death sentence on the two, that it should not be carried out in the courtyard of the Justice buildings but in the camp before the assembled 3000 prisoners – preferably with the rope on the gallows.

Heil Hitler!

Yours H. Himmler![43]

Gürtner replied, denying that he had encouraged Himmler to change his service instructions, and saying that the case in question would have turned out no differently had they remained unchanged. The only remedy was to guard the inmates in such a way that opportunities and therefore attempts to escape were decreased. And he concluded, significantly, 'Because from men who have nothing to lose, but hope to gain their freedom with an act of violence, one must expect every self-liberating act.'[44] Did he believe that all cases recorded as 'shot while attempting escape' were genuine, or was he simply playing along with Himmler's form of words to save his face?

One of the escaped murderers was caught in short time and sentenced to death. Himmler wired Gürtner to inform him that the Führer had charged him (Himmler) with the man's execution on the gallows in Buchenwald. 'Request notification as to when the prisoner will be handed over.'[45] Himmler was weekending at his villa in Gmund on the Tegernsee on the day appointed for the Buchenwald execution. His personal secretary, Hedwig Potthast, had accompanied him, and that evening he had her wire his office in Berlin with instructions to call up Eicke and inform him that 'Reichsführer-SS wishes for a precise report over the attitude of the prisoners at the hanging of the murderer Bargatzky.'[46]

Himmler's running skirmish with Gürtner and the legal bureaucracy was paralleled by his struggle with Frick over control of the police. Frick himself had prepared the way for Himmler's assumption of police power by using him – or so he believed at the time – in his own campaign to detach the police forces of the *Länder* from their authorities and transfer them to his own Reich Ministry. Once the essential steps had been taken to create a nationwide force under the Ministry of the Interior Himmler pressed Frick to appoint him Chief of Police. His long-term goal was to merge the police into the SS, so creating a monolithic instrument of internal order. He was supported by Hitler, but Frick, fighting to retain control, insisted – just as Göring had insisted when giving up the Gestapo to Himmler – that the Police Chief should be directly subordinate to himself as Minister of the Interior. Himmler and Heydrich, who undertook the detailed negotiations, accepted the form of words, knowing that once they took over there would be nothing to stop them doing as they wished.

So, once again, the end was attained with a seeming compromise. As expressed in a decree signed by Hitler and promulgated on 17 June 1936, in order 'to ensure unified control of police duties in the Reich . . . the Deputy Chief of the Gestapo, Reichsführer-SS, Heinrich Himmler, is hereby appointed Chief of the German Police within the Reich Ministry of the Interior.'[47] In this capacity he was 'personally and directly subordinate' to the Minister of the Interior. In practice Himmler paid as little attention to the phrase 'within the Reich Ministry of the Interior' as he did to his nominal subordination to Göring in the affairs of the Gestapo and the concentration camps. As 'Reichsführer-SS and Chief of the German Police' he acknowledged only one superior, Adolf Hitler.

*

Within days of his official appointment Himmler had established a new structure for the unified Reich force: he amalgamated the criminal detection and Gestapo positions throughout the Reich into a Sicherheitspolizei – Security Police – under Heydrich, all rural and urban uniformed police, with the exception of the traffic police who came under the Ministry of Transport, into a single Ordnungspolizei – literally 'order-keeping police' – under Daluege. Typically he kept the two separate and, instead of establishing a unified Police Head Office, dealt with both branches through his own personal office headed by Wolff – so setting up an interesting three-way rivalry in this area, Heydrich–Daluege–Wolff.

As Police Chief his goals were practically limitless. He saw his task as preventing crime before it happened by shutting away habitual criminals, preserving the *Volk* from contamination by shutting away subversives who might corrupt them, picking up vagrants, the 'work-shy' and 'anti-socials' and putting them to useful work in his camps, and in addition supervising public morals. Abortion and homosexuality concerned him particularly; in a speech over the radio in January 1937, he put these two topics high on the list of his 'tasks for the future', only behind getting the traffic police into his own hands.[48]

> We have already set out to tackle these abominations [*Schleusslichkeiten*] rigorously and with deep seriousness, in the bitter knowledge that a growth or even just a continuance of these two epidemics must bring any *Volk* to the abyss. I refrain from giving figures, but know that the number of crimes in these areas, although lower in Germany than in most European and foreign countries, is nevertheless shockingly high.

He was not so reticent about figures when he addressed his Gruppenführers the following month:[49] there were 2 million registered members of homosexual clubs, he told them, and experts working on the question believed there were between 2 and 4 million homosexuals in the country. Taking the lowest possible figure they had to reckon that 7–10 per cent of the 'sexually capable men in Germany – that is men over sixteen years old – ' were homosexual. That meant, if it remained so, that 'our *Volk* is being destroyed by this epidemic.' A *Volk* whose sexual management and equilibrium were disturbed in this way would not endure, he went on, and if one added the disequilibrium between the sexes caused by 2 million soldiers killed in the war it could be seen that Germany was out of order and tending towards catastrophe.

There were homosexuals, he said, who considered that what they did was their private affair and of no concern to anyone. This was not so. Nothing in the sphere of sex was the private affair of an individual, but concerned the life and death of a *Volk* and its prospects for world mastery. 'The *Volk* that has many children has the qualifications for world power and world mastery. A racially good *Volk* that has very few children has a certain ticket to the grave – for the loss of significance in 50 to 100 years, for the funeral in 200 to 500 years.'

After a detour into masculine- and feminine-run states – theirs being a masculine state which they should hold on to with a grip of iron, since the organisation of a masculine state was best – he explained how homosexuals in positions of influence, instead of choosing subordinates for their professional competence, chose them because they were homosexual. This was an argument Hitler had used years before to Diels; he had lectured him on the role of the homosexual in history. Now Himmler used precisely the same analogy as Hitler had to explain the point. Diels, who could not have heard or read Himmler's talk, described Hitler saying: 'Look, if I have the choice between a lovely but incompetent girl as a secretary and one who is capable but hideous, I decide all too easily in favour of the lovely incompetent.' So it was with homosexuals appointing men to posts, he went on; if they were to acquire influence the National Socialist state would soon be in the hands of 'these creatures and their lovers'.[50]

Himmler told his Gruppenführers:

We are all men here, consequently it is safe to say – the moment you have to select a stenotypist and you have two candidates before you, one fearfully hideous fifty-year-old who does 300 words, a sheer genius in this sphere, and another racially good, pretty twenty-year-old who does a bare 150 words, you will – [in response to his audience] I must completely misjudge you – probably with the most serious air and with a thousand moral reasons – because the other is old and therefore could become ill more easily – I know take the lovely young twenty-year-old, who does fewer words.

Good, one can laugh – that [example] is harmless and has no significance because if she is pretty she will soon marry and moreover the position of a stenotypist is not important for the state. . . .

The moment, however, that this principle of selecting not purely on performance, but – I should like to speak now in all seriousness – on an erotic principle, a male–female, a sexual principle in a masculine state of man appealing to man, the destruction of the state begins. . . . I should like to mention in this respect that I believe there is scarcely any post in the inhabited world today which has gathered so much practical knowledge in this area of homosexuality, abortion and so on as we in Germany in the Secret State Police. I believe that we can truly speak as the most experienced people in this area.

Himmler was seldom content with making a point once. He continued at length to explain how the man appointed for his sexual bent would act in the same way when he came to make an appointment. Thus in a masculine state if you found one man of such an inclination in a position 'you could with certainty find three, four, eight, ten and still more people of the same bent.'

He added that the homosexual was a pathological liar. He, Himmler, had not known this at the beginning, he went on, since to a normal person it was so alien. He and Heydrich and a couple of other colleagues really had to learn in this area from vile experiences. Now he no longer asked a homosexual if he could give him his word, for the homosexual in the instant he said something was convinced it was true. Interestingly, this is exactly what Professor Gebhard had said of Himmler himself.

'In my experience homosexuality leads to an absolute, I should almost like to say mental irresponsibility and madness,' and, he went on, the homosexual was naturally the most suitable object for blackmail, first because he was liable to prosecution, second because he was a flabby fellow, lacking in will power. He also had an insatiable need to communicate information in all areas, especially sexual areas. One generally found that those who were caught gave all the names they knew. There was no loyalty in the love of man for man. The homosexual talked endlessly in the hope of saving his own hide.

> We must be clear about it, if we continue to bear this burden in Germany without being able to fight it, then it is the end of Germany, the end of the Germanic world. Unfortunately it is not so simple for us as for our ancestors. With them these few individual cases were of such an abnormal kind. Homosexuals, who were called *Urning*, were sunk in a bog. Herr Professors who find these bodies in the swamps are certainly not aware that in ninety cases out of a hundred they have a homosexual before them, who with his clothes and all was plunged in the bog. That was not a punishment, simply the extinguishing of an abnormal life. . . .
>
> Unfortunately I have to say it – this is no longer possible for us. In the framework of the SS I should like to speak quite clearly. I expressly emphasise that I know precisely what I am saying. This is obviously not for discussion at Führer conventions, but you can explain it in the course of conversations.

What he had to say was that homosexuality in the SS was declining. They had some eight to ten cases a year in the entire corps, and he had decided how to deal with them.

> These people will obviously be publicly degraded and dismissed and handed over to the court. After the expiration of their court sentence they will by my regulations be taken into a concentration camp and in the camp they will be shot while escaping. In each case that will be announced on my orders to the unit the man belonged to. In this way I hope to worm out this type of person from the SS to the last man, in order that at least the good blood we have in the Schutzstaffel and the blood we shall draw in for Germany will be kept free.

Of course that did not solve the wider problem in Germany. He explained how the evil had been allowed to grow in the years before they took power. In the first six weeks of his time in Berlin they had prosecuted more homosexuals than had been brought before the courts in the last twenty-five years. They should not forget that unfortunately the German population was two-thirds urban; the problem did not exist in the villages. Despite the priests and despite Christian morality, despite thousands of years of religious instruction the villages retained a natural and healthy order. So he turned again to discussion of the blood laws of their forefathers on the land.

Eventually returning to the point he suggested that homosexuality was caused by the exaggerated masculinity of the whole of German life: 'We militarise impossible things.' He deplored especially the militarisation of women and girls – especially girls – and the foolish attempt to make them into logical thinking instruments, which was 'in general possible only if we so masculinise them that in time the sexual difference, the polarity disappears'. Then the way to homosexuality was not far. He admitted that when it was said about them abroad, 'You can really be nothing but military,' it was in part true.

The way to alter the excessive military and male orientation of German life and German youth was to bring up SS men and youths – so far as they had influence over them – as knights and cavaliers who treated women respectfully. They must, however, draw the line at going as far as the Anglo-Saxon nations, especially America where men were in slavery to their womenfolk, 'the best example of a female tyranny!'

The subjection and undervaluation of women he traced to the Christian Church. He was becoming incoherent now, or so it appears from the text, asserting that the whole trend of Christianity went to show that it was directed at the destruction of women in order to emphasise their lesser value. 'The whole tenor of the priesthood and the whole of Christianity' was, according to his 'firmest conviction', that of 'an erotic male fraternity' (*Männerbund*) associating 'for the formation and maintenance of this Bolshevism'. Whatever that meant, he substantiated it, he said, on the history of Christianity in Rome, which he knew very precisely.

I have the conviction that the Roman emperors, who exterminated [*ausrotteten*] the first Christians, did precisely what we are doing with the communists. These Christians were at that time the vilest scum, which the city accommodated, the vilest Jewish people, the vilest Bolsheviks there were. The Bolshevism of that time had the power to grow large on the dying body of Rome. The priesthood of this Christian Church, which later in unending battle subjugated the Aryan Church, was engaged from the fourth to the fifth century in demanding the celibacy of the priesthood. They based themselves on St Paul and the original apostles who represented the woman as something sinful and tolerated or recommended marriage as a legal way out of whoredom – that is in the Bible – and represented the procreation of children as a necessary evil. This priesthood pursued this path consistently through those centuries until in the year 1139 the celibacy of priests was put into effect.

Further, I have the conviction that merely for the few who do not wish to reconcile themselves to this homosexuality – especially for the parish priests who in my estimation are to an overwhelming extent, over 50 per cent, not homosexual, while I assume that in the monasteries homosexuality amounts to 90–95–100 per cent – there is a way out created for them to procure the necessary women and females in the oral confession box.

Were they to pursue the priests like other German citizens, he said, he could guarantee 200 or more cases in the next three to four years. Trials were not lacking because they lacked cases but because they simply did not have enough officials and judges. But he hoped that in four years conclusive proof would be furnished that the Church leadership and priesthood were to an overwhelming extent an erotic homosexual male fraternity, 'which on this basis has been terrorising people for 1800 years, claiming from them the greatest blood sacrifices, sadistically perverse in its manifestations'. This brought him to the witch and heresy trials of the middle ages and the burning of some 5000 to 6000 German women – not, he emphasised, German men.

The whole tirade provides a vivid glimpse into Himmler's mind. The content, the abnormal time spent on 'erotic male fraternities', the imagery of putrefaction, even the rambling, disordered thought progression surely indicate a disordered and tortured psyche: the parading of enemies, intermixing them until they seemed facets of a single mask, homosexuals, Jews, Bolsheviks, priests – 'the vilest Jewish people, the vilest Bolsheviks there were', like parasites 'growing large on the dying body of Rome' (exactly the kind of image used in Goebbels' propaganda films), like parasites 'exterminated' precisely as he and his Gruppenführers were dealing with communists; then there was the characterisation of the Church as a homosexual club seeking the degradation of women, and the suggestion that their Germanic forefathers had dealt simply with homosexuals by sinking them in bogs. With these glimpses into Himmler's soul it cannot be doubted that the goals he was to pursue a few years later were direct expressions of this inner turmoil and were present, even if not precisely formulated, in 1937 – had been present at least since he had come under Hitler's spell and been appointed Reichsführer-SS. The cleansing of the German nation to which he had set his hand was nothing less than the physical elimination of all enemies within: Jews, Bolsheviks, priests, homosexuals.

A more interesting question than the state of Himmler's mind, which is amply documented by his actions, concerns the state of mind of the listening Gruppenführers. It goes without saying that no leader can carry his troops with him unless he appeals to their sense of their own collective worth, their idealism, their hopes and fears. Had his audience felt that he was indulging fantasy, he would have lost them.

Had they not inhabited the same world they would have recognised the meanness of his vision and he would have earned their ridicule by his attempts to twist history. He did not lose them; he was able to repeat the same leitmotifs in speech after speech without fear of ridicule. And to judge by their actions and, for instance, Stroop's awed respect, he inspired them with his own nightmare. How much he acted as a conduit liberating and conferring respectability on their subconscious hatreds – removing the public censor – how much his own inner rage contributed to their hate are questions that can never be answered. But Wolff and Heydrich and the top circles of SS leaders who heard these lectures year after year did not consider their Reichsführer insane, and when, later, they indulged an orgy of hate and physical extermination they did not do so merely because he had ordered it. They were a part of the process; they, as much as the Führer, Adolf Hitler, had made their contribution. In many ways Hitler's dictatorship was more genuinely democratic than the 'democracies' it opposed. It was an expression of the collective *demos*.

Himmler eventually returned to the point in his talk – how they were to combat the exaggerated 'masculinising' of society and the consequent tendencies towards homosexuality. He urged them to see to it that their men met girls to dance with at the summer solstice festival, and to ensure that when winter dances were arranged for the young recruits they did not invite 'any bad girls, but the best', and when they gave their SS men opportunity to dance with the girls, the men should be 'merry and bright' (*frohlich und lustig*). He regarded these remedies as especially important for keeping the men away from homosexuality. There was, however, another positive reason: to prevent them from meeting and so marrying girls who were not racially valuable.

'*Meine Herren!*' he concluded this part of his address, 'misconducted sexuality is the most lunatic arrangement one can conceive. To say we behave like animals is a slander on animals; because the animal does not do such things. Therefore, this question of correctly oriented sexuality is the vital question for our *Volk*.'

Whatever Freudian meanings may be read into that extended lecture – only a fraction of which has been reproduced here – the state of Germany, most notoriously the state of Berlin, before the Nazi take-over had given objective grounds for concern. A young Englishman, John Heygate, in search of pleasure in Berlin in 1929 had been saddened and depressed by what he found. The capital had been 'rotten', not simply with the professional vice to be found in every city, but with 'something more, a something which could be directly attributed to the effects of an unsuccessful war, and the disintegration of a nation which had only fifty years of political unity behind it'.[51] The city had become 'the European market of bodies'. Young girls and boys from the provinces, desperate for money, were being sucked in to sell themselves and take part in the perverted or sadistic practices that had always flourished in military-minded nations. So degraded was the picture, Heygate formed the impression that Germany had not only lost the war but, in its hopelessness and distress since, had lost its virtue: 'A whole generation of growing-up girls and boys came to think that it didn't matter to Germany and so it didn't matter to themselves, in what way they used their lives, provided merely it brought them money. . . .'[52]

Himmler and the Gruppenführers who listened to his homilies were not simply indulging their subconscious fantasies, or if they were they were doing so as part of a great historic pendulum, a great movement of national cleansing. The chosen scapegoats were Jews, priests, Bolsheviks and, of course, the perverts themselves.

From homosexuality Himmler passed on to the equally 'vital question' of abortions. Here, too, he was happy in his inner circle to give figures: there were 600,000 to 800,000 abortions a year in Germany, and, what was even worse, some 300,000 women became sterile each year as a result and were consequently 'lost as future mothers'. Moreover some 30,000 to 40,000 each year died from having abortions.

'Look here,' he went on, 'it could be said, "How is it that we as SS and you as Reichsführer-SS concern yourselves with these things? They have absolutely nothing to do with us and you!"' In the first instance, he agreed, they were not of direct concern. It had been his view from the beginning that as Police Chief he could take care of 'exceptional cases of asocial people by prohibition and police deployment', but when it came to great questions, 'the great question of hunger on account of a misdirected economy, the great question of misdirected sexuality, the great question of – shall we say – mass desertions', he could never deal with them with the police. His choice of 'mass desertions' as one of the great questions, and the manner in which he dealt with it are as revealing as his earlier imagery.

> In Germany I can round up 100, 3000, 5000 deserters in the individual towns. That is 5000 individual cases. I can, if there are 200,000 deserters, hold them in check for a time with Totenkopf battalions and shoot them down. But then the time has come to reflect over what is fundamentally amiss here, what should be altered so that these defects do not appear in the populace which itself is brave and decent. Something must have been done positively wrong by the leadership.

That, he said, was precisely how it was in the matter of abortions. The fundamental reason was that the German people had become atomised. They had gone to the towns where they lived as single people, split from their families. To them it was immaterial whether they had children, or if they wanted children it was for egotistical reasons.

> How was it with the man in the past? He was incorporated horizontally in the natural fabric of the *Sippe*, village communities, *Gaue*, and he was incorporated vertically as a member in a long chain with the belief that he would always be reborn in his *Sippe*, on which account – you will find with our ancestors that grandchildren would frequently be named after their grandfather – it was always asked of fate that a man might have a son so that he would not be reborn in an alien *Sippe* with another name.

In his rambling discourses Himmler frequently seems to have been under the influence of some recent event or idea that had been revealed to him. In this case, he was reading the manuscript of a book entitled *Irdische Unsterblichkeit* (*Earthly Immortality*), with the subtitle *German Belief in Reincarnation in the* Sippe, sent to him by the author, Professor Doctor Karl Eckhardt. His own knowledge of the subject was such that he was able to point out to Eckhardt that he should not include 'the thoroughly misleading term *Seelenwanderung* – transmigration of souls – in his work'; this had never been a Germanic belief, only rebirth in the *Sippe*. Nevertheless, he thought the work a 'hugely valuable contribution'[53] and later ordered 20,000 copies solely for the SS. He had second thoughts, however, and true to his method of proceeding cautiously and not running ahead of opinion and so bringing ridicule on the SS, he cancelled the order.[54]

In his speech to the Gruppenführers he said that the question of reincarnation was one which could be discussed for hours. It was as impossible to prove scientifically as it was to prove Christianity or the teachings of Zarathustra or Confucius, but it had a great advantage: 'A *Volk* that has this belief in rebirth and that honours its ancestors, and in so doing honours itself, always has children, and this *Volk* has eternal life.'

So far as abortions were concerned, the task was on the one hand to act relentlessly against the practitioners and on the other hand to give every aid and encouragement to the education of the people in their heritage, and get them to return to the land.[55]

He had much else to say during the course of his immensely long speech on Germany's need for children and racially valuable blood. He pointed to the landed nobility:

> If you look at the individuals, you must notice that there is damned good blood there – and further you must notice that the Party has not gained this good blood. That is a sobering observation. The Party says they are reactionary. Fine, they may be; obviously no one knows that better than I. I believe that I, as chief of the German Police, know that better than anyone in Germany, but I would place the highest possible importance on winning these people over. Since for all that one says these people are reactionary, they are enemies of the state, they are not erased from the world – they are there. If I win them over, then I shall have won a great deal of good blood for the movement. And if I speak from the viewpoint of the Schutzstaffel, I shall have won a great deal of good blood that I should very much like to have in the SS.

This was to be accomplished by going into society and talking to these people, for hours if necessary, to win them over to the *Weltanschauung*, which he asserted was by no means far removed in its fundamentals from their own (the nobility's) *Weltanschauung*. And they must win over the sons and daughters of these people.

If it was his endless repetitions, year after year, of the importance of racially valuable blood, his endless denunciations of racially inferior ideological enemies, which explain the deeds of which the SS became capable – as has been asserted – the areas in which his exhortations had no effect have to be explained. There were examples in this speech. Referring to the debts a number of them had run up during the 'time of struggle', he told them that in the long term this was not permissible: 'In this area also we must arrive at a way of life during the first ten years in which it will be manifest that an SS man buys nothing for which he cannot pay. That further an SS man never buys on hire purchase – he can save up the money beforehand and then buy; further that it is recognised that the SS man is the most honourable human being that can be found in Germany – the most honourable that one can imagine.'

He had set up an account, he told them, which would be used to settle SS debts, first the senior officers', then gradually those of the whole SS. His negotiators would mediate with the creditors to secure a settlement; creditors were usually happy if, for instance, on a debt of 3000 Marks they could get repayment of 1500, 1600 or 1800 Marks, then write off the rest in their books. Those SS officers and men who had their debts paid off in this way would have to give a pledge that neither they nor their wives would resort to hire purchase again, nor run up further debts.

> We must progress so far in a couple of years that one can assume from the start that an SS man has no debts, an SS man can be trusted completely with the greatest and smallest things, because he is unconditionally honourable. We must progress so far. That is to say, when we have gone, this foundation must have been laid, so that the SS can march into the future with this treasure, with these qualities of integrity, honour and keeping one's word.

No doubt Himmler believed this at the time he said it. Yet to do so he had to shut out from his conscious mind the fact that his chief adjutant, his 'Wölffchen', had built a ten-roomed luxury villa with its own foreshore and beach on a prime site on the Tegernsee which he had no hope of paying for on his salary – despite having bought the land and negotiated the contract on favourable terms by virtue of his position in the SS. Wolff ran up a debt of over 150,000 Marks, which became the subject of a Party court case two years later. Himmler wrote to the chief Party judge to say that he was convinced Wolff was honourable and the only reproach that could be brought against him was that he could not take sufficient trouble over the house because he had too much work.[56] The dispute lasted into 1941 when SS negotiators succeeded in having the debt written down to 21,500 Marks. Himmler gave Wolff 20,000 Marks from his treasury accumulated from Freundeskreis donations, and prevailed on the Party treasurer to advance the remaining 1500 Marks from Party coffers.

Such brazen corruption in a large affair concerning his closest companion and confidant was matched by an infinite number of lesser corruptions at all levels in the concentration camps, from the Kommandants who had furniture, clothes, boots made for themselves or their wives or mistresses by craftsmen inmates, or sold products of the camp workshops for their private profit, down to individual guards who accepted bribes for withholding punishment.[57] It was rife in the SS departments concerned with Jewish emigration, and the police officials and border guards who administered it. When, in the following year, 1938, the Jewess Bella Fromm was persuaded she must leave the country, the jewellery, much of it consisting of family heirlooms, which she took with her was confiscated at the frontier and she was required to sign a form declaring that she was a Jewish thief trying to rob Germany by taking German wealth from the country.[58]

Stephen Roberts, the Australian academic who wrote in 1937 that he was convinced no one he met in Germany was more normal than Himmler, had found him 'much kinder and much more thoughtful for his guests than any other Nazi leader, a man of exquisite courtesy and still interested in the simple things of life. . . . He joins lustily in the songs of the Blackshirts and is as natural at a camp *Bivouak* as he is uneasy at formal public functions.'[59] This was the impression Himmler liked to give. No doubt it was how he thought of himself and how he wanted the knights of his Order to behave. Yet in the real world the Order was a huge system of corruption from top to bottom, the knights as greedy as anyone for show and status. And in the real world Himmler had to care for their desires. SS salaries were low, and to ensure loyalty had to be supplemented partly by 'expenses' from the special account 'R' accumulated from Freundeskreis donations, partly in the form of exclusive facilities, SS clubs (*Heime der SS*), hotels, resort amenities, hospitals, even tailors and shoemakers, as a result of which the SS regarded itself and was regarded by the people as distinct. One minor official recalled after the war that 'scarcely anything isolated the Nazis, especially SS staffs, from the population as much as the four car wheels. There were relatively few cars then in the Reich, but these people were continually under way in their cars.'[60]

Thus while he appealed to their idealism as an elite Himmler ensured they were an elite in more down-to-earth ways. Everything suggests that this was not cynicism, but a natural blending of his driving fantasy with the wiliness and compulsion to 'fix' things which he had always shown. It was the same seamless fusion between the two planes that characterised his treatment of the 'sub-humans' at the other end of the scale.

This was demonstrated very clearly in his first large-scale action as Police Chief, a nationwide round-up of professional criminals. He ordered the preparations in early 1937 directly the separate criminal police forces had been unified organisationally. The chief of the former Prussian criminal Police Office – renamed Reich Criminal Police Office – SS-Gruppenführer Arthur Nebe, circulated all regional offices with a request for 'speedy transmission of a list of all the criminals in your district who . . . have to be regarded as professional and habitual criminals or as habitual offenders against morality and who are at large.'[61] On 9 March, a few days after his exhaustive lecture to the Gruppenführers, Himmler gave the executive order for a lightning strike, and some 2000 people selected from these lists found themselves arrested and thrown into *Schutzhaft* in the concentration camps which had been prepared to receive them. There they remained at Himmler's pleasure without redress. Many of the most brutal among them readily lent themselves for use as foremen – Kapos – of work detachments, creating another layer of psychic and even physical stress for the political prisoners.

The concentration camp population had reached a low point of some 7500 distributed in three large camps, Dachau, Sachsenhausen, Buchenwald for the men, and one, Lichtenburg, used from summer 1937 exclusively for women. One of the advantages of increasing the number of inmates was that it justified an increase in the strength of the Totenkopf units guarding them. Himmler aimed to use these units as the spearhead of his force for maintaining internal order in occupied territories in the coming war – so he told the Army chiefs to reassure them, and it is borne out by his remarks to the Gruppenführers about rounding up deserters. Yet an increasing military element in Totenkopf training and increased exchanges of personnel between the Totenkopf and the SS-Verfügungstruppe suggest that Himmler was already planning to combine elements of his camp guard units with his special front-line soldiers in war.[62] He used every device to achieve increases in the strength of both specialised formations.

A more immediate advantage of the increase in numbers inside the camps was the larger workforce provided for various economic enterprises he had taken over or set up as SS firms. The most labour-hungry of these was a real estate and construction company which acquired land, often from Jews or Jewish firms, and built houses and other facilities for the SS and the Party. The following year, 1938, he formed the German Earth- and Stone-works Company and set up three new camps, Flossenbürg, Mauthausen (near Hitler's birth-place, Linz) and Gusen, all close to quarries in order to use the inmates to excavate building stone and produce bricks and other construction materials for his companies. To provide more inmates Himmler widened the list of 'anti-socials' to be arrested arbitrarily: tramps and vagabonds, beggars – even those with a fixed address – gypsies and people who travelled from place to place like gypsies if they showed no will to work regularly, pimps who had been involved in legal proceedings even if not convicted and who still associated with procurers and prostitutes, or people under strong suspicion of procuring, and finally people who had demonstrated by numerous previous convictions for resistance, causing bodily injury, brawling, trespass and similar 'that they do not want to adapt themselves to the orderly *Volk* community' were all specified in a decree of December 1937.[63]

Little over a month later he extended the list to include the 'work-shy', which he defined as men of working age, certified fit by a doctor, who could be shown to have turned down work on two occasions without good reason, or who had started work only to abandon it soon without good reason.

In this way he acquired the slaves – for that is literally what they became, lacking the most elementary rights of free people, and that was how they were worked, as an expendable resource under the most pitiless camp regimes – to man the civil engineering operations which helped provide funds for increasing SS strength and facilities. At the same time these funds gave him the means to retain his grip on his people, and increase his freedom of manoeuvre outside Party and state authorities. His total disregard of the state legal authorities by this time is demonstrated by the way he cut through all conventional forms of justice to define categories of people he wished to arrest.

Inside the camps the prisoners reflected his obsession with order and his compulsion to classify: they formed a living card index, displaying their category in coloured patches sewn on the left breast of their jacket and the right side of their trousers – red triangles for 'politicals', green for criminals, pink for homosexuals, black for the vagrants, the work-shy and the unco-operative who were known as 'anti-socials', purple for Jehovah's Witnesses, whose beliefs prohibited them from bearing arms, yellow for Jews.

He had absolute power over them.

'There will be very many whom we should never let out,' he told his Gruppenführers during the anniversary celebrations of the beer-hall putsch in November 1937,[64]

> for let us be clear about it – over the coming years and decades broad masses of our people will always at one time or another be susceptible to the poison of Bolshevism, which will be offered in ever new forms and in homeopathic doses in the most sophisticated propaganda. If we let their officials out then they [the people] will succumb to the poison; however, if we take away the heads and the leadership, lock them up, then in serious times the good spirit in the German – even he who was a communist in all seriousness earlier – will gain the upper hand and he will obey the good spirit. If we were not to do that, I must say, I would already, or at least at the first emergency, be very pessimistic.

'My dear Lehner Toni,' he wrote to a Party comrade whom he had committed to Dachau for alcoholism at Hitler's request, 'Obviously you will be released. The date I must reserve to myself. . . .' It would only be, he continued, when he was convinced that Toni had completely renounced alcohol. 'The punishment was not imposed by the Führer to hurt you, but to turn you from a way that had brought you and your family to the abyss.'[65]

In addition to the closed triangle, 'police – concentration camps – SS', now spread over the Reich and interlocking with it at every point, was his original intelligence service, the SD. Heydrich, whom he had engaged to set up the service, remained its chief. The headquarters were at the Hohenzollern Palace, 102 Wilhelmstrasse, backing on to the same green area as the Gestapo building, No. 8 Prinz Albrecht Strasse, where, wearing his other hat, Heydrich was chief of the Sicherheitspolizei (Security Police), or *Sipo* – the newly merged Secret State and Criminal Police. Himmler also had offices in both buildings. From 102 Wilhelmstrasse Heydrich controlled SD offices in every SS district and sub-district (*Ober-* and *Unterabschnitt*) and the nets of V-men (agents) radiating from them.

While the 'police – concentration camp' system was concerned chiefly with eliminating overt opposition to Hitler's Reich and forcing conformity, or *Gleichschaltung*, by the threat of the whispered, unknown terror behind the wire, the SD monitored every area of national life, not least its original targets, the Party and the police. Heydrich appointed SD officials to high positions in the police forces he controlled, or recruited existing officials into the SD. He also recruited officials of Daluege's Ordnungspolizei into the SD, and increased the number over the years, selecting 'the most ruthless, most unprincipled people'.[66] Besides providing information this net ensured several lines of authority outside the official channels, which allowed him to bypass the state and regional bureaucracy still enmeshed in police procedures, to act directly on the orders of Hitler via Himmler. Daluege was doing much the same in a less ordered framework by recruiting police officials into the SS – waiving normal SS entry qualifications if this were necessary. The double penetration of the police served Himmler's long-term goal of merging the force wholly into his sworn, ideologically committed Order of political soldiers.

Besides internal surveillance, where Office II (*Inland*) worked closely with corresponding departments of the Gestapo, the SD deployed a net of foreign- and counter-espionage agents from Office III (*Ausland*). In this field it worked in co-operation with the armed services counter-espionage division, or Abwehr, whose chief from January 1935 was Heydrich's mentor in the spying game, Wilhelm Canaris, now promoted rear admiral. Prior to his appointment there had been considerable friction between the Abwehr and the Gestapo, and there seems little doubt that Himmler and Heydrich used or even managed the resulting ill-will to manoeuvre Canaris into the post. Heydrich, at any rate, was involved in the affair which led to the dismissal of the former Abwehr chief and after Canaris' appointment in his stead Heydrich and Canaris resumed or more probably continued their close personal relationship. Both moved home almost simultaneously to the Schlachtensee district of Berlin, where their gardens abutted; they rode together in the park every morning, accompanied by Heydrich's chief of SD administration – Office I – Dr Werner Best; and Heydrich again played first violin in Erika Canaris' evening string quartets.[67]

Their political views were in complete harmony. Whatever Canaris may have come to think about Hitler later, at this period he was a devoted, unquestioning disciple, and the National Socialist slogans he injected into his first directives in office surprised and alarmed his professionally apolitical staff. By engineering his appointment it appears that Himmler succeeded in penetrating the citadel of the only real power in the state which matched 'Party–SS–police' power, the power, moreover, which contained 'reactionaries' at its core, and in which other 'reactionary' elements reposed their trust. If it is going too far on the evidence to state that Canaris was indeed Himmler's most important V-man inside the Wehrmacht, it is nevertheless certain that the Admiral, while by nature far more complex than either of the 'black *Diaskuren*', was a convinced National Socialist, and from the beginning he and Heydrich worked in close co-operation. After the war Lina Heydrich characterised Canaris' relationship to her husband as paternal. Himmler, for his part, had an 'almost superstitious respect' for Canaris as 'the born spy'.[68] And the basic formula by which the three main intelligence services of the Reich – Abwehr, SD and Gestapo – divided off their areas of responsibility was arrived at within two weeks of Canaris moving into his office at 72–76 Tirpitz Ufer. As Heydrich's latest biographer, Edouard Calic, points out, this is in itself highly suggestive.

From its inception the SD had been concerned with the ideological enemies – Jews, freemasons, Jesuits, Bolsheviks – and these demons continued to exercise Heydrich as much as they exercised Himmler. A keen young Nazi from Austria named Adolf Eichmann, who had applied for service in the SD to escape the crushing monotony of military training in SS-Standarte Deutschland at Dachau, found himself accepted and posted to the 'Freemasons' section at the Wilhelmstrasse Palace. At first he worked in a huge room stocked with filing cabinets, sorting and filing cards on freemasons worldwide. His chief was an SS-Sturmbannführer with a goatee beard, Professor Schwarz-Bostowitsch, an expert on masonry, who struck him as 'outlandish and very funny'.[69]

After three weeks he was transferred to a neighbouring department where a freemasons' 'museum' was being formed from books, cult objects, medallions, photographs taken from masonic lodges throughout the Reich. His new task was to classify, catalogue and label thousands of seals and medallions. Later this 'museum' was removed to the Prinz Albrecht Strasse building. The Swiss representative of the International Red Cross, Carl Burckhardt, described being shown around it by Heydrich. In one great hall glass-fronted showcases surmounted by different national flags held handwritten lists of names – 'The freemasons of all countries,' Heydrich explained. He opened a door and they passed through into another room, windowless and quite dark. Heydrich switched on a violet light and 'slowly all manner of cult objects stood out from the shadows along the walls. Bleached as a corpse in the wan light Heydrich stepped through the room talking of the world conspiracy, the extent of its dedication and at the peak of the occult hierarchy the Jews leading it towards the total destruction of all life.'[70]

After 'Freemasons' Eichmann was transferred to 'Jews' – SD Office II 112 – where he was given a book by Theodor Herzl advocating the establishment of a Jewish state in Palestine and told to abstract its arguments for the instruction of the SS in general and the SD in particular.

From this beginning he became the department expert on Zionism and Jewish emigration. Like the 'Freemasons' the 'Jews' office was engaged in building up a card index of all prominent Jews in the Reich and abroad. In co-operation with the Jewish desk in Gestapo Department IIB it carried out surveillance of Jewish associations and gatherings, monitored the Jewish press, held courses for officials manning the Jewish desks of the SD regional and sub-regional offices, who were required to send in monthly situation reports, and prepared handbooks on the Jewish question for the instruction of the SS.[71] These were simple tracts, characterising the Jew as a parasite living on the productive efforts of the German people, a rootless, wandering bloodsucker forcing people into economic bondage and carrying out a planned violation of Aryan womanhood:

> It is known that the Jew prefers blonde girls. He knows that the women and girls he dishonours are forever lost to their *Volk*. Not because their blood is thereby debased. But the dishonoured girl is spiritually destroyed. She is seized by the greed of the Jew and has lost all sense for the noble and pure.[72]

This aspect of the Jewish danger was very real to Heydrich. There was a law against sexual relations between Germans and Jews, and when in May 1937 the Gestapo office at Neustadt reported serious violations in Jewish sanatoria, hotels and pensions between guests and German employees Heydrich directed that every case should be examined after the court judgement to see whether, having completed his sentence, the culprit should be taken into *Schutzhaft*. His directive continued: 'Moreover, I request immediately after the conclusion of a case of racial violation in which a man of German blood is sentenced, the Jewess concerned is to be taken into *Schutzhaft* and this is to be reported here [Sicherheitspolizei, Berlin] immediately.'[73]

Other departments of SD *Inland* dealt in the same way as the Jews' and freemasons' departments with communists, social democrats, the Church, reactionaries – chiefly to be found in the higher ranks of the Army and among the landed nobility – registering the personal details of the individuals concerned in similar giant card indexes. In addition, all professional, cultural, sporting and youth organisations of the Party and the state and regional bureaucracy were infiltrated and kept under surveillance. Since in many areas this duplicated the work of corresponding Gestapo departments which had executive powers for arrest and *Schutzhaft*, the SD – in part no doubt as a result of Parkinson's Law, chiefly because of Himmler's obsessive empire-building and his determination to retain his grip on all the strings of intelligence – developed into a comprehensive information service, which was given the task of instructing 'the Reichsführer-SS, the state leadership and the leadership of the Party on the political situation in the Reich and the mood of the population'.[74]

Heydrich's, and it can be assumed Himmler's, purpose went far beyond a mere report to the leadership on the state of public opinion: SD *Inland* and the Gestapo were envisaged as twin pillars of thought surveillance and control. Thus in September 1937 Heydrich directed the District SD-Führers to report on 'how the National Socialist *Weltanschauung* prevails in the individual spheres of life, what opposition there is and in that case from whom . . .'.[75] Such findings were then passed to the relevant Gestapo positions for action. However, such was the hysterical state induced in the German nation by this time that, as during the witch craze and the height of the Inquisition in Spain, and often for similar venal reasons, denunciations from ordinary citizens seem to have been as common as confidential reports from SD agents.

SD Office III (Foreign) in addition to its intelligence duties gathered information on prominent personalities and ideological enemies in neighbouring countries for use in the coming war of conquest. Adolf Eichmann described to his interrogator after the war how in early 1938, some three months prior to the 'annexation' of Austria, everyone at SD headquarters was taken off normal duties and put to work in three shifts filling in cards for 'an enormous (rotating) circular card file several yards in diameter, from which a man sitting on a piano stool could operate and find any card he wanted thanks to a system of punch holes'. Each card listed an Austrian individual, his address, Party membership, whether he was politically active, a Jew, freemason, Catholic or Protestant and any other details which could be gleaned from membership files, annual reports, directories and similar material brought across the border by agents.[76]

On the basis of the information gathered and filed, plans were worked out for the internal conquest of the countries to be annexed or overrun. Just as the Army general staff planned the coming war of *Blitzkrieg* in all detail, so Heydrich and the intellectuals he had collected in the SD planned the political, economic, racial and class reorganisation necessary to subjugate the conquered populations. The plans were referred to as 'solutions': 'the solution of the Czech. problem', the 'solution of the Russian problem'. Fundamental to each 'solution' was the elimination of the leadership classes, representatives of the ideological enemies and Jews, and the control and exploitation of the economy for the German Reich. According to Edouard Calic the plans provided for the elimination of whole ethnic or social strata through hunger, slave labour, the spread of epidemics, sterilisation and chemical means.[77] In view of the means that were eventually employed and the means Stalin was already using to subjugate the Russian peasantry and in particular the population of the Ukraine – a savage onslaught of terror and deliberate starvation which claimed an estimated 14 million lives between 1930 and 1937 – there is no reason to question this.

SD Office III also carried out covert operations abroad, its agents liaising with activists in the German minorities in neighbouring eastern countries to co-ordinate their subversive or provocative activities with

Hitler's diplomacy. It trained and deployed hijack- and murder-squads on specific targets abroad, equipping them with the necessary kits of weapons, explosives and fake papers from its own laboratories and workshops. Thus, just as in the very early days of the SD Heydrich had planned and carried through the suborning of leading personalities and faked the communist 'provocations' by which Hitler came to power in the Reich, so now, with his greatly expanded service, he planned and carried out the external 'provocations' by which Hitler extended his power over neighbouring countries. If Hitler is regarded as the ego or will of the Third Reich, Heydrich and the SD can be likened to the nerve- and reasoning-centre, structuring the Führer's basic methods, which never varied.

Such was Himmler's empire by 1937. It had grown so rapidly and penetrated so far into every area of internal life and every aspect of foreign intelligence that it was far from an integrated structure. The different threads of finance and industry, police and concentration camps, intelligence and subversion abroad, ideological knighthood and front-line soldiery, SS discipline and mothers' welfare, Germanic heritage, racial breeding and moral cleansing only really met in his personal office.

The compulsion to manage, order and manipulate which had resulted in this apparently eccentric, even crazed structure – which yet had a terrible symmetry – drove him continually to meddle in affairs outside his direct responsibilities, enormous as these were. He encouraged and financially supported research into the genetic and cultural causes of homosexuality, instructing the Gestapo to provide the professor conducting the study with names and addresses of known homosexuals in his area; similarly he supported research into criminal families, and into the castration of sexual offenders.[78] He entered into a dispute between the chief of the Party Office for *Volk* Health, Dr Gerhard Wagner, and one of his own favourites in the field of race hygiene, Dr Gütt, over the administration of the sterilisation laws for the hereditarily unhealthy.[79] When it came to his attention that the Reich Association of the Child-abundant (Families) was not fulfilling its purpose of assisting and encouraging racially valuable parents in the lower-income groups to have large families, and of educating the most capable children of such stock in special National Socialist schools, he recommended that one of his own men, SS-Obergruppenführer Heissmeyer, take over as chairman: '. . . I should be glad if the Reichsbund der Kinderreichen were under Heissmeyer, because I believe it to be important that the SS, which is so very much occupied with race and family questions, takes a leading part here.'[80]

When in February 1936 the Economics Minister and Reichsbank President, Hjalmar Schacht, a man whose National Socialist loyalty he distrusted, made an after-dinner speech favouring tradition and criticising the innovation-mania of the Party, he forbade publication in the press.[81] When a court of honour acquitted an officer who had had a year-long affair with a Jewess on the ground that he had not realised she was

Jewish but believed she was a negro half-caste, he drew the matter to the attention of his ally, Göring.[82] He could not take direct action since the armed services were outside his jurisdiction. After an SS-Sturmbannführer had been seriously ill with a heart condition he forbade him to smoke for two years, after which he was to furnish a doctor's certificate of health, 'on which I will decide whether the smoking prohibition is to be lifted or to remain in force'.[83]

He was continually coming up against Alfred Rosenberg because of their mutual spheres of interest in the Germanic heritage and the new Germanic cult. 'I certainly do not, when I see someone else digging, cause the SS to start digging there,' he replied hotly to one rebuke from Rosenberg about Ahnenerbe archaeological excavations near a dig of his own. Rosenberg evidently took this as a humorous comment, since Himmler wrote next: 'Witticisms I did not write in my letter and I am sorry that you came to this erroneous view.' He believed, he went on, that there was a lot that had to be cleared up between them, and proposed that their adjutants agree a date for a meeting.[84]

Foreign policy was another area in which he took a hand. Since he had scarcely travelled outside Germany and his historical reading was entirely German-centred, his views on other countries were shallow, and often amusing. One of his ideas was that the English upper classes retained good figures because they ate porridge for breakfast; as a result the SS and the pregnant women in Lebensborn homes had to start the day with porridge. However, the overall principle of Hitler's foreign policy was simple enough: to avoid a two-front war while the German Army thrust east, England had to be detached from France and won over to benevolent, anti-Bolshevik neutrality. By 1935, like Hess, Rosenberg, Ribbentrop and other unofficial ambassadors to England, he was actively involved in promoting Anglo-German friendship. With a Swiss-born US citizen named de Sager as his intermediary he made contact with pro-German elements in England – not lacking at that period – and with the help of the Wolffs spent several weekends at his villa at Gmund on the Tegernsee playing host to a Member of Parliament, an admiral and others whom he supposed influential. An inspection of Dachau was usually included in the entertainments. Two officers representing the veterans' association, the British Legion, agreed after their visit that it was indeed wise for racially and politically inferior elements to be isolated in camps.[85]

His attempts to cultivate English connections began even earlier through the Christian evangelical movement, Moral Rearmament. Founded by the American Frank Buchman, the movement was particularly attractive to upper-middle-class Englishmen, and became known from its most fertile early recruiting ground as the Oxford Group. No doubt Himmler's conviction that all Englishmen of this type were honorary secret agents was what impelled him to penetrate the Group – this was certainly his reason later –

yet he must also have seen an opportunity to bring influence to bear on an important section of English opinion.

His attempts to recruit one of Buchman's German disciples, the Silesian aristocrat's daughter Frau Moni von Cramon, give an interesting glimpse of his style and method. First she was told she was to be arrested since an anti-Nazi pamphlet had been found in her house. Next a Silesian SS leader – Udo von Woyrsch perhaps? – arrived to ask her if she could introduce him to the family of a girl he had set his eyes on. She told him of her imminent arrest, and he promised to intercede with Himmler. She was driven to Berlin and found herself ushered in to Himmler's office. Himmler left her at one end of the room while he stood by his desk, looking through a file. Taking a photograph of Buchman from it, he asked her if the man was a Jew. She replied that she didn't know; she did not think so; she would ask him.

'Do you think he will tell you?'

'If he knows, why shouldn't he?'

'What is the relationship between the Oxford Group and the Jews?'

She could not answer, she replied, because the Group had no rules or statutes. He asked her how many times she had been to England that year.

'Three times, I think.'

'You're wrong. Four times.'

He then told her the exact state of her bank balance, and asked how she afforded these journeys. She replied that she had sold her grand piano. She had faith in God, she added, and believed He gave people what they required when they served Him.

'I believe in God, too,' Himmler said seriously. 'I believe in miracles. I'm Party member number 2. We were seven men who had faith that this National Socialist ideology would win. Now we are the government. Isn't that a miracle?'[86]

His self-promotion to Party member number 2 is interesting, suggesting that he already saw himself as Hitler's right hand, above the Deputy Führer, Hess, and the nominal successor, Göring. Did he see himself, as he was apparently seen by many in 1936, as Hitler's natural successor?

Later Frau von Cramon worked for him for a while, setting up social welfare services for women and children, while Buchman himself, realising 'what it would mean for the world if Himmler were to be changed',[87] made strenuous efforts to convert him to the moral absolutes of his movement. But the two were so similar in the messianic certainty of their beliefs that they made not the slightest dent on one another. Meanwhile Himmler had Frau von Cramon and all German offshoots of the movement under surveillance and he dismissed her when he learned she had warned a friend who was helping Jews in Berlin. Nonetheless, the fact that both she and Buchman were able to spend some considerable time with Himmler socially, hoping for his conversion, is an indication of the reasonable, even charming exterior he could assume – in the words of Stephen Roberts quoted previously, 'much kinder and much more thoughtful for his guests than any other Nazi leader, a man of exquisite courtesy . . .'.[88]

In addition to his duties and those hobbies and enquiries which he raised into duties, he was much concerned with sport. Sport was taken very seriously in the Party as a whole. In the *Weltanschauung* its demands served in peacetime as a substitute for the natural struggle for existence; in practical terms it served to produce a physically fitter nation more capable of withstanding the rigours of the coming war years. Besides, strength and form were requirements of the Aryan myth. In political terms success in sport at international level raised German prestige abroad – which was suffering from reports of Jew-baiting and cruelties in concentration camps – and raised morale at home, again diverting attention from less satisfactory areas. Himmler applied all these views to his beloved SS. It appeared to him axiomatic that as the racially selected elite the SS must produce the finest sportsmen, and to encourage all-round fitness he made promotion dependent on the attainment of the sports 'badges' awarded by the German Sports Association for standards of achievement. He explained his ideas to a gathering of Hitler Youth in 1936:

> Why do I place such value on the performance badges? First, because sport and the performance badges again select and kick out the man who does not achieve. Second, because I thereby avoid us all becoming bureaucrats who, because they have so much to do, never take bodily exercise. If now that becomes a must, then as an old Nazi one just gets down to it. [Applause.] Further, I avoid in this way having a leadership corps which at the age of forty or forty-five puts on paunches. [Applause.] Further, I make sure that everyone has to train in some field. I also make sure that the consumption of alcohol and nicotine will be somewhat reduced.[89]

This was the speech in which he claimed to have taken part in the first war. 'We who as front-line fighters learned to booze and smoke . . .', he said, explaining that if one was in battle, did not know whether one would survive the next hours, was hungry by day and had nothing to eat, then one could very easily get used to smoking and boozing. The idea of the sports badges was to avoid that. What he said next seems equally to have been designed to demonstrate his hardness to the youngsters. He told them that his method of handling someone in the SS who got drunk and brawled or made a fool of himself was very simple. The man was reprimanded, then given the alternative: 'either you show me that you can handle alcohol and adjust yourself to us, or you are handed a pistol and have to make an end. You have twenty-four hours to consider it.'

The themes of sport and sports badges occurred frequently in his speeches during the mid-thirties. In November 1937 he reminded his Gruppenführers that their own promotion depended on acquiring the badges: 'If we require our men to take the sports badge, then in exactly the same way it must be required from the leaders. Please attend to this.'[90]

The traumas of his treatment on the parallel bars at the hands of Herr Haggenmüller at the Wilhelm Gymnasium must have approached very close to the surface of his mind as he lectured his people. Perhaps it is not surprising that he had to bolster his ego with suggestions that he had fought at the front and there learned to 'booze and smoke'. Just as his features were far from the Nordic ideal, his body was not designed for sport. There are photographs and cine films of him in running shorts and vest, or a bare top revealing heavy breasts, thick middle, large backside, very short arms and stodgy legs, and a generally unathletic appearance. In the films, he smiles a good deal as he encourages his sportsmen, an incongruous, even embarrassing avuncular figure among the vigorous youth.

According to his first biographer, Frischauer, he had a part of the park behind the Prinz Albrecht Strasse building converted into a sports field with running track and jumping pit, parallel and horizontal bars, and devoted an hour almost every day to training for the sports badge. Wolff stood by to encourage and time his efforts. 'He displayed much energy,' Wolff said after the war, 'and persevered with the strength of despair.'[91] It took him months to approach the necessary standards, however, and it was not until the end of 1937 that he finally submitted himself to the test. Wolff took charge of the stopwatch, so his story went, and ensured that Himmler passed. Whether his tale is true or not – and it is not clear how he could have ensured Himmler's success on the bars – it is surely a valid description of their relationship.

Expansion

Himmler said in 1935 that he required ten undisturbed years to establish the SS as an Order. This sounds like the time-scale Hitler was working to – thus the notes of a top-level meeting Hitler convened in November 1937: 'should the Führer live [i.e. survive], it is his unalterable resolution, at the latest 1943–5, to solve the German [living] space question.'[1] The similarity in dates may be coincidence. However, the rearmament programme needed this length of time to mature without a major European war so it is probable that Himmler accepted Hitler's assurance on the time-table. Neither was to be granted so long. For the resolution in blood of 30 June 1934 had not been final, and beneath the obvious changes and rhetoric of National Socialism the struggle between the old financial and power groupings intensified, forcing ever more radical solutions.

At the heart of the financial–industrial argument was Germany's dependence on imports of foodstuffs and raw materials. Hitler was pressing rearmament at the expense of exports, hence sucking in raw materials from abroad without earning the foreign exchange to pay for them, and Schacht as Minister of Economics and Reichsbank President was forced to employ ever more desperate sleight of hand to ward off shortages. From at least early 1935 he was warning that the speed of rearmament had to be restrained and in May 1936 he insisted that the programme had to be stopped or it would result in inflation and the collapse of his fiscal policy.[2] Hitler did not listen. He preferred the advice of his own Commissioner for Economic Policy within the Chancellery, Wilhelm Keppler, who advocated reducing the need for imports, hence foreign exchange, by producing synthetic fuels, rubber and other necessities for rearmament at home with indigenous materials instead of buying in from abroad. They would be far more costly as a result, but this mattered only if Germany were competing in the world market. Were Germany to be decoupled from the world market it would become a purely internal transaction. The increased costs could be offset by holding down consumer goods and living standards in general.

The difference between Schacht and Keppler was basically the difference between the banking–industrial grouping tied in with US and British capital, and the opposing groupings led by IG Farben, who wanted to decouple Germany from the US-dominated world market and create a financially independent European bloc. It is evident that, whether or not

Keppler had been a cleverly camouflaged IG Farben V-man all along – as Gossweiler asserts he was – he was now undoubtedly representing the IG Farben-electrochemical viewpoint. Further, he was chairman of the board of one of the concerns which would gain from such a programme. This was Braunkohle-Benzin AG, created by Schacht's Ministry in partnership with IG Farben and various mining interests to produce petrol and lubricating oils by the hydrogenation of coal. The others on the board were the pro-Nazi Dr Krauch of IG Farben, Dr Koppenberg of Junkers-Werken, General von Vollard-Bockelberg, and Fritz Kranefuss, Keppler's close colleague and Himmler's adjutant.

The duo Keppler and Kranefuss leads directly to Himmler's industrial–financial Circle of Friends – Keppler as the original founder and administrator, Kranefuss as his protégé who was now taking over the leading role in the Circle. It seems probable, therefore, that Keppler was not simply representing the IG Farben line – and his own personal interests – but was spokesman for an economic consensus arrived at in this Freundeskreis, whose strongest supporters like Kurt von Schröder, the original mediator between the power groupings, were convinced National Socialists. The Nazi *Weltanschauung* and the IG Farben-led drive for a closed European economic bloc merged naturally, and nowhere is such a fusion more likely to have taken place than in this SS-oriented group. Himmler was no friend to Schacht. Later he recalled at the dinner table that Schacht, besides being an accomplished liar, had never said 'Mein Führer!' when greeting Hitler, always 'Herr Chancellor!'[3] It seems likely that Himmler's industrial–financial supporters had arrived at a consensus in line with the IG Farben–electrochemical viewpoint and acted as a pressure group against Schacht's attempts to pursue conventional economic policies within the constraints of the world market. The penetration of this consensus is shown by the fact that the Dresdner Bank, formerly linked to US capital, was now committed to the goal of economic self-sufficiency. The key director, Karl Rasche, who worked with the Party to undermine Schacht's policy, was a member of the Freundeskreis.[4]

Imports of foodstuffs were as central to the question as raw materials for armaments. The allied 'hunger blockade' during the world war had left a deep scar on the nationalist psyche: it was credited with having so lowered the morale of the population as to have been a chief cause of the revolution of 1918. One of Hitler's fundamental arguments for conquering *Lebensraum* in the east was to acquire an agricultural base which would allow the Reich to be self-sufficient in foodstuffs and so able to withstand any future blockade by sea. When in the autumn of 1935 the distortions caused by rearmament and the shortage of foreign exchange combined with the results of a poor harvest to create a crisis in the pricing and supply of foodstuffs, it touched a raw nerve. Adequate food supplies for the *Volk* had to be preserved at all costs. Failure could result only in Bolshevism.

The autumn food scarcities were followed by a full-scale foreign-exchange crisis in the early summer of 1936, and brought the Schacht–Keppler, world-market versus economic self-sufficiency arguments to a head. Hitler decided in favour of Keppler. Instead of slowing down rearmament and paying some attention to profitability and market forces, he appointed Göring economic supremo of a Four Year Plan to step up rearmament and mobilise the economy for war – and in order to gain a short breathing space to set up a massive production programme for synthetic materials and place even stricter controls on imports. Göring, once representative of the heavy industrial Thyssen–Schacht axis, had come under the influence of IG Farben, the light industrialists and the Deutsche Bank largely through his responsibility for commercial and military aviation. The speed with which he had built up the Luftwaffe and the consequently prolific consumption of raw materials had brought him into conflict with Schacht – over foreign exchange – and the Army leadership – over allocation of resources – and turned him into a vigorous exponent of economic self-sufficiency. Hence his appointment.

The memorandum in which Hitler argued the Four Year Plan shows that it was intended as an interim solution only, to save foreign exchange for the purchase of foodstuffs until the time came to strike east for living space. The 'final solution' lay as it always had 'in an expansion of *Lebensraum*' to provide a sufficient 'raw-materials and foodstuffs base'.[5]

It was entirely in character that Hitler sought to meet the crisis by will power, advancing rather than retreating from the unalterable aims of the policy which had caused the crisis in the first place – namely rearmament for the conquest of *Lebensraum*. And since his arguments in the memorandum express ideological views identical to those in *Mein Kampf* and in his second book, and his speeches, it can be argued that the decision to increase the pace of rearmament, to put the economy on a controlled war footing and to take the first steps in decoupling Germany from the world market emanated from his ego, his will and his *Weltanschauung* more or less unaided – except perhaps by Göring's ambition.[6] Nevertheless, in its synthetics' production programme and its general economic aim of exploiting eastern Europe for the Reich within an independent economic bloc outside the US-dominated world economy, the plan might have been dictated by the experts of IG Farben. Hence it is possible to see it both ways: the bankers and industrialists had been brought into line (*gleichgeschaltet*) by the prospect of rich pickings in eastern Europe and the 'Aryanisation' of Jewish firms and were dancing to the Führer's pipe, or the now-dominant banking and industrial consensus, having achieved their aims in the suppression of the trade unions and the subordination of the workforce by the Party, were thrusting the Führer out ahead, as they had originally thrust him into power. Probably both views are aspects of the same phenomenon. Germany was on the march to avenge Versailles and take its promised place in the sun.

What is not in doubt is that the losers were the Schacht–Thyssen–US and British capital grouping and their allies in the Army leadership, the

Junker landowning class and the higher state officials, lumped together in Party jargon as the *Reaktion*. None of these groups opposed the goal of the policy – German hegemony in Europe from the Atlantic to the Urals – but all had reason to be alarmed at the radical means and their own loss of power to radical Party elements. An IG Farben – Reich Agricultural Ministry – SS consensus was a threat to the traditional landowners. The higher state officials from the same background who ran the administration and the foreign office under the present regime much as they had under the Hohenzollerns and the Weimar Republic were thoroughly alarmed by the financial and diplomatic irresponsibility of the new course. The Army leadership, the natural power support and hope for the *Reaktion*, was alarmed by the unpreparedness of the armed services to meet the early European war the policy seemed destined to provoke. Moreover they and the upper tiers of officialdom were profoundly disturbed by the way the SS had swollen to fill the revolutionary vacuum left by the SA, and was creating the seeds of a state within the state able to bypass official channels and act directly on the wishes of the Führer. The Army leaders were also deeply suspicious of Himmler's encroachment on the Army's preserve as sole arms-bearer of the nation, and were equally alarmed by Göring's take-over of the economy. Von Blomberg and the head of the Army Economics Department, General Georg Thomas, had fought side by side with Schacht against Göring's encroachments. Schacht's fall signified their own loss of control over the armament industries and economic mobilisation. It was symbolised in summer 1937 by the founding of the state-owned and -run mining, smelting and armaments complex, the Reichswerke Hermann Göring, which was to become a giant monument to national self-sufficiency.

Thus a loose 'opposition' had formed – not an opposition to rearmament or to the fight against Bolshevism or to the necessity to drive east and eventually claim the world, rather an opposition which disliked the encroachment of the Party and the 'Führer principle' of command into every sphere, and feared the wanton course on which the nation was embarked, stiffened here and there by those who were genuinely repelled by the amoral and brutish values being foisted on the nation.

This internal opposition turned naturally to the potential foreign opposition, chiefly American and British financial and diplomatic circles, in order to alert them and enlist their aid. One of the first emissaries was Karl Goerdeler, ex-Burgermeister of Leipzig and formerly Commissioner for Hitler's price control policy. He arrived in London in the early summer of 1937 and succeeded in impressing the Foreign Office official most strongly associated with anti-German sentiment, Sir Robert Vansittart, with the necessity to deal firmly with Hitler in order to weaken his grip on the nation and give the more liberal opposition elements their chance to depose him. Vansittart failed to convince the Foreign Secretary, Anthony Eden, who squashed Cabinet discussion. After London, Goerdeler continued his mission in the United States. Writing his 'Political Testament' in New York, he described Germany as being in 'a condition of outlawry, of moral decay, of economic fantasy and financial wantonness', and warned that the outside world had to expect 'every atrocity and every frightfulness. For National Socialism has masterfully deceived at least 80 per cent of the German people and much of the outside world.'[7]

It was, of course, Himmler's task to penetrate the opposition and keep its interlocking circles under surveillance. Precisely who his agents were is impossible to determine. Few from the opposition survived and those who did had good reason to lay false trails. The most likely suspect on the edge of the leading group formed in Canaris' staff in the Abwehr is the Chief of Criminal Police at the Ministry of the Interior, SS-Gruppenführer Arthur Nebe. He was a pure opportunist with no moral feelings about the regime or its methods – as demonstrated by his activities later in command of an extermination troop in the east. He had been one of Himmler's principal accomplices inside the Gestapo during the take-over struggle and there seems nothing in his modest background or his character to suggest why he should have decided to join the reactionaries – from a socially more elevated milieu – at the very time his patron, Himmler, and the Nazi message itself was in the ascendant.

Nebe was introduced to the head of the opposition group in the Abwehr, Major-General Hans Oster, by another of Himmler's accomplices in the take-over of the Gestapo, the legal officer Hans-Bernd Gisevius. After Himmler's take-over, Gisevius was transferred with Nebe to the Criminal Police Department of the Ministry of the Interior. He was one of the few to survive the war and much of the resistance legend comes from his post-war writings, according to which he and his friend and colleague, Arthur Nebe, belonged to Oster's network of informants about the activities of the police and the Gestapo. It is more likely that Nebe at least acted as a double agent for Himmler, feeding Oster selected material to work his way into the resistance.

It is even probable, as suggested earlier, that Canaris himself was one of Himmler's plants in the reactionary camp. There is no question of Canaris' loyalty to Hitler at this stage, nor of his extreme nationalist and anti-communist views and activity. Moreover as a naval officer and son of an industrialist he had no particular class or family ties to the gentlemen with uniforms and monocles. On the other hand he had a close personal relationship with Heydrich, and he attended at least one meeting of the Freundeskreis of industrialists as Himmler's personal guest. He was aware that, while Army leaders either venerated Hitler for what he had done for German pride and their own goals, or at least tolerated him, they despised and feared the revolutionary aims of the Party. He knew Oster as a particularly biting critic of the Party, who had gathered a circle of like-minded men in the Abwehr. According to his latest biographer, Heinz Höhne, he was, however, 'broad-minded (and careless) enough to let Oster carry on in his own way'.[8] It may be, as Lina Heydrich asserted,

Heinrich Himmler as a child,
with his elder brother,
Gebhard, and their parents.

The Himmler family during the latter part of the First World War. *From left:* Frau
Himmler, Ernst, Professor Himmler, Heinrich, Gebhard.

The twenty-three-year-old Himmler carries the Imperial Ensign for Ernst Röhm's Reichskriegsflagge during the 'Beer Hall Putsch' of 1923. 'One could see how secure the flag felt in his hands and how proud he was of it. I go up to him, incapable of speaking a word . . .' (Mariele Rauschmayer).

Himmler after his appointment as
Reichsführer-SS, 1929.

Nazi leaders with the Munich area Army
Commander, General Ritter von Epp, in
1930. *Front row from left:* Himmler, Frick,
Hitler, von Epp, Göring. *Second row:*
Mutschmann, Goebbels, Schaub; in the
doorway is Dr Fritsch.

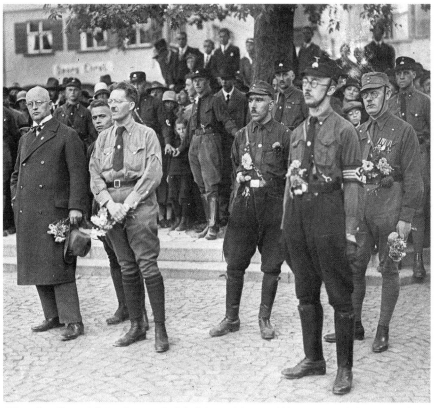

Himmler *(front right)* as Deputy Reichsführer with two of his men, providing protection
for a street meeting addressed by the Nazi Party Treasurer, Franz Xavier Schwarz.

Göring, establishing his own Political Police in Prussia (Gestapo), appoints the shaven-headed Himmler as Chief of Bavarian Political Police, April 1933.

Wilhelm Canaris, famed chief of the Abwehr (military intelligence and counter-intelligence), here as a naval commander in his younger days.

After the *Machtergreifung*, 1933. Hitler and Göring in the centre, Himmler beside them *(right)*; *back row:* Goebbels *(fourth from left),* Röhm *(centre)*; Darré, Hess *(right)*.

'Der treue Heinrich' stands at the shoulder of his superior, SA Chief of Staff Ernst Röhm, in 1933.

Himmler's former chief, Gregor Strasser, murdered, like Röhm, in the bloody purge of 30 June 1934.

After the purge of Röhm, Strasser and other 'enemies of the State', Göring and Himmler share a joke with Hitler, 1934.

Himmler with his wife Marga and daughter Gudrun at Kassel airport, 1935. A few paces behind is 'Wölffchen', with his wife Frieda and their daughter.

The rivals: Heydrich *(standing, left)* reports to Himmler, 1938; Karl Wolff *(standing, right)* listens.

The devoted father with Gudrun ('Puppi'), 1938.

Himmler addresses guards during an inspection of Dachau concentration camp, 1938.

Himmler and, a pace or so behind, Heydrich in Vienna after the Anschluss, March 1938.

that Canaris was simply a born intriguer, who played a double game for its own sake. On the other hand, if he wished to keep himself intimately informed of the generals' opinions, he could have chosen no better way than to encourage and appear to support Oster. The subsequent retreat of the generals before Hitler and the successive failures of the opposition are easier to account for on the assumption that he was working in concert with Himmler and Heydrich against internal as well as external enemies of the regime than on the assumption that he was simply broad-minded and careless in his attitude towards the dissidents within his own organisation.

This is especially so in the celebrated affair of von Blomberg and von Fritsch – respectively Minister of Defence and Army Commander-in-Chief – and Hitler's take-over of supreme command of the armed forces. The conventional version of the story starts with a meeting Hitler called on 5 November 1937 to explain his strategy to his service chiefs; the meeting is usually known after the name of his adjutant, Colonel Hossbach, who took notes. Attending were von Blomberg and von Fritsch, Göring as Commander-in-Chief of the Air Force, Admiral Raeder as Commander-in-Chief of the Navy, and the Foreign Minister, von Neurath. Hitler harangued them for over four hours, starting with his usual premises about Germany's need for *Lebensraum*, then outlining his programme for attaining it in two stages, first 'in foreseeable time' the incorporation of Austria and Czechoslovakia into the German Reich and the drive to overrun eastern Europe, next colonies overseas and 'world power'. It appears he had given up hope of winning England over to his design – which is not surprising since he had kicked over the pro-US and British capital grouping the previous year – for he told them that German policy had to reckon with 'two hate enemies, England and France', who would not welcome a German colossus in the middle of Europe.[9] Reminding them, nevertheless, of the huge risks Frederick the Great and Bismarck had run in the cause of German greatness, he declared his intention of solving the *Lebensraum* question at the latest by 1943–5. By then German rearmament would be approaching completion with modern weapons. After that period the situation could only change to Germany's disadvantage as their enemies' rearmament caught up. A solution before this period could be expected, however, if foreign political circumstances appeared favourable, possibly as early as next year, 1938.

The world view he outlined, with the western colonial powers England and France regarding Germany with jealous eyes and determined to stunt her growth by preventing her access to world trade, if necessary instituting another hunger blockade, conformed to the German naval view in which Raeder had been indoctrinated from his earliest days at sea. When Hitler promised him an increase in his steel quota from 40,000 to 75,000 tons and assured him that he would not involve him in a war with Great Britain before 1943, he appeared satisfied. Von Blomberg, von Fritsch and von Neurath, however, did not believe that Great Britain and France would stand by idly and allow them to carry out the preliminary expansion of the Reich into Austria and Czechoslovakia. According to the accepted story it was their remarks at this meeting which showed Hitler how much they distrusted his reckless forward policy. If so, he was badly informed about the attitude of the *Reaktion*.

In the light of his invariable method of dealing with men who were not prepared to submerge all critical faculties before his genius, the 'Hossbach' meeting is more likely to have been one stage in a scheme to isolate elements he already wished to dispose of, and tempt them into an exposed position from which they could be picked off. The timing was probably connected with plans to incorporate Austria into the Reich. Von Blomberg had proved unreliable during the march into the demilitarised zone of the Rhineland in defiance of treaty terms the previous year. Fearful of an impending French attack which the German forces had no prospect of withstanding, he had repeatedly urged retreat. Perhaps Hitler needed a completely reliable Army leadership for the march into Austria. More probably it was the other way about. The favourable foreign political constellation, in particular the increasingly close ties with Mussolini, which allowed him to plan the take-over of Austria was seen as the moment to deal with the potentially dangerous centre of resistance to his regime in the Army High Command – as before he had dealt with Stennes, Strasser, von Schleicher and Röhm – and impose the Führer principle on this reactionary power base.

His chief fellow conspirators were once again Göring and Himmler. Göring had ambitions to take over from von Blomberg as War Minister; Himmler deployed the SD and SS, as in all previous 'solutions', as respectively the general staff and the unconditionally loyal guard of the Führer. Heydrich was once again in charge of the detailed planning, of both the external strike against Austria and the internal strike against the Army leadership. He appears to have been aided by extraordinary luck. Both von Blomberg and von Fritsch seem to have delivered themselves without resistance into his hands. But it is equally possible to see their downfall as the result of his shrewd assessment of their individual weaknesses.

Von Blomberg – a handsome widower and known ladies' man – was destroyed by his marriage to a girl who was found afterwards, so it was alleged, to have been a prostitute. She was a stenotypist named Erna Gruhn, whose mother had once run a dubious 'massage parlour'. The circumstances of her meeting with von Blomberg make it entirely possible that she was planted on him: while the War Minister was convalescing at a hotel in Thuringia the hotel manager, apparently thinking he looked lonely on his own at dinner, asked if he would like an introduction to one of the young lady guests. Thus he became acquainted with Fräulein Gruhn, soon his mistress. He grew so fond of her that he asked Göring what the Führer would think if he were to marry her – he a noble and the first soldier in the Reich, she an ordinary girl of the people. Göring was shortly able to tell him that nothing would delight the Führer more; it would be a public demonstration of the new classlessness of society. That was Wolff's story.[10] Like most of his stories it is possibly true but probably truer if turned round 180 degrees. One of von Blomberg's nicknames was 'Hitler Youth Quex' – after the enthusiastic young hero of a propaganda film – and it is far more likely that Göring planted in his mind the idea of the Führer's pleasure if he were to marry the girl. Frau von Blomberg told Edouard Calic that Göring had suggested to her husband in December 1937 that he might like to legalise the affair with his young secretary.[11] Perhaps he added that, since she was of good Aryan stock, he would be setting a splendid example to the *Volk*. Göring did not think in these terms but his allies Himmler and Heydrich undoubtedly did. However that may be, Hitler and Göring both appeared to think so well of the match that they agreed to be marriage witnesses at the wedding, which was fixed for 12 January 1938.

Another strand of Wolff's post-war account is that von Blomberg's naval adjutant, von Friedeberg, suggested discreet enquiries be made with the police about his future bride. Why is not clear, but Gisevius has a story about a young lover of Fräulein Gruhn who drew attention to her past; Göring caused him to be posted to South America.[12] According to Wolff, von Friedeberg found himself posted to Kiel before the police had replied to his enquiries. These stories would not be worth the mention were it not for the fact that von Friedeberg was later on very close terms with Himmler. In any case, the marriage took place. The Defence Minister departed on his honeymoon, and then by chance a criminal police official named Hellmuth Müller was handed a file of pornographic photographs for reproduction for records. They showed a girl named on the back as 'Gruhn, Erna Margarethe'. Müller was sure he had recently heard that name . . .[13]

It is unnecessary to detail the rest of the preposterous story hatched after the war to explain how Müller discovered that Erna Gruhn had a record for soliciting in a public place and theft in conjunction with sexual intercourse and hurried to offload the dynamite on his chief, Arthur Nebe; how the white-faced Nebe – 'Good God, Müller, and the Führer kissed that woman's hand!'[14] – instead of telling his own chief, Heydrich, hurried to the Berlin Police President, Graf Helldorf, who had the inspiration of asking von Blomberg's colleague, General Wilhelm Keitel, whether the Erna Gruhn in the photographs and von Blomberg's new lady were one and the same; and how Keitel, who had not seen her, suggested that Helldorf ask Göring. It is unnecessary because it is a childish fabrication. Probably there were such photographs. According to Müller's post-war explanation the girl in the pictures was wearing pearls – nothing more, but suggestive; for it would have been easy for Heydrich's SD experts to create a photo-montage with the face and neck of Blomberg's new wife superimposed above the pearls on another body below. However that may be, had Nebe sidestepped Heydrich by going to Helldorf and then Göring with the pictures it would have cost him his job and almost certainly his life. He could have done so only under instructions from Heydrich. The reason for the instructions was to spread rumours in the Army High Command to undermine von Blomberg's position before the actual dénouement. Keitel was the conduit to the officer corps; Göring was the agreed line to Hitler.

When the 'shocked' Göring took the file on Erna Gruhn to the Reich Chancellery to show it to Hitler on his return from the Obersalzberg, he took another file with him, also prepared by the criminal police in collaboration with the vice department. This showed that in November 1933 von Fritsch had indulged in a homosexual act with a professional male prostitute in a dark corner of the Berlin Wannsee railway station. The charge rested on the depositions of a professional blackmailer named Otto Schmidt, who had been caught two years after the incident during Himmler's drive against homosexuals. It was a framed charge, resting on a similarity of names. The man Schmidt had seen at the Wannsee station was a retired officer with a monocle named von Frisch, but it was not difficult for the Gestapo to convince Schmidt that he should implicate General von Fritsch. So Hitler had the ammunition with which to ask for the resignations of both his Defence Minister and his Army Commander-in-Chief. He did so two days later on 26 January. Von Blomberg agreed to go, but von Fritsch protested his innocence, and Hitler had his file sent to the Reich Minister of Justice, Dr Gürtner.

It is typical of Heydrich's method that whispering campaigns preceded the resolution of his intrigues. In this case towards the end of January 1938 there was every possible scope with both senior soldiers of the Reich implicated in scandals which, if made public, would sully the sacred honour of the officer corps. On the other hand von Fritsch's papers were with the Justice Minister, who had long been fighting a losing battle with Himmler. He could be expected to try and use them against the Gestapo, for it was not difficult to conclude that both generals had been 'framed' by Himmler and Heydrich, especially perhaps as Goerdeler and others had been warning the Army leadership for months of the danger of an SS coup.[15]

A group including Schacht, Goerdeler and Gisevius, supplied with information by the police officials Arthur Nebe and Graf Helldorf, and by Dr Gürtner's personal adviser Dr Johannes von Dohnanyi, who had been gathering a dossier on SS murders and brutalities in concentration camps, joined with Oster at the Abwehr to try to push the Army leadership into a pre-emptive strike against Gestapo headquarters in Berlin. When they found von Fritsch and his Chief of Staff, Beck, and other senior officers unwilling or perhaps unable to think in terms of 'mutiny and revolution',[16] they turned to regional Army commanders. As might have been expected, they proved equally reluctant without a directive from Berlin. Admiral Raeder also turned them down. He had been bought off with the increased steel enabling him to dream of a gigantic – in real terms fantastic – fleet to break out of the grip of the Royal Navy and launch Germany on her world-oceanic destiny.

It is as impossible now as it must have been then to disentangle truth from rumour and the deliberate disinformation inspired by Heydrich. However, if one examines two key figures, on the one hand Arthur Nebe, the most important defector from the enemy camp, on the other hand Canaris, chief of intelligence in the Army camp, the suspicion emerges that both were playing a double game on behalf of the conspirators against the Army leadership and the opposition in general.

Canaris and Beck had been opponents for some time. Canaris, as a convinced National Socialist and adherent of the Führer principle, supported a new Wehrmacht command structure introduced by von Blomberg and von Reichenau to realise the Führer principle in the armed services. Its core was a Wehrmachtamt whose purpose was to co-ordinate and eventually control the three largely autonomous fighting services. It was staffed by young officers enthused by the Hitler cult and devoted to developing new forms of organisation and leadership on National Socialist principles, and it had already acquired so many functions it was referred to as the Oberkommando der Wehrmacht – OKW – or Armed Services High Command.[17] Beck, as Chief of the General Staff of the Army, traditionally the premier military power in the land, naturally opposed the new department, which encroached on his domain and threatened his influence and his ambitions to become principal military adviser to the Führer, and in war operational commander of the armed forces as a whole.

Beck also clashed with Canaris in the intelligence field. He placed less reliance on Abwehr reports than on information from his military attachés abroad and he sought new sources outside the Abwehr network. To add to the tension between the two, they were by temperament and conviction poles apart – Beck an ultra-conservative and naturally pessimistic critic of Hitler's high-risk economic and diplomatic policies, Canaris at this stage at least an enthusiastic supporter of Hitler who could describe a unified Wehrmacht imbued with the Führer principle as 'the strongest manifestation of the National Socialist will to power'.[18] It is probably also relevant that Canaris came from the parvenu service, the Navy, a stronghold of National Socialism from the earliest days, whose grand ambitions seemed about to be realised under the Führer.

In the Blomberg–Fritsch crisis, one of the extraordinary aspects of Canaris' role is his apparent lack of all prior knowledge. His Abwehr Department III was responsible for counter-espionage in the armed services, arms- and munitions-producing firms and government departments. The chief of the department, Major Rudolf Bamler, had a network of informants throughout the Reich similar to the network deployed by the SD, and he worked closely with Heydrich and the Gestapo. Yet at the time that Göring was wresting control of armaments production from the Army's ally, Schacht, and concentrating all economic power in his own hands against the interests of the Army Economics Department under General Thomas – thus at the time the Party and the Party-oriented financial groupings were triumphing over the Army and the conservatives – at a time when von Fritsch and Beck were fighting back against the Führer principle as it applied to military strategy and Goerdeler was warning the Army of an impending SS coup, and the lover of von Blomberg's future wife was being despatched to South America, and von Blomberg's adjutant, von Friedeberg, was being posted to Kiel, Canaris, the master spy, is supposed to have been taken entirely by surprise.

He was in Spain when von Blomberg married Fräulein Gruhn and although he returned to Berlin on 22 January he did not learn the facts of the case against her until the 27th, the day after the Defence Minister's dismissal. His informant was Gisevius, whose source was Nebe.[19] The next day, 28 January, amid the confusion of rumours, Hitler informed General Keitel, chief of the OKW – the former Wehrmachtamt created expressly as an instrument of the Führer principle – that he (Hitler) would take over von Blomberg's responsibilities as Supreme Commander himself, and he asked Keitel to remain as his Chief of Staff. Hitler went on to say that von Fritsch would also have to go because of offences against morality; the papers were with the Justice Ministry. Keitel, who did not consider 'deserting his Führer in his hour of need', informed his department heads, then told Canaris, with whom – unlike Beck – he was on the closest and most trusting terms. A bare recital of these facts suggests that Canaris was an accomplice in the move to shift aside the traditionalist Army leadership represented by von Fritsch and Beck – who was now left in limbo – in order to bring the OKW into play in the role for which it had been designed originally, and which he approved, as conduit for Führer commands. The alternative is that he and his Department III chief, Bamler – in contrast to Oster a believer in National Socialism – were thoroughly incompetent, indeed asleep.

Nebe's role is, if anything, more dubious. As chief of the Criminal Police, whose officials were, according to the accepted version, responsible for preparing the files on both Erna Gruhn and von Fritsch, he was aware of the pending crisis for the Army leadership some time before Canaris returned from Spain and Hitler returned from the Obersalzberg. Yet he transmitted the information about von Fritsch, again via Gisevius – this time to Oster – on the 28th, after Hitler had told Keitel that von Fritsch would have to go. In short, according to the accepted version in which Nebe was acting as an informant for the opposition, both his warnings came days after he himself knew of the threat, after the blows had fallen and far too late to be useful or even news. The only reasonable explanation is that he was working his passage into Oster's circle of the opposition as Heydrich's plant. Subsequently he assisted Canaris in investigations to uncover the real von Frisch, who had committed the indecent act in the dark corner of Wannsee station. Thus Canaris was able to prove his own – and Nebe's – energy and enthusiasm in support of the Army against the machinations of the Gestapo.

Alas, it was too late. Hitler had taken over the Wehrmacht; Keitel and his OKW were loyal to him; von Fritsch was in disgrace on indefinite leave pending the findings of a Reich court of honour – convened eventually with Göring as president – and before Canaris could prove von Fritsch's innocence and the false witness, Schmidt, could be made the scapegoat for the whole affair by being forced to admit he had lied, Hitler had taken over Austria. With this triumph on top of his previous record of success against the 'Versailles powers', he was unassailable. Von Fritsch could be satisfied that his honour was cleared, but neither he, not Beck, nor Oster had any chance of instigating an Army putsch against the regime.

For all the subsequent discussion of missed opportunities, the traditionalist Army leadership never had a chance. It was like a venerable tree, presenting a magnificent, unchanging outward appearance, but rotted away at the core, and ready to come crashing down in a gale. The lower ranks contained many officers who accepted the Hitler cult. The OKW was a germ cell of National Socialism within the War Ministry. Moreover the Navy and the Air Force were pro-Hitler. Von Fritsch and Beck and Thomas were isolated long before the intrigue which brought home their impotence. In any case their background, the whole Prusso-German military ethic, made it unlikely that they would or could plan and stage a revolt against the head of state to whom they had pledged their oath of allegiance. The intrigue itself was a skilful blend of falsehood and innuendo grounded on the characteristics of the victims. It was possible to imagine that von Fritsch, a bachelor, might have had the tendencies alleged. He had befriended two Hitler Youths and had been in the habit of instructing them in history and geography, punishing inattention by striking their bare calfs with a ruler, a fetish which Heydrich's agents had picked up. Fräulein Gruhn's mother did have a dubious past. So the ground had been cut from under and around the victims and they had been left suspended in uncertainty tinged with guilt and surrounded by Heydrich's inspired rumours while changes in the structure of the High Command were put through without them.

Meanwhile Heydrich's *provocateurs* joined members of the conservative opposition in inciting Oster and senior generals to stage a coup on their behalf. Had they done so Himmler would have had the evidence he needed to act against them as traitors. As it was a number of senior officers showed their political unreliability and on 5 February, when Hitler formally announced the retirement of von Blomberg and von Fritsch on health grounds, he retired sixteen other generals and transferred over forty to different commands. At the same time he announced that the OKW – under General Keitel – would assume the responsibilities of the War Ministry, and he himself would take over as Supreme Commander of the Wehrmacht. It was as complete a victory as 30 June 1934, without any of the blood and evil publicity of that coup; it had equally profound consequences: the stronghold of establishment opposition had been emasculated and brought under the Führer principle. Keitel's nickname was, or soon became, 'Lakaitel' – meaning lackey. The man appointed to succeed von Fritsch as Commander-in-Chief, von Brauchitsch, was little better able to stand up to Hitler. In any case the chain of command had been altered decisively against him and Beck. The Army was no longer master in its own house and no longer provided a unified centre of resistance to the Party and the SS. On the contrary – if the analysis of the intrigue given here is correct – one of the most profound consequences for the opposition was that Oster's circle had been entered by Nebe, Helldorf and probably other agents of Himmler and Heydrich, while Canaris, by his support for Oster and his energy in working with Nebe to uncover von Frisch and save von Fritsch's honour, had established his own credentials in the opposition – credentials which fifty years later he still retains.

Schacht had asked Hitler's permission to resign as Minister of Economics at the end of August 1937 since, he wrote, 'the fundamental differences in our economic policies are insurmountable.'[20] Hitler let him go at the end of November that year. Now he appointed in his place Walther Funk, whose economic views were precisely in line with Keppler's, and who in any case entirely lacked the strength of character necessary to stand up to him or to the real economic dictator, Göring. At the same time von Neurath was replaced as Foreign Minister by the amateur England expert von Ribbentrop, and three ambassadors of the traditional school in Vienna, Rome and Tokyo were replaced by more committed men.

The secret SD situation report for the leadership at the end of that year drew attention to these personnel changes of 5 February as the most important internal political event of 1938, which had been interpreted by the conservatives – termed the Rechtsbewegung, or rightist movement – as a 'blow in the face'. The extent of SD penetration into the various groups of the opposition is suggested by the sentence 'The future plans for opposition nourished in many connections in these circles were thwarted.'[21]

Göring's reward for his part in the successful intrigue was promotion to field marshal and senior military officer of the Reich. Himmler's reward was the vengeance he had taken on those elements who opposed his military ambitions for the SS, and the knowledge that he would now be able to increase the Verfügungstruppe and the Totenkopfverbände. His bad conscience over the affair is shown by an incident which took place a few weeks afterwards. He and Wolff ran into von Blomberg unexpectedly in the Hotel Vier Jahreszeiten in Munich. 'What do we do now?' he asked in dismay. Wolff suggested acting as if nothing had happened; that, as it turned out, was the correct course, for von Blomberg greeted them genially, apparently still unaware of the machinations behind his downfall.[22] Von Fritsch had no illusions about Himmler's involvement; according to Wolff he kept silent because he had been threatened with proceedings for 'calf-fetishism' if he talked.[23] At the start of the war he took an early opportunity to find death on the battlefield.

Preparations for the annexation of Austria were under way at the time the problems of the Army leadership and Foreign Ministry were brought to a successful 'solution'. As mentioned, Heydrich's officials in SD headquarters at 102 Wilhelmstrasse were working round the clock in three shifts to complete the details for the huge, circular punched-card personnel index on Austria. Wilhelm Keppler was shuttling to Vienna as chief liaison with the underground Austrian Nazis. He kept them in line with the overall plan worked out by Heydrich's general staff through control of their funding which came largely through the SS and the Freundeskreis.[24] As an indication of the extent of financial involvement in the plans, as early as 1937 Keppler was working with Emil Meyer and Dr Karl Rasche, the representatives of the Dresdner Bank in the Freundeskreis, to 'Aryanise' – or free from Jews – the affiliated Austrian Mercur-Bank.[25] The Aryanisation of banks and industrial concerns – well under way in Germany itself – was an important strand of the strategy for taking over the Austrian and Czechoslovak economies for the German war effort.[26]

The 'solution to the Austrian problem' was worked out with a mixture of internal penetration and subversion, military threat and verbal bullying. What is notable in view of the changes in the Army High Command and organisation that immediately preceded it is the smooth liaison between Himmler and the OKW in the integration with Army mobilisation of SS infantry and motorised regiments, Totenkopf formations and police. Equally notable is Canaris' co-operation. When, on 13 February, nine days after the purge of the generals, Hitler instructed Keitel to exert military pressure on Austria, Keitel immediately called Canaris in. Canaris made various proposals for shamming military preparations by disseminating false reports via agents and border personnel, and Keitel phoned them through to Hitler the same day. Hitler approved them and instructed Canaris to take personal charge of the operation – which he did with gusto. It was the game he loved best. Later, while waiting at Munich airport with his department chief for south-east Europe, Major Pruck, he happened to catch sight of Heydrich's right-hand man, Dr Werner Best, head of the legal and administrative departments of the SD. To Pruck's astonishment – so he said after the war – Canaris not only started talking to Best, but sat with him throughout the flight to Berlin, describing every detail of the campaign of deception he had just initiated.[27] Why this should have surprised Pruck is not clear: Canaris, Heydrich and Best took regular morning rides together in Berlin.

To anyone viewing the preparations for Austrian Anschluss without knowledge of the post-war legends about Canaris and the German resistance to Hitler, the whole sequence of events starting with the dismissals of von Blomberg and von Fritsch would point to the conclusion that Himmler, Heydrich, Canaris and Keitel had been joined in a common purpose from the beginning – to bring the Army into line as a pure expression of the Führer's will in time for the planned incorporation of Austria. The fact that the planning for both internal and external intrigues was being carried out at the same time under the same team led by Heydrich at SD headquarters would indicate the same conclusion. Perhaps this is too simple a *post hoc* view, but perhaps the obvious explanation should not be despised because it is so simple.

Himmler was intimately concerned with the Anschluss since it was his task to carry out the cleansing and disciplining of the population in Austria – *Gleichschaltung* – as he had in Germany, also because he controlled the underground Austrian SS under Ernst Kaltenbrunner which represented the chief internal threat to the government. The unfortunate Austrian Chancellor, Kurt von Schuschnigg, was squeezed between the prospect of a violent putsch from within or compliance with a demand backed by threats from Hitler that he hand over his Interior Ministry – thus the police – to the pro-Nazi Minister, Seyss-Inquart. This was bound to lead to a Nazi take-over by the back door after the pattern of the earlier Hitler–von Papen administration in Germany. Schuschnigg made a valiant attempt to shake free by appealing to the people in a snap referendum only five days ahead to decide whether they wanted union with Germany. Hitler reacted swiftly by ordering a real (as opposed to the previous sham) mobilisation for an invasion of Austria on Saturday, 12 March – the day before the referendum was due to be held – then began raising the pressure via Seyss-Inquart, Keppler, the German military attaché in Vienna and Göring down the telephone line from Berlin. The final demands were for Schuschnigg's resignation and Seyss-Inquart's appointment as Chancellor. Otherwise the German Army would invade. Meanwhile Nazis throughout Austria were mobilised to demonstrate and seize public buildings. Shortly before midnight on 11 March the Austrian President agreed to Seyss-Inquart's appointment. Instead of calling off the invasion, due to begin in a few hours' time, Hitler instructed his forces to go ahead, adding, 'It is in our interests that the whole undertaking proceed without the use of force in the form of a peaceful entry march greeted by the people.' However, any resistance was to be broken ruthlessly by force of arms.[28]

Canaris had alerted his network of *Spannungs* – or 'tension-period' – agents throughout Europe. Their duty was to report any signs of mobilisation, and he waited with his staff at Abwehr headquarters for their messages. Those from England and France were naturally the most critical. Hitler himself took care of the other possible source of interference, Italy, with a direct appeal to Mussolini. Himmler concentrated on Austria. He was wearing a new-style SS uniform that was to become standard for foreign ventures, not in the distinctive black with silver trim, but in the traditional Army field-grey. Wolff, Heydrich, Daluege, other senior officials with him and his escort commando of armed Verfügungstruppe – and along the border the SS regiments waiting to cross with the Army – wore the same field-grey, another indication that the operation had not been hurriedly stitched together in the five days since Schuschnigg called the referendum. Donning field-grey again must have been a significant moment for Himmler. He must also have felt some considerable apprehension: this was his first taste of real active service, and the situation appeared fluid up until almost the last moment.

He was waiting with his entourage at the Prinz Albrecht Strasse headquarters; on receiving reports of Schuschnigg's capitulation he and his small staff and escort commando sped to Tempelhof aerodrome, where two Junkers Ju-52 transport aircraft were waiting. They flew to Munich, where further reports indicated that Seyss-Inquart and Kaltenbrunner, whom he had appointed Police Minister, had the security situation in hand; they took off again for Vienna, landing at the commercial airport at five in the morning of the 12th. A reception committee headed by Schuschnigg's former Police Minister was waiting respectfully, and after Himmler had inspected a police guard of honour his party was driven in to the capital in an official convoy. He took over the Hotel Regina for himself and his staff, the Hotel Metropole for use as Gestapo headquarters, then almost immediately left with Wolff to travel by car back towards the border to meet Hitler entering with the Army – a remarkable indication of his confidence in the control Seyss-Inquart and Kaltenbrunner had achieved only a few hours after the official climb-down by the Austrian President. It was not misplaced. The German troops were met with joyous demonstrations as they marched in, and he and Wolff had no difficulty in joining Hitler before he made an emotional home-coming to his boyhood town, Linz.

To be with his Führer at this momentous time was important to Himmler. Although an 'old fighter' from the 'time of struggle', he was not in Hitler's intimate circle, and needed to bring himself to attention at every opportunity. Emotionally, he needed to drink at the fountainhead of power; politically, in the Byzantine atmosphere which Hitler created around himself, he needed to impress the leader with his contribution, and especially in this case when he had personally penetrated the hostile citadel ahead of the Army, and left it in the charge of his officers. He wore field-grey, and his chief rival, Göring, was in Berlin.

The following day he and Wolff were in Hitler's entourage as the Führer visited the grave of his parents, and again the next day, 14 March, as Hitler made his triumphal entry into Vienna, then spoke from the balcony of the ancient palace of the Habsburgs to enthusiastic crowds below. Canaris was also present to experience this historic moment which, as he expressed it in a lecture scarcely more than a month afterwards, 'uplifted every German heart . . . one nation, one Reich, one Führer.'[29]

By this time Austrian communists, monarchists and other ideological opposition leaders were disappearing into *Schutzhaft* as their German counterparts had after the *Machtergreifung* in Germany, and Austrian SA and SS men enrolled as auxiliary police were unleashing pent-up pack brutality on their hated enemies, the Jews. Jews were forced on their knees to scrub the pavements and made to clean out lavatories with praying-bands. Most of the opposition leaders were sent to concentration camps in Germany; a few especially important ones were locked up in the servants' quarters in the attics of the Hotel Metropole, now Gestapo headquarters. One of these was Louis Freiherr von Rothschild, head of the Vienna branch of the great banking family. Wolff had a story about Himmler's first visit to him. Apparently confused by Rothschild's appearance, which did not conform to his image of a Jew, his bright blue eyes and the cool way he was regarding him, Himmler said stupidly, 'Do you know who I am?' Rothschild replied with his name and rank.[30] Himmler inspected the garret and gave instructions for new furniture and a new lavatory seat and basin to be provided.

After the war Wolff was at pains to suggest that he had assisted Dr Kurt Rasche of the Dresdner Bank in obtaining Rothschild's release against the machinations of Heydrich, who wanted to extort millions in ransom. The facts are that Dr Rasche was negotiating with the Rothschild family on behalf of Göring, offering Louis von Rothschild's freedom in exchange for the return of his assets from London, where he had transferred them to protect them from a Nazi take-over. No doubt Rasche had to talk to Wolff since Rothschild was Himmler's prisoner. Rasche brought the negotiation to a successful conclusion, thus gaining entry into a substantial section of Austrian and Czechoslovak banking and industry. With other confiscations achieved by Aryanisation, this was integrated via the Reichswerke Hermann Göring into the Four Year Plan.

Before leaving Austria, which was incorporated as an SS administrative district under the old name, Ostmark, Himmler looked for a site for a new concentration camp which would further his own economic enterprise, the German Earth- and Stone-work Company. He found it on slopes above stone quarries near the Danube village of Mauthausen and gave instructions for the area to be levelled and enclosed with walls and guard towers for the characteristically rectilinear-pattern camp pioneered at Dachau. A labour detachment was sent from Dachau to begin the work.

He could be confident there would be no shortage of inmates when it was completed. For the moment, the Austrian opposition to union with Hitler's Reich had been overwhelmed by the surprise achieved and the sheer speed and efficiency of Heydrich's measures against the leaders and their organisations, but there were no illusions in the SD about the extent of the potential resistance when the Austrian nationalists and monarchists and the communists regrouped. Within the former circles the most significant movement was the 'Legitimacy', comprised almost entirely of nobles, officers and a portion of the clergy. The aim of the movement was to recreate an Austrian middle-European empire under the slogan of 'a supranational community of different peoples guaranteeing justice and peace' and ruled by the Habsburg heir, Otto von Habsburg. The movement had ties to the *Reaktion* in Germany, especially to those monarchists and Catholics in Bavaria who still dreamed of a south German–Austrian – and perhaps Polish – Catholic federation separated from the Protestant north. However, in Himmler's and Heydrich's minds the Austrian rightist groups were funded and guided by the international Jewish conspiracy: as it was expressed in the SD review of 1938, 'the universal ring stands over the external national or patriotic camouflage'. Otto von Habsburg, it continued, had taken up residence in Paris 'where he works with the newly formed *Volksfront* of Emigrant Austrians to agitate under the slogan "Jewish–Clerical–Legitimate" '. This work, the report continued, was financed almost exclusively from Jewish capital, mainly from Holland.[31]

Of the many Austrians arrested by Heydrich's teams in the wake of the Anschluss and transferred to Dachau, one, Maximilian Reich, has described an inspection by Himmler shortly after their arrival.[32] The prisoners had been paraded on the *Appelplatz* for him.

'Austrians!' he had begun. 'You know you are guarded here as prisoners in protective custody [*Schutzhaftlingen*]. That is to say we want to do everything to grant you protection—'

The guards about him shook with laughter.

'There are several kinds of *Schutzhaftlingen*,' he went on. 'First the professional criminals who have committed a small murder, a small break-in or something of that sort. These are really the most decent *Schutzhaftlingen*. The second group consists of political prisoners. This is a more evil company and we want to bestow on *you* our special protection—'

Again he was interrupted by laughter and applause from his entourage.

'Then comes the third group. It represents the refuse of humanity, the carrion of our social life, bloodsuckers, exploiters – in short, Jews.'

The applause from around him was more boisterous than ever.

'And if I say there is still a fourth group,' he went on, 'which considered from a human standpoint comes far beneath even the Jews, I can spare myself any further characterisation of this rabble – they are the communists.'

That ended his address. He began inspecting the ranks of his prisoners. Each one he stopped before was required to give his name and occupation; usually Himmler returned some ironic remark drawing laughs from his escort. He stopped before Maximilian Reich and it was then, as Reich gazed into the eyes behind the glittering pince-nez, that he recalled a buzzard he had seen once toying with a mouse in its clutch, apparently enjoying its distress.

The acquisition of more and more enemies was a natural product of Hitler's success. In its turn it made the threat of the world conspiracy against Germany appear even more real, the National Socialist message more relevant, the need for indivisible unity behind the Führer more necessary. In the summer of 1938, Himmler spelled this out before several classes of the National Socialist schools for political education (NAPOLA).

We as a *Volk* of 75 million are, despite our great numbers, a minority
in the world. We have very, very many against us, as you yourselves as
National Socialists know very well. All capital, the whole of Jewry, the whole of
freemasonry, all the democrats and philistines of the world, all the Bolshevism of
the world, all the Jesuits of the world, and not least all the peoples who regret not
having completely killed us off in 1918, and who make only one vow: if we once
get Germany in our hands again it won't be another 1918, it will be the end.[33]

The chief principle of unity and strength against this world of enemies
was, of course, the blood. Now that the expansion of the Reich had
begun, Himmler set up a new department, the SS Ergänzungsamt –
literally Replenishment Office – to systematise the acquisition of the good
blood he intended drawing into the SS from every area conquered. The
present SS recruiting system in the Reich did not satisfy him, and he had
been pondering the problem for some time, as he wrote in a memorandum
outlining the tasks of the new department.[34]

The first necessity was to find out how many racially suitable inhabitants
there were in each area from which general SS – as opposed to specialised
Verfügungstruppe or Totenkopf *Standarten* were drawn. The areas should
be arranged so that each *Standarte* had approximately the same reservoir of
racially good stock. Then it was the duty of the chief of the Ergänzungsamt
'in personal discussion with the district, sub-district and *Standarten* Führers'
to encourage them to 'find, seek out and gain for the SS individually valuable
young men'. Each *Standarte* was to have its own recruiting desk.

Only in this way will it be possible really to unite in the SS the best
blood-nobility of the German *Volk*. In this activity it is incumbent on the
Standartenführer as well as the recruiting desk personnel to be acquainted
with every individual locality, so that one knows: in the places a, b, c the
population is of eastern, wendish, mongolian type, so that there is no question
of us recruiting there. On the other hand places d, e, f have a mixed population,
thus one could draw some men from there for the SS. Then again in places x, y
pure Germanic farmers are gathered, thus an area in which one can recruit to a
significant extent.[35]

He was in competition with the other armed forces for young men,
and the chief immediate task of the Ergänzungsamt was to spearhead and
co-ordinate a drive to ensure that as many of those valuable youngsters who
qualified for the SS were not lost to the other arms. His remarks on this
point reinforce the impression that he was using the Totenkopfverbände
as a backdoor way of augmenting the numbers of Verfügungstruppe, the
front-fighting units, which were to become known later as Waffen-SS. To
keep up the fiction that they were trained simply as camp guard units
he had had to accept that Totenkopf men were liable to call up for
military training like all other young men in the Reich. Members of
the Verfügungstruppe were not so liable since their training was officially

military, and to avoid Totenkopfverbände men being called up and possibly
ensnared in one or other of the armed services and losing their allegiance
to the SS – as had happened – he encouraged their temporary transfer to
the Verfügungstruppe, insisting that individual corps spirit should not be
allowed to stand in the way of such transfers. He also warned against the
tendency of the specialised units to look down on the general SS: 'the
SS Verfügungstruppe . . . forgets that this general SS is the core body from
which they have come and from which they must always be replenished,
and that the SS Verfügungstruppe without the general SS would become
sooner or later a mere division of the Army which happened to wear
black.'[36]

Another point which concerned him was that, in recruiting for the SS,
those who failed to pass the selection should be treated with the utmost
tact, not made to feel outcasts.

Necessary rejections of young men, who have for the most part set their heart
on admission to the SS, must – even if it entails more trouble – occur in such a
way that these young men are not only not offended, but are heartened. The
grounds should never be given as racial unsuitability, they should always be
made out as one or other physical shortcoming.[37]

The danger of provoking racial discord within the *Volk* was something
that evidently concerned him at this time. In his speech to the National
Political Schools he stressed that Nordic blood should never be allowed to
create a division in Germany:

It is not permissible that anyone who believes his external appearance
especially racially desirable should fancy himself to be more valuable and
better than someone else who, if you like, has dark hair. Were we to allow
that then the consequence would be that in the shortest time, in place of
the social class battle which has been overcome, a racial class battle would
emerge, a difference between high and low which would be a misfortune for
our *Volk*.[38]

It was indeed a ticklish point, not only in terms of the *Volk*. It could not
escape notice that few in the top leadership conformed to the racial ideal
in any way: Hitler, Hess, little Dr Goebbels and, of course, Himmler had
dark hair.

The Anschluss with Austria – where Himmler lost no time in raising a
new Totenkopf *Standarte*, Ostmark, to be based at Mauthausen, and a
new Verfügungstruppe *Standarte*, Der Führer – was the prelude to the
take-over of Czechoslovakia; had the dice fallen differently the one might
have preceded the other. A campaign of unrest by German natives of the
Sudeten region of Czechoslovakia had begun the previous autumn: their
leader, Konrad Henlein, demanded autonomy for the region. Goebbels

fanned the German press into a blaze on his behalf. On 28 March, a fortnight after the Anschluss, Hitler and Henlein met and adopted the simple
plan used in Austria to raise demands which would prove unacceptable
to the government. When the diplomatic outlook appeared favourable a
pretext would be created for the German Army to march in to protect the
interests of the so-called Sudeten Germans. Keitel was instructed to draw
up the necessary military plans and Canaris to send in undercover teams.
His Abwehr Section II was responsible for sabotage, subversion and special
duties, particularly the mobilisation of German minorities abroad – the so-
called *Volksdeutschen* – and had been especially active in Czechoslovakia.
Now Canaris sent combat and sabotage teams across the border to establish
ammunition dumps, prepare for the seizure of key bridges, railway stations
and border towns and liaise with reliable groups of Henlein's men to stage
uprisings on day X. On 1 April, Canaris was promoted vice-admiral.

In May the Czech government paid Heydrich and Canaris out in their
own coin. Learning that an SD-inspired uprising by the Sudeten Germans
was set for the eve of municipal elections on the 22nd, they ordered
partial mobilisation, manned the frontier posts and launched a campaign
of disinformation alleging German divisions concentrating on the border
for a surprise attack. The alarm in London and Paris was such that the
British Ambassador delivered a warning to von Ribbentrop that France
had obligations to Czechoslovakia and if these had to be fulfilled the British
government 'could not guarantee that they would not be forced by events to
become themselves involved'.[39] On top of this and another warning from the
Foreign Secretary Lord Halifax the next day, the Czech government put it
out that their mobilisation had deflected Hitler from his planned invasion;
every newspaper outside Germany took up the theme that the democracies
had brought Hitler to heel.

The effect on Hitler was dramatic. Already in the 'Hossbach' meeting
the previous November, Hitler had referred to Germany's 'two hate enemies
England and France'; now this had been demonstrated; they had humiliated
him in concert with his intended victim. The rebuff acted as a goad: he
determined to build a huge fleet against England – the fatal error he had
discerned in the Kaiser's policy – as well as impregnable land fortifications
on the border with France, the West Wall, increase the Luftwaffe mightily
and meanwhile smash Czechoslovakia. That he came to these decisions
within a day of the crowing in the western press is evident from the fact
that his naval adjutant wired Admiral Raeder on the 24th with proposals
for an enormous acceleration of naval construction and a summons to a
conference on the 28th.[40]

Up to this point war with England had been a taboo subject with the
naval staff. This changed after the meeting on the 28th, which Göring,
von Ribbentrop, von Neurath and from the Army von Brauchitsch, Beck
and Keitel also attended. On his return Raeder ordered a paper from his

operations staff on the possibility of waging naval war with Great Britain, and from this there emerged a design known as the 'Z Plan' for a vast fleet headed by a squadron of the most powerful battleships to date; Hitler approved this early the following year.[41] Meanwhile Göring increased his plans for the Luftwaffe to provide for 2000 heavy bombers capable of reaching Russia, Great Britain and even the United States, together with 5000 medium bombers, and he expanded the plan for explosives production to the astonishing total of 61,400 tons a month, including 9300 tons for 'chemical warfare'.[42] Plans for motorising the Army and modernising the railways were stepped up and the engineer Fritz Todt was charged with the construction of the West Wall fortifications and a new autobahn network. Göring's recent biographer, Richard Overy, draws from these programmes the 'inescapable conclusion' that Hitler was preparing for a major war with 'some or all of the great powers in the mid-1940s'.[43] The chiefs of the German armed forces certainly believed this. Raeder's fleet chief, Admiral Carls, commented: 'War against . . . half to two-thirds of the whole world has inner justification and prospects of success only if prepared economically as well as politically and militarily. . . . The will to make Germany a world power leads of necessity to suitable preparations for war. . . .'[44]

The programmes had the opposite effect on the few realists left in positions of power. The steel and raw materials requirements alone placed the plans beyond the limits of rationality. The fuel needed for Raeder's Z Plan ships exceeded Germany's total oil consumption for all purposes in 1938, and if the fuel requirements for Göring's 7000-bomber fleet, his fighter fleets and von Brauchitsch's twenty motorised Army divisions were added it became plain that the plans were fantasy – the arms necessary to overrun the world were only realisable after the world had been overrun. Even the expenditure planned by the Wehrmacht in the event of war breaking out in 1939 exceeded the German national income. Göring was prepared to increase the money supply and the national debt. Orthodox economists like Hjalmar Schacht, still head of the Reichsbank, predicted a period of desperate inflation and financial chaos.[45]

With this quickening of the internal tempo of revolution came another, more serious round of Jew-baiting. Almost certainly there was a connection: Jews were, after all, considered to be the wire-pullers behind the international conspiracy against Germany, and Jews were immediately accessible within Germany as defenceless targets for vengeance. It is surely not coincidence that the first burning of a synagogue took place in Munich, spiritual headquarters of the regime, on 9 June, thus little more than a fortnight after the Czech rebuff; it was followed by the arrest of over 2000 Jews throughout the Reich, who were thrown into concentration camps.[46] On 28 June Bella Fromm found the entire Kurfürstendamm shopping centre of Berlin plastered with anti-Jewish graffiti and cartoons. Travelling into the poorer quarters of the city where small Jewish shopkeepers plied their trade she found havoc: 'Everywhere were revolting and bloodthirsty pictures of Jews beheaded, hanged, tortured and maimed, accompanied by obscene inscriptions.'[47] Gangs of Hitler Youth roamed, breaking up shops, looting or throwing the merchandise into the road and terrorising the owners. 'Spontaneous' street violence was accompanied by official Gestapo round-ups from cafés and bars known to be patronised by Jews.

Besides the vengeful, sadistic aspects the inspired campaign had the practical aim of convincing Jews that they should leave Germany. This aim, of course, stood at the heart of the ideology. It was necessary to eliminate the Jews from the Reich – subsequently from Europe – not only because they were behind the international conspiracy against Germany but because their blood must not taint the racial stock – nor of course should the blood of any *minderwertigen* elements. Nazism was practical race hygiene.[48]

There can be little doubt – though much over-pedantic argument – that Hitler at least already had in mind the ultimate solution to the problem, which was to use the upheavals and cheapening of human life that would occur in the coming war years physically to exterminate the Jews. He is known to have indicated such an intention in respect of the incurably ill as early as the Nuremberg Party rally in 1935;[49] there is only the memory of those who overheard him to indicate that he did not include Jews among the categories to be eliminated, and these memories have proved most selective. Stephen Roberts, visiting a museum of Party relics in Munich in 1937, had been shown a wooden sculpture which he was told by the curator had decorated the table at which Hitler founded the Party in 1920. It was a gibbet with a 'brutally realistic' figure of a Jew hanging from it. 'Is it not funny?' the curator asked.[50]

Considering the numbers involved, such a final solution was not possible in peacetime. Even a boycott of Jewish shops organised during the street terror immediately after the *Machtergreifung* had been answered by threats from abroad, especially from the United States, of a counter-boycott of German goods. Consequently the strategy had been adopted of gradually stripping Jews of their livelihood by banning them from the civil service, professions and occupations while Aryanising Jewish businesses and imposing a wealth tax. In addition cinemas, theatres, restaurants, bathing beaches, villages, even towns displayed notices ranging from 'Jews not wanted here' to 'Jews forbidden' or 'Jews enter this place at their own risk'.[51] Those who had not emigrated because they lacked the money or the skills to sell abroad or who refused to believe the ultimate intent had gravitated to the cities, where they scraped a living among their own; as the SD secret report for 1938 put it, the progressive exclusion of Jews from working life and the emigration of wealthy Jews had caused an increase in the destitute Jewish proletariat which 'by far surpassed the number of those earning a living'.[52]

The most surprising thing to Stephen Roberts as he toured the country was the general consensus among Germans that the persecution was a good thing. He met no one who adopted even an apologetic attitude to it; on the contrary they gloried in the persecution and 'looked forward to the day when not a single Jew would survive in the Reich'.[53] Bella Fromm's diary and other Jewish memoirs indicate that this is too wide a generalisation; as with the opposition, there were individuals and groups whose attitude was grounded on morality, often Christian morality, who did not run with the pack. Nevertheless there is no reason to question Stephen Roberts' general statement written before the terrible events which have since coloured all recollection, that all Germany was behind Hitler in the campaign against Rassenschande, or race defilement. Roberts spoke to peasants and great industrialists, Army officers and factory labourers; all approved of it.

The same applied in Austria. The Zionist expert at the SD Jewish Department II 112, Adolf Eichmann, had been sent there during the preparations for the Anschluss; now he was running a Central Office for Jewish Emigration in Vienna which processed the complicated emigration transactions on a production-line basis. He created an 'emigration fund' which forced contributions from wealthy Jews, contributions from Jewish organisations abroad and the proceeds of foreign lecture tours given by members of the Jewish community to gain the foreign exchange which all host countries demanded from immigrants. Eichmann was so successful that he aggravated the difficulties already caused in outside countries by the flight of Jews from Germany. Their arrival in Poland for example had ignited an explosive Polish hostility to their own Jews – far more numerous than those in Germany – and Polish Jews had joined the general exodus from Europe. Thousands had sought refuge in Palestine, alarming and setting off riots among the Arab population whose land was threatened. An international conference on the problem was convened at the Lake Geneva resort of Evian that summer but arrived at no solution. As the SD report expressed it, 'with the exception of America, basically no country declared itself unconditionally ready to take in as many Jews as required. . . .'[54]

The 'actions' of that summer – as pack bullying was designated – so far as they were not simply inspired by the wound administered to Hitler's ego by the Czechs, were engineered deliberately to induce more Jews to emigrate and to force international opinion into a more receptive mood for taking them in.

Meanwhile Himmler, Heydrich and Canaris continued undermining the Czech state from within, and Heydrich prepared for the elimination of the internal opposition after the take-over. Thus in June he drafted outlines for the SD mission 'in case CSR' (Czechoslovakia):

> The SD follows, if possible, immediately behind the troops marching in and takes over, analogous to its functions in the Reich, the security of political life and simultaneously, so far as possible, the security of all firms necessary for the economy and therewith of necessity the war economy.[55]

The compilation of a great card index was under way in SD headquarters Section III 225, with notes on:

arresting	observing
disbanding	confiscating
removing from office	police surveillance
	withdrawal of papers etc.[56]

The country was divided on the map into SS districts and sub-districts to which SS-*Standarten* had been assigned. Joseph Stroop, recently promoted Standartenführer, had been appointed to command Abschnitt XXXVII centring on the town of Liberec. Since completing a six-week course at the SS-Führer school at Dachau in February, he had been familiarising himself with the topography of his future command area and lists of opponents against whom he would need to act.

General Beck, meanwhile, feeling himself left out of the preparations and still believing that Britain and France would not stand by while Czechoslovakia was overrun and that the German armed forces would be crushed in a two-front war, started writing critical memos like those he had drafted after the 'Hossbach' meeting. These had no effect on Hitler's determination, so he tried to organise a mass resignation of the Army High Command and, when this failed, an Army coup against the SS and the Gestapo. According to his deputy, General Franz Halder, he was urged on this course by Canaris and Oster. When he failed to persuade von Brauchitsch and the commanding generals into taking such a step he resigned. By this time it was August. Halder succeeded him as Chief of Staff.

Now, as Hitler and Henlein, the SD and Abwehr Section II stepped up pressure on the Czech government, the German opposition groups were provoked into action to save Germany from what they saw as a suicidal course – or alternatively they saw their opportunity to remove the regime. It became a repeat of the situation in 1937 after Schacht's resignation and leading up to the Blomberg–Fritsch crisis and the Anschluss. The same personalities took the lead; on the civil–financial side Schacht, Goerdeler, Gisevius, von Dohnanyi, from the Army leadership Beck, Halder and several commanding generals including von Witzleben, von Brockdorff-Ahlefeld and von Hase, encouraged and co-ordinated at Abwehr headquarters by Oster under Canaris' benevolent eye, and supplied with information about the police and Gestapo – so far as that could be gleaned – by Nebe, Graf Helldorf, and in addition the Berlin Police Vice-President Count von der Schulenburg.[57] Practically all these men were involved in the later attempt on Hitler's life on 20 July 1944.

As before, the conspirators tried to alert and obtain support from foreign, especially British, governing circles. Goerdeler contacted Sir Robert Vansittart, who sent an emissary to Germany at the beginning of August.

Goerdeler told him Hitler was determined on war, and as before he urged the British government to take a firm line and announce their intention of preserving Czechoslovakia if necessary by force of arms. Hitler had changed in the past months; he now felt he was a god, Goerdeler said. He was mad. The only man who had any influence with him was Himmler and Himmler's power was growing to such an extent that he would soon become virtual master of Germany. However, if the peace could be preserved by Great Britain holding firm on Czechoslovakia Hitler would face a financial crisis, the conditions for the people would deteriorate, Himmler would need to become Germany's Robespierre, and there would be a revolt led by the generals and the leading industrialists.[58]

This assessment is confirmed by others and by the economic facts of life for the German people, whose living standards had actually deteriorated with the concentration on armaments, and for the industrialists outside the Freundeskreis consensus – and probably many inside who were coming to realise the extent to which the war economy was leading to state control – as much as for the generals who feared they were being drawn into a world war they could not win. It seems clear that the pressure on Hitler to advance was created by these internal conditions as much as by his ego or his *Weltanschauung*. He needed a foreign success to preserve his aura and bind the people to him as the saviour of Germany as much as he needed Czechoslovakia for its economic and strategic position. For the same reasons he needed ideological enemies. It was an ever-tightening spiral that could lead only to increased internal repression and foreign adventures. And the tighter this spiral became the more he had to rely on Himmler.

It is impossible to say how finely balanced the position was or what might have been the result had the British government followed the Goerdeler–Vansittart line, for it did not. Other emissaries from Germany were in London that summer, some like Princess Hohenlohe representing the essential reasonableness of Hitler's case with regard to the Sudeten Germans and his limited and peaceable intentions. In the context of a general European war they were, of course, peaceable. This was the message the British Prime Minister, Chamberlain, his principal adviser on foreign affairs, Sir Horace Wilson, his Foreign Secretary, Lord Halifax – a friend of Princess Hohenlohe – and large sections of the governing classes and the British people wanted desperately to hear. This was one of the foundation stones on which Hitler rested his Czechoslovak policy; the other was the weakness he saw in the French body politic.

Canaris appears to have been playing both sides. While Abwehr Section II stoked up the situation inside Czechoslovakia he sent his own emissaries to warn London and acted as intermediary between Oster and Halder in the preparations for an Army coup against Hitler. It is possible he had become convinced of the mortal dangers into which Germany was being led and was keeping his options open for a jump either way. On the other hand few were better informed than he, Himmler and Heydrich that 'appeasement' was ascendant in London – it is interesting that both Chamberlain and Sir Horace Wilson were members of the Oxford Group – and Canaris' special envoy on behalf of the 'opposition', von Kleist-Schmenzin, reported in August that his arguments had got nowhere with Chamberlain. From the trend of his message he might almost have been sent to London to muddy the waters for the Goerdeler–Schacht group. Once again there is more than a suspicion that Canaris remained a convinced supporter of the Führer, and that his 'opposition' activities were designed to incite and uncover anti-Nazi generals, delivering them to Himmler who could seize them if they decided to act – so winning great sympathetic support for Hitler and the regime – or mark them if they did not, holding them to the line in future by the threat of his surveillance and their own knowledge of guilt.

Detailed plans for the coup were drawn up between Oster, Halder, the commander of the Berlin military district, von Witzleben and his deputy, von Brockdorff-Ahlefeld. They involved assault troops launching simultaneous attacks on the Chancellery, Göring's palace, Gestapo, SD and police headquarters, outlying police stations, the barracks of the SS-Leibstandarte Adolf Hitler in Lichterfelde, SS barracks at Sachsenhausen, the occupation of the German broadcasting station and telephone and telegraph exchanges; Hitler, Himmler and the other leaders were to be arrested and a military dictatorship proclaimed. Von Brockdorff-Ahlefeld inspected the target localities in company with Gisevius before working up the detailed deployment of the assault squads.[59]

The plan assumes significance when compared with the coup that was attempted eventually on 20 July 1944, but little otherwise can be taken at face value. Hitler's and Himmler's method in successive coups was always to draw their opponents into the open. No one will ever know who the double agents were in this deadly dangerous game nor the twists and turns of the plot. It is not inconceivable that there were those in 'opposition' circles who were inciting Hitler to a forward policy in order to draw him into a false move, not inconceivable that Himmler himself was keeping his options open as it seems he probably had in the plots against his previous chiefs, Röhm and Strasser.[60] Gisevius, who was urging the generals to strike against Hitler without delay, wrote that the question was open then 'and is today not fully answered' as to who was playing with whom, and who was outmanoeuvred.[61] All that can be certain is that things were not as they appeared and that Himmler and Heydrich lurked behind some of the figures in the 'opposition'.

Meanwhile there was the annual Party rally at Nuremberg. This had developed into a week-long military–theatrical orgy of solidarity, overwhelming in its effect on participants and spectators. At the rally in 1937 Himmler had awarded Stroop the signal honour of leading the SS and police parade. It was a highlight of his life:[62] 'a fantastic distinction'. Years later in his prison cell he confessed that a sunny September day always aroused in him the recollection of that most wonderful experience, 'the colours of the *Standarten* and the uniform of the Führer . . . the roared "Sieg Heil!" from thousands of voices . . . the roll of the drums. This concentrated power. . . .' Himmler marched alone at the head of the SS bloc, Wolff following, and Stroop came fifty paces behind; behind him was a great rectangle formed by the *Standarte* bearers, 'especially selected, tree-tall men', above their heads a forest of black, white and red swastika banners and eagles . . .

'Look, Moczarski! This is how we marched! This is parade step!'[63]

The sense of massed power and participation in great events heralding a heroic future was particularly tangible after the Anschluss at the September 1938 rally. Only a few foreign observers formed a different impression. One was the travel-writer and journalist Robert Byron, who had persuaded Hitler's English admirer, Unity (Bobo) Mitford, to include him in her party. He himself was strongly anti-Nazi. He kept a diary: 'I expected to get the impression of a vigorous evil which must be destroyed at all costs – and perhaps I do. But that is subordinated to the negativeness and vacuity of it all. It is not so much intellectual poison as intellectual and spiritual death – a greater death than physical death. . . .'[64] Two days later he attended the Party congress, sitting (thanks to Bobo's influence) in the front row immediately facing the Party leaders on the dais so that every time he raised his eyes he met those of Goebbels or Himmler or Hitler. That evening he recorded his impression of the leaders who had been so close to him: 'Himmler terrifying, he sucks his teeth and keeps them bared. The Führer is peculiar for the pink and white podginess of his face. . . . eyes like peas, but a good-humoured face obviously very moved by music.'[65]

Later in the week Byron attended the SS bivouac which Himmler hosted every year. Himmler himself received the guests – who undoubtedly included many of the Freundeskreis. Byron noted his 'very small hand, a sort of doll's hand'. Later that evening Bobo's father, Lord Redesdale, also in Munich, was telephoned by an Oxford Group spokesman, saying the Group wanted to 'change' the Führer. Bobo said she did not want the Führer changed. 'No, damn it,' Redesdale agreed, 'I like the feller as he is.' Byron entered in his diary: 'Himmler apparently dotes on the Oxford Group and writes to its English members discussing their troubles with them. Frau Himmler has a twitch of the face.'[66]

Marga Himmler had invited the wives of the highest SS generals to the Party rally that year and was managing them. When Lina Heydrich and Frieda Wolff tried to escape and enjoy themselves in the predominantly masculine gathering she called them to order. They complained to their husbands and they, according to Wolff, had the temerity to raise the matter with Himmler. 'So ist sie eben!' he shrugged helplessly. 'That's just the way she is!'[67]

No one in his close entourage was surprised, Wolff said after the war, when Himmler sought spiritual and sexual relief with his secretary, Hedwig Potthast. She was twelve years younger than he – thus twenty-six

in 1938 – the daughter of a sergeant-major in the Army. It is usually held
that she became his mistress only after the outbreak of war – according
to Wolff, in 1940. She was already a part of his personal entourage. She
accompanied him, for instance, when he weekended at his villa at Gmund,
and there are handwritten notes 'for Frl. Potthast' on some of the typed
file notes of his conversations at mealtimes which were started in February
that year.[68] Like the notes of Hitler's table-talk made during the war, these
consisted of his observations on subjects as inconsequential as the number
of words in the average German's vocabulary or incidents from his own
childhood.

Probably Hedwig, known familiarly as 'Häschen', was not his mistress
yet. It appears that he had one, but at this time it was probably the ageing
Munich concert singer Karoline – 'Nini' – Diehl,[69] a poisonous woman who
later married the infamous medical experimenter, Sigmund Rascher, and
goaded him on in his abominable research.

Byron's description of Himmler sucking his teeth and keeping them
bared at the Party congress suggests the strain he was under. No doubt
the embarrassing figure Marga cut beside Wolff's and Heydrich's attractive young wives provided niggling background tension, but undoubtedly
Czechoslovakia and the impending generals' revolt caused him desperate
anxiety. Even with hindsight the decision for war or peace appears to
have been balanced on a fine edge. Hitler and Himmler believed that the
western democracies would crack, but they needed all their nerve to sit it
out impassively while their agents fed the flames inside Czechoslovakia and
– it must be assumed – incited the generals to conspire. Both plots matured
as the rally ended. In his speech, on the final day, 12 September, Hitler
worked up to an impassioned pledge to stand by the Sudeten Germans.

Afterwards Hitler retired to his eyrie on the Obersalzberg. Next day, 13
September, Henlein's men launched their planned provocations. The Czech
government proclaimed martial law, and with the prospect of the German
Army crossing the border to aid the Sudetens, the French government
cracked: six of the Council of Ministers voted for standing by their treaty
obligations to support Czechoslovakia in the event of a German attack,
four voted against. The Prime Minister, Daladier, sent an urgent message
to Chamberlain: 'Entry of German troops into Czechoslovakia must be
prevented at all costs.' Chamberlain determined to fly to meet Hitler.
Meanwhile an impetuous break-away group from the generals' conspiracy
led by Gisevius, Oster and Friedrich Heinz – to every appearance one of
Oster's most resolute anti-Nazi colleagues in the Abwehr – also resolved
to avert war, prepared to launch an immediate coup against Hitler. It is
difficult to see how they could have reached him in the inaccessible fastness
of the Obersalzberg and protected by SS, but the story goes that they were
forestalled in their attempt only by news of Chamberlain's flying visit.

Chamberlain and Sir Horace Wilson saw Hitler alone at the Berghof
above Berchtesgaden on the 15th, and over tea in the study agreed in

principle to a separation of the Sudeten Germans from Czechoslovakia. For his part Hitler agreed to give peaceful negotiations a chance before his Army marched. As soon as the two Englishmen had returned to London to gain agreement with the French and Czech governments over practicalities, Hitler ordered the campaign of unrest by Henlein's men to be stepped up. Canaris, who had made arms and Abwehr 'safe houses' in Berlin available to the Gisevius–Oster–Heinz conspiracy against Hitler, and who was still liaising between Oster and Halder in the larger generals' conspiracy, busied himself supplying a Freikorps of émigré Sudeten Germans with arms, intelligence and funds. On the 19th they began a series of bloody border incidents. When Chamberlain flew back to see Hitler at Bad Godesberg on the 22nd carrying an agreement that he and Daladier had forced on the Czech government to transfer the Sudeten districts to Germany Hitler rejected it and, on the strength of the casualty toll among the Sudeten Germans in the border clashes, raised impossible demands which had to be met by 1 October; otherwise his Army would march. It was the technique he had used with Schuschnigg. He aimed at control of the whole of Czechoslovakia, not just the Sudeten areas, and had, or thought he had, taken the measure of the English Prime Minister and his adviser, and of the fear of war among the peoples of the western democracies. Newsreels of this meeting show Himmler fussing in the wings like a good and faithful servant to his master.

The result of the meeting at Bad Godesberg was the opposite of that which Hitler intended. Chamberlain and Halifax took *his* measure. Halifax informed the Czech government that there was no longer any objection to them mobilising, and he approached Russia, which had been left out of the discussions so far despite being pledged by treaty to come to Czechoslovakia's aid if France did so. The Soviet Foreign Minister, Litvinov, said that his government would honour its obligation. The British fleet was mobilised; the French mobilised half a million men; Anglo-French staff talks were resumed; and on 26 September Wilson, who had been sent to Berlin alone to try and talk Hitler out of his apparent determination to settle the dispute by force, was instructed to deliver a message that France intended supporting Czechoslovakia if she were attacked, and this would inevitably bring in Great Britain.

The momentum towards a European war in which Germany would be engaged on three fronts and blockaded by the western navies heartened the internal opposition. On the 27th Hitler drafted preparatory orders for the mobilisation by the 30th of five Army divisions and fourteen reserve divisions at the jumping-off points for the Czech operation. Oster and Halder took this as proof that Day X was fixed for 1 October, the deadline Hitler had given Chamberlain and the date towards which OKW planning had been directed from the start. Halder went to the Commander-in-Chief, von Brauchitsch, with the orders as proof of Hitler's intention to lead them into a war which they could not survive, and succeeded in winning him over to the conspiracy. Hitler, however, was already pulling back. In a letter to Chamberlain, also on the 27th, he said he pledged the safety of the Czech population in the areas to be occupied, declared himself 'ready to give a formal guarantee for the [territorial integrity of the] remainder of Czechoslovakia' and practically invited the British Prime Minister to continue his good offices.[70]

The British government needed no second invitation to avert war. Another meeting was convened with Hitler with extraordinary haste, this time bringing in Mussolini and Daladier. Before it began at the Brown House in Munich at 1.30 p.m. on the 29th, Mussolini had been provided with a memorandum drawn up largely by the German Foreign Ministry outlining terms scarcely different from Hitler's ultimatum to Chamberlain at Bad Godesberg, but extending the time-scale of the hand-over of Czech territories in four stages with fixed dates. When Mussolini read these out at the meeting neither Chamberlain nor Daladier had any difficulty in agreeing since they had been proposed originally to the German Foreign Ministry by the British Foreign Office after gaining French consent. Hitler had no difficulty in agreeing since he had caused the memorandum to be sent to Mussolini in the first place. The most important point was that the first stage of the hand-over was to take place on 1 October, the day Hitler had promised to march in.

The following morning, 30 September, Chamberlain proposed to Hitler that they make a joint declaration that the agreement just reached was a symbol 'of the desire of our two peoples never to go to war with one another again'. Hitler was happy to sign. Chamberlain flew home and as he emerged from his aeroplane cheered by waiting spectators as a peacemaker, he waved the declaration crying, 'I've got it.' It seems he had few illusions, though.

General Alfred Jodl, Keitel's Chief of Staff at OKW, wrote in his diary: 'Czechoslovakia as a power is out. . . . The genius of the Führer and his determination not to shun even a world war have again won a victory without the use of force. The hope remains that the incredulous, the weak and the doubters have been converted and will remain that way.'[71]

The incredulous, the weak and the doubters were indeed converted. The generals' conspiracy dissolved like snow in the sun of the Führer's genius. Now it is difficult to assess if it really existed outside the imaginations of a few individuals like Oster and Beck and Gisevius. Baron von Weizsäcker, State Secretary at the Foreign Ministry, was one of Canaris' confidants in the 'conspiracy', allegedly urging the British government to stand firm against Hitler's demands. Yet von Weizsäcker was one of the principal authors of the memorandum which was delivered to Mussolini before the Munich meeting. And, like Canaris, he had thrilled to the Anschluss, writing home ecstatically from Vienna of 'the most noteworthy day since 18 January 1871'[72] – Bismarck's foundation of the Reich. Another aristocratic 'conspirator', the Police President Graf Helldorf, had made a name for himself as a Jew-baiter in the early days after the *Machtergreifung*. Now he was using his position to seize the passports of wealthy Jews wishing to emigrate, after which he sold them back to the owners for exorbitant sums of up to 250,000 Marks. By the nature of things the traditional power elite of the *Reaktion* was concerned with its own position and Germany's: their opposition was to a second world war and what was seen as inevitable defeat.

The Munich settlement was the final turning point for the *Reaktion*. If they ever really had an opportunity after their step-by-step retreat, they had missed it. Munich was the final turning point for Hitler. He had met the leaders of the western democracies and made monkeys of them. He had proved that tactics of deception, threat and histrionics worked at the highest levels of European diplomacy. His will had broken the bonds of reality; everything was possible. The paladins who surrounded him assured him of it. After Chamberlain left the conference, von Ribbentrop, perhaps influenced by the old gentleman's black suit, announced that they had England's obituary notice: 'Meine Herren, die Todes Anzeige Englands ist getroffen!'[73]

Munich was a turning point for Chamberlain. Hitler's occupation of the Sudeten territories, which he had pledged as the limit of his territorial ambition, was the test of his good faith. When it became obvious he had failed the test Chamberlain was left with two options: to guarantee the countries of eastern Europe in the way of Hitler's further advance or, in von Ribbentrop's imagery, hand in Great Britain's obituary notice as a world power; but this latter was not really an option. And Munich was the turning point for Europe. Goerdeler informed his British liaison a fortnight after the conference that war was now inevitable.[74]

Meanwhile the spasmodic Jew-baiting of the summer was superseded by a nationwide 'action'. The pretext was the murder of the Third Secretary at the German Embassy in Paris by a young Jew. This bore the hallmarks of one of Heydrich's 'provocations'. During the preparations for taking over the Sudeten territories Hitler had suggested the murder of the German Ambassador in Prague as a suitable pretext for intervention; the proposal had been the subject of discussions between Canaris and the OKW. Thus, there was nothing novel about the idea of procuring the murder of a German diplomat. If he were politically 'not reliable', as appears to have been the case with the Third Secretary at the Paris Embassy, vom Rath, it was twice justifiable. No proof was found at the time linking Heydrich's agents with the murderer, Herschel Grynszpan, and probably no proof will ever be found. The suspicion rests chiefly on Heydrich's record of similar provocations and the fortuitous timing.

Grynszpan had been a student in Paris for two years. He had been brought up in Hanover, where his father, originally a Polish Jew, had settled in 1911. In the evening of 27 October 1938, the Grynszpan family in Hanover was rounded up, together with several thousand other Jews who had originated in Poland, and taken by train to the eastern border, where they arrived on the 29th. They were searched and relieved of any money they had over ten Marks, then forced towards the Polish border about a mile distant. Years later Grynszpan's father recalled: 'the SS men were whipping us, those who lingered they hit, and blood was flowing on the road. . . . they treated us in a most barbaric fashion – this was the first time that I'd ever seen the wild barbarism of the Germans.'[75]

The Poles allowed them in, but there was nowhere for the thousands to be accommodated, nor any provisions for them. They had to find shelter from the wet autumn weather in stables and pigsties. Somehow or other Grynszpan managed to write a postcard to his son, Herschel, in Paris, describing what was happening to them. Herschel received the card and, desperate to bring the sufferings of his people to the attention of the world, bought a pistol, went to the German Embassy and emptied the barrel into vom Rath, leaving him in a critical condition. Such were the facts. There is no evidence linking Grynszpan with Heydrich's agents. All that can be certain is that a great 'action' against the Jews had been planned, that Himmler and Heydrich initiated the expulsion of the former Polish Jews, that postcards were used in later deceptions by Heydrich – to suggest that murdered Jews were alive and well[76] – and that the 'outrage' in Paris, which occurred on 7 November as the Party stalwarts were coming together in Munich for the annual Bürgerbräukeller celebrations, was immediately taken up by Dr Goebbels as proof of the world conspiracy of Jewry against the Reich.

If any proof is needed of Himmler's complicity it is contained in the address which custom demanded he make to his Gruppenführers on the night of 8 November.[77] It was his hardest, most specific, most unequivocal speech yet, filled with the prevailing sense of triumph in the wake of the Anschluss and Munich, and expressing the heady feeling that this was but the start, the essential base and beginning of their task as *Herrenvolk*. It was a call to arms – ruthlessly – against a world of enemies:

We must be clear that in the next ten years we face unprecedented conflicts of a critical nature. It is not only the battle of the nations, which have pushed forward only in the case of the opposition, but it is the *weltanschauliche* battle of the entire Jewry, freemasonry, Marxism and churches of the world. These forces – of which I assume the Jews to be the driving spirit, the origin of all the negatives – are clear that if Germany and Italy are not eradicated, *they* will be eradicated [*vernichtet werden*]. That is an elementary conclusion. In Germany the Jew cannot hold out. This is a question of years. We will drive them out more and more with an unexampled ruthlessness. Italy is going the same way and Poland does not want the Jews. The struggle concerns these vital questions.

The other states, Sweden, Norway, Denmark, Holland, Belgium, are today naturally not anti-semitic but they will become so with time. We are sending our best propagandists in there. The moment the Jewish emigrants to Switzerland, to Holland and so on establish themselves in their typical occupations, suddenly patriotic anti-semitism will begin. If out of ten barristers in a Swiss town three are Jews, the Swiss barristers certainly have no more bread, and where the purse begins to pinch even an advocate will suddenly on those grounds become an anti-semite.

Furthermore, Czechoslovakia has become anti-semitic, all the Balkans are anti-semitic, the whole of Palestine is engaged in a desperate struggle against the Jews, so that some day there will be no place in the world left for the Jew. He says to himself, this danger will only be removed if the source, if the originating country of anti-semitism, if Germany is burnt out and destroyed [*ausgebrannt und vernichtet*].

Be clear about it, in the battle which will decide if we are defeated there will be no reservation remaining for the Germans, all will be starved out and butchered. That will face everyone, be he now an enthusiastic supporter of the Third Reich or not – it will suffice that he speaks German and had a German mother.

He continued at length about many other things, about the blood and about loyalty, about duty and obedience, hardness and decency. He laid it down that in coming wars of life and death between peoples an SS man should never be taken prisoner; he had to make an end of himself beforehand. And referring to their duty to prevent treason and revolution within, he told them that while they wanted as individuals to be humanly kind and decent, when it came to preserving a *Volk* from death they must be without any pity. 'Then it is a matter of indifference if in a town 1000 [people] have to be put down. I would do it, and I would expect you to carry it out. About that there is no doubt.'

Finally he returned to an earlier theme, that in the recent crisis over the Sudetenland, while the behaviour of the people had been splendid, that of the intelligentsia had been pitiable, 'pitiable individually, pitiable in its bearing, pitiable in its courage'. This reference to the opposition indicates that whatever his own feelings at the height of the crisis, whether or not he had ever considered jumping the other way, outwardly he had preserved absolute loyalty to the Führer.

The passage in the middle of the long speech about the Jews' intentions towards the German race was psychologically revealing in its language – *vernichtet*, 'wiped out' or 'annihilated'; *ausgebrannt*, 'gutted'; and *ausgehungert und abgeschlachtet*, 'starved out and slaughtered' – precisely the intentions he had towards the Jews. He said nothing about the next stage in this strategy which was to be set off when vom Rath died of his wounds, since there were many honorary SS officers from all walks of life in the audience and the fiction was to be maintained that the 'action' was 'spontaneous'. His words had been chosen carefully. No doubt they sent frissons of anticipation down the spines of those active Gruppenführers in the know.

The 'action' began the following evening after news of vom Rath's death. In every city and town and most villages in the Reich, parties of SA, SS and Hitler Youth in plain clothes, already briefed on their targets, went on a rampage of arson and destruction of synagogues, Jewish shops, businesses and homes, rounding up Jews and humiliating, beating and in several cases killing them. Wolff knew nothing of the start of this, according to his account, nor did Heydrich, according to his widow's account. Wolff was in the Hotel Vier Jahreszeiten preparing to call Himmler for the SS recruits' oath-taking ceremony, which took place every 9 November at midnight before the Feldherrnhalle where the martyrs of the 1923 putsch had fallen. Heydrich was celebrating with some senior SS officers in the Nobel Hotel. He was telephoned from Berlin by Heinrich Müller, his Gestapo chief, with the news that roving bands of youths were destroying Jewish businesses. What should be done? Heydrich decided he must speak to Himmler; he went to see Wolff. Himmler was with Hitler in the salon of the Führer's Prinzregentenstrasse flat and was not pleased when Wolff called at the door and asked to speak to him before the due time of departure for the oath-taking ceremony, 11.30. Wolff's report visibly astonished him, though. He went back into the salon to tell Hitler, and Wolff was called in shortly to find Hitler incensed by the news, which had obviously come as a complete surprise . . .[78]

This would not be worth repeating were it not for the glimpse it affords of the rivalry Himmler had built into the SS command structure. Even Heydrich had to seek an audience with him through Wolff, and Wolff jealously guarded his right of access. As for Hitler, perhaps he did feign surprise. He undoubtedly sanctioned the action – Himmler would not have dared to incur the international odium it was bound to bring down on the Reich without reference to his Führer – but it is notable that, as with the 'final solution' to the Jewish problem later, there was no Führer decree or order, not a single slip of paper – or none that has been found – to connect Hitler with the proceedings in any way. Officially it came as a huge surprise.

Probably there was no formal order. It is even very possible that Himmler or Heydrich proposed the action since the campaign against Jews was the SD's affair – or Göring perhaps proposed it because he needed funds and more Aryanised businesses for the war economy. But it is equally likely that in the wake of his Munich triumph, which was not so much of a triumph as he would have liked since he had not been allowed to 'smash' Czechoslovakia completely, Hitler called for vengeance against the Jews – or, in Himmler's invariable phrase, 'desired' it. Wherever the idea for the 9 November pogrom originated, any suggestion that it was a spontaneous uprising is given the lie by the text of messages sent out that night. The first was from Heinrich Müller at the Gestapa, Berlin, to all Gestapo offices; it was transmitted at five minutes to midnight on the 9th, and marked 'immediate and by the quickest route – SECRET!'

1) Actions against Jews, especially against their synagogues, will take place throughout the Reich shortly. They are not to be interfered with; however, liaison is to be effected with the Ordnungspolizei to ensure that looting and other significant excesses are suppressed.

2) So far as important archive material exists in synagogues this is to be secured by immediate measures.

3) Preparations are to be made for the arrest of about 20,000 to 30,000 Jews in the Reich. Above all well-to-do Jews are to be selected. Detailed instructions will follow in the course of this night.

4) Should Jews in possession of weapons be encountered in the course of the action, the sharpest measures are to be taken. Verfügungstruppen der SS as well as general SS can be enlisted for all actions. Control of the actions is to be secured in every case through the [Ge]Stapo. Looting, larceny etc. is to be prevented in all cases. For securing material, contact is to be established immediately with the responsible SD *Ober-* and *Unterabschnitten* leadership.

Addendum for Stapo Cologne: In the Cologne synagogue there is especially important material. This is to be secured by the quickest measures in conjunction with SD.[79]

This message was followed an hour and twenty-five minutes later by a more detailed wire to all Gestapo and SD district and sub-district offices from Heydrich – 'lightning, urgent, immediate attention':

Concerning: measures against Jews in the present night.

On account of the assassination of the Leg. Sec. v. Rath in Paris, demonstrations against the Jews are to be expected throughout the Reich in the present night – 9/10.11.38. . . .[80]

The wire went on to direct all Gestapo chiefs to contact the political leadership of their area – the *Gau-* or *Kreisleitung* – in order to co-ordinate the execution of the demonstrations. They were to bring the police chiefs in to their discussions:

the political leadership is to be informed that the German police have received the following instructions from the Reichsführer-SS and Chief of Police, to which the measures of the political leadership should be adapted appropriately:

a) Only such measures should be taken as will not endanger German life or property (i.e. synagogue burning only if there is no fire-danger to the surroundings).

b) Businesses and dwellings of Jews should only be destroyed, not plundered. The police are instructed to supervise this regulation and to arrest looters.

c) Especial care is to be taken that in business streets non-Jewish businesses are absolutely secured against damage.

d) Foreign nationals – even if they are Jews – should not be molested. . . .

Subject to these guidelines, the message continued, the police were not to prevent the demonstrations. Archive material and cult objects were to be seized and handed over to the responsible SD office.

5) Directly after the termination of the events of this night, the employment of the officials deployed [for the demonstrations] permitting, as many Jews – especially the well-off ones – are to be arrested as can be accommodated in the available prison space. Above all only healthy, male Jews, not too old, are to be arrested. Immediately after execution of the arrests contact is to be made with the appropriate concentration camp regarding the quickest committal of the Jews to the camp. Special care is to be taken that the Jews arrested on this order are not maltreated.

6) The content of this order is to be passed on to the responsible inspectors and commanders of the Ordnungspolizei and to the SD-Ober- and Unterabschnitten, with the rider that the Reichsführer-SS and Chief of the German Police has ordered these measures. . . .

The terror experienced by German Jews over the next hours and days cannot be described. Perhaps it cannot be imagined by those who have never found themselves in a suddenly primaeval night hunted or running the gauntlet of a mob baying for blood, with nowhere to turn – the authorities last of all – no succour in the alien darkness. A British diplomat in Berlin wrote of the forces of mediaeval barbarism let loose.[81] That implies a belief in moral progress that was evidently misplaced; in the light of flaring synagogues and burning books and Torah scrolls and pools of blood in the streets it was apt as an analogy.

The 'healthy, male Jews, not too old', transported to concentration camps were herded inside from the buses by the guards who tripped, kicked and struck them with fists and rifle butts. One inmate of Buchenwald, Gerd Treuhaft, recently recalled the first night after the Jews' arrival: '. . . SS guards entered, picked Jews at random, and took them outside to be whipped with steel rods or battered to death with clubs. Throughout the night we heard shots and cries of mortal terror.'[82]

By 12 November Buchenwald was full and a message went out to all Gestapo offices that no more transports should be sent there apart from those already under way.[83] It was probably because of the way the camps were filling up that Himmler that evening ordered the release of all Jews over fifty years old who had been taken into *Schutzhaft* in the recent action.[84] The reason, quite obviously, was to make more space available for younger men more able to do hard, physical work. The same day Heydrich represented him at an inter-ministerial meeting chaired by Göring to agree on the administrative steps necessary to complete the work begun in the action. Heydrich pressed for decrees barring Jews from public transport, hospitals, schools, anywhere they would come into contact with Germans, in brief to drive them into ghettos. Göring thought such measures should be introduced in succession; for the present he seemed more concerned with Jewish business and property. 'Another question, *meine Herren*,' he said, 'how would you judge the situation if I announced today that as a punishment for this [damage] a contribution of a billion [Marks] were to be imposed on the Jews?'[85] According to his statement after the war, he had agreed the figure with Hitler and Goebbels two days before – thus while the terror raged on the streets. The 'fine' of a thousand million Marks was promulgated by government decree that day, 12 November; it was to be collected in the form of a 20 per cent levy on Jews whose wealth exceeded 5000 Reichsmarks. In addition Jews were forbidden to run retail or transport businesses or to pursue a trade. The only place they might have in German life was as subordinates.

Two days later Heydrich ordered the release of all Jews possessing the papers necessary for emigration and due to leave the country within three weeks so that they could meet their travel arrangements. At the same time he gave instructions that those Jews whose businesses were in process of Aryanisation should be allowed out of *Schutzhaft* on short-term 'leave' in order to execute the legal formalities. The following day, 15 November, it was announced that Jewish children were debarred from attending German schools. Over the next weeks the net was tightened in other areas.

The guiding purpose of the pogrom and subsequent legislation is made clear in the SD secret report for the leadership:

> The action manifested itself in general in the destruction or burning down of synagogues and the demolition of almost all Jewish businesses, which were thereby forced to sell up. In part the homes of Jews were affected in the action. . . . In resisting a number of Jews were killed or wounded.[86]

The report did not detail the exact extent of the damage or the number of deaths but an idea of scale can be gleaned from Heydrich's report to the ministerial meeting on the 12th: 7500 businesses destroyed, 267 synagogues burned or damaged, 177 of them totally destroyed. Some ninety-one Jews were killed, but this figure was soon overtaken by the number beaten or otherwise done to death by the Totenkopf guards in the concentration camps – according to some accounts more than a thousand.[87]

The report merely stated that 'in order to strengthen the compulsion to emigrate' 25,000 male Jews had been taken to concentration camps 'for the moment temporarily'. The report concluded: 'In summary it can be stated that Jewry – so far as German nationals and stateless persons are concerned – has finally been excluded from all areas of the German community so that only emigration remains to the Jews to safeguard their existence.'[88]

Reichskristallnacht (as the pogrom came to be called) and the subsequent legislation provoked an international outcry, but again no practical steps were taken which even approached the scale of the problem. Within Germany it brought home to individual members of the former power elite just how powerless they had become. Ulrich von Hassell, one of the diplomats sacked in the February purge, wrote in his diary of the horror felt by all decent people at the shameless persecution of the Jews. Talking with two of his friends about how they could make a practical expression of their abhorrence, he concluded that there was no way: 'Without power one has no effective means; the only consequence would be to be silenced or worse. It is precisely the educated world which was in a good strategic position at the beginning, which has long lost it through its own guilt.'[89]

On 4 December, a week after this diary entry, Goerdeler again appealed to the British Foreign Office for support to enable the liberal elements in Germany to overthrow the regime; his arguments, as summarised by his English intermediary, Vansittart, started with the premises:

> a) Himmler is the real master of Germany. . . .
>   b) We [the British] must recognise that we are dealing with gangsters, of the most depraved type. . . .[90]

However, Goerdeler went on to make several demands which aroused Vansittart's suspicion that he was 'a mere stalking horse for German military expansionism'.[91] These included British aid in returning Danzig and the 'Polish corridor' to Germany, the return of colonial territory, a loan of four to six billion gold Marks 'to secure a stable and international basis for German currency' – a sign of Goerdeler's alliance with Schacht – and the foundation of a new League of Nations by England, France and Germany. Several other emissaries from the German opposition, described in British Foreign Office parlance as 'so-called moderates', made similar pleas. They served to increase suspicion of German aims at all levels and Lord Halifax was advised that 'there might be the greatest danger in identifying ourselves with those who may be plotting revolution in Germany.'[92] When Goerdeler sent another messenger with an urgent request for a reply to his proposals by 18 December, hinting that von Fritsch would lead a generals' revolt some time between that date and the end of the month, the chief of the Secret Intelligence Service, Admiral Sir Hugh Sinclair, was asked his opinion. He was sceptical. That evening the proposals of the German opposition were placed before Chamberlain by the Foreign Office official Sir Alexander Cadogan. Afterwards Cadogan noted in his diary: 'He would have none of it, and I think he's right. These people must do their own job.'[93]

Towards the end of December von Hassell talked with a member of the opposition, the Prussian Finance Minister Dr Johannes Popitz. Popitz had contacts with Himmler, and von Hassell, greatly puzzled by Himmler's attitude to the persecution of the Jews, asked him what he knew. Popitz told him that Himmler had created a sophisticated alibi. He had told Hitler – in writing or by telephone – that he could not carry out the orders for the pogrom. On receiving no reply, he had felt bound to carry them out; but he could now say that he had done what he could.[94] Evidently he was able to deceive even those members of the 'intelligentsia' he despised about his true fanaticism and his intentions with regard to the Jews. In part, this was probably caused by the frightfulness everyone discerned in Heydrich. Sheltered behind such a demon – and other very obvious gangsters in the hierarchy – Himmler could pose as one of the few moderate and conciliatory, even civilised, Party leaders.

Popitz told von Hassell that he had said to Göring that those responsible for Kristallnacht must be punished. 'My dear Popitz,' the Iron One had replied, 'do you want to punish the Führer?'[95]

Taking Popitz's words at face value, for they were recorded in December 1938, it is astonishing that members of the Prussian administration could have remained in ignorance of the character and aims of the Party and its leaders up to this late date.

Kristallnacht was scarcely over before Heydrich was preparing to complete the take-over of Czechoslovakia. Himmler meanwhile went on long leave to Italy; such was his anxiety that one of his leading SS-Führers might cut him out with Hitler that he appointed no deputy to act in his absence.[96] It was another manifestation of his contradictions that while he appeared to Goerdeler and others to be the real master of Germany he was so unsure of his position that on his return he continued to take every opportunity to bring himself to Hitler's attention and to propose schemes which arose as much from his need to impress as from his fanaticism. Thus, as he and his rivals, Göring, Goebbels, von Ribbentrop and, recently, Martin Bormann circled around each other, their competing fantasies drove out what was left of reality about the Führer.

Himmler was also very anxious about his health at this time; he was suffering severely from the stomach cramps which had always afflicted him; at times they became so bad they almost reduced him to unconsciousness, and sometimes they lasted for days, leaving him utterly depleted.[97] Although they were almost certainly caused by the old internal tensions, aggravated by his accretion of powers and responsibilities and anxieties about his rivals, he feared the pains were symptoms of cancer; his father had died of cancer of the stomach glands. According to Frischauer, it was Karl Wolff, faced with the Reichsführer's fits of despair at these attacks, who called in a Swedish chiropractor named Felix Kersten, then enjoying a considerable reputation in social circles.[98]

Before Kersten was allowed to examine him, he was sworn to absolute secrecy. The reasons went beyond the need for the chief of the SS and the police dictator of Germany to appear physically beyond reproach; they touched the core of the racial message of National Socialism: the Aryan was by definition fittest of the fit. And here, surely, we are back at the nub of the contradictions which drove Himmler: for, as Kersten saw to his surprise when he met him for the first time, he corresponded not at all with the image he had expected; he was small, 'weak-chinned' and 'far from being an athletic type, cramped, instead of being loose and elastic'.[99] Had he not known who he was he would have taken him for a city clerk or schoolteacher; as for his racial aspect 'one would almost say that there was something oriental in his broad cheekbones and round face.' If, in addition to these imperfections it were to become known that he spent considerable periods doubled up in helpless agony, his credentials for selecting and preaching, bearing down hard and punishing his Nordic elite as they wanted to be hardened and punished must have appeared doubtful.

There was another reason which was purely political: Kersten discovered this early the following year when Himmler asked him to examine von Ribbentrop. Himmler had already spoken to von Ribbentrop and told him that Kersten treated him for rheumatism; now he instructed Kersten to say nothing about his stomach pains. Von Ribbentrop must think he was perfectly strong; if he were to find out he was ill he would intrigue and snipe at him even more than at present.[100] There is no doubt – although Kersten did not say so – that the chief reason Himmler was prepared to help the Foreign Minister by sending Kersten to him was that he hoped to gain inside information himself.

It says much about the strains at the top of the Nazi hierarchy that Kersten found von Ribbentrop suffering severe headaches, giddiness, partial loss of vision and stomach pains. Hitler himself had suffered from sharp, cramping pains in his right upper abdomen since about the time of the *Machtergreifung*, and since 1936 had been taking capsules prescribed by his personal physician, Dr Morell, consisting of bacteria cultured from the excrement of a Bulgarian peasant.[101]

Kersten practised a form of physio-neural therapy which aimed to affect the tissues and blood vessels beneath the surface. As he explained it, psychic occurrences such as excitement, fright, worry, overwork, depression exercised a constant and often fatal effect on the vaso-motor function of the blood vessels; it is evident that several or probably all of these psychic conditions were factors in Himmler's cramps, and from the first Kersten was able to bring him relief. Himmler asked him to stay on as his personal attendant, but he refused. It was not until German forces overran Holland, where Kersten had made his home, that Himmler secured him permanently. From then until the end of the war he was in almost constant attendance, indispensable for his soothing touch. He became a father confessor with whom Himmler could discuss most of his ideas and problems in a neutral atmosphere without stress; Himmler came to call him his 'magic Buddha'.

For this reason Kersten's observations on Himmler's relationship with Hitler, carrying the weight of long and intimate experience, are important. It seems from these that when Himmler spoke of the Führer as sent by Providence to lead the Germanic race, he meant it literally, consequently when in discussions and speeches he used the phrase – as he so often did – 'the Führer is always right' that was what he believed; it was self-evident from Hitler's status as Germanic leader. Even if he could not understand certain decisions, or thought they were wrong, he yet believed they had a transcendent quality; it was only his own lack of vision that prevented him from seeing their essential rightness. 'Simply an indication that Hitler might have a different opinion', Kersten wrote, 'sufficed to make Himmler hesitate and postpone a decision until he had been able to make sure of Hitler's attitude.'[102] More surprising still, Himmler was in a state of fear before his audiences with the Führer. No one who had not seen it with their own eyes would have believed it, Kersten wrote, 'nor would anybody believe how Himmler rejoiced if he came out of the interview successfully or, better still, received a word of praise.'[103]

For his part, despite his shortcomings as an Aryan, Himmler inspired loyalty at every level of his SS, not only among those of limited education like Stroop and Höss who formed some 40 per cent of the Führer-corps, but among those from socially more fortunate backgrounds like Karl Wolff. How else is one to interpret a passage in a remarkable letter Wolff wrote to his wife in February 1939?

> Fate has placed me as the closest colleague of an unparalleled man, the RFSS, whom I not only revere immensely on account of his quite extraordinary qualities, but of whose historical mission I am utterly convinced.[104]

The historical mission was, of course, the racial mission of the SS since Wolff went on to say how deeply depressed he was by the thought that his sons – who had their mother's brown hair and eyes – would not pass the selection procedures that would be developed in the SS over the next years, 'the more so since theoretically I could donate racially more highly qualified children to the *Volk*'.

In fact he had done so already by his mistress, the Gräfin. Heydrich had arranged for her to have the child discreetly in Budapest. It had been a boy – Widukind; he was faultlessly blond and blue-eyed. Leaving aside Wolff's marital problems, and making every allowance for his need to cite Himmler as mentor in his racial task, it appears that he did have enormous respect for him. This arose in part from Himmler's role as the most effective instrument of current racial theory which so suited Wolff. Yet there must have been more. The absolute conviction, the hard will, the ordered analysis followed by unequivocal decrees, the painstaking hours of work that Himmler put in and demanded from his subordinates inspired respect. But Himmler also exerted charm; there are too many accounts of his seemingly genuine concern for his people and their families to doubt this. Without these qualities it is difficult to imagine how he could have built up and retained his tight grip on all the instruments of national–racial and political control, the SS, SD, police and concentration camps.

Those outside observers who had not heard his secret speeches to his leader-corps always did find it difficult, if not impossible, to imagine; George Ward Price of the *Daily Mail*, who had attended Nuremberg rallies and SS bivouacs, and had had many talks with Himmler, 'never ceased to wonder that this mild-looking, mild-mannered, rather self-effacing man should have it in him to wield the great power that is his.'[105] Stephen Roberts described him in similar vein as lacking any distinction in appearance, 'modest in manner. His very indefinite features and his glasses make him look rather insignificant, more of a student than an agitator.' Roberts was not deceived by any other aspects of the Nazi regime or intentions, yet he entirely failed to penetrate Himmler's camouflage:

> it is ridiculous to view him as a young man carried away by his inordinate power and revelling in his lust for blood. Actually he sets an example of quiet dignity and simplicity of life that is often lacking in Nazi Germany, and remains entirely unspoilt, living like a clerk in a simple Berlin flat.[106]

By this date Himmler owned a splendid villa in the fashionable Berlin suburb of Dahlem alongside the other Party greats, as well as his country home on the Tegernsee, and – far from shunning grandeur – the seat of his Order, Wewelsburg, still under construction by forced concentration-camp labour, was as bizarre and extravagant a folly as anything Göring conceived. Unlike Göring's conscious attempts to act out the Wagnerian life, Himmler insisted that his own fantasy remain secret. Secrecy had been a principle of the knightly Orders. During a three-day visit to the castle in mid-January 1939, the Gruppenführer in charge, Taubert, asked Himmler what attitude he should take to requests to inspect the castle. Inspections did not come into consideration, Himmler replied shortly. If anyone were invited it must come as a special honour. He had in mind inviting one or another of the generals at some later date; the Reichsleiters, higher Party officials, would be invited too.[107]

The focal point of Wewelsburg, evidently owing much to the legend of King Arthur and the Knights of the Round Table, was a great dining hall with an oaken table to seat twelve picked from the senior Gruppenführers. The walls were to be adorned with their coats of arms; although a high proportion lacked these – as of course did Himmler himself – they were assisted in the drafting of designs by Professor Diebitsch and experts from Ahnenerbe. Below the hall in a circular cellar, known as 'the realm of the dead', was a shallow well-like structure in simple stone where, on the death of one of the knights, his arms were to be burned. The rooms allotted to the knights in the castle each commemorated different Germanic heroes and were decorated and furnished in period and provided with books and documents on their subject. For the entrance hall before these rooms Himmler intended a great triptych, to encapsulate his ideas on the meaning and purpose of the Order, as his instructions to the painter make clear:

> a) The attack of an SS troop in war, in which I envisage the representation of a dead or mortally wounded old SS man, who is married, to show that from death itself and despite it new life springs.
> b) A field in a new land being ploughed by a defence-corps farmer [*Wehrbauern*], an SS man.
> c) The newly founded village with the families and numerous children.[108]

Himmler's quarters in the castle were dedicated to the tenth-century Saxon King Heinrich I, known as 'the Fowler', who had checked the incursions of Magyar horse archers from the east and laid the basis of the German confederation of princes which became, under his son Otto, the Holy Roman Empire. On the thousandth anniversary of the Fowler's death in July 1936 Himmler had inaugurated a solemn remembrance festival at Quedlinburg, once Heinrich's seat; and in 1938 he had founded a King Heinrich Memorial Institution to 'revive the spirit and deeds of the King for our time'.[109] It was said that he thought he was the reincarnation of Heinrich I. It is doubtful if he believed in reincarnation in such a direct sense, as opposed to the physical transmission of the blood of the *Sippe* through generations, yet he liked hearing that he was called 'King Heinrich'; and certainly he saw himself as the embodiment of the Fowler's aims in the consolidation of Germany against the hordes from the east.

During this visit to Wewelsburg he told Taubert that he wanted for his rooms 'if possible' a long and narrow Gobelin tapestry 'with the figure of a fully developed virginal girl, a future mother', and on the opposite wall in stone 'the figure of a mother with a half-grown lad, who is becoming a man'.

He also told Taubert he desired a strongroom in the castle for a gold- and silver-treasury, 'first out of tradition, and second – one must be clear about this – as a reserve [*Notgroschen*] for bad times'. Reaching a room on the first floor he said he had a thought, whose realisation would prove very expensive: 'I should like to install a planetarium in the castle.' Exactly where this should be located he was still not sure.

Just as Stephen Roberts failed to discern this fantastic side of Himmler's nature, he missed the dark side. Neither he nor any other foreign observers were unaware of the tortures taking place in Gestapo cells or of the knock on the door in the early hours of the morning, which Germans had to fear, or the merciless treatment inside concentration camps, yet he and most others, it seems, failed to make a direct connection between Himmler's character and the methods and instruments of his will.

Towards the end of January 1939 Himmler made a public wireless broadcast in his capacity as Police Chief. It was the sacred duty of the police, he said, to protect the life and health of fellow Germans from misfortune, crime and injury; in the process many measures had to be taken which would place demands on the discipline and perhaps on the comfort of the individual. 'Many hard punishments must be executed which will affect the individual concerned and his family painfully, but which in the interests of the higher purpose are not only justified but must be demanded.'[110]

He reiterated his promise not to wait until crimes were committed before arresting criminals, and pledged that, in order to protect the populace, professional criminals who had been sentenced many times would be pursued more ruthlessly than before and isolated in concentration camps. He added that these camps were, contrary to the slanders in the foreign press, models of cleanliness, order and instruction; sharp and strong disciplinary measures were employed, to be sure, but treatment was just and the inmates learned trades through their work and training. 'The motto which stands over the camps runs, "There is one way to freedom. Its milestones are: obedience, zeal, honesty, order, cleanliness, temperance, truth, sense of sacrifice and love for the Fatherland." '[111]

It was the day after this broadcast, on 30 January, the sixth anniversary of the *Machtergreifung*, that Hitler in the course of his usual Reichstag speech issued his notorious public warning to the Jews. He wished, he said, to be a prophet: 'If international finance-Jewry in and outside Europe should succeed once again in plunging the peoples into a world war, then the result would not be the Bolshevisation of the earth and thereby the victory of Jewry, but the annihilation of the Jewish race in Europe.'[112]

The machinations to undermine the Czechoslovak state from within matured in March and the pattern of events that had preceded the Anschluss and the acquisition of the Sudeten territories was repeated: inspired press reports of atrocities against ethnic Germans, the massing of German forces on the border – with SS-Verfügungstruppe formations filling in gaps in Panzer divisions – and verbal bullying reached a climax as Hitler threatened to flatten the capital with Luftwaffe bombs. In the early hours of 15 March, the Czech President gave in and signed away what remained of his country. German troops had already crossed the border. The citizens of the capital, Prague, awoke to find swastika standards and field-grey steel-helmeted soldiers in the streets. Behind the columns came Heydrich's SD-Einsatz staffs, mixed teams of police, Gestapo and SD officials armed with lists prepared from the great card index in SD Section III 225, who directed Einsatzkommandos in the arrest of suspected leaders and ideological enemies, and established police, Gestapo and SD headquarters in what was shortly declared the Reich Protectorate of Bohemia and Moravia. Behind them came representatives of the SS-Ergänzungsamt to gather in all 'valuable' blood. The economy and the valuable armaments industry were incorporated into Göring's war economy. Farmland owned by Jews or ideological enemies was confiscated by officials of the settlement office of the RuSHA run by the impoverished noble, SS-Oberführer von Gottberg, whom Himmler appointed chief of what had been the Czech Land Registry; the farmland was then handed to SS families.

A large bank in the capital was commandeered for Gestapo headquarters. A British agent who had occasion to visit this sombre building a few months later has described the high hall and corridors which seemed dark even on a sunny day – perhaps, he thought, because of the black guards everywhere, two of whom, one on each side, escorted him to the official he had come to see.

In crossing the hall it was impossible not to think of the cellars underneath, where perhaps at that very moment human beings were being flogged to death for no other reason than that they were Czechs, Jews or Communists. The top floor was also used for prolonged forms of torture, because cries and shrieks behind shuttered windows were not likely to be audible at that height from the street.[113]

Himmler and Wolff, uniformed in field-grey again, entered the capital in the Führer's motor column, as they had entered Vienna; they and Martin Bormann were in his close entourage as he moved into the ancient Hradcany Palace and they shared his triumph as he looked out on his prize from an upper window, bareheaded, with balled fists.'Here I stand, and no power on earth will remove me from here.'[114] The moment made an indelible impression on Wolff, no doubt on Himmler and Bormann as well. For Hitler, it was another demonstration of his divinely ordained mission, and another proof that the western powers dared not oppose him.

The effect on the western governments was, of course, the reverse. For Chamberlain it was an especially brutal slap in the face, and from the moment that news of the coup reached London the policy of appeasing the dictators was buried. The first intelligence reports based on the movement of German Panzer and motorised divisions within Czechoslovakia suggested that Hitler's next move would be south-easterly through Hungary to Rumania in concert with Bulgaria.[115] In the search for a joint Anglo-French strategy to meet such a thrust, a pact with Soviet Russia was considered. It was a distasteful idea. Chamberlain distrusted the Bolsheviks, with some reason, and grossly underestimated the strength of the Red Army; besides it reminded him too much of the coalition policies which had culminated in the First World War. He preferred to encourage a Polish–Rumanian mutual assistance pact to be guaranteed by Great Britain and France. He was warned of the danger of excluding Russia, and the Chiefs of Staff advised that the western powers could help neither Poland nor Rumania to resist a German invasion. Nevertheless, when on 29 March the US Ambassador to London, Joseph Kennedy, gave Lord Halifax an 'urgent message' that Hitler's policy was aimed at Poland – a suggestion that seemed to be confirmed by other reports – Chamberlain was spurred to action. Meanwhile rumours of an imminent German attack on Danzig were affecting the stock market and the Cabinet debate which the Prime Minister called took place in an atmosphere of crisis. He pushed through his solution, and on 31 March told a hushed House of Commons that, should Poland's independence be threatened, Great Britain would come to her aid.

Canaris was with Hitler when the news of Chamberlain's speech was brought to him. The Führer erupted in an outburst of rage which caused the Admiral to doubt his sanity.[116] Afterwards ascending to the Berghof to brood on his response, he ordered Keitel to prepare orders for a possible attack on Poland. Keitel had the draft orders, codenamed 'Case White', ready by 3 April; preparations were to be completed by 1 September. On 6 April Chamberlain's Commons statement was formalised in a British guarantee to Poland. On 11 April Hitler signed 'Case White'.

The following month Himmler and Wolff joined Hitler's special train for a journey to inspect the West Wall fortifications, a complex of anti-tank obstructions and concrete gun emplacements stretching from the Belgian frontier to the Swiss border. The inspection lasted five days from 14 to 19 May; on the return journey on the 20th they stopped at the Army exercise ground at Münster where Himmler had arranged for a demonstration by his SS-Verfügungstruppe Standarte Deutschland. The regiment was commanded by a former Reichswehr officer, Felix Steiner, who had radical ideas about the training and equipment of more mobile, independent and aggressive troops, and Himmler had invited a number of generals to see the show. They were inclined to be superior about SS soldiers.

They watched an astounding demonstration. It was a full-scale infantry assault on entrenched and wired positions prepared by Army artillery batteries laying down a barrage of live shells, and carried through with the use of live machine-gun and rifle ammunition and live hand-grenades. The generals were visibly impressed. Hitler was delighted in more ways than one. Himmler received permission to form an SS-Verfügungstruppe division, and Keitel was ordered to have guns and equipment made available for the necessary SS artillery regiment.[117] According to Wolff, only two men were wounded by splinters during this demonstration, but casualties were not always so light during SS training with live ammunition. Himmler's response when tackled on this question was that 'every drop of blood spilled in peacetime saved streams of blood in battle.'[118]

There was a sense in which the SS-Verfügungstruppe had been created as a blood sacrifice – that at least was how Himmler had rationalised it to his Gruppenführers in his speech preceding Reichskristallnacht the previous November.

> the Verfügungstruppe is created to go into the field, to go to war. If I designate the total task of the SS together with the police – SS and police are to become increasingly united, and they will become so – as guaranteeing the internal security of Germany, then it is only possible to perform this task if a part of the Schutzstaffel, this *Führerkorps*, stands at the front and bleeds. Were we to bring no blood sacrifice and were we not to fight at the front, we would lose the moral obligation to shoot people who sneak home and are cowardly. That is the reason for the Verfügungstruppe, which has the very noblest task, to be permitted to go into the field.[119]

Himmler used this argument repeatedly, and there is no doubt he saw it as valid, yet it was also a very useful way to damp Army suspicions that the Verfügungstruppe was the thin end of the wedge of an SS take-over of the military. Given Hitler's and Himmler's revolutionary views, their distrust of the officer corps and their method of proceeding step by step, fatally weakening opponents before striking them down when they could no longer resist, there seems every probability that the long-term goal was indeed an SS take-over of the Army. But that was for after the war. In the meantime, the generals were an unpleasant necessity.

Three days after the stunning demonstration on the Münsterlager manoeuvre ground, Himmler and Wolff were present when Hitler took the leaders of the armed forces into his confidence about the meaning of 'Case White'. 'Danzig is not the object,' he confided. 'It is a question of broadening our *Lebensraum* in the east.' His object would be to isolate Poland; if this should not be possible, however, it would be better to attack in the west, settling the Polish problem at the same time.[120]

Through the summer, as the military preparations went forward, and Canaris filtered teams into Poland to reconnoitre key points in the communications system, and Heydrich prepared the provocation which would justify the attack, Hitler repeatedly assured Admiral Raeder, anxious for his infant fleet, that he need not fear war with England until 1942–3 at the earliest.

Part Two

THE TESTING TIME

8

War

The precise timing of the outbreak of the Second World War owed nothing to rational calculation, except perhaps on Stalin's part; but his role remains largely hidden in the Kremlin archives. Of the two other principals, Chamberlain and Hitler, neither wanted a general war; nor did their advisers, nor their military, nor the British or German people, nor the French government and people, who found themselves sucked along in the British wake, nor of course the Poles, who were the first victims. The situation had been created by Chamberlain's reckless pledge to Poland; the western powers' inability to support that pledge in any practical sense left an opening on the game board of eastern Europe between the two major powers who claimed that sphere, Germany and Russia. It was their moves, specifically their non-aggression pact, that decided the date and initial direction of the European war.

To suggest that this pact between ideological enemies was due to the diabolic cunning of either Stalin or Hitler is to accord more historical weight to individual 'genius' than even the Führer can bear. For instance, as early as 16 June, Sir Robert Vansittart told Lord Halifax that he had learned from his German informants, 'The military are delighted to have got Hitler on the path of an agreement with Soviet Russia. . . .'[1] Hitler knew he could not carry the generals into a two-front war, knew in any case that a two-front war would be the end of him militarily, yet in the summer of 1939, when Chamberlain followed his pledge to Poland by opening negotiations with Russia – which if successful would make the two-front war inevitable in 'Case White' – there was no talk of a generals' plot to unseat him. Even that apologist for the German 'resistance', Professor Gerhard Ritter, concedes that the opposition members who crossed to England in 1939 had nothing to say about a generals' revolt. On the contrary, the British pledge to Poland had made it easy for Goebbels to whip up hostility to England and so reduce the chances of an internal revolt.

The reason there was no danger from the *Reaktion* in 1939 as there had been in 1938 was that nationalism had become stronger than dislike or distrust of the Austrian Corporal – this because Chamberlain's pledge and the old bogy of 'encirclement' by England had forced German foreign policy back to something the traditional diplomats and generals could appreciate, not ideological – but *Realpolitik*. *Realpolitik* dictated an accommodation with Soviet Russia.

There is no doubt that Hitler would have preferred an agreement with England. That comes through as plainly from the records of the bewildering number of unofficial mediators between England and Germany during this fateful summer of 1939 as from the pages of *Mein Kampf*, and all subsequent speeches. But when it became clear to Hitler that the price for agreement with England was disarmament, hence the end of his aim to carve out an eastern empire by military force, he had only two options, outside the two-front war he was determined to avoid: either renounce his sacred mission or come to terms with his mortal enemies in the Kremlin to secure his eastern flank. The former was impossible personally and politically. The latter it had to be. He hoped, he even expected, that when England saw the Russian sword snatched from her hand and understood that she had no prospect of intervening effectively in eastern Europe she would renege on her pledge to Poland; if not he would finish off Poland in short time with a *Blitzkrieg*, then loose his Luftwaffe and Panzers in the west to smash France. Having secured his western flank, he could proceed with his real aims in the east. It was a circuitous route to Moscow and the Urals, hazarding much to chance and his enemies, but he could hope that once his tanks stood on the Channel coast England would see reason.

As for Stalin, he had no illusions about Hitler's ultimate aim. In order to parry it he had an obvious interest in embroiling Germany in war with the western powers: in the best case both sides would bleed and exhaust themselves; in the worst case it would give his military and industrial expansion programmes a year or two more. Also he could hope that by allying with Germany he might divert Germany's ally, Japan, from striking north – against Russia – into the alternative policy of a strike south against the British and Dutch colonies. It is interesting that President Roosevelt in Washington watched the game being played between Hitler and Stalin while Chamberlain and most of his advisers slept. But there was nothing Chamberlain could have done in any case to retrieve his initial slip, nothing Roosevelt could do with the American people so firmly in the grip of isolation. The war was engineered in the negotiations in Moscow and Berlin which divided Poland and eastern Europe into spheres of interest between them. If history has recorded that Stalin was the shrewder player and Hitler the bigger dupe, this again places more responsibility on individuals than they can bear. If Hitler was duped, it was by his own people who needed to pay homage to a warlord able to lead them into the sun of a greater Germanic empire; his personal tragedy was that he had come to believe them.

Yet, of course, at core Hitler was an ideologist. It is said that he and Nazism represented nothing more than the lust for power or the lust for destruction. Both are no doubt true at a subconscious level; Robert Byron smelled this at the 1938 Nuremberg Party rally when he recorded 'the negativeness and vacuity of it all. It is not so much intellectual poison as intellectual death – a greater death than physical death.'[2] But if it appeared that this urge to destruction was not wrapped up in powerful ideological symbolism it was only because the implications of the ideology and the steps along the path could not be stated publicly, or only in guarded or coded ways. In closed gatherings they were openly expressed, as Himmler's secret speeches to his Gruppenführers show. It is clear from these that race was the heart of the creed. It is clear from Wolff's reaction – to take one example – that the creed carried a terrible conviction, as powerful as Marxism, and clear that like Marxism it was believed to rest on 'scientific' principles, which justified it and justified any methods used in pursuance of its goals – although this was a very circular argument. Hitler was Himmler's mentor. His ideological graph shows a straight line from *Mein Kampf* to his final political testament twenty years later in the ruins of Berlin; any apparent deviations such as the Nazi–Soviet pact were purely tactical. Thus to view the Second World War only in terms of power politics and continental strategies, industrial production figures and numbers of men and tanks and aircraft and the careful weighing of chances – as the majority of the traditional career diplomats and generals and industrialists perhaps did – is to miss the key area, indeed the area without which the war would not have broken out when it did. The professional men of the *Reaktion*, whom Hitler despised for their rational and negative arguments, thought Hitler mad not simply because the people had raised him into a god but because he was a prophet.

In *Mein Kampf* Hitler had put in place of liberal, democratic claims for the rights of man 'only one most sacred human right . . . namely to ensure the preservation of the best of humanity in order to make possible a nobler development of this nature'.[3] Naturally this best, indeed only genuinely human, type was the Aryan, 'the Prometheus of mankind, from whose luminous brow the divine spark of genius flew to [light] all ages . . .'.[4] And naturally the antithesis of the Aryan was the Jew, who had lived through all ages as a parasite in the body of various host states, and whose final goal was 'the victory of democracy, or, as it is understood, the rule of parliamentarianism'.[5] The Jew was at the same time the carrier of Marxism; indeed in Hitler's prose the two terms seem interchangeable. Thus he described the German Marxists of 1918 as being guilty of high treason for causing revolution at home and treading over 2 million war dead for the sake of clambering into government office, then he went on:

If at the beginning of the war or during the war one had held twelve or fifteen thousand of these Hebrew *Volk*-corrupters under poison gas such as hundreds of thousands of our very best German workers from all strata and occupations had to endure in the field then the millionfold sacrifices of the front would not have been in vain. On the contrary, twelve thousand scoundrels removed at the right time would perhaps have saved the lives of a million respectable Germans of value for the future.[6]

That this was no mere flourish is suggested by his sections on practical race hygiene. Starting with the premise that the Reich had the task of gathering and preserving the most valuable stock of original Germanic racial elements and slowly and surely raising these to the dominant position – which was of course the blueprint for the SS – he stated that only the hereditarily sound should be allowed to propagate. The wishes and egos of individuals had to yield before the state, the guardian of the thousand-year future. The state had to place 'the most modern medical means in the service of this perception';[7] it had to declare the diseased and genetically unsound impotent and render them so practically:

> He who is bodily and mentally not sound and deserving [*würdig*] may not perpetuate this misfortune in the bodies of his children. The *völkisch* state has to perform the most gigantic rearing-task here. One day, however, it will appear as a deed greater than the most victorious wars of our present bourgeois era.[8]

Here, the idea of *völkisch* or racial purity has been inserted into the argument about *genetic* health. It is neither a Freudian slip nor careless writing, but a carefully coded message, as the inclusion of the word *würdig*, almost equivalent to 'valuable', indicates. Sterilisation laws to deal with the hereditarily diseased, mentally deficient, schizophrenics, epileptics and numerous other categories had, of course, followed within weeks of the *Machtergreifung*, and the slow but systematic exclusion of Jews from German society had begun, culminating with the nationwide orgy of destruction of Jewish property in November 1938. On 30 January 1939, the Jews had been warned that if they provoked world war it would result in the destruction of Jewry in Europe.

On 18 August 1939, three days after Hitler had been convinced – by talks between the German Ambassador in Moscow, von der Schulenburg, and a new Soviet Foreign Minister, Molotov – that Stalin was ready to do business,[9] a secret circular went out from the Reich Interior Ministry which marked the beginning of a programme of 'euthanasia' for mentally ill or deformed children up to three years old. Doctors would be required to report all such cases to the health authority on special forms; the forms would be forwarded to a panel of three medical assessors who would adjudicate over life or death by appending '−' or '+'. Should all three place a '+', a euthanasia warrant would be issued, signed by Reichsleiter Philipp Bouhler of the Führer's Chancellery, or SS-Oberführer Dr Viktor Brack, head of the Chancellery's 'Euthanasia' Department II.[10] And so it happened: infants marked for death were transferred to what were referred to as Children's Special Departments in politically reliable clinics, there to be given a 'mercy death' by injection or in one institution at Eglfing-Haar simply starved by a progressive reduction of diet.[11]

The children's euthanasia programme was typical of Hitler's cautious, step-by-step method of initiating policies which ran counter to current religious or moral values. It was designed deliberately to gain experience in procedures and methods and to habituate staff to radical acts, in this case acts contrary to their professional training. By beginning with abnormal infants the way was opened for the removal of older abnormal children, abnormal adults and finally adults selected for race. These steps followed quickly, cloaked, as Hitler intended, by the dislocations of war. Other typical features of the children's programme were the use of the panoply of officialdom to confer legality and euphemism to ease practitioners' consciences.

The euthanasia action was ordered by Hitler himself and was executed by high officials of his Chancellery, yet Hitler instructed Bouhler that 'the Führer's Chancellery must under no circumstances be seen to be active in this matter,'[12] another leitmotif of his programmes when they were contrary to conventional 'bourgeois' morality. Despite this Hitler did sign a decree for an adult euthanasia programme directed against 'lebensunwertes Leben' – literally 'life-unworthy life' or 'beings unworthy of existence' – a concept pioneered by two German professors as early as 1920. The decree appears to have been issued at the end of October backdated to the outbreak of war, 1 September 1939, and was typed on Hitler's personal headed paper. Addressed to Reichsleiter Bouhler and Hitler's personal physician, SS-Obersturmführer Dr Karl Brandt, it charged these two with 'enlarging the authority of certain physicians to be designated by name in such a manner that persons who, according to human judgement, are incurable can, upon a most careful diagnosis of their condition of sickness, be accorded a mercy death'.[13]

A similar system of special forms and adjudicating medical experts who appended their '−' or '+', was followed and those patients who drew the '+' were removed to special 'sanatoria' to be granted the 'mercy death'. The instruction sheet accompanying the special forms which were sent out as early as 9 October listed the patients who had to be reported under four divisions; first came schizophrenics, epileptics and sufferers from senile disorders, paralysis, encephalitis and terminal neurological conditions generally; next, patients who had been in institutions continually for five years; next, the criminally insane; finally, patients 'who do not possess German citizenship or are not of German or kindred blood'. These latter were to be designated by race and nationality. The purpose of including them is made clear by the examples listed to help doctors with the forms: 'German or kindred blood, Jew, Jewish *Mischling* [cross-breed] 1st or 2nd degree [i.e. half- or quarter-Jew], negro, negro *Mischling*, gypsy, gypsy *Mischling* etc.'.[14] Thus, there can be no doubt that this adult euthanasia programme, later designated 'T4' from the Chancellery offices at Tiergartenstrasse 4, Berlin-

Charlottenburg, from which it was run, was designed from the beginning with racially as well as mentally and physically 'life-unworthy life' in view. It was in the 'sanatoria' to which T4 patients were transported for their 'mercy death' that the gas chamber camouflaged as a shower room was inaugurated.

These programmes did not spring up suddenly with the outbreak of war; they had been discussed in a small circle for years and prepared in detail for months; Hitler had given oral orders for implementation at the latest in July 1939. Towards the end of that month fifteen to twenty directors of mental institutions and experts in the field had been invited by Bouhler to Berlin and initiated into the plans.[15] Bouhler had told them that, by killing a portion of the mentally ill, necessary hospital space and medical personnel would be released for the treatment of the wounded in the coming war. No one would be forced to participate. All present nevertheless agreed that they would. According to post-war testimony they were told only of 'euthanasia' for the mentally ill; in that case it is difficult to understand why the 'euthanasia' questionnaires contained questions about race.

At about the time of this meeting or soon afterwards Bouhler's associate in the programme, Viktor Brack, charged the chief of Criminal Police, Arthur Nebe, with the task of finding and testing a suitable killing method. Obviously Nebe's superiors, Heydrich and Himmler, were informed. Nebe entrusted the task to the head of the Chemistry and Physics Department of his Criminal Technical Institute (KTI), Dr Albert Widmann. According to Widmann's post-war testimony Nebe asked him if the KTI could supply large quantities of poison; when he asked the purpose: 'To kill people?', Nebe replied, 'No, to kill animals in human form, that is to say the mentally ill. . . .' Widmann already had experience with the effects of carbon monoxide (CO), and he advised the use of this gas.[16] By the time prototype gas chambers had been completed in the autumn of 1939, the offensive against Poland had been unleashed; the plan to release hospital space for wounded soldiers was carried out on Himmler's orders by Heydrich's Einsatzkommandos removing mental patients from institutions in Pomerania and West Prussia and killing them with a single shot in the back of the neck.[17] At the same time the Einsatzkommandos were rounding up Jews for abuse or massacre in every Polish town and village they entered.

The genetic and racial health or 'purity' of the *Volk* was as integral and inseparable a part of the scheme for eastern conquest as the destruction of Bolshevism, the desire for *Lebensraum* or the drive for raw materials, a master thread in a closely woven and comprehensively Germanic 'system'. At the psychic level it was probably *the* master thread. The psychiatrist Robert Jay Liston, who spent almost ten years studying the central role of German doctors in the Nazi extermination programme, concluded: 'Rather than medical killing being subsumed to war, the war itself was subsumed to the vast biomedical vision of which "euthanasia" was a part. Or to put the matter another way, the deepest impulses behind the war had to do with the sequence of sterilisation, direct medical killing and genocide.'[18]

Hitler's inner compulsion to begin his mission in the east was formalised on 15 August, the day von der Schulenburg's discussion with Molotov convinced him he would secure the agreement he wanted with Stalin. He fixed Day Y for the 26th or 27th; military, naval and air commanders were recalled from leave; Canaris received orders to send Abwehr 'K' (combat) and 'S' (sabotage) teams across the Polish border; Heydrich, who had begun final preparations for the 'provocation' exactly a week before, was given the night of the 25th/26th as his target date. Gisevius came to von Hassell in a state of great excitement: Hitler wanted to loose the blow against Poland; he did not believe the western powers would attack. Von Hassell found that difficult to credit.

The Führer was high above the world in his eyrie on the Obersalzberg. Next morning, 16 August, he was joined by his close entourage for a celebration of the twenty-fifth anniversary of that day in 1914 when an unknown Austrian artist scraping a living painting view cards had signed on in Munich as a volunteer with the Bavarian Reserve Infantry Division 16. On the 22nd, he addressed senior generals and admirals: 'I shall supply a propagandist reason for starting the war. The victor will not be asked, later on, whether he told the truth or not. . . .'[19]

Von Ribbentrop flew to Moscow the following morning, and after conversations with Stalin and Molotov put his signature to the non-aggression pact with the Soviet Union. A secret protocol divided Poland between them along the Narev, Vistula, San river line, declared Lithuania in the German sphere and the two northern Baltic states, Estonia and Latvia, in the Russian sphere as well as Finland and on the southern flank the Rumanian province of Bessarabia. The same day the British Ambassador Nevile Henderson flew to Hitler to convey a letter which Chamberlain had addressed to him on the 22nd, after learning of the prospective German–Soviet agreement and the fact that circles in Berlin believed it would preclude intervention by Great Britain on behalf of Poland. 'No greater mistake could be made,' Chamberlain wrote; 'it cannot alter Great Britain's obligation to Poland.'

After relieving his emotions on Henderson in 'violent, recriminatory and exaggerated language' Hitler retired to compose a reply. This pinned the blame for the crisis on those who had consistently opposed any peaceful revision of 'the crime committed by the Versailles dictat' and reiterated protestations that he had fought all his life for Anglo-German friendship. Should there be any change in the present British attitude nobody would be happier than he.

The following evening Hitler flew back to Berlin, and next morning, the 25th, Himmler and Wolff joined other Party leaders in the Reich Chancellery to await his final decision on war or peace. Provisionally the attack on Poland had been fixed for the 26th at 4.30 a.m.; to meet this

timing the executive order had to be given by three o'clock that afternoon. It
is notable that Himmler appears to have played little part in the decisions of
these fateful days.[20] Göring, von Ribbentrop, von Weizsäcker of the Foreign
Ministry, Keitel, Bormann had been at Hitler's side; Goebbels had whipped
up the press against the Poles. Himmler had remained working feverishly
in Berlin, co-ordinating his Verfügungstruppe and reinforced Totenkopf
battalions and SD–Security Police Einsatzkommandos with the Army
command. If he exercised the malign influence on the Führer attributed to
him by Goerdeler and others of the opposition, it does not seem to have
amounted to more than agreement on the measures necessary to subjugate
Poland after military victory: on the one hand to harness ethnic Germans,
or *Volksdeutsche*, and to Germanise, or *eindeutschen*, suitable Poles who
appeared to have Germanic blood; on the other hand to liquidate the
Polish leadership classes, nobility, officers, clergy, teachers, intelligentsia.
Jews also were to be removed but because of the huge numbers involved,
over three million, considerably more than in the Reich itself, they were in
the first place to be rounded up and driven into mass ghettos. In this sense
Himmler and Heydrich, who were responsible for the detailed planning of
these actions, may be said to have contributed to Hitler's decision since
subconscious blood-lust rationalised as purification appears to have played
a larger part in the decision for war than serious consideration.

It is said that Hitler was blinded by the success of his previous
bloodless victories and the godlike status he had attained, and simply lost
the patience he had displayed in previous crises. But that is another way of
saying that he wanted war – for he had been warned. Another explanation
is that the war economy, by then reaching the levels of production attained
in the final year of the First World War, was forcing an inflationary crisis – as
Schacht and Goerdeler certainly believed – and Hitler was pushed into war
as an alternative to domestic trouble. Göring's recent biographer, Richard
Overy, has found little evidence in support.

Whatever explanations are accepted, Himmler had no overt influence on
the outcome. Undoubtedly his hard views reinforced Hitler's own desire for
war; they were blood-brothers, each with his score to settle with the world,
but, in the vital matter of when and how, Himmler was content to bow to
his Führer's genius. He had been briefed on his task in Poland before Hitler
harangued the generals at the Berghof on the 22nd. 'Close your heart to
pity,' Hitler had told the military chiefs. 'Act brutally.'[21] He was warning
them of what was to be expected from Himmler's Einsatzkommandos behind
the lines.

Some time after midday on the 25th word went around those waiting
in the Chancellery that the British Ambassador had been called for an
interview with the Führer. Sir Nevile arrived at 1.30. He found a different
Hitler, who 'spoke with calm and apparent sincerity'. Once the question of
Danzig and the Polish 'corridor' through Prussia had been settled, he said, he
was ready personally to pledge the continued existence of the British empire

and to place the power of the German Reich at its disposal, provided only that some limited colonial demands were met and his obligations towards Italy were respected. Once the Polish question was settled he would make no further demands since he preferred to end his life 'as an artist and not as a warmonger'.[22] When Henderson left there was less than half an hour before the deadline.

It is a measure of Hitler's uncertainty that three o'clock struck, and he had still not given the word. Two minutes later the doors from his study opened, and he emerged before the expectant gathering to announce 'Fall Weiss!' – 'Case White!'

It is not clear why he said it. He had not succeeded in detaching England from Poland; Henderson was due to fly to London the following morning with his latest proposals; Göring's unofficial peace ambassador, the Swedish businessman Birger Dahlerus, had only just landed at London–Croydon airport to begin his work with Lord Halifax. The decision seems explicable only in terms of the excitement and strain in which Hitler had been living the past fortnight and his habitual response in crisis to take up advanced, exposed positions. In any case he soon rescinded the order. Some time after 4.30 he received news that Great Britain and Poland were about to sign their pact, and shortly after six he was handed a message from his friend Mussolini to say that Italy could render Germany no assistance in the event of a conflict with Poland; she had neither the military nor the economic strength to resist an Anglo-French attack. Hitler was shattered. Sending for Keitel, he told him to hold everything. 'I need time to negotiate.'[23]

Countermanding orders were passed down to all units massed around the borders. The clandestine preparations were less easy to halt; one of Canaris' combat teams inside Poland could not be raised by radio, and one of Heydrich's SS teams in Polish uniforms began a mock skirmish in the woods around the German customs post at Hochlinden. Otherwise, the aborted attack was more or less concealed from the world, although it was evident to every German citizen that something was up; because of military requirements trains no longer ran to time-tables, petrol stations had nothing to sell, and on the 27th a system of rationing for food and clothing came into force; moreover, the Nuremberg Party rally was cancelled. During the next few days as official and unofficial negotiations for a bloodless solution continued unabated between Chamberlain–Halifax–Henderson and Hitler–Göring–Ribbentrop, with the Polish and Italian governments also involved, Hitler somehow returned to his original determination. On 31 August he gave the word again for 'Case White'.

Heydrich's special 'provocation' teams reassembled to await the code-words to begin their work; they came through some time after ten that night. SS-Sturmbannführer Alfred Naujocks, veteran assassination-squad leader, took over the German radio station at the border town of Gleiwitz, and a Polish-speaking member of his team broke into the broadcast in accented German, 'This is the Polish rebel force. Radio station Gleiwitz is in our hands. The hour of freedom has struck!'[24] A Polish prisoner who had been anaesthetised and brought to the station was shot; his dead body was photographed *in situ* for the press. Meanwhile the team of Polish-speaking SS men in Polish uniforms who had already performed a dress rehearsal on the night of the 25th, attacked the German customs post at Hochlinden again and an opposing SS team uniformed as border police counter-attacked and chased them off. A third team brought a dozen or so inmates of Sachsenhausen concentration camp, referred to in the orders as *Konserven*, or 'tinned food', to the scene. They were dressed in Polish uniforms supplied by Canaris' agents and were either shot before they got there or shot on arrival, and left lying to be photographed. Another Polish-speaking SS team attacked and wrecked the German forestry station at Pitschen, smearing ox-blood over the walls and floor.

At 4.30 next morning, 1 September, without a declaration of war, German forces began the assault much as von Reichenau had described *Blitzkrieg* to Winterbotham five years before, Luftwaffe and Panzer columns acting in concert to overwhelm and cut through the defences. They struck east from Pomerania, west from East Prussia and in the south von Reichenau crossed the border from Silesia. SS-Verfügungstruppe were incorporated into three of the five armies: Felix Steiner's Standarte Deutschland together with the newly formed SS artillery *Standarte*, the SS reconnaissance battalion and an Army Panzer regiment formed the 4th Panzer Brigade under the command of the Army General Kempf. SS-*Standarte* Germania formed part of the army moving in from East Prussia, the Leibstandarte Adolf Hitler and an SS engineer Battalion part of Reichenau's Tenth Army from Silesia.

An hour later Hitler broadcast to the nation that Poland had refused to negotiate and had violated the frontier; there had been fourteen border incidents during the night. 'In order to put an end to this lunacy I have no choice than to meet force with force.' Later that morning he mounted the rostrum in the Kroll Opera used to house the Reichstag since the fire, and repeated that he had been forced to take up arms in defence of the Reich. From now on he was just the first soldier in the Reich. He had put on that uniform that was most sacred and dear to him – the parallel with Himmler's early diary entries springs to mind – and he would not take it off again until victory was secured, or he would not survive. His jacket was field-grey; it resembled that of an officer in the SS-Verfügungstruppe without distinguishing flashes.

Two days later Chamberlain finally gave up hope of halting the attack by negotiation and resigned himself to war. An ultimatum was drafted and Sir Nevile Henderson was instructed to call on von Ribbentrop at nine the following morning, 3 September, to present it. Von Ribbentrop was at the Chancellery with Hitler. When the ultimatum was brought in and translated, Hitler sat silent and immobile; after what seemed an age, he turned to his Foreign Minister with a savage look, 'What now?'[25]

Henderson had the impression when the ultimatum expired two hours later that the mass of the German people were 'horror-struck at the whole idea of the war which was being thus thrust upon them'.[26] The American journalist William Shirer formed a similar impression as he looked at silent groups in the Wilhelmplatz; the people seemed stunned, unable to comprehend that Hitler had led them into a world war.[27]

Of the armed services, the one least prepared for the announcement was the Navy, which still had years to make up before it would be in a condition to challenge the Royal Navy. Raeder recorded his despair for the file: 'Today the war breaks out against England–France, which according to the Führer we need not have reckoned with before about 1944 and which until the last moment the Führer believed he should prevent. . . .'[28]

What Himmler's reaction was to this first major setback for the Führer's policy is not recorded. He was still in Berlin; he could not have failed to be aware of the atmosphere of 'utter gloom and depression' which struck Henderson everywhere he went: 'The whole effect was one of apathy and unhappiness, or bewilderment.' But faintheartedness was what the SS had been formed to counter. Now the peacetime training in hardness and total dedication to duty had to prove itself.

'The Reichsführer-SS', Eicke lectured the officers of the replacement concentration camp guard units that day,

> desires from every SS-Führer model duty-consciousness and commitment to *Volk* and fatherland to the point of self-sacrifice. Now in this war the SS has the main task of protecting Adolf Hitler's state, above all from every internal danger. A revolution as in 1918 is out of the question. Every enemy of the state, every war-saboteur is to be liquidated. The Führer desires from the SS that they protect the homeland from all hostile intrigues.[29]

Only the SS, he went on, could protect the National Socialist state from internal threat; other organisations lacked the necessary hardness.

On the evening that he delivered this address at Sachsenhausen the first war-saboteur was delivered to the camp. He was a communist who had been denounced for refusing air-defence work at the Junkers factory at Dessau. He had been taken to Gestapo headquarters, Berlin, for interrogation, and a report laid before Himmler, who had ordered his immediate execution. According to the secret mobilisation orders Himmler had promulgated, all executions he or the Gestapo decreed had to be carried out in the nearest concentration camp.

The prisoner arrived in shackles between two Gestapo officials, and the Kommandant was handed a brief warrant stating that the named man was to be shot on the orders of the RFSS; he was to be informed of this in the *Arrest* cell, and was to be executed one hour afterwards. Rudolf Höss, as adjutant of the camp at that period, carried out these instructions to the letter, using a firing squad he selected from three older NCOs and giving the condemned man the *coup de grâce* himself with his revolver. Over the following weeks he had to repeat the performance almost daily, chiefly on men condemned for refusing call-up or as 'war-saboteurs'. This he gleaned from the escorting Gestapo officials; the execution warrants themselves carried no details of the offence.

After the final break with the western powers there was nothing to keep Hitler in Berlin, and he left on 5 September with Keitel and the OKW staff in his special mobile headquarters train for the eastern border. Among the liaison officers from all branches of the services and major ministries, Karl Wolff was aboard as Himmler's eyes and ears. Göring left Berlin on the same day with his Air Staff in his special train *Asien*, and Himmler with his staff in his special train 'Heinrich', which he shared with von Ribbentrop and the Secretary of the Reich Chancellery, Dr Lammers. The train was equipped with a telegraph and wireless *Zentrale*, giving the three leaders complete communication and information facilities wherever they stopped, and several compartments were furnished as offices. One of Heydrich's young protégés, Walter Schellenberg, described the activity here:

> The rattling of typewriters and the loud voices of those who were dictating created an almost unbearable din even when the train was standing still, but it grew quite intolerable on top of the noise of the wheels. So I made myself a work table, using a crate covered by a blanket in the spacious sleeper that had been reserved for me.[30]

Schellenberg, whose task was to deal with incoming SD courier mail and maintain the closest touch with Heydrich in Berlin, reported to Himmler every morning. He found it unnerving: the eyes behind the pince-nez were seldom visible. The expression was equally impenetrable, and since he made no comment it was impossible for Schellenberg to tell what he was thinking or even if he were interested. Later, after Schellenberg had worked himself into his confidence – one of his particular *fortes* – Himmler began to probe and promote discussion, as much it seemed to 'display the universality of his own interests and knowledge' as to test Schellenberg's views. Schellenberg felt as though he were back at school facing his old headmaster. Still Himmler expressed no opinion on the specific reports. Schellenberg came to realise that this 'air of aloofness, of being above ordinary conflicts', was a characteristic of Himmler's indecisive nature, which had become a feature of his whole method of control. When something went wrong a subordinate could always be blamed.[31]

Though it may appear strange that the man who expressed such extremes of certainty in his secret speeches to his Gruppenführers and took such draconian decisions over the fate of individuals or groups was basically indecisive, there are too many independent accounts of this to doubt it. The two men who were probably closer to him for a longer period than even Karl Wolff, the chief of his personal staff, Dr Rudolf Brandt, and his 'magic Buddha', Felix Kersten, both referred to his vacillating nature and inability to make up his mind.[32] Yet this apparent contradiction is surely one of the keys to understanding him: was it not because he was so little able to make up his mind that he needed a creed to hold on to and a master to obey? Was it not because he was unsure of himself, indeed almost certainly thought of himself as a little worm beside the 'old fighters' of the Party and the Aryans with whom he surrounded himself, that he not only conformed to, but exaggerated, the prevailing Germanic myths and the Freikorps spirit of hardness and ruthlessness?

In his secret speeches and talks with his Gruppenführers who adhered to the same creed, he could escape to his ideal world in which everything dovetailed into place and there were no half-tones, only Germanic heroes and deepest villains. Then he had no need for judgement or decision; everything followed from the very few, very simple premises. Again, when he was faced with an obvious enemy of the *Volk*, whether a saboteur or a 'race-defiler', there was no need for decision; that was dictated by the creed. But in the real world of half-tones and insidious corruptions there were seldom such obvious situations and he shrank back into his uncertain self or sought instructions from his Führer. Kersten had no doubt that his severe stomach convulsions were not due to a poor constitution or overwork, but were 'the expression of this psychic division, which extended over his whole life'. He soon realised that he could bring him relief but never achieve a cure, for the cause of the convulsions was constantly being aggravated.[33]

Hitler displayed similar indecisiveness before large decisions as the rationally inexplicable course of events between 24 August and his final order for 'Case White' on 30 August indicates. He, too, so lacked powers of judgement that he had to cling to his simple creed and despise the conventionally educated who brought logical arguments to bear on real problems. The story of the Third Reich suggests that his scorn was not misplaced. Yet, although the Reich was a harmonisation of countless strands of Germanic and European history, the specific forms of aggression, in particular the monstrous crimes now launched in the east, seem to have arisen not so much from a warrior caste confident in its strength as from the pathology of weakness and inferiority. It is surely no accident that the three leaders who increased their power from the outbreak of war until the final collapse and who kept the Reich on its straight course for destruction, Hitler, Himmler, Goebbels, had the best reasons for feeling inferior.

The Luftwaffe and Panzer and motorised columns sliced the Polish defences and advanced at speed, bloodied but seldom seriously impeded by the ill-equipped and numerically inferior defending forces. The Luftwaffe early established total command in the air; after that Poland was lost. The leaders' trains followed the advancing front, 'Heinrich' often closing up on the Führer's train so that Himmler could attend a headquarters conference or accompany Hitler on a tour to the front. Schellenberg has described these journeys by car, starting usually at nine or ten in the morning, equipped with sandwiches, thermos flasks of hot tea and cognac, and returning to the trains towards nightfall. Great stretches of countryside appeared untouched by war, but on the roads the column of cars passed continuous streams of lorries, armoured cars and tanks, and coming in the opposite direction prisoners 'exhausted by battle, strain and hunger'. Where the Polish lines had held, the ground was churned for short stretches by shells and bombs, trees and houses razed as in the first war battlefields Hitler had known.

Heydrich's Einsatzkommandos were following the advancing armies, rounding up Jews, aristocrats, priests and the professional classes in every community they entered. In some cases they took their victims to 'reception centres' for execution, in some cases simply stood them against a wall and shot them or hung them in rows from long beams in the market place; on other occasions they made deadly sport, chasing Jews through the streets or into synagogues, hurling grenades in after them, setting fire to buildings and burning them alive. They were assisted in their task by fanatic ethnic Germans, formerly a minority in the Polish state created by Versailles, who had some scores to settle with the Poles and who were formed into so-called 'self-protection' formations. Like Wolff,[34] Schellenberg in his post-war account made no mention of this deliberate mass murder in the interests of German mastery and race hygiene, nor the grisly evidence of it he must have seen on these tours with Himmler.[35]

As Heydrich expressed the plan to his SD and Security Police departmental chiefs and Einsatzgruppen commanders on 21 September, the Polish nation was to be expunged from the map, the Polish people, deprived of their leaders and educated classes by physical liquidation, were to be incorporated into the German economy as migrant workers – except those to be reclaimed for the Reich because they possessed Germanic blood. The migrant workers were to find a home in the southern region of the former Polish state around Cracow.

Precisely what Heydrich said about Polish Jews will never be known, but as summarised in a secret circular he made a distinction 'between 1) the ultimate aim which requires a long period of time, and 2) the stages in the implementation of this ultimate aim, to be carried out on a short-term basis'.[36] These preliminary stages included clearing Jews completely from the western areas of the occupied territory and concentrating them in the east in large cities at railway junctions or along railways 'so that future measures may be accomplished more easily'. Property and land belonging to Jews was to be expropriated. Confronted with this document after the war, Adolf Eichmann could think of no other explanation for the term 'ultimate aim' than physical extermination, and had to agree that 'this, call it basic, conception was already firmly established at this date, 21 September 1939.'[37]

By this date the Polish war was over bar pockets of resistance in Warsaw and a few other isolated areas. The Russians, alarmed at the speed of conquest, had already begun moving into their allotted regions and within a week their forces met the Germans at the agreed dividing line, which was moved somewhat further east during negotiations in Moscow on the 27th and 28th; this was in return for Hitler giving up his claim to Lithuania. On the face of it Stalin seemed to have gained by the new arrangement, which brought the Soviet empire to the very borders of East Prussia. It is doubtful if Hitler gave it a thought; he was resolved to unleash his armies against Russia at the first opportunity. In the meantime he needed a quick settlement in the east in order to convince the western powers that there was no point in continuing the war – or more probably while he struck west to smash France and drive Britain from the continent in order finally to free himself for the real war for the east.

Meanwhile Warsaw fell. On the same day, 27 September, Heydrich's SD and Security Police Offices were merged into a single Reich Security Head Office (Reichssicherheitshauptamt) or RSHA – not to be confused with the long-established RuSHA, the Race and Settlement Head Office. The merger had been under discussion for most of the year. It was a step, a very small one, on the road to Himmler's ultimate goal of complete fusion between the security services and the SS, and it was obviously precipitated by the key role of the SS in the subjugation of Poland. Yet it scarcely addressed the problem of executive unity; the Ordnungspolizei, which remained under Daluege, the ethnic German formations and the Totenkopf police reinforcement units, who came to play a major role in the further enslavement of the Poles, remained outside. It was a typical Himmler compromise, sacrificing administrative clarity to caution lest any single authority gain enough power to challenge his overall leadership. Since he was aping, consciously or unconsciously, the game Hitler was playing in the Reich as a whole between the Party organisation, the original state bureaucracy, the armed forces, the SS and special commissioners created for particular areas, the tangle of competing authorities became ever more hopelessly confused as the Reich expanded. Consciously or unconsciously both he and Hitler needed this confusion not simply as a safeguard against the growth of overmighty subjects, but on the psychic level as reassurance that they alone – Hitler in the Reich, Himmler in the SS and police – were in control and able to cut through the web of competing interests to offer the definitive solution.

Occupied Poland was an example. It was divided into four main administrative districts: in the north and west three *Gaue*, Greater West Prussia, Greater East Prussia and the Warthegau (which included Poznan and Lodz), each controlled by a Gauleiter appointed by the Party; while the whole south-east was designated the General Gouvernement Polen, administered by a governor-general. However, these Party functionaries had no direct authority over either the military forces responsible for the internal security of occupied territory, or the SS and security forces who had to carry out the special measures ordered in the occupied east. In these vital areas the Gauleiters had to work at first through the commanders of the military districts and Heydrich's Einsatzgruppen commanders, later through Himmler's regional representatives styled Höheren SS und Polizeiführer (Higher SS and Police Leaders) – HSSPFs. Powerful as the HSSPFs were in theory, they lacked real authority over the organs of the RSHA – the SD, Gestapo, Criminal Police and foreign intelligence service – under Heydrich – or even the Ordnungspolizei or Totenkopf formations. The result, as in the Reich itself, was a network of rivalries in which the more forceful character, the more wily politician or the one with the most direct wires to the highest authority prevailed. It was the survival of the politically most adaptable, which in the atmosphere set by the highest leadership and the Party *Weltanschauung* meant the most radical.

This tendency was especially marked in the wake of the lightning victory over Poland. Thus there is little sense in seeking a point source for the extreme, insanely counter-productive 'solutions' to the problems of the Jews, Poles and other subject populations in the east – whether they were handed down as 'the Führer's wish' or passed up to him by his Bormanns, Goebbels, Görings, Himmlers, Heydrichs – or whether, as has been alleged by apparently serious scholars, the 'final solution' to the Jewish question emerged from the exigencies of war and the zeal of technicians at the base of the pyramid. These questions have no meaning. Everything that had happened, everything that was to happen was implicit in the *Weltanschauung*, and the Reich was no longer, if it had ever been, tied to the earth or bound by space or time; it rode the spiral of its own fantastic imagery, taking Hitler up with it and looking to him to draw it higher. Anyone who retained some grip on the logic of resources and production, or the law, or old religious and moral certitudes and tried to tether down a corner here or there simply lost his hold. Of course, this had been so for years. But it is only perhaps now, in the war years, that we can discern the extent of the illusion. And it is now that the leaders can be seen, not as individuals with particular characteristics exercising free will in their own free orbits, but as interdependent, intermeshing parts of the machine of revolution.

The Himmler we have watched growing from a mother's boy, suffering in the school gym, the *Star* of his class, tormented by adolescent failure, the Heini who fixed things, who saw his fraternity colleagues home when they were drunk, took cakes to the destitute old lady, was moved by the story of the Christ-child, vowed he would always love God, was perhaps a part of the Reichsführer-SS, but he was not him. The Reichsführer was created from that 'Himmler' in conjunction with the Nazi Party – it would be truer to say that the several Reichsführers-SS were joint creations of that Himmler and whichever group he found himself in.

The question, therefore, of whether Himmler, Heydrich, Hitler or anyone else was ultimately responsible for the policy of removing the

Polish leadership and using the rest as slaves for the Reich, and of physically exterminating European Jewry – if that was what Heydrich had meant by 'ultimate aim' in his circular of 21 September – has no meaning. There was no entity 'Himmler' capable of being viewed in isolation; if there had been it is apparent that that 'Himmler' would have had neither the self-confidence nor the power to have ordered helotry and genocide. We are peering dimly into a madhouse, but it is a communal asylum, and the inmates go home in the evening and discuss homeopathic medicine or read their children bedtime fairy tales. We are not dealing with individual psychopaths; we are not dealing with a Reichsführer who was merely the sum of Heinrich Himmler's genes and experiences, a man who could be described as either 'indecisive' or 'ruthless' or labelled with any of the attributes he has been given here. We are dealing with something which was infinitely greater and infinitely less than the sum of 'Himmler's' characteristics, a corpuscle in the bloodstream of the German experience circulated by forces over which that 'Himmler' had no control and was, by the nature of his involvement, totally unaware. The same can be said of the 'Hitler' precipitated into the Polish war by his lust for blood, and the 'Heydrich' who reported to the RSHA departmental chiefs – so Schellenberg minuted on 27 September – that 'of the Polish leadership, there remained in the occupied area at the most 3 per cent.' The rest had been subjected to 'special treatment' – a term that Heydrich or someone else in the SD or Gestapo had coined for cases which, because of their seriousness, danger and propaganda consequences, 'deserve to be considered for elimination, ruthlessly and without respect of persons'.[38]

Rudolf Höss was shocked to find an SS officer from the Berlin Gestapa brought to him for execution. He knew the man well; the officer had regularly brought war-saboteurs and draft-dodgers to Sachsenhausen for Höss's firing squad; he had brought one down the previous day and afterwards he and Höss had taken a meal together in the Mess. He was in his middle thirties, married with three children. Now Höss learned that he was to have brought a communist to the camp that day for shooting, but had softened to the man's plea for a final leave-taking with his wife and escorted him home. There, while he and his subordinate talked to the wife in the living room, the communist had escaped. When he reported this he was arrested and tried by court martial. Within an hour the death sentence had been pronounced; both Heydrich and Heinrich Müller interceded for him with Himmler, but Himmler would not hear of mercy; the first serious dereliction of duty by an SS-Führer in the war had to be punished severely.

Höss read the brief warrant to the man in the *Arrest* cell, and went to summon his three-man firing squad.

He went, calm and composed, to his death. How *I* however could have given the firing order *calmly* I still cannot conceive. The three men who fired did not know whom they had to shoot and that was good, perhaps they would have trembled. I was so agitated inwardly I could scarcely place my pistol to his temple for the finishing shot. Nevertheless I managed to pull myself together so that the others noticed nothing untoward. . . . This shooting remains with me always in connection with the continual demands for self-conquest and uncompromising hardness.[39]

On 5 October Hitler entered Warsaw for his triumph; Himmler and Wolff accompanied him as they had accompanied him for his triumphal entries into Vienna and Prague and most recently Danzig. Afterwards there was a discussion about complaints by the military of the brutal activities of the Einsatzkommandos, and in some instances actual interference with their tasks. Canaris was responsible for at least some of the Army sensitivity. Heydrich had told him early in September that his groups had orders to kill aristocrats, priests and Jews, and Canaris had instructed his agents in the field to keep an eye on the Einsatzkommandos and submit detailed reports of their activities; he had used these to alert the generals to the atrocities committed in their areas.[40] This seems to have been the turning point in his attitude towards Hitler – although with such a complex personality it is hardly possible to be sure. At least from this time on his feelings for the Führer and the Party which he and the Navy had done so much to promote from the very earliest days became increasingly ambiguous. He remained a committed nationalist, but, ever more pessimistic about the methods of National Socialism, he lapsed like thinking members of the *Reaktion* into despair. He more than any knew their impotence before the Führer myth and the momentum of National Socialism, especially among the younger generation; he more than any knew in detail the extent of the abominations practised in the east. He confided in private, 'Our children's children will have to bear the blame for this.'[41]

Canaris was actually occupying the most exposed outpost at the front line of the older Germany. It is not surprising he remains an enigma. Just as there was no single entity 'Hitler' or 'Himmler' there was no 'Canaris': the daring young first war naval intelligence officer and U-boat commander, the ruthless anti-communist, anti-Versailles, anti-Republican activist of post-war, now a small, white-haired, rather round-shouldered and even shabby-looking admiral with an occasional lisp and a deliberately casual, ambiguous manner had dissolved behind the manifold faces of the master spy who was both chief of the Wehrmacht intelligence services and confidant, aid and shelter for the most active groups of the rational opposition to Hitler and all his works. It is unlikely he knew who he was himself, understandable that his devotion to his pet dachshunds became obsessive, and that we can still wonder whose side he was really on. He registered a mild complaint with Keitel about the Polish policy early on when he visited the Führer train on 12 September, pointing out that 'The world would ultimately extend responsibility to the Wehrmacht because these things had happened under their noses.'[42] Keitel appeared not to understand since the Führer had arranged for the SS to carry out the tasks specifically so that the Wehrmacht would not have to dirty its hands.

That seems to have been Canaris' single official attempt to bring his objections to bear at the highest level, even though his subsequent tours through Poland, especially the burning ruins of Warsaw, left him, as von Hassell noted in his diary, 'utterly shattered'. He knew Heydrich and Hitler and the roots of the policy in the Nazi creed too intimately to expect to influence them directly – knew besides that here as in most of its institutions and methods Nazism aped Bolshevism; the mass grave of Polish officers discovered later in Katyn Forest in the Russian-occupied zone came to symbolise this truth. Consequently he sought to work through the sense of honour and the practical common sense of individual corps commanders by supplying detailed reports of the horrors. One report was instrumental in preventing, at least for the time, the activities of Himmler's friend SS-Obergruppenführer von Woyrsch, commanding the Einsatzgruppe operating in the area of the Fourteenth Army.[43]

On 5 October, while Hitler and Himmler were discussing these problems in Warsaw after the victory celebrations, the Gauleiter for Greater West Danzig, Albert Forster – no friend to Himmler – was especially vehement in his complaints about Army interference in the 'pacification' policy in his *Gau*. Hitler needed no prodding to remove the generals from their civil responsibilities – effected over the following weeks. Himmler suggested that he himself take overall responsibility for race policy in the area; this was the SS mission. Two days later he was appointed by Führer decree Reichskommissar for the Consolidation of German Nationhood. His duties were itemised as, first, the repatriation of ethnic Germans from abroad, in the first instance from the Baltic states now assigned to the Russian sphere; secondly, 'the elimination of the damaging influence of such portions of the foreign population as constitute a danger for the Reich and the German community' – this meant a continuation of existing policies for the elimination of the Polish leadership and Jews; thirdly, the formation of new German settlement areas, both for the home-coming ethnic Germans and for Germans from the Reich.[44]

This did nothing to eliminate conflict between the different authorities, indeed exacerbated them by imposing a mass resettlement policy right across the regional divisions and the claims of the war economy. Adolf Eichmann, who had conducted the successful business in Jewish emigration from Vienna, subsequently from Prague, was transferred back to head a Central Office for Jewish Emigration in Berlin. His chief task now, instead of promoting emigration from the Reich to Palestine, the USA and other countries overseas, was simply to deport Jews to the occupied east of Poland as the first, preliminary stage before what Heydrich termed the 'ultimate aim' of the Jewish policy. He was given target dates by which Vienna, the Protectorate and regions of Germany were to be rendered *judenfrei* – free of Jews. He ran into trouble immediately. Hans Frank, Governor-General of the General Gouvernement, considered that he had too many Jews already. Some quarter of a million had managed to escape into the Russian zone of occupation in the first weeks before the border was effectively patrolled, but Jews from the northern and western *Gaue*, evicted from their homes to make accommodation available for the Baltic ethnic Germans, were being driven into labour camps or ghettos in his region. He refused to allow in the transports from Vienna and ordered Eichmann's arrest if he ever set foot in the General Gouvernement.[45]

By December Frank calculated he had some 2.5 million Jews in his domain, 3.5 million if half-Jews were counted as well. As in Germany these were deprived of their normal means of livelihood. In consequence as winter gripped they began to die of exposure and malnutrition; others were worked in forced labour gangs in sub-zero temperatures to the point of exhaustion, a policy refined deliberately into working to death, or 'liquidation through work'. For Frank Jews were simply an intolerable burden on his administration and food resources. He noted in his diary that 2.5 million could not be shot, nor could they be poisoned. 'We shall have to take steps, however, designed in some way to eliminate them.'[46] It is probable that this was an accurate expression of Himmler's and Heydrich's aims in the 'ultimate goal'; it is probable that there was a direct link with the Nebe–Widmann experiments in the use of carbon monoxide gas for killing *lebensunwertes Lebens* (life-unworthy life). Prototype gas chambers had been completed already under the supervision of another of Nebe's officials, Kriminal Kommissar (and SS-Obersturmführer) Christian Wirth of the Stuttgart Kripo, the first in a converted coaching shed in the grounds of Grafeneck Castle in Württemberg, another in an abandoned prison at Brandenburg-on-Havel, near Berlin.[47] It was Christian Wirth who would be sent out later to former Poland to create the death camps in what became known as 'Operation Reinhard' or the 'final solution' to the Jewish question. It is a *post hoc* argument to suggest that the 'euthanasia' programme and the gassing experiments were designed for genocide from the start; yet given that race was the core of the Nazi *Weltanschauung*, given that the first 'euthanasia' questionnaires listed 'Jew, Jewish *Mischling* 1st or 2nd class, negro, negro *Mischling*, gypsy, gypsy *Mischling* . . .', given Heydrich's September 1939 circular distinguishing between the 'short-term' and the 'ultimate' aims of Jewish policy, given the Nazi predilection for deception and the gaps in the memories of those who took part in genocide, it is surely more likely that the Nebe–Widmann–Wirth gas-chamber experiments were designed from the beginning for the use to which finally they were put.

Be that as it may, more serious for Eichmann in the long run than the obstruction of individuals like Hans Frank was the conflict between his part in the 'resettlement' policy and the requirements of the war economy. Here, as in all other areas, confusion ruled. Theoretically Göring exercised central direction through a so-called Ministerial Council for Reich Defence, which had been revitalised by Hitler on 30 August; a council was of course a contradiction in the Führer state, and in practice this one merely served as a conduit of information for Göring who made decisions in the light of overall directives from Hitler. In September, no doubt in preparation for the strike west after finishing with Poland, Hitler called for 'the complete conversion of the economy to wartime requirements'.[48] If carried through to its conclusion this involved breaking off the Four Year Plan programme for the construction of the huge steel and synthetic raw materials plants designed to lay the basis for a long-war economy in the mid-1940s; without this foundation it would be impossible to provide the quantity of weapons ultimately necessary for world war. Yet the volume of materials and skilled labour devoted to the Four Year Plan programme seriously cut into the immediate, short-term production of armaments. Göring made his decisions as chairman of the Reich Defence Council in his Four Year Plan hat, and they mirrored this insoluble dilemma. Hitler had simply bounced himself into the European war five years too soon.

In addition to this basic problem Göring had no administrative network to execute his policies at local level, whereas the Wehrmacht, whose priorities often differed from his, had local armaments Inspectorates. This led to massive confusion and inefficiencies in the early months. However, the fundamental dilemma facing Göring was the conflict between mobilisation for total war and the tenets of Nazi ideology. This showed itself in reluctance to recruit women for war work – since their task was to bear Germanic children and bring up families – and above all in the racial policy which it was Eichmann's task to carry out. This also provided a source of conflict between the Party and the Wehrmacht Economics Department which strove to retain Jews in the war economy for their industrial and craft skills. An authority on the German mobilisation for total war, Ludolf Herbst, has gone so far as to assert that racial policy, namely the elimination of Jews and gypsies and the enslavement of foreign peoples for labour under Germans as a practical manifestation of the master-race theory, doomed the Nazi war effort from the start: 'The war was therefore lost before it began, and would only be ended by abandoning the validity of the racial concept of total war.'[49]

This was impossible since race was the foundation stone of Nazi ideology and the underlying cause of the war in the first place. And it was impossible for Göring since he was as psychically dependent on Hitler's good opinions as Himmler, and was ensnared, like Himmler and the others at the Führer's court, in the remorseless round of over-bidding. As in the matter of immediate armaments or building up the industrial base for the future, Göring could only compromise. His compromises and the Wehrmacht's practical approach to labour requirements for the war economy placed real difficulties in Eichmann's path.

Himmler's own difficulties with the generals over atrocities in Poland were brought to a head by the Army court martial of a private of the SS Artillery Regiment, and a military policeman, who took it upon themselves to herd a working party of some fifty Jews into a synagogue and shoot them.[50] That one of the accused was a member of the Military Police indicates the extraordinary ambiguity of Canaris' position, and indeed of the Wehrmacht's. For the Geheime Feldpolizei (GFP) – Secret Field Police – was controlled by the Abwehr, but was trained in large part by Gestapo officials, and its duties in the operational theatre corresponded to those of Heydrich's Einsatzgruppen behind the lines, namely 'to investigate and combat all activities damaging to the nation and state'.[51] As this example indicates, they were liable to interpret their instructions in the same way as the Einsatzkommandos. The Army court martial found both men guilty of manslaughter; the military policeman was sentenced to nine years' penal servitude, the SS man to three years' imprisonment. Neither served a day of their term since the sentences were dissolved in a general amnesty.

Nonetheless Himmler took the opportunity to press for the SS to be removed from the jurisdiction of military courts. This was effected by a decree of Göring's Reich Defence Council on 17 October; while still subject to the military penal code, members of the SS and 'police groups on special tasks' would in future be tried only by special SS courts.[52]

Himmler was also in dispute with the generals about the performance of the SS-Verfügungstruppe in the Polish campaign. They had suffered relatively far greater casualties than Wehrmacht units; the Army put this down to bad leadership, specifically to inadequate officer training, and used it as an argument for disbanding the SS fighting troops. Himmler argued that his formations had been incorporated in strange units under Army commanders who often assigned them the most difficult tasks. There was much truth in this; it was also true that the SS considered themselves elite soldiers and their whole training and ideological preparation had stressed heroism, self-sacrifice and the *Draufgängertum*, or dare-devil spirit, of the Freikorps; on its own this was sufficient to explain a higher casualty rate in such a war of movement. In any case Himmler naturally pressed the case for complete SS divisions under their own commanders. Probably he had already obtained Hitler's approval for such a step as early as 1938 when he gained permission to increase the Totenkopf formations to 40,000–50,000 men in the event of war.[53] Now he was authorised to form three SS fighting divisions and an enlarged *Leibstandarte*; these were, however, to be distributed among different Army corps and were to remain under the operational command of the Army leadership.

He combined the existing *Standarten* into the SS-Verfügungsdivision, charged Eicke with the formation of a Totenkopfdivision from existing Totenkopf formations reinforced by Verfügungstruppe veterans and men from the general SS, and formed a Polizeidivision from members of the Ordnungspolizei, thousands of whom were not SS men. It is interesting that, after barely a month of war, he was compromising the ideals of the Order, for members of the SS-Polizeidivision did not have to measure up to either the physical or the racial standards of the SS, indeed they were not necessarily admitted into the SS as individuals although serving under the SS standard. It was at this time that the term 'Waffen-SS' was coined to describe the SS combat units; it occurs in a handbook of instructions issued to the SS recruiting offices dated 29 October.[54]

In the competition for recruits Himmler and the chief of the Ergän-zungsamt, Gottlob Berger, met the stubborn resistance of the Army, as they had at each stage of their intrusion into the generals' sphere, and had to use subterfuge and every resource of under-age and over-age men, ethnic Germans and later 'Nordic' volunteers from the Low Countries and Scandinavia to build up the Waffen-SS and reserves and replace the concentration camp guards and police units recruited for the field forces.[55] Inevitably the original ideals of the Order, especially physical and racial standards, suffered. This was largely concealed by propaganda. No doubt Himmler excused it to himself as necessary improvisation in war; that was what he liked to tell his officers who raised difficulties in other spheres.

Towards the end of October, as German forces were being regrouped for the lightning blow Hitler hoped to strike against France before the end of the year, Himmler broke his own rule about not proceeding too fast and too far ahead of opinion. He promulgated an SS order which not only provided grounds for ridicule but roused anger and concern, much no doubt genuine, much blown up by the generals in their running battle with him.

Set in old Germanic type,[56] it was addressed to 'the entire SS and police', and opened with a favourite aphorism of Hitler's: 'Every war is a blood-letting of the best blood.' The necessary death of the best men was not the worst aspect; much worse was the lack of children caused by soldiers not being able to propagate while at the front, while after the war children could not be propagated by those who failed to return.

> The old wisdom that only he who has sons and children can die peacefully must in this war again become reality for the Schutzstaffel. He can die peacefully who knows that his *Sippe*, all that he and his ancestors have wanted and striven for, is continued in his children. The greatest gift for the widow of a man who falls in battle is always the child of the man she loved.

Next came the paragraphs that caused the rumpus:

> But beyond the boundaries of otherwise perhaps necessary bourgeois laws and customs, even outside marriage, it can be a lofty task for German women and maidens of good blood, not lightly, but in deepest moral seriousness, to become mothers of children of soldiers called to war, of whom fate alone knows whether they will return home or fall for Germany.
>
> Also the men and women, who serve the state in the homeland, have at this precise time the sacred obligation to become again mothers and fathers of children.

Did the juxtaposition of these two paragraphs signify that it was the duty of men at home to have relations with the wives and sweethearts of those at the front? it was asked. The assumption that that was the intended meaning was easy for those who had not seen the original order, those who wished to cause the Reichsführer mischief, or those who were simply scandalised by the encouragement of the SS and police to sexual licence. Already rumours were circulating about the Lebensborn homes.

The order went on to assert that in past wars many soldiers with a sense of responsibility had not had children because in the event of their death they had not wanted to leave their wife to bring up the child in need. 'You, SS men, need not have these doubts and worries'; Himmler pledged that 'for all children of good blood born in and out of wedlock whose father had fallen in the war' he would personally commission a representative as guardian 'in the name of the Reichsführer-SS'. The SS would stand by these mothers and care for the education and material needs of the children up to maturity. Further, the SS would care for the mothers-to-be and for their children born during the war in or out of wedlock if they were in need; and after the war, if the man returned, the SS would guarantee financial aid on a magnanimous scale upon a reasoned application.

He ended in grand style, difficult to render in English:

SS-Men
    and you, mothers of these children hoped for by Germany, show that you,
    in belief in the Führer and in the will to eternal life of our blood and *Volk*,
    as gallantly as you are prepared to fight and die for Germany, are ready to
    transmit [future] life for Germany.

This stirring admonition to heroism on the field of Venus transcends his usual homespun or alternatively terse communications. Perhaps one of the more poetic experts of the Race and Settlement Main Office prepared the drafts; perhaps he was in a mood of temporary exaltation.

The order itself was wholly in line with his beliefs; it could not be faulted on logical grounds, and would have passed as self-evident and proper had he expounded it in one of his secret speeches to his Gruppenführers. Why he was so imprudent as to have it printed and promulgated is another question. 'Colossally simple!' was his answer when he sought to explain it afterwards: the proportionately very high losses in the Polish campaign had persuaded him of the need for it.[57] At the sub-rational level the answer may be that it was yet another manifestation of the desire for blood and death which lay at the root of this war. Perhaps it was also an expression of the thwarted sexuality that surely drove him, probably Hitler and perhaps the entire male collective of the Nazi Party, even all strata of this masculine, warrior state.

In Poland both 'negative' and 'positive' sides of Himmler's racial task were driven forward. Officials of the Race and Settlement Main Office and the Volksdeutsche Mittelstelle – the SS agency through which ethnic German minorities had been incited and co-ordinated with the programme for Reich expansion – and an earlier association of ethnic Germans abroad, the VDA, harnessed now to his new office for the Consolidation of German Nationhood, planned and ordered great movements of settlement and deportation. Totenkopf police reinforcements were drafted in to serve with the local ethnic German 'self-protection' units as the whips of eviction and the guns of order. On 7 November the mass expulsions of Jews and Poles from the western occupied districts began; forced marches over frozen terrain, train journeys in trucks left for days on sidings without heat and with no provision for the occupants accounted for more suffering and mass death than the original work of the Einsatzkommandos. Arbitrary shootings and beatings went on alongside the systematic cruelties.

Other officials of the Race and Settlement Office drafted plans and lists for reclaiming for the Reich Poles with German forebears or the appearance of Aryan blood. Others screened prospective German settlers from the Baltic provinces, from the Reich, from the Russian-occupied east of Poland, even from the South Tyrol, and allotted the vacant homes and farms, and appointed managers for the estates whose owners had been shot. Meanwhile Göring's officials appointed managers for the Jewish firms now Aryanised, and for Polish industries to be incorporated into his Four Year Plan. Himmler and the SS were in the forefront, but after the military conquest all agencies of the master race played their part in the rape of Poland.

Professor Stanislaw Lorentz of the National Museum in Warsaw received a visitor in early November, Professor Dagobert Frey of Breslau, a fellow art historian whom he knew well; that summer of 1939 they had travelled together to an international congress of art historians in England. Now Frey came, not in friendship, but simply to present him with a list of the pictures he required. Later Lorentz watched Frey vandalise Warsaw Castle: baroque ceilings, stucco decoration, carvings and sculptures were cut out of the ancient seat of the Polish monarchy for transport to the Reich. 'I can still see Professor Frey . . . admiring the beauty of a neo-classic fireplace . . . and in my presence giving the order for it to be torn away from the wall.'[58]

Heydrich meanwhile was preparing a provocation to precede the strike against the west. Canaris was in on at least one part of the game. The Abwehr office at Stuttgart had been running a supposed anti-Nazi German émigré in Holland since 1937; the man had succeeded in convincing the head of the British Secret Intelligence Service in Holland, Captain Payne-Best, that he was in touch with the internal German opposition to Hitler, and in October, such was the close collaboration between the SD and the Abwehr, Heydrich inserted Walter Schellenberg into the plot to play the part of a Wehrmacht officer, Captain Schaemmel, supposedly in close touch with the

'General' leading the Army opposition. This was a comparatively easy task since Heydrich probably knew as much about the opposition groups and their aims as they themselves. Schellenberg adopted a monocle and played his part skilfully, requesting British support in the overthrow of Hitler and a secret agreement which would result in a peace treaty once the generals had seized power – precisely what the real opposition had been angling for. Finally he promised to bring the 'General' over the border to meet Payne-Best and the head of British intelligence in western Europe, Major Stevens. The meeting was arranged for the afternoon of 8 November at the Dutch border town of Venlo at a café called the Bacchus, hard by the customs post.

The other arm of the provocation – which Canaris may or may not have been a party to – was prepared in the Bürgerbräukeller, Munich, where the annual celebration of the beer-hall putsch was due to take place on the same date, 8 November. No proof has been found to link Heydrich with the drama here, but everything points to his directing hand. The usual lone scapegoat was procured, in this case a cabinet-maker and former communist named Georg Elser – as described by Gisevius a lean figure with dark-blond hair brushed back from a raw-boned face, intelligent eyes and the long, delicate hands of a craftsman.[59] According to Pastor Niemöller, who spoke to him afterwards while both were inmates of Dachau, he was actually an SS-Unterscharführer (sergeant).[60] Two men – Heydrich's agents presumably – gave him the task of building a time bomb into a panelled pillar close by the podium in the Bürgerbräukeller from which Hitler was due to address the Party comrades.

On 7 November Alfred Naujocks, Heydrich's murder squad chief, who had been given a leading role in the provocation before the Polish campaign, took a troop of sixteen SS men in armoured cars to the border before Venlo and laid low. Next day Schellenberg postponed his meeting with the British intelligence officers until the 9th. That evening, 8 November, Hitler delivered his speech in the Bürgerbräukeller, but it was noticed that he cut it shorter than usual, and instead of staying to reminisce with the 'old fighters' as was his invariable custom, he left in some haste to catch an ordinary scheduled express train for Berlin. No doubt this could be explained by the demands of the war; indeed Hess had been scheduled to stand in for him originally because of his responsibilities. It was, or should have been, more difficult to explain why all the top men like Himmler, Bormann, Frick, Rosenberg, as well as a number of old comrades who were unlikely to have had such pressing reasons of state, left with him. About thirteen minutes later the explosive concealed in the pillar went off, bringing down a part of the ceiling and the joists, killing seven, and seriously injuring sixteen of the 'old fighters' who had stayed.

News of the explosion was brought to Hitler when the train reached Nuremberg. According to a secretary his eyes flashed with excitement,

'Now I am content! The fact that I left the Bürgerbräu earlier than usual is corroboration that Providence intends to let me reach my goal.'[61] During his speech he had made a similar reference to his belief that Providence willed all that happened to him, and Goebbels made much of the miracle in his directives to the press. Heydrich directed a whispering campaign at parish priests to try and induce them to spread from the pulpit the idea of divine intervention.

Elser, meanwhile, had been arrested. On the night of the attempt, ostensibly while fleeing to Switzerland, he was caught by an auxiliary border policeman while outside an inn trying to listen to the announcement of his deed on the radio. Inside his lapel was a communist badge and in his pocket a picture postcard of the Bürgerbräukeller with the pillar in which he had concealed the bomb marked with a red cross. Not unnaturally he was sent to Gestapo headquarters for questioning. The next day at Venlo Payne-Best and Stevens fell into the trap laid for them. No sooner had their car appeared at the Café Bacchus, where Schaemmel/Schellenberg was waiting, than Alfred Naujocks and his SS team crashed the border barrier in an armoured car driven backwards in order to make a smart get-away. After a brief exchange of fire during which the accompanying Dutch military intelligence officer was mortally wounded, the two Britons were snatched and driven into Germany before the border police realised what was happening.

The timing of the Venlo incident makes it probable, if not certain, that it was deliberately engineered so that the British secret service could be enmeshed in the bomb plot against the Führer. And since Naujocks' team was in position from 7 November, giving the lie to Schellenberg's assertion in his memoirs that the decision to seize the British officers was only taken after the explosion in the Bürgerbräu, it follows that both incidents were engineered at the same source. Moreover the bomb plot bore Heydrich's signature; it was a virtual repeat of the Reichstag fire with blood and death to give added authenticity. And it is significant that the responsible security officials were never disciplined. Himmler appointed a top-level commission of enquiry headed by Arthur Nebe, but its conclusions omitted any mention of the wholly uncharacteristic slackness there must have been in surveillance and inspection of the hall prior to Hitler's speech. The assumption is that it was not slackness, but complicity.

Himmler released the commission's findings on 21 November. Georg Elser, it appeared, had constructed and planted the bomb singlehanded, but the plot had been masterminded by Otto Strasser from Switzerland, and commissioned and paid for by the British secret service, specifically its west European *Zentrale* in The Hague. By bringing in Strasser and the British, Himmler and Heydrich were able to involve the German reactionary opposition. As contained in a propaganda leaflet for Switzerland Himmler's statement ran:

On the grounds of information from German emigrants which was as criminal as it was absurd, the British government and its intelligence service were of opinion that an opposition existed in the state, in the Party and in the Wehrmacht which aimed to bring about a revolution in the Reich. In these circumstances officials of the Sicherheitsdienst of the SS were commissioned to make contact with this British terror- and revolution-*Zentrale* in The Hague. In the belief that they were actually dealing with revolutionary German officers the representatives of the British intelligence service disclosed to the German officials their views and plans, indeed in order to maintain a permanent link with these ostensible German officers they gave them a wireless apparatus tuned to England through which the German Geheime Staatspolizei [Gestapo] have up to now maintained contact with the British government.[62]

On the 9th 'Mister Best und Kapitän Stevens' had attempted to cross the border into Germany and had been arrested by officials keeping them under surveillance, and delivered to the Gestapo.

This complex 'provocation' served any number of useful purposes. If Hitler meant to loose the blow against the west on 12 November, as he had determined apparently as early as 22 October, it was evidently intended to provide the necessary pretext to violate the neutrality of Holland, the haven for the British 'terrorists', and at the same time unite the people and Army behind the Führer for a general European war which they did not relish. If one can believe the SD internal report of 10 November – although this was put out by Heydrich's own organisation not entirely from disinterested motives – the latter aim was achieved in full. 'In many schools the hymn "Nun danket alle Gott . . ." was sung' in gratitude for the Führer's deliverance and as details emerged during the course of the 9th the population talked bitterly about the English and the Jews. Among the working classes the bitterness was recorded as especially great; there was talk of Göring laying London in 'ruins and ashes' with his bombers; 'no stone should be left on another.'[63]

It appears from this that if the main purpose was to provoke hatred for England, unite the people behind the Führer, create a pretext for attacking through the Low Countries, where the main thrust was indeed planned at that date, and cow the generals who believed a winter offensive to be madness and were again plotting to unseat Hitler[64] the Bürgerbräu–Venlo provocation was brilliantly successful. And in the atmosphere of fear and suspicion created deliberately by the Gestapo, it was evident to von Brauchitsch, Halder and the other senior generals who had dusted off and reworked the 1938 plans for an Army putsch that the bomb attempt against Hitler could easily be turned to use by Himmler and Heydrich as the pretext for a pre-emptive SS strike against them. This prospect became even more real when it was learned that two senior British intelligence officers were being interrogated by the Gestapo. The members of the 'reactionary' opposition in touch with the British government and all in the conspiracy with them felt under threat.

There is no doubt that Hitler and Himmler were aware of the 'defeatism' in the Army High Command, little doubt that Himmler was informed about the generals' plans and, had Hitler wished it, could have implicated them in Elser's bomb attempt. Perhaps this was the chief purpose. Perhaps the threat was sufficient and there was no necessity to carry it out. For three days before the Bürgerbräu explosion von Brauchitsch had made a final appeal to Hitler to call off the western offensive, receiving such a verbal onslaught that he had emerged shaken and broken in resolve. Hitler had told him he knew all about the spirit of Zossen (Army Headquarters), and intended ruthlessly to stamp it out. Brauchitsch's anxiety in the wake of this dressing-down had infected Halder, who ordered his deputy, von Stülpnagel, to destroy all the paperwork for the planned putsch.[65]

There was every reason for their nervousness. Apart from the threat of an imminent SS strike in the manner of 30 June 1934, there were the hard facts, as expressed by one of the most ardent conspirators, General Thomas of the Army Economics Department, that nearly all the younger Army officers and 75 per cent of the population were behind the Führer.[66] And at the psychic level there was the tradition and indoctrination of the officer corps in absolute loyalty to the Supreme Commander, who was of course Hitler; at a more conscious level there was the legend of the 'stab in the back' by which communists and defeatists at home had sabotaged the 'undefeated' Army in 1918. It is difficult to imagine that the generals could have carried out their plans. Nevertheless Himmler and Heydrich might have considered the situation more finely balanced than it appears with hindsight, or might have provoked it deliberately to remove the potential leaders of revolt. Karl Wolff said after the war that he believed the Bürgerbräu bomb prevented an attempt by the generals to arrest Hitler.[67]

On the other hand it is possible that Hitler really did intend a surprise attack against the west that November. Motorised and armoured units were still refitting after the Polish campaign; there was an insufficient number of divisions; the weather and ground conditions were likely to be unfavourable for an attack through the Low Countries; and the ammunition available was scarcely sufficient for a month's fighting. Yet, inflated by his lightning victory in Poland, Hitler might have considered these objections outweighed by the advantage of surprise. In that case the provocation might have been designed primarily to produce a pretext for attack in the west, and it was only his characteristic hesitation before decision, bad weather and the generals' opposition that caused postponement until the following spring.

The other arm of the provocation led to Switzerland; this was where the scapegoat, Elser, was supposed to have been seeking asylum, and where his puppet-master, Otto Strasser, was living and operating his anti-Nazi propaganda station. Directly Himmler made known the findings of his special commission into the bomb-attempt the German government requested Strasser's extradition. Strasser fled to France. It is possible that Heydrich, who was certainly after Strasser, was also seeking to confuse the west about the direction of the German attack – through the Low Countries or through Switzerland. A leaflet campaign he conducted in Switzerland supports this interpretation.[68] Canaris' and Heydrich's campaign of deception before the attack in the west was a masterpiece, which contributed largely to the speed of victory, and it may be that the Bürgerbräu–Venlo provocation was intended as the opening shot. It put British intelligence in Europe out of action for a while and made it certain that future approaches by the real German opposition would be treated with the utmost suspicion. The most active opponent of the regime in the Abwehr, Colonel Oster, had already passed information about the date and direction of Hitler's intended attack, and he continued to do so through Holland and the Vatican as other dates were set. These proved as false as this first alarm, and his information too became suspect. There seems no doubt that at this stage the two German intelligence services outplayed the British service which Canaris and Heydrich both respected so much. The attacker always has the advantage; later the positions were reversed.

Meanwhile Elser was taken to Sachsenhausen to ensure his silence, thence to Dachau, where he was kept in solitary confinement in otherwise privileged conditions in a cell converted from two single cells and fitted out as a carpenter's shop. He practised his craft, sang mournful songs to the accompaniment of a zither, and whenever he had a fleeting chance of talking to a fellow inmate told how he had been taken to the Bürgerbräukeller over a period of several days and made to construct a carefully concealed cavity for an explosive charge in one of the pillars of the saloon.[69]

In Poland in mid-winter, the bitter cold was harnessed to murder. Two days before Christmas 1939 an official in von Ribbentrop's Ministry in Berlin wrote to his mother trying to describe to her how he found it necessary to anaesthetise his mind to what he had to live with: 'An example: I sit at table with a man whose duty it will be, in the Jewish ghetto of Lublin, to let a great part of the Jews deported there freeze to death and starve according to programme.'[70] The official, Albrecht Haushofer, son of the 'geopolitician' Karl Haushofer, who had had such influence on Hitler's views through his pupil Rudolf Hess, was himself a quarter-Jew, and survived in official Germany only because of Hess's protection; nevertheless his tortured feelings were not untypical of those thinking Germans who knew what was being done in their name and felt powerless either to intervene or to escape responsibility. 'I can only live in two different forms,' Haushofer's letter continued, 'as a mind in the service of lying or as a body in the service of murder. Both can be endured, but only when one no longer feels it.'

The Commander-in-Chief, East, General von Blaskowitz, felt a more immediate responsibility for the crimes committed in his region, particularly as he was powerless to control the Higher SS and Police Führers in overall command of the units responsible. He prepared detailed memoranda on the incidents and the effect they had on the morale of his officers and men and forwarded them to Army High Command. At Abwehr headquarters a young lawyer, Hans von Dohnanyi, who had compiled a file of SS crimes within Germany, added Polish atrocities to the dossier; he intended it for use when Hitler and the Party leaders were brought to trial after their arrest by the generals. Meanwhile the accusations were used by the Army High Command in its fundamental struggle with the SS. Himmler deputed Karl Wolff to smooth over the difficulties. When he had satisfied himself about the nature of the complaints Wolff arranged a meeting between von Brauchitsch and Himmler alone. It took place over tea on 24 January 1940.[71] Only the results are known, but the trend of Himmler's defence can perhaps be inferred from a speech he made to a gathering of Gauleiters the following month.[72]

Obviously it is possible in the east with the trains – but not only the evacuation trains – that a train freezes up and the people freeze. That is possible, that happens unfortunately with Germans as well. You simply cannot do anything to prevent it if they travel from Lodz to Warsaw and the train remains standing ten hours on the track. You cannot blame the train or anyone. That is just the climate. It is regrettable for Germans, it is regrettable for Poles, if you like it is even regrettable for Jews – if anyone wants to pity them. But it is neither intended, nor is it preventable. I consider it wrong to make a great *Lamento* about it.

Those who say, yes, it is cruel that the Poles in Posen were fetched from their houses inside three to four days and marched off, may I kindly remind them that in 1919 our Germans were driven on a punishment trek across the bridges with 30 kg of luggage. Our Germans were driven out of Posen and West Prussia by the western European culture-*Volk*, the French, without even so much as 30 kg of luggage. We have really no need to be crueller; however, we do not need either to play the great, wild, dumb German here. Therefore one does not get excited about it.

Then – [the reproach] that many things have to be done on the march. Yes, dear God, I cannot alter it. Unfortunately I was not even able to alter the fact that Germans had to march on foot. Therefore I will worry myself about the Germans first. If I can alter it for them, I certainly shall. And then, if I have time and opportunity I will very gladly also alter it for Poles and Jews. But that comes last in the line. However, to make a great agitation and spread tales about cruelties now, here in Berlin – that I consider wrong.

I will in no way deny that in the east – it is very well known to me – this or that excess occurred, where there was boozing, where people were shot drunkenly, people who would perhaps have been among those shot in any case, who however should not have been shot by people boozing – where looting occurred in the whole east, at times in a way, I must say, such as I had not imagined possible, by every possible office, by all possible people in all possible uniforms. But one does not excite oneself unnecessarily over that. In my view one has to grasp the nettle. Where there is such a case, one must calmly establish it . . . and then the man will be seized. The question is merely whether one puts one's back into [solving the problem] or does not put one's back into it.

It is interesting to compare this with some words he had to say to the officers of the Leibstandarte Adolf Hitler that autumn 1940 about events in Poland,

where, in a temperature forty degrees below zero we had to drag away thousands, tens of thousands, hundreds of thousands – where we had to have the hardness – you should listen to this, but forget it again at once – to shoot thousands of leading Poles, where we had to have the hardness, otherwise it would have rebounded on us later. In many cases it is much easier to go into battle with a company of infantry than it is to suppress an obstructive population of low culture or to carry out executions or drag people away. . . .[73]

He did admit in his earlier speech to the Gauleiters in February 1940 that in the beginning very drastic measures had been necessary; they had had to take 'the leading heads' from the enemy, 'the Polish intelligentsia. They had to go.' Undoubtedly he told von Brauchitsch the same thing. Even the 'reactionary' von Hassell, returning to Berlin four days after the discussion, was given a graphic description by Goerdeler of how Himmler 'with wagging pince-nez and a dark expression on his common face had said he had been charged by the Führer to take care that the Poles could not rise again. Therefore extermination policy.'[74]

Wolff had suggested before the 24 January meeting that the Army let the SS have their dossier of atrocity reports so that enquiries could be instituted. Von Brauchitsch and Himmler agreed this; Himmler promised that his legal officers would examine every accusation and where necessary the culprits would be brought before an SS court and judged rigorously.[75] It was perhaps a way out for von Brauchitsch, but he could not have expected Himmler to court-martial the HSSPFs and all the other SS-Führers down the line who had been carrying out his orders.

The compromise did not have the desired effect; the ill-feeling rumbled on, and in March Himmler came before a gathering of senior generals to try to work them round to his view. His notes for this contained such phrases as 'execution of all potential resistance leaders' and 'we must remain hard'.[76] How many he convinced is impossible to determine, but during the questioning afterwards he was not given a particularly tough time and was able in his homely way to skirt around all ethical issues as simple necessity to prevent a later serious uprising. He admitted 'excesses'; they were being looked into and those found guilty would be punished severely. In any case, as he had stressed, he had been commissioned for the task by the Führer and did nothing the Führer did not know about. Because the person of the Führer must not be connected with the policy he was ready to take responsibility before the world.

Precisely what the policy was at this stage had been revealed in his speech to the Gauleiters the previous month;[77] so was the justification – or it may be thought rationalisation – of the policy. This took the form of a lecture on the historical origins of the problem. If one cuts through the pedantic and condescending explanations he wove around each step in the story, it is interesting for the light it throws on the absolute centrality of race.

'Originally,' his explanation started, 'we, a Germanic–Nordic master caste, took overlordship as princes and rulers of the peoples of the east – partly on the request of the people themselves, who called for someone to govern them – "We cannot govern ourselves, we want someone who will create order among us." '

In those days there had been a clear racial cleavage between the rulers and the ruled; then over the course of centuries the master caste had intermarried with the daughters and handmaids of the subservient races in order to found an *Unteroffizier* class. This half-breed class had risen gradually and begun to intermarry with the master caste, at which point the blood of rulers and ruled became intermixed. Then – as his audience knew from their history – these eastern peoples had been unable to manage things for themselves any longer and they had called in Germans as colonists. It was not long, however, before the German colonists, cut off from their spiritual home, became absorbed into the countries they had gone to, and forgot that they were Germans. Not only did they forget their Germanhood, but by virtue of their blood they became the best nationalists of their adopted country, the most idealistic, the most decent, the most reliable soldiers.

> We must be clear about one thing. We are firmly convinced of it, I believe that exactly as I believe in God, I believe that our blood, Nordic blood, is actually the best blood on this earth. As long as we look back, as long as we consider our present – how the far-distant future will be no one knows. In hundreds of thousands of years this Nordic blood will always be the best. Over all others, we are superior. . . .

From this it followed that their most dangerous enemies were those of their own blood who had adopted foreign nationalities, especially when they were in commanding positions; as examples he named from the Polish campaign General (Juliusz) Rommél, the defender of Warsaw, Admiral (Josef) Unrug, defender of Hela, and General (Viktor) Thommée, the defender of Modlin, who was of Huguenot descent, 'also our blood, Germanic blood'. They must therefore take note: 'It is only our own blood – dangerous in history and dangerous on this earth – that can endanger us. Consequently we have to see that now, while we are strong, we do our utmost to recall

all our blood and that we take care that none of our blood is ever again lost abroad.'

Having established blood as the fundamental question, he came to the methods by which he aimed to tackle the problem. They were various. And it was then that he admitted it had been necessary in the beginning to remove the Polish leadership class – 'and may I request that that is intended only for this small circle'. He had been told this was unGermanic, and that the German troops themselves would be injured – presumably von Blaskowitz's complaints about the morale of his soldiers. But of these clever people who complained and gave him advice none, he believed, had been present at the *Exekution*. He could have meant the execution of the policy, or the execution of the victims, but both came to much the same thing as his next words indicated:

I can say to them: it is horrible and frightful for a German if he has to see it. That is so, and if it were not horrible and so frightful for us then, indeed, we would no longer be Germans, certainly we would not be Germans. Just as it was horrible it was necessary – and will in many cases still be necessary to carry it out. That is to say, if we now lack the nerve, then these bad nerves will affect our sons and grandsons. . . . We do not have the right to do that. Because if we live in this present time, having been educated by Adolf Hitler and having the good fortune to be permitted to work for Germany in Adolf Hitler's Reich or under the guidance of Adolf Hitler, then I must say we cannot be weak.

An *Exekution* must always be the hardest thing for our men. And despite it, they must never become weak, but they must do it with tightly clenched lips [*zusammengebiessen Lippe*]. In the beginning that was necessary. The shock which the Poles had to have, they have had. Now I believe, for the moment, nothing will stir in West Prussia, Posen and the new provinces. It may be the Pole is very tough in conspiracy, all Slavs can be; it may be that it has to happen again. Then it will happen again.

This passage raises the question of whether he had been present himself at any of the executions. The impression he conveyed, without actually saying so, is that he had been. After the war Wolff told a highly coloured story about the first mass execution Himmler witnessed; it was during the Russian campaign in the late summer of the next year, 1941: 'I knew from his own mouth', Wolff's tale ran, 'that, up to this moment, he had still not seen any men killed.'[78] Himmler was not above implying things in his speeches which were not true – for instance that he had learned to 'smoke and booze' at the front in the first war. However, none of Wolff's post-war statements can be accepted if they involve his own defence, as this one did. The question must remain open, although in view of Himmler's later insistence on seeing for himself the early stages of the final solution of the Jewish question and the more horrible medical experiments, the presumption must be that he did insist on witnessing a mass execution during the Polish campaign, particularly as at the deepest levels – if the analysis given here is correct – death was what his war was all about.

One of the main problems he faced, he told his audience, was the small proportion of Germans in the conquered area. He estimated the total population of the two new *Gaue* added to the Reich – Danzig–West Prussia and the Warthegau – and the two existing *Gaue* which had been enlarged – East Prussia and Silesia – at some 16.5 million, of which only 7.5 million were Germans. In the General Gouvernement Polen, out of a population of some 14 million, only 90,000 were Germans. The rest were Poles, Ukrainians, Gorales, Lemken, a few White Russians, some 2.5 million Jews; 'There will be more [Jews].'

The first stage of his solution, which had already commenced, was to empty the four *Gaue*, West Prussia, Warthegau, East Prussia and Silesia, of all foreign or half-breed stock and push it into the General Gouvernement. This would be replaced by homecoming ethnic Germans and Germans from the Reich; thus 'those who are now Reichsstatthalters and Oberpräsidents of the new provinces will be able to appear before the Führer one day and report that their province has now over the course of years become German.' The existence of the General Gouvernement as a receptacle for the unwanted was, he told them, the essential key to the solution. In an obvious attempt to ingratiate himself with Hans Frank, he went on: 'our work, the work of these four Reichsstatthalters and my work, would not be possible if there was not on the other side in the General Gouvernement a Governor-General who was also a National Socialist, who had taken on himself now this highest negative task of relieving us of all that we turn out of our provinces.'

In the further stages of the scheme, which had not, he admitted, been worked out in detail, he looked forward to concentrating German settlement in the new provinces in 'islands' dividing the occupied area in both north–south and east–west directions – he made an analogy with the way the German armies had divided the enemy forces during the military campaign. The final stage was to Germanise the spaces between the islands, leaving of course a reserve in the south of the General Gouvernement for that residue of uneducated and unGermanic Poles and other breeds who were to provide the itinerant manual labour force for the Reich.

His words on the treatment of Polish workers to be sent to the Reich show that slave labour was not something forced by the exigencies of war, but was implicit from the beginning in the plans for eastern colonisation. The 'master race' was a literal concept.

It has been represented to me, we should screen these Poles, we should only allow in racially valuable and decent, orderly people. I have turned myself against that because we simply cannot do it. I cannot screen one million people in four weeks because I do not have the people to do it at present. One person cannot examine, shall we say, two to three hundred men in a day if his judgement is to have any value. Otherwise the danger would arise that they would be inspected carelessly and it would be said, 'Yes, the man is all right [*in Ordnung*],' then he has the rubber-stamp that he is all right. Therefore I will do it another way: the Poles will be fetched here *en masse* and treated as Poles *en masse*. They will have to wear plainly visible markings on jacket and shirt. There will be no intercourse with Germans; it will be an absolutely clear separation; they are agricultural labourers who make themselves available for private contract.

If now these Poles want to or should spend an evening some time in an inn in a village – I am against having an inn taken over especially for the Poles – a Tuesday or a Wednesday or any other evening will be agreed on for the Poles to go to the inn; then, however, no German goes inside. That is what I propose, and it must be absolutely clear and absolutely clearly carried out.

I now intend therefore, if a Pole has intercourse with a German – has sexual intercourse – then the man will be hanged and indeed before his own camp. Then, you know, the others will not do it. Moreover, we will make sure that a sufficient number of Polish women and girls come over with them, therefore there can be no possible talk here of necessity.

[German] women (in sex cases with Poles) will be strictly taken to court and where the facts of the case are insufficient – there are always such borderline cases – taken to a concentration camp. We must do that if these one million Poles and the hundreds of thousands of other foreign workers are not to cause inconceivable damage to our blood. There is absolutely no point in theorising. It would be better if we did not have them – we know that – but we need them.

Coming to his plans for the year ahead – 'on the assumption that the whole year is war' – he would, he said, be proceeding with the emigration of the Jews. The numbers he would be able to deal with depended on three factors: the food situation and the 'absorption capacity' of the General Gouvernement, and the transport available. At first he would concentrate on bringing the Jews out of the four eastern *Gaue*, then out of the Reich, then from the Protectorate of Bohemia and Moravia. He did not want to raise false expectations, however. It was true he had removed Jews from Pommern, but that was only because there was no room there for returning Baltic Germans. At present the question did not arise for other *Gaue* in the old Reich. 'Therefore no false hopes, *meine Herren.*' He went on to tell them that the emigration of Jews to Palestine and to South and North America continued despite the war. 'This is one of the most essential things. Really nice and droll [*nett und neckisch*]' – and he explained the system by which Jews travelled abroad to raise the foreign exchange which it was necessary for each Jew to put up before being admitted as an immigrant abroad. He did not explain the currency manipulations, tax-clearance certificates and other devices by which Jews of any substance were milked before being allowed to emigrate; most members of his audience would have known these things. He hoped despite the Anglo-French naval blockade to keep up a rate of emigration of 6000–7000 Jews a month; that was, he estimated, about 80,000 during the course of the year. He passed on to the question of the gypsies. There were only some 30,000 in the whole of the Reich, but racially they caused very great damage, and he hoped to get them out in the course of the year.

He said nothing of what was to happen to the Jews or gypsies once they had been concentrated in the General Gouvernement – unless perhaps in answer to questions afterwards, not transcribed – although it was evident that the number able to emigrate abroad was a mere handful compared to the millions who would find themselves transported to Poland. Nor did he use the words 'ultimate aim' or 'final solution'. He was more concerned to describe the positive aspect of his task, which was to ordain, after the victory of the sword, 'the victory of the blood', not in the 'foolish form' of German colonisation in preceding centuries but by 'the real Germanisation of the land, the real *völkisch* occupation of the new provinces'; as a result of this he hoped to see the landscape and even the climate transformed by the planting of woods and trees. He admitted that he could not do it all himself; he would need the help of all the Gauleiters and all ministries and agencies. He saw his task as setting the general rules and guidelines, concerning himself with all questions that arose and making his wishes known in order to avoid overlapping between different ministries and departments.

> I believe the business we have out there is so exalted, so great, so unique and many-sided that no one will concern himself about someone else taking away his work. I propose that we be pitiless in the settlement [policy] because these new provinces must become Germanic, blond provinces of Germany – must become National Socialist provinces. Here, from the start, we want no false people settled. Therefore it is my iron determination not to admit those willing to buy, who would like to buy a farm out there but who are not convinced National Socialist – [that is] not merely inclined to National Socialism but inwardly convinced – who are in fact absolutely stiff-necked, reactionary people who reject us. . . . The new provinces must really be a Germanic blood-wall, must be a wall within which there is no blood-question, no children-question, but where one day that question will again take precedence and we will become a *Volk* of abundant children [*kinderreiches Volk*].

He passed on to the problems of screening people for their racial value, a task they would only be able to complete in peacetime, and he concluded with an appeal to all those present to look on the east as a godchild which the Führer had donated to them as representatives of the German people; they should wish to present it to the Führer in the shortest possible time after the war as Germanised in blood and peoples. 'We want to lay the most fundamental groundwork so that in decades this land will not only have been conquered by Adolf Hitler, but in truth by the German people with its living blood. It will be so steeped in it as to serve as a source of new blood for all future ages. That I see as the task, and here I request all help from you.'

The speech again reveals how the simplicity of his premises and the narrowness of his vision allowed him to cut through all complexities and competing necessities to arrive at fundamental solutions. But, despite being tedious, long-winded and schoolmasterly in exposition, there is little doubt that he reflected the convictions of his listeners, and the general hubris after the Polish victory and the quiescence of the western powers.

Himmler's immense tasks did not prevent him concerning himself with such questions as whether to ask for Russian assistance for an SS expedition to Tibet to examine relics of their Aryan forebears,[79] or badgering the State Secretary in Göring's Air Ministry, Colonel-General of the Air Force Erhard Milch to make sure that he did not build the runways of one of his new aerodromes over an outstanding prehistoric cultural monument in Schleswig-Holstein. In this positive task he was successful and must be credited with preserving a site of true archaeological importance.[80]

Nor did he lack time to write what seems to be a semi-frivolous letter to one of his favourites, the SS cavalry officer Hermann Fegelein serving in the occupied east. The semi-frivolity appears in the date, 31 February 1940; the content was entirely serious.

It had come to his notice, he started, that Fegelein was having considerable difficulty carrying out his work because of the severe weather, and that he was often cut off from his units for days at a time by blizzards and snow drifts. He knew from his own experience that such circumstances, away from the bustle and temptations of city life, gave one the time for serious reflection.

and now your opportunity for mature reflection is so favourable that these lines of mine ought to influence you in a thoroughly positive sense. Undoubtedly, despite the severe weather, you have received the Reichsführer-SS order of 28 October and learned thereby how the Reichsführer-SS feels about the children-question and what he expects especially from his Führerkorps.

The purely external circumstances are now so favourable for you, dear Fegelein, that you can only concern yourself with the question of the next generation in the context of marriage. . . . you have now had sufficient time to seek out a wife, and the war is no excuse in this respect, but rather a circumstance which makes the solution of this question appear even more urgent.

The Reichsführer-SS does not want you to marry straightaway in the former Poland, but he does expect you to make use of the lovely spring that is sure to follow this hard winter to make serious efforts to find a wife and to report your engagement to him by the end of May.

With best wishes and Heil Hitler![81]

The file copy was endorsed: 'Letter was not sent. Fegelein was with RFSS and Gruppenführer Wolff on 9 March, and took cognisance of the contents. He stated that he would become engaged in the near future.'

This was not the only matter discussed between them that day. Himmler had just received a report from Gestapo headquarters in

Munich alleging that Fegelein had sent goods looted in Poland back to the SS cavalry school in Riem, from where many items had found their way to members' homes. A search of the school had disclosed a lorry, a six-cylinder Mercedes trimmed in black, another in dark brown, a two-seater Stoda cabriolet, 50 lb of coffee, fourteen packets of cocoa, a chest of tea, two chests of chocolate, clothes, furs and other goods.[82]

Fegelein told Himmler that these things had been distributed by SS Standartenführer Spacil, commissioned as chief of administration. He also told him that the whole Munich Gestapo action had resulted from von Eberstein's hostility towards him personally. Himmler accepted his explanations. A few days later he wrote to Heydrich laying down a regulation that, if in future an SS barracks were to be inspected, prior application should be made to him (RFSS). He also asked for the names of the SS-Führers in whose private apartments Polish goods had been found. He would then decide on the action to be taken. So far as Fegelein was concerned he continued to back him even when Munich raised accusations of looting money. Finally he wound up the case: he was certain that Fegelein had taken the money for his cavalry school.[83]

Racial Warrior

Winter melted to lovely spring. Preparations for the western offensive, codenamed 'Case Yellow', neared completion. The plans had been altered by now, the main thrust through the Low Countries downgraded to little more than a feint to draw the allies into Belgium while the weight of armour pushed through Luxemburg and the wooded hills of the Ardennes, thence across the rolling countryside of Picardy to the Channel coast to confuse and split French forces and catch in the pincers the allied armies lured into Flanders. Canaris and Heydrich had the vital task of misleading enemy intelligence in that direction. At the same time they had to conceal an offensive due to be launched before 'Case Yellow'; this was a seaborne invasion of Norway and Denmark codenamed 'Weser Exercise'. It had been rendered necessary by the discovery of British plans to occupy Norway under the pretext of sending aid to the Finns, who had been attacked by Stalin. German armament production depended on the import of Swedish iron ore carried in ships down the Norwegian coast and across the Baltic, hence 'Weser Exercise' was literally vital. Since it hazarded Raeder's still minute Navy and the troop transports to the overwhelming weight of the guns of the Royal Navy, it was equally vital to conceal the preparations under the guise of troop movements for the western offensive.

In Berlin and Zossen moods fluctuated between expectation and high nervous tension. It is scarcely too much to say that success or disaster depended on the Abwehr. Had Canaris sought to ruin Hitler, this was his opportunity, yet of course the little Admiral would have had to betray his beloved Navy at the same time. He was inextricably caught in the snares. As it was Oster, who was not of course a naval officer, did reveal the plan through his Dutch and Vatican contacts in good time; he was not believed. In view of the previous false alarms he had sounded, there was no reason why he should have been believed. In this, as in the successful deception for 'Case Yellow', the origins can be traced, at least in part, to the disruption of British intelligence and the discrediting of the German opposition by the Bürgerbräu–Venlo provocation.

The SS field divisions were not involved in 'Weser Exercise'; all were committed for the western offensive. Incorporated as they were in different army groups under Army command they were still not accepted by the generals. Himmler's chief of procurement, Oberführer Gärtner, was experiencing all the difficulties in procuring arms and equipment that the chief of recruitment, Berger, still met in his struggle for men. The SS was assigned lower priority for the supply of artillery than even the reserve divisions of the Army. Himmler's motives were distrusted – with reason – and having allowed him a foot in the door with his field troops the generals were fighting to keep control of SS weapons and preserve the advantage in heavy guns and tanks that would be decisive if it came to a showdown after the war.

While supporting his subordinates in the in-fighting in Berlin, Himmler made frequent excursions with 'Wölffchen' to encourage his field troops drilling along the West Wall, inspect his concentration camps, and check on the migrations and Germanising programme he had set in train in the occupied eastern provinces. A journalist, Hanns Johst, who shared one of these eastern journeys, has left a description of how Himmler liked to stop the car, jump out and scramble over the fields beside the road. Bending, he would take a pinch of earth between his fingertips, 'sniff it thoughtfully with inclined head, crumble it between his fingers and then gaze out over the wide, wide expanse full to overflowing of this good productive soil', musing on the trees and bushes and hedgerows that would soon transform the scene and provide protection from the devastating winds, increase the formation of dew, promote clouds and rain and so increase the economic viability of this 'now all German earth'.[1]

Not all prospects were so pleasing. The Governor-General, Hans Frank, was still making difficulties about the numbers of Jews dumped in his province; worse, in Danzig–West Prussia Himmler's HSSPF, Obergruppenführer Richard Hildebrand, told him that the Gauleiter and Reichsstatthalter, Albert Forster, was taking short cuts in the 'Germanisation' of the *Gau* by admitting to the German citizenship list Poles whose blood was suspect. Himmler let it be known that he would send in his race experts from the RuSHA to examine all newly enrolled German citizens.

'If I looked like Himmler I would not talk about race!' Forster said when he learned of the threat. The remark soon got to Hildebrand, who reported it to Wolff, and Hildebrand was called to Berlin to give an account to Himmler in person. According to Wolff's post-war yarn, there was discussion of a duel with pistols and of standing Forster before a Party court. Himmler, however, had no desire to provoke a quarrel with the Party and merely had some witnesses to the slander make statements for the file. This rings true; accumulating evidence for use later was his trademark.[2]

On 8 April 'Weser Exercise' was launched; Hitler was in a state of high nervous tension, and had to be held to the mark by his headquarters staff, but complete surprise was achieved and Oslo, Bergen, Trondheim, Stavanger and Narvik were occupied virtually unopposed; counter-attacks over the next days by the forces gathered for the British Norwegian venture were repulsed. By 20 April, when Himmler and Wolff appeared at the Chancellery to congratulate Hitler on his fifty-first birthday, the Scandinavian position was secure and the Führer was happy to approve Himmler's request to form another SS field regiment from the Nordic men to be found in Denmark and Norway.[3] Berger was directed to set up a recruitment office to attract volunteers in Oslo, with a branch in Copenhagen, and on 30 April orders were issued for the establishment of SS-Standarte Nordland.[4] At the same time Berger took advantage of the prestige following the run of German success to set up his campaign to draw in German blood from other areas; by May he was attracting a stream of ethnic Germans from the Balkans, especially Rumania. A file of extracts from letters of the Danish and Norwegian volunteers for Nordland indicates how the propaganda for a new order in Europe, to be formed of peoples of a common Germanic bloodstock, appealed to much youthful idealism.[5]

Gärtner achieved a similar success in the struggle to equip the SS divisions. He had been working for some time to circumvent the Army procurement departments by ordering directly through the Ministry for Munitions headed by the construction supremo Fritz Todt; the SS quarries and building materials concerns, concentration camp and Polish slave labour provided him with ample bargaining counters. The deal was struck in early May. Todt agreed to take care of an SS shopping list for 50,000 rifles and carbines, together with bayonets, pistols, submachine and machine guns, artillery, anti-tank guns, millions of rounds of ammunition and 250 field kitchens, in return for which Gärtner agreed that he would be provided with 20,000 Polish factory workers. Gärtner reported to Himmler that now the whole SS armament problem could be solved with or without the Wehrmacht.[6]

The triumph was shortlived; in mid-June the Army reasserted its control over SS arms and equipment, and it was another two years before Himmler was able to turn the tables again by forging an alliance with a new Minister of Munitions, Albert Speer. This episode, and similar difficulties Berger experienced directly the Army discovered the extent of his recruiting successes – no less than 59,526 men for the field divisions between January and 30 June 1940[7] – indicate the complex power balance between the Party, the Army (and to an extent the Air Force and the Navy), the SS and the civilian agencies involved in the war economy. Although he controlled the police and terror apparatus of the state and enjoyed the dictator's wholehearted support, Himmler was unable to ride roughshod over the generals or indeed the Party; he still had to gain his ends by manoeuvre and political jobbing as he had from the beginning; he still lost many tricks.

Undoubtedly Hitler needed the generals for they commanded the finest military machine in the world. Himmler's few SS-Verfügungs formations were insignificant in military terms, their leadership and training suspect.

There was probably more to it, though. There are signs that he was running too fast at this period and making too many enemies, not simply through his plain ambitions for the SS, but because his ideological vision cut across too many practical areas. This was especially so in the occupied east. He was continually refining his ideas about his task here, and in early May he promulgated a regulation which united the eastern Gauleiters, Wehrmacht procurement officials, Todt's officials and Göring's Four Year Plan officials against him. It was a wildly impractical order which, if carried out, meant uprooting the 'racially valuable' Poles who were to be 're-Germanised' and transferring them to a 'pure German environment' in the old Reich so that they could lose their Polish ways and Polish consciousness. The Reichsstatthalters of West Prussia and the Warthegau, Forster and Greiser, raised the loudest objections to this interference with their already depleted workforces, and they gained powerful allies. Again Himmler had to admit defeat. A later report put it: 'Solely on the grounds of work-deployment – so far as serious interference with essential war-production is to be reckoned with – families capable of "re-Germanisation" were left in place in the eastern area. They were, however, designated for a later transfer to the Old Reich.'[8]

On 9 May, the day he issued the unworkable order, Himmler left in 'Special Train Heinrich' for the west. He had been recalled from Poland for 'Case Yellow' three days before. Wolff, wearing the uniform of a general of the Verfügungstruppe, travelled again as his liaison officer with Hitler's special train to the headquarters complex codenamed 'Felsennest' – or 'crag-eyrie' – in the Eifel massif south-west of Bonn. 'Heinrich' drew up some forty miles to the east in the Westerwald near Altenkirchen.

Of Himmler's field formations, only the Leibstandarte and one regiment of the Verfügungsdivision, Der Führer, were accorded the honour of a place in the first wave of the assault. Both were incorporated in the northern Army Group, 'B', and stationed on the Dutch border. The remainder of the Verfügungsdivision was in the rear ready to follow when the frontier had been breached. Himmler had tried hard to gain a place for Eicke's Totenkopfdivision in the first wave so that they could establish their moral right to carry out harsh internal pacification duties and redeem their unsavoury concentration camp reputation. Army High Command had denied him; both the Totenkopf and Polizei divisions were held in reserve.

The attack began against the neutral Low Countries at 5.35 in the morning of 10 May. Again Oster of the Abwehr had passed the word through his contacts; again his warning was virtually disregarded. In any case the speed and violence of the assault by every conceivable arm was sufficient to surprise and overwhelm any preparations that might have been made. Stuka dive-bombers screamed vertically on enemy and neutral Dutch and Belgian airfields; Panzer and motorised units broke across the borders; Army airborne infantry and Luftwaffe paratroops spread far and wide in the interior to seize key bridges and forts, assisted by Abwehr commandos, the so-called Brandenburgers, already inside in the uniform of Dutch policemen. The Western allies responded on cue, advancing north-east into Flanders. As Holland and Belgium were overrun, the tanks of the central Army Group, 'A', massed in a column 100 miles long, cut through the Ardennes and raced for the Channel coast. Surprise was complete; confusion was heightened by radio broadcasts ostensibly from French stations, actually directed by Schellenberg, designed to mislead the allies about the direction of the main thrust; they caused such panic among the French population as to hinder allied troop movements behind the lines. The British Expeditionary Force and the northern French divisions were cut off and encircled and began to retreat towards the coast.

By this time the Totenkopfdivision had been taken out of reserve and, like the Leibstandarte and the Verfügungsdivision, pressed into the attack across Flanders and the Pas de Calais. Towards the end of this push, as the British 2nd Division dug in stubbornly to buy time for their comrades to retire on Dunkirk, the first mass atrocity in the west occurred. It was on 27 May after some of the fiercest fighting of the campaign. A company of the Totenkopfdivision, which had taken heavy casualties forcing canal crossings near Béthune, accepted the surrender of some 100 men of the 2nd Royal Norfolks surrounded in a farmhouse near Le Paradis, then machine-gunned them in cold blood; wounded survivors were shot at close range or bayonetted. The following day the 2nd Battalion of the Leibstandarte carried out a similar massacre of eighty unarmed British prisoners in a barn near the village of Wormhoudt in Flanders. The episodes did nothing to assist Himmler's relations with the Army. They were also doctrinally unnecessary since the victims were neither Slavic *Untermenschen* nor Jews, but representatives of those blood-brothers of the Germans with whom Hitler and Himmler still hoped to come to terms after the French had been defeated. Despite Army calls for an enquiry, the Obersturmführer who ordered the massacre at Le Paradis was not court-martialled and went on later to command an SS regiment; nor was any action taken against the Leibstandarte commander. The incidents indicate the revolutionary spirit in which Himmler's field formations had been indoctrinated.

After the British Expeditionary Force in the north had been rescued by an extemporised flotilla of small craft from the Dunkirk beaches, all SS divisions, including even the Polizei, were pulled in for the drive south to complete the rout of the French armies; all displayed reckless élan in attack and defence, and as in the Polish campaign bled in proportionately greater numbers than the Army formations. All took thousands of prisoners.

Himmler, meanwhile, with Wolff by his side, had been driving around Holland and Belgium in the wake of the conquest. He was especially happy to see the good racial composition of the Dutch population, noting 'a gain for Germany'.[9] After dining with the commander of the Leibstandarte, Sepp Dietrich, he returned to the Felsennest on 25

May and gained Hitler's permission to raise an SS field regiment – to be called Westland – from Dutch and Belgian volunteers. Berger was instructed to establish a recruiting office in The Hague with a branch office in Antwerp.

Himmler also took the opportunity to present Hitler with a memorandum containing his latest thoughts on the treatment of the foreign peoples in the east.[10] 'The Führer read the six sides,' he noted afterwards, 'and found them very good and correct.' The first principle he established in the memorandum was that the individual nationalities, Poles, Jews, Ukrainians, White Russians and the rest, must be splintered into innumerable particles so that they would lose their national consciousness and any interest in unity. Members of these races should be used as police and town officials, but not allowed to attain any higher position than local police chief or mayor. Meanwhile genetically valuable elements from the 'racial brew' should be fished out and brought to Germany for assimilation.

The 'school question', he went on, was fundamental both for the racial sifting of youth and for the eventual elimination of national consciousness in the various racial groups, including the largest, the Poles themselves.

> For the non-German population of the east no higher school is permitted than the four-class *Volk* (or primary) school. The aim of this *Volk* school has to be exclusively:
> Simple calculations up to 500 at the highest, writing one's name, a precept that it is a Divine Commandment to obey Germans and to be honest, industrious and trustworthy. I do not consider reading necessary.
> Apart from this school no school should be permitted in the east. Parents who want a better education for their children from the beginning, both in the *Volk* school and in a higher school, must present a petition for this purpose to the Higher SS and Police Führer. The decision will be made on whether the child is racially immaculate and suitable for our conditions. If we recognise such a child as of our blood, the parents will be notified that the child should attend school in Germany and remain in Germany permanently.

Here is Himmler's guideline for the treatment of every question – individual fate is of no concern beside the good of the German nation:

> Cruel and tragic as this may be in each individual case, if one rejects the Bolshevic method of physical extermination of a people from inner conviction as unGermanic and impossible, then this method is really the most lenient and the best.
> The parents of this child of good blood will then be faced with the choice of either surrendering the child – in which case they will probably procreate no further children so that the danger of these sub-human peoples of the east obtaining a leadership-stratum of equal quality to us through such people of good blood will be removed – or the parents commit themselves to

go to Germany and become loyal citizens. One has a strong lever over these people in their love for their child, whose future and education will depend on the loyalty of the parents.

He went on to stress that these children and their parents should not be treated as lepers when they came to Germany, but – with changed names – should be helped to become loyal Germans:

> because we believe that they are really our own blood, which has found its way into a foreign nationality through the mistakes of German history, and we are convinced that our *Weltanschauung* and our ideals will re-echo in the racially equal souls of these children.

If these measures were carried out consistently over the next ten years, with regular annual screenings of all six- to ten-year-old schoolchildren to pick out those with good blood, the people of the General Gouvernement would be reduced to a 'blinded, inferior-value population' consisting of all the elements expelled not only from the eastern provinces but from the old Reich itself. He ended:

> This population will be available for Germany as a leaderless work-*Volk* of annual itinerant labourers and for special tasks (streets, quarries, construction); they will thereby eat and live better than under Polish rule with their own lack of culture and, under the strict, consistent and just control of the German peoples, be called to co-operate on the Germans' eternal cultural exploits and building works, which so far as the mass of crude work is concerned are perhaps only possible with their labour.[11]

The memorandum dealt with the situation within the borders of the occupied east as they were at that date, so it does not seem that Himmler guessed – despite the extremely favourable progress of the western campaign – that the real thrust for eastern *Lebensraum* would follow in the immediate future.

The interesting question about this memorandum, however, concerns his plans for the Jews. The only detailed reference to them came in the passage referring to the necessity for taking away all national consciousness from the various racial groups: 'The concept "Jews" will be completely eliminated, I hope, through the possibility of a great exodus of all the Jews to Africa or otherwise into a colony.'[12] In view of what actually happened to most Jews, another phrase he used assumes significance – 'if one rejects the Bolshevic method of physical extermination of a people from inner conviction as unGermanic and impossible'. Taken at face value these two passages seem to indicate that at this date, May 1940, he intended to solve the Jewish question, not by physical extermination, which would be unGermanic, but by forced emigration to some colonial territory. The French colony of Madagascar was talked of in this context, indeed Heydrich had Eichmann's department work up details to give it the semblance of authenticity. It must have been known, however, that a Polish Commission of Enquiry had investigated the possibility in 1937 and concluded that the island could accommodate at the absolute maximum only 15,000 European settlers.[13]

Apart from this memorandum, the signs indicate that physical extermination of the Jews had been decided on long before this date. Jews had already been rounded up and shot in local actions in Poland; they had been deliberately frozen to death in railway wagons; deliberately worked to death in labour camps and they were dying of starvation in the ghettos in which they were being concentrated in the major towns of the General Gouvernement. Even more suggestive – for Poles too had been shot and frozen to death – was the separate status Jews, gypsies and negroes had been accorded in the medical questionnaires from the very beginning of the T4 euthanasia programme in October 1939. In April 1940 the Reich Interior Ministry ordered that all Jewish patients in mental institutions and sanatoria in Germany be card-indexed and in June the first gassings of Jewish mental patients took place in Castle Grafeneck in Brandenburg, one of four T4 killing centres which had been set up in different regions of the Reich; two more were added in 1941.[14]

Heydrich's officials had taken a major role in the practical side of the 'euthanasia' programme; mention has been made of the Arthur Nebe–Albert Widmann carbon-monoxide experiments starting in the summer of 1939 and the gas chambers constructed under the supervision of Kriminal Kommissar Christian Wirth. The first demonstration gassing for Bouhler, Brack and other officials of the 'euthanasia' programme had taken place in the disused prison at Brandenburg-on-Havel in the first half of January 1940. Two or three cells had been knocked into one chamber and fitted with a system of perforated pipes leading in from an adjacent cell which housed the cylinders of CO gas. Some eighteen or twenty patients had been used as the test subjects. They entered the chamber naked; the door was locked and Widmann turned on the gas, watching its effects through a small observation window. After about five minutes all were dead; the door was opened, the chamber aired and SS men entered with specially constructed trolleys to deliver the corpses to cremation ovens.[15]

It was apparently Philipp Bouhler who suggested after this successful demonstration that gas chambers should be camouflaged as shower rooms with the carbon monoxide entering through the pipes and nozzles. Wirth carried this out at Castle Grafeneck, where he was sent to set up a special registry to fake death certificates; he added a 'changing room' as ante-room to the 'showers' to complete the deception. Besides issuing certificates with false causes of death, numbered and dated to conceal the group nature of the operation, Wirth's registry sent out letters of condolence to next of kin citing the fictional cause of death. Himmler was deeply involved since the SS administered both the crematorium orderlies and the camouflage ambulance service, the Public Welfare Transport for the Sick Company, which brought the patients from the institutions to the killing centres.

In May 1940 Wirth had been appointed Kommandant of another 'euthanasia' centre, Castle Hartheim in Upper Austria, some twelve miles from Hitler's home-town, Linz, thus near Mauthausen concentration camp. The gassing process had been duplicated here, but was being mismanaged. Wirth brought order to the system, and in June he was appointed Inspector of the Euthanasia Killing Centres. A photographer he employed at Hartheim to take pictures of the victims' death struggles and often their brains after dissection – pictures which were sent to Berlin as 'scientific material' and no doubt used for propaganda purposes in SS publications – was interviewed by Simon Wiesenthal after the war. He provided a picture of good living for the staff and sexual promiscuity: 'everybody was sleeping with everybody else'. Then he said, 'One thing I couldn't make out. About thirty or thirty-five patients were gassed every day in the cellar. Yet they had at least eighty employees and some came down to the cellar to watch. What did they need eighty people for?'[16]

Knowing that Wirth later commanded the first extermination camps in the east and that his predecessor and successor at Hartheim, Franz Reichleitner and Franz Stangl – both also police officers – went on to command extermination camps, Wiesenthal concluded that Hartheim and the five other chief 'euthanasia' killing centres had been training schools for the genocide programme; it seemed to explain how the men who had to carry out mass killings day after day, month in month out, were put through their paces *psychologically*, for it had always been a puzzle why none of the executives of genocide had cracked under the strain.

In fact there were several cases of 'unsuitable personnel' transferred from the death camps in Poland to other duties; other men developed psychosomatic diseases and some suffered nervous breakdowns. In any case it does not follow that the killing centres were designed from the start as psychological testing and training centres. For one thing it is not clear what date the Hartheim photographer was referring to; he was first employed in 1940, but the large staff may have been a later feature; alternatively the staff may have been assembled for another purpose such as sterilisation or sterilisation experiments. This is made more probable perhaps by the remark 'everybody was sleeping with everybody else' – many there were women. Nurses were used for the sterilisation programme. Moreover the SD confidential report for 13 March 1940 stated that card-indexing of the population of the Ostmark (Austria) necessary for the execution of the laws for the prevention of hereditarily diseased offspring was well under way and some 2000 cases were immediately available for the hereditary health court to adjudicate. However, the report continued, it was not intended to begin the action in too sharp a form 'in order to avoid a probable backlash of public opinion during the war'. This was expected chiefly from Church circles, already conducting a whispering and poster campaign against the hereditary-disease laws. It was, therefore, only possible for the present to carry out 'the urgent sterilisations'. What constituted urgency was not disclosed. It is possible, of course, that 'urgent sterilisation' was a euphemism for T4 'euthanasia'.[17] Yet this is unlikely since the sterilisation programme continued throughout the war alongside 'euthanasia' and later genocide, and Himmler for one remained deeply interested in sterilisation as a way out of his racial problems.

In addition to gas chambers, there were gas vans whose occupants could be killed by the driver throwing a switch to divert the exhaust into the gastight body of the vehicle. Himmler's HSSPF in the Warthegau made use of this equipment in May 1940 when, as he put it in his subsequent report, an itinerant T4 special unit – Sonderkommando – assigned to him by Heydrich's RSHA 'successfully evacuated' – read exterminated – '1558 mental patients from the Soldau transit camp'.[18] The mental patients had been brought to Soldau from institutions in East Prussia and the Sonderkommando, named after its commander, Lange, took from 21 May to 8 June to liquidate them with the vans. This Kommando's vans were used subsequently at the first of the extermination camps in the east.

It has been suggested that the use of gas for mass killing followed psychological and morale difficulties experienced with the Einsatzkommandos who had to perform the executions. This hardly seems to accord with the fact that gassing experiments preceded the outbreak of war, but it can be argued that these were strictly for the 'euthanasia' programme and the method evolved and the officials trained in it were naturally employed for genocide later, after the decision had been taken to liquidate European Jewry.

Against this argument there is Hitler's, Himmler's and Heydrich's – indeed all leading Nazis' – obsession with Jews as parasites living on and debasing the blood of Germany and Europe, who had to be extirpated lest they bring about the total degeneration of their host. As suggested, the war was a race war and the elimination of the chief racial polluters was among the main war aims. On the other hand, finding a colony for the Jews in Africa or elsewhere was not only impossible given the numbers involved – and the proven obstacles to international co-operation for this purpose – but was actually undesirable since it would amount to the foundation of an independent Jewish state; Nazi doctrine was opposed to this on principle.[19] Moreover, if it was the aim to transport all Jews *en masse* to an extra-European destination, why did Heydrich find it necessary to stipulate the strictest secrecy in his directive of 21 September 1939, detailing the 'short-term' steps necessary before the 'ultimate aim' in the Jewish question? If the ultimate aim was emigration there was no need for secrecy.

Hence the talk of a 'Madagascar plan' or an African colony tends to confirm rather than refute the suspicion that extermination was planned from the beginning. It was spread about openly. Hans Frank noted in his diary after a conversation in July 1940 with the HSSPF East, Frederik-Wilhelm Krüger, and the Reichsstatthalter of the Warthegau, Arthur Greiser: 'it is planned in the shortest possible time after a peace treaty to transport the entire Jew clans in the German Reich, in the Gen. Gouvt. and in the Protectorate to an African or American colony. . . .'[20] It is not difficult to find why a cover story had to be invented. Apart from the need, as with the sterilisation campaign, not to upset the Churches and the vast numbers of their followers within the Reich, there was intense sensitivity about American reactions. An American-based committee[21] was funding the continued emigration of Jews, which Himmler found so 'very nice and droll'; more important, President Roosevelt was supporting the British war effort and only looking for a suitable pretext to bring the United States in openly on England's side. Von Ribbentrop's Foreign Ministry officials were so anxious about American opinion they had set up a special desk to monitor the activities in Poland for anything that might damage Germany's good name.[22]

Whether the extermination of the Jews was planned from September 1939, probably a good deal earlier, rests ultimately on the psychic make-up – or pathology – of Hitler, and to a lesser extent of Heydrich – since the threads of the Nebe–Widmann–Wirth experiments led to Heydrich's RSHA. There can be little doubt about Hitler's attitude: he had expressed it plainly in *Mein Kampf*; even before that, when he founded the Nazi Party, if the Curator of the Party museum in Munich was to be believed. And on 30 January 1939 he had given international-finance Jewry a very public warning that if they were to bring about a world war it would mean the destruction of the Jewish race in Europe, a prophecy he was to repeat. There can be little doubt either about Heydrich's methods. A deception like the Madagascar plan was in his style. The extermination programme as carried out was based entirely on deception; the idea of a colony to be set aside for the Jews was likely to have been the first step, not simply to hoodwink the Jews, but to deceive the officials and people of Germany and world opinion. Meanwhile, to judge by his provocations, he would have been training special teams to carry out the 'ultimate aim'. If this was indeed the pattern, the T4 programme was conceived from the beginning as the experimental and psychological school for the executives of the 'final solution' – as indeed it became.

It was especially valuable in turning doctors into killers. In his psychological study *The Nazi Doctors*, Robert Jay Lifton has pointed to the necessary involvement of German doctors in every stage of the 'final solution'; 'the imagery of killing in the name of healing' – that is to say purifying the race – was crucial, and he concludes that 'the destruction of the boundary between healing and killing' was at the heart of systematised genocide.[23] It was in the euthanasia programme, starting with very young children with serious disabilities, progressing to 'life-unworthy life' adults that the transformation was effected, and a sufficient number of doctors were chosen or chose themselves for the work of mass-killing healthy adults in the name of racial purity. This explanation for the T4 killing centres seems more in line with Hitler's intentions, with Nazi *Weltanschauung* and with Heydrich's methods than the idea of rather haphazard experimentation coming in useful later when it was realised that something had to be done about all the Jews concentrated in the east. The Jews were concentrated there by Himmler's orders for a purpose.

In this light Himmler's use of the 'African colony' solution in his memorandum about the treatment of the eastern peoples only indicates that he was a party to the deception plan. It was also important that no documentary evidence link the Führer with any of the killing programmes. Yet at the same time he rejected physical extermination of a people 'from inner conviction as unGermanic'. It is possible that he found no problem with the Jews since they were not a people but – in Nazi eyes – merely battened on other peoples, and the phrase in the memorandum refers to the Poles and other national groups. Alternatively, Himmler knew that Hitler wished for the physical extermination of the Jews, but really did believe it represented a Bolshevic and unGermanic solution, and was trying to make the point. This hardly seems to accord with his absolute belief in the Führer's genius, or with the terrible anxiety he experienced if he thought he might be out of favour.

The simple answer to the question of Himmler's attitude at this date is that the memorandum was not about Jewish policy and does not give his views; it was about the treatment of the peoples who were to remain in the east. The Jews were not to remain. He gave the agreed, coded solution to their problem and left it at that, while declining physical extermination for the Poles and other racial groups. Copies of the memorandum went to Hans Frank and the four Gauleiters and Reichsstatthalters of the eastern provinces, to the head of Hitler's Chancellery, Lammers, the Minister of Agriculture, Walter Darré, Hess's secretary Martin Bormann, Heydrich and the chief of Himmler's own Office for the Consolidation of German Nationhood, SS-Brigadeführer Greifelt, who communicated the contents to the HSSPFs in the east. The chiefs of various SS main offices like the RuSHA were also shown the memorandum, although not allowed to make extracts or copies; they had to memorise the general lines. With all these recipients, some of whom were not privy to the 'ultimate aim', Jewish policy could not be spelled out, especially as they were told that 'The Führer has acknowledged and agreed the paper as the guideline' for the east.[24]

The inability of the western allies to stem the advance of the German armies across France inspired Mussolini to enter the war on Hitler's side, fulfilling the earlier promise of a central European 'Axis' of the two dictatorships. On the same day, 10 June, the French government abandoned Paris; four days later German troops entered the capital. On 16 June the French Premier resigned, to be replaced by Marshal Pétain, who immediately entered armistice negotiations. The terms Hitler imposed were extraordinarily moderate considering the huge war indemnity the Germans had hoped to claim from France in the first war, the humiliation they had actually forced on Russia at Brest-Litovsk in 1918 and Germany's own humiliation at Versailles. No doubt the final settlement would have satisfied Hitler's lust for vengeance, but in the meantime he had to consider Stalin, who was quietly enlarging the Soviet empire at his back, and the British empire and Navy, active around his flanks and tacitly supported by Roosevelt. He expected that after the French defeat the British would realise the hopelessness of their position and respond to his peace overtures; he did not want to encourage the 'warmongers' around Churchill by driving the French too hard and perhaps pushing them into taking their Navy over to Churchill and carrying on the fight from overseas. He contented himself with reclaiming Alsace-Lorraine, occupying Paris and north-east France and, in order to widen his naval- and air-strategic position, occupying the Channel and Biscay coastal areas down to the Spanish border. He left Pétain's government in Vichy central and southern France, the French fleet and all her colonies.

He contrived to express the vengeance in his soul, in the German soul, by having the armistice signed in the clearing in the forest of Compiègne outside Paris where the armistice ending the first war had been signed, and in the same railway car, fetched from its museum. Strangely Himmler was missing from this, Hitler's greatest triumph. It was apparently due to ill health. Kersten had joined 'Heinrich' shortly after the launch of the western offensive, and had been treating him and his confidential secretary and chief of his personal staff, Dr Rudolf Brandt.[25] During the week of the armistice – signed on 22 June – Kersten was also treating Hess for 'severe stomach pains' caused apparently by tension and excitement over events in France; Hess assured Kersten they would soon make peace with England.[26]

Himmler had told Kersten the same thing in February; the Führer would be magnanimous, he had added. When Kersten had asked why England should give up her traditional policy of preserving the balance of power on the continent, Himmler had told him that things were different now: National Socialism had opened everyone's eyes to the real laws which governed life – the laws of race. The English were a Germanic people; real hostility between peoples of the same blood was out of the question. It was only the small ruling group backed by the Jews who wished to preserve the old policy, and when the Führer made peace with England he would demand the expulsion of her Jews.[27]

Himmler had gone on to prophesy that Kersten would live to see Adolf Hitler, Führer of the greatest Germanic land power, received on a state visit to London by the King of England, leader of the greatest Germanic sea power, there to conclude a just peace for the worldwide Germanic race. It is more than possible that he had the former Edward VIII in mind for this scene. Edward – now Duke of Windsor – had been forced to abdicate as much probably for his political and pro-Nazi views as for his insistence on marrying an American divorcée. At the time of Himmler's comments Windsor was serving on the British Military Mission in France. Since then he had crossed into Spain and there he had become an object of intrigue, von Ribbentrop, Himmler and Canaris all attempting to win him over for the Führer.

At every level in the Reich, hubris fed on the prospect of the German millennium. On the day the armistice was signed Göring charged the Economics Minister, Funk, with the planning of an integrated European economy incorporating all the occupied countries under German direction.[28] Admiral Raeder was quicker off the mark; as early as 3 June his operations division had produced a memorandum on strategy after 'the won war', which started with the premises that all peoples in the occupied countries should be politically and militarily dependent on Germany, with France so militarily and economically crippled she could never rise again. A colonial empire should be fashioned in central Africa stretching from the Atlantic coast to the Indian Ocean, and overseas bases acquired in North and South America, Asia and Australia. A world map produced by the naval staff at this time shows the great German world empire, including a great part of Africa, in blue opposing the remnants of a British empire in red now controlled from Washington.[29] When Raeder made one of his regular reports to Hitler on 11 July, he carried a memorandum detailing the gigantic fleet that would be required after the war to command the 'economic and military sea communications' of this vast German world empire.[30]

On the same day the secret SD report on the people's mood began with 'the chief question which stirs the whole German population: "When will the real war against England start, and how long will it last?" '[31] To judge by these reports the people had been growing ever more impatient for 'retaliation' against England, seen as the instigator of the war; rumours about peace negotiations through the mediation of the Duke of Windsor in Spain had been circulating since at least the first week in July, to the dismay of 'the overwhelming part of the population' who wanted to see England brought to account. The most frequently heard view was 'It would be lamentable if England were not smashed to pieces.'[32] In view of the manipulation of the news to create this public mood, it is interesting that by 15 July the people were feeling uncertain about Russia, and rumours were circulating of a race between Russia and Germany for the Rumanian oil fields.[33] By the time Hitler came to make a much heralded speech to the Reichstag on 19 July the burning questions which the people hoped he would answer concerned an ultimatum to England, peace negotiations with England, the start of the assault on England, the Balkan question and relations with Soviet Russia.[34]

It is not surprising that, when Heydrich returned to his desk after setting up an SD and Gestapo *Zentrale* in Paris under the French-speaking

SS-Standartenführer Helmut Knochen, Himmler charged him with drafting plans for the control of Great Britain after occupation.

But Himmler's major preoccupations at this time were with the situation in the east. Despite the ideological drive and 'decency' he attempted to inculcate in his SS leaders, Poland and the Protectorate had degenerated into mires of corruption trampled by rival robber barons. Earlier in the year he had found it necessary to suspend the head of the Resettlement Office, von Gottberg, and consign several SS-Führers to *Schutzhaft* for misuse of their powers in Aryanising and otherwise confiscating land and handing it to SS families; afterwards he had transferred the Central Land Registry from the RuSHA to his Office for the Consolidation of German Nationhood.[35] Other SS-Führers and HSSPFs had used the resettlement programme to set up *wild* concentration camps as in the days immediately after the *Machtergreifung*, and run businesses with camp labour. In the ghettos being formed in the major cities SS-Führers engaged in even more lucrative 'black' economic enterprises employing Jewish labour or took the equivalent of 'protection' money from entrepreneurs setting up workshops with Jewish craftsmen.

Meanwhile productivity in the official SS economic enterprises employing concentration camp labour suffered from the combination of inadequate rations and brutality handed out by the camps' administration. Since Eicke had taken his Totenkopfdivision to the front, he had been succeeded by his former Chief of Staff, Richard Glücks. Glücks continued along the lines Eicke had laid down; inmates were 'the enemy'; the utmost hardness was necessary in dealing with them. On top of this, over-age 'old fighters' from the General SS, ethnic Germans, youngsters and others called in to replace Eicke's corps of camp guards lacked training and experience. Höss, who had been given the task that spring of converting a former Polish artillery barracks at Auschwitz into a camp for 10,000 inmates, recalled after the war the inadequate human material he had to work with; junior officers and even the professional criminals sent to him as Kapos, or foremen, were not only incapable but displayed a 'conscious negligence and malevolence that simply forced me to do the most important and urgent things myself'.[36]

The problem was especially acute after the fall of France since one of the expressions of euphoria was an upsurge of interest in building; and building materials were the chief concern of the SS companies employing concentration camp labour. Not only had Hitler revived the plans of his architect, Albert Speer, for setting the thousand-year Reich in monuments of stone, but a massive residential building programme was needed for ordinary German families whose task, in the ideology, was to be fruitful and multiply and so produce the real condition for world mastery after the won war. House-building, like all consumer products, had suffered in the run-up to the war and there was an enormous deficit to be made up if parents were to have decent conditions in which to bring up large families of healthy children. In Berlin, for instance, it was reckoned that if a two-and-a-half-roomed flat with kitchen was taken as the minimum for family life, two-thirds of Berliners lived in what was termed 'family-unworthy accommodation'.[37] Himmler had grandiose building plans of his own for large SS families and barrack complexes as well as farmhouses and buildings for the German communities he intended planting in the occupied east; as he expressed it to the officers of the Leibstandarte later that summer, his programme was not conceivable – no one was going to donate money for it – without putting to work 'the refuse of humanity, the prisoners, the professional criminals' in his camps. After the war, he confided to them, he wanted to form guard battalions of Waffen-SS and post them for three months at a concentration camp; it would be the best instruction they could have in the ways of the *Untermenschen* and *Minderrassentum* – those of inferior race.[38] With this attitude at the top it is not surprising that Glücks followed doggedly in Eicke's footsteps and that at the bottom the guards and Kapos made merciless sport working political and racial prisoners beyond endurance at the quarries, murdering them on the one hand while on the other selling their meagre rations and exploiting those they found with skills.

Himmler had already begun regularising many of the *wild* camps; he now opened a new camp for Scandinavian, French, Dutch and Belgian political prisoners by extending an offshoot of Sachsenhausen at Neuengamme outside Hamburg, which had been producing bricks for the German Earth- and Stone-Work Company since before the war; another camp was opened by the site of stone quarries near Natzweiler in Alsace, and another by a granite quarry at Gross Rosen in Lower Silesia for the Poles expelled from the new *Gaue* added to the Reich. At the same time he formed an SS holding company (Deutsche Wirtsschaftsbetriebe) to co-ordinate investment and supervise the various SS firms; but he did nothing to integrate the camp administration with them. He was aware that if he did so it would be said that he arrested people only for use as workers, but no doubt his chief concern was as always to keep power divided. Glücks' Inspectorate, which had been a branch of the SS Main Office, was transferred into a new SS-Führungs (Command) Main Office, together with the High Command of the General SS and the old Verfügung-struppe, now officially designated Waffen-SS.[39]

The two other Main Offices with a direct interest in the camps were Heydrich's RSHA, whose officials executed the policy of enslavement and liquidation in the east and also had the duty of seeking out corruption, not least within the SS itself, and the Economics and Administration Main Office (WVHA), under a thrusting former naval Paymaster-branch captain named Oswald Pohl. His officials sat on the boards of the SS companies employing camp labour and indeed invested their own capital gained through corruption in these firms. So the conflicts between Himmler's enslavement agencies and Göring's Four Year Plan officials, the Army Economics Department Inspectorates and the provincial Gauleiters and Reichsstatthalters were matched within the SS by similar conflicts between the WVHA and Glücks on the one hand, and the WVHA and RSHA on the other. While conducted in terms of ideology or pragmatism these struggles were more concerned with the vast power conferred by control over millions of helots and the fortunes and possibilities for patronage which this conferred. The dichotomy between this real state of affairs, which Himmler used as a source of motivation and power balance within his empire, and the ideal state of 'decency' and order in his mind's eye perhaps contributed to a deterioration in his health noted at this time.

In mid-July he left Berlin to tour Burgundy with Wolff. Away from the problems that occupied him every day until late in the evening he relapsed into those deep and comfortable recesses of his mind where since childhood he had woven history and ideals together. Viewing the towns they drove through as conquerors and the fruitful summer countryside as part of that Burgundy which, after the partition of Charlemagne's empire, had stretched from the Mediterranean to the Low Countries, he dreamed of recreating something like it in modern form as an SS state annexed to the Reich, but autonomous with its own government, laws and fighting services. He would be Grand Master, Wölffchen his Chancellor. It would act as a buffer to ensure that France would never rise again and at the same time as a field in which pure SS theory could be practised without being undermined by the Party or state bureaucracy. It would be a model state, he told Wolff, an example to the world.[40]

They flew back to Berlin for Hitler's appearance at the Reichstag on 19 July. The imperial capital was *en fête*, something the Berliners had become used to, but this time the mood in the streets, beflagged and garlanded with flowers, matched the festival atmosphere. In the evening Himmler, Wolff and Heydrich took their place among the Party dignitaries in the Kroll Opera for the speech that Germans by their radios throughout the Reich and the occupied countries were waiting to hear. The Führer did not disappoint. It was accounted one of his best performances. There was no hysterical baying, little shouting; his voice was low and controlled, his hand gestures as eloquent as his changing expressions, now martial, now reasonable or, with a turn of his head and eyes, ironic. The American journalist William Shirer, watching from the gallery, was forced to admire his artistry: 'so wonderful an actor, so magnificent a handler of the German mind . . .' he noted.[41]

The military were there in force, the first balcony alight with uniforms, gold braid, crosses and orders. Hitler brought them into his act, promoting no fewer than eleven generals, including two Luftwaffe generals, to field marshal. The Army had suffered many humiliations at his hands since 1933; surely this was the greatest. They believed they were honoured; caught up in the spirit of his performance, perhaps Hitler believed it too, but in the cold light of will he had merely gauged their price: victory and glory. After the generals it was Göring's turn; he was promoted from field marshal to Reich marshal.

One who was not taken in by the show was Halder. Shirer, watching his 'classically intellectual face' as he congratulated the younger generals promoted over him, thought he was hiding his true sadness. What Himmler and Heydrich felt is not recorded; neither gained rewards. Heydrich, who had done more than anyone to create the preconditions for the generals' lightning victory, was not mentioned in the speech; 'Party Comrade Himmler's services' in organising the security of 'our Reich' as well as the units of the Waffen-SS were recognised in one brief sentence. Himmler could take comfort in praise Hitler bestowed on 'the valiant divisions and regiments of the Waffen-SS' – a term which now passed into general use to describe the SS field regiments – and for the share of medals allotted to his field commanders: Sepp Dietrich, commander of the Leibstandarte, Steiner of the Standarte Deutschland, Keppler of Der Führer, together with three other commanders, received the Knight's Cross, the highest basic order of the Iron Cross.[42] Nevertheless, Himmler and the SS as a whole were left in the shadows on this day of triumph rather as they had been after the *Machtergreifung*, while Göring and the generals basked in the Führer's favour.

According to the subsequent SD report, the speech was received by the people with tremendous emotion and enthusiasm, but one point caused almost equal surprise. This was when Hitler, adopting a tone of utmost moderation, almost despair, felt it his duty 'before his conscience to appeal once more to reason and common sense in Great Britain' to put an end to the war. Despite the rumours that had been circulating beforehand, this public offer of peace was apparently the 'astonishment of the hour' and the chief talking point of the population, who regarded it as almost too magnanimous since, if England were spared her just punishment, she would in a few years instigate another war.[43] Those Germans Shirer spoke to did not share this view; apparently they wanted peace and simply could not understand why Britain did not throw in the towel.[44]

Meanwhile the intrigue around the Duke of Windsor, now in Portugal, moved towards a climax. At the end of the month Churchill sent Sir Walter Monckton and intelligence officers to extricate him from the toils of Himmler's and von Ribbentrop's agents. He was persuaded to take up an appointment as Governor of the Bahamas, a thankless post near bottom in the order of British colonial governorships but intended to remove him from the German sphere. He and his Duchess sailed most reluctantly on 1 August; 'that bloody British government', she wrote from aboard ship.[45]

By this time Churchill had rejected Hitler's 'last appeal to reason'. Hitler concluded, reasonably and rightly, that this stubbornness could be caused only by expectations that Russia and the United States would enter the war against Germany. He outlined these views to a small group at the Berghof on 31 July. After expressing scepticism about the possibility of invading England – indeed virtually ruling it out – he stressed that Russia was the factor on which England placed most hope; if Russia were removed from the reckoning British hopes in America would also disappear since America would have to cope with a Japan whose weight had increased on the Far Eastern board. He concluded that if Russia were smashed, England's last hope would be extinguished:

> Decision: in the course of this dispute Russia will have to be removed. Spring 1941.
> The quicker we smash Russia, the better . . . May 1941. 5 months for execution. . . .[46]

For those like Canaris with grave doubts about the wisdom of launching German forces into the distances of Russia before England had been subdued, it was already too late. The mass of the German nation was ready to believe Goebbels when he assured them that the generals and the Reichsführer-SS saw in Hitler the greatest German leader and the greatest warlord of all time. The younger officers especially believed it. As for the generals, even the usually over-optimistic Goerdeler told von Hassell in early August that he now expected nothing from them.[47]

A witticism going the rounds in Berlin that autumn had Goebbels complaining to Hitler that he had not been promoted.

Hitler: 'Don't worry – after the war Göring will be World Marshal and you will be Half-world Marshal.'

'And Himmler?'

'Underworld Marshal.'[48]

It was perhaps Himmler with his mystical sense of the past who first compared Hitler to the twelfth-century German soldier king and crusader Friedrich I of Hohenstaufen, known as Barbarossa. Certainly Goebbels' representative, Karl Böhmer, announced to the foreign press at a daily conference that autumn that Hitler was Barbarossa's reincarnation.[49] The idea of linking the two may also have been a part of the great deception which Hitler, von Ribbentrop, Canaris and Heydrich were preparing for Stalin.

Preliminary intelligence work and planning for the assault on Russia had begun in early August in both the Army General Staff under Halder (OKH) and Keitel's OKW, and was carried on side by side with planning for an invasion of England and an indirect attack on British sea routes through the Mediterranean by the capture of Gibraltar and Suez. In September Mussolini launched an assault from Libya on the British forces protecting Egypt and the Suez Canal, and in October he attacked Greece. Hitler affected surprise and anger, but it is probable that the operation had been agreed mutually to enable him to move his forces eastwards ostensibly in support of his Axis ally, ostensibly to gain Greek airfields and naval bases from which to attack the British Middle Eastern position, hence the vital Suez Canal, at the same time allowing the Luftwaffe to operate against

British bases threatening the Rumanian oil fields – even more vital to the German war effort than the Canal was to the British. Thus a convincing picture was built up of an indirect strategy of closing the Mediterranean to the British and protecting vital Balkan resources from British attack.

Meanwhile at the end of September a three-power pact was signed between the two Axis powers and Japan; Russia was invited to join, in order to form a four-power anti-British bloc stretching from Tokyo to the shores of the Atlantic, and on 12 November Molotov visited Berlin to discuss the proposition. He was treated by Hitler to an extravagant 'worldwide perspective' of the partition of the British empire and the exclusion of the USA, and von Ribbentrop provided him with a draft treaty and protocols defining each of the four powers' share of the real estate: for Russia it was to be a drive southwards to the Persian Gulf area and the Indian Ocean. Since this denied her historical and obvious present interests in the Balkans and eastern Mediterranean, it was not a serious proposition, although both Hitler and von Ribbentrop did their utmost to make it appear so. Later that month Halder's staff set up war games to determine the basic lines of advance for an attack into Russia. The results were incorporated in Directive 21: 'The German armed forces must be prepared to crush Soviet Russia in a rapid campaign even before the end of the war against England. . . .' This was issued by Hitler on 18 December and required preparations to be completed by 15 May 1941; the day before issuing it Hitler changed the codename from 'Fritz' to 'Barbarossa'.[50]

Those in the Russian intelligence and foreign services familiar with early European history would have known that Friedrich Barbarossa had led the Third Crusade through the Balkans and Asia Minor with the aim of wresting the Holy Sepulchre in Jerusalem from Saladin. Hitler had done all in his power to suggest that a latter-day 'Barbarossa' might be aimed in the same direction to wrest the Middle East from Great Britain and sever the imperial link with India.

In one important sense, however, 'Barbarossa' was not a misleading title; Hitler may have convinced himself and his inner circle and military staff under Keitel that a pre-emptive strike against Russia was necessary before the Red Army was ready and before Stalin began exerting pressure on the Reich through Rumanian oil and the other vital raw-material supplies. He may have convinced himself that Churchill and Stalin had already come to a secret agreement, but there is no doubt from his subsequent orders to Himmler and Heydrich that the deeper reasons for the campaign were ideological: 'Barbarossa' was the crusade against Jews and Bolsheviks he had promised and prophesied.

It was a colossal gamble: he had to crush the Russian armies before winter. The military precedents were not good, nor indeed the implications of the name chosen for the venture: Friedrich Barbarossa's crusade had been a failure; Friedrich himself had drowned in Cilicia. Nevertheless he, Adolf

Hitler, was recognised as the greatest warlord of all time, and for once his military advisers, including even Halder, were if anything more sanguine about the risks than he. And so he made his final throw; and so, with the eye of hindsight and knowledge of his habitual response in difficulties, it appears inevitable.

Himmler had begun preparing for the Russian campaign in early August at the same time as or even before the preliminary planning started in Keitel's and Halder's staffs.[51] His creation of the SS-Führungs Main Office as Waffen-SS High Command was no doubt connected with this since his concern to increase the strength of his fighting divisions was intensified by the chances of glory to be earned in the east. He wanted his SS troops to shine. He wanted the reflection to give him lustre among his rivals at the Führer's court where he was taken for granted, so he felt, as agent for all negative tasks which needed doing but could not be spoken of and which earned him and his Order little honour, chiefly fear and repulsion. This is supposition, but it accords with the views he expressed.

In his struggle with the Army that autumn and winter for men for new field divisions, he and Gottlob Berger used much the same tricks as before; the under-age youths and over-age General SS 'old fighters' who had replaced Eicke's original Totenkopf units were in their turn formed into field regiments, and Berger led a renewed drive to recruit volunteers of Nordic blood from all over Europe. A training camp 'Sennheim' was established in Alsace where foreign recruits went through a six- to eight-week course to learn German.[52] By these means the Waffen-SS was doubled to the equivalent of six field divisions by the start of the Russian campaign. Including all reserves, it still numbered scarcely 160,000 men though, a minute fraction of the Army of some 3 million poised for the assault.

There is no doubt that Himmler supported and looked forward expectantly to the conquest; Kersten recorded many talks during treatments that winter when his patient outlined his plans for settling a new farming aristocracy in the east. The nobility degenerated directly it lost touch with the soil from which it had sprung, Himmler told him, especially when it received no fresh blood into its ranks; had the English system been employed of continually reinforcing the nobility from below, the German upper classes would be less degenerate than they were today. The new ruling class had to be brought into contact with the soil and avail themselves of its renewing strength. The only question was how this should be done. As a first step he proposed that all intellectual, industrial and political leaders should be endowed with a farm which they would not be allowed to sell. Spending their holidays there, they and their families would gain a wonderful experience of the land which would last the children throughout life. Some posts would carry with them automatic tenancy of a state farm in the vicinity.[53]

Another day he mused about the English system whereby the eldest son inherited everything and the other sons and daughters had to earn their living, thus re-entering and bringing their good blood into the national life. That, he suggested, might be called conscious racial breeding. After the war he looked forward to radical measures in this area: only the owner of an estate would be allowed a title; the former aristocrats would be judged on their National Socialist reliability and the proofs they had given of it during the war.[54]

When Kersten pointed out that this new aristocracy might not be or even wish to be farmers, and might mismanage their estates, Himmler answered that naturally this point had been considered; the farms would be looked after by a manager appointed by the government.

'Then, Herr Himmler, you are simply providing your ruling class with a country house on the cheap.'[55]

Himmler agreed there were difficulties; they would need to find a way around them. After a lapse of five days he returned to the argument; the appointed farm manager – and he had in mind wounded members of the Waffen-SS as first choice for these posts – would have the task of taking the owner or tenant under his wing and initiating him, and especially his children, into farm management and country lore. It would all take time and a great deal of patience, but if they only succeeded in bringing one son or daughter in every state bureaucrat's family back to the land they would have achieved an immense amount. These youngsters would then be trained in agricultural colleges and assigned farms in the east. 'So we will enable our leading families to escape from the evils of civilisation in the city.' Thus, he concluded, the Germanic race would flourish again and its existence would be guaranteed for a thousand years. Kersten noted after this conversation that Himmler always pursued a subject obstinately until he had reached the conclusion he wanted.[56]

Discussing these ideas in a group of high-ranking SS leaders after dinner a few days later, Kersten found that they all shared their chief's enthusiasm. Simply to mention the land was to rouse their instant approval. Their eyes shone and they talked in almost identical phrases, which had the effect, it seemed, of magical incantations: 'back to the land', 'own your own land as a free man', 'a new ruling class', and above all 'the SS looks after everything.' Kersten found himself wondering whether it was the sense of confinement in which Germans lived in apartments in cities, coupled with Germanic romanticism, which caused this passionate yearning for country life. In any case Himmler had harnessed it to his purpose. Each of these hard-headed men believed they only had to do their duty and they would literally be led to the promised land. Each 'already saw himself as a gentleman farmer in the east with a Germanic family of at least seven children'; each saw 'King Heinrich' as the guarantor of this paradise.[57]

It is evident that the eastern enslavement and extermination policy had as much to do with these utopian goals as with race, at least with the majority of practical and ambitious SS leaders. Even for Himmler eastern racial policy was closely tied in with his early Artamen Society ideals and with the aspirations of the frustrated small businessmen, shopkeepers and tradesmen who had provided the initial backing for the Nazi Party long before big business and finance.

So far these sections of the middle classes had been ill served by the regime. The war economy and consequent cut-back of all consumer products had tended to concentrate businesses and forced many small men to the wall; the Jewish businesses expropriated in the Aryanisation processes had tended to go to the larger capitalists. The middle-class movement saw its salvation in the SS plans for the east. The leader of the Reich Associations for Commerce and Trade, Franz Hayler, knew Himmler well as a fellow Bavarian and had a high honorary rank in the SS. Hayler's chief business manager, SS-Gruppenführer Otto Ohlendorf, was chief of Heydrich's SD-Inland as well as a section leader in Funk's Economics Ministry. Above all Himmler himself took a direct interest on both ideological and practical grounds in the middle classes who were to take the place of the liquidated or enslaved Jewish and Slavic traders and craftsmen to provide the backbone of his eastern Germanic settler communities. In November 1940 the General Secretary of the German Trades Association stated that his group acted 'in constant touch with the Reichsführer Himmler'.[58] And in December Ohlendorf spoke before another commercial group of the huge numbers of independent people in trade and commerce who would be needed alongside the farmers in the east: 'In the final analysis it is these three [groups] together who will form the reservoir from which over and over again people will emerge who will give to this German *Volk*, and thus the white race, its appearance and character.'[59]

The related topic of women and large families also occupied Himmler's mind that winter, as indeed it occupied many in leading circles. The numbers available for colonisation did not correspond to the vast areas that were to be carved out in the east. On 17 January 1941 Kersten recorded that Heydrich was closeted with Himmler all morning, the red light over the door signifying that he was not to be disturbed. When at length Heydrich emerged and Kersten was able to start his treatment he found Himmler in buoyant mood. He had, he said, been discussing details of new marriage laws whereby divorce would be legal if after five years a couple were childless. Kersten said he knew of many happy marriages without children. Whether Herr and Frau Müller were happy or not was of little account, Himmler replied; the good of the Reich came before the happiness of individuals.[60]

He began to tell Kersten of ideas he had discussed with Hitler for setting up a Women's Academy for Wisdom and Culture to educate women specially selected for intellect, quick wit, grace of body, complete political reliability and Germanic appearance.

'You mean that only blonde, blue-eyed women will be admitted?'

'Naturally. Of course I know some brunettes have outstanding intellectual qualities and great charm, but we have to make a logical start.'[61]

Describing the Academy, Himmler made it sound like a cross between a finishing school and a training college for the diplomatic service. The young women's intellects would be honed by studying history, foreign languages and daily games of chess, their physical grace by sport, especially fencing, riding, swimming and pistol practice; they would also have special courses in cookery and housekeeping. Then, on passing an exam they would graduate with the title of 'Chosen Woman'. Their primary duty afterwards would be to marry Party and SS leaders. Too many of the top men in the Reich had married during the 'time of struggle' and the women who had been perfectly appropriate to conditions then had failed to rise with their menfolk and fill their new station in life. On public occasions they made the wrong impression; the men took mistresses; scandal was the result. The 'Chosen Women' on the other hand would set an example and be a permanent ideal for the whole nation. The present leaders' wives would be granted a respectable pension, he concluded.[62] Later the word *Domina* was spoken of as a title for the first or senior wife.

Kersten questioned him during treatment the next day on how much choice of husband the 'Chosen Woman' would be permitted. She would have a right of refusal, Himmler replied, provided that she chose a partner from the appropriate circle of rank and position within a given time limit; if she failed to do so within the time the right of choice would revert to the men. The Führer had placed him in charge of the project and final decisions on marriage would rest with him. In the SS, he added, promotion to the higher ranks would be made dependent on marriage to a 'Chosen Woman'.

Kersten realised that what he was really aiming at was racial breeding: by seeking to eliminate chance in the selection of mates for his exemplars of Nordic manhood, providing them instead with wives chosen for the highest mental and physical gifts, he would create a new upper class and seedbed of a higher Germanic type. Expounding these themes he gave Kersten the impression of a preacher of fanatic faith and scholar combined, pedantically directing his listener in the findings of the latest research.[63]

The idea of fulfilling their racial mission with a second wife perhaps appealed as much as a farm in the east to the SS leaders. Certainly it did for 'Wölffchen': he had of course been worried for some time about not passing on sufficient of his pure genetic material through a suitable Nordic partner; more practically perhaps, his mistress, the Gräfin, who had by now borne him two children, wanted to marry him. Racially she was immaculate – she would make the ideal second wife, but she did not want to share him with Frieda. In any case the new marriage laws, while favoured in the Führer's immediate circle, had not been promulgated and he was forced to choose. He came down on the side of the blonde Gräfin, no doubt expecting Himmler's blessing, and asked for permission to divorce. Himmler refused him. He did not want a scandal. Later perhaps – under cover of a great victory – it might be possible . . .[64]

Himmler himself was carrying on what his earlier biographers, Manvell and Fraenkel, were told amounted to a bigamous marriage with his personal secretary Häschen Potthast by this time.[65] A note he had written to Heydrich the previous year indicates her acknowledged position in his intimate circle; it closed 'Many heart-felt greetings from Wölffchen, Rudi Brandt [head of his personal office], Häschen, especially however from me'.[66]

This picture of staff cosiness was an illusion so far as the relationship between Heydrich and Wolff was concerned. According to Brandt there was intense antagonism between the two; both felt themselves Himmler's natural successor. Heydrich, however, recognising that he could do nothing about Wolff's close attendance on his master, affected friendliness.[67]

All testimony suggests that the relationship between Himmler and Häschen was a loving one on both sides. A girl who joined Himmler's secretarial staff two years later and lived for long periods in his special train noticed that he kept Häschen's photograph in his desk and often, when he was working, took it out to look at it.[68] And immediately after the war, when she must have known she would not see Himmler again, Häschen confessed to the aviatrix Hanna Reitsch 'how much she loved Himmler, and how good he had been to her'. Lina Heydrich told Himmler's biographer, Fraenkel, how he had become more relaxed and human as a result of his affair with Häschen. At one time, she said, he had wanted to divorce Marga to marry her. Häschen had stopped him for Marga's sake.[69] It is more likely perhaps that he stopped himself for the reasons he had refused Wolff permission to divorce. There must be no malicious gossip around the person of the Reichsführer; he above all had to set an example of decency. That is conjecture.

On 30 January 1941 Hitler made his annual speech to mark the anniversary of the *Machtergreifung*. Maintaining the public deception that England was the only target, he lavished much time and scorn on the island and its leading clique; yet there were traces of his real ambivalence as he described how often he had proffered the olive branch: 'No man can offer his hand more often than I have. But if they want to exterminate the German nation, they will have the surprise of their lives.' Afterwards he turned to the Jews, reminding his audience of his prophecy in 1939 about their fate if they should instigate a world war: 'the coming months and years will show that I was right. . . .' And when Judaism had ceased to play a part in Europe, he concluded, those nations who still opposed Germany would recognise the danger within. 'Then they will join us in a combined front against international Jewish exploitation and racial degeneration.'[70]

Himmler was suffering bouts of crippling headaches at this time. They were so bad that they affected his eyesight, preventing him working, and Kersten's magic fingers were indispensable.[71] After one treatment Himmler showed him dozens of boxes of headache remedies that had been prescribed for him formerly; doctors were simply salesmen for the pharmaceutical industry, he said, chemists their clerks. It was another area he intended transforming after the war. He would take young, open-minded doctors into the SS and have them trained in natural healing.[72]

During the discussions they had on nature cures and homeopathic medicine Kersten was astonished by Himmler's knowledge. Himmler tended to exaggerate, as always, but it was clear from the way he talked in detail about the properties and methods of application of numerous herbs still in use among the Bavarian peasantry that it was more than simple enthusiasm; the annotations he had made in ancient herbaries on his bookshelves testified to his deep study of the subject.[73] Although Kersten did not reveal it in his memoirs, Himmler presumably mentioned the herb and spice gardens, hothouses and laboratories he had created outside the concentration camp at Dachau. They were managed by an SS company called the German Research Institute for Nutrition and Food, formed in 1939. Known in the camp as the Plantage, these gardens employed thousands of the inmates, who were worked in the habitual cruel fashion in all weathers and not infrequently drowned exhausted in the irrigation ditches.[74] The company was among the most profitable of the SS undertakings and grew prodigiously over the coming years, taking over estates in other parts of the Reich and supplying spices which had become unobtainable from the usual sources because of the war.

Himmler intended the new camp at Auschwitz to be the centre for agricultural experiments for the conquered east. Höss described in his memoirs his first meeting with Himmler after he had been appointed Kommandant. Himmler had shown not the least interest in his difficulties in constructing the camp or feeding the inmates: as Kommandant that was his affair; it was wartime; everything had to be improvised. But when they came to plans for making the Auschwitz camp *the* agricultural research station for the east and erecting great laboratories and plant- and animal-breeding departments, Himmler had become a changed man, going over every detail at such length that his adjutant had to remind him eventually that his next visitor was waiting.[75]

Himmler paid his first visit to Auschwitz on 1 March 1941. Among his entourage were the Gauleiter, Bracht, and the HSSPF for Upper Silesia, Schmauser, the chief of the Concentration Camp Inspectorate, Glücks, Karl Wolff and senior executives of IG Farben, who intended building a giant synthetic oil and rubber plant there to exploit Silesian coal, using the water from the Sola which flowed past the camp into the Vistula, and the camp inmates as labour force. In negotiations with Himmler's Economics and Administration Main Office (WVHA) the company agreed to pay three Marks per day to the SS for each unskilled inmate, four Marks for each skilled inmate and one and a half Marks for each child they employed.[76] Oswald Pohl, chief of the WVHA, seems to have convinced them that they could expect 75 per cent production efficiency from their slaves as compared with free workers. In the event the ratio proved to be under 33 per cent.[77]

Before the visit Glücks had warned Höss he should not bring anything disagreeable to the Reichsführer's notice. Höss complied while the other visitors were present, but afterwards, when alone with Himmler and the Silesian HSSPF, SS-Obergruppenführer Schmauser, driving around the camp and outer environs, he took every opportunity to point to overcrowded huts, lack of water for sanitation and lack of drainage and sewerage plant. In consequence, he said, his medical staff had to contend with constant epidemics. Himmler did not want to hear. When Höss asked him if deliveries of prisoners could be stopped, he flatly refused; the security police actions he had ordered must go ahead; Höss was to see to it that he was ready for the consignments. More, Himmler told him to begin the construction of a vast new camp to accommodate 100,000 prisoners of war.

Himmler would not have said the prisoners would be Russians since the campaign to suggest that the movement of troops east was to deceive the English was at its height; moreover the separation of planning and administration had been a feature of Himmler's organisation from the beginning, and no one was told more than they needed to know. He simply informed Höss that in addition to becoming an agricultural research centre, his camp was designated as a huge prisoner–armaments *Zentrale*, and they drove out some two miles to the west away from the Sola river towards derelict farm buildings of what had been the village of Brzezinka; the inhabitants, like the inhabitants of six other communities occupying a fifteen-square-miles 'camp sphere of interest', had been resettled. This, Himmler decided, was where the new compound, named in German Birkenau, should be sited. He wanted it outside the main camp and away from main roads, and laughed off all Höss's and Schmauser's objections about the lack of construction materials, water and sewerage plant: '*Meine Herren*, it will be established. My reasons are weightier than your attempts at obstruction!'[78]

In addition he charged Höss with increasing the size of the main camp for a peacetime complement of 30,000, and making 10,000 prisoners immediately available for the construction of the IG Farben plant.

Before leaving, Himmler visited Höss's family at the Kommandant's house. All traces of irritation disappeared and, as always on these occasions when talking with SS wives and children, he was the soul of amiability; moreover 'one had the feeling', Höss wrote, 'that it was not merely politeness.'[79] Finally he told Höss to extend his house to make it more imposing for representational purposes.

So the inspection ended. Höss, who had been convinced that, when Himmler saw for himself the inadequate facilities and appalling conditions in the camp, he would take steps to have the necessary material and personnel supplied, was left without illusion. Neither the Reichsführer nor Glücks would help him. He was on his own. 'I went to work grimly. No SS man was spared, no prisoner. The potential at hand had to be utilised to the limit. I was under way almost continually to buy materials of every sort, to *steal*, to confiscate. Yes, indeed, I had to help myself!'[80]

He admitted discreetly that a good deal of his success in gathering materials was due to his good relations with industry; what this meant was that he provided IG Farben directors with favours derived from his control of the slave labour force, and they returned them by virtue of their great purchasing power in the war economy. So consciously or unconsciously, Himmler's methods led necessarily to corruption and mercilessly forced labour during which prisoners, in over-abundant supply, were treated as an expendable resource.

In March and April Kersten again recorded Himmler suffering very bad health. At times when reading the memoirs of those who had or felt they had things to hide about their own activities in the Third Reich one gains an impression of the writer attempting to plant a coded message for posterity between the lines of his account. This may be imagination. Yet that feeling comes very strongly through Kersten's record of Himmler's sufferings in the early spring of 1941. The reason for his ill-health, according to Kersten, was an order he had received to 'resettle' the entire population of Holland – over 8 million people – in east Poland. It is unnecessary to probe whether Hitler did give such an order, and if so whether – like the Madagascar plan – it was an elaborate disinformation campaign to cover the imminent 'resettlement' of the Jews or the troop trains to the east, since it would have been plain madness to cripple the transport and administration systems and above all the war economy with the resettlement of an entire country at the very moment he was embarking on the greatest gamble of his life, the Russian campaign. What has survived of the 'General Plan' for the east which Himmler, Rosenberg and others initiated at this time shows no trace of Dutch settlers.

A more likely cause of Himmler's emotional tension or excitement at this period is the instructions he had been given by Hitler to wage a war of extermination against Bolshevism and Jewry behind the Army's advance into Russia. Kersten's first reference to his sufferings – after accounts of crippling headaches in early February – was on 10 March: 'In the last few days Himmler has been very unwell. . . . I've repeatedly told him that he is trying his nervous system too severely. . . .'[81] Later in the war he recorded reminding Himmler that his health had never been so bad as in March and April 1941; Himmler agreed. This was the time the ideological war was being prepared. Thus on 13 March special instructions were issued by the OKW to be attached to Directive 21, 'Barbarossa': 'In the Army's area of operations the Reichsführer-SS has been given special tasks . . . resulting from the necessity finally to settle the conflict between two opposing political systems. . . .'[82]

The nature of these special tasks is revealed in a later summary of Heydrich's orders to the Einsatzgruppen commanders who had to carry them out. All officials of the Comintern, officials of senior and middle rank in the Communist Party and the central, provincial and district committees, People's Commissars, Jews in the service of the state or Party and other extremist elements, saboteurs, propagandists and so on were to be executed. Purges initiated by anti-communist or anti-Jewish elements in the newly occupied countries were to be secretly encouraged, every precaution being taken, however, that these people could not say they were acting under German orders.[83] There is no doubt, either from the testimony of those involved or the massacres that subsequently took place, that Heydrich gave oral instructions to execute all Jews, whether members of the Party or not, since, he said, Judaism was the source of Bolshevism 'and must therefore be wiped out in accordance with the Führer's orders'.[84]

The same month Himmler called Heydrich, Wolff, Daluege, Berger and the Ober- and Gruppenführers who would be commanding Einsatzgruppen or taking over as HSSPFs in the conquered east to Wewelsburg to initiate them into the secret plans. This seems to have been the only occasion when the castle served the purpose for which he intended it. During his speech he told them that the Führer had decided to unleash the blow against Russia in the summer. The aim was to smash the Soviet system and reduce the Slav population by some 30 million. There is no record of his speech, only the testimony of one of the Gruppenführers present, but his reference to the wholesale reduction of the Slav population agrees with conclusions set out by Göring's economic staff in a directive two months later: famine would claim 'many tens of millions of people', this concluded,[85] when foodstuffs from the overrun agricultural regions of the Soviet empire were diverted to the Reich. Himmler included Jews among the indigenous peoples to be starved or slaughtered to make way for the Germanic settlers.[86]

This, then, was the period at which Kersten was at pains to insist Himmler suffered more than usually severe nervous strain. It is possible that having been briefed by Hitler and in his turn briefing Heydrich and his Gruppenführers on the manner of the round-ups and killings necessary, the grossness of the task came home to him, provoking heightened conflict between an inner aversion to such unGermanic indecency and the hard outer shell adopted as Reichsführer-SS – between ideals and the methods of attainment. This is the impression he sought to give Kersten when he told him – according to Kersten much later that year, 1941 – that he had been charged by the Führer with the physical destruction of the Jews.[87]

When Kersten remonstrated, Himmler was silent for a while, gathering his thoughts. Then he gave the standard Party lecture on Jews constantly overturning all stable systems through political, economic, intellectual and artistic revolution, causing the rottenness on which they thrived; they dominated the world through the press, cinema, art and commerce and induced the destructive spirit which caused disunity and war. They bore the blood-guilt for millions, in recognition of which other peoples in the past had undertaken their partial extermination. There would be no end to war waged as a business concern until the last Jew had disappeared from the world, and the invisible Jewish empire was no more.

'It is the curse of greatness that it must step over dead bodies to create new life,' he had concluded on that occasion. 'Yet we must create new life, we must cleanse the soil or it will never bear fruit. It will be a great burden for me to bear. . . . Earlier I had other things in mind, but the urge to atonement and self-defence overwhelmed me. It's the old, tragic conflict between will and obligation. At this moment, I'm learning how terrible it can be.'[88]

From this it seems plain enough that it was a conflict between his orders and an inner aversion to mass slaughter and genocide which brought about his partial collapse, Yet Kersten was in a sense party to his master's acts, and would have attempted to distance himself by distancing Himmler, so far as possible, from the ultimate decision for genocide. Himmler's previous speeches on the Jews, especially that on 8 November 1938 before Reichskristallnacht – with its brutal imagery of mass slaughter and race annihilation, suggest there were clamouring devils inside him excited by such pictures. It is scarcely possible to account for his career otherwise. It is probable, therefore, that what he rationalised as 'the old, tragic conflict between will and obligation' was a more fundamental conflict between the two parts of his own personality, the weak, insecure, indecisive core and the hard outer carapace he had grown to conform and compete in the exaggeratedly masculine society of the Freikorps men who became the Nazis. And if one accepts and applies Klaus Thewelweit's conclusions about Freikorps man to Himmler and assumes that he also was divided between 'a [female] interior and a [male] exterior' which were mortal enemies, it is easy to imagine that confrontation with the scale and unprecedented nature of the task entrusted to him – and no doubt claimed eagerly by him – would have triggered a nervous crisis. The reasons he gave Kersten about the Jews constantly upsetting all 'stable' systems and thriving on 'rottenness', the necessity to 'cleanse' the soil and 'step over' dead bodies to create new (orderly) life tie in precisely with Thewelweit's analysis of the subconscious of Freikorps man.

It is still not clear why the emotional conflict should have afflicted him particularly at this time. The campaign to eradicate the Polish intelligentsia and Jewry and impose racial laws had been continuing since the first *wild* excesses in the wake of conquest, and had been given additional impetus in summer 1940 after the fall of France.[89]

That spring, 1941, von Hassell heard that 180 Polish agricultural labourers had been hanged on Himmler's orders for intercourse with German women. Von Hassell's informant had remonstrated with the Reichsführer and pointed out that it would be impossible to recruit Polish workers under these conditions; Himmler replied that he had examined every case thoroughly himself. 'I have had the photographs brought to me and established that hanging was justified in each case from the racial viewpoint.'[90]

Whether the photographs were of the men before or after hanging is not clear from von Hassell's account. What is clear from this and other reports is that the cruel task Hitler had entrusted him within Russia differed from the continuing task in Poland only in scale.

It may be that his serious ill-health that spring was caused simply by overwork and the strains of his many conflicting responsibilities. He and Heydrich had to fight for the SS sphere against Göring, who claimed industry and agriculture in the areas to be occupied, and against Rosenberg, whom Hitler had decided to lift from comparative obscurity and appoint Minister for the eastern territories; Himmler had to struggle constantly against the Wehrmacht claims for jurisdiction over the conquered populations in the west as well as the east, and he had to support Berger in his war of attrition over men for the Waffen-SS. Yet these were the ordinary problems of the Führer principle of government. He was used to them; they may have been exacerbated that spring during the planning for the eastern campaign but they did not end when Kersten recorded his recovery – they became more complex.

Another possible reason for his emotional disturbance is anxiety about the gamble on which Hitler was embarked. Through Heydrich and Schellenberg he knew of the extreme pessimism of Canaris and the conservative opposition about the imminent two-front war – in reality a two-front *world* war since the United States was openly siding with and supplying Great Britain. He would have been aware of the fine margins and balances between deliberate disinformation and real security leaks by internal enemies in the campaign of deception on which military success in Russia depended. There are even signs that he was probing the possibility of the British government offering peace terms provided that Hitler was removed as head of state. Certainly he knew of the opposition's renewed moves in this direction.

The attempts had been given added impetus in January that year when Carl Burckhardt, Swiss President of the International Red Cross and an intermediary with London, had conveyed the sensational 'unofficial' news that the British government was prepared to negotiate peace terms on certain conditions, which included the reinstatement of Holland, Belgium and most of Poland – but not with Hitler.[91] Burckhardt had expressed an interest in meeting Albrecht Haushofer. Since the failure of the intrigue around the Duke of Windsor, Haushofer had been attempting to set up negotiations between his patron, Hess, and other English circles which he thought might be favourable to peace talks. Besides working for Hess and von Ribbentrop, Haushofer was a member of the Wednesday Society to which von Hassell and others of the intelligentsia and conservative opposition belonged. He had been introduced by a lawyer named Carl Langbehn, an acquaintance of Himmler's who had a house not far from his on the Tegernsee and whose daughter was a friend of Himmler's daughter, Gudrun. It is possible that both Langbehn and Haushofer were plants of Himmler's inside the opposition, although the tortured quarter-Jew Haushofer at least was no simple double agent.

Haushofer travelled to Switzerland on 28 April to see Burckhardt, who later described him to von Hassell's wife, Ilse, as having come with a 'double face' – that is on behalf of both Hitler and Hess *and* the opposition. Burckhardt also told her that he had been approached by a V-man of Himmler's to find out whether the British government would be prepared to make peace with Himmler instead of Hitler, news which von Hassell – probably more in hope than knowledge – took as 'a new proof of the inner fragility in the Nazi circle'.[92] It is possible, therefore, that Haushofer talked to Burckhardt with a triple face – especially as it is suspected that Himmler's V-man to Switzerland was Langbehn.

It is difficult to imagine Himmler considering an SS putsch to overthrow Hitler, the greatest warlord of all time. Yet in view of his record for striking down patrons to whom he had pledged equal loyalty it is not impossible. In any case his sufferings continued and the treatments did not prove as effective as usual; on 6 April Kersten recorded him as reduced to despair and begging him to do all in his power since he (Himmler) could not give up now, 'it would be a terrible blow for the Führer.'[93] Kersten advised him not to put too much strain on his nerves. Still his stomach cramps grew worse, and ten days later Kersten was called in three times, the last time at ten in the evening when he found him lying out twisted with pain and exhaustion.

'Please help me,' he implored, 'I can't bear any more pain.'[94]

That was the climax of the attacks. Kersten credited his recovery the following day, 17 April, to a decision by Hitler to postpone Dutch resettlement until after the war.[95]

Since this is scarcely credible, and since genocide was not postponed, it may be that Himmler's spring crisis had more to do with Hitler's foreign and military difficulties which seemed to resolve themselves at about the time of his recovery. If so, it was probably not the difficulties which caused his nervous prostration so much as the support they afforded those who regarded a two-front and naval war against England–USA–Russia as disastrous folly, and believed peace with Great Britain or her subjugation must precede 'Barbarossa'; this would be especially so if Himmler were flirting seriously with the opposition at this stage.

The difficulties had started with the failures of their Axis partner in North Africa and Greece. British forces had pushed the Italians back from Egypt across the Libyan desert to Benghazi; a British expeditionary force had been landed to help the Greeks, and Royal Air Force units had been established in Crete. As suggested, it seems at least probable that Hitler had prompted Mussolini's two thrusts as part of his own grand deception: he had provided for an army group to be concentrated in Rumania ready to help the Italians in Greece and an armoured division to be held ready for despatch to North Africa at the time the planning for 'Barbarossa' had been taking firm shape in November. On 3 February 'Operation Marita', the German invasion of Greece, had been made an official part of the

'Barbarossa' camouflage,[96] and on 15 February further guidelines for the camouflage were issued which directed, first, that the impression of an impending invasion of Britain should be heightened and Operation 'Marita' exaggerated, and, second, that during the final period Stalin should be persuaded that the troop build-up for 'Barbarossa' was 'the greatest deception operation in the history of warfare', namely camouflage for the final preparations for the invasion of England.[97] At this date 'Barbarossa' had been scheduled for 15 May.

'Operation Marita' involved the co-operation of the Balkan states through which the German Army Group was to advance on Thrace. Hungary and Rumania had accepted the status of satellites, and pressure was exerted on Bulgaria and Yugoslavia to join the three-power pact; Bulgaria soon acceded and on 25 March Yugoslavia also came in. However, President Roosevelt's special representative, later head of the Office of Strategic Services (OSS), the legendary William J. Donovan, had been stirring up anti-Nazi sentiment and promising US largesse throughout the Balkans. On 26/27 March Serbian nationalists staged a coup and took over the government of Yugoslavia. Apparently in a fit of pique that anyone should dare to interfere with his schemes, Hitler had decided to smash Yugoslavia. Plans drawn up in haste to combine this operation with 'Marita' had put 'Barbarossa' back a few weeks.

It is usually assumed that the time lost – eventually five weeks – was a result of this impulsive decision. However, it is equally possible to see the postponement as another brushstroke in the grand deception. A large part of the success of the deception before the French campaign had been because so many leaks by Oster and others had proved false alarms; it was an obvious ploy to build false alarms into 'Barbarossa'. By this stage the intelligence services of every major power, including Japan, knew that Hitler was going to attack Russia; the only question was when, and it must have been assumed that the security leaks known to exist would have alerted Stalin to 15 May. It is unlikely therefore that this was ever intended as the real starting date. Moreover it was a Thursday; since the first of his 'Saturday Surprises' before the war, Hitler had always staged his dramas at weekends, and usually attacked on Sundays. There was a Sunday later in the summer with connotations which would undoubtedly have appealed to his sense of destiny, 22 June, first anniversary of the French armistice in the forest of Compiègne, and within a day of the anniversary of Napoleon's crossing of the River Niemen into Russia with the Grand Army in 1812. Probably Hitler had had this date in mind all along.

Meanwhile an armoured division had been despatched to North Africa under General Erwin Rommel, one of Hitler's most enthusiastic supporters. He had taken command of all Axis mobile forces in Libya and on 31 March had begun a lightning offensive which drove the British back to the borders of Egypt inside a fortnight. In the early hours of 6 April German forces, including the Leibstandarte and SS-Division Das Reich had entered Greece and Yugoslavia, and bombers had taken off for the Yugoslav capital, Belgrade, in an operation codenamed 'Punishment'; like Warsaw before it, the practically defenceless city was subjected over the next week to systematic devastation. On the 13th an assault group of SS-Division Reich entered and took the surrender, but when Canaris flew in two days later the city was still in flames, deprived of all essential services, littered with corpses, overhung with the cloying smell of death. Two days later the Yugoslav forces capitulated. Similarly in Greece the German columns carried all before them.

Such was the position as Himmler recovered his health on the 17th. In North Africa, Greece and the Balkans the Führer's will had proved irresistible; within four days the British began evacuating Greece; on 27 April German tanks rumbled into Athens.

An even more favourable development was the prospect of success in the attempt to make contact with British circles thought to be favourable to peace or – depending on how this operation was conceived – to throw dust in Stalin's eyes. Impenetrable mystery surrounds this still but a few points seem certain: Carl Burckhardt was a willing intermediary with London since he was appalled by the widening of the war and hoped to bring Germany and Great Britain together before the USA and Russia were drawn in; the British secret service was involved, since in March and April Albrecht Haushofer's pre-war friend and chosen British contact, the Duke of Hamilton, was interviewed by intelligence officers who wanted him to travel to Portugal to meet Haushofer. Himmler and the SD were involved since Heydrich and Schellenberg had played a part in the original Lisbon intrigue around the Duke of Windsor and Heydrich probably had a role in the attempt Hess made to fly to Britain. Finally there are the facts of Hess's mission.

Hess, the pupil of Haushofer senior, the geopolitician whose views on expansion eastwards into the 'heartland' of Europe he had helped feed into *Mein Kampf*, had always been convinced that peace with England was a necessary precondition for the strike east; since the fall of France at least he had been working to bring it about, and since September 1940 had been learning to handle a new two-seater Me-110 fighter–bomber made available for him at the Messerschmitt works outside Augsburg. Presumably even at this date he had the idea of flying across the Channel as a personal peace plenipotentiary. In April 1941, after Burckhardt had received approaches from London, Hess had several meetings with Albrecht Haushofer,[98] and on 28 April – as noted previously – Albrecht travelled to Switzerland to meet Burckhardt on behalf of Hess, the Wednesday Society opposition and perhaps also Himmler – if Himmler was working on an alternative line to Hitler. Afterwards Ilse von Hassell gathered from Burckhardt that he was of opinion that Great Britain was still prepared to make peace on reasonable terms, but not with Hitler and 'perhaps not for much longer'.[99]

On 10 May Hess made his spectacular flight across the North Sea. It was a brilliant technical achievement; he succeeded in finding and parachuting down within twelve miles of the Duke of Hamilton's home, Dungavel House, near Glasgow. Yet if this was a serious attempt at negotiations between the German government and English circles thought favourable to peace it was astonishingly misconceived even for a regime intoxicated by the conquest of western Europe. For after Hess had revealed his identity to the Duke of Hamilton the terms he proposed were such as had been rejected time and again by successive British governments back to the Kaiser's era – namely if Germany were allowed a free hand in Europe, Great Britain could retain her empire and have a free hand overseas. Moreover none of Germany's conquered territory would be given up, and Churchill and the British government who had planned the war would have to be replaced; the Führer would not negotiate with them. Finally there were threats: should Great Britain continue the war the Führer would blockade and starve the population to death, besides devastating London and other cities by bombing.[100] These were standard tactics in dealing with Germany's small neighbours, but to apply them to a proud imperial power was psychologically so inept as to cast doubts on the seriousness of the mission – the more so as Britain was supported in all but name by the United States with her vast potential for war production, and the British intelligence services knew that England was about to be granted a reprieve as Hitler turned east against the Soviet Union; this indeed was the double bluff being fed all the world's intelligence services. On both practical intelligence and psychological grounds, therefore, the mission could only fail, and Churchill's reported comment when he heard of the visitor's arrival, 'Well, Hess or no Hess, I'm going to see the Marx Brothers,' was wholly appropriate.

If the attempt was not genuine, it must have been part of the grand deception for 'Barbarossa'. Heydrich flew reconnaissance flights over England and Scotland in the week prior to the attempt and he was in the air on a secret mission over the Channel on the evening of the flight,[101] which raises the question whether the affair was not his most bizarre 'provocation'. The idea is lent support by official rumours soon circulating to the effect that Hess had been lured into a trap by the British secret service. Hess was known to favour friendship with England, hence his entrapment and disappearance from the higher councils left the Führer with no obstacles to proceeding with the assault on the island empire – so Stalin was supposed to assume.[102] Or alternatively his flight was intended to be seen by Stalin as part of 'the greatest deception operation in the history of warfare', namely the real bluff to convince the English that the German build-up in the east was indeed preparation for an assault on the Soviet Union – rather than camouflage for the invasion of Great Britain – for had not the Führer's Deputy flown over in a desperate last-minute attempt to save Germany from a two-front war? The new date for 'Barbarossa' had been set on 30 April, but Stalin's attention would still be fixed on 15 May, only five days away.

*

While it seems Himmler was preparing to lose this latest of his close colleagues that spring, he was also taking steps to anticipate the eastern campaign by starting to weed out Jews and other racially unwanted elements from the concentration camps. Bouhler, director of the T4 euthanasia campaign, made his experts and killing facilities available to clear the camps of the seriously ill, physically and mentally; as with T4 itself race was a factor in selection. Probably Höss's protests about the epidemics at Auschwitz played their part here. This euthanasia programme is usually known by the code number used in the camps' books to record deaths from this cause, '14 f 13'. It was often subsumed in correspondence under Heydrich's general cover phrase for execution, 'special treatment'.

Initial selections were made by the camp doctors who filled in forms similar to T4 questionnaires, but shorter; the final assessment, '+' or '−', was made by panels of T4 psychiatrists who visited the camps. It is doubtful if even at the beginning they did much more than rubber-stamp the camp doctors' lists; certainly with Jews 'it sufficed', one of the assessors wrote cheerily to his wife, 'to take the reasons for arrest from the papers and transfer them to the questionnaires.'[103] This young psychiatrist, Friedrich Mennecke, found his work rewarding at first: examining some 400 prisoners in Sachsenhausen on 4 April, he wrote of his 'very very interesting task';[104] by the end of the year, however, he was processing questionnaires at record-breaking speeds, 230 in one day on 1 December, 80 in under two hours on the morning of the 2nd – a rate of over 40 cases an hour for special treatment. And by this time disillusion had set in. Yet he did his work. The desensitising process which allowed him to sheaf through forms instead of examining individuals, and to separate what Robert Jay Lifton terms his 'medical killing self' from his everyday, family-loving self, was an essential feature of the programme of genocide as developed. Since Himmler was advised by Professor Werner Heyde, a psychiatrist of some prominence, whom he put in charge of the '14 f 13' programme, and Heydrich was advised by another senior psychiatrist, Professor Max de Crinis of Berlin, it is not far-fetched to suppose that this preliminary desensitisation or numbing of SS and T4 medical staff was conceived as a necessary prelude to genocide.

The numbing of public opinion to the hounding of Jews, so far as that was necessary after the pre-war campaigns, had begun the previous year, 1940, with two anti-semitic feature films, *Die Rothschilds* and *Jud Süss*. The latter was particularly effective, according to the SD secret report. A combination of fine acting, realism and 'loathsome episodes' apparently made people feel they wanted to wash their hands as they came out of the cinemas, and it prompted parents and the educated classes to ask themselves whether, in view of its 'extraordinarily strong psychological effect', children should be taken to see it; almost universally the answer was no. It provoked anti-Jewish demonstrations; in Berlin there were calls of 'Drive the Jews out of the Kurfürstendamm! Out with the last Jew from Germany!'[105]

These two had been followed at the turn of the year by a documentary of 'political enlightenment' called *Der ewige Jude* (*The Eternal Jew*) which achieved notoriety through its scenes juxtaposing Jews and sewer rats. Himmler and Heydrich and perhaps Christian Wirth, commander of the killing centre at Castle Hartheim, helped Goebbels' people by producing the malnourished, twisted and deformed specimens presented as typical Jews. Its release was preceded by enormous publicity, perhaps overdone, since according to the SD report for 20 January 1941, many people thought it had little new to offer, coming as it did so soon after the major film *Jud Süss*; there were reports from west Germany of cries from the audience, 'We have seen *Jud Süss* and have now had enough of this Jewish filth [*Dreck*].' The repulsiveness of the scenes disgusted people, especially one showing Jewish ritual slaughter of animals, and caused them to advise their friends not to see the film. Nevertheless others found that the images left them with a clearer, more convincing picture than many anti-Jewish tracts, and the statistical data and maps representing the worldwide influence of Jews made a great impression; people were 'astonished at how openly the Jewish influence and predominance in the USA had been demonstrated'.[106]

In May SS-Oberführer Josef Stroop felt he could no longer bear the taunts of his comrades about his Christian name – even the wife of the Gauleiter of his district called him teasingly 'Juzik, Juzik!' – and he went through the legal formalities of changing his name to Jürgen.[107]

The same month, during the final preparations for 'Barbarossa', the emigration of Jews from the Reich and occupied territories including France was banned. The instructions that went out to the consulates from the Central Office of Emigration cited Göring's authority, presumably to keep Hitler's name out of the affair, for the reason given was 'the doubtless approaching final solution [*Endlösung*]'.[108] Later that month Schellenberg circulated the Security Police departments in the same way: all Jewish emigration had been banned because of the 'zweifellos kommende Endlösung.'[109]

On the 27th Himmler discussed a new method of mass sterilisation of women with a gynaecologist, Professor Clauberg, whose acquaintance he had made after Clauberg had cured an SS-Führer's wife of infertility the previous year. Himmler's obsession with increasing the population extended to the whole process of childbearing and it was no doubt in answer to his questions that Clauberg had described his treatment based on preparations he had developed to clear the fallopian tubes. Their conversation then progressed – it was said that Himmler directed it[110] – to the possibility of reversing the process by developing a substance to block healthy tubes, so allowing the possibility of non-surgical and cheap mass sterilisation. Clauberg had gone away to put his mind to the problem; Himmler had funded him from one of his special SS accounts.

Like many of the key figures Himmler harnessed to his purposes, Clauberg seems to have been an ugly, unbalanced man with a previous history of violence; although very short and fat, he attempted to give himself the airs of a Prussian officer, and succeeded only in looking unpleasant or, to his experimental subjects, terrifying. By the time he came to see Himmler on 27 May 1941, he had developed a caustic solution which when injected inflamed and blocked the fallopian tubes; having inflicted extreme pain and distress on large numbers of animals, he was ready to begin on human subjects. Himmler was happy to provide them from the women's concentration camp, Ravensbrück, but unusually does not seem to have made himself clear. Clauberg left the meeting thinking they would be sent to his clinic at Königshütte; Himmler thought Clauberg had agreed to conduct the experiments at Ravensbrück. Two days later the Chief Doctor of the SS, Ernst-Robert von Grawitz, had to write to tell Himmler that Ravensbrück was out of the question: the Professor needed to keep a constant eye on the progress of his subjects. Von Grawitz continued:

> In view of the unprecedented significance which such a technique would have in the sense of a negative population policy and the consequent importance of promoting with all means a perfect solution to the problem, allow me, Reichsführer, to propose that Professor Clauberg establish a suitable research Institute in or near Königshütte and incorporate in it a women's concentration camp for about ten persons.[111]

Eventually a compromise was achieved whereby Clauberg was given facilities within the new camp at Auschwitz–Birkenau, closer to his clinic than Ravensbrück was, where he experimented on young married Jewesses selected from the transports that were, by then, arriving from all over Europe.[112] Later his experimental block was moved to the main camp at Auschwitz.

At some time in that summer of 1941 Höss was ordered to report to Himmler in Berlin. Since Himmler spent a great part of his time after the launch of 'Barbarossa' in his 'field headquarters' near Hitler's command post in East Prussia it seems possible that Höss saw him in June at a date before the 22nd. There Himmler told him the Führer had ordered the *Endlösung* of the Jewish question. 'We – the SS – have to execute the order,' and he added that since the existing liquidation sites in the east – by which he must have meant the T4 killing centres and the mobile gas-van Kommando – did not have the capacity for the intended large-scale actions, he had decided to use Auschwitz, 'first on account of the favourable position in regard to communications, secondly because the area that has been decided on there lends itself to easy isolation and camouflage'. He had intended, he said, to appoint an HSSPF to oversee the task but had decided against it because of the conflicts of responsibility that would ensue; Höss must undertake it himself.[113]

It is a hard, tough task which demands the commitment of the whole person without regard to any difficulties that may arise. You will be given details by Sturmbannführer Eichmann of the RSHA who will come to see you in the near future. The departments taking part will be informed at the appropriate time. You have to maintain the strictest silence about this order, even to your superiors. After your discussion with Eichmann send me plans of the intended plant immediately. The Jews are the eternal enemies of the German people and must be exterminated. All Jews we can reach now, during the war, are to be exterminated without exception. If we do not succeed in destroying the biological basis of Jewry, some day the Jews will annihilate the German *Volk*.[114]

After the war Höss recalled that Himmler had been extraordinarily and unusually serious and taciturn when giving him the order. The whole interview had been short and strictly matter-of-fact. Höss said nothing of his own response. He travelled straight back to Auschwitz.[115]

Eichmann came to see him a short time afterwards. During his interrogation before his trial in 1960 Eichmann said that he had been told about the *Endlösung* by Heydrich: ' "The Führer has ordered physical extermination." These were his words. And as though wanting to test their effect on me, he made a long pause, which was not at all his way. . . .'[116] He thought this had been two or three months after the beginning of the Russian war. Heydrich had then told him to go and see Globocnik, the HSSPF in Lublin, from whence he had been taken to the extermination camp, Treblinka. Since Treblinka did not come into operation until 1942, he was evidently confused about dates or deliberately confusing the issue in order to put back the date of his own knowledge and complicity. He was in charge of the Jewish department IV B 4 of the RSHA, concerned with all aspects of Jewish resettlement, hence must have known at the latest in May that Jewish emigration was banned because of 'the doubtless approaching final solution'; it is unlikely that he would have been left in the dark for a further four or five months about the nature of this solution, highly unlikely that a man of his indefatigable zeal who by his own account was making frequent inspection visits to the Polish ghettos at this time for his immediate superior, Gruppenführer 'Gestapo' Müller, would not have realised from the overcrowding, starving and death he saw there that the final solution was and could only be extermination. Given the conviction and thoroughness with which the programme was devised and executed and given his key role, this four to five months' gap in his knowledge is virtually impossible. No doubt he was informed by Heydrich, but that is likely to have been in the spring of 1941, May at the latest. The probability is that he visited Höss at Auschwitz in June.

According to Höss, Eichmann first informed him of the order in which the Jews in the different regions were to be transported to his camp and the approximate numbers involved; then they discussed how they were to be liquidated. 'Only gas came in question since to remove the anticipated multitudes by shooting would be absolutely impossible and, in respect of the women and children, would impose too great a strain on the SS men who would have to carry it out.'[117] Eichmann told him about the gas-vans and the carbon monoxide used in the shower rooms of the T4 killing centres; neither method seemed capable of dealing with the huge numbers they were contemplating, and they failed to reach a conclusion. Eichmann, Höss recalled, wanted to find a gas that would be easy to obtain and would not need any special plant to produce it on site. That was how they left it; Eichmann would report to Höss again when he had found the appropriate gas. They went out to inspect the site by the old farm buildings in the north-west corner of the proposed new camp, Birkenau. It was isolated, well screened by trees and hedges, yet close enough to the railway to bring up a branch line for the transports. They estimated there was sufficient space, once they had built gas-tight chambers, to kill about 800 people at the same time. There were meadows beyond where the bodies could be buried in long mass graves; they were not thinking of cremation then. So it was left for the moment. Eichmann could not tell him when the action was due to start: everything was in preparation; the Reichsführer had not yet given the order to begin.[118]

Meanwhile the leadership of the armed services had also been initiated into the necessities of the ideological struggle. Heydrich had undertaken the detailed co-ordination of the Einsatzgruppen with the armies they were to follow.[119] Hitler had given the senior commanders of all three services a two-and-a-half-hour harangue in the great hall of the new Reich Chancellery at the end of March. Generals and admirals, sitting in orderly rows of seniority, had listened in silence as he demolished any notions of humanity or chivalry so far as the war in the east was concerned. Bolshevism was a social crime; it had to be destroyed and its functionaries and intelligentsia eradicated so that a new intelligentsia could not arise. Halder noted some of the points afterwards in his diary: 'It is a war of extermination. If we do not so regard it we will, it is true, defeat the enemy, but in thirty years time the Communist enemy will confront us again.' Commissars and GPU people were criminals and had to be treated as such; in the east harshness now meant lenience in the future; leaders had to sacrifice their scruples.[120] The necessary sacrifices had been codified over the following weeks and in early June they were issued as an order to remind military commanders that they were fighting an ideological war: commissars and political functionaries of the enemy were to be segregated from other prisoners and handed to the SS for liquidation; they were not to be sent back to the rear, where they would subvert the others. Von Hassell, hearing of this, noted that von Brauchitsch and Halder had opened the door for the Army to take on 'the odium of the murder factory', hitherto borne by the SS alone.[121]

There is an inexorable quality about the German revolution only brought into starker relief by von Hassell and the relatively few, powerless individuals comprising what he referred to bitterly – in English – as 'His

Majesty's most loyal Opposition'. The nation, it seemed, was a living organism which, temporarily thrown into disorder by the shock of defeat in the first war and its aftermath, had healed itself naturally, discharging the foreign bodies from its system, and was again what it wanted to be or dreamed it had been, only stronger and harder over the scar tissue. The leading classes, the officer corps, the diplomatic corps and higher civil service, the *Herr Professoren* and *Herr Doktoren*, the medical profession, the legal profession, the art historians, big business and finance, and the chains of petty officialdom and the people had sunk their individual selves and their doubts to follow the strong leader they found they wished to revere as the greatest warlord of all time. It was the spiritual triumph of the Prussian warrior caste. It had created the German nation scarcely seventy years before. Now obeisance to authority, orderliness, industry and hard soldierly virtues were raised to mindless extremes – parodies of the original code – and the nation was welded together as it had never been under Prussian rule. It prepared under the new revolutionary leaders – for the most part neither Prussian nor conforming to the tall, high-craniumed, industrious, austere knight–landowners of the dream – for the final, decisive battle with the Slavs for command of the 'heartland' of Europe; from thence the world. In the beginning was the idea. This was the genetic material which ordered the cells in the organism of the state.

Exactly how Stalin evaluated all the intelligence about the imminent final showdown with this living body will not be known until the Kremlin files have been disentombed. He had freed himself that April from the danger of a two-front war by means of a neutrality pact with Japan. More accurately, the previous September at the time of the three-power pact with the Axis the Japanese military groups favouring a 'strike south' against British imperial possessions and the USA had won their argument with those in favour of a 'strike north' against the Soviet Union. Hitler had hoped and worked for this; he saw Japan diverting his western opponents and freeing his hands to finish off Bolshevism. His pleasure was a symptom of the military's under-estimate of the Red Army and the Soviet war economy, and Göring's gross under-estimate of the US economy. As it turned out, it was the Russian forces in the east freed by the Japanese strike against Britain and America that tipped the balance against the German *Blitzkrieg* that winter.

According to the SD secret report for 17 April, some of the public – not the majority, who thought Japan was protecting her rear for an assault on the USA – viewed the Soviet–Japanese pact as a sign that Russia would turn against Germany, an interesting idea in view of Heydrich's deception that German troop movements were conditioned by the Russian threat.[122] By early June the public had become preoccupied with the events in the war against Britain in the eastern Mediterranean and the Atlantic, and 'America's intention to widen the war'. When the battleship *Bismarck* was sunk soon after she had herself sunk the pride of the Royal Navy, the battlecruiser *Hood*, it was widely believed that American bombers were responsible, and 'renewed hate and anger broke out against this country [the USA] and its government.'[123] Meanwhile relations with Russia were perceived as improving, and rumours spread that Stalin would be visiting Berlin shortly to bring the Soviet Union into the three-power pact.[124] By 16 June the rumours of Stalin's impending visit to the Reich had strengthened.[125] By contrast the public was deeply anxious about American policy; the US Navy had become involved in the escorting of merchant shipping destined for Great Britain, and German credits in the United States had been frozen. A more direct US involvement in the war was feared.[126] It is clear that Dr Goebbels was playing a key role in the deception: German attention, no less than Russian, was being directed west. Faced with the hostility and growing involvement of the United States, how could Germany risk war with the Soviet Union as well?

This, then, was the underlying assumption Stalin was being fed. It is not surprising if it fooled him. The British Chiefs of Staff Committee, supplied with comprehensive intelligence of German troop concentrations and the lengthening of runways in the east, still refused to believe until almost the last moment that Germany was about to commit herself to an attack on Russia while Great Britain remained undefeated.[127] Why should Hitler answer British prayers? Stalin had the same intelligence about troop movements; he had accurate summaries of Directive 21 ('Barbarossa'), copies of a Russian phrasebook being printed in quantity for the German Army with questions like 'What is the name of the Party District Committee?';[128] and he had been supplied with numerous dates for the beginning of the German offensive ranging from 15 April to the week of 15 June; the British Ambassador in Moscow had somehow picked the correct date, 22 June, six days before Hitler, and helpfully passed it on.

Stalin regarded warnings received from Churchill and Roosevelt with intense distrust as Anglo-American provocations designed to upset the fine balance of his relationship with the Reich. Yet his master spy, Richard Sorge in Japan, had reported that Hess had been sent to Britain in a last-ditch attempt to negotiate peace before the attack on Russia, and war was inevitable.[129] He had even received a warning from the German Ambassador in Moscow, the supposedly anti-Nazi von der Schulenberg. This was perhaps the cleverest and most decisive stroke. For von der Schulenberg had advised in early May – the time of Hess's mission – that Stalin's best hope of preserving peace in eastern Europe was to engage Hitler in protracted negotiations and appease him. Apparently this convinced Stalin that Hitler was bluffing to force concessions; so the seed was planted in his mind that Hitler would make demands or at least stage a provocation before striking. The best guess about why, when the attack was launched, the Red Army and Air Force were caught completely off guard, many of the front-line officers even on leave in Black Sea resorts, is that the seed had taken root and Stalin was convinced there would be demands followed by an ultimatum.[130] There was none. The bolt was launched – in the first grey light of dawn – from a clearing sky. This was the ultimate surprise – on top of the surprise that Hitler could contemplate war with the three major world powers. Perhaps it should not have been: Hitler's entire career and successes had been built on surprise and disregard of conventional thinking. It seems that Stalin with all his intelligence sources, perhaps because of them, failed to read the character of his enemy.

The German people were utterly astonished. Yet it was not for long. If the next SD secret report is to be believed, the initial shock gave way within hours, the very afternoon of that fatal Sunday, 22 June, to the unanimously held conviction that the Reich government could not have acted otherwise. That was what Hitler told them. There was 'especially strong sympathy for the Führer, who had had to keep silent so long before his *Volk*'.[131]

10

Endlösung

As the Russian campaign was launched, Himmler despatched Wölffchen as his eyes and ears with the Führer to the command post known as the 'Wolfschanze' – 'the wolf's lair' – hidden in the forest near Rastenburg, East Prussia. He set out in 'Special Train Heinrich' to a command post codenamed 'Hochwald', near Lötzen some twenty miles east of the Wolfschanze and only about thirty from the border with Soviet-occupied Poland. This too was in a pine forest; it consisted of simple wooden barracks by a railway siding where his train 'Heinrich' stood with its communications *Zentrale*, offices, sleeping accommodation for staff and guests and restaurant car in which, according to an account from later in the war, one found all those called to an appointment with the Reichsführer drinking 'the good coffee' while they waited, sometimes for days. His own office was at the end of one of the barrack huts among the pines. It was here he received the reports of the special groups carrying out ideological war behind the advancing fronts.

There were four of these Einsatzgruppen: 'A', under one of Heydrich's SD men from the 'time of struggle', now SS-Brigadeführer Franz Stahlecker, was attached to the northern Army Group driving through the Baltic provinces for Leningrad; 'B', under the chief of the criminal police in the RSHA – and opposition informant – SS-Gruppenführer Arthur Nebe, was attached to the central Army Group advancing through White Russia towards Moscow; 'C' and 'D', under SS-Oberführer Dr Otto Rasch and SS-Gruppenführer Ohlendorf, the intellectual chief of SD-Inland and responsible for the secret SD public opinion reports, were attached to the southern Army Group striking through the Ukraine for Kiev. The groups comprised the mix of Gestapo, Kripo (Criminal Police) and SD officials and Ordnungspolizei whose combined operations had been refined in every country Hitler had taken over. In addition this time each group had a striking force of Waffen-SS troops; there were also three newly formed police regiments equipped with armoured car and anti-tank platoons operating under HSSPFs assigned to the conquered areas and these could be called upon, as could reserve units of front-line divisions of the Waffen-SS. The regular sources of extra manpower, however, were the indigenous communities. Hatred of the Russians was exploited in the Baltic provinces which had been annexed so recently and ruthlessly; so were similar feelings in the Ukraine, millions of whose people had been liquidated by starvation or deportation in the cause of Stalin's agricultural policy. Religious, ethnic and language differences and anti-semitism in the regions overrun were all made use of: Latvian, Lithuanian, Estonian, Ukrainian and even Polish volunteers were sworn in as auxiliary police and proved as enthusiastic hunters, guards and killers of men, women and children as the SS men who had been indoctrinated specially for the task.

If history had never seen such mighty forces, armour and firepower engaged, neither had it seen such sustained murder stretching the breadth of a continent in wake of conquest. Because of the complete tactical surprise achieved the early advance was swift, thousands of prisoners were caught and the thousands of Jews who had succeeded in fleeing east during the conquest of Poland found themselves trapped together with those resident in the territories so suddenly overrun.

Waffen-SS units were incorporated in all three advancing army groups, in the north the Totenkopf and Polizeidivisions, in the centre SS-Division Das Reich and in the Ukraine the elite Leibstandarte and the Nordic volunteer division Wiking. Numerically they scarcely counted among the 3 million men of the Wehrmacht but their fanatic commitment to the ideological war probably gave them significance out of proportion to their numbers. Besides carrying out the Commissar order for liquidating Communist Party functionaries at prisoner collection points, they murdered prisoners wholesale and on occasions civilians too. Just how normal or exceptional these orgies of butchery were is difficult to determine. Merciless barbarity was displayed by both sides; the Russians tortured and murdered German prisoners. It is impossible to disentangle reprisal and counter-reprisal. Nevertheless the terrible reputation the Waffen-SS gained can scarcely be accidental. Himmler's pride in the fearful name his elite guard carved out speaks for itself. Two years later, after units of the Leibstandarte and Totenkopf in particular had massacred – according to the Russian accusation at Nuremberg – 20,000 civilian inhabitants of Kharkov and shot and burned alive prisoners of war,[1] Himmler addressed the divisional officers there, exhorting them to bring up their young recruits in the same spirit:

> We have only one task, to stand and pitilessly to lead this race-battle. I say now once more what I have already said today to men at another position: the reputation for horror and terror which preceded us in the battle for Kharkov, this outstanding weapon we want never to allow to diminish, but only want to strengthen it. The world may call us what it will. . . .[2]

Earlier in his address he had stressed that the decision of the war lay there in the east, where the Russian enemy, 'this 200 million Russian *Volk* must be militarily and humanly annihilated and bled to death.'

Behind the advancing fronts a motorised SS infantry brigade formed

from two Totenkopf regiments and an SS cavalry brigade roved inde-
pendently of the Army High Command against Russian forces which had
been bypassed by the Panzer columns. They also co-operated in the work
of the Einsatzgruppen, the three police regiments and the locally recruited
auxiliary police formations against guerrillas, communist functionaries and
Jews. In the early police reports the victims were described variously as
'Jews', 'Jewish plunderers', 'Jewish Bolshevists' or 'Russian soldiers'. By
far the greater number were Jews.

'Gestapo' Müller sent the chief of his Jewish department, Adolf
Eichmann, east to report on the killings. He travelled first to Minsk and
visited the place of execution outside the city. At his trial after the war,
he described young riflemen with Totenkopf collar patches shooting down
at people in a pit already full of corpses. From Minsk he drove to Lvov
(Lemberg) where a similar mass execution had just finished. The pit had
been covered over, but blood was gushing out, 'how shall I say . . . like a
geyser'.[3]

Accounts of scenes as Jews were rounded up and marched in groups to
woods or meadows or disused fortifications outside the towns, ordered to
undress and hand over money and valuables, then conducted in single file,
holding hands sometimes, to long graves that had been dug, or anti-tank
ditches, old fuel pits, mine workings or cliffs, men, women, children and
babes in arms, and there shot in cold blood by execution squads with rifles
or machine pistols, and the next group ordered up and shot to fall on the
warm bodies, many still alive and jerking, or perhaps on a layer of sand or
earth or lime that had been shovelled on top of the expiring heap, then the
next group . . . leave a numbing impression of the deliberateness of this
first *wild* phase of the *Endlösung*. For every account that has survived there
were a hundred other unrecorded scenes in villages and small towns and
forest hide-outs where Jews were found and chased, corralled into barns or
synagogues or derelict buildings, and clubbed or shot or burned to death.
It was a giant semitic hunt from the Baltic to the Black Sea, which neither
words nor pictures nor any imagination can encompass. Jewish babies were
held by the ankles and whirled against boulders or brick walls or hurled from
windows so that their skulls smashed like eggshells. This was the quickest
way to dispose of them.

'What can they be thinking?' an SS non-commissioned officer wrote in
his diary after setting down a description of Jews digging the mass grave
in which they would be interred. 'I believe each still has the hope of not
being shot. I don't feel the slightest pity. That's how it is and has got to
be. . . .'[4]

The Commissar appointed for occupied White Russia that July, Wilhelm
Kube, was a virulent anti-semite; he was shocked nonetheless by the manner
of the round-ups and executions; he thought them unworthy of the German
cause and extraordinarily damaging to German reputation. Examples of
'bodenlosen Schweinerei' (boundless filthiness), as he expressed it in his

reports to the Ostministerium, included the employment of a Jewish married couple, both dentists, to break out the gold bridges and crowns and fillings from the teeth of their fellow Jewish victims as they were herded into the Minsk courthouse jail some two hours before the 'actions', and burying alive severely wounded Jews, 'who were then able to work their way out of their graves again'.[5]

Kube was one of those who later attempted to save Jews by having them employed in 'essential war production'; like most others who tried the same means of salving their conscience or sense of decency, he was defeated by Himmler's zealots, in his case the Security Police and SD commander for White Russia, SS-Obersturmbannführer Dr Strauch.

In the initial stages the overall commander of the extermination force, Einsatzgruppe B with headquarters in Minsk, was Arthur Nebe. Himmler visited Nebe on a journey of inspection in late July or early August. The tally of executions by 7 August was reported as 37,810,[6] not high by the standards of other areas, but sufficient to cause the HSSPF of the region, von dem Bach-Zelewski, a nervous breakdown some weeks later.

Nebe met Himmler accompanied by Karl Wolff when they flew in to Minsk airport in one of Himmler's Ju-52s; they were driven to his headquarters, formerly Stalin's police headquarters, where all officers and NCOs of the Einsatzgruppe had been mustered for Himmler to address them. What he said was not recorded; there is only Wolff's recollection, tailored to fit his story that the visit was on account of Hitler's orders to step up action against Russian guerrillas behind the lines.[7] It is more likely that Himmler wanted to satisfy himself about the methods of mass execution which were, once again, raising Army complaints, and it is probable if not certain that Nebe had laid on a special demonstration for him. By Wolff's account it happened by accident: they learned shortly after the address that 'a hundred Jewish spies and saboteurs' were due for execution, and Himmler decided they should witness it. 'It is well that I can see it myself for once.'[8] And so, Wolff maintained, Himmler first saw the human results of his orders. Up to that moment Himmler, he knew 'from his own mouth', had never seen a man killed.

They were driven to an open field, in the middle of which two graves had been dug, each some 25 feet long by 6 feet wide and 6 feet deep; a twelve-man firing squad was drawn up by one of them. The victims had been taken to a wood about half a mile distant, the Security Police captain explained, for they would be brought up in batches, and those waiting would not hear the shots.

A truck drove up with the first batch, 'ragged forms, mostly young men, some with tears running down their cheeks', two of whom, while being hustled from the lorry to the grave, threw themselves down, 'clasping their police escorts around the knees, pleading for their lives'. This description by Wolff, in stark contrast to so many other accounts which bring out the mute, numbed dignity with which many Jews, men, women and children, faced their incomprehensible end, is perhaps the most sickening of Wolff's entire post-war tissue of evasions. If on this occasion two youths were allowed such time-wasting antics before the Reichsführer, it is certain from a host of eyewitness accounts of other executions that many more did not give the guards this satisfaction.

The Jews were driven in to the grave and made to lie down on the earth bottom on their stomachs. Wolff's account is silent about what they wore, although the adjective 'ragged' suggests old rags; the probability is that they had been made to leave their clothes in the wood and hand their money to the non-commissioned 'treasurer' of the Kommando. Himmler had taken a position at the edge of the trench from which he could see the length of it and was gazing down at the victims, both arms folded across his chest, his lips pressed tightly together, his dark brows lifted.

The police Captain brought the execution squad to the ready: twelve carbine barrels pointed down.

'Fire!'

The salvo rapped out, followed by a rattle of bolts, and another salvo, and another . . .

Wolff watched Himmler jerk convulsively and pass his hand across his face and stagger. He went to him and drew him away from the edge. Himmler's face was almost green; he took out a handkerchief with trembling hands and wiped his cheek where a piece of brain had squirted up on to it. Then he vomited.[9]

The dynamics of the situation are against Wolff's flying piece of brain, and it is unlikely that Himmler so far lost control as to stagger and vomit. Otherwise he would hardly have stayed while the next truck loads were despatched, then have had the face to give the squad a talk on the sacred necessity of their task – hard as it was – which according to other participants strengthened the men in their resolve to do their duty.[10] That he was shocked, and blanched, is probable. It may even be that this demonstration decided him that another method had to be found. Yet it is more likely, as suggested earlier, that gas had been decided on long since, and he had already ordered Höss to extend Auschwitz for extermination.

On the last day of July Göring signed an instruction prepared by Heydrich, which charged him (Heydrich) with all necessary organisational, technical and material preparations for 'a total solution of the Jewish problem in all territories under German control', asking him to send draft details 'for the achievement of the final solution to which we aspire'.[11]

This was the second instruction from Göring mentioning the *Endlösung* – the first had been in May when he ordered a halt to Jewish emigration. No doubt he issued it wearing his hat as Controller of the Four Year Plan rather than as second man in the Reich. Aryanised Jewish firms and Jewish labour were enmeshed in the war economy and he expressly exempted Jews working in the armaments industry from deportation to the east, hence at least for the time being from the 'final solution'; it was not until the following summer when there were more slave labourers and his own position in the hierarchy was falling that he bowed to Himmler's pressure to release Jewish armaments workers. His July 1941 instruction to Heydrich may be said to mark the organisational beginning of the systematised programme of genocide – as opposed to the *wild* initial pogroms – distinguished by the use of gas – as opposed to shooting – and known after its guiding brain as 'Operation Reinhard'.

Besides controlling the Four Year Plan and the Reich Defence Council, Göring had been charged shortly before the launch of 'Barbarossa' with the exploitation of all economic resources in Russia. If ideology was at the heart of the drive east, the need for oil from the Caucasus and wheat from the Crimea were the immediately vital practical goals. SD public opinion reports for the spring and summer of 1941 reveal how tightly German civilian food rations were stretched,[12] while synthetic production of oil could not begin to meet the needs of war for several years yet. It is another manifestation of the impossible situation on which Hitler had been impaled, or impaled himself when he went to war five years too soon, that while the thrust of the Southern Army Group in Russia was designed primarily to capture the oil fields, the long-term synthetic programme intended to free the Reich from dependence on foreign oil continued to divert skilled manpower and vital raw materials from immediate armaments.

Yet of course ideology and human and material exploitation were all faces of the same German drive to conquest. If Göring was more representative of plunder, Himmler of racial policy, their aims were identical; if they were rivals for power, their officials co-operated closely on the use of concentration camp and slave labour for the war economy, and in the depopulation policy for the east. It was Göring's purpose as much as Himmler's to empty the east for German settlers, leaving only a proportion of the indigenous peoples as uneducated labourers for new German colonial masters. His officials were instructed to leave the Russians as little food as necessary to keep a sufficient number of them alive as a workforce.[13] His special 'Plunder Kommandos' operated behind the Army, locating Russian machines and tools and materials which could be of use in German industry and sending them back to the Reich. The Army also had an interest in Russian workshops and materials for its immediate repair and maintenance needs, and Rosenberg as the new Minister for the Occupied East had an interest in racial and population policy. Thus, as in Poland, a four-way internal power struggle followed conquest. In the long run Himmler, with his control of the police and paramilitary security forces, was bound to gain the upper hand. In the meantime a bitter jest that started in Poland that June, spread east through the other occupied regions. Q: What is it called when someone steals? A: Kleptomania. Q: What is it called when a whole people steals? A: Germania.[14]

*

At Auschwitz that late summer and autumn Höss received regular transports of Commissars and Russian Party functionaries for liquidation. They were shot by his execution squads at gravel pits near the administrative building in the main camp or in the courtyard of Block II. In early September, however, while he was away, his deputy, SS-Hauptsturmführer Karl Fritsch, decided to experiment with a prussic acid gas called Zyklon B that was stored in the camp in crystal form for use against vermin. The victims, some 600 Soviet functionaries who had been taken prisoner and 250 patients from the camp hospital blocks, were crammed into the cellars of Block II, whose windows below ground level had been stopped with earth. An SS man trained as a disinfector and wearing a gas mask moved down the passageway throwing in crystals of Zyklon B, then locking the cell doors. Some prisoners survived the first dose apparently and more crystals had to be thrown in. Nevertheless the experiment was judged a success and Höss told Eichmann about it when he next visited the camp. They decided that this was the gas they had been looking for.

Meanwhile Höss extemporised a gas chamber in the mortuary of Crematorium I to deal with the parties of Russian prisoners and Jews sent to him. The door was made airtight with rubber and screw fittings and secured by heavy bolts against pressure from the victims inside. The parties for liquidation were gathered in the mortuary yard and told, as in the 'euthanasia' process, to undress and leave their clothes tidily before going in to shower and be disinfected. When all were inside and the door had been bolted, 'disinfectors' in gas masks on the roof opened tins of Zyklon B and poured the contents down holes drilled through to the chamber below.[15]

The crematorium was already working at capacity with victims of typhus and tuberculosis, most of whom were despatched by the camp doctors with phenol injections, both to prevent overcrowding in the medical block and as a means of preventing the spread of the epidemics. As in the 14 f 13 programme Jews were especially vulnerable. At first the doctors injected the phenol – or experimental substances such as petrol, hydrogen peroxide, sodium evipan, cyanide – into the vein in an aura of medical professionalism, but it was not long before they were injecting straight into the heart to speed up the process. 'The executioners used to boast about their records,' one doctor testified after the war. ' "Three in a minute . . ." '[16] During his death agony, the victim was lifted by his armpits and thrown on to a pile of corpses in an adjacent room. Far from preventing the spread of epidemics, this method increased it: realising that a visit to the medical block with the symptoms of fever was to invite 'mercy killing', the inmates kept the early signs to themselves.

Phenol injections, gas vans, shower rooms in the formerly T4, now mainly 14 f 13 killing centres and Höss's Zyklon B chamber accounted for a very small proportion of the murders in the east that autumn. By far the greater number of victims, the vast majority of whom were Jews, were despatched – or wounded and subsequently buried alive – by gunshot. The

Einsatzgruppen, now deploying large, trained and enthusiastic formations of auxiliary police recruited from the indigenous peoples, and for large actions assisted by Waffen-SS or regular Army units in reserve behind the front, even on occasions by Luftwaffe squadrons, performed prodigies of sustained slaughter.

At the end of September individual records were broken at Kiev. The city's Jewish community was assembled at various collection points on the usual pretext that they were to be 'resettled'. They were then taken to the neighbourhood of a ravine on the outskirts of the city named Babi Yar. They had been instructed to bring their jewellery with them; now they were told to deposit it on the other common pretext of certain formalities, and made to undress. Afterwards they were driven in batches through a corridor of Ukrainian auxiliaries with sticks and dogs to the edge of the ravine and there cut down by the execution squad with machine-gun fire. After two days of this work more than 33,000 corpses and half-dead lay below; the cliffs were detonated to entomb them.[17]

One of Canaris' aides who sent back a report of this action wrote of scenes so horrific they could not be described, while the effects on the German execution squads were such that they could only normally carry out their duty with the aid of alcohol. General Georg Thomas, chief of the Army Economics Department, returning to Berlin from the east, told von Hassell that the most repulsive cruelties were continuing, 'above all against the Jews, who are shot down in rows without shame';[18] he was possibly referring to Babi Yar. Von Hassell and the opposition had been receiving reports of horrific massacres from the start of 'Barbarossa'. That month Canaris had made a formal complaint to Keitel as he had during the Polish campaign. It had been drafted by Count Helmuth von Moltke of his International Law Department – a leader of the Christian opposition grouping known as the Kreisau Circle – and it referred to the arrangement Heydrich had negotiated whereby Gestapo and SD officials sieved through Army prisoners of war for 'carriers of Bolshevism' – including Jews – and took them for summary execution. This time Keitel understood exactly what Canaris meant. 'These objections accord with soldierly conceptions of a chivalrous war,' he noted. 'What matters here is the destruction of an ideology.'[19]

Himmler was on an inspection tour in the Baltic provinces at the time of Babi Yar. Before that he and Heydrich had spent two days at the Wolfschanze conferring with Hitler and Bormann, chiefly about the Protectorate of Bohemia and Moravia; sabotage and slow-work threatened the important contributions of the former Czech armaments industry to the war economy. Finally the decision had been taken to send the Reichsprotektor, von Neurath, on leave on health grounds and install Heydrich in his place with the title of Deputy Protector and the task of re-establishing discipline – as he expressed it in his inauguration address to his officials on 2 October, making the Reich 'Herr im Hause'. While Heydrich set about administering immediate shock treatment by means of hangings and deportations to concentration camps, Himmler and Wolff travelled to Kiev to inspect Rasch's Einsatzgruppe C, then further south to Ohlendorf's group D. There is no record of another demonstration execution for them, but Himmler again gave encouraging talks to the Kommandos about the hard necessity of their task for the Fatherland.[20]

The initial belief in a swift collapse of the Soviet colossus had faded, yet ultimate success was not doubted. The early spectacular rate of advance had been slowed; the Russians, conjuring up fresh divisions, were inflicting enormous losses, and winter, which would halt everything, was only a few weeks away. Yet the central Army Group was within striking distance of Moscow, in the north Leningrad was under siege, and in the south the advance towards Stalingrad had reached the eastern extremity of the Sea of Azov. Looking ahead to the occupation of the Caucasus the following year, Himmler ordered Jürgen Stroop to prepare himself in the strictest secrecy for the post of HSSPF in the region. Stroop received the commission on 20 October. 'This date I shall never forget,' he told Moczarski while he awaited execution after the war; the pride in his voice was unmistakable.[21]

Heydrich had not given up control of the RSHA when he took over from von Neurath in Prague, nor his overall direction of the *Endlösung*, indeed of the whole eastern policy. Himmler had two departments working on plans for the colonisation of the east, his Staff Main Office for the Consolidation of German Nationhood and the Race and Settlement Main Office (RuSHA), but Heydrich's SD-Inland Department known as Volkstum (Group IIIB), under SS-Oberführer Dr Ehlich, took a leading role. Himmler believed the east belonged to the SS, Heydrich knew that the RSHA would deliver it. There is an example of this in his report after a meeting he held on 4 October – two days after taking over in Prague – chiefly about the establishment of police bases and settlements in the east and the provision of construction materials for Albert Speer's building programme. Representatives of Rosenberg's Ministry for the Occupied East (Ostministerium) attended; Heydrich was supported by Dr Ehlich. At some point the Jewish question was raised, no doubt in connection with the labour force necessary, for in his report Heydrich expressed concern about the great number of cases in which representatives of the economy especially were claiming Jews as an indispensable workforce, 'and no one was striving to replace Jews with other workforces.' This, he went on, 'would defeat the plan for a total evacuation [*Aussiedlung*] of the Jews from the areas occupied by us'.[22] Whether or not he put these points during the meeting, he did raise the question of whether it was necessary for Rosenberg's Ministry to have its own Jewish experts and case-workers: 'The representatives of the Ostministerium, however, showed little inclination to yield in this question, so that finally, because in any case the treatment of

Jews is handled in every respect by the Security Police, further discussion of the problem was abandoned.'[23]

Apart from showing his very natural attitude towards Rosenberg's lack of effective power, this report, written some weeks after the meeting, on 21 October, shows beyond doubt that *Endlösung* meant the liquidation of every Jew within the grasp of the Reich; there is no other explanation for Heydrich's concern that the claims of the economy 'would defeat the plan for a total evacuation of the Jews'. There was a desperate shortage of labour, especially skilled labour;[24] the few opportunities for Jewish emigration had been stopped by Göring's earlier decree. The only possible reason for taking Jews from vital war work at this time was to kill them. The report confirms that Heydrich was as ideologically committed as Himmler.

Yet 'ideological commitment' at this stage of the war and in this area of the east meant little more than general consensus. The Himmler–Heydrich solutions to the 'population problem' in the occupied areas and the 'biological' problem of Jews and gypsies were undoubtedly radical, but they were agreed by virtually everyone who counted in the top leadership of the Party and the doctors, lawyers, academics and industrialists and managers who served the Party and the SS. They received assent in a significant proportion of those who did not belong to either: von Reichenau, admittedly an early Party supporter, directed his troops in the east to understand 'the severe but just atonement' meted out to 'Jewish sub-humanity', and this sentiment was repeated by von Manstein in an order of the day to his forces.[25] If Himmler and Heydrich on occasions expressed dissatisfaction with their role as hangmen or garbage collectors of the Reich, they had every reason; they were putting into effect, and after the lost war were made scapegoats for, ideas that had taken deep root in the psyche of the *Herrenmenschen*. Their solutions, which strike the chill of disbelief in liberal minds, were commonplace with the officials concerned with the east.

Dr Erhard Wetzel, head of Rosenberg's Race-Political Department, was one such. He was thirty-eight years old, a doctor of law, who had risen to Assessor or lower-court judge by the time of the Nazi take-over of power. Four months later he had joined the Party, and subsequently the Party Race-Political Department. When Rosenberg chose him he was in the forefront of racial theorists. Now in this month of October 1941 he was exchanging letters on the forthcoming 'solution of the Jewish problem' with Hinrich Lohse, Reichskommissar Ostland – comprising the Baltic states and White Russia. One of these, drafted for Rosenberg to send to Lohse, differed from Himmler's, Heydrich's or Eichmann's letters on the topic only by its use of fewer euphemisms. It concerned the gas vans designed by Bouhler's chief executive in the T4 euthanasia programme, Viktor Brack. There were not sufficient of these 'gassing apparatuses', Wetzel wrote, and Brack's view was that 'construction of the apparatuses within the Reich would present far more difficulties than producing them on the spot'. He had suggested therefore sending his experts to Riga – where Lohse had his headquarters. 'I ask you to contact Oberdienstleiter Brack in the Führer's Chancellery through your Higher SS and Police Leaders,' Wetzel continued, adding that Sturmbannführer Eichmann – evidently still an unknown minor official for he explained his position as the 'case-worker for Jewish questions in the RSHA' – agreed this procedure. Then he told Lohse what they had learned from Eichmann at the Ostministerium:

> Camps for Jews will be set up in Riga and Minsk, where Jews from the Old Reich might also be sent. Jews are now being evacuated from the Old Reich to Litzmannstadt [Lodz] and other camps, from whence those fit for work will be transferred to workforces in the east. In the present state of affairs there are no objections to getting rid of those Jews not capable of work with the Bracksian device. . . .[26]

The 'present state of affairs' referred to the public mass executions of Jews in the east: 'such incidents can hardly be tolerated,' Wetzel wrote, and 'with the new procedures will no longer be possible'.

On the day this letter went off, 25 October, Himmler and Heydrich were with the Führer at the Wolfschanze; precisely what was discussed is not known, but both were invited to dinner and notes of Hitler's table talk reveal that he mentioned rumours among the public 'attributing to us a plan to exterminate the Jews'.[27] It may be significant that the war was beginning to go seriously wrong; the campaign against Russia had to be won quickly because a long-drawn-out struggle against the world powers was not economically sustainable. Nevertheless the concentrated blow the generals had wanted to aim at Moscow had been dissipated in the early stages by the drive south for Ukrainian foodstuffs and above all for the oil fields of the Caucasus. Now that Hitler had taken the generals' advice for an all-out push on the Soviet capital the weather had turned against him; heavy rains had made the ground a morass in which tanks and motorised units stuck fast. Meanwhile a guerrilla war had erupted in Yugoslavia. In the Mediterranean the Royal Navy was imperilling Italian supply lines to Rommel's forces in North Africa, and Hitler had diverted U-boats from the Atlantic to help his Axis partner; partly as a result the figures for merchant shipping sunk by U-boats had fallen drastically. Worst of all, the United States had all but entered the war: the US Navy escorted convoys to mid-Atlantic 'meeting points' where the Royal Navy took over; these points had been moved four degrees eastwards as a result of an August conference between Churchill and Roosevelt. Already two US Navy convoy escorts had been attacked by U-boats; it seemed a matter of time only before an incident in the Atlantic battle provoked America to come in openly against the Reich.

Hitler's ingrained response to setbacks was to blame the Jews; perhaps this is why he raised the topic at dinner that evening. It is equally likely that he had been discussing the progress of the *Endlösung* with the two chief executives. Whatever the causes, his remarks which Bormann arranged to have recorded for posterity reveal the yawning tedium of his mind, fixed still on the resentments and received ideas of his adolescence in Vienna, barred and tight-shuttered by endless turgid repetitions. His mind had neither moved nor grown. In providing this insight by handing down his monologues at table Bormann has not only revealed the numbing dullness of his own intellect but that of all who worshipped at the same stale fount. One may imagine the rapt attention with which Martin Bormann and his friend Heinrich – known in his absence as 'the Reichsheini' – listened to Hitler hold forth on the common enemy.

> Before the Reichstag I prophesied to Jewry, if war was not avoided the Jew would disappear from Europe. This criminal race has the two million dead of the world war on its conscience, now hundreds of thousands more. Let no one say to me 'We really can't despatch them into the morass [in the east]!' Who after all worries about our people? It is good if the horror [*Schrecken*] precedes us that we are exterminating Jewry. The attempt to found a Jewish state will be a failure.[28]

Schellenberg has left a vivid picture of Martin Bormann: 'He was a short, stocky man with rounded shoulders and a bull neck. His head was always pushed forward a little and cocked slightly to one side, and he had the face and shifty eyes of a boxer advancing on his opponent. . . . If I thought of Himmler as a stork in a lilypond, Bormann seemed to me like a pig in a potato field.'[29]

Yet they had much mental baggage in common, and it is probable that Bormann was Himmler's only friend in the higher leadership, the only one in the circle close to Hitler to whom he could unburden himself, as he did. He himself was never in that intimate circle. He was too much in awe, too unsure of himself, with too professional a façade perhaps, certainly too busy, and he kept so far as possible to regular hours of work and sleep. Bormann on the other hand was with Hitler constantly and moulded himself to him, gradually making himself indispensable and advising him in many insidious ways. And since he combined this intimacy with the Führer with the leadership of the Party Office, his backroom influence extended over vaster areas than almost any of the prominents on view to the public. Himmler in his role as ideologist and puritanical chief of the Order of the SS, despising the corruption he saw everywhere in the Party, must have found the alliance an uneasy one in many ways, yet in his other character as political gangster and police chief with a file on everyone and a compulsion to extend his empire, there is no doubt that the partnership was of the greatest value to him – as it was to Bormann. Each had mutual services they could render the other.

From the Wolfschanze Himmler travelled to von Ribbentrop's hunting lodge in the Austrian Alps near Salzburg, most reluctantly according to

Kersten, who accompanied him together with the faithful Wolff. Certainly Himmler had no liking for the Foreign Minister, nor respect for his ability; for his part von Ribbentrop suspected, with good reason, that Himmler and Heydrich were attempting to emasculate his foreign intelligence service to advance the claims of the Foreign Department of the SD. That August Hitler had made Himmler and von Ribbentrop sign a conciliation agreement defining their separate areas of responsibility. Among von Ribbentrop's other guests for the late October house party was the Italian Foreign Minister, Count Ciano, who during a pheasant shoot on the first day bagged six times as many birds as Himmler.

'Ciano can shoot the lot himself,' Himmler said petulantly to Kersten afterwards. 'Personally I find no pleasure in blowing the poor creatures to bits. I would never have come to this shooting party if the Führer had not expressly wished me to do so.'[30]

In the evening he retired early to his room, saying he had some papers to work on, but he told Kersten he couldn't listen to the chatter of those two fools. Possibly he was suffering from his stomach gripes, and Kersten followed him up to treat him; it is equally likely that he could not face a second worsting at the hands of these two travelled men and the other guests who talked of race meetings and shooting parties and aristocratic circles in England. He was still essentially provincial; his experience of 'abroad' was still derived mainly from books, state visits to Italy and Spain and tours through occupied countries in the secure isolation of his train or armoured motor column. Von Ribbentrop probably pressed his advantage.

Over the following days' organised sport Himmler told Kersten how much he disliked shooting animals. He liked walking in open deer-stalking country, but when it came to taking aim from behind cover with telescopic sights at a poor, innocent, defenceless creature browsing – did Kersten add the adjectives himself for greater effect when recounting this tale? – it was simple murder. 'I've often bagged a deer,' he said, 'but I must tell you that I've had a bad conscience every time I've looked into its closed eyes.'[31]

'But was not hunting truly Germanic?' Kersten asked. 'Was it not in the blood?'

'You can't catch me with those arguments, Herr Kersten. If our ancestors went hunting they did it because they urgently needed game to eat. I approve of that sort of hunting, and I would take part in it myself.'

What he did not approve of was fat city men donning theatrical hunting costume, driving in large cars at sixty miles an hour to hunting lodges in the country, where they were led down stalking paths by huntsmen who had selected the deer to be shot weeks before. He was especially scornful of Göring's prowess in the fabulously stocked estate the thick one had created for himself. Göring didn't stalk; he was guided to the deer.

'No, Herr Kersten, don't talk to me about this sort of hunting. I don't care for so crude a sport. Nature is so wonderfully beautiful, and every animal has a right to live.'

He progressed in his habitual way from strong disapproval to talk of proscription: after the war he would issue strict regulations to protect animals; children would be taught at school to love animals; societies for the protection of animals would be given special police powers.

Kersten suggested that mass murder of animals occurred daily in the abattoirs and if he thought about such organised slaughter he must surely become a vegetarian and not allow himself to touch another piece of meat.

'Stop! It upsets me to think about it,' Himmler answered.

It was true, he went on, he could be defeated with logical argument. Unlike the Führer he was not a vegetarian but he was ready to become one at any time if that would in any way help to stop the killing of animals. He added that Indian teaching permitted eating the flesh of animals whose death one had not intended oneself. Here he showed himself, as always, well versed in Hindu and Buddhist scriptures.

Kersten laughed. 'That's a fine piece of Jesuitry, Herr Himmler!'[32]

The evacuation of Jews from the Reich had begun, as Eichmann had informed Rosenberg's officials in Berlin, in mid-October. Trains with locked and barred doors had left from Luxemburg, Düsseldorf, Cologne, Frankfurt, Hamburg, Munich, Berlin, Prague, Vienna for the ghettos of Lodz in the Warthegau, Warsaw and Lublin in the General Gouvernement, and Riga and Minsk in the newly occupied Ostland, and they continued to run through November and December. It is a symptom, perhaps, of how successfully German Jews had been isolated economically and socially that despite the stories of mass shootings in the east and, if Hitler's remarks at table are to be believed, of a plan to exterminate the Jews circulating among sections of the population, these Jews deported from Germany, Austria and the Protectorate believed the story they had been fed that they were going to industrial centres in the east where they would be found work. Naturally they wanted desperately to believe. Many seemed to arrive in a pioneering spirit.

There was an element of truth in the deception. In some cities, after the shootings, the Jewish quarters were being turned into 'working ghettos' and there were many Jewish labour camps for the able-bodied. Nevertheless the reality for these western Jews when they arrived was horribly different from expectation. The crowding of families into single rooms, starvation, disease and cold, the daily spectacle of wasted bodies lying frozen and lifeless in the street where they had fallen were matched only by the powerlessness of these enclosed, wired-in pariah communities they were joining and the nonchalant savagery with which their Gestapo, police and SS rulers exercised mastery. Raids might occur at any time of day or night for baiting, loot or reprisal. Women were raped not in the usual way, although that occurred, but with leather-gloved hands groping with merciless disregard for internal injury after hidden money or valuables.

Anyone, man, woman or child, who showed a sign of resistance or failed to respond at once to the whim or order of a high-booted member of the master race or failed to show the necessary servility was shot out of hand. Small children were thrown from upper-storey windows. These, after all, were *Untermenschen*. For those western Jews consigned to Riga, where the Reichskommissar Ostland, Hinrich Lohse, had his headquarters, death came sooner rather than later, and it was probably a mercy.

Himmler was in Munich in early November for the annual Bürgerbräu celebrations, then he followed the Führer to Berlin. It was there, on the 11th, that Kersten while kneading him with his sensitive fingers on his couch managed to dig out the information that the physical destruction of the Jews was planned. That is his account. Given his intimacy with his patient and the long period he had spent on the best social terms with Himmler's circle at field headquarters it is difficult to believe. 'Himmler is very depressed,' he wrote. 'He has just come from the Führer's Chancellery.'[33]

That was probably true. For it was on 10 or 11 November that the newly appointed HSSPF for North Russia, SS-Obergruppenführer Friedrich Jeckeln, reported to the Prinz Albrecht Strasse headquarters and received Himmler's instructions to liquidate all the Jews in the Riga ghetto. 'Tell Lohse it is my order, which is also the Führer's wish.'[34] If it is true that Himmler was very depressed that day and for that reason, and there is little obvious motive for Kersten to have made it up for he did reveal he had been told the forbidden secret, it suggests that despite Himmler's later speeches making light of the liquidation of Jews as purely a matter of hygiene – 'it is not a *Weltanschauungs*-question to rid oneself of lice; it is a matter of cleanliness'[35] – despite this and other speeches before his SS-Führers, a part of him, perhaps much of him, rejected this solution. Yet of course he had to carry it out for it was the Führer's wish.

Jeckeln told Lohse his instructions. On 15 November Lohse asked for a ruling from his authorities at the Ostministerium: were all Jews to be killed 'regardless of economic considerations'? The reply, signed by Ministerialdirektor Dr Otto Bräutigam, chief of Rosenberg's Department I 1 – general political matters – instructed him that economic considerations did not apply to the Jews.[36] Evidently Rosenberg had fallen into line.

Bräutigam's immediate superior, Dr Leibbrandt, had been one of the Ostministerium representatives at the 4 October conference after which Heydrich had expressed concern about the dangers which the 'total' plan for the Jews faced from representatives of the economy who needed workers. On 26 November Himmler at last responded in writing to that report. He was then at the Wolfschanze, where Hitler had returned to direct the final push for Moscow. Whether Rosenberg or Lohse was still raising difficulties about the Jews is not clear, but Himmler told Heydrich that he could not agree that the requirements of the SS extended only to the economic departments of the Ostministerium; they could work together only if Rosenberg's pettiness ceased and he showed the large-mindedness which the Ostministerium 'always stressed as necessary for this great colonial space'.[37]

On 30 November, a Sunday, Jeckeln began the action to liquidate the Riga ghetto. He had at his disposal Dr Lange's experienced Einsatzkommando together with police and Latvian volunteer units. The site chosen lay outside Riga in the Rumbuli Forest; pits designed to hold about 30,000 bodies had already been prepared in the sandy soil somewhat off the road near the station at Rumbuli. As always with prepared actions the Jews were told they were being 'resettled', and to lend credence to the deception were allowed to carry luggage with them as they were marched out of Riga for some five miles, thence off the road on to a dirt track leading into the forest. There they had to leave their luggage. They were marched a little further and told to deposit money and valuables in wooden boxes, further still and they had to remove their overcoats, then their other garments and shoes until they were down to their underclothes. The temperature was a degree or so below freezing and there was snow on the ground from a fall the previous day. The task of the guards shepherding the Jews was to keep them moving at a steady pace up the path, neither crowding on too fast, nor causing delays to the process. The victims could hear continuous volleys of shots from somewhere through the frozen trees ahead.

Finally they were sent on in single file in groups of ten up an incline to the pit where they saw the massed bodies of earlier victims, the first of whom had been taken there directly from one of the trains from Berlin while the Riga Jews were still on the road. No doubt in their daze they saw the spectators standing around the edge of the pit, SS, SD and police officers, members of the Wehrmacht and civilian officials from the city, as they heard orders to jump down on to the corpses. One witness who came on the scene by accident, following the sound of sporadic gunfire and screams, spoke of 'brutal laughter' from the guards. Between six and twelve SD executioners stood on the bodies in the pit with machine pistols set for single shots, directing the victims to lie flat on their fronts in interstices to make the best use of the space; the elderly and very young were assisted by the able-bodied. 'The victims maintained a perfect calm and composure,' according to a man who heard the story from another accidental witness, a captain of the Engineer Reserves, Otto Schulz-Du Bois, who was devastated by what he saw. 'There were no outcries, only light sobbing and crying and soothing words to the children.' It continued all day, even after darkness had fallen.[38]

The similarities between the method used at Babi Yar outside Kiev in late September by Rasch's Einsatzgruppe C and that used outside Riga in late November–December by Stahlecker's Einsatzgruppe A – an initial mass deception, followed by stage-by-stage breakdown into smaller and smaller units wearing less and less until the victims were overwhelmed by their fate – and the similarity with the method of execution witnessed by Himmler himself in July or August outside Minsk by Nebe's Einsatzgruppe

B testify to the preparatory staff work that had gone into the campaign. It would be surprising if it had not been so. Heydrich was in overall command and his operations were invariably meticulous. The group and unit commanders had been put through a special course in the spring that year. If live victims were used, it has not so far come to light, but it would have been out of character if experiments had not been made to test for the most expeditious and economical way of killing and to inure the leaders to their task, and above all perhaps weed out those who showed lack of stomach. It is possible that some or many of those Jews and mentally ill or incurable concentration camp inmates were the guinea pigs.

In December, after the ghetto at Riga had been liquidated entirely, Jeckeln reported the fact by phone to Himmler, and later that month he reported in person to the field headquarters outside Lötzen. Himmler, he told his interrogator after the war, expressed himself 'satisfied with the results', and told him more Jewish transports were due in Latvia; these too were to be liquidated. He was not certain how he wanted this done, by shooting or chasing them into the swamps. Jeckeln, according to his account, advised shooting as the simpler and quicker way.[39] If Himmler was undecided about methods at this stage, it was only because of more complaints about the morale of troops witnessing or forced to take part in mass shootings, and perhaps also because of breakdowns and indiscipline among the Einsatzkommandos themselves. The gas chambers at Auschwitz–Birkenau and smaller extermination centres being prepared in the General Gouvernement were still under construction.

The German armies before Moscow were caught in the grip of winter. It seems extraordinary that although *Blitzkrieg* against Russia had been under preparation from at least 1934, no provision had been made for an extended campaign and the rigours of the eastern climate. No suitable cold-weather clothing had been provided, no ice axes, no lubricants which would work in the extreme temperatures now experienced; fires had to be lit under vehicles before they would start, tank turrets would not turn, horses froze to death, frostbite claimed thousands of troops. Much of this was due to the early confidence and Hitler's refusal to contemplate the possibility of failure. Himmler, however, had taken pains to study the problem of winter clothing and had had the Waffen-SS supplied with furs, many simply stolen from the eastern ghettos controlled by the SS. This must have been a factor, although not of course a deciding factor, in his troops adding to their earlier name for dash in attack a reputation for stubborn defence as fresh Russian armies spearheaded by Siberian divisions in white, quilted uniforms, fully equipped for winter war, launched a massive, surprise onslaught all along the fronts. The commander of III Panzer Korps, General von Mackensen, wrote to Himmler later that December expressing his admiration for the Leibstandarte, which was serving under his command. Every division, he wrote, wished to have the Leibstandarte beside it. 'Its inner discipline, cool

Draufgängertum, cheerful enterprise, its unshakeable firmness in a crisis, even when things become difficult or serious, its exemplary toughness, its camaraderie . . . are outstanding and cannot be surpassed.'[40] Coming from a general of the old school and at a time of near disaster, such praise had been earned.

As the Red Army launched its counter-offensive on 6 December, Japanese naval and expeditionary forces were fanning eastwards across the Pacific for Hawaii and other island groups, and southwards into the China Sea for the Philippines, Hong Kong, Siam and British Malaya with the same insane intent at a surprise knock-out of their opponents, the western democracies, as had betrayed Hitler into the Russian campaign. The blows fell over the next day and night. Previously von Ribbentrop had assured the Japanese Ambassador that, if Japan became involved in war with the United States, Germany would join her immediately, for Hitler hoped that once Great Britain and America were diverted in defence of their Far Eastern and Pacific possessions, he would win a breathing space to complete Stalin's downfall. This would more than compensate for the acquisition of another such powerful enemy. Roosevelt was in any case already fighting him in all but name. He duly fulfilled his promise to Japan, declaring war on the United States on 9 December.

In the midst of danger on the Russian front, Japan's entry into the war caused a burst of manic excitement at Wehrmacht High Command and among the service staffs. Admiral Carls, commanding Navy Group North-east, looked forward to the promised new division of the globe; Admiral Schuster, commanding Navy Group South, broke into verse, enjoining his officers never again to be humble, but to summon the arms of the gods. The Army Commander-in-Chief, now a sick man, the commanding generals in the east and even Hitler himself knew that the rejoicing was at the least premature. It is as difficult as ever to discern Himmler's views from beneath his mask of loyalty, but he knew too much about the new strength the Russians were drawing from their Far Eastern divisions – released by the Japanese strike south – and the desperate situation in which the overextended German forces were placed to join wholeheartedly in the rejoicing. Even before the Russian offensive the Waffen-SS, again taking a far higher proportion of losses than the Army, had over 8000 dead and 28,000 wounded, a casualty list of more than a quarter of the 120,000-strong force that had begun the campaign; the division Das Reich had lost 60 per cent of its fighting strength.[41]

Hitler made scapegoats of the commanding generals, dismissed von Brauchitsch and took over the detailed control of the eastern front himself, since, as he told von Brauchitsch, he knew of no general capable of instilling the Army with National Socialist spirit; Himmler's star rose with the military reputation of his elite divisions, and he spent more time at Führer headquarters in conference with Hitler and Bormann.

*

On 20 January 1942, after two postponements, Heydrich's conference to co-ordinate the various offices involved in the Jewish question took place in the Interpol Building at Berlin-Wannsee. The responsible Party leaders and ministers, Göring, Himmler, Frick, Lammers, Bormann, Rosenberg, von Ribbentrop, the acting Minister of Justice who had succeeded Gürtner and Hans Frank, Governor-General of the General Gouvernement, where the 'final solution' was to be enacted, were absent; they were represented by their State Secretaries, departmental and police chiefs. There were also two more junior officials, Adolf Eichmann, now promoted Obersturmbannführer – who by his own account sat in a corner with a stenotypist 'and no one bothered us'[42] – and SS-Sturmbannführer Dr Rudolf Lange, commander of the Security Police in Riga, who had so recently organised the liquidation of the Riga ghetto; indeed it was his engagement in this action that caused Heydrich to postpone the conference on the second occasion.[43] The minutes prepared by Eichmann employ Heydrich's standard euphemisms throughout but it is difficult to understand why Lange was there or why the conference had to be postponed for him unless he was to explain the practicalities of liquidation. He was expert in both mass shootings and the use of gas vans.

The great majority of the officials gathered at Wannsee had known for some time that liquidation was intended. It is inconceivable that the few who may still have been doubtful did not learn very quickly; the absence of detail in the minutes was a natural precaution taken in all written communications. Hence if it is impossible to know how much practical detail Heydrich or Eichmann or Lange gave, there can be no doubt that this group of fifteen, mostly high officers of state, knew they were discussing genocide on the grand scale. They were given the figures – 5,000,000 Jews remained in the Soviet Union, 2,284,000 in the General Gouvernement, 1,144,700 in the western and Nordic occupied countries, 742,800 in Hungary . . . so it went, making a total of over 10 million European Jews; when Jews in Great Britain and neutral Turkey were added the grand total came to over 11 million.

Heydrich explained that in place of the former solution of emigration the Führer had now sanctioned a further, or wider, possible solution, 'the evacuation of the Jews to the east' – so Eichmann recorded it in his officialese. The Jews would first be brought to 'so-called transit ghettos' for further transport to the east. During the course of it the able-bodied of both sexes would be conscripted for labour gangs to build roads. 'Undoubtedly a large percentage of these will be eliminated by natural attrition. Those who remain alive, certainly the most resistant group, will be treated accordingly since they would constitute a natural selection of the fittest who would form a new cell from which the Jewish race could again develop.'[44]

'What does "treated accordingly" mean?' Eichmann's interrogator asked him after the war.

'Killed. Killed. Undoubtedly.'[45]

Göring's State Secretary for the Four Year Plan Office raised the question of Jews employed in essential war work, and Heydrich confirmed his former agreement that they would not be deported. He also announced a model ghetto he had established at Theresienstadt in the Protectorate where Jews over sixty-five years of age from the old Reich, Austria and the Protectorate and those who had been decorated with the Iron Cross, 1st Class, in the first war might be accommodated. This, he said, would silence all criticism at a stroke.

Finally, after some discussion about whether half-Jews and the Jewish partner in mixed marriages should be included in the solution or whether some compromise such as voluntary sterilisation might be adopted, 'there was a discussion of the various types of solution possibilities.' Here, presumably, Eichmann and Lange were called to speak.

It could be said that the 'final solution' had already begun with the opening the previous month – 8 December 1941 – of the first installation designed wholly and simply for mass extermination. It was sited in a disused fort at Chelmno (Kulmhof) near Lodz in the Warthegau close by the border with the General Gouvernement, and used the techniques of deception developed in the T4 programme. The victims were mainly Jews from the ghetto at Lodz who were told they were being resettled, also gypsies, typhoid cases, the mentally ill, and Party functionaries selected from Russian prisoners of war. They were escorted to a cellar changing room by white-coated guards posing as medical staff, told to deposit their money and valuables and leave their clothes for disinfection, while they were sent on naked in groups of fifty or sixty up an inclined ramp, following a sign 'to the bath'. At the end one of Brack's gas vans, to all appearances a large, grey-painted lorry with steel sides and roof and wooden gratings on the floor, covered by straw mats, awaited them with open rear doors. They were packed inside, the doors were closed and bolted, and the driver in Totenkopf uniform drove off to woods where a work-party of Jews waited by a deep trench they had dug. There the driver stopped and pressed a button to divert the exhaust into the sealed body of the van. At once shouts and screams and a fearful banging on the sides and back doors began.

Eichmann had been sent to report on the operation soon after it started. After the war he told his interrogator something of his experience. He said he could not look inside, he was so shaken by the screaming. He watched the van drive up to a long trench, where the doors were thrown open and the corpses thrown out, the limbs 'as supple as if they'd been alive. Just thrown in [the trench]. I can still see a civilian with pliers pulling out teeth.'[46]

Eichmann's was a distanced, sanitised and deodorised description of the scene as a cordon of guards urged the Jewish work-party with threats and whips to frantic haste in unloading the heaped corpses and examining them for internally hidden valuables and gold teeth fillings – as Eichmann noted, extracted with pliers – before they were tossed by feet and hair into the pit,[47] where other members of the gang arranged them to fill all spaces. No doubt Eichmann's account to the officials at the Wannsee conference was strictly matter-of-fact. Or perhaps Lange, the practical expert with gas wagons, presented the statistical results obtainable by this and other methods. Eichmann would have reported on Höss's use of Zyklon B and the capacity and designed throughput of the new gas chambers under construction at Auschwitz–Birkenau, and the preparation of other extermination centres in the General Gouvernement.

So the conference ended. The delegates moved on to refreshments.

Towards the end of January Hitler returned to Berlin to deliver his annual speech at the Sportpalast in commemoration of the *Machtergreifung* – only eight years before. He recalled the battles of the 'time of struggle' and the repeated severe setbacks, despite which finally the movement had won through. His audience, according to the SD report, drew the intended parallels with the present setbacks in the east. He assured them that the worst part of the battle against Bolshevism was now over. He belaboured Churchill and Roosevelt and turned as he had twice before on this occasion to the Jews behind them and Stalin:

> The war will not end as the Jews imagine it will, with the uprooting of the Aryans, but the result of this war will be the complete annihilation of the Jews. Now, for the first time, they will not bleed other people to death, but for the first time the old Jewish law of eye for eye and tooth for tooth will be applied. . . .[48]

'The renewed denunciation of Jewry and the prominence given to the Old Testament maxim "Eye for eye and tooth for tooth" were interpreted as meaning that the Führer's fight against Jewry would be conducted with inexorable consistency to the end and before long the last Jew would be driven from European soil.'[49] Was this section of the SD report on the effects of the speech simply Heydrich's wishful thinking or did it represent the feelings of most of the people? At all events the speech lifted them from deep misgivings at the latest news from the eastern front and worsening food shortages.

Both Heydrich and Himmler liked to insist that it was the positive, not the negative side of their tasks they relished. After the initial shock treatment in the Protectorate, Heydrich had switched to a social policy designed to win over the workers to German rule through wages and welfare. Meanwhile he retained a key role in planning the colonisation of the eastern occupied territories and the vast road, rail and community building projects which were to be realised there, mainly with concentration camp labour. Despite or because of this Himmler now placed the concentration camp administration in a remodelled Economic and Administration Main Office (WVHA) whose responsibilities covered the administration and supply of the police, Waffen-SS, General SS and the SS construction, real estate and other business concerns. At the head of this organisation was Heydrich's erstwhile naval colleague, now his serious rival, Oswald Pohl. Whether Himmler's motive in thus mightily building up Pohl's power base was to curb Heydrich's growing ambition and popularity with the Führer after his decisive action in the Protectorate and with the *Endlösung*, whether it was to fend off outside rivals from the economic sector, or whether it was just an obvious rationalisation now that camp labour and the SS building materials firms were in the forefront of eastern colonisation plans is not clear.

Even less clear is the underlying nature of the relationship between Heydrich and Himmler. To judge from letters and reports which they exchanged, the partnership was one of mutual trust and on Himmler's part affection. To judge from statements by Heydrich's widow since the war, her husband was secretly contemptuous of the theories which obsessed his chief. This is difficult to believe; all the documentary evidence suggests that he was quite as committed to the Aryan–Germanic virtues and the fight against their eternal enemies. However, her portrayal of Himmler as 'the schoolmasterly type who never looked like a soldier and always wanted to be what he was not', her husband by contrast 'a soldier' who 'did not play with ideas' but 'saw his tasks in concrete form'[50] rings true. Obviously it was so. Kersten pointed the same contrast between the two, Heydrich by far the more dynamic, far superior in exposition and as decisive as Himmler was constitutionally indecisive. Now that Wolff was at Führer headquarters, Heydrich had the right of immediate access to Himmler, even during Kersten's treatments, hence Kersten had opportunity to see him in action. His impression was that the clarity and incisiveness of Heydrich's arguments when he was proposing a course of action simply overwhelmed Himmler – so much so that, after Heydrich had gone and he had had time to reflect, Himmler would often phone through instructions that the agreed measures should not be put into effect until he had discussed them with the Führer. He was, Kersten concluded, simply not in the same class as Heydrich.[51]

Schellenberg, who had equal opportunities to observe both men closely, came to a similar conclusion, indeed he wrote of Heydrich as the 'hidden pivot around which the Nazi regime revolved. . . . He was far superior to all his political colleagues and controlled them as he controlled the vast intelligence machine of the SD.'[52] Many others with first-hand knowledge of the two men have written in the same vein and have credited Heydrich with carrying his mediocre chief up to the power position he occupied; Edouard Calic, Heydrich's latest biographer, has implied this. Obviously it is how it appeared from the outside; obviously too neither man could have been unaware of Heydrich's sharper mind and practical abilities, yet it never showed. Himmler treated his protégé with special consideration and fondness; Heydrich showed him what Kersen regarded as 'quite inexplicable servility'. It was 'Jawohl, Herr Reichsführer!' – when everyone else addressed him simply as 'Reichsführer!' – and 'if that is the Herr

Reichsführer's wish . . .';[53] and if Himmler expressed an opposing view Heydrich immediately adopted it. Whether this was merely outward form – a sign of his diabolical management of people – or whether, like Karl Wolff and Jürgen Stroop, he truly respected his chief for his ideological hardness, wider knowledge in all the ideologically important areas of race, Germanic history and comparative religions, above all perhaps as the founder and head of the Order of the SS, are questions which cannot be answered. Both men were too complicated to conform to such simple analysis. Both were driven characters with deep-seated childhood complexes of inadequacy and they operated within a shifting minefield of power rivalries; neither was what he seemed. Lina Heydrich said of her husband that he also *played* the hard man; 'his apparent arrogance was no more than self-protection. Even with me he expressed no kind word, no word of tenderness. . . .'[54] Himmler and Heydrich were a partnership and after more than a decade of success that virtually moulded the Nazi revolution they knew each other's strengths and weaknesses and each his position vis-à-vis the other as intimately as the partners in a marriage; as in a marriage no doubt the relationship changed and shifted subtly from time to time.

It has been suggested that Heydrich's appointment as Acting Reichs-protektor did give the relationship a decisive shift. Heydrich now had direct access to Hitler. His most conspicuous trait had always been extreme competitiveness. Schellenberg likened him to a beast of prey, possessed of insatiable ambition always to know more than others and to assume the leadership. Another close colleague, head of Department II in the RSHA, SS-Brigadeführer Dr Werner Best, in conversation after the war with Heinrich Fraenkel, confirmed Heydrich's 'insatiable ambition, intelligence and ruthless energy'.[55] He said he was certain that Heydrich aimed to supplant Himmler, perhaps even Hitler. It is possible, of course, that Hitler and Bormann unwittingly furthered this design by attempting to split the 'black Diaskuren' and, with his appointment as Reichsprotektor, raising Heydrich as a counter-weight to Himmler's power. Himmler may have sensed this and acted to build up Pohl and the WVHA as a balance to Heydrich's RSHA. If that was the case there is nothing in the subsequent correspondence to suggest any change in their relationship. The whole area is speculative. If one asks who in the partnership used whom most successfully it is evident that up to the time of Heydrich's death Himmler, who had first recognised the young ex-naval officer's exceptional abilities, had employed them skilfully without ever allowing free rein to what everyone who knew the man perceived as his insatiable ambition. And after Heydrich's death Himmler continued to accumulate power. Yet it is notable that he did so by carrying on the straight path that Heydrich had signposted. In the years of crisis and defeat that soon followed, indecisiveness prevented him, despite his apparent power, from using it except in defence of the *status quo*. If, as Best and others insisted, Heydrich did have ambitions to supplant him – and Hitler – this would have been his time and the ultimate test of the partnership. But by then Heydrich was dead; we can only guess at the chemistry there was between the two.

Probably nothing shows more plainly the dangers Himmler may have faced than the key role Heydrich assumed in Hitler's three master projects, the *Endlösung*, the eastern colonisation and Speer's great building designs for the thousand-year Reich. Certainly nothing is more indicative of his very special place as Himmler's Chief of Staff. His meeting the previous October with the State Secretary, Meyer, and other representatives of Rosenberg's Ostministerium had been concerned principally with '1) the erection of SS and police bases [in the east] 2) the provision of raw material for the erection of settlements 3) the extensive provision of raw material for Speer's special commissions for the erection of great buildings [in Berlin and other cities]'.[56]

In December Heydrich had directed both Pohl and Glücks, chief of the Concentration Camp Inspectorate, to start preparations for the SS building projects, especially post-war reconstruction, by training the better-educated camp inmates in the necessary trades and feeding them better.

Towards the end of January 1942, just before the official transfer of the camp inspectorate to Pohl's main office, Himmler wrote to Glücks to inform him that since Russian prisoners of war could not be expected in the near future, he was sending great numbers of Jews deported from Germany to the camps: 'Arrange to take in 100,000 male Jews and up to 50,000 Jewesses. The concentration camps will receive great economic tasks and commissions in the following weeks. . . .'[57]

On 31 January Himmler wrote to Pohl about the 'absolutely huge buildings we wish to provide for the Waffen-SS, General SS and police'. He was satisfied that the SS concerns could provide the stone and cement, and he believed he could secure the necessary quota of iron through 'very close collaboration' with the President of the Board of the Reichswerke Hermann Göring, the required timber after discussion with the State Secretary in the Reich Forestry Office about the allocation of timber concessions in North Russia – a revealing description of his methods. Like Heydrich, he was thinking largely in post-war terms. He estimated that before the war was over the Reich would have run up an internal debt of some 100 thousand million Marks. Bearing in mind Speer's huge building plans and other cultural and social programmes it would be necessary, he wrote, to adopt 'the greatest Prussian frugality' in their own building. He directed Pohl therefore to begin an immediate programme to train camp inmates for building on a production-line basis. There should be specialists for digging out foundations, specialists for laying foundations and concrete floors, specialists for building walls, for roofing, for window-framing and so on. He anticipated that they must provide 80 per cent of the buildings, fixtures and fittings, including central heating, with concentration camp and other slave workers. Should they not manage it, they would be unable to have 'either decent barracks, schools, office buildings, nor houses for our SS men in the old Reich, nor will I as Reichskommissar for the Consolidation of German Nationhood be able to provide the giant settlements with which we make the east German.'[58]

Building problems were straightforward by comparison with the human (or, as it was perceived, *racial*) questions involved in making the east German. Heydrich must have directed SD-Inland to begin planning some time in the summer or autumn of 1941; by November SS-Standartenführer Dr Hans Ehlich, head of RSHA Department IIIB (Volkstum), had established a figure of 31 million people to be evacuated from the occupied east.[59] Himmler's Main Office for the Consolidation of German Nationhood (RKF) was still planning the Germanisation of former Poland; it was not until January 1942 that the chief of Department II (Planning), SS-Oberführer Professor Dr Konrad Meyer, received instructions to extend his activities to the former Russian areas. The other SS Main Office concerned, the RuSHA, was chiefly involved with the question of reclaiming Nordic–Germanic elements from the indigenous peoples, the process termed *Eindeutschung*. Rosenberg of course claimed the final say in eastern policy for the Ostministerium, and on 4 February, in an effort to harmonise the views of the different authorities, a conference was convened in Berlin under the chairmanship of the chief of Rosenberg's Department I 2 (Ostland), Dr Bruno Kleist. Five other representatives of the Ostministerium attended and four representatives of the three SS Main Offices concerned – two from Dr Ehlich's department in the RSHA, although not Ehlich himself, and one each from the RuSHA and the RKF, although not Professor Meyer; there were also two academic anthropologists, one (Professor Dr Eugen Fischer) a special favourite of Himmler's.

The tensions between Ostministerium and SS officials show clearly between the lines of the report of the sitting. It was noted, for instance, that Obersturmbannführer Heinz Hummitsch of the RSHA, attending in place of Dr Ehlich, 'despite coming from the most interested and strongest office of the Reichsführer-SS, said not a word during the session'.[60] It was also noted that SS-Hauptsturmführer Schubert, representing the RKF, made a point of stressing the unique responsibility of his own department for all the questions under discussion. Both he and the RuSHA representative, SS-Standartenführer Professor Schulz, were agreed that the majority of the eastern peoples were not suitable for *Eindeutschung* and must be expelled to western Siberia. The junior representative from the RSHA rejected forcible expulsion, however; he believed voluntary emigration would be possible. The representatives of the other two SS Main Offices then swung round to the view that the greatest possible voluntary emigration should be encouraged. Since 31 million people were involved, it is difficult to take these arguments seriously. Schubert of the RKF undoubtedly expressed Himmler's and Heydrich's real views when he likened the German occupation of the east to the Spartan occupation of the Peloponnesus eight centuries before Christ: 'The Germans, he declared, must have the position of the Spartans, the existing middle class of the Lithuanians, Estonians and the like the position of the Perioeci ['Periöken' was handwritten in a space left in the typed report], the Russians on the other hand the position of the helots.'[61]

The Spartans were, of course, the ancient Greek warrior caste whose constitution had been idealised by Plato and Plutarch. Spartans had exercised all political power in their realm and owned all the land, which was worked for them – since they had to be free for military service – by the enslaved original inhabitants, termed helots; the Perioeci were a middle class of free men with no political power. It is not surprising that this famed example of a warrior state should have found echoes in Germany. The Prussian elite who had ruled Bismarck's Reich had adopted the ideals of Sparta; Nietzsche had drawn much from the same source. If Himmler read and spoke more of the ancient Indian warriors of the Kshatriya caste and the Vedic scriptures, nevertheless he had absorbed the spirit of Sparta through his pores from earliest boyhood. It is only, perhaps, by considering Sparta, an ancient totalitarian power state where the propagation of children was encouraged by legislation, but infants judged sickly were left out to die of exposure, where boys left home at the age of seven to be schooled communally in hardihood, indifference to pain and submission to discipline as soldiers, where their land was worked by helots – and where one day a year was set aside when helots might be killed legally – that those raised in a liberal democracy, the antithesis to the ideal of Sparta, can begin to see Himmler's ideas in context and understand how they were shared by the companions of his Order. This analogy drawn at the conference by Schubert of Himmler's RKF is useful, therefore, in showing a direct link – or more properly a rationalisation – from Sparta to the SS eastern colonisation policy.

The conference closed with unanimous agreement that the various peoples of the occupied east must be assessed racially in order to judge what proportions might lend themselves to *Eindeutschung*, but the programme should be camouflaged as an enquiry into health. This was of course a well-tried expedient: it had been used in the T4 and 14 f 13 programmes, and Himmler had suggested it to the chief of the RuSHA in October 1940 as a means of investigating the racial composition of schoolchildren in the Protectorate. A form for each pupil should be devised, he had written, which included purely medical questions such as number and type of illnesses, state of teeth, vision and so on together with the important questions, 'exact height, weight, eye colour in three categories: 1) blue, grey, green, 2) brown, dark brown, 3) black; and finally hair colour separated into: 1) blond, dark blond, 2) brown, dark brown and black'.[62] In a letter on the same subject, he required from each child a profile and full face photograph – undoubtedly in order to detect Slavic features such as prominent cheek bones.[63]

Eindeutschung was already well under way in former Poland. After the huge losses of the best young blood on the eastern front it appeared more than ever necessary to reclaim Nordic blood from the conquered peoples, and children of Nordic appearance were made a special target. That February Himmler's RKF sent out a directive to all HSSPFs, with copies to the Minister of the Interior, the Minister for Education, the RuSHA, RSHA and Lebensborn, detailing the correct order of procedure. Although headed '*Eindeutschung* of children of Polish families and from former Polish orphanages', it is plain both from the correspondence and from what occurred subsequently that a similar system was to be adopted throughout the occupied east.

The first step in the former Polish area was the registration by the Youth Office of the Warthegau of all children in orphanages or in the care of foster parents; next the children were to be examined racially by the local officials of the RuSHA and medically by the local health officials; those passing the examinations were to be sent to the *Gau* children's home in Brockau for psychological examination by Frau Professor Dr Hildegard Hetzer. The head of the home, where the children were to remain for six weeks, was also to render a character report. Himmler had to work through the *Gau* administration in all he did, and it was the Reichsstatthalter acting on his behalf who had the final word, on the basis of the various reports, as to which of the children should undergo *Eindeutschung*. Those selected aged between two and six were to be taken into a Lebensborn children's home, whose duty it then was to find childless SS families to adopt them; those aged between six and twelve were to go to state boarding schools in Germany. Children were not to be taken, however, from parents who were themselves racially valuable and capable of being Germanised. Finally: 'Special care is to be taken that the expression "*Eindeutschungs*-capable Polish child" is not used in public to the detriment of the child. Rather the children are to be described as German orphans from the reconquered east.'[64]

By no means all the children taken were orphans; thousands were simply stolen from their mothers in actions designed for the purpose. Selected for fair hair and blue eyes at assemblies in school playgrounds or village squares in Poland and Russia, or even passing in the street, they were sent for further examinations to special homes like that at Brockau where racial experts took measurements of their skulls and limbs and bodies, in girls the pelvis, in boys the penis, and classified them as 'valuable', 'acceptable' or 'not desired' for *Eindeutschung*.[65] There was never any difficulty in placing those accepted because, such was the mood worked up by propaganda, Party and SS members were desperate to do their duty by adopting children of good blood. According to a study of Lebensborn by Clarissa Henry and Marc Hillel, demand actually outstripped supply.[66] Such was the racial hysteria among doctors, psychologists and staff at the homes where the chosen children underwent preliminary Germanising that they not only were told their mother or father was dead – which was too often true – but were fed stories designed to make them reject their parents. They were, of course, given German names and indoctrination designed to instil pride in their new racial identity. The story of one of these children has been told in a recent book by Karl-Heinz Huber:[67] he was a Pole named Alojzy Twardecki. His father had been killed during the German invasion in 1939, and he was taken at the age of two in 1941 – thus before the directive establishing the proper procedures – and given to a Party functionary in Koblenz named Hartmann who brought him up, naturally, as a convinced Nazi. In the final stages of the war the files on the kidnapped children were destroyed, and it was 1950 before Alojzy's mother finally traced and reclaimed him; he was one of very few to be reunited with his real parent.

Himmler meanwhile made a small personal contribution to the renewal of the blood. On 15 February, Häschen Potthast bore him a son, whom they called Helge. Schellenberg claims that since Himmler's salary did not run to a second home he had to ask Bormann for a loan of 80,000 Marks from Party funds to set Häschen up in a house. Both Schellenberg and Kersten made a point in their post-war accounts of Himmler's financial rectitude. But it would be necessary to know more about the terms of the loan to decide whether it supports the idea of his personal probity or merely demonstrates his ability to convince himself that dipping into Party funds to install his second family in a style befitting the Reichsführer-SS was somehow different from dipping into SS funds. Of course it may simply be one of Schellenberg's stories. The villa was among the complex on the Obersalzberg, all of which, including Hitler's mansion, were registered in Bormann's name; perhaps Himmler simply rented a house.

He did not manage to steal many days away from his desk at field headquarters or while attending the Führer, but he now divided his family time between two homes, and wrote letters to make up for his absences. He remained a good father to Gudrun and a considerate husband to Marga.

To judge by his correspondence he continued to devote a large part of his energies to his task as Reichskommissar for the Consolidation of German Nationhood (RKF). In early March, after hearing that Polish girls were being employed as maids in households in Germany without reference to the RKF, he instructed Greifelt to send him a report on how this was possible: 'Only girls of good blood who have been examined by the RuSHA and who are really capable of *Eindeutschung* should be taken into service.' The intention, he continued, was that mothers and expectant mothers of National Socialist families with many children should be supplied with Polish girls as helps; the girls themselves would thereby be brought up as German girls to become German women. The respective HSSPFs should be responsible.[68]

It mid-March he travelled to Cracow and discussed his plans for settlement and *Eindeutschung* in the General Gouvernement with Frank and his ministers. He recommended that in certain districts which he intended Germanising (because he had no doubt the people there were originally of German extraction) a census should be taken of the proportion of blond, blue-eyed children in the schools.[69]

Returning to Führer headquarters, he laid before Hitler a draft regulation for a new definition of 'kindred blood'; Greifelt and RuSHA officials had been working on it since the previous summer. It was entirely tautological, defining Germanic peoples and all those capable of being Germanised as *Stammesgleiches-* (literally, 'equal stem- or stock-blood'), the other European peoples as 'Kindred-non-*stammesgleiches* blood'. Hitler was evidently happy with it, and Himmler issued it over his own signature on 23 March, together with a summary of the three priorities which had to be established for future population policy:

> 1) The special position of the Germanic peoples with the object of fitting spiritually into the unity of the Reich and biologically into a common body of blood;
>   2) The extraction of people or clans capable of *Eindeutschung* from non-Germanic peoples, as is already occurring through my Staff Head Office [RKF] and through my RuSHA;
>   3) The clear demarcation of the non-Germanic peoples, above all the Slavs living in the same settlement areas as us as well as the foreign workers employed in the Reich, with the aim of preventing any mixing of blood.[70]

Himmler still looked on homosexuals mainly in terms of their negative effect on his population policies. He said to Kersten one day that it was his intention to eliminate them entirely from the nation, and he had been considering for a long time whether it would not be best to castrate them all: 'That would help them and us.'[71] Evidently he had not succeeded even in rooting them out of the SS and that month he circulated a 'confidential' reminder to heads of Main Offices about a Führer decree of the previous November: 'a member of the SS or police who commits an indecent act with a man . . . will be punished by death.' His memorandum continued:

> This order is to be made known *orally* to *all* members of the SS and police with the instruction that communications about this outside the SS or police are forbidden. . . . In this connection it should be pointed out that all members of the SS and police must be in the forefront of the fight to eliminate homosexuality from the German people. . . .[72]

Of course the SS was also in the forefront of the struggle to increase the racially valuable section of the population. This was very much on Himmler's mind after the losses on the eastern front, and at some time that spring he gave the administrative head of the Lebensborn homes, SS-Standartenführer Max Sollmann, secret instructions to plan a great

Lebensborn *Zentrale* in Munich. As he explained it to Pohl later, he had in mind 'the approximately 400,000 women there are already who, because of the men who have fallen in the war, cannot acquire husbands'. The building had to be 'decent and imposing befitting the noble idea and the honour of the unmarried mother'.[73] For some reason, he also told his personal secretary, Dr Brandt, to have Sollmann set up a small card index of all Lebensborn mothers with a Greek nose, or a hint of one.[74]

By the end of March the Soviet winter offensive had broken on rocks of 'fanatical resistance' ordered by Hitler; new lines had been established some 100 miles in the rear of the November positions, yet holding key cities and lines of communications for resupply, and the greatest warlord of all time was initiating preparations for a summer campaign to complete what had been snatched from his grasp in December, most importantly the oil of the Caucasus. Without oil the war machine was doomed. The first flecks of grey were visible in his hair.

Himmler could take pride in the reputation his divisions had won in carrying out the 'no withdrawal' orders. The cost had been terrible: the division Das Reich had been cut down to less than half its original size; casualties in the Waffen-SS as a whole totalled over a third of the force assembled in June 1941; 15,000 mainly of the rigorously selected elite of the racial stock were dead. In a major speech to Gruppenführers a few months later Himmler spoke especially of the loss of almost 700 officers, a considerable number of them regiment and battalion commanders:[75]

> It is therefore the first, the best of the young generation of idealists we acquired in 1934 from the first entrants to the *Junker* [cadet] schools at Tölz and Braunschweig, who had risen to battalion commanders and are now dead, lying under the earth. This loss cannot be helped. The reason I mention this to you is that I have to tell you the truth, indeed I must tell you because I have to demand of you in the coming months – perhaps years – that you summon out from every post every person who in general still has two legs and can move. I speak intentionally only of men with two legs; later the time will come when we send out many who have only one arm.
>
> Altogether, however, this winter has given us the critical test. In the Führer's judgement we have passed it and have fashioned renown, name and what is so infinitely important for the coming generations, tradition. Today every member of the German *Volk* knows what Waffen-SS means. Everyone knows what SS means. And in the future those who come after us will be able to build on that which has been created in this year 1942, and will certainly also be created over the coming year; on this a hundred- and thousand-year tradition of this Order of men and knights of the Reich – the SS – can be built.

One of Hitler's favourite aphorisms from Nietzsche hung in every SS barracks: 'Praise be that which toughens!' Even allowing Spartan inspiration, Himmler's words were remarkable for their ruthlessness. The coming years were to bear them out; the one-armed, the over-age and beardless boys would be called into the lines, but to hear the prophecy at this comparatively early stage is like catching the sound of a prayer: 'Praise be that which toughens!' Was this what he read in the grim faces of his audience? Was it what he carried with him from the warlord in the Wolfschanze, or did the words spring fully formed from within?

Whether he demanded sacrifice for its own sake or for the greater cause – and no doubt they were twin faces of the demon within – his ruthlessness was not rhetorical; it showed in his response to practical realities. Early in April he received several reports detailing the cost to the survivors of his eastern divisions in terms of health and morale. One that especially engaged his attention was from the battalion commander of II/SS-Totenkopf Infantry Regiment I, enclosing his medical officer's report on 281 men who had been in the front line – 92 since the beginning of the eastern campaign the previous June, 28 since August or September, 134 since before the turn of the year and 27 in the current year.[76]

After a thorough examination of these men to determine how they had been affected by 'the stresses of battle, the unfavourable weather and the not always sufficient rations', the medical officer concluded that 30 per cent were unfit for the coming campaign and their recovery, 'even with better food and lack of stress, was not to be expected for a long time'. He classified them as 'absolutely inadequate', 'inadequate' or 'wanting'. There were eight under the first heading, showing 'conditions of debility such as I have only seen with asocials during my KL [concentration camp] work'. Those simply classified as 'inadequate' he described as men 'who in consequence of a weak physical constitution from upbringing, despite often showing the best will – but not with all – were not equal to the stresses'. Nearly all in these three categories of inadequacy were from the younger age groups, seventeen- to nineteen-year-olds at the start of the campaign. These results illustrate the difficulty Berger's recruiting offices had had in expanding the Waffen-SS against Army obstruction; the medical officer's recommendations pointed this up vividly: 'Longer barrack training and hardening and above all character and cultivation of will (selection) of the young year groups is required if at all possible. The *weltanschaulich* orientation especially of the *Volksdeutsche* should be given special attention.'

He did point out that after a short rest period and normal food 70 per cent of the men would be fit for duty, and he paid a special tribute to the older SS men, who, 'irrespective of whether active or reservist, have proved themselves the best throughout, and were in all respects an example for all younger comrades, who frequently attempted to match them'.

The accompanying letter from the battalion commander was perhaps more worrying; he wrote that he was not attempting to prove that the battalion was no longer battle-fit – 'it is obviously exactly as battle-fit as all others' – but simply posing the question of how much could be demanded of his men in their present condition in the coming battles of movement. And he described a marked decline in moral standards since the end of November, symptomised by increasing offences against discipline and comradeship; these included thefts of food and valuables, also malingering before front-line duty, self-mutilation and in a few instances desertion. 'Finally, I believe I may be permitted to say that we must lay down much more rigorous standards with new enlistment for the reserve because the quality of the human material brought in lately surely hardly justifies the standard of the Schutzstaffel as "racial selection".'[77]

His remarks touched Himmler on the raw. At the Wolfschanze again at the end of April, he wrote to the commander of the Totenkopfdivision, Eicke, characterising both sets of observations as 'sly perceptions' and truisms; obviously the winter had been unbelievably exhausting for the men:[78]

> Sun, somewhat more quiet after the end of the battles and especial care with the rations at the front which are certainly not bad, as well as, especially in spring and summer, supplies of vegetables will considerably improve the state of nourishment and strength. In the opinion of Dr E one must now say to the Russians: We request an armistice for half a year because we have to allow 30 per cent of our men to rest.

The new reserves, he went on, had to go to the front earlier than he would wish because of the great losses. The ideal would be a training of three to four months or indeed peacetime standards of training: 'Ideals cannot be executed in war, war is a chain of improvisation. He who improvises better, who has on average higher value [men] and whose officer corps has higher morale and the better nerves, wins.' This was a nonsensical over-simplification, omitting the essential arithmetic of industry, technology and size of forces engaged.

He did not need a doctor, he continued, to tell him that the *Weltanschaulich* instruction must be strengthened; doctors should look after wounded legs, arms and heads and not worry about things other people understood better. That he, as Reichsführer-SS, could make better selections of men in peace than in war was clear; 'Unfortunately here also I have to make a compromise – which is certainly not my practice – between the necessary quantity and the best possible quality.' He reserved some of his sharpest comments for the battalion commander's aspersions on the quality of the *Volksdeutsche*, the foreign racial Germans whom Berger had been forced to recruit even for the German divisions of the Waffen-SS:

> If the Herr Battalion Commander is not capable of training *Volksdeutsche* I am sorry for him. According to his theory we can relinquish some 12 million *Volksdeutsche* who are still in the world. However, we will not do this since the *Volksdeutsche* is trainable, though certainly not if one insults him and looks on him and treats him from the beginning as inferior, as this Herr evidently believes he is.

As Himmler wrote, Berger was conducting a drive for *Volksdeutsche* recruits in Yugoslavia. Hitler had granted permission in December for a new SS division to be raised to fight the partisans whose guerrilla raids in Serbia and Croatia were tying down German regular troops. An auxiliary formation already raised from Serbian ethnic Germans formed the nucleus of the new division, which had received its title, SS-Volunteer Division Prinz Eugen, on 1 March. Recruiting proved far more difficult than anticipated and later that year Berger was forced to a compulsory draft, first with threats, subsequently by resurrecting an old military service law for the German community in the occupied parts of Serbia.[79]

Himmler ended his letter to Eicke with the proposition that doctors in the SS should confine themselves to their proper tasks and seeing to the diet and hygiene of the troops; such foolish reports as this should be forbidden as demoralising for the troops. 'I request you, dear Eicke, to speak to your divisional doctors as well as to the commanders in this sense.'

Eicke reported soon afterwards that he had forbidden his commanders to submit such reports in future about the troops' state of nourishment and strength. He had also instructed them and the doctors to pay special attention to improving diet and quarters where possible.

Himmler's response to another complaint which reached him about the same time via the chief of the Reichschancellery, Lammers, was similar. It originated from Warsaw and concerned 'Corruption in the Gouvernement General'. A tenfold inflation – aided perhaps by zlotys and US dollars dropped by Royal Air Force planes – and the German effort to extract everything possible for the war economy had led to widespread barter and black-market dealings. The complaints concerned German soldiers and officials trading cigarettes, captured arms, even vehicles and petrol to Poles, even trafficking with Jews: 'According to regulation every Jew who leaves the Warsaw ghetto without permission should be shot. [But] if he hands over a fur he will not be shot. . . . The trade between Jews and Germans is large. Even responsible officials of the authorities concerned take part.'[80] Himmler sent a copy of this to Heydrich asking him to see to it with less indulgence than formerly that effective discipline and integrity prevailed in Warsaw; and if any reproaches were raised about the conditions there they should not touch the SS.[81]

By this time the final stage of the solution to the Jewish problem was under way in the Lublin region of the General Gouvernement. Himmler had appointed a rabid anti-semite, SS-Brigadeführer Odilo Globocnik, HSSPF Lublin, to be in overall charge on the spot. Globocnik was one of those extreme characters Himmler appointed for especially demanding tasks; he called him familiarly 'Globus' (Globe).The chief technical executive was Christian Wirth, the former official of the criminal police who had designed the camouflaged gas chamber 'shower room' for the T4 euthanasia programme and subsequently been appointed Kommandant of Castle Hartheim killing centre and Inspector of euthanasia killing centres.

More recently Wirth had set up the murder station with mobile gas vans at Chelmno and established the first extermination camp with a fixed gas chamber at Belzec, south-east of Lublin; this camp had become operational – the words mean of course that production-line murder had begun – in March 1942.

The same month Wirth's successor as Kommandant of Hartheim, Franz Stangl, had received orders to report to Globocnik in Lublin. There, in the park-like grounds of the SS headquarters, Globocnik had told him he was to build a camp near the village of Sobibor on the railway line some 100 miles east of Lublin.[82] He was provided with a workforce of Jews guarded by Ukrainians from the nearby SS special training camp at Trawniki. About three days after arriving at Sobibor, so Stangl told Gitta Sereny after the war, his chief lieutenant, Michel Hermann, who had been with him at Hartheim as chief nurse, called him to come and look at a strange brick building which had been erected in the woods by a labour gang of Poles; it reminded them both of the gas chamber at Hartheim. That was Stangl's first intimation of the real purpose of the camp he was building. Shortly afterwards, he was given a more shocking glimpse into his task; he was ordered to report to Wirth at Belzec. 'The smell, oh God, the smell,' he recalled, 'it was everywhere.'[83] He found Wirth standing on a hill by burial pits which had been filled too full; as a result of decomposition below, the upper corpses had been forced up and had rolled out and down the hill. It was then that Wirth told him Sobibor was for the same purpose.

It is difficult to accept this. By Stangl's account he had spent some three hours with Globocnik in the grounds of SS headquarters, Lublin, studying the plans of the camp he was to construct. Since it was designed specifically for production-line killing it is hard to understand how Globocnik could have discussed it with him as something else, or indeed why he should have done. Nevertheless it is not impossible. If Stangl's story was true it does not invalidate the theory that Hartheim and the other T4 killing centres were designed as training schools for racial elimination in the east; it simply indicates that the trainees were not aware that they were being observed and judged for their suitability in the larger programme. It is equally possible of course that T4 was not designed deliberately as a research and selection programme for the larger plan. The answer to the question hangs largely upon when the final solution was decided, if it was indeed synonymous with the 'ultimate aim' Heydrich referred to in September 1939. In any case, if Stangl's story is true it is an indication of the strictness of Himmler's policy never to tell officers more than they needed to know, and an indication of the level of secrecy surrounding the final solution even after it had begun.

Sobibor became operational in mid-May 1942. It worked on the well-tried deception techniques. The victims were told, after they had been ordered out of the carriages, that they were in a transit camp from where they would be sent to work in the east; they were required to hand in money and valuables, then to undress for 'disinfection'. Naked on the path to the 'bath house', women were taken to a barber's hut where their hair was shorn rapidly, to be baled later and sent back to the Alex Zinkfelt factory near Nuremberg in Bavaria for use in the production of industrial felt for insulation, particularly in the Kriegsmarine and the railways, and cold-weather clothing for the forces and quiet boots for the U-boat arm. After the 'bath house', where they were gassed in batches, gold teeth fillings were extracted and the bodies removed by Jewish work gangs and thrown into mass graves.

Höss, who had begun by gassing batches of Russian prisoners and Jews in the extemporised chamber in Crematorium I at Auschwitz main camp, had been forced by pressure of numbers arriving to extemporise another two gas chambers in deserted peasant farmsteads – known as Bunkers 1 and 2, or the 'white house' and the 'red house' – in a clearing near the new camp at Birkenau.[84] The corpses were buried in pits in the meadow beyond.

Another mobile gas-van centre was in operation by this time at a farm called Maly Trostenets outside Minsk. Throughout occupied Europe, from France to Russia, Jews were being rounded up and Eichmann's department was requisitioning trains from the Transport Ministry to take them to these killing centres in Poland. Gypsies were also rounded up for despatch to Auschwitz, where Himmler had ordered Höss to accommodate them in a separate enclosure.[85]

It could be argued that Himmler was squeezed into the extermination programme by Hitler's pressure from above and Heydrich's from below; Goebbels' diary entries for 1942 leave little room to doubt where the policy originated. Thus 27 March: 'The Führer is the moving spirit of this radical solution, both in word and deed. . . .'[86] Himmler himself always spoke of the onerous burden the Führer had placed on his shoulders. Certainly the sight of killing appears to have caused him physical distress. Yet his underlying attitude to the mass extermination now gathering pace may be gauged better from his correspondence about experimentation in the camps – in many ways even more horrifying than extermination – than from his own or others' assumptions about his motives.

His support for Professor Clauberg's sterilisation experiments has been mentioned. At about the same time he was corresponding about sterilisation or castration by X-ray with Dr Viktor Brack, head of the Euthanasia Department at the Chancellery and inventor of the gas van. Brack had then suggested a production-line method of X-ray sterilisation whereby the apparatus would be concealed under a counter to which the victims would be called, ostensibly to fill in a form for two or three minutes, actually to have their genitals exposed to X-rays switched on by an official behind the counter. Brack had estimated that about 150–200 persons per day might be sterilised by such a process, thus with twenty machines 3000 to 4000 a day.[87] In 1942 he returned to the project, as he expressed it, in order to render the large number of Jews employed in labour gangs in the east incapable of propagating. Himmler authorised feasibility experiments at Auschwitz.[88]

Even more indicative of his attitude to non-Aryan life, since it did not involve Jews directly, was his encouragement of medical experiments at Dachau. From the early spring of 1941 he indulged his great interest in homeopathic medicine by having one of the blocks isolated and used for testing homeopathic against conventional medical treatment for tuberculosis. The groups tested were culled from all the concentration camps; when the patients had fulfilled their purpose they were sent off to an extermination centre. He also patronised experiments aimed at immunisation from malaria by providing facilities at the camp and experimental subjects for a world-renowned expert in tropical diseases, Professor Klaus Schilling; the subjects were chiefly young Polish clergy, whom Schilling infected with the disease by means of mosquitoes collected from the marshes of Italy and the Crimea. At his trial after the war the Herr Professor agreed that his subjects had not volunteered, but he insisted that his work had been for the good of mankind, a sentiment with which Himmler would certainly have concurred – although in the narrower context of the valuable races – and which has, of course, provided the justification for all subsequent and previous experimentation on non-human subjects, who also, it must be assumed, were not in many cases volunteers.

The most notorious of the Dachau experiments were conducted or assisted by Dr Sigmund Rascher. He had been recommended to Himmler as early as April 1939 by his very much older mistress – now his wife – the Munich concert singer, Nini Diehl, who had flirted with or had an affair with Himmler earlier. They evidently parted on the best of terms. Rascher was enrolled in Ahnenerbe, given the honorary rank of SS-Untersturmführer and assisted with funds for private cancer research. At the beginning of the war he joined the Luftwaffe as a junior doctor, and in spring 1941 found himself on a course in Munich, at which high-altitude research played an important part, specifically the problem of aircrew without oxygen masks subjected to a sudden drop in pressure and lack of oxygen by the destruction of their pressurised cabin at great height. Experiments had been conducted on monkeys and other animals but none on humans because of the danger. Rascher wrote to Himmler asking whether 'two or three professional criminals could be made available'.[89] Himmler was happy to oblige. An altitude research pressure chamber, a wood and metal cabinet approximately a metre square by two metres high with a window, through which the subjects could be observed, was installed at Dachau; inmates were made available subject to their names being submitted to Berlin for approval – a great number appear from the correspondence to have been under sentence of death, but others must have been chosen for their state of health or physique – and Rascher was given an additional allowance from Ahnenerbe funds.

The start of the experiments was delayed, partly it seems because the director of the Munich aviation institute carrying out the research, Professor Dr G. A. Weltz, feared that his superiors in Berlin might consider the use of human subjects 'amoral'.[90] However, early in 1942 the director of the Aviation Research Institute at Berlin-Adlershof, Dr Ruff, and his assistant, Dr Romberg, arrived in Dachau for a conference with Weltz, Rascher and representatives of the camp administration to agree procedures for the experiments. It is not known whether Ruff had submerged his personal doubts or whether Himmler had exerted pressure via Field Marshal (Luftwaffe) Erhard Milch, Göring's right-hand man at the Air Ministry. Milch's genealogical table showed him to be a half-Jew, although his mother had sworn that his real father had been Aryan. Nonetheless, he was peculiarly sensitive to the kind of pressure Himmler could bring to bear. That there were doubts at least in medical circles in the Luftwaffe is shown by a subsequent letter about the experiments which Himmler addressed to Milch. He referred to 'the difficulties based mainly on religious objections which Dr Rascher encountered in carrying out his experiments', then proceeded to demolish these objections with a sentence which catches precisely his tendency to extremes: 'In these "Christian medical circles" the standpoint is being taken that a young German aviator should be allowed to risk his life, but that the life of a criminal – who is not drafted into military service – is too sacred, and one should not stain oneself with this guilt.'[91]

He estimated that it would take another ten years at least before they could wean people from such narrow-mindedness. Narrow-mindedness was an apt description – although not in the sense intended – since the people who stood on their religious or ethical principles apparently saw no further than human life. Monkeys and other animals already used in the high altitude experiments had to be below the scale at which morality began, as they were for the representatives of the western powers who sat in judgement on the Nazi doctors at Nuremberg after the war – as they are in practice in the canon of medical and pharmaceutical ethics. Here we are at the nub of the problems posed by Himmler's 'criminality'. For there is not much doubt that on the level of reason he believed that his goal was right and that it justified his methods – not only justified but necessitated them. In the context of German society one is again faced with the question: how was he different from the 'amoral', unthinking or infinitely corruptible circles at every level from the most highly educated to the most ignorant and loutish who did his work for him, as the Luftwaffe doctors – Ruff, Romberg, Weltz and others – were to do? It is not a question that the experimental subjects at Dachau would have found difficulty in answering.

The experiments began in March 1942, conducted by Rascher and Romberg. The 'experimental persons' were confined one at a time in the low-pressure chamber and wired up to instruments recording their vital functions. Air was exhausted from the chamber to simulate gaining altitude at about 1000 metres per minute, the subject breathing oxygen from a mask until the chosen test altitude was reached; in other experiments decompression was explosive. Both Rascher and Romberg submitted themselves to an ascent. Rascher went up to a comparatively modest altitude of 12.5 kilometres (7.75 miles) while breathing oxygen but experienced such intense pain reminiscent of the 'bends' that he stopped the test – a forbearance he did not extend to his subjects, some of whom were taken up to 21 kilometres (13 miles), the limit of the apparatus. After his own experience he described feeling as if the whole side of his body were being crushed between presses, his head being blown apart.

At the chosen altitude the subject had to perform six knee bends to represent the exertion needed to leave the cockpit, after which the pressure in the chamber was raised either quite slowly to simulate a parachute descent, or rapidly for a free fall to ground level – in some cases with, in others without, oxygen.[92] Another series of experiments tested the results of prolonged lack of oxygen at altitudes. The pain, especially in descents without oxygen, was intense. Subjects suffered convulsions, breathing difficulties, temporary blindness and paralysis, expressing their agony by crying out, contorting their faces, biting their tongues, foaming at the mouth; some at extremes of low pressure tore at their head and face with their fingers before losing consciousness.[93] From some 150 subjects approximately half died, indeed many of the 'experiments' were no more than a sadistic form of execution. It appears from a letter Nini Rascher wrote to Himmler on 13 April that these 'X' – execution – experiments were carried out by her husband on his own. The letter opened with sickeningly effusive thanks for presents, chocolate and an accompanying letter Himmler had sent and continued: 'My husband is very lucky that you take so much interest in the experiments, just now over Easter he has carried out single-handed only those experiments for which Dr Romberg would have had scruples and shown compassion.'[94]

Rascher had already made a preliminary report to Himmler describing fatalities from experiments at altitudes above six and a half miles.[95] Himmler replied on the 18th assuring him of his great interest in the work, especially it seems the possibility of revival after apparent death which Rascher had touched on. He instructed him to carry on with condemned men and if he succeeded in bringing one of them back to life that man would have to be pardoned – that is his sentence would be reduced to life inside a concentration camp. This was typical of the way his imagination seized on extraordinary but often trivial phenomena.

An Austrian lawyer named Anton Pacholegg, who was held in Dachau on suspicion of contact with the British secret service and was employed as a clerk in the experiments office, stated after the war that Himmler and his staff generally witnessed important experiments and any kind of new experiment.[96] It is probable, therefore, that Himmler viewed a high-altitude test or an execution in the chamber. In any case it can be assumed that, apart from a flood of interim reports from Rascher, he heard details from Wolff and others of his staff who were present on at least one occasion,[97] and also saw photographs and the cine film that was made of the subjects in their agony, perhaps also coloured photographs Nini Rascher took of the autopsies after fatal experiments. Wolff saw the cine film through and told Rascher afterwards that he might be called to show it at Führer headquarters.[98]

Rascher's 'normal' colleagues and co-workers recognised him as a fraud who inflicted unnecessary suffering and fatalities and used his privileged position with the Reichsführer to gain medical reputation and advancement. Even allowing for the post-war attempts of German doctors to saddle him with the odium, it seems certain he had a notorious reputation. It is evident that Romberg disapproved of him; he refused to take part in the more extreme 'tests', and after the series ended in May took no further part in research with human subjects at Dachau. Another doctor who met him described him as 'definitely an unpleasant man, full of inferiority complexes, and without restraints of character'.[99] Dachau survivors described the low-pressure chamber as 'among the most dreaded tortures because of the intense pain associated with "the bends" experienced by the victims'.[100] This is reminiscent of the terror inspired in the women's blocks at Auschwitz by another of Himmler's protégés, the small, 'fat and unpleasant looking . . . more or less deformed' Professor Carl Clauberg, when conducting his experiments in sterilisation by injection.[101]

Nini Rascher had, if anything, a more evil reputation than her husband. Her letters to Himmler reveal her as a shameless scrounger, asking for more money, reduction of taxes, extra fruit allowances, servant girls from the east – in all of which he indulged her – and show her intriguing on behalf of her husband and denouncing his colleagues. One doctor remembered her as 'petite, elegant and lively', another as 'a typical overdressed, ageing mistress',[102] but it is the self-absorption, the ghoulish interest in her husband's macabre work and the cloying flattery of the letters Himmler annotated and preserved that seem to sum up her character.

Such were the people Himmler patronised and indulged: Sigmund and Nini Rascher, Carl Clauberg, Theodor Eicke, Odilo Globocnik; surely it is these and other diseased characters he picked – and who picked him – who provide the clue to the subconscious motivation beneath his idealism. Dr Werner Best told a story after the war about a dinner party at which Himmler had held forth on the superiority of the Nordic races. Best's wife, a brunette, had asked if that were not rather a dangerous doctrine; if it were realised, they would lose the entire leadership, 'The Führer, you, Herr Himmler, Dr Goebbels . . .'

Himmler replied that even in a round skull, such as his own, a long brain could be planted.[103] To account for the results of the Nazi *Weltanschauung*, it is perhaps necessary to see that inside his roundish skull was a diseased brain, behind the seemingly ineffectual exterior the ugly lineaments of Rascher, or Clauberg, and that if the results of his power were everywhere humiliation, torture and death it was because these were the things that, beneath his conscious thoughts, he craved.

Factory Murder

On 27 May Heydrich was due to fly to Berlin to report to Hitler on the progress of the *Endlösung*, arms production in the Protectorate and the employment of concentration camp labour in the war economy. It seems probable that he also intended to raise the question of co-ordinating security throughout the German-occupied territories, west and east, through the creation of a Reichskommissar with powers to override local administrations; obviously his own position and record gave him unique qualifications to fill such a post himself.

If that was his aim, it was not to be. Three agents of the Czech government in exile, trained and flown in by the British Special Operations Executive (SOE), were waiting to ambush his car at a hairpin bend on the road from his residence to his headquarters in the Hradcany Palace, Prague. Elements of mystery surround the final order to the agents, but the most recent study by Callum MacDonald leaves little doubt about the motive. Heydrich had been too successful in breaking up the underground Home Army and pacifying the armaments workers. Consequently the leader of the Czech government in exile in England, Eduard Beneš, needed to build up his declining bargaining position with the great powers, also his own position vis-à-vis the Czech communist resistance. Heydrich's assassination was to be the means. It would be presented as a spectacular act of internal resistance and the fearful reprisals to be expected would spark real resistance, re-establishing his people's hostility to the German occupation and their strength in the allied cause.[1]

It appears that Beneš was also worried by the possibility of a negotiated peace between the western allies and the German conservative resistance, a second 'Munich' at which his country would again be sacrificed. Certainly Hitler's setbacks in Russia had encouraged Goerdeler and others to believe that the generals would come round actively to their side, and talks were proceeding with the west through intermediaries in Switzerland and Sweden. These assumed, as a first stage in a change of German government, Himmler's co-operation in toppling Hitler – indeed without Himmler it could hardly be done. In these circumstances Beneš believed that his people had to demonstrate clear resistance to the occupation.

Heydrich made a habit of travelling to his headquarters in an unescorted, unarmoured open car. Himmler had tried to persuade him to take more security precautions earlier that same month, but with limited success. Heydrich believed he had the Czechs well in hand and liked to demonstrate it; it appealed to his vanity, perhaps also to his sense of danger. On a calculating level he must have reasoned that the vengeance certain to follow an attempt on his life made it unlikely that anyone would try. So it was that on the morning of 27 May his dark-green, open Mercedes was unescorted and still unarmoured as his driver slowed and changed down for the sharp bend where Beneš' agents waited. One gave the signal of his approach. Another at the bend stepped forward, raised a sub-machine gun from beneath his rain coat, aimed and squeezed the trigger. The gun jammed. The third man, waiting in reserve with a specially designed bomb, lobbed it at the car. It exploded under the rear wheel, driving fragments of metal, leather seat-cover, stuffing and pieces of Heydrich's own uniform into his internal organs. Despite this he leaped from the car with pistol raised, giving chase and firing at one of his attackers before collapsing. Afterwards he was rushed to hospital and X-rayed, then operated on by Czech doctors to remove the splinters and fragments.

When the news was phoned through to Himmler at his field headquarters, according to Karl Wolff he broke down in tears. Hitler's first reaction, when he learned of the attempt was to order the arrest of 10,000 Czechs as hostages and the execution of all prisoners already held for political offences. Himmler immediately conferred with him at the Wolfschanze, afterwards repeating the oral order by teletype: the 10,000 to be rounded up were to include the entire Czech intelligentsia as recorded in the card index; one hundred of the most important were to be shot that night.[2] He had already despatched 'Gestapo' Müller and Arthur Nebe to Prague and he told his friend Professor Gebhardt to fly there at once to take over from the Czech doctors.

His feelings after the first shock and anger are difficult to guess for memoirs of the few survivors from this time agree that he had real cause to fear Heydrich's ambition now that Heydrich had direct access to Hitler. According to one account from the resistance, he had been warned by Langbehn that Heydrich planned to supersede him.[3] An Austrian intelligence agent close to Schellenberg wrote that sometimes in drink Heydrich would reveal his aim of bypassing Himmler by becoming Minister of the Interior in charge of the Security and Order Police; Himmler might remain as RFSS, but, without the police and with the Waffen-SS under Army control, he would be shorn of real power.[4] It is evident from Himmler's caution in keeping the Ordnungspolizei from Heydrich under Daluege that he was acutely aware of this danger. Schellenberg himself wrote that it was Heydrich who had reason for alarm at this time; his popularity with the Führer had aroused the jealousy and antagonism of both Himmler and Bormann, formidable in combination, and in his last conversation with him Heydrich had revealed his forebodings.[5]

The first reaction of the Czech population as rumours circulated of an attempt on their Deputy Protector's life was, according to the SD secret opinion report, 'malicious glee and satisfaction'. Only isolated individuals, foreseeing the inevitable consequences, condemned the deed as a crime against the Czech people; the ministers of the Protectorate government, meeting in deep dismay, fully shared this view, and the alarm spread later that day as a state of martial law and a reward of 10 million Crowns – some £125,000 – for information leading to the capture of the perpetrators brought home to all the gravity of the situation and the retribution that would be exacted. The Jews remaining in the Protectorate did not need these indications; they had been seized with apprehension from the first, fearing that the attempt would be made a pretext for getting rid of them. German sections of the population, meanwhile, as enraged as the Jews were terrified, demanded 'the sharpest reprisals and the final dissolution of the Protectorate';[6] that evening sporadic acts of violence by Germans against Czech-owned businesses and restaurants were reported in the town of Iglau.

The great manhunt which followed raised the alarm of the Czechs to panic. The state of fear induced by the Gestapo is illustrated in the next SD report which described the inhabitants of the town of Pilsen raising their arms in the German salute, Heiling Hitler, producing German-language textbooks and political tracts and employing every device to prove their 'German-friendliness'.[7]

It was five days before Himmler visited Heydrich in hospital. What was said is not known since no one else was present at the bedside. Lina Heydrich wrote much later that Himmler told her only that her husband had quoted some lines from one of his father's operas: 'Yes, the world is but a barrel organ, which our Lord God turns himself, and each must dance to the tune, exactly as it stands on the drum.'[8]

If Himmler had been told there was little or no chance of recovery, as surely he was, for Heydrich's internal wounds had become infected and there was no penicillin available to German medicine, it must have been a poignant parting. Whatever his suspicion or jealousy of his more brilliant subordinate, they had worked together almost from the beginning of that heady time when power first shimmered in view. He knew how much he owed to Heydrich's clarity of purpose and iron heart. If he felt some relief that he need no longer fear for his own position he surely felt regret for the protégé whom he had shown so much consideration, and for those simpler years of struggle.

After an encouraging medical report on 3 June, Heydrich succumbed to blood-poisoning and died on the 4th. It is a symptom of the chronic state of suspicion in which the leadership lived that there were whispers about Professor Gebhardt not permitting the removal of Heydrich's wounded spleen where the infection was rooted. Whether Himmler sent him to Prague to try and save Heydrich or to make sure he did not recover is a secret they have taken to the grave; in any case it probably had no effect on the outcome.

He was given a funeral in Prague on 6 June, and three days later a grand state funeral in Berlin. The coffin, draped with a swastika flag with his sword and steel helmet on top, was borne on a gun carriage drawn by six black horses, escorted by an honour company of Waffen-SS led by Himmler – no doubt very conscious of the gap some paces behind where the dead man had marched on so many previous state occasions – from Prinz Albrecht Strasse to the Reich Chancellery, where Hitler opened the solemn rites. The leadership attended in force, Canaris in the front rank, tears running down his cheeks[9] – weeping for yesteryear, the adventure that had gone so terribly wrong, a young naval officer who had played violin sonatas at his home and eagerly drunk in his tales of spies and spying.

Canaris was a broken man. The barbarities in the eastern campaign, the murder factories established by his former disciple offended his notions of honour as much as Hitler's crass military challenge to the world offended his intelligence. He saw nothing to hope or work for, only doom and disgrace, divine retribution on a leadership and state that had offended against the law. He now travelled desperately, spent hours in meditation in Catholic churches, expressed his extreme pessimism in sardonic, defeatist humour or gestures directed at the idiot pomposities he saw everywhere around him. He had lost interest in his personal appearance. He was a mere husk, a tired and grey shell, kept in office by reflex and the loyalty of his staff. If Heydrich's death seemed to remove the immediate threat to his Abwehr, it could only be a matter of time before, leaderless and drifting, it was delivered up to another of Himmler's men.

Himmler, by contrast, appeared actually stiffened by the difficulties on all sides and the ruthlessness demanded. He had intended to address his Gruppenführers and departmental chiefs in Posen to prepare them for the tasks of the coming summer offensive but had cancelled the convention because of Heydrich's assassination and the measures necessary in the Protectorate; now that they were all gathered in Berlin for the funeral he took the opportunity of talking to them on the 9th. Whether influenced by the emotions of the afternoon when he had delivered the eulogy and held the hands of Heydrich's two young sons before the Führer, who had touched their heads, or whether he said what he had been intending to say at Posen, his words were distinguished by savage frankness. During the past winter, he told them, they had stood 'absolutely before a catastrophe, had not the energy and genius of the Führer intervened and mastered fate with an iron hand'.[10] He told them of the high cost of the winter in lives and went on to make the extraordinary prophecy, quoted earlier, that in the coming months and years they would need to fill the gaps with men who might have only one arm. At times he sounded as if he were contemplating another Thirty Years War. This year, he was convinced, would bring many and great successes, but he did not believe it would bring the end of the war. He did not wish, he said, to theorise about how long the war might last; but personally, as a soldier, he was prepared for all the consequences and eventualities of a war which would last for years.[11]

I am totally convinced that in this war it is really a matter of he will win who has the last battalion in the field and holds out. *Meine Herren*, we want to be clear, the battalions of this year can no longer be the battalions of 22 June [1941]. The battalions of June 1943 will no longer be those which we deploy now in June 1942. Should it continue a year longer, so they will decrease somewhat – as will all peoples in this war. It is important only that we always hold the margin we have over our enemies. It is important only that we all see before us an infinitely important task, never to allow the front-line of the Waffen-SS and the police to die out in any way. And if at some time we have to put the sixteen-year-olds, the fifty- and fifty-five-year-olds to arms, then we will do it. It is completely immaterial whether a year-entry bleeds more or bleeds less if it is a question of a whole *Volk* living. You can believe me, in every individual case, the many, many individuals of our worthy youth, the leaders and the men, who one knew and whom one has brought up oneself, cause one bitter sorrow and pain. But war is no matter of sentimentalities. The war will be won because we have here the conflict between Europe and Asia. We have here the conflict between a Germanic Reich and the *Untermenschen*. This we have to win – and we will win it.

He told them to reduce their staffs and departments from the peacetime levels they would like, and seek out every possible man for the front. He was convinced that within a year they ought to have in their staffs only those permanently unfit for service, who for example had only one eye or one foot. It was important that those who led had the opportunity to learn and did not sit on the staffs; the past winter had shown the importance of the older ideologically committed SS men. It was a conflict between the German officer and the Russian commissar. And he stressed the importance of ideological training for the men; he was, he said, convinced that in many, many organisations in Germany they administered but did not lead, commanded but did not educate:

With our *Volk*, and above all with our outstanding [SS] men, we can do everything if we lead them. We can ask everything from them if we educate them, if we give them the great line, over and over again. I should like to interject here – *that* was Heydrich's greatness – when one talked to his people in whatever forsaken corner of the world, in Poland or the Crimea, in Estonia or Serbia, they were all ideologically clear and correctly educated and took the right attitude to all problems. That was not mere guile and not merely great Sherlock Holmes or similar. But they aligned themselves correctly and always gave the right answer.

'For us', he went on, 'there is no word "impossible" ': they could not report to the Führer that they could raise no more men; if he had to he would take the Berlin traffic police from the streets, and the gendarmes from the country districts, let people moan and groan as they would. But 'impossible' or 'We can do no more' were words that he would not utter, he could assure them, for as long as the war lasted nor for as long as he lived, and nor would they.

This was a promise he kept to the letter for so long as Hitler lived. It is difficult, therefore, to know what to make of his contacts with the conservative resistance through Langbehn and Haushofer, to name but two, and the peace feelers the same resistance was putting out to the west, predicated on a strike by Himmler against Hitler. It must be doubted that he acted as a simple *agent provocateur* since he genuinely wanted peace with Great Britain, and it was obviously to Germany's advantage, indeed was beginning to look like a matter of life or death, to have the Anglo-Saxon powers on her side in the struggle with Russia. Hitler could make no peace feelers in his own name: the message from all sources was unequivocal that peace was still possible with a 'decent' Germany, not with Hitler. Was Himmler acting on his behalf to gauge whether some new disposition of government offices or apparent diminution of the Führer's power would satisfy the west? In terms of *Realpolitik* neither Great Britain nor America wanted to see Germany and Europe overrun by Bolshevism. Was he taking a position from which he could jump either way – as it seems he did with Röhm and Strasser – while preaching loyalty to the last man and boy? Was he telling the Gruppenführers what they wanted to hear, and on the other hand when he was with Langbehn, and probably Schellenberg, also telling them what *they* wanted to hear? The previous November von Hassell had noted some remarks of Langbehn's about the changeable spirit of the SS 'in whose breast two souls live in strange admixture: a barbaric Party soul and a misunderstood aristocratic soul'.[12] It is evident that Himmler was always torn between his ideals and the realities of Party corruption; it is possible that his cautious feelers to the opposition were one manifestation of this. Given his powers of self-delusion the potentialities are limitless. For his ideal state and his ideal conditions of victory over Bolshevism there is little doubt he would – in his mind – have sacrificed even the Führer. Meanwhile within the gathering of the knights of his Order his message was loyalty to death.

The second of the points he wanted to stress concerned pessimism; that too was forbidden and impossible, he told them. At present there was no cause for pessimism, but fate might strike them again anywhere and he did not want his commanders 'wandering around with long faces and sad eyes': the mood would seep down through the staff.

Even if it is so desperate – one can do no more than die. I have the conviction now – which we all have – that in the final analysis the others will die sooner than us. In the final analysis we have the thicker skull. We have the better blood, the stronger heart and the better nerves. Good, our comrade Heydrich, our friend Heydrich, is now dead, he lies under the sod. Now the whole SS – and I can assure you that if he lived he would say exactly the same – will march on with beating drums and helmets donned. And if another blow strikes us, we will march on. And if we have attacked ten times, will attack an eleventh time. So long as one man in any position, in a company, in a platoon remains who can crook a finger round a trigger, all is not lost. . . .

These words are remarkable enough, doubly so for the early date; for they express precisely his attitude in the desperate days of early 1945 when all *was* lost – barring a miracle. That he said them in the summer of 1942 when Germany was master of the greater part of continental Europe, before an offensive designed to gain the objects so narrowly missed the previous year, illustrates the simple, unchanging fanaticism of his leadership. Either this caused him to disregard the very different position by 1945, or he lacked the moral fibre to adapt to the changed circumstances and act.

He continued at great length on the harsh necessities of war, repeating his invariable maxim that they must be hard on themselves. As for the quality of the recruits, they must not make a great *Lamento* to him; it was not possible in war to preserve the standards of entry. But while they could not select for positives they could weed out for negatives. 'In every case where a fellow has any weak, asocial characteristics, he will be grabbed and stood up against a wall' – SS argot for execution by shooting.

He warned them of the dangers of alcohol, and the legions of those lost from all ranks on account of drink. They must double the punishment for offences committed in drink, and they must set the example themselves.

If one wanders around dead drunk before one's foreign slaves it makes a really splendid, convincing impression of the master race which has arrived there! If into the bargain one of my commanders is boozing and there is a Ukrainian girl there etc. – so – it comes to other things! *Meine Herren*, that we cannot afford.

After urging them to be more industrious, more duty-conscious and, once again, harder on themselves than ever before, to be shining examples of an unbreakable conviction of victory – 'I say to you we will win, there is no doubt with us' – he turned to the great tasks of peace, first within the SS. The fusing together of SS and police and the education of the leadership corps in military, ideological and political respects would be the immediate aims. It is interesting that from the figures he gave he was not thinking of a greatly enlarged Waffen-SS at this date, only some 100,000 to 120,000 men all told.

The next great task would be to win Germanic people to the Reich.

Germany has a basis of 85 to 90 million people. If we fetch into this Reich the Germanic peoples – and the Führer wants that – that represents an increase of 30 million people of Germanic blood, that represents the core of Europe – exactly as the 90 million Germans are the core of this Germanic Reich – that represents for the future in the northern part of Europe the organisation of some 250, 300, 400 million people, that represents the regulation of the continent, the representation of the rights of the white, Nordic races on this earth. This question of winning the Germanic peoples which we are now already dedicating ourselves to intensely in this war – where history will be written and the basics created in blood – we must dedicate ourselves to for all time. . . .

He urged them to treat young Norwegians, Dutch and Fleming recruits with the greatest understanding and tenderness.

The third great problem for peace was the settlement of the conquered territories. The war had no sense, he told them, unless Bohemia–Moravia, South-east Prussia, Danzig–West Prussia, the Warthegau, Upper Silesia, the General Gouvernement, Ostland (the Baltic states and White Russia), the Crimea and Ingermanland (on the Black Sea) were totally settled with Germans within twenty years. That was the task they must set themselves for the peace – 'should we live so long'. They had to lay the absolutely solid foundations in the era of Adolf Hitler so that even if those who followed showed weakness and stupidity nothing could disturb the greater Germanic *Imperium*.

If we do not make the bricks here, if we do not fill up our camps with slaves – in this context I say things very plainly and very clearly – with work-slaves to build our towns, our villages, our farmsteads without regard to any losses, then after a long war we will simply not have the money to furnish the settlements so that really Germanic people can live there and take root in the first generation.

I said the first great peace task is to overhaul the whole SS and police and to fuse them together. The second task is to fetch in and fuse the Germanic peoples with us. The third task is the settlement and migration of peoples in Europe which we are carrying out. The migration of the Jews will be dealt with for certain in a year: then none will wander again. Because now the slate must be made quite clean.

It was appropriate that he should make this first undisguised reference to the *Endlösung* on the evening of Heydrich's state funeral. It is significant that he felt able to do so in such a laconic way without explanation. Every one of those present knew precisely what was meant. The following month he visited his chief executive in the killing zone in the General Gouvernement, SS-Brigadeführer Odilo Globocnik, who wrote to Wolff afterwards: 'The RF was here and has given us much new work which now fulfils all our most secret desires. I am so very grateful to him for this that he can be certain of one thing, these matters that he wishes will be accomplished in the shortest time. . . .'[13]

Globocnik's words, like Himmler's, like the many and varied euphemisms with which the *Endlösung* was cloaked – yet so openly conveyed between initiates – have the unmistakable smell of a conspiracy undertaken not in guilt but in a shared, breathless spirit of flouting the canon of orthodox morality, of being bound by dark, forbidden knowledge so terrible it could not be written, nor spoken aloud except among those who knew. It must be assumed that those who listened to Himmler that night and shared this overwhelming secret, like Globocnik, were excited by it; otherwise Himmler would not and could not have referred to it in that way.

By *Volk* migration, he went on, he meant the movement of foreign peoples who would be able to work for them later, in other words not Jews but immigrant labourers.

> However, if these want to have children they should have them somewhere else, not with us. Starting families, nest-building and the rest one may and will never tolerate. They will work here and in the winter be transported out again. They can be concentrated in camps. They can have brothels, they can easily have them in abundance, I have nothing against that. But with our German *Volk*, they have nothing to do. Any slave families, of good Polish agricultural worker- and miner-origin we will radically destroy. If they want to breed, they should do it outside. Certainly we need new slaves, but not with us in Germany. There may be no infiltration or suchlike.

The fourth and last task he said he wanted to mention that evening was the honouring of ancestors. They would have to deal with Christianity more rigorously than heretofore. 'This Christendom, this greatest pestilence which could have befallen us in history, which has weakened us for every conflict, we must finish with.' During Heydrich's funeral ceremony, he had affirmed his deep inner belief in God (*Gott*), or fate, or the *Uralten* (original or age-old), calling Him by the old Germanic word Wralda. It was the Christian idea of God which had to be changed for the people. Man was nothing special as the 'megalomaniac doctrine of Christianity' made him out to be; he was part and parcel of the world. They had to anchor him in the eternal chain of his ancestors and grandchildren: 'If we are thus anchored, our *Volk* has eternal life in the blood. Who has ancestors has children and grandchildren. If we always live only in the "I" and "You" of present-day life, we will continually stop and go. In the final analysis that represents the death of the entire *Volk*. . . .' And he returned to the theme of the losses in the winter campaign.

What he did not say in this address is almost as revealing as what he said; he did not mention the Americans or the British, despite the fact that mass 'terror' air raids on German cities provided a constant disturbing theme of discussion among the populace.[14] Nor did he mention shortage of foodstuffs, especially fresh vegetables, and the rising price of basic necessities affecting German housewives – another constant theme – nor the fuel shortage affecting the armed services, especially the Navy and his own anti-partisan units. He did not mention the question of women being urged to work in the war economy, which of course cut right across the grain of his ideology, and his constant exhortations for a higher birthrate. His attention was fixed above these common concerns, on the struggle in the east, the ideology of the blood and the establishment throughout the Reich of the new morality he was trying to implant in the SS:

> All that we do must be accountable to the clan [*Sippe*] and the ancestors. If we do not find this deepest and best of all – because most natural of all – anchorages we will not be capable of overcoming Christendom on this plain and establishing the Germanic Reich as a boon for the world. That is after all our task as a *Volk* on this earth. For thousands of years it has been the task of the blond races to rule the earth and continually to bring to it prosperity and culture [*Glück und Kultur*].

More passionate rhetoric in this prophetic style followed until finally he finished, 'What we do, we do for Germany, we do for the Führer and we do for his Germanic Reich, the Reich on this earth – Heil Hitler!'

As he spoke the village of Lidice in the Protectorate was being prepared for a mass reprisal by one of the usual SD Kommandos of mixed Gestapo, Security Police, Ordnungspolizei, Feldpolizei and Wehrmacht. Heydrich's real assassins had not been tracked down, but a Czech resistance fighter and an illegal radio set had been traced to this small mining village, and Hitler himself had given orders for the community to be erased. The following day all the men and youths were taken in small batches from the barn in which they had been locked overnight, and shot. There were 199 all told. The women and younger lads from sixteen down and children were shipped to a transit camp at Lodz, from whence the women were entrained for the Ravensbrück concentration camp and the children tested for suitability for *Eindeutschung*. No one was anxious to take responsibility for those judged 'non-valuable' and they seem to have been shuttled from camp to transit camp eventually to die, nearly all, from starvation or exposure. Thirteen selected for *Eindeutschung* were sent to a Lebensborn home at Pushkau, and later handed over to German families for adoption.[15] A little over a year afterwards, Himmler wrote an extraordinary letter about these to the administrative chief of Lebensborn, Max Sollmann: 'The children of good race, who obviously could become the most dangerous avengers of their parents', were to be humanely and correctly brought up, and their personalities closely examined.[16] The danger of racially good stock on the enemy side was an idea that obsessed Himmler and had obsessed Heydrich.

Meanwhile on the day of the action, 10 June, Lidice village itself was totally destroyed and burned, and thirty Jews, driven there from the 'show' concentration camp, Theresienstadt, were forced to bury the male corpses.

The Sudeten Germans especially had been disturbed by the lack of immediate reprisals, fearing that Heydrich's assassination might be the signal for a wave of attacks on German life and property in the Protectorate. According to the SD public opinion report, the punishment of Lidice met with their general approval: 'It was a very hard judgement, but they did not deserve anything else' was one comment cited. 'Only a part of yesterday's bourgeoisie were in view of such consequences somewhat "weak in the knees".'[17] Once again one is confronted with the fact that Himmler, the SS and the Nazi Party were not, by this stage of the war, after years of Dr Goebbels' propaganda, radically out of line with general opinion.[18]

Lidice was a comparatively minor, though the most notorious, part of the reprisal measures in the Protectorate: over 13,000 people were arrested and nearly 700 executed or gunned down when eventually the assassins were betrayed for the reward, and surrounded. And in Mauthausen concentration camp nearly 3000 Czechs were killed. The Jews also suffered as they had feared: between 10 and 12 June some 3000 from Theresienstadt were entrained for 'resettlement' at an extermination camp.

On 12 June, two days after the destruction of Lidice, Himmler began a letter 'Lieber Heydrich!' – so it appears from the carbon copy. 'Heydrich' was crossed out and 'Greifelt', chief of the RKF Office, substituted in pen.[19] The letter concerned the 'General Plan East', and the remarkable slip suggests how closely this was tied up with Heydrich in Himmler's mind.

No copies of the plan survived the war; its contents have to be inferred from Himmler's remarks and a memorandum on it by Rosenberg's racial expert, Dr Erhard Wetzel. It provided for fully 'Germanised' settlement areas in former Poland, the Baltic provinces and White Russia up to a line from Lake Ladoga (east of Leningrad) to Bryansk (south-west of Moscow), and in the southern sector taking in the western Ukraine and later the Crimea. Of the 45 million foreign peoples in these areas, it was estimated that 14 million would be capable of *Eindeutschung*, and would therefore remain and become Germanised; the other 31 million 'racially undesired' would be pushed out to west Siberia. Dr Wetzel considered the population estimate far too low; if 14 million were to remain he thought that between 46 and 51 million – depending on whether 5 to 6 million Jews had already been removed – would need to be pushed out. He also dismissed the data on which the racially valuable proportions had been estimated. He made no mention of slave-labour or losses in the slave-labour force in his comments, but it is evident from Himmler's remarks on 9 June that large numbers of the 'racially undesired' were to be employed as slaves in the construction of the settlements and the great arterial highways which were to link the east with the old Reich. Some of the discrepancy between the population figures might be accounted for by the anticipated wastage of slaves.

The plan provided for 840,000 immediately available Germanic settlers and a further million resettlers and overseas *Volksdeutsche* to move in initially, and a further 2.5 million Germans to move east and settle over the next thirty years at an average of 20,000 to 30,000 families a year – some 4.5 million all told to take the place of the 31 million expelled. In his letter to Greifelt of 12 June Himmler said that the plan was entirely to his liking and he wanted to present it to the Führer some time; before that other areas within the proposed greater Germanic Reich now included in the Protectorate, Austria and Alsace-Lorraine should be incorporated. He also wanted the time-scale shortened to twenty years. When amended thus, a 'Total Plan East' should be submitted to him in draft form showing the requirements in people, workers and money over five-year periods. 'Then if something is really impossible we must reconcile which things can be struck out.'[20]

Although Himmler still spent a great deal of time at Führer headquarters, it was not until mid-July that he found Hitler in a receptive mood to listen to his ideas about eastern settlement. The summer offensive had been launched by then, Sebastopol had already fallen, and Hitler had flown with his headquarters staff to a new command post, codenamed 'Werwolf', at Vinnitsa in the Ukraine south-west of Kiev. On the day of his arrival, 16 July, Himmler drove up to talk about a number of points from a field post he had taken up at Zhitomir. Afterwards he broached his plans for eastern colonisation. As he described them later to Kersten they involved communities of soldier–farmers (*Wehrbauern*) filling a belt several hundred miles deep along the borders. Each settlement would consist of thirty to forty farms of up to 300 acres each. Besides maps of the settlement areas, he showed Kersten, and presumably Hitler, ground plans of a typical *Wehrbauern* village he had had prepared. It focused on Party headquarters, which served also as entertainment and instruction centre. Close by was a cinema and the manor house, to be occupied by an SS or Party leader chosen for his qualities as man and soldier. He would be head of the community – both Burgermeister and Party leader, thus achieving a fusion of state and Party – and military commander of the farmers and their sons who would form a unit of approximately company strength disposing of machine guns, automatic rifles and grenades. A tank force would be incorporated in a group of such units at battalion level.[21]

Hitler, so Himmler told Kersten when he arrived back at his Zhitomir headquarters, listened attentively, asking questions and drawing his attention to points which needed further consideration, but in general approving. Himmler was so excited that Kersten could not relax him sufficiently for a successful treatment.

'This is the happiest day of my life,' he said. 'Everything I have been thinking and planning on a small scale can now be realised. I shall set to at once on a large scale. . . .'[22]

The next day, 17 July, although Kersten did not mention it, Himmler visited Auschwitz. He was accompanied by the Gauleiter of Upper Silesia – where the camp was situated – the HSSPF of the region, the chief of Pohl's Works Department, SS-Gruppenführer Heinz Kammler, and others probably including Karl Wolff, although Höss did not mention him. Höss conducted his important visitors to the officers' mess to show them plans of the camp and its manifold offshoots, thence to the Works Office, where Kammler explained the construction in progress with the aid of plans and models, not disguising the difficulties they were experiencing, presumably through shortage of engineering and special materials. Himmler asked questions but made no comment on the difficulties. It is probably an indication of his priorities that they then toured the farm and agricultural experimental laboratories, workshops, barns and plantations outside the main camp. The head of this department, SS-Obersturmführer Dr Joachim Caesar, showed them the plant- and animal-breeding research in progress, the rubber plants from which it was hoped to harvest rubber and the herb gardens worked by gangs of prisoners. No doubt after some refreshment Höss took over again to conduct the party through the various sections of the camp, the Russian, the gypsy and the Jewish compounds. As on Himmler's earlier visit, Höss was at pains to point out the overcrowding, the primitive and totally insufficient washing and lavatory facilities in the long timber barrack huts laid out in regular ranks. He took Himmler to the hospital blocks to show him the emaciated creatures suffering epidemics, caused in part by poor nourishment and insanitary crowded conditions and, he believed, by the discharge of untreated sewage into the River Sola running alongside the main camp. The camp doctors detailed the very high illness and mortality figures.

Höss did not reveal whether they discussed medical experiments. Himmler had given the final approval for sterilisation and castration by X-ray research 'of major dimensions' at a meeting in Berlin ten days earlier,[23] and the first 100 female 'experimental-persons', mainly Jewesses, had been taken from the women's barracks to the hospital block on 10 July. In view of his extraordinary interest in sterilisation and the minutiae of procreation and fecundity and his habit of inspecting new experiments at Dachau it would be surprising if Himmler did not enquire about progress during that first week and ask to see the apparatus. Höss merely said that after the hospital block, when he took him to inspect the facilities and work in progress at Birkenau, Himmler had heard enough of hygienic and construction difficulties, overcrowding, sickness and mortality rates and told him vehemently he wanted to hear no more about his problems. 'For an SS-Führer there are no problems – his task is continually to remove problems himself immediately they appear! Over the *how*, *you* blow your brains out, not I!'[24] Kammler and the site construction manager with him received the same message.

At Birkenau Himmler was shown the changing room and adjacent gas chamber known as Bunker No. 1, disguised like the T4 installations with pipes and shower nozzles, all kept spotless and bright by a Sonderkommando of Jews to lull the next party. The pressure had eased somewhat in the last week as Himmler had allowed the able-bodied to be selected for work gangs. The first such selection had been made on 11 July;[25] prior to that every train-load had been taken straight to the bunker. Himmler also inspected the construction site for a specially designed combined 'underground changing room–gas chamber–crematorium' complex which would be the ultimate in production-line killing and disposal. Höss was still having bodies buried in mass graves, but it was cumbersome and unhygienic in view of the numbers involved, and shortly after the inspection Himmler ordered him to burn them instead. He did so first on great open-air wood pyres, later in pits, but this too proved unsatisfactory and at certain wind directions the stench of burning flesh carried to the surrounding populace, who talked openly of 'Jew-burning'.[26] It was not until the crematoria complexes came into operation the following summer that the whole procedure from unloading the transports to the reduction of the remains to ashes became a completely controlled and efficient factory process.

After seeing the site and work in progress the party drove back to the railway platform or 'ramp' just outside Auschwitz station to view the organisation of selection and killing from the start; the branch line taking wagons right in to Birkenau itself was a later refinement.

Two trains rolled in together that afternoon; they carried the first two consignments from Holland and each contained about a thousand mainly German Jews who had sought refuge there; they had been told they were being taken for labour service in Germany. Waiting for them on the platform were the duty camp doctor, SS and Ukrainian guards, several with dogs, and work parties of shaven-headed Jews in vertical-blue-striped prison garb with the yellow triangle on their sleeves. Trucks were drawn up nearby to take those selected for death, and an ambulance painted with red crosses in which the 'disinfecting' staff carried the canisters of Zyklon B – such was the macabre sense of humour with which the deception procedures were invested. Perhaps it was part of the 'imagery of killing in the name of healing' the body of the *Volk* which Robert Jay Lifton concluded from his study of Nazi doctors was the crucial step in the development of production-line murder[27] – or merely subconscious reaction to the incomprehensible where everything was turned on its head.

As the wagons clanked to a halt the guards moved into a violent routine designed deliberately to stun the senses and create an impression of urgency with no time for thought. Unbarring the doors they banged on the coachwork yelling, 'Juden, raus, raus, raus . . . [Jews, out, out, out . . .] alles raus . . . schnell, schnell, schnell . . .', and hurled threats and imprecations, wielding dog whips or steel-charged leather batons to hustle them out and move the slow along. The bewildered occupants, who had been incarcerated for two days on the train, were formed into lines in small batches of five or so, while their luggage was thrown out on to the platform to be collected by the Jewish work-parties. The groups were moved along the platform towards the doctor, who looked at each person and nodded his head to one side or the other or pointed his finger to separate the young and fit for the labour gangs from the too young, or too old, weak or ill-looking. The able-bodied were divided by sex and formed into squads to march to the Jewish compound at Birkenau, there to be tattooed on the arm and have their body hair shaved; those selected for death were crammed into the trucks. From the total 2030 people on these two transports watched by Himmler, the majority was passed as fit, and only 449 men, women and children were driven to Bunker No. 2 in the clearing.[28]

Himmler's party followed. In the changing room the victims were instructed to undress, and leave their clothes in orderly piles, remembering exactly where they had left them so that they could retrieve them quickly after they had been through the shower and delousing room; there were numbers on the walls above the benches to help them. Every effort was made to suggest normality. Even the Jews of the Sonderkommando who assisted at this stage – later to gather up the clothes and take them to the store – had every reason to conspire in the pretence and prevent panic and the inevitable violence that would ensue. Women and children went out first naked in batches following the signs 'to the bathroom'. It is highly unlikely that on this occasion, with the top brass watching, they were harassed, pinched or fondled by leering guards, but that was sometimes almost the last experience young Jewesses carried out of the world. The men, generally fewer in number since the able-bodied had been selected for labour, followed the women and children in to the chamber by the single entry door. After the last one a guard standing just inside the door to preserve the aura of normality, stepped out and closed and bolted it. The great strength of the method, one survivor of a transport reflected, was its 'unbelievability'. Even those who were warned in whispers on the 'ramp' by the Jews gathering up the luggage could not believe it – even later when the sweet smell of burning flesh hung on the air.

Directly the door had been closed 'disinfectors' stationed on the roof above opened canisters of Zyklon B and tipped the crystals down shafts into the chamber; they formed gas immediately. Those standing next to the shafts collapsed while the others began to scream and fight for air, soon clambering up and over each other and forming a struggling pyramid in the centre of the chamber. There was an observation window in the door through which the duty doctor observed the scene to decide when all had succumbed; no doubt Himmler watched through this. The time taken depended on the temperature and humidity, also on the state of health of the victims. Höss wrote that 'the screaming, the elderly, the ill, the frail and children collapsed first';[29] after some twenty minutes there was no further movement. 'He [Himmler] viewed the extermination process in complete silence, saying nothing at all. Several times he watched me unobtrusively and the Führers and Unterführers taking part.'[30] He was obviously gauging the effect of this method on the operators since the terrible effects on sub-stantial proportions of the Einsatzkommandos engaged in mass shootings, especially where women and children were concerned, may have been the chief reason for using gas on a large scale.

The duty doctor gave the signal about half an hour[31] after the gas had been thrown in. Entry and exit doors were opened, the ventilating plant switched on and the waiting members of the Sonderkommando jumped into their routine, pulling out bodies, searching for hidden valuables, opening jaws to discover teeth with gold fillings – which were knocked out with pliers and hammers and thrown in a box – passing bodies of women and girls to the barbers who cut off their hair. Having been processed the corpses, which according to Höss showed no discolouration or visible changes, were pulled away to the prepared mass graves.

A survivor of one of the later Jewish work-parties whose duty was to take the bodies from the gas chambers at Auschwitz gave the film-maker Claude Lanzmann in Lanzmann's documentary *Shoah* a very different account of the state of the corpses. The sight as the chamber was opened was unbearably gruesome, one that he could never grow accustomed to. Bodies were pressed together in the pyramid of death, and as the door was released upper ones fell out like blocks of basalt. Many were battered and bloodied from the death struggles; the weak and old and children at the bottom of the pile, covered with blood, vomit or excrement, were sometimes so pressed and crushed as to be unrecognisable.[32]

Meanwhile the work Kommandos from the undressing room and from the 'ramp' were delivering the victims' clothes and luggage to the huge warehouse known as 'Kanada' and nearby huts erected to take the overflow; prisoners working at long tables sorted the items and searched for hidden money and valuables. The different garments and articles were then stored to be sent to new settlers or German families who had lost their possessions in air raids; the money and jewellery were packed up and sent to the WVHA in Berlin, from whence foreign exchange was negotiated in Switzerland; the gold was melted down for use by the SS dental service; clocks and watches were sent for sorting, valuing and repairing at workshops set up for the purpose at Sachsenhausen camp, after which they were stored for Himmler's disposal to deserving units of the Waffen-SS on the eastern front or to U-boat crews. Nothing was wasted. The operation netted huge sums for Himmler's special accounts and for the Reichsbank. The foreign exchange was particularly valuable.

Within Auschwitz it was a source of corruption on a colossal scale which Höss found impossible to put down despite the death penalty for any SS man or woman stealing Jewish property or taking bribes from prisoners who took money, watches or rings while sorting. Höss put most of the escapes from Auschwitz down to bribes from this source.[33]

Omitting for the moment a visit to 'Kanada', Himmler and his guests went directly from the gas chamber to inspect the IG Farben 'Buna' synthetic oil and rubber plant which had been erected largely by camp inmates. This involved a drive back past Auschwitz station and over the River Sola. Himmler asked the IG Farben managers about the work of the slave labourers they hired from the concentration camp. He was told that it was poor; despite knowing that a cut-back in prisoners' rations was planned, Himmler instructed Höss to see that performance improved. Exactly how Höss was to manage it was, again, his affair.

Before dinner in the mess that evening Höss presented his officers to Himmler, who showed his invariable interest in their families and service experiences. During the meal he quizzed Höss about several of them, and Höss took the opportunity, as he had during his last visit, to represent their incapacity and to ask for better replacements and an increase in the number of guards. 'You will be astonished', Himmler replied, 'what impossible types of Führers you will have to manage with soon! I need every Führer, Unterführer and man who is capable of front-line duty for the front.'[34] For the same reason, he told Höss, he could not expect any strengthening of the guards; he would have to employ every technical means in their stead, and use more dogs. The SS Commissioner for Guard-dogs would visit the camp in the next few days to introduce him to a new-style sentry routine for dogs. Höss was to use every means, *'every means'* he repeated, to prevent escapes.

After dinner the Gauleiter asked Himmler and his guests and Höss and his wife back to his residence in Kattowitz. There Himmler became a changed man. He was geniality itself, especially to the two ladies in the company, radiating bonhomie and talking on a wide variety of topics; children's education, new houses, books, pictures, his travels to the front with the Führer and experiences with Waffen-SS units, avoiding only any reference to their day at Auschwitz, and refusing to be drawn on service matters. Höss described him conducting the conversation in 'best sparkling form'; he had never seen him like it before.[35] Himmler drank a glass of red wine and smoked a cigar, again surprising Höss although it is apparent from Kersten's record that he allowed himself these relaxations over dinner in the evening. The party broke up amiably rather late.

There is no doubt from this and other accounts that Himmler could shine at social events when the company was congenial to him. He was not the invariably grim fanatic or 'crank' depicted in so many post-war memoirs. Of course on this occasion most of the guests were directly subordinate to him and could be expected to share his opinions; nevertheless he was obviously cheerful and expansive. Höss's description of the evening which so surprised him actually tallies with Kersten's account of dinners with Himmler, his staff and guests at field headquarters; service matters were not discussed, neither was there any small talk. Himmler liked to raise historical themes, especially it seems the great movements of the Germanic tribes, the settlement policy of Henry the Fowler, Genghis Khan and his methods of government, but he did not do all the talking; he drew the others in, reserving for himself only the formulation of practical lessons from the case discussed. As for women, Kersten reported him as always extremely respectful towards them and when talking about them. He hated obscenity or *double entendres*; he regarded these as insults to his own mother. He was very fond of children, a characteristic noted by most others who knew him, and was always ready to give time to widows and war orphans, indeed his staff were forbidden to turn them away. 'Compared with their sacrifice,' he would say, 'the half-hour which I sacrifice to them is such a small matter I would be ashamed if I failed to listen to them or give them the feeling there was somebody to whom they could turn.'[36]

Of course it cannot escape attention that the evening on which Höss first experienced Himmler's best social form followed hard on his inspection of the extermination of 449 people, naked women and children leading the procession to the chamber.

Himmler was staying with the Gauleiter, and next morning took the opportunity to discuss the *Volksliste* of those passed for *Eindeutschung*, and resettlement measures in the *Gau*. Then he was collected by Höss and the HSSPF and escorted to Auschwitz for a second day of inspection. He toured the kitchens, the butchery and bakery, the workshops and stables, and saw the sorting work on the Jews' possessions in 'Kanada' and the women's camp – where again Höss attempted vainly to impress him with the overcrowding and inadequate hygiene facilities. Himmler had reserved to himself the right to approve the corporal punishment of women, and now he asked for a demonstration so that he could judge the effect. A professional prostitute under sentence for thieving in the camp was brought out, strapped to the *Bock* and beaten across the bare buttocks. Twenty-odd years later, after Wolff had been tried in a Munich court for abetting the murder of Jews and sentenced to fifteen years' imprisonment – very few of which he actually served – he was reading through the judgement against him and making defiant marginal comments when he came to the accusation that in a concentration camp he had watched a woman beaten; he noted: '5 strokes!'[37]

After annulling the sentences of some women for minor offences and talking with a group of female Jehovah's Witnesses – a sect whom he admired for the strength and resolution with which they stuck to their beliefs, even though he had to incarcerate them for pacifism – Himmler had a final discussion with Höss in his office. He told him that he had seen all the shortages and difficulties he faced, but there was nothing he could do. They were in the middle of a war and had to learn to think in the context of war. The actions he had ordered could not be stopped simply because of lack of barrack space. Eichmann's programme would continue and would increase from month to month; the extermination of Jews incapable of work had to be continued ruthlessly. He also told him that he must exterminate all gypsies not capable of work. This seems to have come as something of a blow to Höss; the gypsies were his favourite prisoners. They were as trusting as children, he wrote. If he went into their compound, they emerged from their barracks at once, playing their instruments and having their children dance. Never had they looked at him with dark, hate-filled eyes. Himmler's original idea had been to gather all gypsies together for genealogical research into their branches and clans, for he believed they were probably direct descendants of the original Indo-Germanic peoples; after the war he had intended that they should live in their own reserve.

Evidently with the exigencies of the war and the extreme shortage of rations they had come into the category of 'useless eaters'. It is unlikely though that he made the decision to exterminate them without reference to Hitler; that had probably been one of the topics discussed at Vinnitsa on the 16th.

Himmler went on to tell Höss that his camp was to be made a centre for armaments production. Kammler would assist him with the necessary buildings. The construction of the crematoria complexes at Birkenau was also to be pushed forward, as were the agricultural research programmes; he needed the results most urgently. Finally he said he was satisfied with all he had seen in the camp and, thanking Höss, he promoted him Obersturmbannführer. Before leaving, he visited Höss's house and spent some time talking to his wife and children, once again in best social form.

It seems from both Höss's and Kersten's accounts of this period in mid-July that Himmler was in a stimulated, heightened mood. Days later he was still talking to Kersten about the vast proportions of the work now beginning in the east. If they succeeded, then all the fighting and sacrifices made sense, for they would have created security for the Germanic race against the threat from Asia. He was even prepared to allow the English and Americans to settle, provided they passed the racial test. They would construct a great Germanic international to set against the Jewish and communist international; the assault of Asia would break against the Germanic armed peasantry.[38]

The day after completing his inspection of Auschwitz Himmler wrote to his HSSPF East in Cracow, SS-Obergruppenführer Friedrich-Wilhelm Krüger, instructing him that the 'resettlement' of the entire Jewish population of the General Gouvernement was to be completed by 31 December. The measure was necessary because of the essential ethnic division of races and peoples in the new ordering of Europe as well as for the security and cleanliness of the German Reich and its spheres of interest. Any relapse in this regulation would signify a danger for the peace and order of the total German sphere of interest, a focus for the resistance movement and a centre of moral and physical plague.[39]

In the conditions created by the occupation and ghettoisation policies, these arguments were valid. Escaped Jews formed active resistance bands in the countryside, while the Jews herded into the towns, prey to extortion and pawns to be bargained for, were a major source of corruption – not in the sense Himmler intended, but because they formed defenceless reservoirs to be milked for personal profit. Nowhere was this more evident than in Warsaw, where over half a million were crowded into a few blocks in the city centre.

A gas-extermination camp had been constructed to clear this ghetto. It was sited near a little railway halt called Treblinka some forty miles north-east of Warsaw on a line crossing the main Warsaw–Bialystok railway, sufficiently close to both cities to run a train shuttle service, sufficiently distant not to draw attention to its operations; for as always the smooth running of the action would depend on deception. Christian Wirth had been in overall charge of construction, as he had been for Belzec and Sobibor, which it resembled. The Kommandant was a young Austrian medical doctor, Irmfried Eberl, another graduate of T4, who had commanded both the Brandenberg and Bernburg euthanasia centres. Although medical doctors were indispensable in the processes of the extermination camps from selection of the able-bodied to gassing the weak and unfit, Eberl was unique in being appointed a Kommandant.

The action began on 22 July. The chairman of the Jewish council in the Warsaw ghetto was told that all his people were to be deported to the east without exception; the first 6000 were to be ready at four o'clock that afternoon, and a similar number every day thereafter. His wife would stand surety: any failure to meet the quota and she would be the first one shot.

Franciszek Zabecki, the traffic supervisor of Treblinka station and a member of the Polish underground Home Army, heard the first train at about 9.30 the following morning, 23 July. It was not the noise of the engine, he told Gitta Sereny after the war, but cries and the sound of shooting that first alerted him. The train had taken over twelve hours for a journey which normally took two and the carriages were so packed that when it came into view it was surrounded by 'a kind of fog' coming from the windows. It was a hot day and guards with guns were sitting on the roofs of the carriages, sleeves rolled up.[40] As at Belzec and Sobibor the barred, barbed-wired carriages were shunted up a spur line to the camp platform where a few SS, but chiefly Ukrainian and Latvian SS auxiliaries, with dogs and whips waited together with a Sonderkommando of Jews for the luggage; the doors were unbolted and the occupants bullied out with blows and cries of 'bremse, bremse', Ukrainian for 'quick'. Men and women were separated, made to hand in their valuables, undress and leave their clothes, then driven naked with dogs and whips if necessary in batches of fifty or sixty up an open sloping track some thirteen yards wide screened either side by high barbed-wire fences, camouflaged with branches of fir trees towards the gas chambers at the top – a way variously known as 'the funnel' ('Schlauch'), 'the last road' ('die letzten Weg') and 'the path up to heaven' ('Himmelfahrtsweg'). The old and infirm were led off to the *Lazarett* or infirmary – again the macabre reversal of life outside – an open pit of corpses where they were killed with a single shot in the back of the neck, and thrown in. The men were sent to the gas chambers first since they took less time; the women took longer as their hair was shorn in the chamber itself by a team of some sixteen or so Jewish barbers working at a rate of two minutes or less per person. Finally the barbers left with potato sacks full of hair; the door was closed and a diesel engine was started whose exhaust led into the chamber. Cries and screaming began immediately and the desperate fight for breath.[41]

Meanwhile clothes and luggage were being taken to the sorting huts by the work-parties; the dozen or so now empty wagons were shunted back up the spur line, full wagons from the waiting train hitched to the engine and drawn down the spur to the ramp for the process to begin again with the next victims.

After some thirty minutes the chamber doors would be opened; the dead 'stand pressed up against each other like pillars of basalt' – the description of the SS chief disinfection officer, Dr Kurt Gerstein, after watching an extermination by the same process at Belzec.[42] He continued:

> Even in death one knows the families. They squeeze each other's hands, clenched in death, so that there is difficulty tearing them apart in order to evacuate the chamber for the next consignment. The cadavers, damp with sweat and urine, legs spattered with excrement and blood, are hurled outside. Children's corpses fly through the air. There is no time, the whips of the Ukrainians sough on the work-Kommando. Two dozen dentists open the jaws with hooks and look for gold. Gold left without gold right. Other dentists break the gold teeth and crowns from the jaws with pliers and hammers.
>
> Among it all the chief, Wirth, leaps about. He is in his element. Some workers check genitalia and backsides for gold, diamonds and valuables. Wirth calls me over: 'Feel the weight of this tin of gold teeth, that is only from yesterday and the day before!' In an unbelievably common and incorrect style of speech he says to me: 'You will no way believe what we find every day of gold and diamonds and dollars!' And now he led me to a jeweller who had to look after all these treasures and had me look at them. . . .

The scene Himmler witnessed after the opening of the chamber doors at Auschwitz must have been much as described by Gerstein. SS men transferred from the T4 programme and the Ukrainian, Latvian, Estonian and other foreign SS auxiliaries who formed the majority of the death camp guards had been trained in common procedures at the special camp at Trawniki, established the previous autumn expending Jewish prisoners in practice.[43] The sight seems to have made little obvious impression on Himmler as Höss recorded merely that he watched the entire procedure up to the evacuation of Bunker No. 2; 'he had nothing to object to but nothing to say about it either.'[44] And that evening he had been in the best of humour. Whatever the interpretation of this, there can be no doubt about the effect the experience had on Gerstein. He was so shattered by what he saw at Belzec and Treblinka that, meeting the Secretary of the Swedish Embassy, Baron von Otter, on the night train back from Warsaw to Berlin, he poured out the details with tears in his eyes, begging him to report them to his government and the allies. He also tried to inform the Vatican through the Papal Nuncio in Berlin.[45]

Gerstein was both an SS medical and 'disinfectant' officer who carried out his duties with zeal, and a Christian and active member of the Protestant Church's opposition to Nazism. He committed suicide in captivity in 1945, since when the springs of his double life have defied explanation. Yet perhaps his was merely an extreme example of the personality split caused in some degree in everyone caught up in a system that upset all normal canons of behaviour.

Treblinka had been operating for less than a month when Gerstein visited it, but the work was continuous from 6.00 a.m. through to the evening, and the corpses lying close-packed in the long mass graves numbered tens of thousands. No one had registered them; no one knew the exact count except Franciszek Zabecki, who made it his business to be at work as long as the transports rolled in, and noted the numbers chalked on the outside of each wagon by the officials who sealed them at the point of departure. Before the camp was shut down, his tally had passed the million mark.[46] At Gerstein's visit in August it was several tens of thousands.

Among the tasks Gerstein had been given by Globocnik was to devise ways of disinfecting the accumulations of the victims' clothes so that they could be distributed to new settlers and others. At Treblinka he found himself confronted by 'veritable mountains of suitcases, textiles and underclothes'. He and his travelling companion were invited to eat in the mess which was furnished 'in typical Himmlerian old-German style'. He found the meal simple, but ample. 'Himmler himself had ordered that the men of this Kommando should receive as much meat, butter and other things as they wanted, especially alcohol.'[47]

That July the Governor-General of the General Gouvernement, Hans Frank, had commissioned Krüger, Himmler's HSSPF East, with the tasks of recruiting Poles and other non-Germans for the labour gangs required in the old Reich and bringing in the harvest in the General Gouvernement itself. Himmler also wrote to Krüger to instruct him how to set about these other tasks. What had to be shown, he started, was that 'not only England can govern great masses of peoples with a wafer-thin upper class, but we can too.'[48] He should make use of the 'vassalage of the Poles and Ukrainians to the Church' and their love for their priests and other village notables, who should be made answerable for the harvest and the good behaviour of the members of the labour gangs with their lives. Further the priests especially were to be rewarded financially for the good work of their flock and on the other hand fined for workers' absenteeism or laziness. As an example he suggested that, with the harvest and other agricultural produce, 20 per cent of any surplus above the target quota should be allotted to the priest concerned in kind, then bought back from him. To ensure that none was stolen the reward should only be paid after the produce had been delivered to the railway collection point – the 'spiritual tax-gatherer himself' to organise the transport there.

He went on in a particularly revealing sentence, 'The priest who is won over in the first year I have for ever, because he has to fear the revenge of his neighbours and the populace and moreover will not allow the lovely profit to slip through his fingers.'[49]

Summarising, he expected Krüger to ensure 100 per cent work quotas from the labour gangs required in the Reich together with 100 per cent coverage of the labour requirements in the General Gouvernement itself by recruiting 'all the tramps and idlers hitherto active in the resistance movement'. So far as foodstuffs were concerned he expected 120–125 per cent of the target requirements. 'A shortfall or non-achievement is out of the question.' What he wished to avoid was 'the smallmindedness of stupid German bureaucracy'; the great thing was to get the harvest in in huge measure without creating an organisation to do it. Success was the sole criterion. 'Every method which guarantees or increases success is right.' He forbade copying or making notes of his letter; the content was to be conveyed orally to those officials who needed to know.

Another example of his methods which he dictated at some date that month – the day is missing on the carbon copy – went to the RSHA, Berlin, which was still without a successor to Heydrich:

> I direct that a *Vertrauensnetz* [network of agents] is to be organised in the whole occupied Russian eastern area, above all among women and girls.
> The inducement for the co-operation of the women and girls must and will be anxiety about the eradication of the family, the killing of the fathers, brothers, friends, fiancés, husbands as well as sons, the aspirations of the women finally to obtain tranquillity after Bolshevism, and on our side the promise really to protect the women and families and finally to secure peace for them.[50]

Himmler was extraordinarily active during this summer and autumn of 1942. Kersten reported that to the horror of his staff he customarily worked almost every day to two or three in the morning;[51] a reading of only a fraction of the reports and correspondence that passed through his office at this period, the summaries of meetings he chaired and the instructions he handed out makes it evident that he must have done so. He was not a nocturnal person as Hitler was becoming, yet several of his interviews were conducted at night; still it seems the number of officers and officials drinking coffee in the restaurant car of his Ukrainian field headquarters as they waited to see him did not diminish. It was the high point of German conquest; from the North Cape of Norway to the Pyrenees, from the Baltic to the Black Sea, Europe quivered under the black boot; in North Africa Rommel was at El Alamein, poised to cut the Suez Canal; from Werwolf in the Ukraine the greatest warlord of all time – abbreviated by the irreverent to 'Gröfaz' – was directing mighty offensives for the oil region of the Caucasus and the great port of Stalingrad on the Volga; Russian armies were in retreat. Himmler's letters and notes of his remarks at this time are full of confidence; the often dark moods of the spring and early summer had gone. It may be that Heydrich's departure had freed his spirit, it may be that the tasks he had won for himself in the east filled his horizons. He was at full stretch but at full power, and evidently relishing it. He treated Rosenberg and his Eastern Ministry with scarcely concealed contempt.

His chief tasks as he saw them were to secure the homeland from the spiritual disintegration into Bolshevism that had preceded the collapse in 1918 – and his Jewish policy was a part of this task – to secure the occupied areas from growing resistance and partisan movements and of course to resettle, reconstruct and racially Germanise the east. Focused as he was on these major goals, he still had time for his other interests and lesser affairs. In July he was trying to decide on a suitable runic logo for Lebensborn;[52] adjudging patterns of beakers for use at SS christening and marriage ceremonies;[53] reading and annotating a report by his police chief in Taurien, an administrative area embracing the Crimea, which described an inspection of 'the old Gothic hill town and fortress of Mangup Kale';[54] reading the final report by Drs Ruff, Rascher and Romberg on the results of their high-altitude experiments at Dachau;[55] arguing with the Minister for Food that prostitutes for the foreign workers in the Reich were a necessity – 'if I did not furnish bordellos these millions of foreigners would run loose with German women and girls' and it was therefore in the German interest that the prostitutes should have sufficient food rations – and occupying himself with a host of other questions.[56]

He was also editing an SS propaganda pamphlet more extreme and aimed at a lower intellectual level even than his 1936 booklet on the Schutzstaffel; it came out later that summer under the title *Rassenpolitik* (*Racial Policy*) 'Compilation and publishing: Reichsführer-SS/SS Hauptamt'. The picture above this attribution was of a full-frontally naked, long-headed Nordic man with sword – a perfect revelation of the fantasy in which he and the pamphlet dwelt.[57]

He had little time to spare for his two families. On one occasion when he got away to his villa at Gmund on the Tegernsee one of the senior SS officers he took with him was astonished to find Himmler's daughter Gudrun reciting grace before meals, so Kersten recorded. He learned from a member of his close staff that Himmler believed it wrong to face children with problems of faith and new forms of belief which were still evolving. When they grew up they could decide for themselves; until then they should not be uprooted from their familiar world.[58]

In early August Kersten found a chance to tackle Himmler on his own attitude to religion and survival after death. It was obvious, Himmler said, that everything did not end with death; nevertheless it was difficult to imagine what form survival would take. And he referred Kersten to the Indo-Germanic peoples' belief in rebirth, the form of which was affected by the *Karma* a man acquired through his deeds.

Kersten asked him if he were not frightened when he considered the things he had to do sometimes and Himmler told him not to look at things from such a limited and egotistical point of view.

'You have to consider the Germanic world as a whole – which also has its *Karma*. A man has to sacrifice himself, even though it's often very hard for him. He ought not to think of himself. Of course it's pleasanter to concern yourself with flower beds rather than political refuse dumps, but flowers themselves won't thrive unless these things are seen to. I try to reach a compromise in my own life. I try to help people and do good, relieve the oppressed and remove injustices whenever I can. Do you think my heart's in all the things which have to be done simply from reasons of state? What wouldn't I give to be Minister for Religious Affairs, like Rust, and be able to dedicate myself to positive achievements only!'[59]

He sheafed through a collection of sayings he kept by him as an *aide-mémoire* to find a short passage from a translation of the *Bhagavad-Gītā*, one of the episodes of the Hindu epic, the *Mahābhārata*. The book was one of his particular favourites and he never went anywhere without it, he told Kersten. This is important for any attempt at understanding what Himmler believed he was doing. For, while the *Bhagavad-Gītā* lends itself to almost as many interpretations as there are seekers after the truth, its resonances abound in Himmler's speeches and conversation. There is, for instance, the system of four social classes, Brahmans, characterised by calm, self-restraint, asceticism, long-suffering, uprightness, wisdom and religious faith; warriors (*Kshatriya* caste) characterised by courage, ardour, endurance, unwillingness to flee in battle, generosity, noble pride; peasants and artisans who work in the fields or in trade; and finally serfs who have no other duty than to serve others.[60] It is not difficult to see his plans for the east in these terms, nor his admonitions to his Gruppenführers and the Waffen-SS, and his own attempts at asceticism, simple decency and higher wisdom.

It is probable too that his belief in immortality had as much to do with the *Bhagavad-Gītā* as with the old Germanic idea of rebirth in the *Sippe*. In the Hindu doctrine the individual self was a timeless, eternal element, a minute part of God Himself, which was constantly reborn in a material body and constantly re-died. The form of its existence, indeed the necessity for its continued existence, was bound up by the *Karma* built up through its embodied deeds; the more bad *Karma* the more unpleasant it was going to find the next incarnation. Salvation came only with perfection; then this element outside time broke its link with its time-bound materialisations, hence with suffering and pain. While there were many paths to perfection, in essence they involved a man doing his caste duty in a disinterested, - passionless way, dedicating it only to God. And here, perhaps, is the key to the picture of Himmler, by nature a squeamish man, forcing himself silently to watch an extermination at Auschwitz. Performance of duty detached from passion was indeed what he continually sought from his staff at the death camps.

A man whose mind was undismayed by sorrow, who had no further longing for pleasure, nor passion, fear or wrath was called a man of steadied thought, a silent sage – thus spake Lord Krishna in the *Bhagavad-Gītā*.

Krishna was an incarnation of the One God, Vishnu, who took on flesh and blood, age after age, 'for the protection of the good, for the destruction of evil, for the setting up of the law of righteousness'.[61] It was this point which Himmler wanted to impress on Kersten, and he read out to him, 'Whenever the law of righteousness withers and lawlessness arises, I will be born anew.'[62] That, he said with the utmost earnestness, suited the Führer absolutely; the Führer was one of those brilliant figures who always appeared at times of crisis for the Germanic world. It had been ordained by the *Karma* of the Germanic peoples that he should come to save them by waging war against the east.

The words Himmler quoted were spoken by Lord Krishna to a warrior, Arjuna, before the great battle on the field of righteousness that forms the theme of the *Bhagavad-Gītā*. Arjuna did not wish to fight. Krishna encouraged him to because ultimately that is what had to happen; it was the *Dharma* – comprising law and fate and duty. He was trying to show Arjuna the true structure of the universe and his place in it as a mere pawn moved by all-powerful God. Again, it is easy to imagine Himmler drawing a parallel here with his own fate and manifest duty, as he seems to have been doing when telling Kersten that a man had to sacrifice himself, though it was often hard; it is easy to imagine him seeing the struggle for the east as akin to the battle and fearful slaughter on the field of righteousness.

Kersten recorded another conversation with him about reincarnation on 12 September. He is supported by one of the file records made of Himmler's table talk; this is for the midday meal the next day, 13 September, and it shows that the subject was very much on Himmler's mind at the time and had formed the topic of a previous discussion.[63] This table 'conversation' reads like one of his speeches and contains the same preoccupations. They had to find their way back to honouring their ancestors, he said, so that a man wanted to continue his line and become the ancestor for his grandchildren. It was the only way to prevent the *Volk* from dying. And they must have sufficient children. Already the Russians formed a mass of 200 million against their own 80 million. With Russian fertility and their own over-refinement, not to say degeneracy, they could expect in twenty-five to fifty years that 80 million Germans would face 240 million or more Russians, and these would be merely the outposts of Asia with its one or two milliards (thousand millions) who would simply, on present trends, bowl them over.

With the person of the Führer fate has compensated us for the want of sufficient men. This, however, occurs only once every 2000 or 5000 years in the life of a *Volk*. As the [downward] course of our *Volk* has been checked in this way by fate, we now have the duty to do something ourselves, not only to hold the position, but to go on upwards.

We will win the war, that is self-evident, but the more difficult task will be to hold the Reich afterwards.

What the Führer has achieved and probably will achieve in practice inside a generation is tremendous – to bring our diminished Reich after the Versailles shame-treaty back to its pre-war footing and then to augment it further and create the greater German Reich. After the greater German Reich comes the Germanic Reich, then the Germanic–Gothic Reich reaching to the Urals, and perhaps then even the Gothic–Frankish–Carolingian Reich. Yes, I believe we even have a claim to that, which others have not yet realised.

Early the following month he travelled to Rome. The highlight of his three days there was an audience with Mussolini. He gave the Duce the Führer's greetings, which he followed, as Hitler had told him to, with an exposition of the situation on the eastern front. Afterwards they discussed the difficult supply position to North Africa and the U-boat campaign against British shipping. Finally Himmler launched into a dissertation on the Jews. They were removing them from Germany and all German-occupied countries since they were the carriers of sabotage, espionage and resistance and formed groups of bandits or resistance fighters. In Russia a 'not inconsiderable number' of them had had to be shot, male and female, since even women and children had become intelligence gatherers and messengers for the partisans. Politically active Jews were confined in concentration camps, others employed on road-building in the east – where since they were not used to work they suffered very high mortality. Old Jews were accommodated in the ghetto-town of Theresienstadt, received their pensions there and lived their own lives according to taste. They had tried to drive other groups of Jews over to the Russians through gaps in the fighting fronts, but the Russians did not want them and usually shot them.[64]

Whether Mussolini was deceived by this farrago of half-truths evading the central fact of the *Endlösung* may be doubted. Himmler described him as very friendly and in best form.

After his return, he reported having gained a very favourable impression of all he had met and seen. So long as the Duce lived, he believed, the Italians would hold 'firm and unshakeable' to the Axis.

12

The Herrenmensch

Himmler's observations on Italy were to prove as wrong as his predictions about the Reich. Not only was Hitler fighting three great powers with superior resources in men, materials and productive capacity, but he was continuing to pay a heavy price for becoming enmeshed in world war several years too soon, before Göring had integrated the satellite economies or come near the goal of self-sufficiency in raw materials. The conflicts between immediate arms production or expanding the industrial base for later massive output had not been resolved, nor could they be in the changing crises of a great war and the occupation of ever larger areas. It would have been impossible without the competing lines of authority built into the Führer system, without active and passive resistance in the occupied countries, without the attempts of the German industrial elites to look after their own capital interests and profits. Göring was bound to fail and by the nature of the system his rivals, Speer, Minister for Armaments and War Production, and in the wings Himmler and the RSHA and WVHA, were bound to contribute to his downfall and enlarge their own spheres at his expense. They were pulling in opposite directions already. While Göring attempted to exploit the resources and industries of the occupied areas Himmler and Speer's plenipotentiary for labour recruitment, Fritz Sauckel, were directing labour from these areas into the Reich to replace men drafted for service in the forces.

The position was aggravated by the warrior ethic. Civilians were second-class citizens in the eyes of the military, hence scientists and production engineers, who should have contributed to rationalisation and acceleration of production, simply bowed to their military masters' demands for excellence and the constant modifications called for from the fighting fronts. This made planning for long production runs impossible; quantity, so desperately needed in the race against their superior foes, took second place to quality. Richard Overy has produced telling figures in his recent biography of Göring: in 1940 while Germany spent an estimated $6 billion on armaments against Great Britain's $3.5 billions, Britain produced 50 per cent more aircraft, twice as many heavy vehicles, twelve times as many armoured cars, more ships and almost as many tanks and guns.[1] In the vital matter of aircraft production Germany was overwhelmed: in 1942 the allies produced 100,000 aeroplanes, Germany and her Axis partners 26,000. The position was actually worse than the figures indicate, since the German provision of engines and spares was less and there was a lower ratio of serviceability.[2] Also so many of the splendidly trained pilots of the early war years had been lost that it was proving difficult to staff even the training schools with the right material.

Göring reacted to these difficulties in his habitual way by bullying, threatening and further interfering with the aircraft manufacturers. To try and retrieve his position with Hitler, he denied intelligence reports of enemy production and made fantastic projections of his own future output, thus adding to the sense of unreality at Führer headquarters. Nevertheless his stock had fallen drastically, and Hitler acted as he had with the generals, virtually taking over tactical control of the air forces on the eastern front, and making all major decisions about aircraft production. His natural inclinations in favour of attack against defence and in favour of terror as the ultimate argument, together with his unscientific faith in scientific wonder weapons which would outweigh mere numerical superiority, exacerbated the already desperate situation; it was eventually to leave the Reich defenceless in the air. The one miracle weapon that could have saved Germany, the atomic bomb, was not taken seriously enough to be accorded the priority it was given in Britain and America – where, of course, Jewish physicists who had fled from Germany played a leading role. Thus rank amateurism, fed on the myths of the warrior caste, spread from on high. At the level of the bureaucracy all was meticulously in *Ordnung*; at the planning levels above all was chaos. And for the leaders themselves there remained only the myth. It is no coincidence that the dogma of the quality of the man and the blood was heard more frequently and given more emphasis the longer the war lasted. Numerical superiority was of no account, Göring told a gathering of Gauleiters late in 1943; 'the man has always been of most value for us. If you look at the American and English prisoners you really have to say: the superiority of the German is still very great.'[3]

This was a gross distortion, as the listening Gauleiters must have known very well. Reports had been coming in from wherever British prisoners of war were employed warning of the dangers to morale caused by the appearance and confidence of the Britons. In the agricultural regions – thus an SD secret report of 8 February 1943 – the mental agility and arrogance tempered with certainty shown by British prisoners of war had allowed them to gain a position of superiority over the local population, and they were using it to spread insinuations that Germany was bound to lose the war and it would not be the last shell but the last tin of meat which would be decisive.[4] From Upper Silesia there were frequent reports of the 'magnificent' physique and the 'proud and self-confident manner' of British prisoners of war, and repeated comments from the locals to the effect: 'Such men have to be treated as enemies whereas Italians, Japanese and so on have to be labelled as friends of the German *Volk*.'[5] The contents of their

Red Cross parcels also created a spirit of envy among the population where shortage of food formed a constant theme in conversation. The British even bartered for sexual favours with Red Cross soap, chocolate and white bread.

From Danzig came reports that British prisoners of war were subverting Polish workers on the *Volksliste* for *Eindeutschung* by telling them that Germany would lose the war and Poland would be reconstituted. Everywhere, it seems from a reading of the SD reports, British prisoners were staging acts of passive resistance and even sabotage in the factories and farms. Their work-performance was 25 per cent that of a German doing the same job; they refused to follow the instructions of German foremen or overseers and would take orders only from their own NCOs. 'These, however,' ran one naive comment, 'see their task in the first line as restraining the British to the lowest possible work performance.'[6] It was recommended that in all areas where British prisoners were employed greater emphasis should be placed on the education of the local German population regarding their attitude to foreigners, especially advising them about the British mentality.

The first visible sign of the fate about to overwhelm the Reich had already appeared in the night skies, heralded by the drone of a thousand aero engines and imprinted on the wan, drawn faces of mothers and children sheltering beneath the smoke and smouldering rubble below the 'terror' fliers. The next signs were in North Africa. That autumn of 1942 a new commander of the British Eighth Army, Montgomery, proved at Alam Halfa that he was a match for Rommel, and at El Alamein on 23 October turned to the attack. He had built up a powerful matériel superiority; the Axis supply lines across the Mediterranean had been lacerated. By the beginning of November Rommel was facing annihilation and on the 2nd on his own initiative, against orders, he began to withdraw. Hitler reacted as he had the previous winter during the Russian counter-offensive, instructing him to hold his ground and prove that the stronger will would prevail over the big battalions; Rommel had to offer his men only victory or death. He made a vain and costly attempt to do so but was soon in full retreat. Three days later an Anglo-American invasion force under the supreme command of the US General, Eisenhower, landed along the coasts of French North Africa at the eastern end of the Mediterranean. Complete surprise was achieved by precisely those methods of deception and confusion which had served Heydrich and Canaris so well in the early phases when Hitler called the tune.

Hitler was on his way to Munich to deliver his annual Bürgerbräu speech when he received the news. He had been subject to extremes of mood for weeks. It is arguable whether these amounted to a personality change induced by disease or perhaps by the drug Metamphetamine, which apparently he received intravenously every day from his personal doctor, Morell, and also took orally,[7] or whether it was simply an exaggeration of personality traits and egocentricity fostered over years by his paladins and now, because of anxiety, overwork and above all perhaps the inkling that he had lost his gamble, allowed free rein. But all in his proximity had occasion to notice the change.

His reaction to the allied landings in North Africa on 8 November appears to have been one of relief that at last suspense was over, and it was not Norway or the second front in Europe that the western allies had chosen. At any rate he was in good form for his speech at the Bürgerbräukeller. He radiated confidence, intimated that he had not been unprepared for the landings, and gave an optimistic assessment of the eastern campaign. He also hinted at secret weapons to retaliate on England for the 'terror' raids on German cities. 'Our engineers and researchers have not been asleep,' he assured the 'old fighters' as well as Germans listening by their radio sets the length and breadth of the Reich. And yet again, as after all setbacks, he reminded them of his 1939 prophecy regarding the Jews; of those who had laughed then 'countless no longer laugh today; and those who still laugh today will probably not be laughing for much longer either.'[8]

Again there is a correlation between an actual record and Kersten's memoirs. For immediately after the 9 November celebrations Kersten noted Himmler saying that since the landings in North Africa the Führer had given orders to proceed ruthlessly against the Jews.[9] Again he apparently told Kersten he had never wanted to destroy the Jews. This time he blamed Goebbels; he himself had wanted to deport them all to Madagascar. He was in an agitated state over the course the war had taken and was suffering badly from stomach cramps. 'The allied landings have clearly dealt him a shrewd blow in the belly,' Kersten commented.[10]

Himmler visited Rome in the middle of the month, no doubt to satisfy himself about measures to monitor the now 'defeatist' mood of the Italian government and, perhaps, the lines of communication suspected between the Abwehr and the Vatican. Scarcely had he returned to his field headquarters in East Prussia than news came of a third unexpected blow, which soon assumed far more ominous dimensions than the events in North Africa. On 19 and 20 November the Russians launched massive armoured thrusts against Rumanian divisions on the northern and southern flanks of von Paulus' Sixth Army then waging a hand-to-hand battle in the ruins of Stalingrad. Cutting through, both arms raced to link up behind von Paulus, and so close to his headquarters that he was forced to transfer to a railway station at Gumrak some 100 miles to the west of the city. Again, complete tactical surprise had been achieved. By the 22nd the German Sixth Army was virtually surrounded and severed from land supply lines.[11]

Hitler was at the Berghof when the first news came through on the 19th. He was at first unable to give any coherent direction, then in the evening of the 22nd he sent a radio message instructing von Paulus to set up a circular defence and hold Stalingrad and the Volga front at all cost. The same evening he left by train with Keitel, Jodl and his adjutants for the Wolfschanze, where he arrived the following evening. Halder had warned of over-extension resulting from two simultaneous offensives in the east, since when he had been sacked; Hitler now reassured Halder's replacement, a younger staff officer named Zeitler, that he had done all he could; he added, 'One finds one's own true greatness in the hour of deepest misfortune – like Frederick the Great.'[12]

Himmler appears to have recovered from his ill-health by this time. He told Kersten that Hitler hoped to come to an understanding with the English and Americans as soon as he could persuade them that the war was not being waged against their world position, but against the world's enemies, the Jewish Bolsheviks.[13] It was a theme he returned to in mid-December after coming from a meeting with Hitler. He was visibly agitated, evidently suffering under the weight of some oppressive knowledge. Kersten waited as he paced back and forth. Finally Himmler told him: the Führer had assured him very seriously that the war with Russia might last ten, possibly thirty years. And behind Russia stood the hordes of Asia whom the Bolsheviks were training and arming to descend on Europe and conquer the entire continent to the Atlantic. Germany was the advance guard of Europe; Hitler had staked her whole manpower and resources in the struggle and were they to be exhausted in the war against Russia, America and England would have to replace them if they did not want to be destroyed themselves. It was something they did not yet understand; the time was coming when they would.[14]

Himmler believed that the Anglo-Saxon powers would be forced to negotiate when they saw the extent of the Bolshevik threat to Europe – despite their repeated refusals to talk while Hitler remained in power. From von Hassell's diary it appears that Himmler's – and the opposition's – agent, Langbehn, was talking at about this date 'with an official Englishman in Zürich and an official American in Stockholm with the approval of the SD'. Von Hassell gained the impression from these talks that England's concern about Bolshevism and her eastern empire had made her ready to negotiate provided there was a change of regime, and that the same went for the United States, which did not want chaos in Europe and required a free hand to deal with Japan in the Pacific.[15] It was no doubt knowledge of this that caused Stalin to put out what appeared to be genuine peace feelers via an Abwehr Russian expert named Edgar Klaus stationed in Stockholm. 'I guarantee', Klaus told Canaris, 'that if Germany agrees to the 1939 frontiers you can have peace in a week.'[16] Naturally peace on Russian terms was the last thing Hitler wanted – or Canaris, who remained violently anti-communist – and although there were talks between officials of von Ribbentrop's office and the Soviet Foreign Commissariat the following year, they came to nothing.

Hitler's health was another matter causing Himmler grave anxiety at this time, if we are to trust Kersten's record. Almost certainly we can, since the Führer's health was causing Hitler himself and his personal doctor, Morell, grave concern. Hitler had become a chronic insomniac and suffered bouts of agonising headaches above the eyes which grew especially severe at night and when he lay down. A recent study by Leonard and Renate Heston has pointed out that these signs are characteristic of sinus trouble.[17]

More serious, his blood pressure was on the borderline of hypertension. He had also developed a tremor in his left hand and arm. However, the major factor weighing on his and Morell's minds was an expert report on an electrocardiograph tracing of his heartbeat taken in July 1941; this diagnosed coronary sclerosis – disease of the arteries supplying the heart muscle with blood. Their anxiety on this score is evident from the fact that it was at this period, late 1942, early 1943, that Morell began taking Hitler's electrocardiogram at unusually short intervals, at least once a month, sometimes once a week. Electrocardiography was still at an early stage, and modern experts shown the tracing of July 1941 regard it as normal, and subsequent changes, also diagnosed at the time as coronary sclerosis, are regarded as 'non-specific' – that is not attributable to any discernible cause.[18] His tremor, first observed at this time, might be ascribed to the amphetamines which Morell was probably injecting, as also his moods of elation and 'grandiosity' marked from this time. His insomnia may have been due to his unhealthy regime with scarcely any exercise, combined with an overload of stress as the real world outside Germany began to break in to his cocoon of fantasy. He confessed, and it could in any case be guessed, that as he lay trying to sleep images of the arrow-covered maps of the evening situation conference obtruded behind his lids.[19]

None of these explanations matters in the context of the time; both he and Morell believed he was suffering from a progressive heart disease which might cut his life short at any moment. Since he was convinced that his life was of the utmost importance for Germany, this knowledge undoubtedly increased his stress and the symptoms of personality change – especially since to preserve his image and protect him from criticism it had to be kept secret. Precautions were taken to conceal the electrocardiograph sessions even from his closest aides, and it seems probable that he took amphetamine orally disguised as vitamin tablets labelled 'Vitamultin'.[20]

That is the background to Kersten's record of 12 December 1942: Himmler, again in a nervous, restless mood at his field headquarters near the Wolfschanze, asked him whether he could treat a man suffering 'severe headaches, dizziness and insomnia'. When Kersten said that naturally he would have to examine him first, Himmler swore him to secrecy, then went to his armoured safe and took out a black file; inside was a twenty-six page manuscript which he handed to Kersten. It was a top-secret report on Hitler's health and medical treatments from the time he had been in hospital after being gassed in the first war. According to Kersten this revealed that he had exhibited symptoms associated with syphilis; these had recurred in 1937 and since early that year, 1942, there were certain indications that he was suffering from progressive paralysis.[21]

Kersten said he was a manual therapist; he could not treat mental disease, whereupon Himmler grew very agitated: this was no ordinary patient, but the Führer of the greater Germanic Reich in the midst of a life-or-death struggle which he alone could win. They had to try every means to keep him going – 'I refuse to believe that this is the end, that the Führer's mind will give way – the mind that has such mighty achievements to its credit.' He continued at length, evidently easing his anxieties, for he concluded that he had to trust Morell to keep Hitler going until he had won the war. Taking the file back from Kersten, he replaced it in his safe.[22]

It seems probable that this report emanated from one of the other doctors at Hitler's court, all of whom distrusted Morell's qualifications and found him personally repellent. As for syphilis, the Hestons' study finds against this diagnosis on the grounds that Hitler showed no signs of dementia and in particular no memory loss, nor the eye signs usually associated with neurosyphilis.[23] Again, this judgement has no bearing on Himmler's state of mind at the time. This was aggravated some days later when Kersten warned him of the grave consequences for the German people of having at their head a man suffering progressive paralysis; it might weaken his judgement, impair his critical faculties and even produce delusions. According to his account he told Himmler that he was unable to understand how he could take the easy way out and simply leave Hitler's treatment to Morell, for there was no way of telling whether the orders Hitler issued were decided in periods of rationality or were products of an ill mind.[24]

Himmler was constitutionally incapable of making a decision on an issue of this magnitude; he evaded it by saying that they could not make a change in the middle of a great war – the *Volk* would not be able to stand the shock. Here he touched on a valid issue. The SD secret public opinion reports make clear just how much the German people still believed in Hitler. Goebbels had built him into a demi-god; if this myth were removed the consequence could be a complete collapse of morale among ordinary people who were not members of the Party. Kersten apparently turned this round by saying that Goebbels was adroit enough to find a way of presenting the matter to the people, and they – and indeed the allies – would welcome the chance of peace which Hitler's departure would allow. It was up to him (Himmler) to make the first move though. He had the SS.

'That's exactly it, Herr Kersten. I cannot make a move against the Führer – I who am Reichsführer-SS, whose motto is "My honour is my loyalty".'[25]

Whatever part Himmler had been playing before in encouraging the peace-feelers to the west, from now on the pressures on him to effect Hitler's removal as a precondition for negotiations increased almost by the week. On the one hand were reports from Führer headquarters and his own observations of Hitler's behaviour which must have tended to confirm the diagnosis in his secret medical report; on the other hand the situation was worsening on every front, naturally strengthening the opposition's call for Hitler's removal before it was too late, naturally converting others, especially in the Army and the industrial community, to the same view.

On 27 December Zeitler told Hitler that unless he ordered a withdrawal on the Caucasus front he would be faced with another Stalingrad. Hitler agreed, later retracting, but by then the movement to shorten the lines was under way. This was followed by a setback at sea in the closing hours of the year. A force headed by two heavy cruisers deployed north of Norway against a convoy taking arms from Great Britain to Russia was beaten off in a brilliant escort action. Hitler threw another exaggerated rage and told the headquarters naval liaison officer to call Admiral Raeder, tell him he had decided to lay up all the big ships, and summon him to the Wolfschanze. When Raeder came he was lectured for an hour and a half without pause on the history of the German Navy, its inglorious role in the first war, the mutinies which had provoked revolution and, coming eventually to the present, the total uselessness of large ships which needed smaller ships and aircraft to protect them; he reiterated his decision to do away with the big ships, use their heavy guns ashore and their crews to expand the U-boat service. Raeder stood the impassioned onslaught in silence, then tendered his resignation. Hitler immediately changed his tone, but Raeder stood by his decision. In his place Hitler chose the thrusting commander of the U-boat arm, Admiral Karl Dönitz, who had impressed him as much by his fanatical commitment and optimism when reporting at Führer headquarters as by the successes his boats had achieved against allied merchant shipping. Bar the 'miracle weapons' under development, U-boats were Hitler's last hope for bringing the Anglo-Saxon powers to terms by cutting the Atlantic supply lines on which they depended.

Meanwhile von Paulus' position at Stalingrad became ever more impossible. Göring, anxious to improve his stock with Hitler, had promised (against all the advice of his air staff) to supply the Sixth Army by air. This proved impossible. By early January 1943 the Army was slaughtering its horses for food as it retreated eastwards into the frozen ruins of the city. Göring's ploy rebounded on him; his reputation declined to vanishing point and Hitler was able to make him scapegoat for the now inevitable disaster. Göring went into a physical decline, retiring for longer periods to his palace, Karinhall, to dress up in outlandish costume with his close entourage, shoot driven beasts and dope himself to ease his unbearable sense of failure.

Hitler's moods were swinging with particular violence at this time and Himmler suffered from his tongue on 15 January, according to a letter Martin Bormann wrote to his wife Gerda the next day. The cause of Hitler's displeasure is not known. It is possible that it had something to do with Himmler's failure to nominate a successor for Heydrich as chief of the RSHA, for a couple of days later Himmler told Bormann he had decided to appoint the HSSPF Vienna, SS-Obergruppenführer Ernst Kaltenbrunner, and Hitler had given his consent.[26] It was an unexpected appointment, bypassing the favourites, especially Schellenberg. No doubt

Himmler brought in the scar-faced giant Kaltenbrunner because he was relatively unknown and outside the established circle of the Heydrichian chiefs, 'Gestapo' Müller, Arthur Nebe, Otto Ohlendorf, Schellenberg and the rest, another example of his rule never to allow overmuch power to any one of his chiefs or Main Offices. The fact that it had taken him seven months to think about a successor suggests that he was not anxious to have anyone in charge of this most powerful of all his departments.

That is speculation. All that is known is that Hitler was acting in a fraught and manic way and he dressed Himmler down over something, leaving him, in Bormann's words, 'deeply offended, and apparently not just since yesterday. . . .' Himmler complained to Bormann of unjust treatment at Hitler's hands going back years; while others had been favoured he, Himmler, had been considered good enough only to raise divisions. Bormann tried to remonstrate that this single criticism had to be set against the constant praise 'the chief' always expressed when talking about him to third parties. It was no use. 'H.H.'s criticism was so very bitter, and at times so acid, that in other circumstances I should have had no choice but to get up and say: "I am sorry, but I must take my leave from you and take off your uniform. The Führer is the Führer, and he is beyond all criticism." '²⁷ As it was, he wrote, he made allowances because of Himmler's state of nervous strain and his consequently distorted view of things. Nonetheless, he found his 'chilly way of criticising unpleasant'.

By 18 January von Paulus' diminishing pocket at Stalingrad had been reduced to ten miles by five; his divisions had been reduced to a third of their original strength; the survivors were digging into the iron ground, preparing to carry out their Führer's order to fight to the last round and the last man. The final act began four days later. Soviet tanks pushed forward under a barrage of fire, overpowering the defenders, on occasions literally grinding them into their foxholes. Finally von Paulus signalled Führer headquarters that the suffering of his troops through hunger, cold and epidemics was no longer bearable; to continue fighting in these conditions was beyond human strength. Hitler signalled back that capitulation was out of the question. 'The Sixth Army will do its historic duty at Stalingrad to the last man. . . .'

It is instructive that when talking to the Italian Ambassador Hitler compared von Paulus' men to the Spartans who had stood and died to a man at Thermopylae; the Sixth Army would show the world the true spirit of National Socialist Germany and its loyalty to the Führer.

In the early morning of 1 February Hitler was roused from his bed with the news that von Paulus had surrendered. In fact an isolated garrison in the southern sector of the city was still holding out, and operations did not cease until the following afternoon after a pulverising bombardment by Soviet artillery, 300 guns to a kilometre. Then silence fell over the smoking ruins and the bodies and wounded in the stinking cellars and the still tanks and abandoned guns, rifles and equipment of what had been the German Sixth Army.

'The man should have shot himself,' Hitler said at the situation conference after the news of von Paulus' surrender came through, 'just as the old commanders who threw themselves on their swords when they saw their cause was lost.'[28]

A week later, Karl Dönitz, newly promoted Grossadmiral, attended his first conference at the Wolfschanze as naval Commander-in-Chief. The Navy had, of course, been most intimately concerned with the growth of the National Socialist Party from its beginnings, and had produced its two most brilliant spymasters, Canaris and Heydrich; now in Karl Dönitz it made an equally significant contribution in the final dying contortions of the movement. For behind the aggressively confident, tight-lipped façade of an incorruptible sailor, possessed of what former superiors had reported on as 'iron will-power, goal-oriented certainty and unwearying toughness . . . inner enthusiasm for his profession . . . and absolute reliability'[29] Dönitz was basically insecure and as emotionally dependent as Himmler on a martial creed to adhere to and a war father to venerate. Hitler, now with bowed back and unhealthily pouched face and trembling hand, suffering the blinding headaches and occasional giddiness which seemed to confirm the doctors' diagnosis of arterio-sclerosis, feeling he perhaps had little time to complete his earthly mission, intuitively sensed Dönitz's dependence and played up to the paternal image expected. Dönitz responded with burning commitment. He was by nature inclined to see his own goals more clearly than difficulties or possible difficulties which might be raised by his opponents. This natural optimism combined now with the desire to impress his war father and gain his good opinion with his determination and will to victory was exactly what Hitler needed after Stalingrad; the relationship was a success from the start.

Hitler had little confidence in his own grasp of naval matters. Dönitz was adept at presenting concise, apparently objective reports; he was able to dissuade Hitler from scrapping the big ships, while at the same time gaining the quotas of men and raw materials to build up the U-boat arm with which he genuinely believed he could win the war in the west. Hitler was happy to give him his head. He did not interfere as he did with Army and Air Force units in the east. Meanwhile U-boats replaced the rockets under development at Peenemünde as the 'miracle' that would turn the war in his favour against the bigger battalions.

Himmler, however sore he may still have felt at the lack of recognition he was accorded, also benefited from the setbacks and Hitler's increased suspicion of all generals. The Waffen-SS had won Hitler's confidence the previous winter with their units' fanatical resistance even in defeat; since realising that Russia was not crumbling, rather the reverse, and foreseeing a long struggle ahead, Hitler had decided to expand and strengthen the Waffen-SS divisions to form an ideologically committed, hardened nucleus on which he could place absolute reliance. The elite SS divisions Leibstandarte, Das Reich and Totenkopf, refitting in the west, were equipped with an increased number of the latest tanks, artillery and armoured personnel carriers and redesignated SS-Panzergrenadier divisions; in December Himmler was authorised to add two SS divisions of this type, the 9th and 10th, which were named Hohenstaufen and Frundsberg. There were insufficient volunteers to fill the enlarged force and replace the losses from the other SS units fighting with Army Group North and in the Caucasus and Finland, and Berger was forced to conscript young Germans who fulfilled the entry requirements, another landmark in the dilution of the original concept of the Order.[30]

The newly equipped Panzergrenadier divisions in the west were transferred to the southern sector of the eastern front where von Manstein faced a Russian offensive rolling on from Stalingrad towards Kursk and Kharkov, second city in the Ukraine. By 15 February the SS divisions, threatened by an encircling movement, were forced to pull back from Kharkov, leaving the city to be re-entered by the Russians the following day. But on the 20th von Manstein used them as one claw of an armoured counter-attack; the Russians, who had misread the preparatory movements, were caught off balance still going forward and were in their turn threatened with encirclement and forced to withdraw, and in March the SS-Panzerkorps – Leibstandarte, Das Reich, Totenkopf – fought its way back to take Kharkov in a grim and devastating battle replete with atrocity. This was the occasion for Himmler's words, quoted earlier, about 'the reputation for horror and terror which preceded us in the battle for Kharkov, this outstanding weapon which we want never to allow to diminish . . .'.[31]

Hitler was elated by the victory after what had seemed an irresistible Russian advance, and was confirmed in his faith in the SS. Already a further two divisions had been authorised, a Panzergrenadier division Nordland to be formed by merging foreign volunteer regiments, and another from seventeen-year-old volunteers from the Hitler Youth named SS-Division Hitler Jugend. Army resistance was now breached, and through that summer and autumn further divisions were raised by drafting ethnic Germans or men of Germanic appearance from all the occupied eastern regions; the 16th SS Division designated Panzergrenadier was named Reichsführer-SS.

Himmler was also able to extend the tentacles of the SS further into the economy. He had already infiltrated most economic agencies with his own men or attempted to gain influence with officials by granting them honorary SS ranks. Now, with the decline of Göring's prestige, he was able to bite deep into the Reichsmarschall's empire. Göring was in any case heavily dependent on the SS for supplies of slave labour especially for his synthetic plants and aircraft factories, and in an effort to make a come-back at court, he judged it expedient to cultivate Himmler; he thus contributed to the growing influence of the SS in the economy.

Another reason why Göring allied with Himmler was to beat off his other rival, Albert Speer. All three had the same basic aim, to rationalise and centralise the war economy for 'total war'. This was more than a propaganda slogan. The muddle between competing authorities in the economy was as great as that in every other sphere of the Reich: the Army and the Navy still insisted on control in their own areas, although Dönitz was soon to ally with Speer and turn over shipbuilding to Speer's ministry in return for a guaranteed programme; Göring was in control of aircraft production, the Four Year Plan office and the integration of industry in the countries under German occupation – again Speer was able to take over most of this empire later that summer.

There was also the Reich Economics Ministry with authority over thousands of concerns not designated 'armaments' firms, yet producing arms, uniforms or parts for the war economy. It was this uncoordinated confusion of 'planning' and the scope it gave private industrialists to play one authority off against another in their efforts to build up their own assets and profits which Göring, Speer and Himmler meant to end by centralising control under their own agencies. As Göring sank into a grotesque caricature of his former self – according to his biographer Richard Overy the result of 'his underlying belief that the war was now lost' as much as his fall from grace at the Führer Court[32] – it resolved itself chiefly into a struggle between Speer and Himmler, with Bormann throwing his power on to one side or the other. If the ostentatiously formal address, 'highly esteemed Party-comrade Bormann' with which Himmler opened a letter in March is anything to go by, the two were not on comradely terms at this time. The letter was in response to complaints from Bormann that the SD was meddling in Party affairs.[33]

So Himmler continued the burrowing, political-jobbing tactics to increase his areas of control, which were surely second nature. Yet he was beset by doubts. This did not show in the front he presented. Through 1943 he grew if anything more extreme in his demands for fanatical commitment to the Führer and the National Socialist state, more vehement in his conviction of final victory and the establishment of the greater Germanic Reich stretching to the Urals, more draconian in his orders for action against resistance movements everywhere, more urgent in calls to accelerate and finally complete the annihilation of the Jews.

In January he commissioned the SS Inspector for Statistics, Dr Korherr, to compile accurate figures of the *Endlösung der europaïschen Judenfrage*, and released the RSHA from responsibility for records; it was to hand all records to Dr Korherr.[34] In February he visited Treblinka and Sobibor; here a demonstration had been prepared for him. He landed in his Junkers at an extemporised strip, the Kommandant, Polizei Hauptmann Franz Reichleitner, and his officers lined up to receive him; thence he and his aides and accompanying officials were conducted on a tour of the 'work Jews' ' barracks in 'Camp 1', then on to 'Camp 2', the mustering place for the victims for liquidation. For this occasion the 'Gasmeister', SS-Oberscharführer Erich Bauer, had selected some 300 young and comely

Jewesses; they had been fed and accommodated in the camp overnight. Now they were brought forward, ordered to strip and herded up the 'Himmelfahrtstrasse' from 'Camp 2' into the gas chamber at 'Camp 3'. The door was closed and they were gassed as a special offering for the Reichsführer.[35]

Whether Himmler appreciated the spectacle, what he may have said or left unsaid, is not recorded. All that can be stated from eyewitness evidence is that he accepted Reichleitner's invitation to dine with his officers afterwards, and they were delighted and excited by this mark of approval from on high. The mess tables were decorated with flowers; 'delicacies and egg brandy' were prepared in the mess kitchen. A Jew helping in the kitchen who was ordered back to barracks when the guests were reported returning from the inspection, on the way found himself face to face within a metre of the party: 'At the head the bespectacled figure of Heinrich Himmler stood out, and around him were the officers who had accompanied him [on a previous visit] . . . among them Adolf Eichmann. . . .'[36]

Five killing factories had been established by this date – not counting the smaller, earlier ones like Chelmno and Maly Trostenets which used or had used gas vans, or training camps such as Trawniki; they were Treblinka, Sobibor, Majdanek, Belzec – which had been closed down permanently in December 1942 – and Auschwitz–Birkenau. Birkenau was designed as the largest, but only gradually attained full capacity through that spring and summer of 1943. The first two of the new complexes of underground changing room/gas chamber/electric lift/crematorium ovens – the ultimate in production-line murder – came into operation in late March, the third in April and the fourth towards the end of June.

Korherr submitted his first report on 23 March. It showed that up to the end of 1942 almost 2 million Jews had been 'evacuated' and/or submitted to 'special treatment'. Since the figures for occupied Russian areas were incomplete, the true number was probably greatly in excess of this. On 9 April Himmler wrote to Kaltenbrunner, his new chief of the RSHA, to say that the report would be useful at a later date 'especially for camouflage purposes' – whatever that meant – but at present it should neither be published nor passed on. 'The essential thing, in my opinion, remains that as many Jews as humanly possible shall be shipped to the east. . . .'[37] The following day he passed instructions to Korherr to amend the wording so that 'special treatment' did not appear; instead 'transport of Jews from the eastern provinces to the Russian east' should be used, after which the report should be re-submitted. Meanwhile Korherr had been instructed to prepare an abridged version 'for submission to the Führer'.[38] Because Hitler's eyesight was poor and he refused to wear glasses (since this would affect his martial image), such reports were typed on a 'Führer typewriter' with especially large characters. According to Eichmann, at his interrogation after the war, he borrowed a 'Führer machine' from Gestapo headquarters at Prinz Albrecht Strasse for Korherr's report. The report was returned to him later with Himmler's notations: '1) Führer has taken cognisance; 2) Destroy' – so Eichmann recollected some eighteen years afterwards.[39]

Professor Fleming, in his study of Hitler's responsibility for the *Endlösung*, has commented on this correspondence as showing 'the cynical, grotesquely naive game played between the Führer and the Reichsführer-SS – like a pact agreed between schoolboys adhered to in deadly earnest . . .'.[40]

The fatuity of this pact to prevent the Führer of the greater Germanic Reich from being implicated in the crime is pointed up by the SD report for 19 April, the day Korherr sent a copy of the abridged, Führer version to Himmler's secretary, Brandt. The discovery in Katyn Forest in former Poland of the mass grave of some 12,000 Polish officers murdered by the Russians had just been made public; commenting on the reaction to this news, the report indicated that in some sections of the population it was being said that 'we have no right to get worked up over these Soviet measures since on the German side Poles and Jews have been done away with [*beseitigt*] to a far greater extent.'[41] This argument, the report went on, was being used especially vehemently in intellectual and confessional (religious) circles. This is the first time the physical annihilation of Jews and Poles was mentioned in the SD reports; presumably it was considered sufficiently widely known to be stated without euphemism.

Opposition circles apparently believed that the news of the grisly find in Katyn Forest was being exploited deliberately to distract attention from military reverses in North Africa. Opinion abroad, the SD report continued, was divided but it was thought that it opened the possibility of a fundamental change in the attitude of the western allies towards the Soviet Union.[42]

Here we are back at the question of Himmler's concealed doubts and anxieties. For on the one hand he could observe at close quarters Hitler's swings of mood. These veered between extreme depression and withdrawal after Stalingrad – causing Morell to announce that the Führer was suffering a manic–depressive illness and to advise a three-month rest – and what Speer described as unreasonable optimism, and Hitler's valet as periods of high optimism despite increasingly grim reports, interspersed with periods of depression.[43] On the other hand Himmler was very aware that the 'defeatism' in intellectual circles of the opposition had spread to large sections of the population.

Thus in March the SD opinion report, in attempting to describe the mood of the people, had distinguished between those who were 'very cast down', indeed 'defeatist', and others who spoke of 'all being lost', but who nonetheless did their duty 100 per cent, concealing their anxieties behind an 'upright and optimistic demeanour'. What is surprising is that already at this date 'in the event of a lost war the hope of a partition of Germany between Soviet and Anglo-American spheres of interest' was being discussed. In south Germany there was talk of creating a new Kaiserreich under Anglo-American protection[44] – no doubt the old separatist tendency asserting itself in the altered conditions. Another trend, caused by Speer's efforts in particular to convert the economy to total war, was the fear among the bourgeoisie that National Socialism was growing indistinguishable from Bolshevism; in face of the growing concentration of state capitalism there were prophecies of 'the ruin of the middle classes'[45] – literally the opposite of what Himmler had hoped to achieve.

Through the summer the situation deteriorated rapidly. First the Anglo-American armies in North Africa forced the surrender of the Axis Army which Hitler had been reinforcing – involving a loss of men and matériel comparable to that at Stalingrad. Next the Allies invaded Sicily as a stepping-stone to Italy, and towards the end of July Italian disaffection towards the war and Italy's German ally resulted in the overthrow of Mussolini and the fascist government. These shocks were compounded by continuous Anglo-American 'terror' air-raids on German cities, especially Hamburg, where firestorms were created of devastating proportions, sucking trees, roofs and people into the flame centre; rumours spread of riots among the civil population being put down by police, SA or the Wehrmacht. There were even rumours of a 'November-mood' – November 1918 – and the German people being unable to endure the continuous bombardment from the air.[46]

By the end of July 'the idea that the form of government in the Reich, regarded as unshakeable, could alter suddenly even in Germany' was 'very widespread'. Allied to this there was much talk of corruption in Party and industrial circles, and 'altogether of a corrupt system' and increasing rumours about Göring, von Ribbentrop or other leaders fleeing Germany. The SD report for 2 August recorded the latest witticisms: Hitler, it was said, had withdrawn to write a book called *Mein Irrtum* (*My Mistake*); Hitler and Goebbels had gone down in a capsized U-boat – they had not been rescued, but the whole German people had been saved.[47] There was widespread cynicism about German news bulletins. In western areas people were toying with the idea of an American occupation, saying it would not be so bad, 'perhaps even better than at present'. All hope of a victorious conclusion to the war had gone – so it appears from these SD reports – and those inclined to be hostile to the Party or cynical about the leaders were secretly looking forward to a turn in Germany like that in Italy when the Party would find itself isolated.

Hitler, Goebbels, Bormann and other leaders had begun to find these SD reports disconcertingly frank and pessimistic; nevertheless, although the list of recipients was narrowed as the situation grew progressively darker, the reports themselves continued to serve as the best guide for propaganda and administrative action to prevent the Reich collapsing internally, and the man behind them, SS-Gruppenführer Otto Ohlendorf, increased his influence the worse the situation became.

Ohlendorf had joined the Party as an eighteen-year-old student in 1925;

after graduating in law and economics his commitment to the ideology had drawn him into politics and in 1936 he had been recruited for the SD as an economics expert. He was already very aware of the discrepancies between the economic practice of the regime and the theory of National Socialism and since that time his intimate knowledge of corruption and inefficiency in the economic direction of the Reich acquired through the network of informants he used for his bulletins had increased his disillusion; it had not, however, undermined – perhaps it had even strengthened – his commitment to the ideals of the movement. Others, like his former teacher and later close colleague, Professor Jens Jessen – a member of the Wednesday Society lunch club to which von Hassell belonged – had moved across to the internal opposition. Ohlendorf remained as an awkward 'conscience' of the movement in the top leadership of Heydrich's RSHA. Himmler, who found him as uncomfortable personally as the other leaders found his reports, called him the 'Gralshüter' – or guardian of the Holy Grail – of National Socialism. It was perhaps because he was an outspoken critic that Heydrich had required him to prove his commitment by leading one of the Einsatzgruppen in Russia behind the advancing armies in June 1941 – so at least it was said.[48] He had performed his murderous duties to the best of his ability, no doubt because he was a convinced believer in the racial core of the creed; he had returned to his desk in 1942 in a stronger position than before.

As the most outspoken critic of the policies and personalities leading the Reich to destruction, Ohlendorf contributed mightily to Himmler's doubts and anxieties that spring and summer, indeed for the rest of the war. As Brandt told Kersten in August, the Reichsführer found Ohlendorf a most inconvenient person since he always spoke the truth regardless.[49] Furthermore, he had a cold and superior manner and tended to lecture from a position of expert knowledge far over Himmler's head. He would have been more persuasive, Brandt said, had he brought him an occasional rune stone or discussed ancient Germanic beliefs. Himmler regarded him as 'the dull Prussian', 'the intellectual'. For his part Ohlendorf told Kersten that what Himmler really wanted was an intelligence service that brought him optimistic reports reflecting his own view of the position. He (Himmler) had immense faith in victory, and he looked at his own reports as the work of defeatists and doubters rather than as indications of where the obstacles to final victory lay. Furthermore, even if he recognised certain criticisms as true, his behaviour was dictated by purely tactical considerations and he did not lay them before the responsible leaders.[50]

'Were he to do so,' Ohlendorf continued, 'he would naturally make bitter enemies of people whose support he needs in other fields. His whole character is against that. I know him well. He prefers to give way and try other methods of dealing with difficulties, but he's only partially successful. Such tactics mean that necessary decisions on important matters are postponed and finally forgotten in the pressure of great events.'[51]

*

Undoubtedly the most important decision in 1943 concerned peace with the western allies – hence, as had been made clear countless times, the removal of Hitler. Alternatively there was the possibility held out by the Russians of peace in the east, but this was of course out of the question in Himmler's ideology. The whole issue of peace with one or other of the enemy groups had been complicated by a decision of Roosevelt and Churchill announced publicly after the Casablanca conference that January that the allies would be content with nothing less than the 'unconditional surrender' of Germany, Italy and Japan. Despite this very public pronouncement mediators were still conducting unofficial conversations between the German internal opposition and the British and American governments that spring and summer, and Himmler's friend, Langbehn, was taking part.

If in previous years Langbehn had been conducting his talks with 'a double face' – for the opposition *and* Himmler – there is every sign that by this date the two were merging together. The traces go back at least as far as the spring of 1942 after the reverses of the first Russian winter. In March 1942 von Hassell had noted that Langbehn assumed Himmler was planning 'diverse things', and it was more realistic to expect action in that quarter than from the generals.[52] At the end of May 1942, when two representatives of the Church opposition, Dr Schönfeld and Pastor Dietrich Bonhoeffer, travelled to Stockholm to meet their western liaison, George Bell, Bishop of Chichester, their message about a strong and organised internal opposition to Hitler included the statement: 'The opposition knows of the threatening rebellion against Hitler inside the Nazi Party by Himmler and his fellows. . . .'[53] The opposition was determined nevertheless to overthrow the whole regime, including Himmler and the SS, and the message called for assistance from the armed forces of the western allies and the neutrals in a police role to secure a new German government.

Meanwhile a new opposition had been forming among staff officers of Army Group Centre in Russia. The leader of this group was Colonel Henning von Tresckow, and he had been brought into the general conservative opposition under the leadership of Goerdeler and the retired General Beck and held together by Oster, still operating from inside the Abwehr under Canaris' protection. Contact between von Tresckow and Oster was maintained by Oster's subordinate and long-time hater of the regime, Hans von Dohnanyi. The military reverses of the winter of 1942–3 led both Goerdeler and von Tresckow to the conclusion that the active generals must now recognise the need for a change of regime. No doubt they did but, like their predecessors in the series of crises that had seemed to offer a chance of toppling Hitler, they were not willing to commit themselves. General von Bock even told von Tresckow that no putsch could be successful without the co-operation of Himmler and the SS.

While von Tresckow and Goerdeler were thus being led by their disappointment with the generals to seek an accommodation with Himmler, the Dresdner Bank director and member of the Freundeskreis, Dr Carl Rasche, whom Himmler had used during the bartering over the Vienna Rothschilds, was seeking contact with the west through his banking connections, specifically to determine whether the allies would negotiate with a German government from which Hitler but not Himmler had been removed. So it was that by the early spring of 1943 both Himmler and the conservative opposition were moving towards a conjunction, which Himmler's most informed advisers, Ohlendorf and Schellenberg as well as the industrialists and bankers in his Circle of Friends, were encouraging by every means.

However, as these twin movements gathered momentum, mischance and a series of tactical errors by Oster threatened the potential alliance. It had started with the arrest of an officer of the Munich Abwehr office named Schmidhuber for illegal transactions in currency, gems and smuggled goods. Schmidhuber was a friend of von Dohnanyi and although his smuggling and foreign-exchange rackets were largely for personal gain he had been employed by von Dohnanyi smuggling Jews out of the country and liaising with the west through his foreign contacts. In order to cover these tracks the Oster group decided to accuse him of working for the British, a fatal mistake which converted a comparatively harmless case of currency and black-market dealing into high treason, and delivered Schmidhuber to the Gestapo. Very soon his interrogator, Franz Sonderegger, was in possession of staggering material about opposition personalities and activities ranging from the Goerdeler–Beck circle, through the Oster–Dohnanyi group in the Abwehr to the liaison officer with the west via the Vatican, and the Bonhoeffer circle's contacts with the west through Sweden and Switzerland. By February 1943 Sonderegger had concluded that the figure masterminding the entire movement was Admiral Canaris himself. He laid his report before his chief, 'Gestapo' Müller, recommending an immediate surprise raid on Abwehr headquarters. Müller had been waiting for just such a chance of sorting out the nest of suspected traitors in the Abwehr since Heydrich's day, and he sent the report up to Himmler. However, to Sonderegger's astonishment Himmler instructed him to drop the case and turn the dossiers over to the legal division of the Wehrmacht; according to Sonderegger's post-war testimony, Himmler wrote on the file 'Kindly leave Canaris alone.'[54]

Discussing this turn of events with his colleagues, Sonderegger learned that this was by no means the first time Himmler had prevented action against the Admiral. In his post-war testimony Sonderegger listed three previous cases, all involving von Dohnanyi or the Abwehr and concerned with conspiracies to assassinate Hitler, where Himmler had stopped the investigation.[55] Schellenberg conveyed the same impression in his Memoirs: he would present reports about the Admiral's betrayals, he wrote, but Himmler, nervously tapping his thumbnail against his teeth, would merely say, 'Leave the dossier here with me. I will bring it to Hitler's attention when the right opportunity arises.' It never did. This happened so often that Schellenberg became convinced that Canaris must have some incriminating information about Himmler; 'otherwise there is no possible explanation of Himmler's reaction to the material which I placed before him.'[56] Schellenberg was in one of the best positions to know, but his memoirs are so riddled with false statements that it is impossible to judge the value of this claim, especially as he was intriguing to take over and merge the entire Abwehr in his own SD.

The more likely explanations for Himmler repeatedly protecting the Admiral are either that Canaris had been Himmler's and Heydrich's man inside the Abwehr from the beginning, and Himmler trusted him to keep a close eye on the activities of Oster and the others, or, as Canaris' biographer Heinz Höhne suggests, both Himmler and Canaris had reached the same conclusions about the hopelessness of winning the war against both east and west and were working on the same lines for Hitler's removal and negotiations with the west. This is certainly true of Canaris; it seems to be true for at least one side of Himmler. It does not, of course, rule out the first alternative. Indeed the total disintegration of Canaris' sense of purpose, even of his personality and appearance, marked by his staff from at least 1942 may have been due to his realisation that in taking up the appointment as Abwehr chief he had made a pact with the devil. By early 1943 he had an air of complete physical exhaustion; his face was tired and hollow, his eyes abstracted; his hand trembled.[57]

Himmler could have expected that by ordering the Schmidhuber files turned over to the Wehrmacht he had buried the case. So no doubt he would have done had not the legal division attempted to forestall any complaints from the Gestapo of a whitewash by keeping them informed; thus Müller was allowed in again. Worse still, the Judge Advocate assigned to the case, Manfred Roeder, was soon convinced that Canaris' organisation was a seat of treason, and suspecting the Geheime Feldpolizei of the same taint – since they were partly controlled by the Abwehr – asked for Gestapo personnel when he decided to make an arrest. Müller was happy to oblige.

So it was that on the morning of 5 April 1943, Roeder called at Abwehr headquarters on the Tirpitz-Ufer, accompanied by Kriminalsekretär Sonderegger, and told Canaris he had a warrant to arrest von Dohnanyi and search his office. The story has often been told how during the search Oster compromised himself by trying to sneak papers from a file and conceal them beneath his jacket, how he was observed by Sonderegger and had to give them up again and leave the room. The papers concerned the Protestant Church's plans to assist in the overthrow of the regime and an outline of a proposed structure for post-Hitler Germany. As a result not only von Dohnanyi, but Bonhoeffer, the Vatican liaison Dr Josef Müller and others were arrested, and Canaris was forced to dismiss Oster, who came under virtual house arrest.

Once again Himmler came to Canaris' rescue. Possibly he used Göring's dependence on him to help have Roeder taken off the case; at all events Roeder was appointed Chief Justice of Air Fleet IV shortly afterwards. The actual instruction to wind up the investigation came from Keitel, who wrote on the top sheet of Roeder's interim report that Himmler had declined to read it and was not interested in proceeding against Canaris; 'the old man should be left in peace.'[58]

Von Dohnanyi's arrest and Oster's removal from office crippled the organisational centre of the conservative resistance. However, von Dohnanyi had already arranged for Langbehn to liaise with Karl Wolff to put out feelers from the opposition to Himmler. That this had gone a long way by spring 1943 is suggested by an entry in von Hassell's diary for 24/25 May: 'Kurzfuss [the code he used for Langbehn] asserted that the highest SS leadership has come to recognise the need to eliminate Hitler'; the 'decent' [*gutgesinnten*], he went on, were having ever more frequent discussions about the possibility, if all else failed, of using the SS to bring down the regime and prevent the internal disorder that must otherwise result. 'Afterwards naturally one wants to eliminate the SS.' The only questions were whether Himmler and his fellows would dare, and if they were to what impression this would make abroad, where the SS was regarded, with justice, as embodying the devil.[59]

Although Langbehn knew Himmler personally, like all who wanted to see him he had to work through Wolff, and there had been a lapse in the conversations since mid-February, when Wolff had become seriously ill. Himmler's old friend, Professor Gebhardt, had taken him into his clinic at Hohenlychen and diagnosed a stone in the kidney (renal calculus), for which he needed an operation; he advised him that the chances of survival were less than even. This spurred Wolff to ask Himmler once again for permission to divorce his brunette wife Frieda in order to marry the blonde Gräfin. Again Himmler refused him, whereupon he went over Himmler's head to Hitler, who gave his blessing. This piqued Himmler, who did not visit him once, only sending Häschen to tell him there was no justification for changing his wife.[60] Wolff did so, nonetheless, a few days before the operation, which he survived.

In late July, when Mussolini was deposed, Wolff was still convalescing. Himmler recalled him, post-haste and irrespective of health, to his field headquarters near Lötzen and told him he was to prepare to take over as his representative in Italy with the title of Highest – instead of the usual Higher – SSPF; he wanted a memorandum on how he would take those thoroughly defeatist people in hand. While preparing it Wolff resumed his conversations with Langbehn, attempting to arrange for Himmler to see a more senior member of the opposition, Johannes Popitz, former Prussian Finance Minister, and provisionally designated Finance Minister in the Beck–Goerdeler post-Hitler government.[61]

It is at this point, with the opposing pressures on Himmler increasing by the day, on the one hand to preserve the internal discipline of the Axis in face of repeated shocks, on the other hand to remove Hitler and install a government with which the west might feel able to talk, that it is legitimate to speculate on which side of the balance Heydrich would have thrown his weight and what might have been achieved. But Heydrich was dead. Kaltenbrunner entirely lacked his intelligence or iron resolution or influence; Schellenberg, at one time the favourite to succeed him, had the intelligence and had been trying since August 1942 to persuade Himmler to offer peace terms to the west from a position of strength before US productive capacity began to overwhelm the Axis, but he lacked the power to do more than prod and urge. The only leader with the power and organisation to bring about a change of regime was Himmler. Thus far he must have been dissuaded by the answers received from the west, for as von Hassell had noted his name was coupled with Hitler's as a synonym for all evil. Together with his constitutional inability to take large decisions, his awe of Hitler (despite the signs of mental instability he could discern) and his addiction to short-term tactical manoeuvring, these dusty answers surely helped to keep him loyal. Yet as Germany's situation deteriorated and with it the mood of the population, despite his outward show of confidence he was inwardly torn between what Schellenberg, Ohlendorf and others represented as his duty to National Socialism and the *Volk*, and the duty to the Führer for which he had pledged himself and his Order.

These opposing pressures heightened through the second half of August. On the one hand he came under Hitler's direct influence during visits to the Wolfschanze on no less than six occasions between 19 August and the end of the month; on the other hand the SD public opinion reports indicated an almost total collapse of morale in the population at large: the report on the 19th suggested that accounts of reverses on the eastern front together with continuous air attacks on German cities had reduced the people in all parts of the Reich to a state of 'oppressed seriousness' or 'anxiety';[62] by the 26th the same causes, above all the evacuation of Kharkov once again and air-raids on the Reich capital, had deepened 'the apprehension and fear in face of what is coming'. The question of what was going to happen ruled 'all conversations about the situation everywhere in and out of homes and workplaces, on the streets and in public houses, often between total strangers'.[63] It is probably no coincidence that Ohlendorf was at Himmler's field headquarters for several days towards the end of the month attempting to win Kersten to his side in his struggle to persuade Himmler of the seriousness of the position. Both sides, it seems, were wrestling for the soul of the hesitant Reichsführer.

During this period, after Wolff had completed his memorandum on how he would take over civil power in Italy, Himmler took him to the Wolfschanze; arriving at the barrier to the inner compound he dropped him and told him he could go swimming: 'I do not need you any more today.' He then saw Hitler alone and presented the ideas in the memorandum.[64]

Wolff's biographer Jochen Lang assumes that he went in alone in case Wolff should reveal a version of his talks with the opposition in order to damage him fatally and succeed him as Reichsführer. One of Wolff's stories after the war was that at the time of his kidney complaint Himmler had tried to induce him to have massage treatment – instead of seeing a doctor – hoping thereby to rid himself of a dangerous rival; Professor Gebhardt seemed to support this suspicion in his post-war testimony. However that may be, most if not all of Himmler's presentations to Hitler were 'under four eyes' only.

On 21 August Wolff told Langbehn he had arranged an appointment for Popitz to see Himmler on the 26th. By this date Hitler had decided on a reshuffle of posts, moving Himmler's nominal superior, Wilhelm Frick, Minister of the Interior and Plenipotentiary for Reich Administration, to the Protectorate to take over from von Neurath, and appointing Himmler Minister of the Interior in addition to his other posts. The changes, which must have caused Himmler some gratification that at last he was being accorded recognition, were announced on the 25th. Outside Germany his appointment was interpreted as a warning to the German people that the Nazi Party was in control and meant to remain so and that the fight would be continued to the bitter end.[65] That this was exactly the interpretation inside Germany is suggested for example by this letter to Himmler from an SA Sturmbannführer:

> Most esteemed and dear Reichsführer!
> Your appointment as Innenminister has been greeted with delight by all decent Party comrades and people. Now finally all the traitors who dare to disparage our beloved Führer will be called to account. Please be cautious so that you are preserved for the Führer and us. I believe the 'right-reaction' is more dangerous than the left. The traitors talk a lot about Germany, but they always mean themselves. What the Führer fought for and gave to the *Volk* should be destroyed. What a pity that in the time of need you cannot have the magnificent Obergruppenführer Heydrich by your side.
> Heil Hitler! Yours, Eugen Spenke[66]

On 26 August, the day this letter should have been delivered to Himmler's headquarters, he received Popitz in his new office in the Ministry of the Interior. He could scarcely have chosen a more significant venue for the meeting with this emissary from the opposition; was it deliberate, fortuitous or perhaps a subconscious signal to his rational self as much as to Popitz? Wolff and Langbehn waited in the ante-room while the two talked. Wolff, according to his post-war account, had had a recording machine built in to Himmler's desk, which worked perfectly. Apparently Popitz began by flattering Himmler's vanity as the guardian of National Socialist values under attack by Party corruption and misdirection of the war effort. The war was no longer winnable, he went on, and if they carried it on as formerly they were heading for defeat or stalemate at best. On the other hand Great Britain and the United States recognised the danger of Bolshevism and were ready to negotiate – but not with von Ribbentrop.[67] In the ante-room Langbehn told Wolff he hoped Popitz would speak out openly; only a frank discussion made sense in present conditions. Popitz was cautious though – for very obvious reasons – and did not say all that was on his mind, particularly about the necessary forcible removal of Hitler and the co-operation he, Goerdeler, Jessen, von Hassell and the others expected from certain generals. Himmler, while remaining as always noncommittal, scrutinising him from behind his pince-nez, showed no sign of disapproving the general trend of the argument, and the following day Wolff arranged with Langbehn for Popitz to see Himmler again to take the discussion further. Langbehn immediately travelled to Switzerland to inform his western contacts of this encouraging news.

On his return he reported to Himmler, who asked factual questions and appeared to treat the project absolutely seriously. Langbehn mentioned the need to eliminate Hitler, but since this had been the constant factor in all talks with the west this could not have surprised Himmler; apparently it did not disturb him either.[68] Whether Himmler had the second meeting with Popitz is not entirely clear for the whole negotiation had to be closed down hurriedly. The story, deriving from the director of US intelligence (OSS) in Switzerland, Allen Dulles, and supported by Schellenberg's memoirs, is that a coded message about Langbehn's mission sent by an allied agency in Switzerland, neither American nor British, was intercepted by the Gestapo, and that 'Gestapo' Müller, who was intriguing against Himmler, passed it to Bormann, who was jealous of Himmler's increasing power. Thus it came to Hitler's attention. In order to clear himself Himmler was forced to order Langbehn's arrest. It is significant, however, that Langbehn was not subjected to 'sharpened interrogation' – the euphemism for torture – at Gestapo headquarters, but was held at Himmler's pleasure in a concentration camp out of Kaltenbrunner's or Müller's reach. Popitz was not even arrested.

It is not necessary to see Himmler's flirtation with the opposition in black and white terms as either a genuine move against Hitler or on the other hand a high-level provocation to probe and keep the leading opposition figures under observation. It is more explicable in terms of his natural bent for intrigue, for playing one grouping against another, for knowing everything, for keeping files on everyone, and for building and maintaining power through his secret knowledge; it is explicable above all perhaps in that byzantine world in terms of his skill in keeping all options open until forced to come down for one side or another. None of this tallied with the legend of 'der treue Heinrich', or with his public face – probably he did not recognise it himself – yet it fits his character better than would a firm decision to act against either his Führer or the internal opposition.

*

While he vacillated, the night over the German people and occupied Europe grew heavier. 'The tyranny, the terror, the loss of values of all kinds is greater than I could have believed possible a short time ago,' Helmuth James von Moltke had written the previous year to a friend in England. Von Moltke was a leader of the religious resistance known after the name of his family seat – passed down from the famous Field Marshal von Moltke – as the Kreisau Circle. A convinced anti-Nazi since before the *Machtergreifung* he had found shelter on the outbreak of war in the international legal division of the Abwehr. In his letter he wrote that an average of some twenty-five Germans were executed every day after sentence by the civil courts, seventy-five every day after sentence by courts martial, and hundreds every day in the concentration camps without pretence of a trial. He went on:

> The constant danger in which we live is formidable. At the same time the greater part of the population has been uprooted and has been conscripted to forced labour of some kind and has been spread over all the continent, untying all bonds of nature and surrounding and thereby loosing the beast in man, which is reigning. The few really good people who try to stem the tide are isolated . . . because they cannot trust their comrades and they are in danger from the hatred of the oppressed people.[69]

He discerned grounds for hope, however, the most important of which was a spiritual awakening among both Catholics and Protestants. The Catholic churches were crowded every Sunday, the Protestant churches not yet, but a movement had begun.

While von Moltke and the Kreisau Circle debated and planned endlessly and vainly with members of the other opposition groupings, knowing they were in constant danger of being denounced as defeatists or caught in treasonable discussions by Himmler's agents infiltrating a gathering, in Munich, birthplace and seat of the Party, another Christian group was acting with the directness and clarity of youth without heed for consequences. It was centred in the University of Munich and called itself the White Rose; its leaders were a student brother and sister, Hans and Sophie Scholl, and a professor, Kurt Huber. They and their fellows perhaps knew they were making a vain affirmation but it was a noble one and in the long view of history will shine with more lustre than the trimming political and military conspiracies with which the German resistance is chiefly identified – a White Rose dewed with tears, visible briefly, pellucidly, as a reminder to succeeding generations that there was courage and faith in the deepest German night.

The HSSPF South in Munich was Himmler's old colleague SS-Obergruppenführer Karl Freiherr von Eberstein. After the White Rose manifested itself with a demonstration, broadsheets and wall-slogans in January 1943, Himmler sent him instructions: he was to remove all visible police measures from the University and merely institute clandestine surveillance by the SD to discover the people behind the movement. 'I assume these wire-pullers are Catholic and reactionary circles.' For the present the Reich student-leader Scheel and *Gau* student-leader Dörfler would impose public order. A copy of the letter was sent to 'Gestapo' Müller.[70]

Two weeks after this, Stalingrad fell. The news came as an extraordinary shock to the whole German people. In the grave discussions of how it could have occurred another question took precedence: how many lives had been lost?[71] The White Rose printed thousands of leaflets and left them around the courtyard of the University.

> Who has counted the dead, Hitler or Goebbels – to be sure neither. In Russia thousands fall daily. It is the time of harvest and the reaper is in full swing among the ripe corn. Grief enters cottages in the homeland and no one is there to wipe dry the tears of the mothers, but Hitler lies to those whose dearest treasure he has robbed and driven to senseless death.
>
> Every word that comes from Hitler's mouth is a lie. If he says peace, he means war, and if in the most sacrilegious way he uses the name of the Almighty, he means the power of evil, the fallen angel, Satan. His mouth is the stinking gate of hell, and his power is debased. Certainly one must conduct the battle against the National Socialist terror-state with every rational means, but whoever today still doubts the real existence of demonic powers has widely misunderstood the metaphysical background to this war. Behind the concrete, behind material perceptions, behind all factual, logical considerations stands the irrational, i.e. the battle against the demon, against the emissaries of the Anti-Christ. . . .[72]

The undercover surveillance Himmler had ordered, or perhaps denunciations by indoctrinated students, led within days to the arrest of Hans and Sophie Scholl and several of their accomplices. They were tortured and executed. Their message outlived them; the leaflets were passed clandestinely, reaching far beyond Bavaria and making such an impression that the students were attacked by the propaganda organs as communists. One leaflet reached von Hassell:

> I have read the simple, magnificent, deeply moral national appeal which brought them to their death. Himmler certainly wanted no martyrs and – a few hours too late – requested postponement of the execution. It is important for the future that such an appeal has seen the light of day. It appears Professor Huber [in the meantime also arrested] is the author. At the execution the worthy siblings Scholl died as courageous and upright martyrs. Report of an eyewitness.[73]

The Munich students provided a spectacular example of resistance put down by the Gestapo; countless other individuals making lone protests or simply giving vent to 'defeatist' sentiments were denounced and suffered the same fate. One example, unnamed, was described in the SD opinion report on the day of the Scholls' arrest. It concerned an official from a department of state in Berlin, travelling by train and discussing the war situation with his travelling companions. 'I can assure you', he said after a long and most open debate, 'with one hundred per cent certainty that we have no *need* to lose this war – we have already lost it!'

A woman in the carriage remonstrated, 'If I were a man I would box your ears,' whereupon he became rude and told her that politics was not a matter for women, they understood nothing about it; he had a high position in Berlin and knew better: he could tell them it was inconceivable they would be able to muddle their way out of the mess they were in.[74]

Below this report was an ominous note that this official's name could be found out and measures had been initiated. Defeatist talk carried a death sentence; on the day in August that Himmler was appointed Minister of the Interior he dismissed an appeal by a Regierungsrat (government councillor) sentenced to death on this ground.

The prospect of German defeat animated resistance movements in every occupied country from western France to Russia, from Norway to Greece and the Balkans. The movements were aided by the allies and by the sheer crassness of Nazi occupation policy: in the east peoples who had greeted German forces as liberators from the oppression of Bolshevism had been turned into bitter enemies; even in the west naked exploitation and pillage, conscription for forced labour and the ruthless taking and shooting of hostages had bred hatred for the *Herrenmenschen*. Himmler and the SS were not alone to blame. Every organ of the Party and the Wehrmacht and the industrial power groupings shared responsibility for displaying what the French after the first war had called rightly the criminal arrogance of the German nation.

It was the military commander of occupied France, Otto von Stülpnagel, who in August and September 1941 had issued what became known as the 'hostages code': all Frenchmen held in custody by the German authorities or on behalf of the German authorities or by the French authorities because of communist activities were to be regarded as hostages responsible with their lives for the impeccable conduct of the population; 'in cases of an incident which necessitates the shooting of hostages . . . the district leader in whose territory the incident happened is to select from the list of prisoners [hostages] persons whose execution he wishes to propose to me.'[75] A similar code had been issued by von Falkenhausen for Belgium and Seyss-Inquart for Holland, neither of whom were SS. Since this policy had proved counter-productive, a new policy of *Nacht und Nebel* (night and fog) had been devised by Hitler and promulgated in all western occupied countries; hostages simply disappeared without the public or relatives finding out what had happened to them or where. This policy was carried out by all German authorities, not only the Gestapo and SD, although they were the final executive.

In the bitter guerrilla warfare among the mountains of Yugoslavia and Greece, it was not only SS anti-partisan units that committed atrocities, executed guerrillas caught in action, deported able-bodied 'suspects' to slave-labour camps, murdered civilians, women and children and razed whole villages to the ground in deliberate terror operations; many Wehrmacht units did the same with equal ferocity. Wehrmacht prison cells were as bare of every amenity and as noisome and lice-infested as Gestapo cells; Wehrmacht prisoners were starved and beaten with as much enthusiasm by the secret military police (Geheime Feldpolizei) as by the SS and SD with whom they co-operated. Wehrmacht prisoners or 'hostages' were transported to slave labour packed in cattle trucks without food or water in the same way as Eichmann sent Jews to Auschwitz. This was not confined to those units engaged in partisan war in the east. A French non-commissioned officer named Paul Roser who refused to work after being taken prisoner – citing the Geneva Convention on the treatment of prisoners of war – described at Nuremberg the way he was sent to a Wehrmacht 'disciplinary' camp at Rawa-Ruska, near Belzec in the General Gouvernement:

> We were stripped of our clothes, of our shoes, of all the food which some of us had been able to keep. We were placed in [railway] cars, in each of which the number varied from fifty-three to fifty-six. The trip lasted six days. . . . we were given soup on two occasions only . . . and the soup was not edible. We remained for thirty-six hours without anything to drink.[76]

Attempts at escape from Rawa-Ruska were punished by guards rushing out on the prisoner 'beating him with the butts of their pistols in the face, with bayonets, with the butts of rifles'; more usually they shot or bayonetted those captured attempting escape. Among the most horrible sights Roser witnessed at this Wehrmacht camp was the arrival of a batch of Russian prisoners of war, survivors of a detachment decimated by typhus:

> It was on a Sunday afternoon that I watched this spectacle, which was like a nightmare. The Russians arrived in rows, five by five, holding each other by the arms, as none of them could walk by themselves – 'walking skeletons' was really the only fitting description. . . . The colour of their faces was not even yellow, it was green. Almost all squinted as if they had not strength enough to focus their sight. They fell by rows, five men at a time. The Germans rushed on them and beat them with rifle butts and whips. . . .[77]

Himmler, the SS, SD and Gestapo were the chief agents of terror which was both cause and effect of the vicious, rising cycle of resistance and oppression throughout Europe. Terror was the method in which the Party was born. Terror begat terror. Yet all three armed services assisted in the restoration of internal discipline by this means and, like the big industrialists, made use of slave labour for their war production, co-operated with the SD and handed over certain categories of prisoner to them 'for special treatment' in full knowledge of the meaning of that euphemism. Himmler was, as he had always been, merely the most extreme, emotionally committed exponent of the orthodoxy of the master race.

The systematic terror of the Gestapo torture chambers is perhaps the most persistent image of this period of growing resistance; the same primitive methods are described by victims everywhere. Arbitrary and indiscriminate beatings with rubber truncheons and whips occur with numbing repetition:

> . . . I had to bend over a bench and the muscles of my thighs and calves were fully stretched. At first I received some thirty lashes with a heavy whip, then another instrument was used with a buckle at the end. I was then struck on the buttocks, on the thighs and calves. To do this my torturer got up on a bench and made me spread my legs. Then with a very thin thong, he finished off by giving me some twenty more biting lashes. When I picked myself up I was dizzy and fell to the ground. I was always picked up again. . . .[78]

This French victim, M. Labussière, listed the methods of torture used by the Gestapo: the lash; the bath, full of cold water into which the victim was plunged head first and held until asphyxiated, then revived by artificial respiration, and if he did not talk he was thrust in again; the electric treatment, in which terminals were placed on hands, feet and genitals; the testicle-crushing press, varied by twisting the testicles; the pulley, for hauling people up by their hands behind their back, jerking them up and down, then leaving them to hang for long periods, often dislocating one or both arms; the soldering lamp, for burning feet or other sensitive spots.

Pins or tapers inserted under fingernails were another standard treatment, and as in the concentration camps sadists invented their own variations and forms of humiliation and psychological torture. M. Labussière was told by his torturer whom he had heard beating a woman, 'It was your wife I have just beaten. I'll go on doing it just as long as you refuse to talk.'[79]

Of all the suffering for which Himmler bore ultimate responsibility as Reichsführer-SS and chief of the German police, by far the greatest in terms of numbers and long-drawn-out deliberate dehumanisation and daily fear and deprivation occurred in the concentration camps. All, barring those in the General Gouvernement used exclusively as extermination camps, had been turned over to the war economy; Himmler and Pohl were attempting to re-educate Kommandants and staff in the new necessities of caring for the inmates to increase their workrate, yet Eicke's tradition was too strong, the facilities and rations available too poor, the human material of the staff and Kapos – many indeed were convicted criminals – too base, the ideology of the master race and the workslave too ingrained to admit of much change except for the worse as numbers of inmates increased. For Himmler had instructed the RSHA to round up as many able-bodied foreign workers as possible for the camps, using a number of pretexts.[80]

Pohl admitted the material inadequacies when addressing a complaint by Albert Speer that April 1943. Speer had expressed dismay at a projected expenditure for work in the concentration camps of 7 million Reichsmarks and using 1000 tons of building materials, over 6000 cubic metres of timber; above all he objected to the workforce involved when what the Reich needed urgently were 'tanks, mineral oil and U-boats'.[81] Pohl pointed out to Himmler: 'Reichsminister Speer appears not to know that we have 160,000 inmates at present and are fighting continually against epidemics and a high deathrate because the billeting of the prisoners and the sanitary arrangements are totally inadequate. . . .'[82]

For something of the reality behind this exchange, here is Madame Vaillant-Couturier testifying to the Nuremberg tribunal. In January 1943 she had been taken from the fortress at Romainville, where she had been held as a hostage, and packed into a railway car with sixty other French women: they were given no food or drink for the next four days during a journey to an unknown destination.

> At the various stopping places we asked the Lorraine soldiers of the Wehrmacht who were guarding us whether we would arrive soon; and they replied, 'If you knew where you are going, you would not be in a hurry to get there.'
> We arrived at Auschwitz at dawn. The seals on our cars were broken, and we were driven out by blows with the butt end of a rifle and taken to Birkenau camp. . . .[83]

On the way they met 'columns of living skeletons going to work'. They were led to the disinfection station where their heads were shaved, and numbers were tattooed on their forearms, thence naked to a steam bath and a cold shower watched over by SS men and women, after which each was given soiled and torn prison clothing. In the living block to which they were assigned, nine had to sleep on a single bunk measuring some six feet by six without mattress or blanket; 'every time one of the nine moved, she disturbed the whole row.' At 3.30 in the morning they were woken by the shouting of the guards and driven with cudgel blows to rollcall, where they waited in the frozen air until dawn at seven or eight o'clock when, after being counted by the Aufseherinnen, the German women guards in uniform, who had cudgels and beat them 'more or less at random', they were led off in work detachments:

> The work at Auschwitz consisted of clearing demolished houses, road building, and especially the draining of marsh land. . . . During the work the SS men and women who stood guard over us would beat us with cudgels and set their dogs on

us. Many of our friends had their legs torn by the dogs. I even saw a woman torn to pieces under my very eyes when Tauber, a member of the SS, encouraged his dog to attack her and grinned at the sight.

The causes of death were extremely numerous. First of all there was the complete lack of washing facilities. When we arrived at Auschwitz, for 12,000 inmates there was only one tap of water unfit for drinking, and it was not always flowing. As this tap was in the German wash-house we could reach it only by passing through the guards who were German common-law women prisoners, and they beat us horribly as we went by. For more than three months we remained without washing our clothes. When there was snow, we melted some to wash in. Later, in the spring when we went to work we would drink from a puddle by the roadside and then wash our underclothes in it. We took turns washing our hands in this dirty water. . . .[84]

The method of feeding was another cause of mortality and epidemics; food was distributed in large red mess tins. Since many of the women were ill and lacked the strength to get up at night and go out to the trench serving as a lavatory, 'the access to which was beyond description, they used these containers for a purpose for which they were not meant.' Next day after being emptied the tins were taken back to the kitchen and rinsed in cold water before the meal was ladled in. Those who grew too weak from illness, exposure, hard work and insufficient nourishment were taken to Block 25.

This Block 25, which was the ante-room of the gas chamber, if one may so express it, is well known to me because at that time we had been transferred to Block 26 and our windows opened on the yard of Number 25. One saw piles of corpses piled up in the courtyard and from time to time a hand or a head would stir among the bodies, trying to free itself. . . . there were rats as big as cats running about gnawing the corpses and even attacking the dying who had not enough strength to chase them away.[85]

A working camp with an even more frightful reputation than Auschwitz, if that were possible, was Mauthausen. Maurice Lampe, who arrived there in a convoy of some 1200 Frenchmen, early the following year, described to the Nuremberg tribunal how they were greeted by the SS officer receiving them: 'I shall quote from memory almost word for word: "Germany needs your arms. You are, therefore, going to work; but I want to tell you that you will never see your families again. When one enters this camp, one leaves it by the chimney of the crematorium." '[86]

Conditions were such in Mauthausen that Himmler decreed no inmates should ever be released. Besides a literal form of 'working to death' in the stone quarries (which had determined the choice of site) or in various workshops erected nearby to utilise inmate labour, Mauthausen was used for the execution of batches of prisoners consigned to the SD 'for special treatment'.

Himmler at the podium. A benign, schoolmasterly style, delivered with a light Bavarian accent.

Sepp Dietrich, commander of the Leibstandarte Adolf Hitler, and Himmler outside Warsaw during the Polish campaign, 1939.

Einsatzkommando in action in Poland, 1940, shooting Polish nationalists and intellectuals.

Himmler inspects a Waffen-SS division in the East.

Punishment posts at Buchenwald concentration camp.

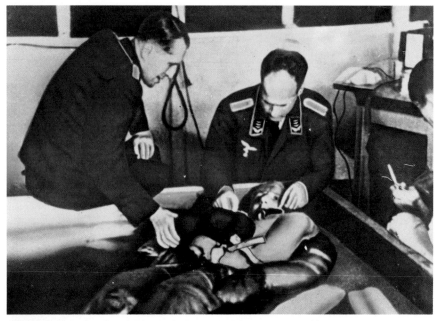
'Resuscitation after freezing' experiments at Dachau concentration camp, 1942.

'Experimental subject' in the high altitude chamber at Dachau, 1942.

Hitler and his paladins, 1943. *From left:* 'the Reichsmarschall' Hermann Göring, Feldmarschall Wilhelm Keitel, Grossadmiral Karl Dönitz and Heinrich Himmler. (Himmler to Dönitz: 'One thing is certain, Herr Grossadmiral: the Reichsmarschall will in no wise be the successor!')

Einsatzkommando in action in the East, May 1943; the victims stand naked at the edge of a mass grave.

Hitler congratulates his most loyal Reichsführer on his forty-third birthday, 7 October 1943, at the field headquarters 'Wolfschanze'; Martin Bormann looks on.

Jews are rounded up for despatch to the gas chamber at Treblinka, during the destruction of the Warsaw ghetto, 1943.

Executions following the Warsaw uprising, 1944.

The empire of the camps, 1945.

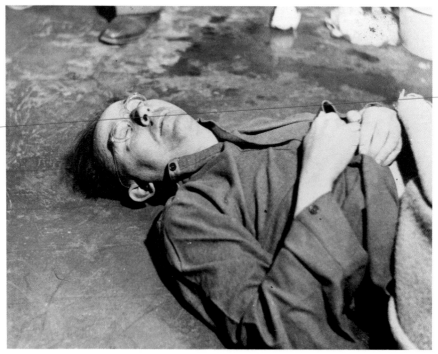

Himmler cheats the hangman, May 1945.

Lampe's first employment was carrying stones up from the quarry which lay in a hollow 186 rough-hewn steps below the camp. On one occasion, while working in a team of twelve, all Frenchmen, under a German Kapo, who was a common criminal, and an SS guard, two of his fellows were murdered within an hour. 'They were murdered because they had not understood the order, given them in German, detailing them for a task.'[87]

Later in the war he witnessed the execution of forty-seven British, American and Dutch airmen who had landed by parachute. They were made to undress down to a shirt and underpants with no shoes, then assembled in front of the camp office and told by the Kommandant that they were all under sentence of death.

> For all the prisoners at Mauthausen, the murder of these men has remained in their minds like a scene from Dante's Inferno. This is how it was done: at the bottom of the steps they loaded stones on the backs of these poor men and they had to carry them to the top. The first journey was made with stones weighing 25 to 30 kilos and was accompanied by blows. Then they were made to run down. For the second journey the stones were still heavier; and whenever the poor wretches sank under their burden, they were kicked and hit with a bludgeon. Even stones were hurled at them. . . . In the evening when I returned from the gang with which I was then working, the road which led to the camp was a bath of blood. . . . I almost stepped on the lower jaw of a man. Twenty-one bodies were strewn along the road. Twenty-one had died on the first day. The twenty-six others died the following morning. . . .[88]

On another occasion which Lampe described, Himmler inspected the camp and was presented with the execution of fifty Russian officers. Himmler watched the beginning of the process as the Russians were called up singly to the execution room, reached by a stairway; he left before the end.

> The Soviet Army officers were called one by one, and there was a sort of human chain between the group which was awaiting its turn and that which was on the stairway listening to the shots which killed their predecessors. They were all killed by a shot in the neck. . . . we saw the condemned men who were waiting on the stairway opposite us embrace each other before they were parted. . . .[89]
>
> As a general rule, all Soviet officers, all Soviet commissars, or members of the Bolshevik Party were executed at Mauthausen. . . .[90]

Mauthausen was but one extreme example of the way in which the ideology of the master race and the dogma of terror, besides encouraging and, for its practitioners, excusing depravity, was senselessly wasteful and counter-productive. Mauthausen had been classed in 1941 as a Category 3 camp for incorrigible criminals and asocials incapable of re-education; while the distinctions between categories of camps tended to disappear in the pressures of total war, Mauthausen preserved a specially vicious aura.

If Himmler's desire to see the killing processes at Mauthausen, Auschwitz, Treblinka and the rest, and the Kommandants' evident desire to please their chief with impeccable demonstrations, reveal much about his psychology – and theirs – the experiments on inmates which he patronised are more revealing still. One which seems to have derived entirely from his complex of subconscious urges since he insisted on it against advice, was carried out by Dr Rascher at Dachau. After the high-altitude experiments had been completed the previous spring, the Luftwaffe had requested another series of experiments to throw light on the problems of reviving aircrew shot down over the sea. It appears that the request may have originated with Generaloberstabarzt Professor Dr Hippke of the Luftwaffe, who asked that three university professors whom he named for inclusion in the research team be investigated for their political reliability by the Gestapo. However, the formal proposal came from Generalfeldmarschall Milch in a letter to Karl Wolff dated 20 May 1942. Himmler gave his approval and the research programme had begun in August 1942. Probably, in accordance with his usual practice, Himmler watched an early demonstration.

Selected inmates, dressed in full flying kit with rubber or kapok lifejackets – or in later series undressed and naked or in special protective suits – wired up with temperature, pulse and other recorders, were immersed in a chamber of ice-cold water – 2.5–12 degrees C – and their struggles observed:

> After five to ten minutes of chilling there was a definite lowering of the intensity of perception of pain. Rigidity of the muscles developed at the same time . . . occasionally interrupted by clonic–tonic convulsions . . . [and] a marked inhibition of breathing. Some subjects said they felt as if an iron ring were being drawn around their chests. Expiration was prolonged and obviously difficult. . . . Consciousness began to cloud when rectal temperature reduced to 31 degrees C. . . . [92]

It took up to one and a half hours for the subjects' temperature to fall to 29.5 degrees, and it continued falling after they were removed from the water. Most subjects were brought down to 26.5 degrees C, then various methods of rewarming were attempted. It was soon demonstrated that death occurred only among those whose lifesaving equipment allowed the back of their head to immerse. The other major finding in the interim report Rascher submitted to Himmler on 10 September 1942 was that rapid rewarming in a hot bath was preferable to slow rewarming by blankets and other means. Rascher concluded that they could 'dispense with attempts to save intensely chilled subjects by means of animal heat. Rewarming by animal warmth – animal bodies or women's bodies – would be too slow.'[93]

Himmler replied on 27 September, insisting that, despite this submission, all possible measures should be tested thoroughly, namely rapid rewarming, drugs, medicines and 'animal warmth'.[94] Animal warmth was a euphemism for the embrace of a woman; it may be that Himmler was running true to his belief in folklore since he had heard that the Frisian islanders resuscitated shipwrecked sailors in this way; it may be that there was more than an element of sexual voyeurism in his instruction. In any case it is noteworthy that it was not Dr Rascher who was keen to perform this trial, but Himmler who instructed him.

Rascher applied to Obersturmbannführer Sievers, chief of Ahnenerbe, to which he was attached, for four female gypsies for this purpose. In the meantime the research team, Professor Dr E. Holzlöhner of the University of Kiel, Rascher and Dr E. Finke, submitted their report on the main series of tests. Eight days later, Himmler wrote to Rascher, trusting that he (Rascher) would receive the credit he was due for this work; perhaps he anticipated that, as happened, Professor Holzlöhner would claim it for himself. His letter continued:

> People who today still disapprove of experiments on human beings, but who prefer to let brave German soldiers die from the consequences of intense cold, are to me nothing but traitors to their country, and I shall not hesitate to supply the names of these people to the authorities who are in a position to take action against them.[95]

He then suggested that the revival of victims in small craft with no facilities for a hot bath might be facilitated with blankets into which warmth packages had been sewn – 'I suppose you know of the warmth packages which we use in the SS, and which the Russians also use.' He concluded: 'I am very curious about the experiments with animal warmth. I personally assume that these experiments may perhaps produce the best and most lasting success. Of course I may be mistaken.'

On 5 November four women from Ravensbrück concentration camp, who had been pressed into service as camp prostitutes, were made available to Rascher, and on 13 November Himmler visited Dachau and witnessed his experiments. It must be assumed that since the main series had been completed the previous month the ones he saw involved the women from Ravensbrück. In his report on the 'animal warmth' experiments, dated 17 February 1943, Rascher described immersing 'the experimental persons in the usual way – clothed or unclothed – in cold water between 4 and 9 degrees C', removing them when their body temperature had dropped to 30 degrees C, by which time all were unconscious: 'In eight cases the experimental persons were laid in a wide bed between two naked women. The women had to snuggle up as close as possible to the chilled people. Then the three persons were covered with blankets. . . .'[96]

Despite the fact that the experimental subjects realised their situation directly as they regained consciousness and snuggled up as closely as they could to the females, their body temperature only rose at about the speed of those subjects who had been wrapped in blankets. Exceptions were provided by four men who had sexual intercourse with the women; after intercourse their temperature rose at a very rapid rate 'which can be compared to warming in a hot bath'.

Another interesting result was that experiments using only one woman showed a more rapid rewarming than with two. One death occurred from a cerebral haemorrhage. Rascher's conclusion from this series of experiments was that animal warmth was a 'very slow' method and could not be recommended except in cases where there were no other possibilities of rewarming.[97]

In the meantime the Chief Physician or Reichsarzt of the SS, Gruppenführer Dr Grawitz, probably piqued by the fact that Rascher and his experiments were controlled within the SS by Sievers of Ahnenerbe – who was not even a doctor – raised the objection that exposure to dry cold might produce different results; this should be tested before any general conclusions were drawn. Accordingly Rascher had done some preliminary tests on this question; in the letter of 17 February 1943, accompanying his 'animal warmth' report, he wrote:

> Up to the present I have carried out intense chilling experiments on thirty human beings by leaving them outside naked from nine to fourteen hours, thereby reducing their body temperature to 27–29 degrees. After an interval which was supposed to correspond to a period of transport lasting one hour, I placed these experimental subjects in a hot bath. In all experiments to date all subjects were successfully rewarmed within another hour despite the fact that their hands and feet were partly frozen white. . . . No fatalities occurred as a result of this extraordinarily rapid method of rewarming. . . .[98]

Himmler was applying for Rascher's release from the Luftwaffe and transfer to the Waffen-SS, where he would have full control over his experiments, and Rascher suggested that directly he was transferred he should continue his researches on people chilled by dry cold at Auschwitz: 'Auschwitz is in every way more suitable for such a large serial experiment than Dachau because it is colder there and the greater expanse of open country within the camp would allow the experiments to be less conspicuous (the experimental subjects bellow when they freeze severely). . . .'[99]

He begged Himmler to give the necessary order so that the remaining winter months could be used for these experiments, 'so important for the Army fighting on land'. Himmler granted him permission on 26 February for 'mass experiments under natural conditions' at Auschwitz or Lublin, and on 6 March Rascher was able to report that he had taken advantage of a spell of heavy frost to freeze a number of naked subjects for fourteen hours at a stretch, bringing their body temperatures down to 25 degrees C; despite frost injuries at the extremities, all had been rewarmed successfully in hot baths.[100]

With the exception of the experiments on rewarming with naked women, which may be ascribed either to Himmler's simple faith in folklore or to sexually sadistic drives – perhaps both – his correspondence makes clear that he believed he had the most valid reason for subjecting his prisoners to this torture by cold, namely to save the lives of German sailors and airmen and his own troops fighting in the east. The subjects, by contrast, were 'criminals' and '*Untermenschen*' – in fact chiefly Poles, Russians and Jews – and to be dissuaded by false humanitarian sentiment was tantamount to treason. Of course, having sanctioned the experiments and witnessed the ordeals the subjects were put through, it was necessary for him to believe this. Yet once again it is notable how many outside the SS, while not expressing themselves in such black and white extremes, were prepared, with or without scruple, to go down the same road – Professor Dr Hippke, Professor Dr Holzlöhner, Generalfeldmarschall Milch and numerous medical researchers.

Meanwhile at Auschwitz the more nauseating experiments into sterilisation by X-ray, suggested by Victor Brack for the negative population policy in the east, were in full swing. The Luftwaffe physician Dr Horst Schumann had been chosen to conduct them. He had a large room in the women's infirmary, Block 30 at Birkenau, where he sat inside a lead-sheathed cubicle to protect himself from radiation, calling in his subjects one by one. They were comparatively healthy young men and women in their late teens or early twenties selected chiefly from the latest Jewish transports, and unaware of their fate. The women had to stand between two plates, the men had to place their genitals on a plate; Schumann then switched on the machine, which hummed. After some five to eight minutes, by which time many received burns, the machine was switched off. Subsequently the women's ovaries were removed and sent for pathological examination; the men were forced to ejaculate with a crude wooden device, and afterwards had one or both testicles removed and similarly sent away for testing. The doctor who performed these operations was a Polish prisoner, Wladislaw Dering, who passed apparently through an initial stage of terrorised subservience to eager co-operation with the aims of the programme.[101]

His methods were rough and unsterilised. The women were locally anaesthetised with a spinal injection while being held under restraint, after which the operation was performed crudely and with great haste inside ten minutes. Apart from the terrifying experience itself the subjects suffered from debilitating internal infections and complications afterwards and the mortality rate was very high – not that this was especially relevant since all Jewish and gypsy victims and all in possession of state secrets – which these were – were destined for the gas chamber in any case. The extent of Dering's desensitisation and eventual total identification with his masters' policy may be gauged from the fact that he made himself a tobacco pouch from the scrotum of a Jew whose testicles he had removed, which he liked to display to his colleagues.

The aim of the programme was well known in the camp. Madame

Vaillant-Couturier, who was employed for a time in the infirmary and saw the queues of young Jewesses standing before the X-ray room, was told it openly: 'They did not conceal it. They said that they were trying to find the best method for sterilising so as to replace the native population in the occupied countries by Germans after one generation, once they had made use of the inhabitants as slaves to work for them.'[102] Madame Vaillant-Couturier could not possibly have read Himmler's speeches to this effect by the date of the Nuremberg tribunal where she gave this testimony.

In the late spring of 1943 the X-ray apparatus was transferred from Birkenau to Block 10 in Auschwitz main camp, sometimes known as 'Clauberg's Block' since it had been created for his sterilisation experiments into the fallopian tubes. Schumann continued his work here, and other doctors studied pre-cancerous growths of the cervix. Women of all ages, selected from incoming Jewish transports according to the categories required by the experimenters, were housed as guinea-pigs and lived in an atmosphere of perpetual apprehension about what they would be used for next. The appearance of Dr Clauberg himself in the ward produced feelings of terror. One prisoner doctor who had to assist in this work described the block as a cross between hell and a mental institution.[103]

The description could serve for the experimental blocks in all the camps – indeed for the camps themselves – since in the atmosphere created by the ideology of the *Untermensch* and slave anything was permissible. Himmler attempted to maintain control over the purpose of experiments by insisting that proposals be submitted to him for approval,[104] but since his enthusiasms and idiosyncrasies were well known, it was easy to tailor the request to correspond. Dr Josef Mengele, who arrived at Auschwitz towards the end of May 1943, after being wounded on the eastern front, almost certainly had no need to adjust his proposal since his early research work had been concerned with racial differences in bone structure and the hereditary transmission of abnormalities, precisely the kind of enquiries which intrigued Himmler. Moreover it seems probable that Mengele's aims at the camp included determining genetic factors for breeding leaders, or, as a doctor who worked closely with him expressed it, 'to advance one step in the search to unlock the secret of multiplying the race of superior beings destined to rule'.[105] His research was in any case concerned with heredity and involved the detailed study of twins, whom he was able to gather in large quantities from incoming Jewish and gypsy transports. He seems to have been on the 'ramp' so frequently in his fanatic search for twins that many survivors remembered him as the doctor who was present at all selections from the trains, an elegant figure in uniform with decorations and a riding crop, looking at faces and bodies briefly before consigning them 'Links' or 'Rechts' – labour or the gas chambers.

These more notorious medical researches – proving the monumental insensitivity and lack of restraint which may be expected from educated, or at least scientific, men driven by the quest for knowledge and provided with powerless subjects believed to be inferior in an environment insulated from questions – are but a fraction of the number that Himmler authorised in the camps. The more important investigations, especially those concerned with mass sterilisation or increasing the possibilities of procreation, he followed with detailed interest and urged on.

Notwithstanding his interest in the experiments, Himmler's chief concern for the camps at this crisis of the war was their productive potential. He needed increased production, not simply because the parts of aeroplanes, anti-aircraft guns, carbines, shells, grenades, electrical components, uniforms, synthetics, building materials and other products to which the camp labour forces contributed were vital for the war effort, but because production figures were a tribute he could lay before Hitler and a weapon in his power struggles with Albert Speer and the officials of the Economics Ministry. Now he was constantly seeking ways of improving the health of camp inmates through dietary changes. After discussing the problem with Pohl in December 1942, he had sent him a note reminding him of the conclusion – curiously reminiscent of the concerns of the more progressive naval commanders of the eighteenth century:

> Try to obtain for the nourishment of the prisoners in 1943 the greatest quantity of raw vegetables and onions. In the vegetable season issue carrots, kohlrabi, white turnips and whatever such vegetables there are in large quantity and store up sufficient for the prisoners in the winter so that they have a sufficient quantity every day. I believe we will raise the state of health substantially thereby.[106]

He had also instigated dietary experiments in the camps, many of which, like Dachau and Auschwitz, had extensive herb and vegetable plantations. He placed his greatest hopes, though, in a system of rewards for higher productivity. After visiting Buchenwald camp, near Weimar, in March 1943, he wrote a long letter to Pohl betraying great agitation on this point:

> . . . I believe that at the present time we must be out there in the factories personally in unprecedented measure in order to drive them on with the lash of our words and use our energy to assist on the spot. The Führer is counting heavily on our production and our help and our ability to overcome all difficulties, just hurl them overboard and simply produce. I ask you and Glücks with all my heart to let no week pass by when one of you does not appear unexpectedly at this or that camp and goad, goad, goad [*antreibt, antreibt, antreibt*].[107]

He had discovered, he went on, that there was still no camp brothel in Buchenwald. He meant a brothel for the inmates; brothels were one of the normal perks for the SS themselves, and indeed for the Kapos. In the system of inducements for production he intended that the opportunity to visit a prostitute should be the third and final stage of reward for the skilled workers; the first stage he saw as an allowance of cigarettes or extra rations for meeting piece-work targets, the second stage a small wage up to 30–40 Pfennigs a day, the crown of the system a visit to the camp brothel once or twice a week: 'this whole latter complex is not excessively beautiful, but it is natural and if I have this naturalness as a means of inducing higher performance I consider that we are duty-bound to utilise it.' He asked Pohl to devote himself intensively to the whole question of a piece-work system and see whether he could find a man who could develop it throughout the camps in 'a downright artistic manner'. It must be possible for them to bring the same intelligence to the question as the Russians, who were goading their people to the most unbelievable performances and had discovered nothing short of a *perpetuum mobile*. They must have the new system working in the camps by 1 May at the latest.

As in the camp regimes, so in the practical application of eastern racial policy and recruitment into the Waffen-SS, the exigencies of war had wrought extraordinary changes. The chief cause remained shortage of manpower for the eastern front and the consequent need to enlist men from the conquered territories to combat the partisans active everywhere behind the lines. The notorious SS-Sonderkommando Dirlewanger, technically a Waffen-SS formation, was an example of such dilution. The unit had been raised originally from convicted German poachers under a Freikorps veteran named Oskar Dirlewanger; Himmler's recruiting chief, Berger, had rescued him from *Schutzhaft* as a recidivist sexual offender with minors. When the supply of poachers had dried up Dirlewanger had recruited criminals of every description, and finally Russians and Slavs; by early 1943 about half the force was non-German, half convicted criminals.[108]

There were other anti-partisan units formed from collaborators or Red Army defectors, notably the Kaminsky Brigade which operated behind Army Group Centre, and the 1st Russian SS National Regiment commanded by a former Red Army major Gill, who had defected – in his own words – 'not from political motives, but to save my skin'.[109] Instead of rotting from starvation and disease in a Wehrmacht camp or being handed over to the SD for 'special treatment' at Mauthausen or Auschwitz, Gill had elected to go for Gestapo training in 'pacification' measures; afterwards he had recruited a 'national unit' from Russian prisoners of war for operations against Soviet partisans. In the summer of 1943 a higher-ranking Soviet defector, the captured General Andrei Vlassov, was attempting to form from among his fellow countrymen taken prisoner a Russian Liberation Army (ROA) to assist the Germans in removing the Bolshevik yoke from his land. Gill, who had changed his name with his loyalties to Rodionov, was given the task of raising an ROA brigade; this was then committed alongside regular Waffen-SS units under the overall command of Himmler's anti-partisan supremo, Gruppenführer von dem Bach-Zelewski. It was a short-lived collaboration: partisans infiltrated the ROA and Gill–Rodionov was persuaded to purge his treachery by re-defecting; he did so on 13 August by attacking the attached SS units and passing back to the Soviet side, where his formation became the 1st Anti-Fascist Brigade. The other defecting brigade leader, Kaminsky, however, remained loyal to the Germans and later that year his anti-partisan brigade was incorporated officially into the Waffen-SS; Himmler appointed him SS-Oberführer.

An even more bizarre example of the fall from the elite and racial standards of entry for the Waffen-SS occurred in February 1943. Hitler sanctioned the recruitment of Moslems from Bosnia and Herzegovina in order to assist in the fight against their traditional enemies, the Serbian Christians who formed the majority of partisans in Yugoslavia. Moslem volunteers flocked to Berger's standard and when the flow stopped he drafted conscripts to bring the formation up to division strength. After training in the west they returned to the Balkans as the 13th Waffen-Gebirgs (Mountain) Division of the SS, Handschar. They wore a field-grey fez adorned with eagle and swastika and the SS death's-head badge, were allowed their religious observances and, as Himmler told Goebbels, were promised heaven by their mullahs if they were killed in action, 'a very practical and attractive religion for soldiers!'[110] he added. They soon established a reputation for atrocity in the cruel guerrilla warfare of the region.

Everywhere in the east the sharp lines of Himmler's racial ideas were being blurred by the necessities of war. The rival authorities and the opportunities for venality and corruption which the master race theory offered – not least to his own HSSPFs – added to the dilution of ideals. If he acknowledged this to himself or the possibility that the war might not end victoriously, it does not show in the directives which issued from his desk at field headquarters. In January 1943 he had ordered the 'General Plan East' enlarged to take in the Baltic provinces, White Russia and the Black Sea and Crimea regions.[111] The same month he ordered the erection of transit camps for children and teenagers of 'suspects' rounded up in anti-partisan operations, so that they could be racially evaluated and those with good blood reclaimed for the Reich. The 'racially worthless' were to be sent to the concentration camp workshops and factories as apprentices:

> Their education is to consist of instruction in obedience, diligence, unconditional subordination and loyalty towards the German masters. They must count up to 100, learn to recognise the traffic signs and be prepared for their trade as agricultural workers, fitters, stonemasons, carpenters etc. The girls are to be trained as workers on the land, weavers, spinners, knitters and similar occupations.[112]

Warsaw was a particular seat of subversion and racial anarchy. It was a centre for Polish resistance, both the AK or Home Army, directed by the exiled Polish government, and communist groupings; entrepreneurs were growing rich by employing Jewish labour, black marketeers by supplying foodstuffs smuggled in from the surrounding countryside since it was impossible to live on the official coupon rations; German managers were seeking to preserve *kriegswichtig* (war-essential) status by ordering and storing materials for which they had no use; Poles were registering for *Eindeutschung* for the better posts and rations and the use of *nur Deutsch* public facilities; officials were abetting it all; Himmler's SS and police leader there, Oberführer Dr von Sammern-Frankenegg, an Austrian, was amassing valuables, paintings and furs from the ghetto and indulging himself in wine and women on the proceeds;[113] the Wehrmacht Armaments Inspectorate was employing thousands of Jews in workshops and factories.

Himmler had been carrying on a paper battle on this question for months: the previous October he had instructed his HSSPF East, SS-Obergruppenführer Friedrich-Wilhelm Krüger, in Cracow to liaise with Pohl and round up all these 'so-called armaments workers in tailors', furriers' and cobblers' shops' and transfer them to a concentration camp. The Wehrmacht should then give its orders for uniforms and accessories to the SS who would guarantee delivery; he ordered severe measures against those who were merely using armaments work as a pretext for 'supporting the Jews and their businesses'. As for the Jews engaged in 'real armaments concerns' they were to be gathered in special factories which could be enclosed to form a few concentration camp firms. 'We will then endeavour to replace the Jewish workforce with Poles,' since 'one day, according to the wish of the Führer, the Jews should disappear.' Copies of this instruction had been sent to the Quartermaster-General of the Wehrmacht, Eduard Wagner, and the Armaments Inspectorate.[114]

In January 1943 Himmler paid a surprise visit to Warsaw and summoned the local representative of the Armaments Inspectorate, Colonel Fretter, to him. He learned that there were still 32,000 Jews employed in 'so-called armaments firms', some 24,000 of them in textile and leather, a very large number of these employed by one firm, Walter C. Toebbens, operating in the centre of the ghetto. He wrote to Krüger:

> I have charged Colonel Fretter to communicate to the Armaments Inspector, Lieutenant-General Schindler, my astonishment that my instructions respecting the Jews have not been followed.
>
> I have once again stipulated a time limit to 15.2.1943, by which the following are to be fulfilled:
>
> 1) Immediate elimination of the private firms. I consider it unconditionally necessary that the owners who have made themselves indispensable here be called up so far as practicable, and sent to the front.
>
> 2) I commission the RSHA to examine the books of the firm of Walter C. Toebbens most rigorously under a magnifying glass. If I am not mistaken here is a man formerly without means, who has developed in the course of three years into a wealthy owner, if not already a millionaire, and indeed only because we, the state, have driven the cheap Jewish workforce to him.

3) Immediate take-up of the whole 16,000 Jews in a concentration camp, preferably Lublin. Guarantee to deliver to the Armaments Inspectorate the same in regard to quantity and date as formerly. I believe, moreover, that it can be done more cheaply.

4) The same goes for a number of smaller ghetto-firms which make parts of machinery or aircraft, which too can be made in a camp.

5) The residue is to be gathered with utmost speed in some spot in the General Gouvernement so that one has a factory with a couple of 'shops' staffed with only Jewish workers, whose guarding and isolation are to receive the sharpest attention.[115]

By this time the Jews in the Warsaw ghetto had learned of the real destination and fate of those who had been deported to 'the east' and a Jewish Fighting Organisation, ZOB, had been formed. It consisted of twenty-two groups, each some twenty to thirty men and women strong, armed with smuggled revolvers, a few rifles and hand grenades, and Molotov cocktails (incendiary bottles); hundreds of bunker strongpoints had been established, connected by a warren of passages and the city sewer system. So it was that, when Krüger acted on his instructions and sent in a special SS Kommando to close the private ghetto firms and round up further consignments of Jews for Treblinka, it was met with armed resistance. The SS, surprised, withdrew. Three days later they launched a prepared attack under cover of gunfire and grenades, but were again forced to retire with several killed and wounded: this time it was the Jews' turn to be surprised at the ease with which they had repulsed the assault.[116]

On 16 February Himmler instructed Krüger that on security grounds the Warsaw Jews were to be transferred to a concentration camp and the ghetto torn down; otherwise Warsaw, 'a centre of subversion and resistance', could never be really pacified. He told Krüger to submit a complete plan of destruction. 'In any case the former living quarter of the 500,000 *Untermenschen* must disappear, and the city of Warsaw, always a dangerous seat of decay and subversion, be reduced in size.'[117]

He had just instructed his HSSPF France, SS-Brigadeführer Oberg, to submit plans for a similar radical solution to the '*Untermenschen*- and sabotage-nest' of Marseilles. Earlier he had sent Oberg a very hot wire for not flying to Marseilles to see for himself when ordered to act against the subversives there, instead submitting a recommendation to call in the military.[118] Oberg was ordered in peremptory terms to meet Daluege in Marseilles the next day. Subsequently Himmler instructed him to propose a plan at the earliest for the cleansing of the city; it should provide for the arrest of the criminal elements and their transport to a concentration camp – 'I propose a number of about 100,000' – together with the destruction by explosives of 'the underground passages and lairs' of the criminal quarter. He did not wish German lives hazarded: 'The French police and "Garde Mobile" have to be used to the greatest extent. The pigsty in Marseilles is a French pigsty. Only the fact that we must have peace there on military grounds causes me to clear out this pigsty. The French police and France might like to know they should be deeply thankful to us. . . .'[119]

By this time discussions with the Chief of French Police, Bousquet, about the 'removal from France of unwanted elements for us [Germans], such as Jews, communists, de Gaullists', had progressed to the point that Himmler was able to inform von Ribbentrop: 'The French police are ready to gather the Jews to begin with in three Prefectures, from whence we can then transport them to the east.' The Italians, he added, were making difficulties about allowing *their* Jews to be removed; he put it down to Jewish bribe-money to the officials. The same went for Switzerland and Spain. It was his opinion that the French police would assemble the Jews peacefully, then deliver them across the borders to Swiss or Spaniards. He asked von Ribbentrop to let him know what he thought about it all.[120]

Meanwhile in the General Gouvernement Krüger, a former Freikorps officer and expert in street-fighting, gathered intelligence about the defensive preparations in the Warsaw ghetto, and laid his plans. It took several weeks, and it was not until April that he put them before Himmler, telling him, however, that he needed a more resolute commander than the Warsaw SS and police leader, von Sammern. Himmler decided on Stroop, then SSPF in Lemberg (Lvov) with the rank of Brigadeführer, thus senior to von Sammern. While in Lvov Stroop had gained much experience and undoubtedly done all that was expected of him in the ruthless liquidation of the ghetto and in great manhunts and massacres of Polish resistance groups in the countryside and the Jews who had joined them after escaping from labour camps.

Returning from one of these manhunts on 15 April Stroop was told that Berlin had been trying to reach him; he should hold himself ready for an urgent telephone call. After he had bathed and anointed himself with eau de Cologne, his phone rang. An officer at the other end confirmed his identity, then he heard Himmler's voice; he was to report next day to Obergruppenführer Krüger in Cracow to receive instructions, and from thence proceed to Warsaw. Stroop asked if he might postpone it for two days. 'My dear Stroop,' Himmler replied, 'everything, even the most important matters, pales beside the task I have assigned you in Warsaw. The time for the great action has come. Go to Krüger, and on 17 April you must be in Warsaw without exciting suspicion. . . .'[121]

He did as instructed, arriving in Warsaw without the monocle he had adopted, and lying low in secret quarters arranged for him by the chief of Security Police in the city, Dr Ludwig Hahn. Hahn had a network of agents inside the Polish resistance. He was able to tell him that the Jews knew of the coming action and he briefed him on the extensive preparations they had made; it would not be a short operation, he warned. He also briefed him on von Sammern's failings. At this stage it seems, Stroop was being held in reserve while von Sammern led the action.

Next day Stroop, still in disguise, toured around the ghetto area in a civilian car, and inspected the auxiliary troops guarding the exits, whom he termed in colonial African parlance 'Askaris'. They were guards under training at the SS camp at Trawniki, a mixture of volunteers from all the occupied eastern territories, principally Letts, Lithuanians, White Russians and Ukrainians. Stroop described them after the war as 'nationalists and anti-semites, all young people, most uneducated and thoroughly wild'.[122] The bulk of the regular troops detailed for the action were from the Training and Replacement or Reserve battalions of the Waffen-SS. These came under Himmler's – not Army – command, and were scattered all over occupied Europe, west and east, to aid the police in putting down strikes, demonstrations and uprisings. Von Sammern had units from five of these *Ersatz* local Panzer-Grenadier battalions and from the Warsaw-based *Ersatz* Cavalry Division. However, they were made up largely of new recruits with no more than three or four weeks' training. In addition there were available Wehrmacht engineers and an anti-aircraft battery, two SS police battalions, SS Security Police, and units of the Polish police and fire brigade.[123]

That evening Stroop retired to his secret quarters, bathed and rubbed himself with eau de Cologne, dined off rare fillet steak and *pommes frites* washed down with Burgundy – so he recalled in his prison cell after the war – and smoked a fine Egyptian cigarette. Next day, Monday 19 April, was the Jewish feast of the Passover; the assault had been scheduled to mark it. He instructed his orderly to call him at 4.00 a.m.

Von Sammern launched the attack at 6.00 a.m. on the 19th with some 850 SS Panzer-Grenadiers and cavalry and Trawniki guards, spearheaded by a captured French tank and two armoured cars. It is evident from between the lines of the official report that the Jewish Fighting Organisation successfully ambushed this force; 'the deployed tank and both SPW [armoured cars] were peppered with Molotov-cocktails. The tank was set on fire twice.'[124] According to Stroop's post-war account, panic broke out as the armoured vehicles and closed up bodies of troops were assailed from windows and roofs by small-arms fire, grenades and bottles of a flaming benzine and phosphorous mixture, and within half an hour the force was broken, demoralised and fleeing, leaving twelve wounded and the tank and one armoured car out of action.

The telephone in Stroop's secret quarters rang continually. Hahn, Krüger and Himmler spoke to him, all furious at the turn of events. Himmler, whom Stroop knew at other times as 'extremely considerate and tactful [*rücksichtsvoll und feinfühlig*]', used unexpectedly coarse language, he recollected after the war, ordering von Sammern dismissed from his post in Warsaw and from command of the ghetto assault force, which should be withdrawn immediately. In fact, according to Stroop, it had already fled in disarray. Stroop was to take command and begin a new attack in two hours' time.[125]

The picture of Himmler which emerges from his directions to Oberg and Krüger – and indeed to other HSSPFs like Rauter in The Hague who was instructed to take equally drastic action at this time against resistance in Holland – and from Stroop's account of Himmler taking control during the Warsaw action, sacking the field commander on the spot, is very different from the image of the schoolmasterly, homely and cranky ideologist left by the records of his speeches and promoted after the war by intimates like Wolff and Schellenberg for their own reasons. It is evident that he was not only a theoretical extremist, not only a collector of secrets and manipulator and politician of guile; when he saw his duty plain he could be as instantly decisive, radical and iron-hearted as Heydrich. In view of the milieu in which he had risen, the rivals he had surpassed or removed and the extraordinary empire he had built up and now controlled, it would be surprising if this had not been so. His appearance and his usual manner were, as they had always been, the best, entirely natural form of camouflage. His indecisiveness, on which all accounts agree, manifested itself only outside the narrow focus of doctrine, loyalty and duty. But this, too, was a kind of camouflage and a decided advantage in manoeuvre which Röhm, Strasser, perhaps Heydrich and even Hitler himself failed to penetrate. Even in the matter of von Sammern Himmler did not allow his rage to overpower his political instincts. He urged Stroop to the utmost tact lest his dismissal raise difficulties in the 'Austrian' group. 'My dear Stroop . . . von Sammern's self-esteem must not be wounded. The business must be put through silently with *Fingerspitzengefühl* [finger-tip sensitivity].'[126]

Stroop took over command of the assault forces, calmed the men, issued a glass of Schnapps or wine to all who wanted one, called up reinforcements, divided the units into assault groups suitable for house-to-house fighting, and sent them in again. The Jews contested every building. As Stroop's report put it, 'The Jews and criminals defended one strongpoint after another, withdrawing at the last moment through attics or underground passages.'[127] He ordered the sewer system flooded to trap them, but they replied by blowing up the damgate valves. So began a bitter contest between Stroop's forces, on average some 2000 men each day, equipped with rifles, heavy and light machine guns, sub-machine guns, machine pistols, a howitzer, anti-aircraft guns and flame-throwers, against the fighting groups composed of some 1200 Jews of both sexes, assisted by Polish resistance fighters, and armed with a few rifles, but chiefly pistols, grenades and home-made incendiary bottles.[128]

Stroop sent daily teletype reports to Krüger in Cracow which were forwarded on to Himmler, and spoke with him and Himmler by telephone each evening. It often took time to get through to Krüger, but he was connected with Himmler at his field headquarters immediately he rang the SS communications *Zentrale* and gave a single codeword. On the first evening after he had gone to bed and fallen asleep his telephone rang again. He answered with an angry expostulation, then heard Himmler's voice, 'Don't be annoyed, my dear Stroop, that I have woken you. . . .' He went on to say that now he had studied his report and spoken to Krüger he had a comprehensive picture: the day's action was only the prelude to a historic episode that would be known one day as '*Grossaktion* Warsaw' – 'Grand Action Warsaw'. 'You have managed this prelude outstandingly well,' he went on, 'especially after the clumsy attempts of the obtuse von Sammern. Because I love Wagner operas and also rate highly today's National Socialist leaders, allow me to say, play on in the same way, Maestro! And our Führer and I will never forget you.'[129]

On the second day the defenders continued to make such skilful use of the network of intercommunicating passages to regroup and reoccupy buildings which had been cleared that in his evening discussions with Krüger and Himmler, Stroop was given full authority to burn the buildings to force the Jews out into the open and prevent re-entry. Such a policy had not been foreseen apparently by the Jewish leadership, and was horribly successful from the start. Stroop reported on the 22nd: 'Jews in masses – whole families – already gripped by the flames, leaped from windows or attempted to let themselves down with bedsheets tied together. Provision had been made to liquidate these as well as the other Jews immediately. . . .'[130] Not all were shot: '5300 Jews were taken for evacuation and transported out.' As other daily reports and Stroop's post-war testimony revealed, these were sent to 'T 11' – code for the death camp, Treblinka.

From the beginning Stroop recorded 'Liaison with the Wehrmacht perfect'. On the 23rd, after finding that the defenders were taking refuge in a block of buildings housing an armaments firm, he put this to the test, requesting the Wehrmacht to remove the valuable machinery and stock. They had done so by 18.00 the following day, and immediately he had the whole block set alight. He reported:

Only after the streets and all the courtyards on both sides were ablaze did the Jews, some alight themselves, emerge from the block, attempting to save themselves by leaping from windows and balconies to the street after throwing down beds, blankets and other bedroom stuff. Again and again we saw that despite the great fire-danger Jews and bandits chose rather to return in to the fire than fall into our hands. The Jews continued shooting until almost the end of the action. . . .'[131]

The *Grossaktion* was one of the high points of Stroop's life, for after the war he described it enthusiastically to his cell-mate, Moczarski, in day-by-day detail, complete with times of events and the daily numbers of Jews captured, killed or transported to Treblinka. His descriptions were less inhibited than those in his official reports.

'The uproar was monstrous,' he recalled, 'burning houses, smoke, flames, flying sparks, whirling bed feathers, the stench of singed bodies, thunder of guns, cracking grenades, the glow of fire, Jews with their wives and children leaping from windows and burning houses . . . they appeared everywhere in windows, on balconies, on the roofs and ledges. Some shot, others sought to escape, many sang something, probably psalms, many cried in chorus "Hitler kaputt", "To the gallows with the Germans!", "Es lebe Polen!" '

Stroop had worked himself into a state of great excitement as he relived the scene, and he began jumping about the cell, gesticulating with his arms and imitating the sound of his young SS soldiers firing at the silhouetted figures and those jumping to the street, whom they named 'parachutists' – 'Paff! Paff!'[132]

In parallel with the systematic burning, block by block, special groups were tracking down the underground hiding places, many of which were provided with washing and lavatory facilities and large stocks of food; when they found one, the engineers on secondment from the Wehrmacht placed explosives and blew it up, often with the obstinate or terrified and overheated occupants inside. By the 26th Stroop sensed he had begun prising out the 'toughest and most resistant Jews and bandits', and he learned from the statements of some of those captured that many who had not left the bunkers since the beginning of the action had been driven mad by the heat of the fires, the smoke and explosions. The results of that day's action he recorded as '30 Jews evacuated, 1330 Jews fetched out of bunkers and immediately annihilated. 362 Jews shot in action'. His attitude is expressed in a sentence reporting several blocks of houses burned down: 'This is the only way and the method of last resort to force this riff-raff and *Untermenschentum* to the surface.'

It may be, however, that this bravado was primarily intended for Krüger and Himmler, for after the war he admitted to Moczarski that he and his officers had been taken completely by surprise by the toughness and readiness for battle of the Jews. 'We, the old fighters of the first war and SS men of the early days, knew what battle-courage and iron will meant. We had been brought up to discipline, inflexibility and hardness. And the Warsaw Jews gave an outstanding demonstration of this hardness – that was our greatest surprise.' And, he concluded, that was why the ghetto battle lasted for so long.[133]

By the end of April Stroop estimated that he had taken or killed a total of 37,359 Jews; on that day 3855 were entrained for Treblinka. In general, he reported on 1 May, the groups engaged in tracking down the 'so-called bunkers, caves and sewer networks' needed to display 'the most extreme vigilance and effort'. They took to lowering smoke candles into the sewer branches to force the defenders to points in the system where troops had been assembled to capture them. It was also known that many Jews were escaping into the 'Aryan' part of the city, and the Polish police were offered cash rewards for tracking them down, a policy which, Stroop reported on 6 May, was bearing fruit. By this stage he was clear that his troops in the ghetto were catching 'Jews and bandits of the so-called Battle [Fighting] groups. They are without exception young fellows and women eighteen to twenty-five years old.' The girls sold their lives as dearly as the men, and evidently shocked Stroop by their emancipation. They were not human, he told Moczarski, 'perhaps goddesses or devils. Cold-blooded and adroit as circus-artistes. They often shot with both hands. Obstinately and enduringly they fought to the end. And close to they were especially dangerous. . . .'[134] He described one such incident in a daily report to Krüger: a group had been pulled out of a bunker and were no doubt about to be ordered to strip completely, a policy that had been adopted since casualties had been suffered after women produced pistols or grenades from their underclothes: 'one of the women, as so often, grabbed under her dress, pulled an oval hand grenade from her pants and after withdrawing the pin threw it among the men conducting the search, jumping for cover herself like lightning. It was only thanks to the alertness of the men that no casualties resulted.'[135] Stroop told Moczarski that this had led him to instruct his men not to take these girls prisoner and in no circumstances to allow them to approach too close but to finish them off with a machine pistol at a safe distance. This did not appear in any of his reports.

Moczarski asked him whether he had never regretted his life. Stroop was silent for a while. 'Whoever wanted to be a real man in those days,' he said at last, 'that is to say a strong man, had to act as I did. Praise be that which hardens!'[136] This was, of course, one of Himmler's favourite *mots*.

It took almost a month from the start of the *Grossaktion* to smoke out and kill or evacuate the great mass of Jews in the ghetto; a few small groups remained obstinately holding out in still unlocated hideouts or the charred ruins of gutted buildings apparently without access, but as the daily sweeps and searches produced diminishing returns, Stroop sought permission to terminate the operation and leave the few survivors to be picked up when the buildings were finally demolished. Thus his last daily report to Krüger on 16 May: '180 Jews, bandits and *Untermenschen* were annihilated. The former Jewish residential quarter of Warsaw has ceased to exist. The *Grossaktion* was ended at 20.15 with the blowing up of the Warsaw synagogue.'[137]

Stroop's eyes were alight with enthusiasm when recalling the scene from his prison cell. 'Was that a magnificent sight! A fantastic panorama for any painter or theatre-goer. . . .' He was standing with his staff at a safe distance; he had personally detonated the explosive charges packed in hundreds of bore-holes in the foundations and walls of the great building, crying 'Heil Hitler!' as he pressed down on the knob. 'The gigantic explosion ripped the flames up to the clouds. A penetrating report followed, the colours were truly fabulous. An unforgettable allegory of the triumph over Jewry! The Warsaw ghetto had ceased to exist. Because Adolf Hitler and Heinrich Himmler had willed it.'[138]

Stroop was awarded the Iron Cross, 1st Class, for the action. Krüger bestowed it on behalf of the Führer and the Reichsführer-SS at a gala reception in Warsaw. Stroop organised a garden party afterwards in Lazienki Park to which he invited 'generals and leading personalities'; they drank and sang, knit in 'knightly mood as befitted correct SS men. It was a wonderful time. . . .'[139]

Stroop's recollections as a condemned man provide insights into the heady mood and feelings gripping the Third Reich even as late as the summer of 1943 which are missing from the apologias of those who survived to write memoirs and give interviews designed to conceal their own identification with this spirit and lay the odium wholly on Himmler and other 'criminal' Party figures. Stroop is a more reliable guide. Without his recollected pride and delight the sickening barbarities which fill so many hundreds of volumes of testimony and evidence at war crimes trials, indeed the figure of Himmler himself, would scarcely be explicable.

After Stroop had sent a final teletype to Krüger summarising the results of the *Grossaktion* as 56,065 Jews taken or annihilated plus an estimated 5000–6000 annihilated through explosions and fires and 631 bunkers destroyed, Krüger suggested that a complete set of the daily reports be bound and sent to Himmler as a souvenir. Stroop was happy to comply; he had fair copies of the reports typed, wrote a preface giving an overview of the operation and the reasons for it, added lists of his own casualties – sixteen killed, ninety-five wounded – chose fifty-four photographs taken during the action and had three sets of the whole bound as commemorative albums in black pebble leather; the title pages bore the words in bold Gothic script 'Es gibt keinen jüdischen Wohnbezirk in Warschau mehr!' – 'There is no longer a Jewish residential district in Warsaw!' One copy was sent to Himmler, one to Krüger, and Stroop retained one for himself.

The spirit of the *Herrenvolk* was, of course, not diminished by the opportunities for looting. Stroop's and Moczarski's cellmate, the former German lower police official and SS-Untersturmführer Gustav Schilke, well knew from a period he had spent working in Cracow that the money and valuables seized in ghetto round-ups and house searches and in the death camps were by no means all handed in, indeed each man expected to gain from a raid or round-up as of right. He could imagine, he told Stroop, what quantities of money and valuables from the Warsaw ghetto disappeared into the pockets of the SS men, police and Askaris employed in his action. Stroop did not contradict him.[140]

Franz Stangl, who had taken over from Dr Eberl as Kommandant of Treblinka the previous autumn, suggested to Gitta Sereny after the war that the same thing happened at much higher levels. He described the scenes at his introduction to Treblinka, the most horrible he saw in all his time in the Third Reich: corpses lined the railway for miles and at the station itself there were hundreds of bodies which had obviously been lying there for days decomposing in the heat. The smell was indescribable. Telling her this Stangl's face underwent a remarkable change that Sereny had noted before whenever he came to something terrible in his story: 'it coarsened and became slack and confused. The veins stood out, he began to sweat and the lines in his cheeks and forehead deepened. His voice became slurred . . . his face thickened . . . and turned dark red.'[141]

Entering the camp Stangl had found himself wading through money, precious stones, jewellery and clothes strewn haphazardly all over the reception area; beyond the barbed-wire fences around the perimeter he saw tents and camp fires with groups of Ukrainian guards and their prostitutes drunk, singing, dancing or playing music. The indescribable confusion of the camp has been put down to Eberl's administrative incompetence. However, Stangl suggested to Sereny that the complete breakdown in control may have been deliberate in order to make accurate accounting impossible and enable Eberl and Wirth to bypass Globocnik's headquarters and send money and valuables directly to the Führer's Chancellery in Berlin.[142] Sereny received confirmation of at least one such episode from a former Treblinka guard, Franz Suchomel; he recalled stuffing a million Marks into a suitcase which was sent straight to the Berlin Chancellery. 'There were enormous, fantastic sums involved,' Stangl said, 'and everybody wanted a piece of it, and everybody wanted control.' He himself remained convinced that the motive behind the extermination programme was simple robbery.[143]

Stangl appears to have been Globocnik's man; his first task was to sort out the money and valuables. He was still Kommandant when the transports arrived from Stroop's action in the Warsaw ghetto. His successor as Kommandant of Sobibor was Franz Reichleitner, another former policeman and graduate of Castle Hartheim extermination centre.

Shortly before the termination of *Grossaktion* Warsaw, SS-Gruppenführer Frank, the staff officer at Pohl's WVHA headquarters, Berlin, responsible for Jewish belongings handed in, chiefly those collected at the various death camps and in 'special actions', sent a list of the more valuable and useful items to Himmler, requesting decisions about their distribution. The reference was: 'Utilisation of Jewish received and stolen goods', a remarkable reversal of roles – in psychological theory, 'projection'. The first section listed 94,000 men's watches, 33,000 women's watches, 25,000 fountain pens, 14,000 propelling pencils, 3500 wallets, 130,000 razor blades, 7500 safety razors and razors, 400 hair clippers, 14,000 scissors delivered to the main store at Oranienburg camp up to the end of April; the second section listed 7000 men's watches, 8000 fountain pens, 100,000 razor blades, 5000 safety razors, 400 hair clippers and 14,000 scissors as reconditioned and ready for delivery to the store; a further 2500 men's watches per month would be reconditioned and available; 'therefore in this year a further 20,000 approximately'.[144]

From the reconditioned items 100,000 razor blades and 4000 safety razors had been sent already to the canteens – presumably SS – for sale, and 1000 new, or as good as new, safety razors had been distributed to SS hospitals for the men from the front; 250 razors and 400 hair clippers had been sent to the barbers' shops of the concentration camps, and the scissors had been distributed to the Deutsche Armaments Works GmbH against payment and free to Lebensborn and the concentration camp medical departments and barbers' shops.

Frank proposed an immediate distribution of 500 men's watches to each battle division (of the Waffen-SS) and a further 500 on 1 October; he reported that the Leibstandarte Adolf Hitler, Das Reich and Totenkopf divisions had already received 500 each. He further proposed the immediate delivery of 3000 watches to the U-boat arm and another 3000 on 1 October, and 200 watches for each of the concentration camp commanders to hand out to their staffs. Similarly with the fountain pens, he suggested that each Waffen-SS division should receive 300 and the U-boat arm 2000. He requested a decision on the 33,000 women's watches.

He also requested a decision on a number of special items:

a) several hundred very valuable collectors' old gold and silver coins . . . of high collection value.

b) four great chests of valuable postage stamp collections, among them complete collections worth 40,000 Marks and over.

c) about 5000 watches with the most expensive Swiss movements in *pure gold and platinum cases*, in part set with precious stones (gold watches with inferior movements or of clumsy, shoddy form have already been handed over to the Reichsbank for melting down).

He asked whether these gold watches should be handed over to the Reichsbank for foreign-exchange transactions or whether a number of them, 'the loveliest and most valuable pieces', should be held back for special utilisation. There was also a number of gold fountain pens and propelling pencils; 'Should these be handed over to the Reichsbank for foreign-exchange transactions or melting down?'

The proposal to include the U-boat arm among the recipients, otherwise Waffen-SS, concentration camp or other SS organisations, is interesting. The U-boat arm was, of course, an elite, fighting in the most dangerous conditions and the sole force able to pursue an offensive strategy against the western allies. Pohl had close connections with the Navy since he was a former naval paymaster captain. But Himmler had involved himself personally in U-boat affairs as early as February, shortly after Dönitz's appointment as Supreme Commander, when he had arranged a meeting to discuss the possibilities of increasing underwater speed, the vital question on which the future effectiveness of the force depended.[145] As Reichsführer-SS and Chief of the German Police, he had no conceivable official interest in the U-boat arm but it is characteristic of his wide-ranging exercise of energies that he should thrust himself into this vital sphere. It also suggests that he established a very early rapport with Dönitz and the new U-boat commander, Konteradmiral Hanz von Friedeburg. Dönitz's adjutant, Korvetten-Kapitän Hansen-Nootbar, recalled after the war that Himmler was trying very hard to establish a relationship with Dönitz at this time, sending him a spate of invitations.[146] Perhaps the watches were a part of this effort.

However Frank's proposal came about, it seems certain that Himmler gave oral approval. A former petty officer of U-333, who could scarcely have known of the proposal, spoke after the war about returning from a patrol in the summer of 1943 and finding that among the special comforts waiting for such 'front' boats was a wooden chest of watches from which the crew could choose which they wanted. All were second hand, all in good working order; a few, however, were watches for the blind. 'Then we knew exactly. That was too macabre. Nobody should say he knew nothing. We knew at that time where they came from.'[147]

Despite several reminders Himmler did not reply in detail to Frank's proposals until December – almost seven months. Any idea that this could be attributed to stirrings of shame at such mute testimony to the thousands of individual tragedies rather than simple pressure of work or habitual slowness in reaching decisions which did not require immediate action is dispelled by a letter he wrote to Kaltenbrunner on 19 May, five days before receiving Frank's list. This concerned a recent book called *Der jüdische Ritualmord* (*Jewish Ritual Murder*). It was about the Jews' alleged practice of kidnapping children for ritual sacrifice, a myth as old as the persecution of Jewry, which seems to have surfaced during all periods of particularly violent persecution through the ages. Himmler had ordered a great quantity of these books to distribute down to Standartenführer level; he was also sending Kaltenbrunner several hundred copies, he wrote, so that he could give them out to his Einsatzkommandos, above all to the men dealing with the Jewish question. Further, he instructed him to start enquiries into Jewish ritual murder among those communities which had not been evacuated yet, particularly in Rumania, Hungary and Bulgaria, so that he could institute trials, publicise them in the press 'and so facilitate the removal of Jews from the countries'. He also instructed Kaltenbrunner to liaise with the Foreign Ministry to see whether it would be possible to set up 'a solely anti-semitic illegal radio station for England and America'. He was thinking of a 'sensational presentation' of the subject such as the journal *Stürmer* had made during the 'time of struggle'. And Kaltenbrunner should set up a section immediately to monitor English court news and police announcements about missing children 'so that we can then give corresponding short news broadcasts that in the place XY a child is missing and it is probably a case of Jewish ritual murder.' He believed that by this means, and perhaps with a similar station broadcasting 'ritual murder' propaganda in Russian, they would 'monstrously activate anti-semitism in the world'.[148]

Evidently he had made up his quarrel with Martin Bormann for he had a discussion with him about this time on the treatment of the various grades of Jewish *Mischlinge* or cross-breeds, and on 22 May he sent him a proposal on the subject emanating from the 'well-known racial researcher, Professor Dr B. K. Schultz', of the RuSHA, together with a covering note in *Du* terms and beginning 'Dear Martin'. They must, he wrote, execute this matter – but it must be kept strictly between themselves – with a process similar to that which one employed in the selective breeding of plants or animals: 'At least for some generations (3 or 4 generations) the issue from such *Mischling* families will have to be racially examined by independent institutions and in the case of racial inferiority sterilised and so eliminated from further generation. Perhaps,' he finished, 'you would let me know some time what you think about this.'[149]

Meanwhile, in the question of the full Jews he had in his hand in the east, he proceeded as he had with Warsaw, ordering all ghetto Jews to be gathered in concentration camps, and establishing a terminal date, 1 August, after which it was forbidden to remove Jews from camps to work. All private firms employing Jews for Wehrmacht clothing and armaments were to be dissolved and a new concentration camp established near Riga to which these firms were to be transferred as 'pure concentration camp concerns'; Pohl was to see that the Wehrmacht suffered no setbacks in production as a result. Jews from the ghettos who were not needed were to be 'evacuated to the east'[150] – a particularly unnecessary euphemism at this stage since Russian armies were thrusting in from the east and there was no possible way for anyone to be 'evacuated' in that direction.

When Himmler finally gave a detailed answer to Frank's questions about 'Utilisation of Jewish received and stolen goods' in December, he agreed to the proposed distribution to the divisions. He said nothing about the U-boat arm; as suggested this must have been agreed orally. He further agreed to a proposal from Pohl that a number of watches and fountain pens be given out to deserving units of the Waffen-SS at the Julfest – *Ersatz* Christmas festival – in his name. Fifteen thousand of the ladies' watches were to be made available to ethnic Germans coming from Russia for resettlement. The collector's coins he wanted sent to the money museum at the Reichsbank; the gold and platinum watches with the most expensive Swiss movements and the gold fountain pens and propelling pencils were also to go to the Reichsbank for foreign transactions, and he thought that the same use could be made of the stamp collections.[151]

Chief of Intelligence

Himmler's involvement with day-to-day tactics in the Warsaw *Grossaktion* indicates that he did not confine himself to laying out broad policy guidelines. He insisted on making personal decisions on detail; it is apparent from the letters, decrees, orders, memoranda and enquiries that issued from his desk that his addiction to detail was obsessive. Kersten recorded that the long hours Himmler spent at his desk horrified his staff. When Kersten tried to remonstrate on health grounds, Himmler replied, 'History will not enquire how well Heinrich Himmler slept, but how much he achieved. It will be time enough to sleep when the war has been won.'[1] This probably means that, in striving for his ideal world, he had an image of perfection which he had to measure up to himself. Here he was quite different from Hitler, whose incapacity for regular work or concentration of any kind was notorious.

Examples of Himmler's concern for individual SS officers and men and for their standards of behaviour and their chivalry towards women abound in his correspondence; and if a trace of Jewish blood were turned up in the distant ancestry of an otherwise 'decent' man or his wife, he insisted on making the final decision on what was to be done, always trying to temper stern necessity with consideration for the man in his unfortunate position. Similarly with his other great 'positive' task, the Germanising of the east, he concerned himself in difficult cases with the fate of individuals. These named cases convey rather more chillingly than his arrangements for anonymous mass murder, gross as these were, the ice-cold core at the heart of his policies.

Eindeutschung was not proceeding with the simple clarity of his original ideas. It was involving his officials in the same kind of tortuous racial semantics and categorisation as the attempts to define which *Mischlinge* were or were not to be allowed to propagate, while the men on the spot were apt to dilute pure racial policy with more pragmatic considerations. SS-Gruppenführer Arthur Greiser, for example, Gauleiter of the Warthegau, who was attempting to abide by the rules – as he understood them – complained that his programme was being compromised by the policies pursued in the two neighbouring eastern regions, Danzig/West Prussia and the General Gouvernement. There Poles who had been expelled from his own *Gau* were being encouraged to offer themselves for *Eindeutschung*, and being accepted on the *Volksliste* with as little as 12.5 per cent German blood admixture – one great-grandparent of German stock; so he complained to Himmler that spring.[2] Himmler asked Kaltenbrunner to have his staff look into it. The reply, when it arrived, achieved a degree of convolution remarkable even by the standards of German officialdom:

> persons or families will be recognised as of German origin, Group A . . . if they have a racial evaluation I–III and show at the highest 50 per cent foreign origin or respectively with racial evaluation I–III at least 12.5 per cent German blood admixture.
>
> As German-origin Group B . . . the following will be recognised: German origin with racial evaluation IV, who are of pure German descent or have at least three German grandparents and a favourable economic and attitude rating. . . .[3]

Admitting these people to the *Volksliste* was simply the first step provided for in the process to win back German blood after the war, Kaltenbrunner summarised. Such was the official position, or confusion, that February 1943 when five 'special cases' in the General Gouvernement were brought to Himmler's attention. They were Johanna Achidzanjanz from Tomaszow, near Lublin, who was '50 per cent German origin and evaluated racially good', but who refused to learn the German language or to become German. Maria Lambucki, also of Tomaszow, was 100 per cent German descent but had married a pure Pole, now in a Russian prisoner-of-war camp, by whom she had had two sons, Ignatz and George; she too refused *Eindeutschung*, saying that she had married a Pole and did not want him to find on his return that she had become German. Stanislaus Koch, from Sitno, despite 75 per cent German origin also 'refused any connection with Germany'. Brunhilde Muszynski, née von Wattmann, had at first disputed that she was of German origin and had displayed an attitude 'which can be described as hostile to Germany through and through'; it was only after her father had been traced as a Reich-German in Vienna that she had admitted to being of German descent. Her husband had been a Polish officer who had fallen in the Polish campaign, and she wished to bring her children up as Poles. Ingeborg von Avenarius, née Wattmann (sic), while admitting her German origin, refused any connection with Germany, saying that since she had married a Pole she had become Polish not only legally but in thought and feeling, and 'in no way did she wish to bring up her children as German . . .'. She could give no account of the present whereabouts of her husband. A note was appended by the security official concerned that, since this was a case of the 'completely Polishised intelligentsia, special examination is necessary'.[4]

Himmler took only five days to give a decision on these cases from his field headquarters near Lötzen: Johanna Achidzanjanz, '50 per cent German origin but totally Polish-minded', was to be transferred outside the German settlement area of the General Gouvernement:

2. Maria Lambucki from Tomaszow-Lub. is 100 per cent German origin and totally Polish-minded. She has completely denied her Germanhood. I decree her immediate transfer to concentration camp Ravensbrück. Both sons, who are eight and thirteen years old and racially very good, are to be brought to Germany through the agency of the Chief of the Race and Settlement Main Office [RuSHA] with the co-operation of the Security Police, and parted to be placed in two especially well-conducted *Heimschulen* [special boarding schools] as boarders. I request quarterly reports. Writing to the mother is forbidden until further notice, until the mother comes to a realisation of the treachery she has committed. With both racially good youngsters the teachers and fellow pupils must strive to make it clear to them that they are in no way deserters from Polishness but on grounds of their origin and racial worth should merely profess again their own blood, from which they are descended. This must be the fundament for all such work and attempts to win back valuable racial *Volksgut* [*Volk*-stock] that has been politically and nationally washed away.[5]

Stanislaus Koch, who had renounced his 75 per cent German origins, was to be taken into an armaments workshop in a concentration camp, also his (Polish) wife and daughters, if feasible in different camps. Brunhilde Muszynski, née von Wattmann, was also to be taken to a concentration camp, and the origins of her father were to be investigated for suspicion of Jewish blood. Both her children were to be brought into a German family if the family tree were found to be in order, the elder one to be placed in a *Heimschule*. Ingeborg von Avenarius, née Wattmann, was also to be taken into a concentration camp and her children accommodated in the same way.[6]

This decree, which Himmler signed, may be compared to a letter his secretary, Dr Brandt, sent to a Waffen-SS wife, who asked that her husband might be granted leave. It is evident that her request played on Himmler's well-known desire for the procreation of children: Brandt hoped that it would be possible to fulfil her wish: 'I should like, however, to advise you to have a prior examination by a woman doctor in order to ascertain what will be a favourable time for conception because only a leave taken at the correct time offers, by human judgement, a guarantee to a certain extent that you and your husband's wish for a child will be fulfilled.'[7]

The investigations Himmler ordered into the family background of the former German women who had become obstinately Polish, Brunhilde Muszynski and Ingeborg von Avenarius, concluded in December with the finding that their father, Freiherr von Wattmann, was a Jewish *Mischling* Grade II; the chief of the RuSHA, SS-Gruppenführer Hildebrandt, formerly HSSPF Danzig/West Prussia, wrote to Brandt at Himmler's field head-quarters to say that in view of this and a 'total judgement' on the two there 'existed no interest in regaining them for Germanhood'.[8] The Inspector of the *Heimschulen*, SS-Obergruppenführer Heissmeyer, wrote that since their Jewish origin had been ascertained their children could not be taken into a German *Heimschule*: 'what should happen to them?' He reported that Maria Lambucki's children had been placed in different *Heimschulen*, the thirteen-year-old in Elsass and the eight-year-old in Baden, and asked whether the mother should be retained in *Schutzhaft* despite the fact that her children had been regained for Germany.[9]

Himmler's decision took much longer this time; it was not until the end of May 1944 that Brandt conveyed it to the RSHA:

1) Maria Lambucki and Stanislaus Koch should not remain further in *Schutzhaft*.

2) Jechwigs Koch should be placed in a *Heimschule*.

3) Brunhilde Muszynski should be taken into *Schutzhaft*. Both her four- and seven-year-old children are to be sterilised and accommodated somehow as foster-children.

4) Ingeborg von Avenarius is likewise to be taken into *Schutzhaft*. Her children, also, are to be accommodated somehow as foster-children after sterilisation.[10]

Copies of this decree were sent to the RuSHA, the Main Offices of RKF and the Volksdeutsche Mittelstelle, the HSSPF East and the Main Office for nationality questions.

A rather different example of Himmler's decisions on the fate of individual families, also originating in the early spring of 1943, concerned German deserters. Seven men from a reserve unit posted to north Norway, and travelling on what was known as the 'horseshoe line' through neutral Sweden, left the train at a Swedish halt and did not return. Himmler acted immediately the teletype from HSSPF North dated 1 April, 1800 hrs, was brought to his attention. Brandt wired the RSHA, Berlin: 'RFSS wishes immediate ascertainment where the families of the men concerned are domiciled, whose immediate arrest must ensue. In case a Gauleiter should attempt to impede this I ask him to refer to the RFSS.'[11]

Enquiries to the Wehrmacht authorities revealed the addresses of the next of kin of two of the men within a fortnight. This news was communicated to Himmler, and Brandt sent a teletype to the RSHA: 'I now request that the instruction of the RFSS to arrest the families be carried out.'[12] At the same time he instructed the HSSPF Danzig/West Prussia to hunt out the families of the other five deserters; by 28 April these had been discovered. The final document in the dossier is a file note dated 5 June 1943, to the effect that the families had been arrested and transferred to a concentration camp: 'One enquiry still outstanding has been transmitted to the RFSS via SS-Hauptsturmführer Falschlein: what should happen to the property of these families? The proceedings are thereby closed for us.'[13]

Thus the families of Kasimir Gernski, Isidor Lewandowski, Josef Malischewski, Max Ossowski, Jan Schuefelhern, Bruno Schulemalkes and Johann Stefanski found themselves victims of *Sippenhaft*, or arrest of kin, due to the desertion of one of their members; what happened to their property is not recorded. Barbaric as this punishment was – indeed Himmler justified it in a speech by reference to the practices of the ancient Germanic tribes – it did not put a stop to desertion. Early the following year the chief of one of the Party bodies dealing with foreign affairs, the Auslands-Organisation, wrote to say that in the majority of such cases the deserter proved to have a Swiss or a Swedish wife. He saw no alternative to putting these countries out of bounds for soldiers on leave – 'a pity for the decent Germans'.[14]

The extent to which these measures were Himmler's own response to the signs of collapsing internal morale, to what extent they were taken after one of his frequent discussions with Hitler 'under four eyes' – a particularly apt description for these two short-sighted and distrustful men – in order to keep his Führer's approval by demonstrating pitilessness, or indeed to demonstrate this to his staff and HSSPFs, is not revealed in the documents. To guess at the answer is to guess at the whole nature of his commitment to the creed and his complex relationships with his rivals at court and with his Führer. One of his measures that summer as the Anglo-American air-raids took their nightly toll of residential districts and factories alike, with the Luftwaffe unable to offer more than token resistance, can probably be ascribed to Hitler. 'Terror can only be broken by terror' was one of the Führer's favourite aphorisms; there can be little doubt that he gave vent to it often in their discussions of the 'terror-flyers', as the allied airmen were known, little doubt that the subject cropped up frequently since Himmler had taken over responsibility for civil defence and air-raid precautions from the time of the first 1000-bomber raids the previous year. He had also taken to visiting devastated cities in the wake of attacks in an attempt to make up for Hitler's notorious refusal to inspect the damage and give comfort to his homeless and wounded *Volk*.

On 10 August 1943 Himmler circulated a top-secret decree to all his HSSPFs, commanders of Security Police, Ordnungspolizei and SS Main Office chiefs, from whence the instruction was to be handed down to all SS and police departments and responsible officers by word of mouth alone. It ran simply: 'It is not the task of the police to intervene in altercations between German *Volk*-comrades and parachuted English and American terror-flyers.'[15] Thus he condoned and encouraged lynch law by which many allied airmen were killed. Others were deliberately 'shot while attempting escape'.

At the end of September the chief SS physician, Dr Grawitz, passed on a request from one of Hitler's personal doctors, Professor Dr Karl Brandt: research on animals into the phosphorous burns experienced by so many victims of terror air-raids was insufficient; could individual inmates of con-centration camp Sachsenhausen be made available for the tests? Himmler noted in his green pen, 'Ja.'[16]

*

By the autumn of 1943 the military situation was hopeless. The summer offensive, codenamed 'Zitadelle', aimed at enveloping a Russian salient centred on Kursk between Army Group Centre and Army Group South, had been held and turned in armoured battles of unparalleled size and destructiveness. The SS-Panzerkorps, Leibstandarte, Das Reich and Totenkopf divisions re-equipped with the latest models of heavy Tiger and medium Panther tanks and used again as a shock force in the southern sector, had confirmed the Waffen–SS reputation for absolute commitment; after breakthroughs of some 100 miles against equally fanatic resistance, the advance had been halted by Soviet counter-attacks. During mass tank actions, in some cases at point-blank range, and ferocious infantry engagements surpassing even the former standards of the eastern front in savagery and blood-letting, German manpower and materiel had been ground down fatally. By September Russian armies were rolling westwards all along the fronts aided by massed partisan brigades attacking German lines of communication. Hitler's last throw had failed. As the staff officer responsible for the assessment of 'enemy forces east' reported in October, 'in future the Soviet-Russian army will surpass Germany in terms of manpower, equipment and in the field of propaganda.'[17]

Himmler ordered his HSSPF Ukraine, SS-Gruppenführer Hans Prützmann, to liaise with the infantry General Stapf, who had already received special instructions; together they were to do all that was humanly possible to ensure that nothing was left in the Donetz basin of use to the Russians, 'no people, no cattle, no quintal of corn, no railway track; that no house remains standing, no mine that is not destroyed for years, no well that is not poisoned'. The enemy must find a totally destroyed and blackened land.[18]

Meanwhile Italy had collapsed. Hitler had anticipated this for some time; originally he had intended sending the entire SS-Panzerkorps to Italy in the hope that the ideological strength of these 'political soldiers' and their experience in propaganda might hold the disaffected Italians to his cause. He had been dissuaded, chiefly by the Soviet counter-offensive at Kursk, and in the event only the Leibstandarte was transferred. At this stage his faith in the Waffen-SS seemed limitless; it had grown in inverse relationship to the deteriorating situation. On 3 September, shortly before going to see him, Himmler boasted to Brandt about what the Führer had said of the SS at their last meeting. Brandt recorded it in a file note: the Führer had expressed his intention after the war to maintain the separation of the three armed services; 'this is an essential relief for a statesman.' It is safe to assume from this that they were discussing the disaffection now manifest in the Army officer corps, although not in the Navy or Luftwaffe to anything like the same degree. 'In this talk the Führer then made the following observation: "The best thing I shall leave to my successor is the SS." He commented moreover that the armed forces in the Germanic countries must be built up under the control of the SS.'[19]

Plans to disarm the Italian forces and take over the country had been prepared in case of Italy's 'treachery' by all three services and in Wolff's SS and police headquarters. On 8 September, news of Italian armistice proposals was broadcast, and at the single codeword 'Achse' sent out from Führer headquarters the disarming operations were set in motion. They were carried through with extraordinary success and lack of bloodshed; it was a coup reminiscent of Hitler's earlier triumphs over Austria and Czechoslovakia, and within hours he was master of the greater part of Italy. Anglo-American invasion forces landed meanwhile in the south below Naples.

Despite this brilliant but essentially short-term solution to the situation on the southern flank, Hitler faced military defeat: he lacked either the manpower or matériel resources to contain his encircling and closing enemies. In the east massive Russian armies pressed; in the south and west the Anglo-American partnership controlled the seas as they controlled the air above the Reich; Dönitz's U-boat assault had been mastered earlier in the summer, and men and materials were being concentrated in England for an invasion of occupied Europe the following year. Meanwhile German cities, factories and communications continued to suffer merciless bombardment from the air, not least the Reich capital itself; children and women had been evacuated. Yet Hitler had prepared mental lines of defence against the idea of defeat: the earliest, deriving from the *Weltanschauung*, was that if the war were lost the German people had not deserved to win and were not worthy of his genius; more practically he had developed the idea that the eastern and western partners in the enemy alliance must split. The propaganda effort after the discoveries in Katyn Forest had been largely directed to this end, so probably were many of the 'unofficial' approaches seeking an accommodation with one side or the other, east or west, attempting to sow suspicion that if not accepted a deal would be struck with the other side.

Hitler supported his theory of an inevitable split between the allies with examples from history, particularly from Frederick the Great's wars. During a conference with Dönitz in August he had pointed out how often during the darkest hours for a nation unexpected developments brought a sudden turn for the better. In their present situation 'the harder the war becomes for us, the more the divergent views of the allies will grow and reveal themselves.' Already, he said, the British war aim of maintaining the balance of power in Europe had been undone: Russia had been so stimulated as to become a threat of a wholly new dimension. The onslaught from the east could be met only by a Europe united under German leadership and this, he concluded, would be in the British interest as well.[20] There was some evidence for the view that the British and Americans were becoming anxious about Stalin's growing power and ambition, yet it was possible to draw a conclusion diametrically opposed to Hitler's: the worse things went for the Reich the harder both sides would press in from east and west to gain maximum advantage for themselves from the shattered carcase.

Dönitz, Rommel, appointed Commander-in-Chief in Italy, and Bormann all noted the confidence Hitler radiated at the time of the Italian crisis.[21] It probably emanated from amphetamines; it was noticed that at some time in the summer of 1943 he developed a mannerism characteristic of amphetamine use – a compulsive picking at the skin at the back of his neck 'as if he wanted to scratch something off'. This was in addition to another typical sign, biting the skin around the nails of his thumb and first two fingers, which his valet described as his most characteristic habit.[22]

Leonard and Renate Heston conclude in their medical study of Hitler that he had attempted to do without the drug after Morell's discovery of progressive heart disease. This had led to severe withdrawal symptoms about the time of Stalingrad when he virtually retired into himself, suffering deep depressions. Later that spring he had appeared to observers to recover completely, and thereafter he presented a super-confident face to all setbacks, leading the Hestons to the view that he had resumed taking amphetamines, or possibly cocaine, starting each day with an intravenous injection and maintaining 'an equilibrium that maximised optimism and confidence and minimised over-arousal' by carefully regulated oral doses.[23]

If this was the case Hitler achieved his purpose. Thus the day after the Italian treachery Martin Bormann wrote, 'Marvellous to see the Führer's poise in face of fantastic complications in the east, the south, and elsewhere . . .'.[24] Bormann's conclusion was that the time had come to stand fast with iron determination. Dönitz had reached a similar conclusion after a Führer conference in August: 'Everything will depend upon our holding out stubbornly'[25] – to provoke the anticipated split in the enemy alliance.

The signs are that Himmler was as impressed as Bormann, Dönitz and Rommel with Hitler's resonance and grasp of affairs at this time. Long after the war Speer recalled a conference that he and his department chief, Karl Saur, had with Himmler at his field headquarters on 20 August. Himmler had proposed to Hitler, presumably at their meeting the previous day, that in order to preserve the secrecy of the Peenemünde rocket programme then codenamed A4, the parts could be manufactured inside the concentration camps; he would guarantee the skilled engineers and manpower necessary. Hitler latched on to the idea and told Speer to discuss it with him; hence his visit to 'Hochwald' field headquarters with Saur. Himmler told the two that he had assigned the chief of Pohl's WVHA Works Department, SS-Brigadeführer Heinz Kammler, to the project and, growing eloquent about this greatest and most important of armament tasks the Führer had entrusted him with, had boasted that Hitler had placed his hand on his shoulder as he left and said that he relied on him, and he (Himmler) was his guarantee for the punctual and precise execution of the commission.[26]

After the discussion at Hochwald Himmler, Speer and Saur had driven to the Wolfschanze to report back to Hitler, who then demanded an absolute minimum of 5000 A4 rockets within the shortest conceivable time. These were the vertical take-off, guided rockets armed with a high explosive warhead developed by Werner von Braun's team and known later as the V-2. They provided Hitler, and no doubt Himmler, another escape from awful reality: they were 'offensive' not 'defensive' weapons such as fighter aircraft and they answered 'terror with terror'; above all they promised both the 'retaliation' against England the people had been demanding for the bombing of German cities, and such a domination of southern England as to make an Anglo-American invasion of the continent impossible, forcing the western allies to terms. That at any rate was the conviction Hitler expressed to Speer and Himmler that evening of 20 August.[27]

Speer's account has to be treated with caution, yet his account of Himmler's boasting about having the Führer's absolute confidence is exactly in line with Brandt's file note of 3 September, recording Himmler boasting about the Führer's good opinion of the SS. And the following day, 4 September, Kersten recorded Ohlendorf telling him that 'the Reichsführer believes that whatever the Führer orders is for the best and a boon for Germany. . . . The Reichsführer has immense faith in victory.'[28] Ohlendorf was far from intimate with Himmler, and his SD reports were now so pessimistic that many were kept from Hitler – as Himmler explained to Kersten on 18 September, unhelpful details should not be placed before the Führer lest they divert him from his task of leading them to victory. Yet Ohlendorf was in a particularly good position to know Himmler's mind at this time since Himmler was engaged in inserting him into a key position in the Ministry of Economics. This was an intrigue, probably undertaken in collaboration with Bormann, against Speer's growing power; in July Speer had managed to persuade Hitler that all production, not simply armaments, should be concentrated in his Ministry.

All these indications suggest that, hopeless as Germany's military situation appeared to the conservative opposition, to an increasing number of Army officers, to most leading industrialists and to a large proportion of the population, Hitler, Himmler and the other paladins kept out reality with ideas of 'miracle' weapons and of an inevitable split in the enemy coalition.

It was in such a state of mind, probably, that Himmler travelled to Posen in the Warthegau in early October and gave two remarkable speeches. The first was to his Gruppenführers on 4 October, the second and most notorious two days later to a convention of Reichsleiters and Gauleiters. He and Bormann had arranged the convention to rally the Party leaders in this critical situation for the Reich and provide them with information and the confidence to stem defeatism in the country. A very high-level team shared the platform, Dönitz for the Navy, Milch for the Luftwaffe, Speer – now Reichsminister for Armaments and War Production – and five of his departmental chiefs for the whole area of weapons and supplies. Only Goebbels was missing from what might be termed the new 'total war' Cabinet which was to support Hitler in the final phase and keep the Reich on course for destruction.

For the listening Gauleiters it must have seemed a long day: the morning session was taken up by Speer and his production experts; after lunch Milch spoke on fighter production to erect a 'roof' over the country, and after him Dönitz on new designs of U-boats which would be able to take the war to the western allies again. It was not until 5.30 that Himmler rose to make the big speech of the day.[29]

'I speak to you as always as Reichsführer-SS and as a Party comrade,' he began in his homely style. He wished to address certain problems, he went on, which were not immediately connected, first the question of 'bandits, partisans and the whole complex of General Vlassov'; they would have heard about these things endlessly through letters and from men home on leave, but he wished to give them his view, grounded on long experience and, he believed, a very good knowledge of the east and the whole Slavic problem. Complaints about partisans ran like a red thread through the letters from the front. It was said that a 300-, even a 400-kilometre-wide ring of partisans separated the eastern front from the homeland. It was true, he admitted, that the railway lines were 'so and so often broken' and they took 'half a day, a day, at times three days' to repair. Yet, he assured them, the front was starved neither of food nor of munitions.

As Reichsführer-SS and Chief of the German Police I have addressed myself from the beginning of the Russian campaign to the guerrilla danger and organised my forces correspondingly. I have allocated about twenty-five police regiments, two infantry and one cavalry brigades to it. For the first time in the winter of 1941–2, for the second time in the winter of 1942–3 and for the third time in the present heavy fighting on the eastern front I have made over my entire SS formations, namely the brigades and the cavalry division – as it has become meanwhile – to the front in order to help avert difficult situations. The moment I am not facing the partisans they become lively again. I cannot expect them to do away with themselves by suicide.

He left the question there and passed on to talk of General Vlassov and another Russian general captured earlier in the year by SS-Brigadeführer Fegelein – a favourite who had since taken over from Wolff as his liaison officer at Führer headquarters. He digressed in most characteristically ironic vein on how this General had presented Fegelein with his Order of Lenin: in turn Fegelein had presented it to the Führer, who afterwards returned it to him mounted in a silver case.

This General we treated correctly, frightfully politely, frightfully nicely. According-ing to the peculiarity of the Slav, who likes to hear himself talking, if one says 'You know that much better' and if one then hears him out nicely and yet stimulates a little bit of discussion, then the man betrays all his divisions, all deployment orders, all that he intends, in general all that he knows.

The price for this treachery? On the third day we said to this General roughly as follows: it is quite clear to you that you cannot now go back. But you are an important man, and we guarantee that at the end of the war you will be granted the pension of a Russian lieutenant-general and that in the immediate future you will have Schnapps, cigarettes and women – in this way one can have a man very cheaply. He is very cheap. Look here, one has to calculate frightfully coolly in these matters. Such a man costs 20,000 Marks a year. You allow him ten or fifteen years to live, that is 300,000 Marks. If some time we fire properly from a battery for two days, that also costs 300,000 Marks. However, it is risky to make a great political programme out of such a Slav, in the final analysis that rebounds back on us.

He was referring to the Vlassov propaganda for the Russian Liberation Army (ROA) which, he went on, had made him really anxious. 'Russia will never be conquered by Germany, Russia can be conquered only by Russians – that is what that Russian swine Herr General Vlassov volunteered himself for.' Vlassov was asking for men and weapons to launch against Russia, perhaps – 'perhaps also one day more probably against us.' No doubt Himmler was smarting still from the defection of Gill–Rodionov. He went on to translate the problem of recruiting Slavic volunteers into the purest racial terms.

We [Germans], however, have more value than they. Our task in the next generation, in the next century, is as it was in the olden days, to reinstate this Nordic man as the leadership class for all parts of the aristocracy, thereby ruling the world. The moment we begin to undermine and explode this fundamental insomuch as we say to our own infantry that we cannot conquer the Russians and that the Russians can only be conquered by Russians, that moment we begin to do away with ourselves. That is the great danger of the Vlassov movement. On that account it must be prohibited. The Führer has strictly forbidden it and for that reason it has to be intellectually eliminated in our own ranks to the last jot.

Of course in the mixture of Mongolian and Germanic peoples one came across here and there an individual of earlier good race. 'Then we want to take his child and bring it to Germany. If he does not reconcile himself we want to slay him because he is dangerous. Because he will be a dangerous leader for the others. If he is reconciled we want to rear him, as we want all German blood and no other, in the body of our *Volk*, and never to allow him back into this area.'

He passed on to the international conspiracy of freemasons, Jews, half-Jews, Bolshevists, democrats, plutocrats and politicised Churches working against them by encouraging natural subversive movements in all the occupied countries. Enemy support for saboteurs and spies within the Reich was a matter of such delicacy that he could not divulge details, he said; he promised to tell them something about it at a Gauleiter conference after the war. But he assured them they had no need to be worried. He touched on the vital part the concentration camps played in internal security as well as armaments production, boasting that inmates contributed 15 million work-hours a month for Speer's Ministry. Speer denounced this figure after the war as an absurd overstatement.

Having assured them that his security forces were in complete control and 'no uprising, no difficulty' could develop anywhere, he moved on to discuss the extermination of the Jews. Why he chose this time to reveal it openly – so far as this circle of mainly Party leaders was open – is not clear. It may be that he wanted to scotch rumours and give them the facts. It may be that he felt he was far enough down the road to the final goal to be able to boast of his accomplishment; it may be on the other hand that in this critical situation for the Reich he wished to implicate them in the extermination, as it were making them accomplices and subject to retribution if the Reich went down in defeat and the allies fulfilled a promise they had made to hunt down and punish all war criminals. Albert Speer was of this view; long after the war he wrote that he assumed Hitler had asked Himmler to reveal the extermination to the Party leaders to indicate that their bridges had been burned. However that may be, this was, so far as is known, only the second time that he dropped euphemism and spoke frankly about the awesome burden on his shoulders; the first time had been two days earlier to his senior officers.

'I may here in this context and in this closest of circles', he told the Gauleiters,

allude to a question which you, *meine Parteigenossen*, have all taken for granted, but which has become for me the most difficult question of my life, the Jewish question. You all accept it as self-evident and agreeable that in your *Gaue* there are no longer any Jews. All German people – apart from individual exceptions – are clear about it, we would not have endured the bombing war and the burdens of the fourth nor perhaps the fifth and sixth war years to come if we still had this festering plague in the body of our *Volk*. The maxim with its few words, 'The Jews must be exterminated', is, *meine Herren*, easily spoken. For he who has to execute its demands it is the hardest and most difficult task there is.

Look here, naturally there are Jews – however, consider for yourselves, how many – even *Parteigenossen* – have directed their famous petition to me or other offices, in which it is said that all Jews are obviously swine, only so-and-so is a decent Jew, to whom one may do nothing. I venture to assert that according to the number of petitions and the number of opinions in Germany there were more decent Jews than nominally available. That is to say in Germany we have so many million people who have one of the famous decent Jews that this number is already greater than the number of Jews. I simply want to say that because you can establish within the area of your own *Gaue* that even with honourable and decent National Socialist people, each of them knows a decent Jew.

Then he gave expression to that sharing of complicity, that dark thrill of knowledge in forbidden areas that appears to have animated the executives of genocide from the beginning:

I ask of you that what I say in this circle you really only hear and never speak of. We come to the question: how is it with the women and children? I have resolved even here on a completely clear solution. That is to say I do not consider myself justified in eradicating the men – so to speak killing or ordering them killed – and allowing the avengers in the shape of the children to grow up for our sons and grandsons. The difficult decision had to be taken, to cause this *Volk* to disappear from the earth. To organise the execution of this mission was the most difficult task we had hitherto. It was accomplished without – as I believe I am able to say – our men or our officers suffering injury to spirit or soul. This danger was very close. The way between the two possibilities, either to become too crude, to become heartless and no longer to respect human life, or to become weak and crack up in a nervous breakdown – the path between this Scylla and Charybdis is horribly narrow.

The entire property that we confiscated from the Jews – it runs to infinite value – has been passed over to the Reich Economics Minister down to the last Pfennig. I have taken the view: we have the duty to our *Volk*, to our race, if we want to win the war – we have the duty to our Führer, who now for once in two thousand years has been granted our *Volk*, not to be petty here but to be thoroughgoing. But we have not the right to take even one Pfennig from the confiscated Jewish property. I established from the beginning that SS men, even if they only take one Mark, are dead. In the last few days on that account I have signed several – I can say it calmly, it was about a dozen – death sentences. Here one has to be hard lest the whole suffer by it. I have felt myself bound to speak to you, as the highest bearers of the will of the Party, as the highest dignitaries of this political order, this political instrument of the Führer, once quite openly about this question and to say how it has been. The Jewish question in those countries occupied by us will be settled by the end of this year. Only a residue of individual Jews will remain in hiding. The question of the non-Jews married to Jews and the question of half-Jews will be sensibly and reasonably investigated, decided and then solved.

Here, in these few words, we have perhaps the clearest glimpse inside the enclosed mind of the Nazi Party. They are so matter-of-factly uttered and it is so clear they need no explanation among this circle of 'the highest bearers of the will of the Party' including Hitler's closest confidant, Bormann, and the eminent guests, Dönitz, Milch, Speer, that the corporate nature of the aim to eradicate the Jews is plain to see. These few phrases should be sufficient to bury the arid academic arguments between those labelled 'intentionalists' – who believe the final solution was planned and ordered by Hitler – and those known as 'functionalists' – professing to believe that it came about through pressure from below as lesser functionaries tried to evolve solutions to the problem of Jews crowded in the east. The speech surely reveals that it was not Hitler, Himmler, Heydrich alone, nor the officials in the field alone, but the mind and soul of the Party and all those who had been convinced by the Party's message that willed the end of the Jews. Himmler was the flywheel, Hitler the driving belt in this machine with countless cogs and gearings fuelled by hate and the urge to destroy.

'That I had great difficulties with many economic concerns, you will believe,' he went on.

> I have cleared out great Jewish ghettos in the base areas. In Warsaw we had four weeks' street-fighting in a Jewish ghetto. Four weeks! We cleared out approximately 700 bunkers there. This whole ghetto made fur coats, clothes and suchlike. Earlier, if one had wanted to reach in there, it was: 'Stop! You are disrupting the war economy! Stop! Armaments concern!' Naturally that had absolutely nothing to do with *Parteigenossen* Speer [he must have turned towards Speer on the platform]. You certainly could do nothing about it. It is the part of the alleged armaments concerns, which *Parteigenossen* Speer and I want to cleanse together in the next weeks and months. We shall do that precisely as unsentimentally as in the fifth year of the war everything has to be done unsentimentally, but with large hearts for Germany.
>
> With that I should like to conclude the Jewish question. Now you know your way about, and you will keep it to yourselves. Perhaps at some much later date one will be able to consider whether one should say something more about it to the German *Volk*. I believe it better that we – all of us – have borne it for our *Volk*, have taken the responsibility on ourselves – the responsibility for a deed not only for an idea – and that we take the secret with us to the grave.

Precisely what he meant is difficult to know. It was unrealistic to expect that the disappearance of the entire millionfold Jewish race from Europe could be kept a secret; in any case too many people, German managers and workers of all nationalities in the factories at Auschwitz and throughout the General Gouvernement, and soldiers on their way to or from the eastern front, saw the flames and smelled burning flesh as their trains were shunted in the area of the death camps, Polish agricultural workers, prostitutes who clustered around the camps for the pickings from 'confiscated' Jewish valuables, members of the Polish Home Army and communist resistance groups, Austrians from near Mauthausen, all knew rather more than Himmler had revealed to the Gauleiters of the manner of extermination. Indeed the whole world could have known; the fact of genocide had been published in the world press and broadcast by radio. Was the Führer's involvement the secret? If so, Himmler had only stated it by implication, not directly. Perhaps it was simply a theatrical flourish, the seal of a blood pact and a secret that could not be told.

He turned to the problem of defeatism. It had been clear to him when Mussolini had been toppled that a dangerous precedent had been set: '*Also*, a Duce can be arrested, interesting, yes how interesting. . . .' But those tempted to think like that had not taken into account that fascism and National Socialism were not one and the same and that, 'with all honour to the Duce', he could not be spoken of in the same breath as the Führer. Such psychological mistakes would have to be avoided.

He pointed to the success of the security services who had located the place where Mussolini had been held, and of the SS-Kommando under Brigadeführer Otto Skorzeny – whom he did not mention, no doubt because Goebbels had made him into a household name – who had released him from captivity. Freeing the Duce had been only one side of their activity, he went on. The other side had concerned all those who had been encouraged by his downfall to talk of the downfall of the Führer and the Nazi Party. They had been 'sorted out pretty tidily', and handed over to the Minister of Justice.

> On educational grounds these laconic short news items appeared in the paper that this and that *Herr* had lost his head. That was continued for a while. We will never seize every grouser and certainly do not wish to. With all offences it is important that again and again someone is seized. He can be very bad, he can be someone who has had bad luck – that is a matter of indifference. Whoever is seized must atone and pay the penalty – that is indeed the sense of every law – in order that his death be a lesson and a warning to thousands of others so that they in their unreason do not do the same.

The Party, he went on, had the duty to set the example against defeatism, not simply in the literal sense, but inwardly. It also had the duty to set standards of behaviour. And he besought them not only to be models of decent living themselves, but to have the moral courage to act brutally and mercilessly even against Party comrades whose behaviour gave rise to scandal and rumour. He would not trust himself to say this to them if he could not demonstrate that he acted thus in the SS. He had long adopted the practice whereby an SS officer sentenced by court was degraded in front of the assembled troops. For how he asked, could he ask his men to give their lives if they did not respect their officers? He was happy to give officers so punished the chance to rehabilitate themselves as ordinary soldiers at the front. There were worse cases, however, where an officer could only rehabilitate himself through his death. When he was killed, then it was announced that the day before his death he had been reinstated in his former rank and rehabilitated. 'Then at least he has left behind a decent name for his children.'

He turned to his new appointment as Minister of the Interior, and to the natural conflicts between central and regional authority, lecturing them on his ideas of efficient administration, after which he spoke with much pride of the Waffen-SS. He reminded them of the feats of the SS-Panzerkorps in Russia, and spoke of the new divisions he was raising; by the end of the year he would have seven Corps and seventeen divisions, besides a number of 'Storm' and 'Shock' brigades. He had two cadet schools and a third was to follow, and four schools for NCOs. The blood toll they were paying at the front, however, was monstrously large.

> Do not forget that since the summer of 1942 most of my company commanders were twenty-four years old, and are now twenty-three years old, and that on average no company commander is there [at the front] for more than four months. Then he leaves through death or wounding. In the last ten weeks the Totenkopfdivision has replaced all its companies twice and had thirty-two company commanders killed and forty-eight wounded. If I have to give a company to a twenty-one-year-old it is self-evident that he will not have the maturity and quality I otherwise demand of a company commander in the Waffen-SS.
>
> For all that no one should reprove us. With all the insufficiencies which every organisation has, we can affirm – I believe – that we have never been in crisis. Never has our courage failed. Never have we lost our sense of humour. Never! We have truly done our bit according to the law. If a company had five men left and they had the order to fall in, then without a word they lined up again. We have now reconstituted the first company of the Leibstandarte with new men for the third time – the famed first company with the 1.9 metre [about six foot three] tall men which is always on guard.

Altogether, he believed that the Waffen-SS had represented the Party worthily in this struggle and never given it cause for shame.

Finally he looked beyond the months, 'perhaps years', of war ahead of them to the time when they would have to win the peace. He believed it necessary already to reflect on the goals: organising 120 million Germans, pushing out the borders of the German peoples 500 kilometres eastwards, or, as he had expressed it earlier in his speech, 'to reconstruct the Germanic Reich whose borders I am convinced – now you will take me for a crazy optimist – will lie at some time on the Urals', working indefatigably on resettlement, creating powerful national bases in strings of settlements extending in the east, south-east and west as far as German power. Above all the task was to prepare the *Volk* in terms of quality and numbers for the conflicts that their grandsons and future generations would have to face, when not peoples but whole races would be organised and continents would march against each other.

> That will come. If one sees that and if one has it already before one's eyes, then we follow together a self-evident law of nature on this part of the way. If we see this, then belief will never desert us, we will never be disloyal, never be cowardly, never in a bad mood but will endeavour to be worthy to be permitted to live under Adolf Hitler and fight alongside him.

Thus he ended the long speech. In essentials, apart from his startling avowal of the final solution to the Jewish question, it was no different from his speeches at the beginning of the war or, in its statements of the racial and eastern creed, from before the war. Neither the compromises he had been forced to make in every area, nor the advance of the Russians and the prospect of defeat had made him reconsider his goals or the manner of their attainment. To speak of establishing the German boundaries on the Urals when they were retreating all along the front should, on the face of it, have established him in truth as a '*crazy* optimist'. Perhaps he felt that a restatement of Party orthodoxy was the only way to combat defeatism; perhaps he believed Hitler was right about an inevitable split in the enemy coalition; perhaps he had been given some reason to believe that the western powers would do business with him. Perhaps, in Bormann's presence, he felt it necessary to play the old record which he knew would be played back to Hitler. Possibly it was the only one he knew how to play. Or perhaps on these mass occasions his fanaticism and dreams for the future overrode his rational judgement.

Yet the most probable explanation is that he really had convinced himself. To talk of victory in the current situation of the Reich and resettling the east to the Urals was no more fantastic than his pre-war convictions about a world conspiracy against Germany or the purity of the blood of the *Herrenvolk*. As events in the real world outside threatened to obtrude, it was probably natural that he should retreat further into the battened-down, claustrophobic, but familiar and internally safe images of his ideal world. These, after all, had made him someone in the first place; with them he had acquired immense power; without them and without his Führer – perhaps that was impossible to contemplate. They were a part of him, and, the worse things became, the more he needed to cling to them.

It is hard to know how the speech was received since the explosive passage about the Jews meant that all those who heard it and survived the war had to lie. According to the memoirs of the Reich Youth Leader, Baldur von Schirach, an oppressive silence ruled while Himmler spoke, and afterwards, when Bormann invited them to snacks, they 'sat speechless at the tables avoiding one another's eyes'.[30] According to Albert Speer the Gauleiters and Reichsleiters drank themselves into a stupor that evening. When the text of Himmler's speech was discovered, Speer corrected himself: he had driven away from Posen at lunchtime that day and had not heard Himmler; the drunken scenes had been at another Gauleiter conference.[31] Dönitz denied to the end of his life that he had known anything about the extermination of the Jews before the end of the war.

While Himmler was in Posen, Kersten went to Stockholm and made contact with a special representative of President Roosevelt named Abram S. Hewitt. He received much the same message as Langbehn had in Switzerland. The United States was anxious to halt the war, but was not prepared to negotiate with Hitler or the Nazi Party. Furthermore Germany would have to surrender her conquered territories, cut her armed forces to a size that would render her incapable of aggression, and deliver her leaders to a war crimes tribunal. Obviously unacceptable as these terms were, Himmler refused to believe that the western allies, especially the British, could fail to see that if they continued supporting the Russians the consequence would be the Bolshevisation of Europe, and he sent Schellenberg to see what he could do with Hewitt. According to Schellenberg, he had persuaded Himmler the previous year that the occupied countries had to be used as bargaining counters to achieve a negotiated peace roughly on the basis of the Reich borders of 1 September 1939.[32]

Schellenberg flew to Stockholm, but failed to move Hewitt on the political conditions, and the negotiation came to nothing. Both he and Kersten in their post-war accounts depict a Himmler unable to resolve to use his power against Hitler and the Party. Kersten has him saying, 'I can't betray my Führer. Everything that I am I owe to him.'[33] But it is apparent that the terms Hewitt was insisting on destroyed all his aims in the east and, by removing the Party hierarchy, undermined his own position. If he seriously considered betraying Hitler and bringing the war to an end, these were not conditions he could accept. All his inclinations as a politician were to await the favourable moment before moving, and it must have been comparatively easy to persuade himself that the west would see reason sooner or later if the Russians continued their advance. In his memoirs Schellenberg described using all his powers of persuasion to try and bring home Germany's real situation to him, but in vain; 'nothing could break the spell which Hitler still exercised upon those around him.'[34] Of course it may be that Himmler was not only still under the spell of his Führer, but acting on his behalf in seeking unofficial negotiations with the west.

Gottlob Berger, certainly one of Himmler's closest confidants in these latter years, stated in post-war testimony that Himmler expressed the opinion during one of their talks that Hitler had not been normal for some years.[35] This rings true since, of course, Himmler had the secret medical dossier suggesting that Hitler suffered from syphilis and it would be surprising if he had not found out about his diagnosed progressive heart disease and his use of drugs from the same source; this would have caused him to observe Hitler closely. Yet the probability is that all his observations and all the intellectual arguments about Germany's plight he heard from Schellenberg, Ohlendorf, Popitz and Langbehn counted little beside his emotional need for and commitment to Hitler. Probably he committed treason in his mind, but not in his heart. That, of course, must be speculation.

In outward things he adhered rigidly to his goals, continued to expand his influence in other spheres and worked more relentlessly and obsessively than ever. This could have been either desperate reaction to the situation of the Reich, or his means of escape from intellectual doubt and internal schism – the means he had used since adolescence to resolve his psychic conflict. Since he did not revise his strategy or his beliefs it is more likely to have been escape, rationalised as giving his all to ensure final victory.

The most pressing goal, acquiring fresh urgency as the Red Army advanced towards the General Gouvernement, was the elimination of the Jewish race in Europe. Before the Italian capitulation it had proved impossible to convince Mussolini of the necessity of handing over his Jews. Now that Germany was master in Italy and the Duce was reinstalled as a mere puppet, the round-up and removal of the Italian Jews had become a priority; Eichmann's assistant, Hauptsturmführer Theodor Dannecker, had arrived in Rome before the end of September, and some time in early October the chief of the Security Police there, Obersturmführer Herbert Kappler, received orders to arrest the 8000 Jews in the city. Kappler began the action on 14 October by burning the synagogues and ravaging the Jewish quarter. Four days later the first transports of goods wagons crowded with human freight pulled away for the journey to Auschwitz.

On 19 October Wolff, experiencing, as he put it 'indescribable happiness' at his first independent command as Highest SSPF in Italy, and rejoicing in 'the trust of the Führer and the Reichsführer',[36] reported to Himmler and both drove to the Wolfschanze to take their midday meal with Hitler. It must be assumed that they talked of the recent action and the prospect of making the whole of Italy *judenfrei*.

Irrational as the final solution had always been, it was now, if possible, more so since it was evident that the Jews of England and the European neutrals were finally beyond their grasp; would not 'the avengers in the shape of the children' grow up in those countries to pursue their 'sons and grandsons'? But faith is not grounded on reason; after the Jews of Italy, it was to be the turn of the Jews of the Balkan allies, and of Greece and the Greek islands.

As with large groups, so with individuals Himmler remained obsessively true to his credo. In August he had had the painful duty of informing the commander of his Waffen-SS division Das Reich, Gruppenführer Walter Krüger, that he could not grant his daughter Elisabeth permission to marry SS-Sturmbannführer Klingenberg. The reason was that the ancestry table of Krüger's wife showed a full Jew in 1711. While it was possible that conception of the progeny might have taken place outside marriage, all concerned were dead, and he concluded that it was impossible to prove.[37] At the end of October, after he had received a petition from Krüger's wife, he wrote to Gottlob Berger to inform him that 'after the most difficult inner struggle and doubts and against my own convictions' he was prepared to allow Krüger's son Gerhard into the SS; he was not prepared, however, to alter his decision about the daughter.[38]

He came to a similar decision in December when three marriage requests were referred to him, one from an NCO, two from brothers who were officers, all three of whom had a common ancestor named Abraham Reinau, born a Jew in 1663 and baptised in 1685. All three

proved themselves in the field and made a 'racially good impression';
in no case was the 'Jewish blood admixture discernible in the genetic
characteristics [*Erscheinungsbild*, thus accurately "phaenotype"].'[39] The
files were sent to him by Obergruppenführer Richard Hildebrandt, chief
of the RuSHA, together with an opinion from the head of his Race Office,
Standartenführer Professor Dr Schultz, to the effect that the chromosomes
deriving from the Jew would have disappeared by the third generation. In
view of this Hildebrandt suggested that the genealogical investigations for
the SS as a whole be limited to only six generations of forebears. Himmler
gave his consent to marriage in all three cases, but wanted the files laid
before him again for reappraisal after the war. He was already decided,
however, that whatever his final judgement the children of these three
would not be accepted into the SS, nor, if female, permitted to marry a
member of the SS. He was scathing about Professor Schultz's opinion; if
the Jewish chromosomes had disappeared by the third generation could one
assert that the chromosomes from all the other forebears had disappeared
in the same way? One thing was clear to him: 'Herr Prof. Dr Schultz' – a
few months ago a favourite of his – 'is not suitable as chief of the Race
Office.'[40]

His methods remained as constantly devious as his beliefs: in September
Hitler's personal physician and General Commissioner for Health and
Hygiene, SS-Brigadeführer Professor Brandt, had reported to him that
the Bishop of Münster, Clemens von Galen, was raising doubts about
the evacuation of patients from mental institutions in areas subject to
air-raids. In 1941 von Galen's sermons about the 'mercy killing' of the
mentally ill had contributed to official instructions to end the euthanasia
programme – then largely superseded by '13 f 14'. Himmler had wanted
to arrest von Galen then, but had not done so for fear of the disaffection
this would have caused throughout Westphalia. Now Himmler instructed
Kaltenbrunner that, when the next parish priest in Münster died, suspicions
should be cast on the Bishop in the same way as he was casting suspicion
on the evacuation policy. 'It should be said that the priest concerned was
done away with by his [the Bishop's] adherents because he had said this or
that against the Bishop at some time.' He asked Kaltenbrunner to let him
know as soon as a death occurred which could be utilised in this way.[41]

Meanwhile Himmler's scheme to insert his adherents into the Reich
Economics Ministry matured. The ground had been cut from under
the Minister of Economics, Funk, by Speer's success in centralising all
production in his own Ministry; like Göring before him, Funk in decline
appears to have seen Himmler as his best hope in his rivalry with Speer.[42]
Consequently he was happy to reorganise the Economics Ministry during
November and December 1943, with two leading members of Himmler's
Circle of Friends, Hanz Hayler and Otto Ohlendorf, in key positions, Hayler
as State Secretary, Ohlendorf – who retained his position in the RSHA –
as chief of a newly created Main Department II, with responsibility for the

key areas of general economic policy, rationing and supplies for the civil population. Himmler had reasonable grounds for interest in these areas since, as the revolutions at the end of the first war had demonstrated, supply of food and internal security were closely related. However, in his study of economic policy in the Third Reich, Ludolf Herbst has concluded that Himmler also saw in Funk's loss of power a chance for the SS to gain a base for use in the long term against Speer's position and to impose ideological goals on economic policy.[43] Speer seems to have apprehended this; he had already persuaded Hitler to commission him with the task of rebuilding the German cities after the war, apparently to make his rivals aware that he was not just there for the duration.

It is striking that at this time when all resources were being mobilised at last and at a desperately late hour for 'total war', the phrase 'after the war' sounded more frequently in leading Party circles. Perhaps it resulted from the hope that since the war could scarcely now end victoriously, Hitler would achieve one of the political masterstrokes on which his pre-war fame had been built. Hitler, of course, contributed to the mood with his conviction of a coming split in the enemy coalition. To judge from his correspondence, Himmler fully accepted the idea. Whereas the previous winter he had been speaking of a seven years' or perhaps even another thirty years' war, references to the post-war years now began to appear more frequently in his letters and decrees. In October he had threatened a forty-four-year-old bachelor, SS-Hauptsturmführer Franz Schwarz, that if he was not married by the end of the war he would be dismissed from the SS.[44] In January 1944 he instructed the Lebensborn manager, Max Sollmann, that rations for the mothers must be reduced 'for the duration of the war', in particular the oatmeal porridge must be made with water, not with full or skimmed milk.[45] The same month he concerned himself with the defensive villages inhabited by an armed peasantry (*Wehrbauern*) which were to serve as the Germanic bastions of the occupied east after the war.[46]

In February he wrote to SS-Gruppenführer Taubert, in charge of the SS castle, Wewelsburg, saying that despite much work he had time to reflect on this and that, and would not like his various ideas and thoughts to be forgotten – in which context:

> . . . I was reminded that in peacetime we could perhaps designate Wewelsburg: Wewelsburg – *Reichshaus der SS-Gruppenführer* [imperial residence of the SS-Gruppenführers].
>
> I request that you lay this note before me again on the outbreak of peace.[47]

In March Hitler told him of a curious phenomenon: the deeper the bulbs of the meadow saffron grew, the harder the following winter; conversely the shallower the bulbs grew, the milder the next winter. Himmler wrote to SS-Oberführer Professor Dr Walther Wüst of Ahnenerbe, informing him of this so that he could add it to the scheme of systematic weather research planned for after the war.[48]

By April 1944 the indications are even clearer. He wrote to Brigadeführer Wilhelm Keilhaus at the SS-Führungs (leadership) office that 'the most urgent task in the intelligence area after the war even in the Armistice period will be the establishment of an SS and police telephone network extending to the nethermost Gendarmerie and border police stations.'[49] Even more significantly he asked Berger to prepare the Reichsminister of Post, Ohnesorge, for the fact that he would ask him to erect this telephone net as a first priority after the war.

Another indication is contained in a file about a Castle Grünwald, near Munich, birthplace of Ludwig the Bavarian, one of Himmler's heroes – as he told Pohl, Ludwig had been 'outlawed by the Church and was without doubt a great German Emperor'. Learning of the owner's death early in 1944, he asked Pohl to make covert enquiries about purchasing the castle for the SS since he had a mind to establish a school of National Socialist ideology there some time.[50] By May Pohl had managed to find out that the heirs had no intention of selling. Himmler nevertheless instructed him to obtain an option for the WVHA 'in case the owners should think of selling the castle before the end of the war', and asked him to take the next opportunity to speak to the Reich Treasury Minister about the purchase.[51]

The most remarkable manifestation of planning for peace occurred in the Economics Ministry. While the industrial leaders were co-operating with Speer and raising war production to record levels – thus by July 1944, despite bombing, armaments production was practically three and a quarter times that of January 1942[52] – they had no illusions about the approaching end. And threatened on the one hand by the debilitating industrial results of central planning and controls in the war economy, on the other hand by further revolutionary trends unleashed by the failure to achieve war aims in the east, they sought to protect themselves as a group in the difficult transition from war to peace which they saw close ahead. Their chosen vehicle was the Economics Ministry; it had close connections with the Reichsbank, was responsible for foreign trade and exchange and credit policy, and was perceived as the rival of Speer's centralising Armaments Ministry. For their part Hayler and Ohlendorf, now the real powers in the Economics Ministry, had every reason to co-operate with the great financier–industrialists to secure their own – or SS – primacy in the industrial sphere after the war. From secret beginnings in the winter of 1943/4 Ohlendorf took over co-ordination of the economic planning groups, using his department in the RSHA as cover. Thus while the industrialists were putting their all into Speer's 'total war' effort and Himmler was stating and restating his belief in ultimate victory, Ohlendorf was erecting a *Zentrale* for post-war economic planning and survival inside the most powerful SS organ, the Reich Security Main Office.[53]

This coincided with a new sense of purpose and determination in the military opposition. It crystallised around Colonel Claus Schenck, Graf von Stauffenberg, appointed Chief of Staff to the head of the General Army Office (Allgemeine Heeresamt) in October 1943. He had been seriously wounded in North Africa that spring, losing his left eye, his right hand and two fingers from his left. Long aware of the need to remove 'the brown pest', the shock of his injuries or the long period for reflection during convalescence, coinciding with the rapid slide in the situation of the Reich, had left him with the conviction that he had to do something to save the Fatherland and further senseless sacrifice of life. His appointment gave him the opportunity, for the General Army Office was in the old War Office building on the Bendlerstrasse, Berlin, headquarters of the Replacement (or Home) Army and since the break-up of the Oster group at the Abwehr, centre of the Army conspiracy against Hitler. Moreover his chief, General Olbricht, was a member of the Wednesday Society and a leading conspirator.

Von Stauffenberg was a south German aristocrat of unquestionable lineage, romantic good looks and abilities which had led superiors and contemporaries to predict a brilliant future for him in the Army. He brought a youthful dynamism and passion which the movement entirely lacked in the higher echelons and virtually took over the practical planning for an Army take-over of power. He also brought with him high-minded, romantic – or, as Canaris believed, woolly and dangerous – socialist ideas which led him to widen the net of civilian collaborators from the former conservative groupings around Goerdeler, Popitz, von Hassell and the others to include former politicians and trade unionists of the centre and left. This caused deep schisms and unease, indeed the only points on which the disparate civilian and military opposition groupings were united were that the war could no longer be won militarily and that the Nazi regime had to be removed as a precondition for peace negotiations.

The longer von Stauffenberg discussed the change of government necessary in order to make the Reich acceptable to their enemies as a negotiating partner, the clearer it became to him and his brother Berthold, serving in the legal department of naval headquarters, that Hitler had to be killed, not simply arrested or replaced. All their plans were directed towards Hitler's assassination as the necessary precondition for an Army take-over and the neutralisation of the SS.

Meanwhile Canaris fell. Abwehr intelligence had been deteriorating for a long while. The enemy held the initiative everywhere and it showed particularly in the field of deception. The more apparent it became that Germany faced defeat the less tolerant neutral governments were to German undercover activity. This applied even in Spain, formerly the happiest of hunting grounds for Canaris; allied pressure threatened his entire network. In North Africa Abwehr stations had been overrun, and in Italy, now the focus of attention, there were insufficient local agents because of a long-standing prohibition on spying on their Axis partner. Canaris' record there was one of repeated failure.

The incident which brought about his downfall was almost an anticlimax. Von Ribbentrop complained to Hitler that Abwehr sabotage aboard British ships in Spanish harbours endangered his Spanish policy; as a result, on 8 February 1944, Hitler decreed that all such acts of sabotage had to cease. Three days later news came of an explosion in a British ship loaded with oranges in the port of Cartagena. Apparently Himmler's liaison at Führer headquarters, Hermann Fegelein, took advantage of Hitler's eruption of rage to suggest that the Abwehr simply be handed over in entirety to the Reichsführer-SS. Hitler nodded, sent for Himmler and commissioned him to form a unified intelligence service from the SD and Abwehr.[54] Thus it seems that it was von Ribbentrop who played the final card removing Canaris from the game; he did not do so on behalf of his arch-rival, but Himmler, who had protected the Admiral for so long against enemies within the RSHA, simply swept in the winnings.

Negotiations between Kaltenbrunner, 'Gestapo' Müller and Schellenberg on behalf of Himmler on the one hand and Keitel and Abwehr department chiefs on behalf of the OKW continued for weeks. Himmler compromised as he had throughout his career, giving up some purely military intelligence, counter-espionage and sabotage functions to OKW personnel for the sake of the major prize of assimilating virtually the entire existing Abwehr departments, outstations and personnel into a 'Military' Section VI of the RSHA under Schellenberg, who thus became chief of a vast unified Reich intelligence service. The final agreement was signed between Himmler and Keitel on 14 May 1944.

Canaris, after a period under virtual house arrest, was rehabilitated by Hitler in June, and appointed to head the OKW special staff for trade and economic warfare, a redundant office at this stage of the war. Why Hitler brought him back has been a puzzle to his biographers. Perhaps, once again, Himmler interceded for him; perhaps it was because his contacts with the west were felt to be still of value.

Thus as the situation of the Reich crumbled through the winter and spring 1943–4 and the opposition organisation spread wider and grew desperate for action before it was too late, Himmler mightily extended his own influence. At the same time the department chiefs of his most powerful organ, the RSHA, Ohlendorf and Schellenberg, were at one with the great industrialists, the conservative resistance and the Army opposition centred on the Bendlerstrasse in the realisation that a political solution had to be sought with the western allies. Himmler was equally clear about this. So for that matter was Hitler; it had been his aim from the beginning. Yet repeated soundings had shown that the west was not prepared to talk with him.

On the other hand it was plain that an Army attempt to seize power was fraught with extraordinary difficulties: the comparatively small circle of officers in the know in key positions might be posted elsewhere before Day X; staffs and units were penetrated by indoctrinated National Socialist education officers; to initiate wider circles to prevent confusion when the putsch was launched invited exposure. Besides, a putsch by the Army alone, or units of the Army alone, must lead to civil war with the SS, security services and police on the side of those loyal to Hitler. It was evident that the SS had to take part in the change of regime. Since the SS was guardian of the ideological purity of the National Socialist state, this was the ultimate paradox – not perhaps to Himmler or Ohlendorf, who considered the Party corrupt, but a paradox and colossal danger for the opposition groupings. To a greater extent probably than at any time since the threatening SA 'revolution' of 1934, Himmler held the key to power in the Reich.

It appears there were four attempts to assassinate Hitler during this period:[55] on one occasion a bomb was smuggled aboard his plane before he flew, but the detonating mechanism failed. Whether the other three attempts aborted because of Hitler's habit of changing his schedules at the last moment in order to foil planned attempts, because of ill luck, or because Himmler learned about them and had Hitler change his itinerary is unclear.

All that seems certain is that there were manifold contacts and exchanges between Himmler's agents and the conservative and military opposition, between his agents and mediators with the west, between his chiefs in the Economics Ministry and RSHA and the secretly 'defeatist' financiers and industrialists, and that his industrial Circle of Friends contained many who were planning clandestinely with Ohlendorf for a post-war integration of the German economy with the west, and were still contributing large sums to his special SS account: in September 1943 1.1 million Marks went in, 200,000 of them from the banker von Schröder himself; as he wrote to Himmler, 'we are very happy to be able to perform a certain help in your special tasks.'[56] At the same time all the leading members of the opposition were kept under close surveillance by the SD and Gestapo and were acutely aware of it. On both sides it was an intricately hazardous game. Himmler sat in his field headquarters, one imagines, with a Sphinx-like gaze behind the pince-nez.

At the same time he was bending every effort to ensure that the Reich could hold out: he urged Pohl to build factories for the production of war materials in natural caves and underground tunnels immune to enemy bombing, and instructed him to hollow out workshop and factory space in all SS stone quarries, suggesting that by the summer of 1944 they should have 'new cavemen' installed in the greatest possible number of such 'uniquely bomb-proof work sites'. The plans to use natural caves came up against the usual rivalries from competing authorities with the same idea. Nevertheless Pohl's Works' Department chief, Brigadeführer

Hans Kammler, succeeded in creating underground workshops and living quarters from a cave system in the Harz mountains in central Germany in what Speer, writing to congratulate him, called 'an almost impossibly short period of two months' – a feat, he continued, 'unsurpassable even by American standards'.[57] This complex, known as 'Dora', was to take over from Buchenwald the secret production of parts for the A4 or V – 'Vegeltungs' (Retaliation) – rockets for which Himmler had assumed responsibility in the summer. The urgency with which this programme was pressed forward was, of course, fully in line with the desire for negotiations with the west, designed as it was to force them to the negotiating table.

Kammler, whom Speer described as making 'an extremely fresh, energetic and ruthless impression – comparable to Heydrich's', went on to build further underground factories at a similarly astonishing speed and with the expenditure of thousands of slave labourers, many of them Jews from Hungary.

Thus far the Hungarian government, like the Italian government previously, had preserved its Jews from the extermination machine, but in March 1944 Hitler ordered the military occupation of the country to prevent its defection from the Axis, and Eichmann went in the next day with a Sondereinsatzkommando to seize able-bodied Jews for labour, the rest for annihilation before the Red Army should overrun the death camps in the General Gouvernement. All those not selected for labour were sent to Auschwitz in May, where as Höss recorded they were despatched at a speed not attained hitherto, 'something over 9000' every twenty-four hours, taken from overcrowded incoming transports, gassed and burned in the crematoria.[58]

The extermination of Hungarian Jewry coincided with a bizarre proposal to trade them with the west in return for merchandise and foreign exchange. Eichmann, at his interrogation in 1960, said that, so far as he remembered, the scheme originated with Himmler.[59] It is equally possible it originated in Schellenberg's fertile mind, either to put Himmler in a better light with the western allies, as Kersten seems to suggest in his diary notes for June[60] – at which date he was treating Schellenberg as well as Himmler – or to probe and exacerbate the tensions between the western allies and the Russians. The choice of location for the negotiation tends to support Schellenberg's involvement; it was Turkey, where he and von Ribbentrop had or believed they might have acquired an agent, codenamed 'Cicero', with access to the most secret despatches of the British Ambassador at Ankara, Sir Hughe Montgomery Knatchbull-Hugessen. It is probable, if not certain, that 'Cicero' was actually controlled by the British secret service. While 'Cicero' resigned from Sir Hughe's service towards the end of April the plan, co-ordinated with the secret Zionist organisation Vaadah, must have been hatching before this was known.

A Hungarian Jew named Uyell Brandt, travelling on a German passport as Eugen Brandt in a German plane, and accompanied by a Gestapo agent, arrived in Istanbul on 19 May claiming to represent Hungarian Jewry, and reporting to the Jewish and allied authorities that the Germans were prepared to evacuate a million Jews to Spain and Portugal in return for 10,000 motor lorries – for use on the Russian front only – and certain other commodities or foreign exchange; failing an agreement all Jews remaining in Hungary, Rumania, Czechoslovakia and Poland would be annihilated.[61] The offer was regarded with extreme suspicion. In Washington it was felt that Eichmann and possibly Himmler might be seeking to obtain foreign currency for their own use after Germany's defeat; in London it was regarded as a 'sheer case of blackmail or political warfare', designed to embroil the UK and US governments with the Soviet government 'by representing to the latter that the former were negotiating with the enemy'.[62] The Russians were informed immediately and replied that any parley with Hitlerite Germany was inadmissible; nevertheless, the British and Americans kept the negotiations open, playing for time for several months. In fact it could scarcely have been a genuine offer since, as Höss recorded, this period in the summer of 1944 saw Auschwitz's highest ever daily figures for annihilation, while all able-bodied Jews were employed building underground factories or in other concentration camp work.

This last phase of Nazi power in Europe saw the logic of the *Weltanschauung* reach its apotheosis. The oil of the Caucasus, the minerals and industries of the Donetz basin, the fertile agricultural lands of the Ukraine, eastern *Lebensraum*, all the ostensible targets of Hitler's assault, had been lost during the Soviet advances of the winter and spring, together with almost a million German and Axis troops; four out of thirteen German armies in the east had been smashed, another virtually annihilated in the Crimea and forced to evacuate by sea. A Russian thrust deep into the Bukovina region of northern Rumania had split the defence of the southern area; intelligence experts of Foreign Armies East predicted a continuing Russian advance without pause from this salient north-westerly into the southern flank of Army Group Centre, the last bastion of German strength in the east. In the west Rommel awaited the Anglo-American invasion forces massed in the southern counties of England. The transport systems of France and the industrial regions of Germany were under constant allied air attack.

The seriousness of the position was clear from Hitler's appearance; shocked visitors to the Wolfschanze or the Berghof saw 'an old, stooping man with an unhealthy, puffy face',[63] whose left leg, arm and hand shook uncontrollably. Yet, sustained by will – or amphetamines – and his most loyal inner circle, Bormann, Himmler, Goebbels, Dönitz and Speer, he saw the turning point in his fortunes within grasp: a rush programme of new jet fighters, the 'Vergeltung' rockets, new U-boats with unprecedented underwater speed would prevent or defeat the allied invasion and allow him to transfer his western armies east for the decisive battle to break the

'exhausted' Russians. This was the phantom shimmering in the close air at
Führer headquarters. Of all those who helped create and uphold it Himmler
and Speer were the key figures since they were entrusted with production
of the necessary 'miracle' weapons.

The other phantom there had a long, narrow skull, blue eyes in the visage
of a warrior; purged of the blood of inferior races this pure Aryan German
could endure all that fate hurled at him and emerge victorious by virtue of
his innate qualities. Here Himmler was the key figure, the *Endlösung* the
talisman and proof.

'Of this you can be sure,' he told a gathering of generals and
members of the Führer headquarters staff in early May 1944,[64] 'had
we not eliminated the Jews from Germany we would not have been able
to endure the bombing despite the decency of the German *Volk*. That is
my conviction.' And he reminded them of Hitler's prophecy before the
war that if the European nations were incited into another world war, it
would not be the German peoples who were exterminated, but the Jews.
Then he repeated the claim he had made to the Gauleiters in Posen the
previous October:

> The Jewish question in Germany and the occupied countries has been solved.
> It has been solved in accordance with the struggle for survival of our *Volk*, in
> which the survival of our blood was at stake, without compromise. I tell you
> that as comrades. We are all soldiers, whatever uniform we wear. You might
> like to sympathise with me and imagine how hard it was to fulfil this soldierly
> order that was given me which I followed and carried through out of obedience
> and the most complete conviction. If you say, 'The men – that we understand
> – but not the children,' then may I draw your attention to my earlier remarks.
> In this showdown with Asia we must accustom ourselves to the groundrules and
> consign to oblivion the morals of past European wars which are dear and much
> closer to us. We are, in my opinion, even as Germans with all our deep heartfelt
> good-natured feeling, not justified in allowing the hate-filled avengers to grow up
> so that our children and grandchildren have to settle with them because we, the
> fathers or grandfathers, were too weak and too cowardly and left the children
> for them.

His use before these generals and members of the Führer headquarters
staff of the phrase 'this soldierly order that was given me' is surely crucial in
reinforcing the truth of his claims on other occasions that he had been
ordered to eliminate the Jews by the Supreme Commander, the Führer.

Later that month he spoke again to a group of generals, repeating his
words about the Jewish question having been solved according to order
without compromise. This time a record of the speech reveals that the
words were greeted with applause,[65] another clue to the wide circle of
agreement about the purpose and ends of Jewish policy. It was the Army
which had been to a large extent responsible for calling forth the Party
in the first place; it seems that the *Weltanschauung* was a more faithful

reflection of their desires than they were afterwards prepared to admit; Himmler was, as he had always been, the extreme conformist.

'I believe, *meine Herren*,' he went on, 'you know me well enough to realise I am no bloodthirsty fellow [*blutrünstiger Mensch*], and not one to take pleasure or amusement in whatever tough thing I have to do. On the other hand, however, I have such good nerves and such a large sense of duty – that I may lay claim to for myself – that, when I recognise something as necessary, I carry it out without compromise.'[66] And he repeated his earlier remarks that it would have been cowardice not to have dealt with the women and children, only to allow them to grow up to take their revenge on their own sons and grandsons.

The following month and before yet another audience of generals, he repeated his claim to having solved the Jewish question without compromise. Had he not done so, had there been Jews in the cities, the German people could not have endured the bombing terror – 'which in the last analysis is organised by the Jews'.[67]

These speeches are curious in their mixture of bravado, self-justification and appeals for understanding about the nature of the task he had been ordered to perform, the courage and hardness required to do away with women and children. His motives for revealing the fact of extermination outside Party circles little more than six months after telling the Gauleiters it was a secret they should take with them to the grave must remain speculative. As with his revelations to the Gauleiters, it may have been to draw the generals into complicity and show them that their bridges were burned. It may simply have been an expression of the radicalism called forth by the desperate situation, intended to bolster morale: now that the Jewish problem had been solved, the cleansed Reich would overcome its other enemies. It may have been a genuine expression of pride in what he had achieved in the face of enormous moral and practical difficulties. Perhaps it also arose from a subconscious longing to rationalise what he knew to have been a crime of historic dimension – and given his devout Catholic upbringing can it be doubted that deep within, entombed by reinforced structures of dogma and reason, but quickening and twisting in the night, was a core of primal, childlike understanding that he had sinned, sinned in the sight of the Lord.

Whatever the mix of motives, the speeches are true reflections of the way in which the ultimate crisis for Nazi power saw the ultimate expression of the *Weltanschauung* and of the urges underlying the whole drive to power and conquest, the Freikorps' urge to war and destruction, the Freikorps' fantasy of women, the pure and chaste of their dreams, and on the other hand the aggressively sexual 'red women' – Jewesses – to be raped and murdered to conquer the softer feminine side within and render the world safe, clean and masculine again. And so the gas chamber–crematoria complexes at Auschwitz reached peak capacity that summer, and at the same time the numbers of *Untermenschen* working and dying as slaves for the master race rose prodigiously. These Dantesque mills of death also managed to reflect the chaos of competing authorities institutionalised both in the Reich and in Himmler's empire. Höss, who had been transferred from Auschwitz to the Concentration Camp Inspectorate under Glücks, and was thus in a position to see the full picture, wrote of this period in his memoirs:

> The harder the war became the more ruthlessly the Reichsführer-SS demanded the employment of prisoners. . . . Chiefly they were sacrificed for armaments. The concentration camps stood between the RSHA [of Kaltenbrunner] and the WVHA [of Pohl]. The RSHA delivered prisoners with the goal of extermination; whether immediately through execution or by the gas chambers or whether somewhat more slowly through epidemics (brought about through the indefensible conditions in the concentration camps which one purposely did not want to improve) made no difference. The WVHA wanted the prisoners preserved for armaments [work]. Because however Pohl allowed himself to be discouraged by the Reichsführer–SS, demanding continually higher work numbers, he gave unintentional support to the purposes of the RSHA, in that his pressure to fulfil the demands meant that countless thousands of prisoners had to die, because in practice all the necessary living conditions for such masses of prisoners were lacking. At the time I suspected this connection but could not and did not wish to believe it. Today however I see the picture more precisely. That and nothing other was the real background, the great shadow that stood behind the concentration camps.[68]

The pressure exerted on the concentration camp Kommandants by Himmler through Pohl extended beyond numbers of prisoners, to their hours of work. Thus at the end of April 1944, Pohl issued an instruction that 'work must be, in the true sense of the word, exhausting in order to obtain maximum output. . . . The hours of work are not limited. The duration depends on the technical structure of the camp and the work to be done and is determined by the camp Kommandant alone.'[69] This hints at the irrational. The previous month Albert Speer had placed workers engaged in fighter aircraft production on a seventy-two-hour week. It soon became apparent that this carried the danger of lower performance through increased sickness, nervous strain and difficulties at home.[70] By advocating working prisoners literally to exhaustion and without adequate hygiene or food, Pohl wrote them off as an expendable material; he must have done so moreover – since he was not a fool – without real expectation of increased productivity. Thus it seems that the great armaments and 'miracle weapons' programmes designed ostensibly to meet the military crisis were another expression of the urge to destroy and kill. It is small wonder that, according to Albert Speer's calculations, each concentration camp worker produced between one-sixth and one-seventh the output of a normal worker in a private factory.

Degraded, undernourished and terrorised as were the prisoners who worked in Siemens' electrical factories, IG Farben's synthetic plants, on the assembly lines of the armaments and aircraft magnates, or in the camps' own factories and workshops, those employed in the underground complexes suffered even more abject conditions of slavery. Speer, who in his post-war accounts attempted to distance himself from the horrors he had been a party to, admitted he had been told by the Chief Physician of the Todt Organisation after an inspection of the V-weapon factories in the Harz mountains that he had seen Dante's Inferno.[71] He himself described 'expressionless faces, dull eyes in which not even hatred was discernible, exhausted bodies in dirty, blue-grey trousers'. The air in the cave was 'cool, damp and stank of excrement. The lack of oxygen made me dizzy. . . .' He was reminded of a visit he had made to the caves of Syracuse dug out thousands of years before by Greek prisoners of war; the scenes he saw here were more terrible than those he had pictured in his imagination then.[72]

For a prisoner's view, here is Dr Alfred Balochowsky, a Russian-born, naturalised Frenchman arrested in France in July 1943, who arrived at Dora, the Harz cave complex, via Buchenwald camp, in February 1944:[73] 'After our arrival, we spent a whole day and night without food in the cold, in the snow, waiting for all the formalities of registration in the camp. . . . ' They found that their block leaders were criminals convicted by German courts before the war, who had been consigned to concentration camps for life after completing their prison sentences. They had no hope of ever getting out. They were distinguished by the criminal's green triangular badge with a black 'S' for 'Security organisation' (*Sicherheitsverband*) superimposed.

> These criminals, however, thanks to the support and co-operation they were offered by the SS management of the camp, now had the chance of a career. This career consisted in stealing from and robbing the other prisoners, and obtaining from them the maximum output demanded by the SS. They beat us from morning till night.
>
> We got up at four o'clock in the morning and had to be ready within five minutes in the underground dormitories where we were crammed, without ventilation, in foul air, in blocks . . . into which 3000 to 3500 internees were crowded. There were five tiers of bunks with rotting straw mattresses. Fresh ones were never issued. We were given five minutes in which to get up, for we went to bed completely dressed. We were hardly able to get any sleep, for there was a continuous coming and going, and all sorts of thefts took place among the prisoners. Furthermore, it was impossible to sleep because we were covered with lice; the whole Dora camp swarmed with vermin. It was virtually impossible to get rid of the lice. In five minutes we had to be in line in the tunnel and march to a given place.

For these deathly pale, overtaxed, filthy and verminous moving skeletons the only inducements to work and obedience were the blows of their criminal overseers and summary executions with the bodies left dangling in the tunnels as a warning.

Himmler explained the Kapo system in the camps as a whole to the generals in his June speech. These approximately 40,000 German political and professional criminals were – he asked them not to laugh – his *Unteroffizier* corps for the whole camp community. Laughter. Each Kapo was responsible for seeing that his thirty, forty or one hundred prisoners performed their work, committed no sabotage, were clean and left their beds tidy; it could not be more orderly in a recruits' barracks. 'He must also drive his men,' he continued. 'The moment we are not satisfied with him, he is no longer a Kapo, he sleeps among the men [of his block] again. That they will kill him in the first night – that he knows. The Kapo is given certain privileges. I have not – I may say this in all plainness – to devise a welfare system here, but I have to bring in the *Untermenschen* from the streets and set them to work for Germany – for victory.'[74]

About the time Balochowsky was accustoming himself to the regime at Dora, Himmler requested his manager of the Lebensborn homes, Max Sollman, to open a file on the 'Question of procreation of girls or boys', and dictated a note to open it: Berger had told him of an old custom practised in his native Swabian Alps by parents wanting a male child. Both husband and wife took no alcohol for a week during which the wife fed herself well and did no work or anything causing strain; after this the husband left home at twelve noon and walked to Ulm, twenty kilometres distant, and back without stopping at an inn. 'After the return of the man from his route-march, procreation took place. The result was always supposed to be the birth of a son.'[75]

Himmler may have been led to reflect on the question by the continuing heavy losses in the east, or by his own prospect of becoming a father again. Häschen was four months pregnant.

Meanwhile through the spring and early summer Ohlendorf's reports on the mood of the population sounded ever more pessimistic. Shortages of accommodation in the cities due to the destruction wrought by bombing caused concern, as did shortages of clothes and vegetables – especially root crops like carrots and turnips due to the absence of labour for planting – but overshadowing everything were the twin questions of the terror air-raids and the impending allied invasion. In early May 'increasing nervousness among the women due to the continuing [air] alarm' was reported yet again. Mothers were spending night after night in the shelters. '"Where is our defence?" is an ever-repeated question.' Things could not continue in this way for much longer, it was felt; the pressure was building up to some violent discharge.[76]

The next report placed the invasion at the centre-point of all conversation. Was it coming or wasn't it? Between this and the air terror the population was under great strain: things quite simply could not continue as they were. By 1 June, 'deep attacks' by enemy planes strafing individuals in the roads and workers in the fields were causing as much stress as the continuous bombing.

The Plot against Hitler

The SD reports conveyed an impression of imminent collapse in civilian morale. In Switzerland Allen Dulles of the OSS was gaining a similar picture of demoralisation in the German foreign service through secret diplomatic and military documents brought to him by a clerk in the Foreign Ministry, Berlin, named Fritz Kolbe – codename 'George Wood'.[1] Dulles was also receiving reports of the opposition plans for an assassination of Hitler and an Army take-over of power, together with the familiar enquiries about the terms on which the western allies would be prepared to negotiate peace or an armistice with the new government. Roosevelt would not move from the publicly stated three-power position of unconditional surrender and no separate peace. Like the siblings Scholl of the White Rose, Fritz Kolbe stands out from the men of affairs and intellectuals and the new military converts to opposition by the apparently splendid simplicity of his motives. Working entirely alone, he was impelled by the conviction that only total military defeat would remove the Nazis from power. A large part of the opposition, however – especially the newer converts – was as 'realist' in its motivation and as crass in its assessment of the outside view of Germany as the regime itself. They believed that if they succeeded in removing Hitler and forming a new government Germany could become an acceptable negotiating partner and they might play on western fears of the Bolshevisation of Europe to obtain:

> an honourable peace without occupation, without ceding territory or war contributions, without political encirclement and economic fetters. If need be the cession of East Prussia could be considered as compensation to Poland as well as a declaration of the independence of Austria.
> Opposed to such a view there is only the English mentality which regards Germany as incorrigibly aggressive. In reality it was only the peace of Versailles which called forth ideas of aggression. . . .[2]

This propaganda pamphlet found in the effects of one of the conspirators, Ulrich-Wilhelm Graf Schwerin von Schwanenfeld, a liaison between the military and civilian opposition groupings, might have been written by Schellenberg, Ohlendorf or a member of Goebbels' office. Leaving out the Kreisau Circle and other religious groupings and individuals like Oster and

Goerdeler, who had been aware from the beginning of the moral dimension
to the struggle, the military men and politicians of the opposition who sought
at the eleventh hour to save the Fatherland from inglorious defeat and the
subsequent partition and occupation promised by their enemies, held the
same view of power-political realities and intended the same political solution as Hitler and Himmler while, like resistance historians since, speaking
of honour.

Like Himmler, von Stauffenberg could not believe that the English at
least did not understand the imminent danger of a Bolshevik Europe. But
nor, apparently, did he understand the weakness of Germany's bargaining
position. Towards the end of May he proposed conditions for an armistice
in the west: on the allied side an immediate cessation of the air war, renunciation of invasion plans and the avoidance of further sacrifice of lives, on
the German side a new free government which would evacuate all occupied
areas in north, west and south, leaving 'permanent defence capability in
the east' along the 1914 borders, retaining Austria and the Sudeten area,
and gaining a part of the Tyrol. These ideas were virtually the same as
Schellenberg's – if his memoirs are to be believed – and von Stauffenberg's
final proposals were in line with Ohlendorf's: 'energetic reconstruction
with co-operation in the reconstruction of Europe, self-settlement with
the criminals in the *Volk*' (the present regime presumably): 'regaining
honour, self-respect and esteem'.[3]

Had it been stalemate, such terms – which von Stauffenberg told
Goerdeler would be on Churchill's desk in about eight days – might have
been 'realist': with Germany's military, diplomatic, economic, manpower,
moral and morale position eroding it was self-delusion. It was probably a
delusion to believe that the Nazi regime could be replaced by a new 'free
government' in any case.

As for the British they were as sceptical about the approaches of the new
opposition as they had been of the old: they had every reason to believe
the German nation incorrigibly militaristic, nationalistic, mediaeval in its
savagery. Von Stauffenberg and his colleagues should not be blamed for
failing to perceive this since they had been subject for years to propaganda
and could equate the allied bombing and strafing of civilians, women and
children, with German crime in the east. Moreover post-war German
historians of the resistance also – and with far less excuse – overlook
the odium which surrounded the very name of Germany. The British
and Americans were determined not to repeat the mistakes of Versailles:
the German nation was to be divided so that it could never again support
militarism or have the industrial capacity to sustain aggression. Since the
allies were in a position to achieve this their posture was as 'real' as von
Stauffenberg's was 'unreal'. Moreover the proposals from the opposition did
not differ greatly from Himmler's proposals, and were frequently conveyed
via the same channels; the Swedish bankers Jacob and Markus Wallenberg,
Himmler's curious friend Langbehn, his Freundeskreis colleague Karl

Rasche, and others whose ultimate allegiance was obscure. Everyone in the higher positions in Germany right up to Goebbels and Hitler was aware that a political solution had to be found and – since the vast majority was anti-communist – had to be found with the west. There was no reason for the allies to believe that the new government promised by von Stauffenberg would be more than a cosmetic exercise to give military nationalists, bankers and industrialists time to reconstruct.

At some time towards the end of May or beginning of June the Inspector of Armoured Troops, General Guderian, talked to Himmler about the need to replace staff officers who had been too long away from the front and were slow in coming to decisions. This included the Chief of Staff to the head of the Replacement Army, General Friedrich Fromm, and he suggested that Himmler bring this to Hitler's attention. Himmler asked whom he proposed as the new Chief of Staff: von Stauffenberg was the best horse in the stable, Guderian replied. Himmler agreed immediately – so the Minister of Finance, Schwerin von Krosigk, recalled in his memoirs.[4]

If correct, this was a significant conversation, for as Chief of Staff von Stauffenberg would have personal access to Hitler, and it is difficult to believe that Himmler was not aware by this date, eight months after von Stauffenberg's appointment to the Bendlerstrasse, that he was the new dynamo of the military opposition. It is equally difficult to believe that Guderian did not know. He had been approached by the opposition the previous year and had declined to join them, yet like the other generals he despaired of Hitler's strategy of trying to hold every yard of ground in the east, and his true position can best be described as enigmatic; he would have welcomed a military take-over if it could be accomplished without civil war. Fromm, who naturally had a say in the appointment of his own Chief of Staff, had been initiated into the opposition the previous year. He condoned rather than actively supported it, and was described by one member of the conspiracy as a man who would act in the uprising when he saw that it had succeeded.[5] He evidently agreed to von Stauffenberg's appointment; it was to begin on 15 June, officially on 1 July.

The picture which suggests itself is of these three opaque characters, Himmler, Guderian and Fromm, all aware of the need for Hitler's removal, and aware of von Stauffenberg's burning desire to accomplish it, agreeing tacitly and without revealing their motives or feelings to one another, to give the young Colonel his head. Whether or not this or the conversation recorded by von Krosigk occurred, it is a useful illustration of the reality behind events: there was a consensus for change, but the system was frozen in place by terror; even Himmler, master of terror, was frozen by that side of his emotional nature which needed to give loyalty to a creed and a strong master and that side of his rational nature that hesitated to come down on one side or the other while there was a chance of waiting to take advantage of events. So he and the military tiptoed around each other, waiting and hoping for the catalyst, von Stauffenberg.

In Himmler's files there is a message from January 1944 that can be construed as confirmation that he knew about the new centre of military opposition in the Bendlerstrasse building; yet it tantalises by its incompleteness and omission of names. It is a 'strictly confidential', 'immediate' wire to Himmler from the Ministerial Director at the Propaganda Ministry, SS-Brigadeführer Dr Werner Naumann: 'The General whom you mentioned to me recently laid before Generaloberst Fromm on 13 December 1943 a report on his measures after the serious air attacks on Berlin which came into my hands by chance today. . . .'[6] Naumann quoted a part of this report which pointed out that the military command (Generalkommando) had not made use of 'command over all the power-resources of the state, the Party and its affiliations' since co-operation with the Gauleiter of Berlin (Goebbels) as Commissioner for Reich Defence was conceived to be the best solution, 'and all measures were agreed in daily consultation with the Gauleiter'. Naumann had laid this report before his Minister, Goebbels, who had sent for General Fromm immediately,

> and pointed out to him in unmistakable style that the ideas of the named General about the command structure after a 'catastrophe' in Berlin were downright 'fantastic'. He requested Fromm instantly to point out to the named General and in addition to all the commanders of the Generalkommando, that we are not living in the Kaiser's Germany, but in a National Socialist *Führungs*-state and that the Party would never give up its claim to control.
>
> Generaloberst Fromm took notice of this statement and gave his assurance that this opinion had come into being without his knowledge and against his orders. He would see that the General concerned was instructed over the actual [command] relationship at once.

Naumann ended his wire by stating that his Minister would now take special interest in the command regulations after an air attack on Berlin; 'He has commissioned me, esteemed Reichsführer, to bring this to your notice.'

Obviously 'the named General' came under Fromm as Chief of Army Armaments and Commander of the Replacement (or Home) Army. The most likely candidates seem to be Major-General Hellmuth Stieff, Chief of the Organisation Department of Fromm's command and an early collaborator with von Stauffenberg, or Lieutenant-General Paul von Hase, the commander of Berlin, also in the conspiracy; it is unlikely that von Stauffenberg's immediate superior, General of Infantry Friedrich Olbricht, would have prepared a report on measures taken after the Berlin air-raids, although it is by no means impossible. Nevertheless it is evident that Himmler had his eye on at least one of these senior staff officers, and the overwhelming probability is that he was fully aware of the nest of conspirators there.

*

Schellenberg's unified intelligence service was no more successful than Canaris' Abwehr in penetrating the bluffs and double bluffs of western deception. When General Eisenhower launched the invasion armada for the coast of Normandy in the early hours of 6 June 1944 the allies achieved complete strategic and tactical surprise. Dönitz, whose U-boats and special small craft were supposed to play a key – and suicidal – role in the critical initial stages while the troops were being landed, was on holiday with his family in the Black Forest. Rommel, commanding Army Group B on the Channel and North Sea coasts, was at home on his way to report to Hitler at the Berghof. The OKW staff thought the landings probably a feint and did not rouse Hitler. It appears that the naval staff were first to recognise the situation for what it was; by 11.15 a.m. when Dönitz arrived back at the headquarters camp outside Berlin known as Koralle, there was no doubt that, as it was expressed in the war diary, 'the war has entered its final stage for Germany.'[7]

The troops landed under cover of a massive naval bombardment and overwhelming air superiority. The short supply route between the Isle of Wight and the assault beaches was protected by such naval and air strength that Dönitz's forces had no chance of entering the corridor let alone hindering the build-up of troops, armour, ammunition and supplies. By 10 June Dönitz's staff conceded that the allies were established ashore; 'the second front is at hand.'[8]

In the German population, and no doubt in the armed forces, news of the invasion came as a sudden break in the tension. The SD public opinion report likened it to 'a cleansing thunderstorm'. Most people, it suggested, received the news 'with satisfaction and pleasure'; 'positive circles' were convinced 'that we will be able to expel the enemy who have landed and they see in this the possibility of winning the war.'[9] The following week came news that the secret rockets had been launched against London and southern England. 'I give you wonderful news,' said one Party comrade to a colleague, recorded in the opinion report. 'The retaliation is under way!' ('Die Vergeltung geht los!'). Another compared the rocket attack on the south of England to the snapping shut of a mousetrap; another expected the war to be over by Christmas.[10] There is a note of hysteria in these wild surges of public opinion and by the end of the month, predictably, the mood had swung right down again. The causes were listed in the SD report of 28 June as disappointment after the exaggerated hopes placed both in the V-1s and in the prospect of throwing the Normandy invasion forces back into the sea, the successful start of the Russian summer offensive and continuing heavy air attacks over the Reich.[11]

Pessimism was even deeper among the generals, extending, according to one account, to Hitler's highest staff officer, Keitel. Rommel and the Supreme Commander, West, Field Marshal von Rundstedt, travelled to the Berghof on the 29th intending to put the true facts before Hitler, but were not invited to eat with him and at the evening situation conference they were silenced by a monologue on the 'overall position' and new 'miracle weapons' which would bring about a sudden turn of events such as had occurred on the death of the Tsarina in the Seven Years War. The deployment of these weapons, Hitler said, would herald 'final total victory'.[12] Afterwards Rommel told Keitel that Hitler was living in a fantasy world; to talk of total victory was absurd: total defeat faced them and the only way to maintain the front in the east and prevent chaos in the Reich and further destruction from the air was to end the war in the west immediately. Keitel promised he would put this to Hitler, then said in a resigned tone, 'I know there is nothing to be done.'[13]

Hitler attempted to stem the defeatism in the High Command in France by replacing von Rundstedt not with Rommel – the expected choice – but with von Kluge, and the commander of the Seventh Army in the Cherbourg sector of Rommel's Army Group B – who had suffered a heart attack – by the commander of II SS-Panzerkorps, Himmler's veteran Verfügungstruppe chief, now Oberstgruppenführer Paul Hausser. He also repeated his eastern strategy of demanding that every fortress, every yard of ground be held to the last man. When the commander of Panzer Group West complained of this static concept, which handed the initiative to the enemy, Hitler accused him of defeatism and replaced him.

Von Kluge, who came to France in a positive frame of mind after an extended briefing at Führer headquarters, was converted within days: a tour of the fronts showed him that his predecessor and Rommel were right and that Hitler was lost in wishful thinking. At Rommel's headquarters on 9 July, he saw Lieutenant-Colonel of the Reserve Dr Casar von Hofacker, from the economic staff of the military governor of Paris, General Karl von Stülpnagel (not to be confused with the former Military Governor of France, Otto von Stülpnagel). Von Hofacker was a cousin of von Stauffenberg and acted as Paris liaison with the Bendlerstrasse conspirators; he was chief adviser to von Stülpnagel, also a committed member of the opposition. He brought with him a memorandum stressing the urgent need for ending the war in the west, if necessary by independent action of the military command in France, and asked von Kluge how long the invasion front could be held. 'Maximum fourteen days to three weeks,' the Field Marshal replied, 'then a breakthrough is to be expected. We have nothing to oppose it.'[14]

Von Hofacker reported back to the centre of the conspiracy in Berlin, where his account of von Kluge's change of heart made a great impression, instilling von Stauffenberg with a sense of renewed urgency. Although the reports from his western contacts were negative about the chances of separate negotiations, he must have drawn encouragement from remarks by Churchill's deputy, Clement Attlee, in the House of Commons on 6 July. Should any section of the German people wish to see a return to a regime based on respect for international law and the rights of the individual, Attlee had said in obvious reference to the opposition groupings, 'they must understand that no one will believe them until they have taken active steps to rid themselves of their present regime.' This, of course, had been the official British attitude since before the war. 'The longer they continue to support and to tolerate their present rulers,' Attlee had continued, 'the heavier grows their own direct responsibility for the destruction that is being wrought throughout the world, and not least in their own country.'[15] The clear hint was endorsed by Churchill himself in the House of Commons on 12 July.

On the same date, perhaps by coincidence, perhaps as a result of personal contacts with the allies across a local armistice line while exchanging badly wounded allied prisoners for German nursing and communications personnel captured in Cherbourg,[16] von Kluge consented to Rommel sounding out the army and corps commanders about their attitude in the event of a military take-over for a separate peace in France. Von Kluge's own attitude was that he was ready to place himself at the disposal of the leaders of the military putsch if Hitler were removed, but beyond that he would not go. By the 15th Rommel had received similar assurances from all his senior officers, including the two most senior Waffen-SS commanders, Oberstgruppenführer Paul Hausser, commanding the Seventh Army, and Sepp Dietrich, commanding the I SS-Panzerkorps.[17] That the commander of Hitler's original elite formation of guards, the Leibstandarte, was apparently prepared to co-operate with the Reaktion in supporting a change of regime is remarkable testimony to the seriousness of the military situation as viewed from France. It is inconceivable that Himmler was not fully informed. According to Stroop, who had good reason to know, he was also fully informed of von Kluge's attitude since he had 'a dependable informant among the most intimate of von Kluge's staff officers'.[18]

Meanwhile in the east the Red Army was on the move in all sectors; Army Group North was in danger of encirclement as the enemy broke through towards the Gulf of Riga and the borders of east Prussia; Army Group Centre had been shattered, losing the greater part of two armies and a Panzerkorps; in the Ukraine a Soviet offensive had been launched for Lvov near the borders of the Protectorate. Fuel shortages and the demands of the western front were hampering German air defence, and the position was aggravated by mounting partisan activity. In both Poland and Slovakia risings against the German occupiers were being planned by nationalist and communist underground forces to take advantage of the approach of the Russian armies.

By rational calculation the war was lost. The opposition might hope that by removing Hitler they could split the enemy coalition and save the Fatherland. Hitler was probably more realistic in thinking it 'childish and naive to expect that at a time of grave military defeat the moment for favourable political action has come. Such moments come when you are having success.'[19] Still clutching desperately at the coming 'miracle weapons' to preserve his own and his paladins' and his people's confidence amid the defeatism and treachery he sensed everywhere, continuing his static defensive strategy of holding every position to the last, he entrusted Himmler with the task of creating fifteen new divisions to stop the gaps torn in Army Group Centre.

Under normal circumstances these new divisions would have been the responsibility of the Bendlerstrasse headquarters of the Replacement Army; so it came about that von Stauffenberg, as Fromm's Chief of Staff, became involved in a common task with Himmler, and on 15 July he flew to the Wolfschanze to take part in a conference on the subject. Himmler also travelled to the Wolfschanze that day. Von Stauffenberg had accompanied Fromm to a number of Führer conferences at the Berghof earlier in the month and it was suggested in subsequent Gestapo reports that he had carried explosives with him but had failed to set them off because Göring and Himmler were absent.[20] The evidence about this 15 July visit is scant and conflicting but it seems that he had the explosives with him again, or they were carried by one of his party, and he told his escorting adjutant, Captain Klausing, that he would 'possibly' make the attempt.[21]

While he was still in the air and some two hours before the conference was due to begin, his former chief, General Olbricht in Berlin, issued the codeword for the first stage of the troop movements that were to start the military putsch under cover of so-called 'Walküre' orders to quell civil disturbance. The conference in the Wolfschanze began at about ten minutes past one; at half-past one von Stauffenberg left and phoned the Bendlerstrasse, apparently to say that the conference had broken off early. He must also have said that he could not make the attempt on Hitler's life – if indeed it had been planned he should make it – for Olbricht counter-manded the 'Walküre' orders and sent the troops back to their barracks. Von Stauffenberg meanwhile went into a special conference, presumably with Himmler, about the fifteen new divisions to be raised for the east. Himmler was certainly at the Wolfschanze that day and his handwritten notes for discussion with Hitler include the questions of the fifteen new divisions, enemy parachute attacks on Führer headquarters, Hungary and the Jews.[22]

It was not until four o'clock that Captain Klausing, waiting for von Stauffenberg with a car ready to drive away, saw him coming from the direction of the conference with Generals Fellgiebel, Army chief of communications, and Stieff, chief of Fromm's Organisation Department at the Bendlerstrasse, both strongly committed members of the conspiracy. On the way to a late midday meal with Keitel, von Stauffenberg said briefly to Klausing, 'It's come to nothing again.'[23]

There are many possible explanations for this second, or perhaps third or even fourth, abortive attempt by von Stauffenberg to plant a fused bomb near Hitler. It may be that it was primarily a test run; the 'Walküre' alert may have been to see how long it took troops from the various training schools and depots to reach the centre of Berlin, while von Stauffenberg probed the possibilities of assassination at the Wolfschanze. Olbricht visited the units which had taken part after cancelling what he explained had been a test exercise, and told the officers they should be ready to respond to a call at short notice, 'be it for deployment in the east, be it on account of an enemy landing in the German Bight, be it to put down civil disturbance, especially in Berlin because of the presence of the many foreigners [workers]'.[24] Two days later he sent Major Oertzen, formerly on the staff of von Tresckow – who had initiated him into the conspiracy – to one of the key units, the Reserve Brigade of the Regiment Grossdeutschland at Cottbus, over sixty miles south-east of the city centre, 'to clarify the question, how long the battle group required after being alerted to civil disturbance to be in the centre of Berlin'. Oertzen also stressed the possibility of civil disturbance caused by the many foreign workers.[25]

On Sunday evening, 16 July, an inner circle of the younger conspirators gathered at von Stauffenberg's brother's house in Wannsee. Apart from the two Stauffenbergs, there were the Grafen Schwerin von Schwanenfeld, von der Schulenburg (Fritz-Dietl), and Yorck von Wartenburg, a leading spirit of von Moltke's Christian Kreisau Circle, Colonel Mertz von Quirnheim, new Chief of Staff in the General Army office at the Bendlerstrasse, Adam von Trott zu Solz from the Foreign Ministry, Colonel Georg Hansen, formerly Canaris' right hand at the Abwehr and now chief of military intelligence in Schellenberg's new regime, and Casar von Hofacker, the liaison with Paris. Von Hofacker reported again on the mood of the High Command in France; the previous day Rommel had composed an 'ultimatum' to Hitler, describing the ultimate hopelessness of the situation on the invasion front and requesting him to draw the appropriate conclusions without delay. He had handed it to von Kluge but von Kluge, not wishing to compromise himself, had not forwarded it to Führer headquarters. Von Hofacker could hardly have known this, but he could report that von Kluge remained as pessimistic as Rommel.

The discussion circled, as it must have done so many times, around the theme of negotiations to end the war. According to Hansen, von Trott asserted that the enemy would be ready to negotiate as soon as the precondition, a complete change of regime, had been met.[26] Von Trott denied this, as might be expected, under Gestapo interrogation, and insisted that it was von Stauffenberg who was convinced that the western powers would be ready to negotiate because of the rapid advance of the Russians. His own recommendation, he said, was that the Army should be in close contact with the SS so that their military–technical expertise could be complemented by 'the greater political knowledge and more elastic mentality of the SS'.[27] Under hostile questioning it is natural to say what the interrogators want to hear; the picture is further complicated by the fact that the only interrogation reports surviving are those which were sent to Bormann and were hence edited and presented to show the view of the conspiracy the SS wished to give.

The following day, 17 July, Colonel Hansen met two of the chief liaison officers with the west, Hans-Bernd Gisevius and Dr Theodor Strünck from the Oster circle. The result of this meeting of Canaris' former officers was: 'All soundings in Switzerland have shown plainly that negotiations with England would be possible,'[28] and the Americans required a rapid termination of the war in Europe to leave them a free hand against Japan. Gisevius left this discussion and drove in Hansen's car to inform the leader of the older, original military resistance, General Beck, of the conclusions.

The same day Berthold von Stauffenberg's immediate chief in the military–political department at naval headquarters, Korvetten-Kapitän Alfred Kranzfelder, had brought von Stauffenberg news of a rumour circulating in Potsdam. A naval officer initiated into the conspiracy had attended a dinner party the previous evening given by Frau von Bredow, and had heard another officer talking openly of a forthcoming attempt on Hitler's life with a bomb at Führer headquarters. Kranzfelder came to Berlin to warn von Stauffenberg of this dangerous lack of security and at the same time to ask whether, in view of the present military situation, there was any purpose in going ahead. 'There is no longer any choice,' Stauffenberg replied. 'The Rubicon has been crossed.'[29]

In France that day Rommel started out early to tour the embattled areas of his front, encourage his men and tell selected commanders of the ultimatum he believed had been forwarded to Führer headquarters. On his way back from his last call, Sepp Dietrich at I SS-Panzerkorps headquarters, his car was spotted by three British aircraft, which dived to the attack. The driver was killed, the car crashed at speed out of control and Rommel was so severely injured that it was thought at first he would not survive. Von Kluge took over command of Army Group B in addition to his duties as Supreme Commander, West.

On the next day, 18 July, von Stauffenberg must have learned that he would be required to report at a conference in the Wolfschanze on the 20th, for he alerted Olbricht and the inner circle of officers at the Bendlerstrasse to the probability of the attempt taking place on that date. A staff officer at the General Army Office, Lieutenant-Colonel Robert Bernardis, was instructed to prepare material for his report on new divisions, and von der Schulenberg, who called in at the Bendlerstrasse at five that afternoon, was told by Mertz von Quirnheim that the attempt would probably take place on the 20th.[30] Von der Schulenberg was deputy to the Berlin police chief, Graf Helldorf, who was also in the plot, and no doubt he informed him. On the 19th von Stauffenberg received confirmation that he was required at the Wolfschanze the next day. Final preparations were put in hand, codewords agreed, and the wider circle of conspirators, military and civilian, were alerted.

At this stage it is worth speculating on how much Himmler might have known. Arthur Nebe, Chief of Criminal Police and opposition informant, told his great friend Gisevius just prior to the 15 July attempt that he was sure Himmler knew nothing of the preparations – that is according to Gisevius' post-war account.[31] Of course, if Nebe was one of Himmler's plants inside the opposition the statement means nothing. He went on to say something rather more interesting: there had been a fundamental change in the popular attitude towards Himmler and, although still feared, he was regarded as the one man amid the confusion who had real power behind him; 'Scarcely anyone could conceive of a change in the situation without the participation of Himmler.'[32] Although similar arguments must have been voiced frequently in the conspirators' discussions, there is scarcely a trace in the Gestapo reports of interrogations of conspirators sent to Bormann; in these Himmler occurs only as a target for assassination. The single exception is the report of von Trott's recommendation that the military should avail themselves of 'the greater political knowledge and more elastic mentality of the SS'.

Nebe's remarks on the people's confusion are supported by the SD opinion reports; they reveal a total collapse in morale. Women were suffering particularly from the desperate situation and complete absence of good news; they were saying they could no longer bear to listen to the armed forces reports. People were willing to respond to Goebbels' appeals to work their utmost for 'total war', but 'only if the burdens are shared equally and the "leading circles" accept the necessary restrictions in the same measure as plain *Volksgenossen*'.[33] The evident failure of the 'Vergeltung' weapons to force the English to terms within a couple of weeks had caused a reversal of feeling; many now described the V-1s as mere propaganda weapons. The Allied air terror and deep flying attacks in broad daylight were regarded with such anxiety that 'perhaps only 60 per cent of the population has a prospect of surviving the war (comment of officers in train)'. Especially striking was an upsurge of interest in astrology, fortune telling and all manner of numerical and alphabetical methods of divining the future.[34]

Such was the deep pessimism and disillusion forming the background to the officers' plot against Hitler. If Himmler's name had not been so unsavoury that the west refused to deal with him, he would have been the natural choice to bring about a change of government – as indeed von Trott seems to have suggested. The almost total whiting out of such a solution in the Gestapo reports to Bormann speaks of the extreme sensitivity of the topic.

On the other hand Nebe's stated belief that Himmler knew nothing of the preparations is so incredible as to undermine his claims to undivided membership of the opposition. Moreover, during these July days his friend Gisevius was in constant touch with Hansen, who was not only Schellenberg's deputy, but working on the same lines as Schellenberg to establish a basis for negotiations with the west. Schellenberg was Himmler's man, and he must have been an extraordinarily poor chief of intelligence not to have known that his deputy and former members of the Abwehr associated with Canaris and Oster were working for the opposition.

Another of Himmler's RSHA chiefs with an internal intelligence service covering the Reich was Ohlendorf. He was attempting to push Himmler in the same direction as Schellenberg, flooding him with the most pessimistic public opinion reports and working in secret with leading financiers and industrialists to prepare a post-war integration of the German and western economies. Several of these industrialists were connected with the resistance, notably Karl Blessing, General Director of Continental-Öl, who was a candidate for Minister of Economics in the post-Hitler government, and Emil Hellferich, Director of Hamburg-Amerika, who was a strong candidate for the post of Minister of Finance. Both men were long-time members of Himmler's Circle of Friends and close colleagues of Keppler and Kranefuss, points which were not mentioned, of course, in the interrogation reports.

At about two o'clock each afternoon the main departmental heads of the RSHA took a working lunch with their chief, Kaltenbrunner, at Gestapo headquarters, No. 8, Prinz Albrecht Strasse. One of these, Nebe, was an avowed member of the conspiracy; two, Schellenberg and Ohlendorf, were seeking the same solution as the conspirators and controlled intelligence services which would have been plainly incompetent not to have picked up the trail of a plot that was talked of openly at Potsdam dinner tables and in Switzerland, Madrid, Stockholm and every point of liaison with the west. The fourth chief, 'Gestapo' Müller, was also in a position to know a great deal since he had infiltrated the communist underground and in early July rounded up several of the former trades unionists, socialists and communists, whom von Stauffenberg had initiated into the conspiracy, apparently at von der Schulenberg's instigation, certainly much against Goerdeler's wishes. The leading figures arrested, Adolf Reichwein and Julius Leber, knew the personalities in the conservative and military groups, for one of the chief aims of bringing them in had been to form a united civilian front from right to left. By the eve of von Stauffenberg's visit to the Wolfschanze they had been in Gestapo hands for a fortnight or more. How much Müller's interrogators had been able to extract from them can never be known; in the French resistance a man was not expected to hold out for more than twenty-four hours against Gestapo methods.

What, then, was discussed at these working lunches during the days leading up to von Stauffenberg's appointment with history? How much did each of the four chiefs know and how much did they divulge to Kaltenbrunner or directly to Himmler? Were they rivals in the deadly power game being played out over the ruins of Berlin, or were they colleagues exchanging information to save their collective skin, working on a common line from Himmler, under Kaltenbrunner's direction? Was each sitting on his own knowledge and seeking his own way out? Between them they controlled the terror state; they were also its victims, in fear of informers and the machinations of rivals. All owed their position to Himmler and knew what they could expect if caught out in double dealing. None has left a truthful record. The answer can never be known, yet in the SS empire it is scarcely conceivable that each did not at least take out reinsurance with the Reichsführer.

Turning to France, it was, according to General Hans Speidel, the SS generals Sepp Dietrich and Paul Hausser who first came to Rommel's headquarters in early July, asking what was to be done in view of imminent catastrophe, and assuring him that they had all SS units firmly in hand – in short that the SS troops would follow Rommel's orders.[35] Sepp Dietrich made his own rules and frequently drew reprimands from Himmler for his independent action, yet it is hardly conceivable that the two most senior SS generals in the field could renege on their oath of loyalty and go over to the *Reaktion* without informing the Reichsführer of the situation. In any case, if Stroop is to be believed, and there was no reason for him to fabricate the story in his condemned cell, Himmler had an informant in the closest personal staff of von Kluge, and knew what was hatching in France – which, of course, was in line with his own aim for negotiation with the west.

So much for speculation. The best guess must surely be that Himmler was fully informed of the progress of the plot, knew that von Stauffenberg was the leading spirit in the young 'Graf's circle', knew he had been called to the Wolfschanze on 20 July – indeed he was working with him to supply reinforcements for the eastern front – and assumed that he would or might make the attempt then. The best guess about his actions, based on the methods he had employed throughout his career, was that he intended remaining on the sidelines, waiting for the work to be done for him, confident in the ability of his organisations to take control in the wake of a successful assassination of Hitler, confident at the least that he had enough cards to be able to bargain with the military to retain his internal power. The alternative would be civil war and the complete collapse of the fronts. This was, no doubt, what the British government and British intelligence hoped to stimulate; probably he or Schellenberg had discerned that too. He had risen to power by lying low in his modest and socially genial camouflage, pretending all things to all parties while secreting information, amassing dossiers, nudging events in the desired direction but keeping his options open and the confidence of both sides, until he could move in decisively one way or the other. All the indications are that he was running true to form in the July crisis of confidence within the Reich.

Stroop, who had been promoted since Warsaw to SS-Gruppenführer and Lieutenant-General of Police, was HSSPF of SS-Oberabschnitt Rhine–Westmark, taking in Lorraine and the Rhineland, where many of the depots and reserve units for Army Group B were located. His headquarters were at Wiesbaden, and there he received a call from Himmler in the night of 17/18 July after von Kluge had taken over Army Group B from the injured Rommel. Himmler instructed him not to leave Wiesbaden but to await a coded message which would assign him an important task. This came in shortly on the telex and Stroop decoded it personally. He was shocked for it concerned the activities of Rommel and von Kluge; a short time later he received a coded dossier on their machinations by radio. Exactly what his own instructions were is not clear, but he took the precaution of moving his wife and children to a secret address, and did not sleep at his own villa.[36]

It is clear, therefore, that Himmler knew treachery was afoot; whether he knew precisely that von Stauffenberg would carry a bomb to detonate at the Führer conference on the 20th is impossible to determine. At all events he did not go to the Wolfschanze that morning, but remained at his own field headquarters some miles distant, where Kersten gave him his usual treatment. It may be significant that Dönitz was due to spend 20 and 21 July at the Wolfschanze, but put off his visit – according to the post-war recollection of his adjutant, because Mussolini was due to arrive that day, and the Duce's presence would shorten the time available for discussion with the Führer.[37] Mussolini's visit had been known for several days though. Dönitz was an ally of Himmler's, a fanatical aid and support for Hitler, and it would have been extremely useful for Himmler to have had the Navy on his side in the event of an SS confrontation with the Army. That Dönitz was tipped off is, however, more speculative even than the extent of Himmler's knowledge of von Stauffenberg's intent.

The aircraft carrying von Stauffenberg, Lieutenant von Haeften – his ADC – and a fellow conspirator, General Stieff of the Army High Command (OKH), touched down at Rastenburg airstrip some five miles from the Wolfschanze at about 10.15 on the morning of 20 July. Stieff and von Haeften drove off to the nearby OKH camp, Mauerwald, while von Stauffenberg was driven to the Wolfschanze. There he breakfasted with a number of other officers, including the adjutant to the camp Kommandant, before being called in to a small conference on reinforcements for the east, where von Haeften rejoined him. At about 11.30 all participants were called to Keitel's office and continued the discussion until about 12.30, when the Führer's *Lagebesprechung*, or situation conference, was due to begin; it had been put forward half an hour because of Mussolini's impending visit.

As they rose to go, von Stauffenberg asked Keitel's adjutant, von Freyend, if there was somewhere he could freshen up and put on a clean shirt – it was a hot and humid day. He was shown to von Freyend's own room nearby, and von Haeften went in with him to assist – in reality to help him prepare the explosive and set the time fuse, an English chemical–mechanical device.[38] It was here that the attempt went wrong. They had two packets of explosive of approximately two pounds each; both would have fitted into the leather briefcase von Stauffenberg was carrying, and it is generally agreed that if both had been used no one would have emerged alive from the *Lagebesprechung*. For some reason von Stauffenberg put only one packet in his case and set the ten-minute fuse; von Haeften retained the other, unfused.

The conference room was at the end of the so-called 'guests' barrack'; it was long and rather narrow – nearly forty feet by fifteen – with a heavy map table down the centre supported on three solid oak transverse plinths. Due to von Stauffenberg's delay the conference had begun by the time Keitel's party entered. Hitler was at his usual place at mid-length of the table facing open windows in the long, outside wall, his back towards the blank inside partition wall; the entrance door from the internal corridor leading to the room was behind his right shoulder and immediately behind General Heusinger, who was making a report on the latest developments on the eastern front. Hitler must have turned as they entered and Keitel presented von Stauffenberg to him, then Hitler nodded to Heusinger to continue. Keitel moved across to take up his customary position on Hitler's left.

Von Stauffenberg squeezed in to the table to the right of Heusinger and his Chief of Staff, Colonel Brandt, which was as near to Hitler as he could get, bent and placed his briefcase with the fused bomb inside on the floor under the table. Straightening, he murmured an excuse about making a telephone call and left. He did not pick up his cap and belt from where he had left them outside lest he arouse the suspicion of the guard–telephonist, Wachtmeister Adam, but walked straight out of the building, thence a little distance past the communications bunker to the Adjutantur, where the chief of communications at the Wolfschanze, Colonel Sander, had his office.

The chief of Army communications, General Fellgiebel, one of the most dedicated members of the conspiracy, was with Sander, as was von Haeften. Fellgiebel went outside when von Stauffenberg appeared, and was no doubt told that the bomb had been planted. They were joined by Sander and von Haeften shortly before the bomb went off, upon which von Stauffenberg and von Haeften went to their car, waiting nearby, and told the driver to take them to Rastenburg airport. They were passed through the first guard point but by the time they reached the outer perimeter the alert had been sounded, the barrier was down, and the guard would not allow them through. Von Stauffenberg left the car, entered the guard room and phoned through to the Kommandant's office, where he found the adjutant with whom he had breakfasted earlier. He explained he had to be at the airstrip in short time to fly back to Berlin. The adjutant, not yet knowing the nature of the incident, and unable to see von Stauffenberg, capless and beltless, accepted his explanation and instructed the guard to let him through. The two officers were driven fast to the airport where their plane was waiting, and they took off for Berlin at about 1.15, some thirty-three minutes after the explosion.[39]

Von Stauffenberg naturally assumed that Hitler had been killed. However, from his position near the right-hand corner of the table, von Stauffenberg had placed the briefcase outside the solid transverse support, and this and the heavy table top itself, which Hitler was leaning over, acted as perfect blast deflectors. Those standing to the right of the support were severely, four mortally, wounded; the others, including Hitler, suffered shock, burst eardrums, burns, but otherwise minor laceration from splinters.

One of the first to gather his wits was the Luftwaffe liaison officer, von Below. While Keitel was assisting the shocked Führer, trousers in shreds, back to his quarters, von Below went to the communications bunker to order a shutdown. He could not do this himself, only Sander could, so he had him called, then told the Lieutenant on duty to put him through to Himmler's headquarters. As the connection was made, Sander appeared, and von Below said to him, 'Attentat auf Führer – Führer lebt. Nichts darf nach aussen drangen—!'[40] ('Attempt on the Führer's life – the Führer lives. Nothing permitted to go out—!'). He was near to or holding the receiver as he said or more probably barked this, and Himmler must have heard. At all events when Sander took the telephone and asked Himmler to come at once, without telling him why, Himmler asked whether all security measures had been taken.[41]

Himmler ordered his car and escort for the drive to the Wolfschanze, then called Kaltenbrunner in Berlin and told him there had been a bomb attempt at Führer headquarters; he was to fly there immediately with a team of criminologists.

At the Wolfschanze, meanwhile, Fellgiebel, who had followed Sander to the communications bunker, thus learning that Hitler had survived, walked over towards the scene of the explosion. There he saw Hitler walking unaided. Fellgiebel's task in the conspiracy was to inform OKH and the Bendlerstrasse when the assassination had been carried out and afterwards to ensure, so far as possible, that the Wolfschanze was isolated from communication. In fact, because of the multiplicity of links and other factors, this was not feasible without preliminary measures which would have drawn the attention of the security services.[42]

Earlier, when he had seen Keitel and von Stauffenberg walking towards the Führer conference, Fellgiebel had alerted his Chief of Staff at OKH, Mauerwald, Colonel Kurt Hahn. After the explosion he had called again to tell him in code that the attempt had been made, and the communications blockade should be put in hand. Now he returned to the communications bunker, where all circuits had been broken on Sander's orders and the personnel had moved their stools back a yard from the switchboard, and told Sander to inform General Walther Thiele, the contact man at the Bendlerstrasse, that an attempt had been made on the Führer's life, but had failed. Sander was unable to reach Thiele, but left Fellgiebel's urgent message with his secretary. A little later, it appears, Fellgiebel did manage to get through to Thiele personally. He also rang Hahn at OKH to say, 'Something frightful has happened. The Führer lives' – a superbly cryptic report. When Hahn asked him what they should do, he replied, 'Block everything!' – in short carry on as planned. Soon afterwards Hahn called Thiele in the Bendlerstrasse and told him this. Thiele, therefore, had authentic news from two sources within about twenty minutes of the explosion. It is impossible to know what he did next since everyone concerned tried to cover the tracks afterwards, but it appears that he may have left the building without saying anything to anyone. Like other conspirators later, he was faced with the awesome decision – to carry on despite the failure of the assassination and the ruthless counter-measures sure to follow, or to attempt to save his skin by distancing himself from the conspiracy. Perhaps he took himself off to consider the position, perhaps he simply lost his head. Alternatively, he may have talked to Olbricht and they both decided to wait until von Stauffenberg's return to clarify the situation.[43]

This was the second failure; it was, of course, consequent on the first. Since communications had been shut down by Sander to prevent news of the attempt leaking, and by Hahn's people to try and isolate the Wolfschanze, and since von Stauffenberg and von Haeften were out of touch in flight on their way to Berlin, there followed a dead period in the early afternoon during which the Bendlerstrasse conspirators knew nothing definite, or at least did nothing. Olbricht could not issue the 'Walküre' orders blind as he had on the 15th since if von Stauffenberg had aborted or failed he could not have explained it away as another 'exercise' within a week. In any case Fromm had not flown to the conference with von Stauffenberg as on the earlier occasion and would not have sanctioned the orders going out before it was certain that Hitler was dead.

The SS and police members of the conspiracy also knew that something had happened. After Himmler's message to Kaltenbrunner from his field headquarters, Kaltenbrunner had called the Chief of Criminal Police, Nebe, and told him to assemble a team of detectives. Nebe was, of course, in the conspiracy. His friend and conspiratorial colleague, Gisevius, was waiting at the Police Praesidium with the Berlin Police President, Graf Helldorf, another conspirator, and according to Gisevius' post-war account he (Gisevius) phoned Nebe shortly before two to ask if he knew anything. Nebe replied guardedly – since phone conversations might be tapped – that a strange thing had happened in East Prussia. Gisevius arranged to meet him at a restaurant they had used before as a rendezvous, but Nebe did not turn up; he had misunderstood and gone to another hotel.[44] Then it was time for Nebe's working lunch at Prinz Albrecht Strasse, one assumes with 'Gestapo' Müller, Schellenberg and Ohlendorf – not Kaltenbrunner, who was on his way with Nebe's detectives to the Wolfschanze. So Gisevius and Helldorf sweated it out on that hot Berlin afternoon, while the leaders of the Bendlerstrasse conspiracy, Olbricht and Hoepner, also went to lunch, and their contact man, Thiele, went no one knows where.

Quite as extraordinary and almost as unbelievable is the story from Himmler's side. He arrived at the Wolfschanze at some time before two o'clock, inspected the site and listened to the reports. No great detective work was required to find the prime suspect. Von Stauffenberg had been missed in the conference room before the explosion as Hitler had asked for information from him, and Keitel had sent someone to recall him. The guard–telephonist, Wachtmeister Adam, believed that von Stauffenberg had done the deed since he had left the building shortly before the explosion, capless, beltless and without his briefcase; the adjutant at the Kommandantur and the guards on both inner and outer control points reported – it must be assumed – that von Stauffenberg and von Haeften had passed out within minutes of the explosion, bound for the airstrip at Rastenburg; it was confirmed from the airstrip that a plane had taken off at 1.15, bound for Berlin–Rangsdorf airport. Himmler already had his eye on Fromm and one of his generals at the Bendlerstrasse, on von Kluge and Karl von Stülpnagel in France, and on Beck, Goerdeler and the older military–conservative conspirators; he probably knew about von Stauffenberg; in any case von Stauffenberg was Fromm's Chief of Staff and was believed to be heading back to Berlin, thus presumably to the Bendlerstrasse. It is inconceivable, therefore, that Himmler did not realise that the bomb attempt was, or at the very least could be, the signal for an Army putsch as the precondition for armistice negotiations with the west. Yet he did nothing. He did not order security precautions at Prinz Albrecht Strasse or Gestapo headquarters in Paris, did not alert the Berlin–Lichterfelde depot of the Waffen-SS Leibstandarte Adolf Hitler, or the Paris SS, did not even order a watch on the Bendlerstrasse it seems. Instructions were sent to 'Gestapo' Müller at some time to have von Stauffenberg arrested when he landed at Rangsdorf, but this was a limp and ineffectual order compared to the absolute control of Berlin inward flights that could have been instituted if he and Müller had intended the action seriously. In the event von Stauffenberg was not apprehended and almost certainly landed at another airport; his driver waited vainly at Rangsdorf until late afternoon. However, the official report of Kaltenbrunner's detective team which was sent to Bormann on 26 July stated merely that von Stauffenberg had departed 'about 13.15 from airport Rastenburg to Berlin–Rangsdorf', with no further explanation.[45]

Thus the hot afternoon ticked away. In the Bendlerstrasse and the Berlin Kommandant's office in Unter den Linden, in Graf Helldorf's office in what remained of the bomb-damaged Police Praesidium, in Nebe's office, in von Stülpnagel's headquarters in Paris and von Kluge's headquarters at La Roche Guyon, and in other offices and homes the conspirators waited tensely for the anticipated call; and in parallel, among Himmler's entourage at the Wolfschanze, at Gestapo headquarters in Berlin and Paris, in Schellenberg's office and Ohlendorf's they were also waiting, while in the air Kaltenbrunner and his team headed for East Prussia and von Stauffenberg headed for Berlin. Himmler, Müller and Schellendorf were, it seems, willing to allow the conspirators the advantage of time and surprise; the conspirators lacked a leader at the centre in the Bendlerstrasse ready to take the leap. That seems to be the picture that emerges.

Yet it is striking that the announcements and instructions which the conspirators had ready and waiting to go out were not hostile to the SS as a whole. It was 'an unscrupulous clique of Party leaders who had never seen the front line', not the SS, who were to be saddled with the odium of attempting to use the death of the Führer 'to stab the heavily engaged front in the back and grab power for their own self-interested ends',[46] and the entire Waffen-SS was to be incorporated in the Army with immediate effect. It is true that any Waffen-SS units whose obedience to the new regime appeared doubtful were to be disarmed ruthlessly, and Gestapo and SD stations and the concentration camps were to be occupied, HSSPFs and Gestapo leaders to be arrested as well as all Gauleiters and leading Party functionaries. Nevertheless it is as if the conspirators believed they could split Himmler's empire and rely on the Waffen-SS and police to assist them. There are riddles and a conflict of signs and events on this afternoon of 20 July that the most meticulous investigators have so far failed to resolve.

Ultimately everything turned on the fact that Hitler was not dead. It was not Himmler, 'Gestapo' Müller or the Leibstandarte who put down the revolt, but doubt in the minds of the conspirators. Fromm was the first leader to renege – not that he ever seems to have been fully committed. The sequence and timing of events are uncertain, but shortly before four Olbricht heard from von Haeften that he and von Stauffenberg had landed, and Hitler was undoubtedly dead. In response either to this call or to a call from OKH at about the same time, Olbricht had the pre-prepared announcements and 'Walküre' orders taken from the armoured safe and sent to the telex coding room below, and other instructions were despatched by hand. He and his Chief of Staff, Mertz von Quirnheim, went in to Fromm, told him that the attempt on Hitler's life had succeeded and that they should now issue the orders for civil disturbance. Fromm wanted confirmation of Hitler's death and since Himmler had ordered the communications blockade lifted at three o'clock Olbricht managed to have him connected with the Wolfschanze. When Fromm learned that Hitler was not seriously wounded he refused to sanction the orders. Nevertheless the action was already under way. About half an hour later von Stauffenberg arrived in the Bendlerstrasse radiating confidence and energy, insisting that Hitler could not have survived the explosion; as Fromm still refused to sanction the orders, Stauffenberg had him arrested and held under guard.

Directly it was realised at the Wolfschanze that orders for an Army take-over of power were emanating from the Bendlerstrasse, signed either by the retired Field Marshal von Witzleben claiming to have taken over executive authority, or by Fromm claiming to have been empowered by von Witzleben – although Fromm himself was under arrest – then by Hoepner, claiming to have taken over Fromm's position, Keitel began issuing countermanding orders. Thus a communications battle developed over the land lines and the air to all Army commands throughout the Reich. Von Stauffenberg fought back energetically by phone as puzzled commanders rang the Bendlerstrasse. Meanwhile the priorities in Berlin itself were not attended to. Partly because of the comparatively small number of officers who could be initiated beforehand and the inevitable delays and confusions this now caused, partly because of the conspirators' determination not to use the gangster methods of their opponents, above all perhaps because of the doubt caused by the failure of von Stauffenberg's bomb and the fact that Hitler, the legal Commander-in-Chief, lived – or the fact that all their training had been in obedience, not revolt – whatever the causes the putschists appeared to lack conviction. The vital communications and broadcasting centres were not occupied, or if occupied were not seized by technical officers;[47] Goebbels, both Gauleiter of Berlin and Propaganda Minister – the ultimate prop of the regime – was not arrested, nor was the RSHA and Gestapo headquarters in Prinz Albrecht Strasse stormed. On the other hand Goebbels, whose role seems almost as equivocal as Himmler's, Müller's or Schellenberg's, did nothing against the putschists. To judge by results, there was a stand-off. It is true that it took over two hours for the armoured troops who were to secure the government quarter to reach the centre of Berlin, but the conspirators appear not to have attempted to seize the initiative with assault teams of the troops already near the city centre or Graf Helldorf's police, while Goebbels and Müller acted as if they had no idea anything untoward was happening.

The fact of Hitler's survival was crucial to Keitel's attempt to retain command at the Wolfschanze, yet it was not until almost quarter to six that Goebbels – apparently on Hitler's personal directive[48] – put out a brief radio announcement that there had been an attempt on the Führer's life but he had suffered only light injuries and had immediately resumed his duties, receiving Mussolini for a long discussion. This was not repeated for almost three-quarters of an hour.[49] And it was not until six or shortly after that SS-Oberführer Dr Achamer-Pifrader, accompanied by his adjutant and two plain-clothes detectives, entered the Bendlerstrasse to ask von Stauffenberg to accompany them to Gestapo headquarters for an interview with Müller. Von Stauffenberg had Pifrader and his escort arrested and placed under guard. If Himmler, Müller and Goebbels had had no inkling of the putsch plans, all this might be explained by the fog of events and natural confusion. Since Himmler and Müller at least had more than an inkling and in any case were aware by this time that treasonable orders were issuing from the Bendlerstrasse, it could only have been tacit collusion or – an even more intriguing theory – an attempt at negotiation. Already, at some time after four-thirty, Thiele – Fellgiebel's contact man at the Bendlerstrasse whose reactions and movements are so uncertain – had called up Schellenberg at the RSHA and asked him if he knew what was actually happening. It appeared to be a putsch, Schellenberg replied.[50] Perhaps Thiele was simply trying to save his skin by laying down a marker of innocence. But both this call and Pifrader's visit hint at lines of communication between the Bendlerstrasse and Schellenberg and Müller as well as Nebe and Graf Helldorf – in fact between the conspiracy and the entire Reich security and police apparatus.

What Himmler was doing all this time is not known in any detail. He escorted Hitler to the platform on the railway line that ran through the Wolfschanze at some time between two-thirty and three to meet Mussolini's train. Wolff arrived with Mussolini; as Himmler's representative in Italy, he was personally responsible for the Duce's safety. Himmler and Wolff then followed as Hitler with singed hair and right arm in a sling led his wide-eyed visitor to the conference room and showed him the bomb devastation. Afterwards they repaired to the so-called 'Tea-house' for a discussion which Mussolini wanted on Italians who had been interned as slave labourers after Italy's capitulation. Here, it must be assumed, Hitler appointed Himmler to succeed Fromm as Chief of Army Armaments and Commander of the Replacement Army. After the war Wolff said that he was one of the few present when this appointment took place, and Göring, also present, went so far as to suggest that Hitler should not stop there, but make Himmler War Minister. Wolff described Himmler saying in a small, hesitant voice, '*Mein Führer*, I can manage that as well.'[51] Wolff cannot be trusted but in the hysterical mood which Mussolini's SS interpreter described afterwards in the Tea-house, it is very likely that Göring did make such a suggestion to prove his own loyalty and ardour to settle with the reactionaries and defeatists in the Army. Himmler would no doubt have masked feelings of elation behind a modest tone. But Hitler would not have considered breaking his careful balancing system by giving the Reichsführer-SS power over the armed services as well. In Wolff's account he merely told Himmler to fly at once to Berlin and settle things at the focal point. 'You have full powers. *Zugreifen!*' ('Go to it!').

The appointment was presumably made after the first orders sent out in Fromm's name proving his guilt – unless, of course, guilt was established by association with von Stauffenberg – thus at some time after four o'clock. The first announcement came in a radio message from Keitel to the commander of Military District IV (Kassel) timed 16.15 from the Wolfschanze. This stated that Hitler was alive, that orders from von Witzleben, Fromm and Hoepner were not valid, and that Himmler was the new Commander of the Replacement Army. Himmler did not leave immediately for Berlin. It is fairly certain that he waited for Kaltenbrunner and his team of detectives, and they did not land at Rastenburg airstrip until 4.30. One anonymous witness saw Hitler giving Himmler a final exhortation on the steps of the Tea-house at about five. This was perhaps the scene Wolff described, ending with 'You have full powers. *Zugreifen!*'

'*Mein Führer*,' Himmler replied. 'You can leave it to me.'[52]

It was about this time that Dönitz, who had been summoned at the same period as Himmler, shortly after the explosion, arrived with his adjutant and joined Göring, von Ribbentrop, Keitel and Jodl for that bizarre tea party which has been described so often – each of them vying with his rivals to protest loyalty to their Führer, who sat silently, cotton wool protruding from his ears, popping coloured lozenges into his mouth until someone mentioned the 1934 Röhm putsch, when he rose suddenly, screaming vengeance on all traitors who had dared attempt to thwart the Providence which had chosen him to lead the German people. He raged, pacing with foam flecking his lips for half an hour or so while the others sat in stunned silence and the Duce watched with bulging eyes.

Himmler and Wolff are not mentioned in the accounts of this episode. No doubt they were on their way by then. Exactly where is a mystery. According to Wolff they flew, as Hitler had directed, to Berlin. By Kersten's account Himmler returned to his field headquarters that afternoon while he was asleep after lunch. He was roused by Himmler's driver shouting 'Attempt on the Führer's life!'[53] Kersten is unlikely to have been asleep at half-past five. Perhaps Himmler returned to his headquarters after meeting Mussolini and Wolff, then drove back to the Wolfschanze, where Hitler confirmed his appointment as commander of the Replacement Army and instructed him to fly to Berlin.

Whatever time it was that Kersten was woken with the news, he went immediately to Himmler's office, entering without knocking. Himmler was standing by his desk, sorting out and destroying papers. 'The attempt was made by a colonel in the Wehrmacht,' he replied to Kersten's questioning. 'Now my hour has come. I will round up all the reactionary gang. I have already given orders for the traitor's arrest.'

Kersten asked how it was possible for the attempt to have been made without his intelligence and security services knowing anything. When Himmler did not reply, he reminded him of the report on Hitler's health some eighteen months back, and asked whether in view of that it would not have been better if Hitler had been killed.

Himmler looked up in horror mixed with anxiety. 'By preserving the Führer, Providence has given us a sign. . . . My place is now at the Führer's side. . . .' He gathered up his papers. 'I am flying immediately to Berlin.'[54]

Either, it seems, Kersten slept late after a heavy lunch, or the observer who saw Himmler taking his leave from the Tea-house was mistaken about the time, or Himmler called at the Wolfschanze briefly on the way from his field headquarters to the airport at Rastenburg. Whenever it was that he and Wolff took off for Berlin, from that point on they are lost to view until after midnight. This is scarcely surprising: Himmler was unlikely to walk openly into the centre of a conspiracy that had sent out orders for the arrest of all Party chiefs and the occupation of Gestapo and SD buildings; and his own aides who survived had no doubt good reason for keeping silent about the ambiguous nature of the SS response that day. He must have gone to earth in some communications *Zentrale* from where he could monitor and direct events. The best guess may be that he was waiting and hoping for the opposition to open talks with the west through Schellenberg's deputy, Colonel Hansen, or Dr Otto John – who had returned from Madrid on the 19th and was in the Bendlerstrasse on the 20th for the express purpose of negotiating with his western contacts on the successful completion of the putsch – or perhaps through von Kluge, general to general, on the invasion front. Von Kluge did call off the V-1 bombardment that day as a preliminary to negotiations. On the other hand Himmler may have regarded Hitler's miraculous escape, as Kersten reported, as a sign from Providence and seen his duty as loyalty. In that case his measures thus far had been unusually inept.

Whatever his precise movements during the afternoon, he did not take off for Berlin until probably half-past five or six, at the earliest. In a speech the following week he said, '. . . I flew to Berlin in the evening of the day of the attempt on the commission of the Führer to root out the conspirators' clique in the Bendlerstrasse. . . .'[55] The turning point came while he was in the air. It occurred in the minds of the officers taking part, chiefly those not initiated into the conspiracy, starting as unease at the nature of their tasks and the provenance of the orders, turning by degrees into the certainty that it was an officers' strike against the regime. When the news spread that Hitler was alive, these men refused to carry out their orders, or actively turned against the conspirators, some because they were convinced Nazis who believed in the Führer, others from terror at the retribution that could be expected for treason.

The first decisive switch was made by the commander of the Wacht-bataillon Grossdeutschland, Major Otto Remer. He had been instructed to seal off the government quarter with his units and allow no one in or out, not even generals or ministers. According to his account, he was suspicious from the start; so was his 'liaison officer to the Reich Ministry of People's Instruction and Propaganda' – a species of political commissar – Captain Dr Hans Hagen. He asked Remer to let him seek clarification from Dr Goebbels or the SD. Remer agreed, and Hagen sped away on a motorcycle to the Propaganda Ministry. No one there knew of anything untoward; Hagen insisted on seeing the Minister, and was directed to Goebbels' residence adjacent to *Gau* headquarters in Hermann Göring Strasse; there he found Goebbels equally ignorant of events. It was five minutes short of half-past five, but Goebbels expressed disbelief when told that the Wachtbataillon had orders to cordon off the government quarter. Either he was in collusion with Himmler and the RSHA and acting a part, or Himmler and Müller had deliberately kept news of the putsch from him; for, as he had stressed to Fromm earlier that year, as Gauleiter of Berlin, he was the supreme authority in the city.

Having alerted Goebbels, Hagen sped away to fetch his battalion commander, Major Remer. By Remer's account, he had established the cordon around the government quarter and was waiting in the ante-room of the Berlin military commander, General von Hase, some time after 6.30 when one of his lieutenants brought him word from Hagen that Hitler was alive, and they were dealing with a military putsch; Remer should come at once to Dr Goebbels. Remer went in to von Hase and asked permission to see Goebbels, but von Hase, a member of the conspiracy from the beginning, refused.

After a word with some of his officers, Remer left to think things out by himself. He reached the conclusion that he should go alone to see Goebbels. Such was his account afterwards. If true this may be said to be the actual turning point of the day; he was undecided, but prepared to disobey von Hase's order. For his part von Hase was aware of Remer's doubts but was not prepared to arrest him; perhaps he felt it impracticable. The conspirators as a whole had had six clear hours since the explosion and had failed to arrest the Gauleiter of Berlin and Propaganda Minister, or prevent him using the Deutschland station to broadcast news that Hitler had survived an attempt on his life. The first bulletin had gone out, as indicated, at 5.42, shortly after Hagen's visit, the second went out about half-past six, probably just before Hagen sent word in to Remer at von Hase's Kommandantur halfway down Unter den Linden.

The dramatic switch when Remer met Goebbels, who connected him on the telephone with Hitler at the Wolfschanze, is well known. It was at about seven o'clock. According to Remer:

> The Führer told me that he was uninjured, and asked whether I recognised his voice. I said yes. The Führer told me of the base plot and said that I should place myself directly under him until the Reichsführer Himmler arrived, whom he had appointed Chief of the Home Army. I had to suppress any and every resistance by all means possible.[56]

It is evident that Hitler did not think that Himmler could have reached Berlin by this time. Flying time from East Prussia was from two to three hours depending on winds and the type of aircraft used.

Doubts resolved, Remer now acted in the most energetic way as the Führer's representative in putting down the revolt. The situation he was faced with was far from straightforward. Rumour was rife but officers from the other Army depots were still following orders from von Hase and the Bendlerstrasse. He withdrew his own units from the cordon and assembled them in Goebbels' garden where Goebbels addressed them on their historic task, then Remer told them he had been charged by Hitler himself to break the revolt ruthlessly. Leaving two companies in defence of the government complex, he ordered a third company to seal off von Hase's Kommandantur, summoned troops and tanks still at the depot, and set about convincing officers from other units that he had a commission from and acted as intelligence officer for Goebbels. All this occupied him some time, during which according to his account he was unaware that the Bendlerstrasse was the focus of mutiny. When this was reported to him he ordered a company to cordon off the block and arrest all suspects. The last instruction proved unnecessary. A group of officers within the Bendlerstrasse but not members of the conspiracy had already taken matters into their own hands. Again it was knowledge that Hitler was alive that impelled their action, although the immediate trigger appears to have been a broadcast at nine announcing that the Führer would shortly make a broadcast and that Himmler had been appointed to command the Replacement Army. By about ten or soon after they had combined to release Fromm and, after a skirmish during which von Stauffenberg was wounded in the arm, Fromm had the principal conspirators under guard.

General Beck, virtually the founder of the military resistance and its senior figure, had come to the Bendlerstrasse that afternoon and was among those arrested. Fromm allowed him to retain his revolver to take his own life, and permitted Olbricht to write a last letter to his wife, then he announced a summary court martial in the name of the Führer, and pronounced sentence of death on 'Colonel of the General Staff Mertz [von Quirnheim], General Olbricht, the Colonel', indicating von Stauffenberg, 'whom I will not name, and Oberleutnant von Haeften.' He ordered their immediate execution.

So the revolt collapsed inwards at the centre. It had already broken down and for the same reasons in the provinces and Vienna and Prague. In France von Kluge had reneged in the same way as Fromm directly he received unequivocal evidence that Hitler was alive. And although von Stülpnagel had achieved a bloodless occupation of the Gestapo and SD headquarters in Paris and imprisoned the men in their barracks, von Kluge's refusal and the collapse in Berlin left him no option but to release them that night.

Olbricht, von Stauffenberg, Mertz and von Haeften were taken down to the courtyard of the Bendlerstrasse building and there shot by an execution squad in the headlights of parked vehicles. They paid the price for their seniors' earlier step-by-step compromise with the monster they had raised. Alternatively they died in a hopeless attempt to save Germany and her good name long after both had been lost irretrievably. They died as brave men, von Stauffenberg crying out at the last, 'Es lebe das heilige Deutschland!' ('Long live sacred Germany!').

Fromm had arranged the hasty execution to clear himself, and he immediately rang through to the Wolfschanze to report what he had done; the mood there was so hostile to him that Keitel and, after him, everyone he asked for refused to come to the telephone. Eventually it was left to Dönitz's adjutant to take the message, and when he relayed it to the assembled company there was an explosion of 'growling rage'.[57] There seems little doubt that Fromm intended the execution of the other conspirators gathered in the building, but Kaltenbrunner arrived at about this time soon after midnight with an SS detachment led by Sturmbannführer Otto Skorzeny, the commando raid expert who had accomplished the release of Mussolini. The conspirators were handcuffed in pairs and taken to the cells at Gestapo headquarters, Prinz Albrecht Strasse. No doubt Kaltenbrunner followed them. Fromm took himself off to Goebbels' residence, where he found Himmler. According to Himmler's account in a speech to the Gauleiters on 3 August Fromm made a 'most peculiar' first impression on both Goebbels and himself. He could not help thinking that some 'uncomfortable partners, not to say witnesses, were quickly being done away with'.[58] Fromm was arrested next day – later to be executed himself.

Remer also reported to Himmler on his measures at this time, about one in the morning of the 21st at Goebbels' residence. His is the first account of Himmler's whereabouts since the anonymous witness at the Wolfschanze at about five the previous afternoon.

The officers' uprising had been wrecked by ineptitude and half-heartedness and turncoats like Fromm and von Kluge, and it had been put down in Berlin by Goebbels and Remer without the assistance of the SS or, it seems, any direction from Himmler or Kaltenbrunner. It may be that Himmler had not intervened because he wanted to avoid increasing friction between Army and SS or even provoking a civil war. This was the impression he sought to convey in his subsequent speeches:

> it was my intention . . . that no one apart from the Army and the companions of the Army should clear out the nest. No hand should be lifted against the Army by another arm of the Wehrmacht. . . . An institution can only be saved for the future after such an inner breakdown and frightful deed, if the organisation itself removes the unworthy members, discharges and stands them against the wall.[59]

This sounds like a convenient justification for his inaction. Had Hitler been killed things would have turned out differently.

In the event Himmler was undoubtedly the chief beneficiary of the failed putsch. In addition to his manifold powers and incursions into every area of economic life, he was now Chief of Army Armaments and Commander of the Replacement Army.

By extraordinary coincidence on the same day, 20 July, Häschen Potthast bore a second child for him at Professor Gebhardt's clinic at Hohenlychen, some ninety miles north-west of Berlin – a girl who was named Nanette Dorothea.[60] That he was at his field headquarters that morning and not by her side is hardly surprising considering the critical situation.

It was not only Himmler who gained by the failed attempt. Hitler's position was strengthened enormously. For the paladins at the Wolfschanze, for Keitel and Jodl and the other military men who could count themselves fortunate at escaping mutilation or death at the hands of a brother officer, for ordinary Germans oppressed, in the words of the SD public opinion report, by 'a kind of creeping panic'[61] at the steadily worsening news from every quarter, the explosion in the conference room acted like a cathartic, releasing pent-up desperation.[62] 'Holy wrath and boundless fury fill us at the criminal attempt on the life of our beloved Führer . . .',[63] Dönitz proclaimed the same night. Jodl told his staff, 'sympathy [with the conspirators] won't do, and the time for lenience is past. Merciless hate to all who oppose!'[64] Others expressed their feelings in maledictions: Bormann proclaimed the plotters a 'reactionary criminal riff-raff . . . with the stature of miniature pipsqueaks [*Miniatur-Würstchen*]'.[65] Von Ribbentrop informed his diplomats of the 'traitorous and criminal generals' who had 'spread their cowardly and defeatist view to contaminate weak characters and draw them into their intrigue . . .'.[66]

Hitler clutched at his escape as a sign. He made the same point to the German people that night over the air as he had to Mussolini while viewing the wreckage: his escape was confirmation from Providence that he should continue precisely as before on his path to his 'life's goal'. To a man, his followers clutched at the same straw. Dönitz, characterising the conspirators as 'an insane generals' clique . . . the tools of our enemies, serving them in characterless, cowardly and false cunning', told the Navy that 'Providence . . . has sheltered and protected the Führer and thereby not abandoned our German Fatherland in its battle of destiny.'[67] Göring, using much the same epithets, proclaimed, 'The Führer was saved by almighty Providence as if by a miracle . . .', and ended with a slightly different formula for believers, 'Long live our Führer, who was so visibly blessed today by almighty God.'[68] Bormann wired the Party leaders, 'The fortunate deliverance of the Führer signifies at the same time the deliverance of the German *Volk*,'[69] and von Ribbentrop described the *Volk* as seeing 'the miraculous deliverance of the Führer from the most extreme danger as a sign from Providence, which desires the Führer to carry through his work . . . victoriously to the end'.[70] Goebbels used the same theme in his propaganda campaign.

While all appear to have been slavishly following Hitler's line, there is every psychological reason to believe that it was a spontaneous group reaction, the more extreme since they dared not admit even to themselves – least of all to themselves – that the conspirators who had threatened their position had been expressing the doubts they themselves held and the anxieties of the German people as a whole. And no doubt because their rage was directed as much at the traitor each perceived within himself, it was accompanied by lust for revenge. Dönitz commanded his men to 'destroy ruthlessly anyone who reveals himself as a traitor!' Jodl demanded of his officers and officials 'merciless hate!' Göring instructed the Luftwaffe to take drastic action in 'rooting out these traitors', who were 'to be arrested and shot. . . . Officers who took part in this crime place themselves outside their *Volk*, outside the Wehrmacht, outside every concept of soldierly honour, outside oath and loyalty. Their extermination will give us new strength.'[71] Jodl expressed a higher aspiration in his homily to his staff – it came straight from the Prussian military code: he was sure they would hold out but 'if fortune should be against us then we must determine at the end to take arms and rally round the Führer, thereby justifying ourselves before posterity. . . . we have to stand before history and before eternity.'[72]

Thus 20 July marked not only the disastrous end of the opposition schemes but the consummation of the Nazi revolution. The officer corps of the Army, the pillar of the counter-revolution, was broken, its honour fatally compromised by a treason, which was compared to the 'stab in the back' of 1918. Four days afterwards Keitel joined Göring and Dönitz in offering Hitler the adoption of the Nazi salute in all arms of the services 'as a sign of the unbroken loyalty to the Führer and the close union between Wehrmacht and Party'. At the same time the inner circle at Hitler's court had become more closely bound to him, less inclined to tolerate their own or others' treasonable thoughts about possible ways out. They had to believe in him; without him their own power dissolved; they were bound to him. They had also come to realise he was their talisman, for Goebbels had anchored his image firmly in the hearts of the *Volk*. The SD public opinion report after the event described the people heaving a collective shudder of relief that the Führer had survived the attempt. 'Almost without exception the bonds to the Führer and faith in the leadership have deepened and strengthened. . . .' It was further reported that Himmler's appointment as commander of the Replacement Army had raised the people's expectation of a 'fundamental cleansing'[73] in all positions into which reactionary elements had insinuated themselves. How much this was a genuine response, how much Ohlendorf's insertion to propitiate his chief is difficult to know. What does seem certain is that it was not simply Gestapo terror that ruled out a further concerted attempt to seize power – although terror was a powerful factor – but a general closing of the ranks against the enemy within. The allies were committed to Germany's 'unconditional surrender'; Germany was now committed to rally round the Führer. Whether there had ever been any realistic way out is doubtful, but after 20 July it is certain there was none.

Himmler's remarks to Kersten on the afternoon of the attempt suggest that he realised this immediately. What were the papers he was destroying? Symbolically they may stand for his bridges. But once again in crisis he kept a cool head. While Hitler, Bormann and the Wehrmacht chiefs were crying vengeance and instructing their people to root out and liquidate any conspirators they could find, Himmler, directly he saw that the putsch had collapsed, sought to conciliate, calm and avoid factions. This is indicated plainly by a telegram marked 'Immediate!' ('Eilt Sehr! Sofort auf den Tisch!') which Bormann addressed to all Gauleiters at 11.35 on the morning of 21 July:

> The commander of the Replacement Army, Reichsminister H. Himmler,
> urgently requests you to halt all further independent proceedings against officers

who showed an uncertain attitude or even those who have to be regarded as open enemies.

The commander of the Replacement Army requests you to send him your records in all cases which in your opinion need to be cleared up. Heil Hitler! M. Bormann.[74]

It was a necessary precaution, as indicated by countless acts of personal vengeance and vendetta which ensued over the following weeks despite this instruction.[75]

Himmler also appears to have talked Hitler out of a desire for great show trials receiving maximum publicity on film and radio, and to have persuaded him instead to have the conspirators handed over to the Volksgerichtshof, or People's Court, for similarly managed sentencing processes but before small audiences selected strictly for political reliability.[76] Since the military could be tried only by their own kind, this involved a prior Court of Honour to expel the conspirators from the service. It is an indication of the depths to which the morale and indeed the honour of the officer corps had sunk that there was no difficulty in assembling a bench of generals under the chairmanship of Field Marshal von Rundstedt – so lately sacked for his own defeatism as Supreme Commander in France – which was willing to expel the required officers solely on Gestapo evidence without hearing their defence.

The same day, 21 July, that Himmler sent his urgent request to Bormann to prevent the Party taking out its feelings on the reactionary elements it loathed, he gave an emollient address to the officers of his new command in the Bendlerstrasse.[77] During the course of it he set out his ideas on a theme he was to develop in subsequent speeches that summer and autumn: what was the sense or purpose of the war? It was obviously something he had to tackle if he was to restore morale and combat the defeatism which he knew from the SD reports was rife throughout the nation, and was likely to be pronounced here in the headquarters of the conspiracy.

It was, he explained, first, to validate Germany as a world power, as the Seven Years War had validated Prussia as a European power; second, to widen and consolidate a Germanic empire from 90 to 120 million people; third, to reorganise this greater Germanic Reich in respect of defence, economics and population – by which, of course, he meant race.

We must be clear about it, this invasion from Asia, such as has occurred this time, will recur continually in 50, in 100, in 200 years. Only we shall not have an Adolf Hitler each time. We must create the preconditions for our *Volk* to enable it to withstand these assaults.

Another necessity of our struggle is the expansion of our settlement space. In the course of the next few years we will at least recover what we have lost in Russia. Defensive borders will be created, the east will be a troop-training area where every division will be able to engage in keen exercises against [partisan] bands at least once a year, or at least twice yearly.

Given the knowledge he had as overall chief of intelligence and chief of the Waffen-SS, given the sober reflections that had led him to seek an accommodation with the west, and the shrunken borders of the Reich Schellenberg had persuaded him to accept for the purpose, such ideas seem fantasy or fiction designed to put heart into his audience. They were the aims he had always advanced, unchanged from the days when Germany had been the hammer; now she was the anvil. The situation deteriorated by the week, but he continued to talk of expanding the borders, and with increasing eloquence pictured the great future of the Germanic Reich. Had he lost himself in fantasy because it was too painful to contemplate the *cul de sac* into which Germany had been led, or because he had no alternative now but to put all his faith in the Führer? Was it a collective fantasy which they all, Bormann, Goebbels, von Ribbentrop, Dönitz, Speer, shared with Hitler and talked up among themselves? Or was he deliberately misleading his audiences?

There is a file note of his conversation at dinner on 17 November 1938, which records him saying to his guests, 'One may never lie, never be inwardly untrue, not in politics, nor in daily life.'[78] There is also Professor Gebhardt's testimony that Himmler always believed what he was saying at the time he was saying it.

Nevertheless, there are signs of deliberate deception at this time: on 26 July, for instance, when speaking to the officers of one of the new divisions raised to plug the holes in the eastern front, he told them that reports suggested the first four weeks of V-1 rocket fire had caused 120,000 deaths in London – a figure, he went on, which absolutely agreed with the number of rockets he knew had been fired.[79] It was a fantastic number. Churchill had reported to the House of Commons under 3000 deaths from V-1s in this period. Lies had always been an integral part of Nazi propaganda. Whether he was convinced that lies were justified by the greater ends they served or whether he had become incapable through his years of power and his closeness to Hitler of separating wish from sober calculation, falsehood is surely indivisible. No doubt all his statements were and had always been compounds of personal fantasy and propaganda fiction blending indistinguishably into each other. Now that reality had diverged so far from Nazi fantasy, it had merely become more obvious.

He had an absolute belief in victory, he told all his audiences, and protested that he had never doubted final victory even for a second – an even more certain proof that he lied knowingly. The grounds for his belief remained as they had been since the Reich was forced on the defensive, the sudden and unexpected turn in the Seven Years War which had allowed Frederick the Great to emerge victorious from a seemingly hopeless situation, the historical truism that coalitions seldom endured throughout the course of great wars, and, most convincing, the divergences in outlook and interest between the Russians and the western powers.

'It is a race now whether the Bolsheviks double-cross the Americans, or the Americans the English – because they are certainly not very united – or whether the English double-cross both the others . . .', he told the officers of the new Infantry Division 545, termed Volksgrenadiers, on 26 July.[80]

> There are hundreds of points of friction. Sooner or later, if we have the nerve – and we have it – one of them will break out of the coalition because the war is senseless for them, above all because they can no longer sustain it inwardly. They can no longer hold their people to it. And when the coalition has come apart, then the war is over, then is our victory. The war is precisely as surely to be won as the world war was in November 1918, January 1919, if only we had had a firm leadership then, a loyalty pervading the whole *Volk* up to the top, and good nerves.

Thus the legend of the 'stab in the back' and the undefeated German Army had become historical truth to be hung like an albatross around the neck of those unborn then.

This time, he went on, they had all the preconditions lacking in 1918. The *Volk* was of unprecedented decency. This noun, *Anständigkeit*, or in adjectival form, *anständig*, occurred repeatedly as a leitmotif throughout his speeches, as it did throughout the protestations of so many who survived the war. In this case he had already told his audience what this 'decency' or 'propriety', 'fairness', 'respectability' of the *Volk* signified: the *Volk* in the homeland differed from its counterpart in 1918 as it had been cleansed of Jews and all criminal riff-raff.

> From this element not the least danger threatens Germany. Because you know indeed – I speak here in this circle to you, my officers entrusted to me by the Führer, completely openly – you know indeed that for ten years, as a precaution, I have locked up what was the scum of Germany, the professional criminals, the asocials, and these are today the most industrious armaments workers on a scale that you as individuals cannot conceive. Of many important weapons and apparatus needed by the Wehrmacht, a third is manufactured in these camps. We are in the fortunate position that we have no more Jews within, so the scum of all revolts has been eradicated in the mass of the people.

The other chief difference from 1918 was, of course, that they had as only once in a thousand years the leader sent by fate, Adolf Hitler.

> I come to something which has indeed echoed through my whole talk. That which I desire from you is that which I carry in myself; a belief shaken by nothing, the belief in the Führer, the belief in the future of this greater German – no, this greater Germanic Reich the belief in our own worth, in ourselves. That is something which I must desire, that without any phrase-making I should like to arouse in you as a sacred flame. It is your most important task, my commanders, that you yourselves at no second and in no hour – however desperate it may appear – lose the belief in final victory, the

belief in our Germanic mission, that you never give expression to inner illusory and deceptive calculations and judgement.

This was surely a revealing sentence.

It is noticeable that with Himmler's increased powers and his new task of raising Volksgrenadier divisions to reinforce the east, he became the subject of heightened propaganda – much of it by SS organs – and the front-line service he had hinted at in his own earlier speeches became established fact. Thus an item broadcast on 24 July had him entering the 11th Bavarian Regiment in 1917 as a cadet 'and in 1918 he came to the front.'[81] The following month the 'Voice of the SS' broadcast, 'In 1917–18 he fought in the German Army, which had to lay down its arms, unbeaten. . . .'[82]

He gave the same impression in his speeches. He stood before them 'as a soldier among soldiers'. He appealed to his new Bendlerstrasse and Volksgrenadier officers as their commander, friend and comrade just as he was, he said, for his own men. 'I know no difference here and I bring my full confidence to this German officer corps, and I know that decency and chivalry are as ever best joined in Germanic peoples. And I should like to give you, the officer corps, a watchword which is an ancient German one. In the middle ages it stood over the offices of the merchant houses, if I translate it into high German: "Honour is compulsion enough!" In that sense we all want to act. . . .'

He was frank about life expectancy on the eastern front. For a company commander it was not more than three months, for a battalion commander at the most four months before he was killed or wounded. To lament this was as foolish as it was unmanly. 'That is war . . .', and he went on to describe how Frederick the Great in the Seven Years War had become so short of men that he had opened the jails, reinforced his battalions with criminals and sent fifteen-year-olds to lead them and the last sons of the nobility – normally reserved so that they might continue their line. 'And [he] held out and won the war in 1763.'

Himmler also appealed to sentiment. He enjoined the officers to inspire their men with 'the sacred fire of real German soldiers' traditional honour' and belief in their Führer and to explain to them what it was they were fighting for. 'Tell him each day to think of his child and his little sister or his parents, his wife – that he protects them, that he protects the purity of our blood and the loveliness of our land, our homeland. . . .'

His final appeal was to philosophy and the ties of race:

so long as the Aryan lives, so long as our blood, Nordic–Germanic blood, lives, so long there will be order on this globe of the Lord God.

And this task, from eternity out into the eternity of our *Volk*, is placed in the hands of each generation, especially ours. And when you see these periods of time, timeless, then I believe that each of you in the hour of difficulty and danger will realise what a short second that is in the life of the earth, in the life of our *Volk*. And during this short second the only thing that matters is that he who lives precisely there [at that time] now does his duty. . . .

And he returned to a favourite theme which he expressed often at this period: 'some time we will come to the end of our existence, hence we want to do everything today so that we are able to say at the end, and our children and grandchildren can say of us: "They were worthy, our fathers, our ancestors, to have been officers of Adolf Hitler, the Führer sent by the Lord God, in the most difficult time for the Germanic *Volk*."'

So he sent his new young Volksgrenadier officers into the savage fighting on the eastern front. There is no reason to doubt the effectiveness of his words; there are ample testimonies to the impression they made on SS and Party listeners committed to the ideology,[83] and these young men had been steeped in it throughout their time at school. Probably he believed in the sentiments as he uttered them. Viewed objectively and with hindsight it is plain that he was sending youth to slaughter for a hopeless cause simply to retain power, and that in the period that he continued to do so between July 1944 and the end of the war the following spring more German cities were reduced to hollow shells of rubble and more of the kith and kin they were ostensibly protecting were killed in the air terror than in the whole war to that date. At the time, however, the only alternative was unconditional surrender, the end of the Nazi Party, the division and occupation of Germany by the enemy powers and the trial of 'war criminals', among whom his own name was second only to Hitler's.

All the historic forces which had impelled Germany to this point, its necessary warrior past and all the philosophers and romantics who had forged from it the Aryan myth, the race-hygiene scientists, the *Herr Professoren* who had interpreted history in terms of Germany's all-conquering mission and *Kultur*, the soldiers and statesmen who had drunk from the Prussian legend and created the myth of the 'stab in the back' and the 'unbeaten German Army' of the First World War – all the forces which had created Himmler's world impelled him on, and without them he was literally nothing. At the same time all the historic forces which that mission had called into being against Germany, and the loathing, and the determination that she should be so dismembered that she could never rise again from a second Versailles to plunge Europe into a Third World War dictated that there could be no softening of the allies' demand for unconditional surrender and the absolute destruction of all that German militarism and Nazism stood for. This was the legacy of history, and the resolution of these opposing forces could only come through further fighting, slaughter, suffering, hate and unbridled destruction.

In this sense Himmler's words were the authentic voice of German destiny, beside which the hopes of the conspirators had been, as he described them, pathetic dreams. Yet they were, of course, also his own dream. He could or would not understand the horror his name evoked, and he continued to seek western contacts where the conspirators had left them. He even convinced himself that the worse things became for Germany, the more the borders were forced in towards the centre, the more coercive power this rump between the advancing armies would acquire: 'A peculiar fact! Each week that passes heightens our political value and increases our [political] force. I might say as an explosive wedge or as explosive to blow the enemy coalition right apart. The coalition of our enemies, England, America, Russia, is and was from the first an unnatural one. . . .'[84]

Consequently it is possible, even probable that when he spoke of pushing out the eastern borders to the Urals, and of the great German future which he saw beyond the hard present, he believed it. Equally, much of the time, and in the small hours of the night, he must have known it was all a chimera. In early September, as the Red Army occupied the Rumanian oil fields and invaded Bulgaria, and Finland dropped out of the war against Russia, he took to his bed with stomach cramps, that sure indicator of his psychic health. Kersten found him in agony with the Koran lying by his bedside. 'I can't bear this pain any longer,' Himmler told him.[85]

Most Powerful Man in the Reich

The dissonance between Himmler's phrases on decency and the inferno they cloaked grew if possible more marked during the death agonies of the Reich after 20 July. The city of Warsaw became a gruesome example. The sight of beaten and demoralised German troops retiring from the remnants of Army Group Centre earlier that summer had heartened the Polish underground, or Home Army, and convinced the commander, General Tadeusz Bor-Komorowski, that the Germans would be unable to prevent the rapid advance of the Red Army across the Vistula to take Warsaw. As Soviet tanks approached the eastern suburbs on 29 July Bor took the decision to stage an armed uprising within the city on the afternoon of 1 August.

It was in many respects a political decision. Stalin had encouraged and supported a rival – virtually enemy – Polish underground, People's Army, and had set up a communist-led Polish Committee for National Liberation as his agency to bring the country into the Soviet orbit after liberation. The Home Army, however, was the fighting arm of the Polish émigré government in London, and their aim in rising against the German occupiers was not simply to help the Red Army liberate the capital, but to be in possession as a conservative–nationalist Polish force opposing the Committee for Liberation and Stalin's plans for a communist take-over when the Soviets entered. Since the Home Army was the largest and most powerful partisan organisation in Europe it represented a serious obstacle to Stalin's plans.[1]

In the event Stalin was aided by Hitler's determination to hold Warsaw, both as communications centre and as bastion of the right flank of the German forces. Reinforcements were moved in from the Baltic and France, including a 'fire brigade' SS-Panzerkorps formed from the elite Wiking and Totenkopf divisions reinforced by the Army's 19th Panzerdivision. The Home Army uprising coincided with the Panzerkorps counter-attacking the Russian forces outside Warsaw, threatening their extended lines of communication and forcing them into a defensive posture. Bor and his approximately 40,000-man underground army were thus left on their own as they attacked German patrols and strongpoints in the city.

It is another indication of Hitler's faith in Himmler that he commissioned him rather than the newly appointed Supreme Commander, East, General Heinz Guderian, to extinguish the uprising. Of course

Himmler was responsible for anti-partisan actions behind the front, yet
the proximity of the Red Army and the fact that Wehrmacht units were
in the city to defend it meant that it was in the area of Army operations.
Here is Himmler's account to Army officers of the circumstances in which
Hitler charged him with the task:[2]

> When I heard the news of the rising in Warsaw I went immediately to the
> Führer. I should like to tell you this as an example of how one should take
> news of this kind quite calmly. I said, '*Mein Führer*, the time is disagreeable.
> Seen historically [however] it is a blessing that the Poles are doing it. After
> five, six weeks we shall leave. But by then Warsaw, the capital, the head, the
> intelligence of this former 16–17 million Polish people will be extinguished,
> this *Volk* that has blocked us in the east for 700 years and has stood in our
> way ever since the first battle of Tannenberg. Then the Polish problem will no
> longer be a large problem historically for our children who come after us, nor
> indeed for us.'

Himmler's appointment was ideological–political; even at this late hour,
he was to resume the programme begun in 1939 to decapitate the Polish
people, leaving the remnants for service as an itinerant labour force for
the Reich. This probably explains why talks some months previously
between representatives of the Home Army and Himmler's security chief
in Warsaw, Dr Ludwig Hahn, to probe the possibilities of a Home Army
alliance with Germany against the communists were stopped by Hitler.[3]

Now, as Himmler told the Army officers in his address, he ordered
Warsaw razed to the ground. 'You may think I am a frightful barbarian.
I am, I may say, if I have no other choice.'

He appointed his veteran anti-partisan commander, SS-Gruppenführer
Erich von dem Bach-Zelewski, to head the operation, providing him
with the notorious Dirlewanger Brigade of poachers, criminals, de-graded
officers, court-martialled servicemen, SS men on punishment and foreigners
on probation for the Waffen-SS; the equally savage anti-partisan Kaminsky
Brigade, recruited chiefly from Ukrainian prisoners of war whose hatred
for Poles equalled their hatred for the Soviets; regular police units from
Posen under the command of the SSPF (SS and Polizei Führer) there,
SS-Gruppenführer Heinz Reinefarth; and part of the 22nd SS-Cavalry
Brigade Maria Theresia, recruited from ethnic Germans in Hungary.
The largest single formation was Kaminsky's, incorporated officially into
the Waffen-SS at this time as the 29th Waffen Grenadier Division Rona
(Russian); Kaminsky himself was appointed SS-Oberführer.

Von dem Bach was provided with artillery, including the heaviest field
service weapon used in the war, the 60 cm (23.6 inch) bore Karl mortar –
which fired a 4850 lb shell capable of penetrating eight feet of concrete –
flame-throwers, gas machines for the sewers, MG 42 machine guns and the
latest 'miracle weapons', remote control miniature tanks called Goliaths.

These tanks were some four and a half feet long, ran on caterpillar tracks and packed 200 lb of high explosive; guided to their target by wire or radio and then detonated, they were ideal for punching holes in street barricades without loss of life from sniper fire. Von dem Bach also disposed of actual tanks equipped with mortars, and could call on the Luftwaffe for Stuka dive-bombers.

Given this formidable arsenal, two pathological commanders, Kaminsky and Dirlewanger, for the largest formations, themselves composed of a lethal ethnic and criminal mix, an SS-Führer, Reinfarth, racially as indoctrinated and ruthless as Jürgen Stroop, and Himmler's orders on behalf of the Führer to level the city – to which he added an authorisation to kill all Poles out of hand[4] – the results were hideously predictable.

Blocks of houses were burned methodically; the civilian occupants were herded into public places, squares, parks, cemeteries, where they were mown down with machine-gun fire, ripped with blast and fragments of lobbed grenades and afterwards burned on mass pyres. Some were ordered to tear planks from fences and hold them against their bodies as they were shot in order to assist the subsequent conflagration. Neither age nor sex was regarded; in that respect the earlier stages of the action resembled the *wild* stage of the mass slaughter of Jews. The testimony of witnesses and survivors is similar. Janini Rozinska, for example, described being hurried along with her two children to a tram depot in Mlynarska Street; there she found herself with some 200 or so Poles corralled by SS and others without SS insignia. A machine gun had been set up and opened fire: 'After the first salvo, wounded began to be visible in the crowd. The Germans then threw hand grenades. . . . My little son was seriously wounded in the back of the head. A grenade had wounded my daughter in the legs, belly and chest. When everybody in the group had fallen, the Germans began shooting at any wounded who raised themselves or moved. . . .'[5]

One who survived a larger mass shooting by falling at the first salvo and pretending death, Waclawa Szlacheta, described a soldier afterwards walking up to a perambulator holding the seven-month-old twins of her neighbour, Jabuczyk, and shooting them both. She was unable, she testified, to state the exact time a German finished off her own daughter, Alina.[6]

Other units meanwhile were storming hospitals, indulging orgies of killing, looting and rape among patients, nurses and nuns alike. Many of the men were drunk. The war diary of the German Ninth Army HQ in the city recorded Kaminsky's Brigade as having 'boozed its way' in from the southern suburbs.

Such methods were militarily indefensible and counter-productive so far as the suppression of the Home Army uprising was concerned. They can only be explained by the savage spirit of racial vengeance and violence spawned in the Freikorps by the humiliation of defeat in the first war, handed down and heightened now by the prospect of defeat in the second. The spirit radiated from Führer headquarters. Again Himmler was carrying out superior orders, again he was passing them down in the most extreme form to men he had handpicked for lack of scruple. Warsaw was again an epitome of the system and his place within it.

The Home Army units were short of arms and soon short of ammunition and food; their lack of artillery and what appears a cavalier approach to tactics meant that they failed to breach the strongest citadels of German command in the city or gain the Vistula bridges that would have opened the way towards the Red Army in the eastern suburbs. Like the Jews before them, their principal tactic was to allow German and 'Ukrainian' units to close before opening sniper fire aimed especially at officers and hurling home-made Molotov cocktails. They sortied and escaped by means of the sewer system. If there was no escape they fought to the last man and woman, knowing in any case that their enemy gave no quarter: prisoners were shot immediately or sent before advancing tanks as human barricades; wounded were shot or sprayed with petrol and burned where they lay like the civilian victims of the executions. For their part, the Polish units gave no quarter either.

For a long time the Home Army received no help from the great powers. Stalin pretended to dismiss their stand as 'reckless adventurism' and refused to drop supplies, send fighters against the German dive-bombers, or even permit British or American aircraft to use Soviet airstrips on supply missions. The US Ambassador in Moscow was told that even damaged aircraft would be refused permission to land. The Royal Air Force managed sporadic drops from mid-August with aircraft based on Brindisi, Italy, but by this time von dem Bach had driven a wedge of destruction right through the city to the Vistula, dividing the Polish-held areas from one another. Only help from the Russian forces in the eastern suburbs could have offset the weight of von dem Bach's technological advantage; this did not come. In his study of the Russian campaign John Erickson concludes that it was not simply Stalin's political motives, but the strategic balance of the Russian armies at the end of a 300-mile supply line and under attack from German armour south of Warsaw that dictated their halt on the other side of the Vistula, and 'it was not simply a matter of being checked before Praga [east-bank Warsaw], but of preparation for a bigger battle that barred the way to Warsaw.'[7]

Meanwhile the Poles, pressed into ever smaller enclaves, clung on with fierce courage. At the end of the month Bor reported to London that the capital had become 'a city of ruins' in which 'the dead are buried inside the ruins or alongside them.'[8] Stalin's inaction and attempts to prevent the western allies helping the Home Army now threatened a major scandal in the west. It was no doubt Himmler's knowledge of the dangerous rift opening out that encouraged him in September to liken Germany's position to an 'explosive wedge' which would 'blow the enemy coalition right apart'.

During the second week in September, Stalin began mending his bridges with the west; he agreed to Anglo-American use of Russian airstrips to supply Warsaw, authorised the Red Army command to send up fighters against the Stukas, to bombard the German positions in Warsaw with artillery and send the 1st (Soviet) Polish Infantry Division – formed from previous Polish prisoners of war – into the eastern suburb of Praga to fight its way to the Vistula. He must have known it was too late. The Soviet Poles succeeded in reaching the river, but the Germans held the western (Warsaw) bank, and blew all bridges across. The commander of the Polish division, General Zygmunt Berling, exceeded his orders by launching improvised amphibious crossings in the nights of 16 and 17 September, establishing minor bridgeheads on the western bank, and linking up with units of the Home Army, but he was not supported by the Russians and was soon ordered to withdraw back across the river.

By this time towards the end of September there was nothing left for Bor but surrender. He was able to consider this because Hitler had been persuaded to grant combatant status to the Home Army; the survivors emerged from the ruins with their weapons and red and white armbands, their wounds and their pride and marched between curious and respectful German soldiers lining the street. They left some 15,000 of their comrades dead beneath the still smouldering debris, together with perhaps 200,000 civilians.[9]

The action cost the German anti-partisan and regular forces 10,000 dead, 9000 wounded, 7000 missing – high losses due in part to the debauched behaviour of Kaminsky's men and the excess *Draufgängertum* enforced in Dirlewanger's Brigade. The rewards bestowed on these two commanders at Himmler's instigation, or at least with his sanction, were for some reason very different. Kaminsky was removed and quietly executed and the results of a mock partisan ambush staged for the benefit of his followers; Dirlewanger received the Knight's Cross. Both von dem Bach and Reinefarth were promoted to the command of Army corps in the final battles in defence of the east.

Meanwhile all remaining civilians were evacuated from Warsaw, the able-bodied to forced labour for the Reich, the infirm to special camps or the gas chambers; some 1000 Jews who had survived Stroop's action or escaped from labour gangs had fought with the Poles and approximately half of them had been killed.[10] *Räumungs* or 'Clearance' Kommandos went into what remained of Warsaw to take out anything of value and they were followed by special teams equipped with flame-throwers and explosive to complete Hitler's order to erase the city. They did not demolish all the walls, but Poles returning after 'liberation' by the Red Army found only tall chimney stacks and rubble behind the blackened and empty façades.

In Berlin during the agony of Warsaw the chief surviving conspirators of 20 July endured personal agony at the hands of Gestapo and Criminal Police officials, and subsequent trial and execution. The lust for vengeance surrounded Hitler; yet again Himmler, as chief executive, contrived to interpret the mood in the most extreme form. On 3 August, before von Rundstedt's Court of Honour had passed its first act of expulsion from the Wehrmacht on twenty-two of the most obviously culpable officers, Himmler had told a gathering of Gauleiters of his intentions towards the leaders of the revolt. Already, he said, he had had the bodies of von Stauffenberg, Olbricht, Mertz and von Haeften disinterred from the spot where they had been buried hurriedly on the night of the execution. 'I then gave the order to have the corpses burned and the ashes scattered in the fields. We do not want the least remembrance of these people – or those who will presently be executed – in any grave or other spots.'[11]

The next step, he went on, was to establish 'an absolute *Sippenhaftung*', by which he meant the arrest of all relations of these men. He had broached the subject of *Sippenhaft* the previous week in his address to the officer corps of the new Volksgrenadier Division.[12] It was an old German custom, he had told them, that the family or clan answered for each member. It was nothing unreasonable. Just as the family of a soldier honoured and endowed by the state benefited, so the family of one who was disloyal had to be drawn to account if they were not able to prove that they had expelled him or her – for it might be the soldier's wife or relatives who were guilty. For all the homely phraseology, it had been a plain warning. With the Gauleiters it was different; he wanted their approval, and he wanted to explain how they should answer fainthearts. For already, he told them, his people had begun arresting the families concerned.

> No one should come to us and say: 'What you are doing is Bolshevistic.' No, do not be touchy. It certainly is not Bolshevistic, but very ancient and was in common use with our ancestors. You only need to look up the Germanic Sagas. If they proscribed a family and outlawed them, or if there was a blood feud in the family, then they were drastically thorough. If the family were outlawed and proscribed, they said, 'This man is a traitor, the blood is bad, there is bad blood in them, that will be eradicated.' And in the case of a blood feud it was eradicated down to the last member of the whole *Sippe* [clan]. The family of Graf Stauffenberg will be extinguished to the last member—

The Gauleiters applauded. 'For it must be a uniquely cautionary example,' he went on, evidently encouraged by the reaction.

> Moreover it will be left to the discretion of everyone in Germany named Stauffenberg – generally speaking *all* who bear the unfortunate names which are mixed up in this treason trial – to propose to change their name, since one cannot expect them to continue bearing the name of a scoundrel and traitor.
>   We shall, however – and this is very important – seize the belongings, the properties of all the families in which a member took a leading part in this conspiracy, and in this disloyalty and sedition.

These threats were fulfilled, not so much systematically except perhaps in the case of von Stauffenberg, but arbitrarily since Himmler refused to set ground rules which might inhibit personal discretion.[13] The Stauffenberg clan was pursued with the utmost rigour; the families of Klaus, Berthold and their brother Alexander, their mother, uncles, aunts, cousins, even in-laws and acquaintances, most of whom knew nothing of the conspiracy, old men and children were all rounded up and imprisoned, placed in *Schutzhaft* or, in the case of youngsters, in Party hostels under new names, or given to foster families. It took months of searching after the war to find them. Probably the distant branches of the other conspirators' families were not hounded so relentlessly. Nevertheless the families of Olbricht, von Haeften, Mertz, Goerdeler, von Tresckow, von Hassell, von Hase, Hoepner, Oster, von Dohnanyi, Bonhoeffer, von der Schulenberg, Schwerin von Schwanenfeld, Hansen, von Hofacker, Yorck von Wartenburg, von Moltke, to name only some of those who have appeared in these pages, were arrested and sent to camps.

Meanwhile a 'Special Commission 20.7.1944' set up by Kaltenbrunner, and consisting of some 400 officials, continued interrogating day and night the widening circle of those they discovered were implicated; the fresh information gleaned each twenty-four hours was summarised by an Obersturmbannführer, Kielpinski, and sent to Bormann with a covering note from Kaltenbrunner. It is notable that, despite Himmler's involvement with many of those arrested, his name appears rarely in the reports, and only in favourable contexts. On 22 July, for instance, the Commission commented on the mood of the population: 'The appointment of the Reichsführer-SS as commander of the Home Army is leading to the hope everywhere that now for once everything will be thoroughly "cleared out"; there is a demand for a general purge.'[14] A precisely similar comment appeared two days later: the Reichsführer was seen as 'a strong man'; it was expected that he would 'finally and ruthlessly make a clean sweep internally'.[15] On 25 July Klausing, von Stauffenberg's escort to Führer headquarters on 11 and 15 July, was reported as saying that the bomb had not been detonated on these occasions because the Reichsführer-SS was not present – testimony that is not supported and indeed contradicted by later reports of the Commission. More strikingly, the author of the report, Kielpinski, surmised without evidence: 'It is probable that the two [sic] explosives which von Haeften threw out of the car on the way to the airport after the attempt *were prepared for the attempt on the Reichsführer-SS*' – italics as in the original.[16] It is difficult to see how a second attempt could have been made on anyone after the bomb in the Führer conference had detonated, and Kielpinski did not suggest how either von Stauffenberg or von Haeften might have contrived to make such an attempt.

Those who knew most about the SS flirtation with the opposition and with the west were either protected by Himmler, or said nothing, no doubt realising it would be their death warrant. It is probably significant that

Canaris was arrested by Schellenberg in person. 'Somehow I felt it would be you,' the Admiral said when he opened the door to him, and after the situation had been explained, 'We'll get over this. You must promise me faithfully that within the next three days you will get me an opportunity to talk to Himmler personally.'[17] Evidently this talk took place. Canaris was subjected to interrogation in September, but was treated, at least at first, with unusual respect, and was not physically tortured; he insisted he had never played any part in the opposition. When Oster's secret files on the pre-war opposition conspiracies were discovered, including a few pages from Canaris' diary, 'Gestapo' Müller reprimanded the official concerned for reporting it to a meeting of the 'Special Commission' without informing him first and told him to make no further reference to the find, even to his friends.[18]

Langbehn was also protected. His membership of various opposition groups and his central role as a liaison with the west were mentioned in a few reports, but his connection with Himmler was stated only once in a summary of Goerdeler's evidence. Goerdeler said he had become acquainted with Langbehn through Professor Dr Jesson, at which time Langbehn had told him of his foreign contacts via Switzerland and Sweden, and of his relationship with the Reichsführer-SS. Goerdeler thought him sinister. 'On the one hand his relationship to the Reichsführer-SS had been important, and at the conference in May 1943 Goerdeler stoutly encouraged Langbehn in the view that the initiative for a rescue action could only derive from the Reichsführer-SS. On the other hand the role Langbehn played appeared to him *dangerous*' – italics as in the original. Goerdeler then stated that Langbehn had told him in August–September 1943 of 'the known discussion' between Himmler and Popitz without divulging details. 'I also did not press him because I fully appreciated his discretion.' However, when Goerdeler learned that Langbehn had been told of the plans for a military uprising he had been alarmed. 'I was shocked and asked myself who could have been so indiscreet as to initiate him and went to Popitz. I tried hard to pose questions about the seriousness of his knowledge, and then told him it was certainly all a nonsense, the generals would never act. I did that because I was never completely sure about the personality of Langbehn.'[19] This summary supported Himmler's own version of his contacts with Langbehn and Popitz, namely that he was leading them on in order to discover the ramifications of the plot.

There were virtually no reports detailing Arthur Nebe's role. According to Gisevius, Nebe fled Berlin after hearing of Graf Helldorf's arrest on 24 July. Gisevius fled with him, and thanks to Allen Dulles' efforts on his behalf succeeded eventually in reaching Switzerland. Nebe, however, was picked up in January 1945, interrogated and apparently executed, although there is no confirmation of this. The first mention of Nebe's name in Kaltenbrunner's daily reports to Bormann occurs in a summary of enemy propaganda dated 16 August. The enemy radio station Atlantik

– run by the British Political Warfare Executive (PWE) – had reported on 7 August that in order to keep the public in the dark about the participation of high SS-Führers in the 'peace movement', the rank and position of SS-Obergruppenführer Nebe had not been disclosed; it also reported that his flight had been assisted by other SS-Führers and police officials.[20] On 11 August the Atlantik station asserted that high personalities in the Party, the economy, politics and 'even Waffen-SS Führers' had belonged to the conspiracy.[21] Von Neurath, Schacht, Graf Helldorf and again Nebe were mentioned, and it was suggested that Himmler's second adjutant had been shot on account of his participation in the conspiracy. It is interesting that the Atlantik station broadcasts were so skilfully woven that Bormann and Kaltenbrunner believed there must be an informer at Führer headquarters, and set 200 signals specialists the task of tracing parallel lines which would transmit conversations to unauthorised destinations – without success.[22] However, when Kaltenbrunner came to make a special report on Nebe for Hitler in March the following year, he gave no details of what the police chief had admitted under interrogation apart from sexual relationships with a wide circle of women; apparently he sought to account for his treachery as the result of a thyroid operation undergone in 1943.

The paucity of information in the reports about those most closely connected with Himmler tends to support popular rumour that SS-Oberstgruppenführer Daluege and Obergruppenführer Kaltenbrunner were implicated in the plot – and, if these two, presumably 'Gestapo' Müller as well. Popular rumour also implicated Keitel, von Rundstedt, von Manstein, von Brauchitsch, von Kluge, Halder, Fromm and von Stülpnagel;[23] it is known that nearly all these were involved and it is intriguing to speculate whether Keitel was really of their number. At all events it was the military conspirators and the traditional ruling class generally, the old enemies of the revolution, whom the SS investigators pursued and destroyed by providing the prosecution evidence at the travesties of trials played out in the People's Court under the turncoat communist, Dr Roland Freisler.

The first eight cases, including von Witzleben, Hoepner, Stieff, von Hase and Yorck von Wartenburg, came before the Court on 7 and 8 August. Hitler had given personal instructions about filming to the Deutsche Wochenschau (newsreel) chief, and Freisler, robed in red, played up to the cameras, adopting what one of the stenographers present described as a 'theatrical, brutal and merciless expression – apparently rehearsed before a mirror – like a second Robespierre'. He shouted the accused down if they attempted an explanation, calling them *Lumpen*, traitors and cowardly murderers; finally in a voice 'that must have been heard like a trumpet in the streets outside he declared all eight accused guilty of the most consummate treachery to the Führer, his followers, all that the German *Volk* was and had, to German history, to all German men and women. . . .'[24]

Hitler had decreed that the accused should be hanged within two hours of sentence, and this too should be filmed for public exhibition. They were taken to the execution chamber of Plötzensee prison in north-west Berlin. It was part of a brick outhouse, furnished with a guillotine, a black dividing curtain, a table for the witnesses, and the executioner's Schnapps, and a wash basin. Eight iron hooks were spaced out along a girder beneath the ceiling. The executioner and his assistants were not strangers to their task: some 2000 victims of the National Socialist state had been beheaded or hanged here since the *Machtergreifung*.

Von Witzleben was the first to be brought in, his hands behind his back and, under the glare of the film lights, hanged with a wire noose. The others were brought in after him one by one. According to an eyewitness, the hangman, known for his humour, had a grin on his face and made witticisms throughout. 'All the accused showed the same fortitude.'[25] The film was processed rapidly and despatched to the Wolfschanze for Hitler's viewing that night, 8/9 August. Such was the spirit of vengeance. Subsequently only the most important victims were filmed as they died; presumably these films too were sent to Führer headquarters, but neither they nor Freisler's exhibitions were shown to the public as the effect on selected audiences made it evident that they had the reverse effect to that intended.

While the interrogations and trials and executions were proceeding, Himmler ordered a round-up of ideological enemies. This had been planned for some time under the codename 'Aktion Gewitter' ('Storm'). The preparatory message went out from Gestapo headquarters, Prinz Albrecht Strasse, to all Gestapo stations on the night of 17 August, signed by Müller:

> RFSS has ordered arrest of all former Reich and Landtag representatives in the Reich of the KPD [Communist Party] and SPD [Social Democratic Party] as well as town councillors of the KPD and SPD. It is immaterial whether there is anything against them at present or not. I extend this arrest-action to the former Party and Union secretaries of the SPD.
>
> The arrest-action must begin simultaneously on 22.8.44 in the early-morning hours. . . .[26]

Those arrested were to be taken into *Schutzhaft*. The only exceptions to be made were those serving in the Gestapo or SD informants' network, those who had become active members of the Party or its affiliates, and those over seventy, or so ill that they were unfit for camp life. The day before the action was due to begin Himmler added all former representatives and town councillors of the Centre (Catholic) Party to the arrest-list, and he requested a short report on the political attitude after the *Machtergreifung* of each individual arrested.[27] The round-up caused alarm in communities throughout the Reich, especially where priests were taken, and the same evening a top-priority message went out from Prinz Albrecht Strasse excluding priests from the action.[28]

The number of those arrested after 20 July has been put as high as 7000; as 'Aktion Gewitter' indicates, most of those rounded up had no direct connection with the conspiracy, but were taken in as a precautionary measure and to indicate to the populace that Himmler meant business. Others were arrested and executed for 'defeatism', but this was nothing new; it had been going on since the first day of the war. The total number of executions officially registered in 1944 was 5764, only 80 more than the official total for 1943.[29] It is uncertain exactly how many were conspirators. Executions of conspirators continued through the early months of 1945 and practically to the end of the war; one authority has put their number at 200.[30] Jürgen Stroop said in his prison cell that the total reached 4500. 'Oh, certainly,' he replied when Moczarski expressed scepticism, 'there was no single garrison in which someone who was guilty or had knowledge of the conspiracy was not found. Each SD office, each branch of the Security Police had to neutralise conspirators, especially those who had camouflaged themselves perfectly. . . .'[31] Moczarski suggested that what Stroop meant was the opportunity was seized to get rid of political enemies, prosecute personal vendettas or remove obstacles to promotion; Stroop did not disagree. The numbers of those executed for their part in the plot, like the numbers who took part or knew about it, will never be established.

Stroop himself was responsible for the arrest of von Kluge. He kept him under continual surveillance in the weeks immediately after the attempt, and found he was maintaining secret radio contact with the British under the guise of fulfilling Red Cross agreements about prisoners of war. On 15 August Himmler called Stroop to tell him that Hitler was replacing von Kluge, who was to be arrested. By Stroop's account he did this the next day as the General was on his way to a meeting with British representatives. After two days of interrogation during which von Kluge denied everything, Stroop left him alone with a pistol to take the honourable way out. He refused, merely writing to Hitler, protesting his loyalty and begging him to end the war. Stroop shot him through the head – thus his account to Moczarski – giving it out, on Himmler's instructions, as suicide.[32]

Later that year, as is well known, Rommel was confronted with a similar choice after recovering from his wounds. For the sake of his family he agreed to take poison. His death was announced as a heart attack and he was given a state funeral attended by von Rundstedt as Hitler's representative. Many other leading figures had already committed suicide without prompting, to save themselves from the Gestapo.

On the day before von Kluge's 'suicide', Himmler wrote a long letter to the chief of Ahnenerbe, SS-Sturmbannführer Wolfram Sievers, and his chief academic, SS-Oberführer Professor Dr Walther Wüst. It concerned a recent learned book on German folklore and justice which had been sent to him the previous month, and it is evident from his detailed comments that he had read it thoroughly. He believed, he wrote, that their forebears enacted their legal ordinances, including marriages, on the ancestor stone at the great burial place of the *Sippe*. 'This is in accordance with the customs of our forebears and their belief: the dead ancestors experienced everything and everyone had to be answerable before them.'

Most of his comments concerned marriage and procreation. Thus he drew attention to a passage about an ancient custom whereby girls went to the ancestor stone at midnight to obtain a man:

> Here I must relate a custom manifestly still alive in our time about the year 1930:
> In Kiel a girl bore a child in hospital. To the question, who the father of the child was, she said it was a child of the stone. When it was looked into more closely it was found to concern the following old custom:
> If there was a girl in a village who had reached marriageable age and not found a man, the father went out on a moon-dark night, that is at new moon, with the girl and the villagers. The girl was placed on the dolmen [stone table] or ancestral burial, the villagers [*Bauern aus dem Dorfe*] stood in a wide circle around this stone, face outward. The father had spoken beforehand with a villager, thus with one from the blood-community. This man took himself from the ring to the ancestral burial and coupled with the girl. The love and sexual act took place on the ancestral burial.
> The interpretation of this is: no good blood may die out without bearing fruit. However, the child must come to such a daughter from a man of good blood from the village and blood-community. What was done was no casual act, but took place in the sight of the ancestors and on the grave of the ancestors.[33]

Referring to another passage about bridal pairs going to the 'bridal stone' at new moon, he said that research with wild and domestic animals would be necessary to find out whether the new moon was indeed a period of special fecundity. Finally, after discussing the etymology of the 'Heisser' stone mentioned in the book, whose origins he believed lay in the word *heischen* or the Bavarian *der Heiss*, he speculated on the origins of the *roter* (or 'red') stone: red, he wrote, always symbolised law or justice:

> The executioner had a red robe, the courts were decked with red velvet or red earth. I believe that in some areas where the material is to be found, the *Gerichtsstein* [Court-of-justice stone] was of red sandstone or similar rock. In the same way I believe that in general the *Gerichtsstein* or *heissen Stein* was known as the *roter Stein* or *roden Stein*.
> This significance of red and justice and its interplay would be an important research project for the Ahnenerbe to tackle after the war.[34]

Himmler had always appeared the most powerful figure under Hitler. It is impossible to say whether he was in practice, and meaningless to ask since he was never prepared to use his power directly to change the course of events; he amassed it to garner more as others amass fortunes and lay them up in securities and bank vaults. He infiltrated and formed alliances and when the time was ripe made spectacular take-overs, and hungered for more empires to topple and dreamed of unlimited authority in a world of Saga, but he did not, it seems he could not, flex the vast network of interlocking force he controlled, except on behalf of his Führer. In this he was Hitler's most inspired and only indispensable choice. Goebbels was brilliant, Speer a technological genius, Bormann the consummate reptile, but without 'der treue Heinrich', the right-hand man who wanted to know everything and manage and control everything, but lacked the decision or ultimate resolve, probably even the desire to be more than the right-hand man, it is difficult to see how Hitler's Reich and his paladins could have survived thus far.

He was not, of course, 'der treue Heinrich' as his flirtations with the opposition and the west demonstrate. Yet neither was he the potential King Heinrich. Had he wished to take over the Reich he could scarcely have had more favourable conditions than those immediately preceding 20 July. It could be said it was the west's failure to treat with him that kept him loyal. But a real quest for supreme power would not have been diverted by the attitude of the enemy. The course of the 20 July conspiracy seems to indicate that he was prepared, as ever, to watch the game and toy with treason, but when the moment came he failed to act and simply allowed power to flow back to its original source. Probably he was relieved inwardly that, by sparing Hitler, Providence had taken the decision out of his hands; he could continue to serve his Führer.

After 20 July his importance as perpetual second man became more marked. His powers had increased dramatically. The Army in disgrace had lost whatever moral and political authority it had retained to that date. By contrast Himmler, whose Waffen-SS grew to thirty-eight divisions – at least in name – had been entrusted with command of the Home Army and with raising the new 'people's divisions'; behind all his titles as Reichsführer-SS and Chief of the German Police, Minister of the Interior, Chief of Army Armaments and commander of the Replacement Army, he was Minister of War in all but name, overall chief of intelligence, chief of the concentration camp labour and industrial complex, and had taken over responsibility for the V rocket production programme; he also retained all racial–colonial responsibilities administered by his Main Office, RKF (Consolidation of German Nationhood), Volksdeutsche Mittelstelle, RuSHA and Dienststelle Heissmeyer. If these decreased in importance as the boundaries of the Reich shrank, his responsibilities for defence increased, first with the formation that autumn of a home militia called the Volkssturm, then with command of armies in the field; at one point he styled himself Supreme Commander, West.

The prestige and influence of the official heir apparent, the Reichs-marschall, Hermann Göring, had fallen away completely by this time and Himmler was considered and undoubtedly considered himself the obvious successor to Hitler; even Hitler appeared to concede this by enlarging his responsibilities to such an extent, and that November he allowed him to make the big speech in his stead at the annual Bürgerbräu celebrations. Hitler judged him more or less correctly. Himmler continued to toy with treason, but he never grasped it. There were plenty of excuses he could make to himself. Why seize power when the west would no more deal with him than with Hitler? Providence had given him a sign. He owed everything he was to Hitler. His honour was his loyalty; how could he of all people betray the Führer? According to all who knew him closely he simply lacked the power of decision.

He was also exposed to the emotional currents in wake of the failed plot. These radiated as much from SS and Party members enraged at the attempted 'stab in the back' and demanding a final cleansing of the reactionary and 'intellectual' stables, as from the Führer and the leaders rallying round him in desperate defence of the power and ideology system that had brought them their positions. In defeat against a world of enemies, the system's ratchet towards extremes increased. From outside with hindsight it is evident that whatever rationality remained was distorted between these tremendous forces and apprehension of defeat. Himmler proved, as always, the supreme conformist.

He and Goebbels, less than twenty years before both ragged, wandering activists for a semi-proscribed, minority cause, putting up at the poor homes of Party members wherever they spoke, became the key figures in the last stand of the system that had grown miraculously from their efforts. Hitler had disappeared from public view. Only the image Goebbels had created of him remained potent. It was Goebbels, appointed Commissioner for 'Total War', and Himmler, in his role as drummer for the new divisions, who sought to mobilise all resources for the war effort and recruit all males at home – then women and girls – for the defence of the Fatherland.

Both took advantage of the propaganda value of the so-called Morgenthau Plan adopted as official allied policy by Roosevelt and Churchill at a conference in Quebec that September. This foresaw, not simply the partition of Germany after the war, but the dismantling of the heavy and electro-chemical industries of the Ruhr and the Saar and the conversion of the country into a land 'primarily agricultural and pastoral in its character'. The aim, natural enough in view of German rearmament in the inter-war years, and indeed before the First World War, was to make it impossible for her to arm a third time for European and world domination. That at least was the declared aim, and in the climate created by the German drive for *Lebensraum* it was more reasonable than it might appear with hindsight – especially, perhaps, as it was precisely what Hitler had intended for eastern Europe. However, the author of the plan, the US Treasury Secretary, Henry Morgenthau, was a Jew; together with inferences about the size of population which a deindustrialised Germany could be expected to support, this was a gift for Goebbels and Himmler in their drive to recruit and whip up a fanatical spirit of defence of the Fatherland. The German press was soon reporting that Roosevelt had 'amplified the plans of his bosom friend, the finance Jew, Morgenthau, and developed a programme of pitiless extermination'.[35]

Goebbels and Himmler were the most visible symbols of defiance. Bormann played his part in the shadows at Hitler's side, filtering the information that reached him, controlling the Gauleiters and the Party apparatus. Speer drove the war economy in face of the crippling onslaughts from the air and fostered group fantasy with production forecasts as overoptimistic as Göring's in better times. Göring and Dönitz shed men from their services to fill the gaps in the fighting fronts and gave Hitler moral support for the strategy of fighting for time until the new weapons could be produced. Keitel relayed the orders of the once greatest warlord of all time to surrender no inch of ground. Von Ribbentrop put out vain peace feelers east and west. These formed Hitler's war council, more separately than together, during the last dying spasms of his Reich; they drew heart from his will – or recognised that there was no alternative. He responded to the fantasy created: the jet fighter aircraft programme that would put a roof over the Reich . . . the new U-boats that would wrest the initiative back from the western allies . . . the V-2 rockets that would pound the British into a conciliatory mood . . . the points of friction between the east and west that would break the enemy coalition apart . . . the miracle of the Seven Years War that would be repeated at the blackest hour for the Reich . . .

For all his public and private assertions of faith in ultimate victory. Himmler was riddled with doubt. Kersten's fingers had relieved him of the worst of the spasms that brought him to his bed in early September, but his private secretary, Brandt, saw him pacing away the night of 9/10 September, unable to sleep.[36] His responsibilities were greater than any single individual could cope with, and the situation was desperate: the western allies had broken out of the invasion pocket and swept across France, had liberated Paris, Brussels and Antwerp and were within striking distance of the Rhine; over that barrier lay the industrial region of the Ruhr, whose loss would signify the effective end of the war. In the east the Red Army thrust towards the Baltic had cut off Army Group North, which was fighting its own separate, defensive battle. Earlier, on 24 July Marshal Rokossovskii's Army Group had overrun the extermination camp at Majdanek; for the first time the unbelievable had become visible. Photographs of gas chambers and crematoria and living skeletons in the camp had shocked the world. In the Balkans on 23 August Rumania had defected from the German alliance and surrendered unconditionally to the Russians. This had fatally weakened Hungary's alliance with Germany. Yet Hungarian oil was vital. Meanwhile at the end of August Slovak partisans had staged a rising potentially more dangerous than the Warsaw revolt. Was Himmler's mind circling tiredly in search of an exit from the tightening noose? Was he perhaps seeing von

Witzleben and the other seven conspirators of 20 July struggling on thin wire in the execution chamber of Plötzensee jail the day before?

On 12 September Kersten, who had begun to use his special relationship as Himmler's 'Magic Buddha' to persuade him to release certain prisoners from the camps, petitioned him on behalf of a group of twenty-seven priests. In the course of the discussion Himmler confessed to the mistake the Nazis had made in attacking the Church; it had proved stronger than they – the Party – but he wondered if, despite all he had attempted against it, there was still room for him inside. Agreeing to release the group, he said, 'When I am dead, will these priests also pray for my soul?'[37]

Four days later he received General Vlassov, the leader of the Russian Liberation Army whom he had spoken of in such sneering tones as a Slavic traitor at the Posen Gauleiter conference the previous October. Since then Berger, Ohlendorf, Schellenberg and other senior SS officers had talked to him, so dramatically had Germany's position deteriorated, and finally Himmler had obtained Hitler's permission to incorporate Vlassov's anti-Soviet formations in the eastern fighting front. The meeting had been fixed for 21–23 July; put off in the aftermath of the bomb plot, it eventually took place on 16 September at Himmler's field headquarters in East Prussia. The two met 'under four eyes', as was Himmler's invariable custom when dealing with important matters, with only an interpreter present.

Vlassov emerged highly gratified by what he had achieved and very surprised. He had expected to meet a bloodthirsty grand inquisitor *à la* Beria, he told his Chief of Staff. Instead he had felt he was talking to a decent, well-brought-up bourgeois.

> Quiet, modest, nothing of the gangster boss like Dr Ley. On the contrary, he was none too self-assured. Not a word about *Herrenmenschen*. No mention of Jews. He more or less apologised for having so long been taken in by *Untermensch* theories. I do not think he is intelligent. He seemed limited, narrow, pedantic. He has a farm – so he is a peasant like myself. He is fond of animals.[38]

Himmler apparently accorded Vlassov full rights as an ally and agreed to him raising ten divisions in the common cause against Stalin. However seriously he meant this remarkable about-turn, Himmler's pact with Vlassov soon fell into the sand of inter-ministerial rivalries and suspicions, and was overtaken by the speed of the German collapse.

At the end of September, Himmler travelled to Bratislava to put his stamp on the suppression of 'Free Slovakia', by that time under overt Soviet control. Originally he had sent the faithful Gottlob Berger to put down the rising as von dem Bach was engaged in Warsaw; now he superseded him with the HSSPF in the region, a typically hardened example named Hermann Höfle, and furnished him with Dirlewanger and his criminals, the blood and ashes of Warsaw reeking in close memory, five Security Police Kommandos, the 18th SS-Panzergrenadierdivision Horst Wessel and the 14th (Galician)

SS-Waffen-Grenadierdivision. In October these formations visited the horrors of a 'rigorous' SS action on the region – as Himmler put it on another occasion that September, 'I will cover you. You can be absolutely certain I will never reprove anyone for excess!'[39] Smoke of burning homes, mass graves of civilians and soldiers, roads jammed with refugees or columns of fearful men, women and children being marched towards internment and forced labour marked the advance of the SS Panzer and police units. By the end of October 'Free Slovakia' had been crushed as a unified force.

On his way back to his field headquarters in early October, Himmler spent a day with Häschen Potthast and his two children at the house on the Obersalzberg. Next day he confided to Bormann that he had accepted no telephone calls but had devoted himself to 'hanging pictures, doing things about the house and playing with the children the whole day long'. He had legalised his paternity of the boy Helge, then aged two, and the baby girl in a document dated 12 September – whether by coincidence or not the day Kersten recorded him wondering whether the Church still had room for him – and had made himself co-guardian of the two children with Häschen.[40] Martin Bormann's wife Gerda, one of Häschen's neighbours in the complex of Party leaders' homes above Berchtesgaden, provides a glimpse of the family in a letter she wrote to her husband on 21 September:

> Helge is a lot taller than our Hartmut but much slimmer and thinner. In his movement and general build he is as much like Heinrich as Hartmut is like you, but I can't see the facial likeness any more. The little girl, however, is ridiculously like her father. Häschen has some photos from Heinrich's childhood where he looks exactly the same. The baby has grown big and sturdy, and is so sweet! All the afternoon she was lying in her basket, sleeping or playing with her little hands. Helge has got some nice carts and a blue wheelbarrow, all the work of the wounded soldiers at Hohenlychen, and the boys were rushing round with them the whole afternoon long. With Helge it is obvious that playfellows of his own age are something new to him. . . .[41]

Häschen, Gerda wrote, was very pleased with the house – completed only recently – and was enchanted with its situation.

Since at least July Himmler had been occupied with the idea of raising a mass levy as an auxiliary to the regular forces for defence of the homeland; it is not clear whether this owed more to the representations of the Army General Staff who were pressing for the same thing, to a defence militia raised in East Prussia by the Gauleiter, Erich Koch, or to parallels he himself had drawn from German history. In the event Bormann ensured that the force, to be known as the Volkssturm, would be raised and administered by the Gauleiters. Himmler, in keeping with his new, heightened persona as spokesman for the Führer and the spirit of defiance, was appointed overall head. And when the scheme was announced over Grossdeutschen radio on 18 October, it was he who explained it to the public.

The broadcast was from East Prussia before an audience of Erich Koch's Volkssturm. Photographs of the hall show Himmler before banked microphones at the speaker's rostrum, an improbable figure under a giant German eagle and swastika banners, flanked by Keitel and Erich Koch, their martial bearing and jutting jaws emphasising the homeliness of his appearance. Surely – this is an impostor.

Proceedings opened with choruses of 'Volk ans Gewehr!' ('People to arms!') after which an announcer read the Führer decree: 'After five years of the hardest struggle and in consequence of our European allies breaking faith, the enemy stands before or at the German borders. He exerts his forces to destroy our Reich and eradicate the German *Volk* and its social order. His final goal is the extermination of the German people. . . .'

Coming to details, the decree prescribed that Volkssturm units to defend 'the native soil' were to be raised in each *Gau* by the Gauleiter; the Reichsführer-SS, as commander of the Replacement Army, was responsible for their military organisation, training, arming and deployment in battle.

After the announcement Himmler started his speech:[42] 'Volkssturm men! Today 131 years ago on the evening of 18 October 1813, after the bloody and extraordinarily changeable battle near Leipzig, the people finally emerged victorious. By this success Germany's soil was swept clean of Napoleon's apparently invincible armed power. . . .' He went on to describe how in the spring of that year the Prussian Landsturm had been raised from ordinary villagers and townspeople, 'armed with every variety of weapon from flintlocks with and without bayonet, spears, pickaxes, pitchforks, swords, scythes . . . etc.' and formed into battalions of fanatical freedom-fighters:

With the words, 'Fatherland! Fatherland!' the Landwehr and Landsturm attacked the better-armed, -trained and battle-hardened enemy in all regions, and over the course of months accompanied by many reverses, drove the French enemy from the Prussian lands. The climax came in the battle of Leipzig famously fought to the end by chiefly Prussian and Austrian soldiers. The Landsturm in half a year had created from an allegedly hopeless situation the preconditions for the Army's important strategic victory at Leipzig, which again was the foundation for the liberation of the Fatherland and winning the whole war.

Now, on 18 October 1944, memorial day of the People of Leipzig, our Führer and highest warlord, Adolf Hitler, calls all German men from sixteen to sixty years of age still at home and capable of bearing arms to the German Volkssturm for the defence of the soil of the homeland.

He went on to describe the very difficult situation of their enemies, who had to force an entry into Germany but whose forces were overstretched everywhere.

Bitter is the extremity of hunger in the Russian lands, whose villages and towns are bled and empty of people. Every method of Jewish–Bolshevic pettiness and terror have to be employed to drive the masses, from lads to greybeards, to the battlefield. . . .

Also for our western enemies the war is becoming ever more difficult. In August, certainly, through the superiority of their air force, they succeeded in breaking through our front in Normandy with the heaviest sacrifices. However, in the course of the last six weeks and against their expectations, the west front has been re-established over a length of 900 kilometres, fortified and made defensively strong. . . .

At the same time in Warsaw, capital of betrayed Poland, the resistance movement burst out in rebellion. They believed Germany had lost the strength to break the insubordination of this city of millions behind the German front. In eight weeks of fighting which cost the Polish people over 200,000 dead and the complete annihilation of their metropolis, the uprising was quashed. It was thanks to German humanity as well, to be sure, as the later prudence of the Polish General Bor, disgracefully deceived and abandoned by his allies, that the last quarter million Polish men, women and children in the middle of the cauldron were enabled to escape certain death in the street-fighting of this blazing hell.

Jewry, freemasonry and democracy, he went on, using trickery and bribery, had been responsible for their allies Bulgaria, Rumania and Finland, laying down their arms; they had thereby committed national suicide. In the west, American soldiers questioned themselves more each day why they should be fighting Germany. The British Tommy 'longed urgently' for the end of the war his leaders had promised him for the beginning of October, the middle of October, the end of October . . . Still he had to fight on. Meanwhile in Germany 'oath-breaking, disloyal and cowardly traitors and defeatists' had conspired against the Führer. Fate had intervened and preserved him for his *Volk*. The Army and its officer corps had been pained by the scandal, yet the German martial tradition was age-old, its eternal models 'great spirits and noble heroes like Prince Eugen and Frederick the Great'.

He passed to the future; new squadrons and parachute divisions would be raised for the Luftwaffe. The Navy, 'unbroken in battle', would tackle the enemy with new means, 'the marriage of the highest technology and unconditionally brave crews' – his code for the new types of U-boat with high underwater speed, which Speer was urging through production.

In this present defensive phase of the war, he went on, 'the worthy women and men' who despite the bombing terror had achieved superhuman performances in farm and factory had to create an impregnable fortification system with spade, shovel and pickaxe. And beyond this it was necessary that the *Volk* support the Wehrmacht through the establishment of the Volkssturm.

As formerly in the War of Liberation the Landssturm, so today the Volkssturm has the task of seizing the enemy fanatically everywhere he breaks through to our home soil, whether by a thrust on land, whether by a parachute drop from the air, and containing him and if possible wiping him out. Our enemy must learn:

each kilometre he wants to advance into our country will cost him torrents of blood. Each town block, each village, each farmstead, each trench, each copse, each wood will be defended by men, young lads and greybeards and – if it has to be – by women and girls.

Even in the area they believe they have conquered, the German will to resistance will flame up again and again in their rear and, like the werewolves, death-defying volunteers will damage the enemy and cut off his life-lines. *Our cursed enemy* must discover and realise that a break-in to Germany, even if it is anywhere successful, will cost the attacker sacrifices equivalent to national suicide. The *Volk* draft will take over the task of helping the Wehrmacht in threatened areas so that they are enabled to arm and regroup and attack the enemy again.

His mention of werewolves was again a code; he had commissioned his former Highest SSPF Ukraine and HSSPF South Russia, SS-Obergruppenführer Hans Prützmann, to set up a secret organisation, Werwolf, to keep National Socialism alive underground if the country were occupied. According to Stroop, who had been initiated by Prützmann the previous month, 'soldiers and civilians, SS people and non-Party, youths and girls, even women and children' were to be schooled in sabotage, the liquidation of enemy agents, poisoning food and water and attacks on transport.[43] It is evident from a letter Himmler wrote to his HSSPF West in Düsseldorf on the day following his radio broadcast that the writ ran to liquidation of German collaborators. Enemy press reports indicated that in many of the places occupied by the Anglo-Americans the population was 'behaving unworthily', he wrote. Therefore he instructed the HSSPF that the guilty persons should be drawn to account directly these places were reconquered, and: 'Already now our organisation behind the American front has to make an educational effect by the execution of the death sentence on traitors.'[44]

He continued his speech to the people as he was wont to address his SS men: they must be armed inwardly with the timeless virtues which alone guaranteed victory. And he gave them 'The new oath':

First, we swear that, like our fathers, we want to be loyal, loyal to the Führer, whom the Lord God has sent us, loyal to the Reich which unites all German stems for centuries and that is and will be as it was formerly the regulating power of the European continent. Loyal to the *Volk* and thereby to ourselves, because we are the most valuable elements to defend and preserve the eternal life of the Germanic peoples, its women and children, and therewith its blood that has created so much that is noble for man.

The second promise was to be obedient to all orders from the Führer and superiors, the third to know that the most powerful forces a people could muster were believing hearts and steadfastness; fourthly they were to declare that they would never entertain any false hopes:

We have learned from the very mouths of our enemies what we can expect, the destruction of our country, the clearance of our woods, the dissolution of our economy, the annihilation of our towns, the burning down of our villages and the extermination [*Ausrottung*] of our peoples. . . .

Never and nowhere are Volkssturm men permitted to capitulate. If at any time a responsible leader believes himself to be in a hopeless position where he must give up the struggle, the usual custom of our brave Navy is valid for the Volkssturm: he must give up the command to that subordinate – even if he be the youngest – who has the will to continue the fight.

He prophesied harder tests in the coming weeks and months, but 'armed outwardly and inwardly, inspired by sacred belief and filled with fanatical determination to spare neither our own nor foreign blood if the welfare of the nation requires it' they would endure and prove unconquerable. And he ended, 'We have the deepest confidence and are convinced that at the end of all difficulties, all sacrifices, all sorrows and struggles, the Almighty will give the Führer and his *Volk* hard-earned victory.'

Erich Koch followed with a short address reinforcing these themes, pledging 'All our belief, all our love, all our strength and all our hate . . .' finally leading that deep-throated, three-fold roar that echoes down the years of 'Adolf Hitler, the Führer of all Germans . . . *Sieg Heil! Sieg Heil! Sieg Heil!*'

The following week the press carried reports of Himmler receiving Army and Waffen-SS men in his special train and bestowing on them in the name of the Führer the 'Close combat' clasp in gold.[45] Linking Himmler with 'the bravest of the brave' and continuing to feature him prominently in the press in this and other martial roles, Goebbels created an impression of Himmler's ascendancy in the councils of the Reich and suggested that he was speaking and acting for the silent and invisible Führer. Whether this was connected with Himmler's continuing attempts to interest the west in a separate peace, or whether it should be taken at face value as the propaganda of total war and defiance of the enemy is unclear. But certainly Himmler made other attempts to open negotiations with the British government in the latter part of October. Wolff's SS and police chief in northern Italy, SS-Obergruppenführer Dr Wilhelm Harster, was one of his emissaries; his go-between was an Italian industrialist with English big-business connections named Franco Marinotti. Their meeting took place at Harster's villa near Lake Como in the afternoon of 24 October.

The offer followed the pattern of SS dealing from the beginning, an undisguised mixture of blackmail and appeals to self-interest – in this case to the financial–industrial interest of the western business community in having a Europe freed from communism. It could be said that this message had not changed in all the years of Nazi power. But first there was the threat: Harster told Marinotti of Hitler's plans for a scorched-earth policy, specifically the destruction of all industry as the German fronts withdrew. However, if the allies were willing to negotiate – and he spoke 'with the approval of the Reichsführer Himmler' – he could offer them the twenty-five German divisions in Italy to maintain order in central Europe (that is stave off Communism) directly hostilities ended along the western front. In return the allies should guarantee the inviolability of the Reich area and its population.[46]

Marinotti was given a safe pass across the Swiss border and on 30 October handed his report of the conversation to the British Consul in Zurich, who forwarded it to London. The offer would have been refused without its provenance; that ensured rejection. Marinotti then approached Roosevelt's chief of intelligence in Berne through an official of the Catholic Church – with equal lack of success.[47]

Himmler's failure to understand the loathing his name inspired in the west was due to his National Socialist vision, aided no doubt by wishful thinking. The hatred for him was propaganda whipped up by the Jews around Roosevelt and Churchill, but once western financiers woke up to the frightful danger of Bolshevism facing Europe they would ensure that the propaganda changed direction; then he might look forward to the British and American press hailing him and the SS as saviours of Europe.[48] This was his hope and it was fuelled by Harster's report which, according to Allen Dulles, gave a distorted view of his own response. Harster claimed that he (Dulles) had Roosevelt's mandate to make contact with SS circles since only the SS could be of value to the United States in its desire to disengage from Europe in order to concentrate its forces against Japan. Contact should be resumed after the re-election of President Roosevelt.[49] Viewed from this angle Himmler's call for fanatical resistance had a certain rationale and was not at all inconsistent with his peace overtures.

As for the odium surrounding his name, Kersten mentioned this during a treatment that winter, and Himmler replied with justification that the west accepted Stalin as an ally, and worse could be said of him.[50] The reversal of US policy over the representation of communists and communism on radio and film which had taken place on the United States' entry into the war – as indeed had happened in Great Britain earlier – the way in which the guidelines about the depiction of their new ally had been followed faithfully, and after the war the employment in western intelligence services of SS officers wanted for war crimes lend added support to Himmler's 'real' view of the world. There is much reason to believe that it was not Hitler and Himmler so much as German military–industrial expansionism that the western allies had set their minds against. They believed that Germany had to be defeated and had to acknowledge her defeat before her leading caste could be re-educated to join the (western) family of nations.[51] There was also the very real fear that any hint of negotiation with Germany might provoke Stalin into changing sides once again. It was these considerations which probably carried greater weight than the emotional momentum of hate and horror, and doomed all Himmler's efforts to failure.

Yet the emotion was real – if not as decisive as the *Realpolitik* – and it is probable that Himmler never admitted this to himself. At all events his attitude towards the Jews did not seem to change; only his policy altered with the changing circumstances: on the one hand Auschwitz and other remaining extermination camps were vulnerable to the next Russian advance; on the other hand he needed all the labourers he could muster, chiefly for a line of anti-tank ditches and fortifications known as the East Wall to hold the Red Army before the Reich. These two factors dictated that the gassing should end, but precisely when he gave the order to stop is uncertain. The Jewish Sonderkommando at Auschwitz–Birkenau got wind of the coming change in early October and, knowing that it meant the end for them, revolted at rollcall on 7 October, throwing themselves on the guard. All were mown down with machine-gun fire. However, extermination at Birkenau continued alongside selection for the labour gangs until the end of October. It was then run down and the demolition of the gas chambers and crematoria and the destruction of camp records began.[52] This probably started earlier at other camps in former Poland.

Höss, in his memoirs, placed Himmler's order to 'discontinue the Jew-exterminations' in the autumn of 1944.[53] SS-Standartenführer Kurt Becher, chief negotiator in the bizarre attempt to barter Jews for trucks, placed it between mid-September and mid-October. His mission to Turkey had led to meetings with representatives of American Jewry in Switzerland, and an agreement to release Hungarian Jews to the Swiss in return for foreign exchange payments – 50 Swiss Francs for each ordinary Jew, 500 Francs for 'prominents' which, according to his testimony at Nuremberg, caused him to persuade Himmler to issue the order forbidding further extermination.[54]

Himmler's aim in bartering Jews for Swiss Francs remains uncertain. It is usually assumed he was playing a double game, on the one hand opening a line of communication to Roosevelt for another attempt at peace negotiations with the west, on the other hand covering himself from Hitler's and Bormann's wrath by presenting it as a means of gaining foreign exchange for the war effort.[55] Certainly he was trying desperately to make contact with both western governments at this period. Not only were there his attempts via Marinotti in Italy and Allen Dulles in Switzerland but he was seeking to persuade the imprisoned Goerdeler to appeal to Churchill via his Swedish contact Jacob Wallenberg and the Zionist leader Dr Chaim Weizmann, and was also trying to reach Churchill via the Swedish engineer Dahlerus, whom Göring had used in 1939 in the last-minute efforts to keep Great Britain out of the war. In addition he was preserving Popitz, Langbehn, Haushofer and other members of the conspiracy with useful western contacts from the death sentence, and was accumulating a collection of important hostages, especially Jews believed to be rich or influential. One was Frau Glück, the US-born sister of New York's Mayor, La Guardia. She was resident in Hungary and during the round-up of Hungarian Jews earlier that summer he had ordered her preserved from transportation to Auschwitz and kept ready to hand in a special camp for 'possible political purposes'.[56]

According to Schellenberg Himmler failed to realise that the release of Jews was important for Germany's foreign policy – he meant relations with the west which he was trying to foster – and seemed concerned only with the effect it would have on Hitler and the Party.[57] Kersten also represented Himmler as terrified of Hitler's response were he to permit a wholesale release of Jews, and Bormann, he said, was ready to stab him in the back.[58]

Bormann's letters to his wife do not give this impression. On 25 October he described an evening at Führer headquarters with Himmler during which they had both been reduced to tears of laughter by his other two guests, Wolff's successor and Himmler's long-term favourite, Hermann Fegelein – who had married the sister of Hitler's mistress, Eva Braun, that summer – and Hitler's military adjutant, General Wilhelm Burgdorf; 'they are like a pair of naughty boys,' Bormann wrote. 'You can imagine what fun we had.'[59] And at the end of the month he told her that at his request 'Uncle Heinrich' was about to be appointed Commander-in-Chief Army Group Upper Rhine 'to put things in order'.[60]

It has been suggested that in proposing him for this post Bormann was trying to ruin Himmler by removing him from the immediate vicinity of Führer headquarters and having him appointed above his competence. This would have been a strange thing to do at such a crisis for the system; in fact Himmler appears to have been the obvious choice. He had been concerning himself all autumn with the strengthening of the West Wall, was commander of the Replacement Army, chief public spokesman for 'fanatical' defence of the homeland, and as a leading member of the regime had a personal stake in ensuring that the Rhine defences held.

Whether Himmler's suspicions of Bormann as revealed to Kersten were the result of his own guilty conscience after the arrival of the first small batch of Jews in Switzerland in November or an excuse for indecision, or whether suspicion was endemic and necessary at Hitler's court – whether he simply knew his man too well – there can be no doubt that he was restrained from making large gestures of mercy for the remaining Jews to redeem himself in western eyes by the fear of what Bormann, Goebbels and von Ribbentrop would be able to make of such a reversal of a basic Nazi tenet. Equally there can be no doubt that he lacked the moral courage to brave his Führer's anger. At the same time all his covert moves and feelers suggest that, behind his rhetoric of fighting to the last to preserve the Fatherland, he was seeking to preserve himself, if necessary at the expense of Führer and Party. This was the tenor of the message conveyed to the British Embassy in Stockholm by Dahlerus that winter. Undoubtedly Himmler was able to convince himself that this was the best and only way now open to save Germany and Europe since the SS was the only force capable of preserving the continent from Bolshevism. Yet it was not a card with any meaning in the world outside his imagination. Moreover the frictions in the enemy coalition from which he hoped so much actually worked against him: Dahlerus' approach and the prospect of garbled versions of it reaching the Russians and Americans caused Churchill to become 'seriously alarmed' and to prohibit further discussions.[61]

Thus at the height of his apparent power in the Reich Himmler was locked into the system which had made him. The high gearing of control by Führer will and the ideological gyro which together had made possible the Party's and the nation's successes against unprepared enemies could not be disengaged simply because the world had been aroused. Schellenberg, Kersten and Ohlendorf might complain of Himmler's indecisiveness, but he was also caught in the machine he had helped to create, whose directional momentum was stronger than any individual however highly placed.

This applied to the destruction of the Jews. His order to cease the extermination had less consequence than the necessary dismantling of the killing factories before the Russian advance. Even if he had wished it he could not have erased the effects of years of indoctrination. His order had no effect on Eichmann's sense of mission, no effect on the desensitised camp Kommandants and guards; if Jews were not to be destroyed directly, they could still be worked and starved to death. Of course this did not apply only to Jews: the whole camp labour–industrial complex under Pohl which consumed workers as an expendable energy resource was raised to heightened tempo by the demand for production to stave off defeat, or by that deeper urge noted by Höss for death. A survivor of both the Auschwitz and Ravensbrück work regimes, Madame Vaillant-Couturier, expressed it in similar terms at Nuremberg: 'the systematic and implacable urge to use human beings as slaves and to kill them when they could work no more'.[62]

A survivor of Buchenwald camp, Dr Victor Dupont, detailed the same phenomenon: until autumn 1944, he stated, labour squads and individuals who had become unfit for even the lightest work were sent to Auschwitz for liquidation, then – and it is apparent this must have coincided with the run-down of the Auschwitz death factory – the killing was done in the sick bay of the camp itself. As numbers grew a special block, 61, was reserved for it.

all those nicknamed 'Mussulmans' on account of their appearance were collected in this block. We never saw them without their blankets over their shoulders. They were unfit for even the lightest work. They all had to go through Block 61. The death toll varied daily from a minimum of 10 to about 200 in Block 61. The execution was performed by injecting phenol into the heart in the most brutal manner. The bodies were then carted to the crematorium. . . . [63]

Dupont went on to describe how even the internees' remains were exploited:

The ashes resulting from the cremations were thrown into the excrement pit and served to fertilise the fields around Buchenwald. I add this detail

because it struck me vividly at the time. . . . Work, whatever it might be, was
the internee's only chance of survival. As soon as they were no longer of any
possible use they were done for.[64]

Increasingly that autumn and winter as the camps, mine-workings and
industrial undertakings in the east were closed down before the Russian
advance the work-slaves were evacuated on foot and death occurred on
the march from hunger, exhaustion and exposure, from blows for those
who dropped out, from the wholesale shooting of groups too weak or ill
to continue.

This was also the fate of thousands of Jews who might have survived
if Himmler's order to cease extermination had been observed in the same
spirit as the original directives for genocide. The majority of European Jews
who had escaped the net so far were in Hungary. After the mass deportations
to Auschwitz organised by Eichmann earlier in the year, the Hungarian
government had refuse co-operation and shipments had been brought to an
end in August. By October, with the Red Army approaching Budapest and
the government about to follow the Rumanian example and secede from
the German alliance, Hitler staged a coup which brought the Nazi-style,
anti-semitic Arrow Cross organisation to power. Immediately Eichmann
returned to Budapest, summoned the leader of the Jewish community
and demanded 50,000 able-bodied Jews for work on the South-east Wall –
fortifications before Vienna – and the fighter-aeroplane programme in the
Reich. This time, he said, they would be deported on foot since transportation facilities were needed for other purposes. Both Becher and another
of Himmler's special 'resettlement commissioners', Dieter Wisliceny, also
engaged in negotiating Jews for foreign currency and merchandise, stated
afterwards that Eichmann's purpose was still to render Hungary *judenfrei*,
if not by extermination, then by deportation to labour and concentration
camps. This seems to be confirmed by a letter written by Hitler's plenipotentiary in Hungary, Edmund Veesenmayer, dated 18 October 1944: 'on
completion of the said footmarch Eichmann intends to demand another
50,000 Jews with a view to achieving the ultimate aim, clearing Hungary
of Jews.'[65] Since he sent children and elderly women who were of little
use in digging anti-tank ditches on the marches, it can be accepted this
was his aim.

Of nearly 40,000 men and boys, women and children rounded up and
sent on a seven or eight days' march to Austria at least 7000 were shot or died
along the route.[66] When news of this reached Switzerland and threatened
to compromise Becher's sale of Jews for foreign currency, he complained
to Himmler, who sent the chief of his Führungs Main Office and Rudolf
Höss from the Concentration Camp Inspectorate to investigate. Both were
appalled by the disorder and piled corpses they found along the road, and
for a while the deportations were halted. Himmler soon sanctioned their
resumption, it appears because the American organisation financing the

rescue of Jews via Switzerland was proving tardy in paying for the first small batch which had arrived. At all events Eichmann, according to the leader of the Budapest Jewish community, demanded a further 75,000 Jews for work in the Reich, threatening that unless the matter of payments was straightened out he would give orders 'to bump off every stinking Jew in Budapest'.[67]

According to Kersten, who learned of these transactions a few days after the resumption of deportation at the end of November, Himmler denied all knowledge when he tackled him. A few days later he admitted that money had been demanded; Schellenberg was dealing with the matter and would see that the money was handed to the International Red Cross.[68] For his part Schellenberg, in his memoirs, represented the whole scheme as a means of gaining touch with the western allies in order to negotiate a truce. Whatever the truth of the affair, Himmler's initial denial of responsibility when questioned by Kersten might suggest feelings of guilt or shame; yet to Kersten he had always expressed regret for the extermination policy while boasting to the Gåuleiters and others he knew to be in sympathy with his rigorous execution of the hard task with which the Führer had entrusted him. He suited his approach to the person or group he was with; the 'true' Himmler varied according to the observer.

For Höss, who had occasion to observe the whole complex of concentration–extermination–armaments camps in the course of his visits of inspection during these closing months of 1944, everything in and of them 'arose solely and simply from the aspiration [*Wollen*] of the RFSS'. No SS-Führer would have dared to thwart or circumvent his intention, he wrote.[69] Eichmann too stressed this during his interrogation: 'I'd like to see the RFSS had he found out . . . that I disobeyed his orders. . . . I'd have been arrested then and there, on the spot.'[70] Höss concluded that 'the whole SS was the tool with which Heinrich Himmler, the RFSS, realised his intentions'; that he was overrun by a stronger force in 1944, 'namely the war', could not alter that *fact*.[71]

A survivor of the Polish camps named Reska Weiss wrote a book called *Journey through Hell* containing a vignette from this period at the end of 1944 which can be paralleled in countless testimonies: it is of a tent containing those too weak and ill to work or move, lying naked and frozen in their own urine and excrement, covered with lice and bites and festering sores, the stench and horror of which 'no stretch of imagination, no power of the written word can convey . . .'.[72] Another survivor, Alfred Oppenheimer, who had been reduced to a 'Mussulman' at Gleiwitz camp by this date, December 1944, testified that on the 25th he and some sixty others were picked out as unfit at rollcall and told they would be going 'to the chimney' in a few days. In the event they were saved by lack of trucks available to take them to Auschwitz.[73] Dr Dupont, who survived Buchenwald, described the effect of camp life as degradation. 'It was done systematically. An unrelenting will seemed to be at work to reduce those

men to the same level, the lowest possible level of human degradation.'
The final stage in this process was setting prisoner against prisoner:

> Let me give a particularly brutal instance. In Kommando A.S.G. which was
> situated at Mansleben-am-See, 70 kilometres from Buchenwald . . . hangings
> took place in public in the hall of a factory connected with the salt mine. The SS
> were present at these hangings in full-dress uniform, wearing their decorations.
> The prisoners were forced to be present under threat of the most cruel beatings.
> When they hanged the poor wretches, the prisoners had to give the Hitler salute.
> Worse still, one prisoner was chosen to pull away the stool on which the victim
> stood. He could not evade the order as the consequences to himself would have
> been too grave. When the execution had been carried out the prisoners had to
> file off in front of the victim between two SS men. They were made to touch the
> body and, gruesome detail, look the dead man in the eyes. I believe that men
> who had been forced to go through such rites must inevitably lose the sense of
> their dignity as human beings.[74]

Another survivor of Buchenwald, Dr Alfred Balochowsky, was employed
manufacturing typhus vaccines which, together with drugs supplied by German industry, notably IG Farben,[75] were used in a research programme on
inmates. He described the method of obtaining twelve cultures of typhus
germ designated BU (Buchenwald) 1–12 with which the experimental
subjects were infected:

> A constant supply of these cultures was kept in Block 46 [the human
> experimental block] by means of the contamination of healthy individuals
> through sick ones; this was achieved by artificial inoculation of typhus germs
> by means of intravenous injections of 0.5 to 1 cubic centimetre of infected
> blood drawn from a patient at the height of the crisis. Now, it is well known
> that artificial inoculation of typhus by intravenous injection is invariably fatal.
> Therefore all these men who were used for bacterial culture during the whole
> time such cultures were required (. . . up to the liberation of the camp) died,
> and we counted 600 victims sacrificed for the sole purpose of supplying typhus
> germs. . . .[76]

To test drugs for use in the treatment of soldiers and civilians
burned by allied incendiary bombs, Russian prisoners of war were taken
to Block 46 and burned with phosphorous; Russians were chosen since
'they had the greatest physical resistance which was obviously superior to
that of the French or other people of western Europe.' Balochowsky saw
photographs, 'and it was not necessary to be a specialist to realise what
these patients, whose flesh was burned to the bone, must have suffered.'[77]
In another series of experiments homosexuals sent to Buchenwald by the
courts were treated with sex hormones; another research programme was
concerned with victims of starvation oedema, or swelling.

Balochowsky also spoke of the practice of skinning corpses, particularly
those with tattoos:

There were always tattooed human skins in Block 2. I cannot say whether there were many as they were continuously being received and passed on, but there were not only tattooed human skins, but also tanned human skins. . . . I saw SS men come out of Block 2, the Pathological Block, carrying tanned skins under their arms. I know from my comrades who worked in Block 2 that there were orders for skins; and these tanned skins were given as gifts to certain guards and to certain visitors who used them to bind books. . . .[78]

A survivor of Mauthausen, Maurice Lampe, recalled that the Chief Medical Officer of the camp had two human skulls on his desk as paperweights: 'These were the skulls of two young Dutch Jews who had been selected from a convoy of 800 because they had fine teeth.'[79]

Such was the empire of the camps: all who were sucked in, whether guards, doctors or inmates, were caught up inevitably in the living nightmare and adapted and lived the parts ascribed and expected of them or went insane or died or were killed, or themselves killed. It was outside imagination, a nether world where primal, forbidden urges for blood, sacrifice and subjection were licensed and given free rein on non-persons; it was the inversion of love, the ultimate fantasy of the superman and the master race where 'sub-humans' were reduced to 'Mussulmen' and 'Mussulmen' were despatched 'to the chimney' and reduced to ashes.

Something which struck Dr Dupont when asked to address himself to the question of responsibility was the similarity of regime in the different camps:

The degree of uniformity in the way in which the camps were run is clear evidence of orders from higher quarters. In the case of Buchenwald in particular, the personnel, no matter how rough it might be, would not have done such things on their own initiative. Moreover the camp chief and the SS doctor himself always pleaded superior orders, often in a vague manner. The name most frequently invoked was that of Himmler. . . .[80]

Eicke, killed in the Russian campaign the previous year, had created and shaped the concentration camps, Höss wrote: 'However, the hard will of the RFSS was always behind him. What came from the concentration camps in war arose simply and solely from the aspiration of the RFSS.'[81] The tenor and content of Himmler's speeches from long before the war leave no doubt that camp Kommandants and guards were fulfilling his express wishes by dehumanising and treating the inmates as fit only for labour and death; he set the example himself by verbal humiliation of the prisoners drawn up for inspection during his visits to the camps.

There can be no doubt either about his attitude towards extermination of eastern Europeans to make room for Germanic man, nor of course about his determination to eliminate the Jews as a race from Europe: 'Anti-semitism is precisely the same as delousing,' he had told his Waffen-SS commanders in

April 1943, 'simply a matter of cleanliness. We are nearly deloused. . . .'[82]
Nor can there be any doubt that his demands for the excavation of
bomb-proof factories in caves and mines and increased production of
V weapons, aircraft and armaments without regard to the conditions
in which his troglodytes lived ushered in a climactic period of slavery,
degradation and death in these final months of the war. The empire of the
sub-humans was his; he had willed it and fashioned it from his vision of a
pure Germanic future; he controlled it. Of all his achievements, this surely
was his monument. Cold stone and wire remain on many of the sites as a
reminder, and gruesome photographs and survivors' accounts are legion.
Yet the extent of that realm he ruled is beyond human measure or recall.

It can scarcely be doubted that it reproduced the dark side of his own
nature, impossible though to believe that it was his creation alone – that such
dehumanisation of guards, doctors and inmates alike can be traced simply
to the self-disgust of the Bavarian schoolboy who believed himself deficient
in physical and martial values or Aryan appearance, or to the bullying of
Professor Himmler, or the gym instructor, Herr Haggenmüller, or to the
girls who rejected a prudish adolescent. He was a conformist. His beliefs
were all around in the intellectual air he breathed. He had never found
difficulty in recruiting lieutenants and functionaries who shared or learned
to share them and most had very different and more successful childhoods
and adolescence. There had never been any lack of rivals establishing camps
in the early days; most had been simple torture chambers. His system had
prevailed because it was the most orderly and efficient. When established
there had been no lack of professors and medical doctors eager to take
advantage of the facilities he offered, no lack of industrialists wishing
to employ his slave labour. The list of factories established close by
concentration camps reads like a rollcall of big business; IG Farben,
Siemens, Krupp, Messerschmitt, Heinkel, Junkers, Saurer . . .

Albert Speer, the very image of rational, technological man, inspected
the cave factories where emaciated, lice-ridden wretches worked on aircraft
and V-rocket parts, inspected Mauthausen, smiled and shook the hand of
the Kommandant, and his conscience was not touched.

Nor was discussion of extermination confined to Himmler or the SS;
all the state secretaries and departmental chiefs who attended Heydrich's
Wannsee conference in January 1942 were initiated into this highest, yet
open state secret, as of course were all their ministers. Part of a record of
a conversation between Goebbels and the Minister of Justice, Dr Thierack,
in September 1942 ran:

> With regard to the destruction of asocial life, Dr Goebbels is of the opinion
> that the following should be exterminated: All Jews and gypsies, Poles having to
> serve three to four years' penal servitude, and Czechs and Germans sentenced
> to death, to penal servitude for life, or to security custody. The idea of
> exterminating them by work is the best. . . .[83]

The applause Himmler received from Gauleiters, Gruppenführers and Wehrmacht officers when he boasted to them of his accomplishment of the hard task with which he had been charged is proof of the level of support he enjoyed. And Höss's phrases about Eicke might be paraphrased: 'the hard will of the Führer was always behind him [Himmler]. What came from the concentration camps in war arose simply and solely from the aspiration of the Führer. . . .' The Führer, of course, expressed the will of the Party. Himmler's creation was the extreme realisation of that will.

The will had been born in frustration, humiliation and desire for vengeance, and as these emotions were heated again in the cauldron of defeat Himmler remained their supreme exponent. Along the borders of the Reich, east and west, labour gangs of prisoners of war, concentration camp inmates, Volkssturm units and others from the local populace, in several *Gaue* including women and children, dug anti-tank ditches and erected fortifications with insufficient materials, plant, transport, rations, water or even technical staff to plan and co-ordinate the lines.[84] 'The work was so strong and so hard and the way they treated us so bad,' one Norwegian internee from an under-Kommando of Neuengamme camp, near Hamburg, recalled, 'about half of the prisoners died of dysentery or ill treatment in the five or six weeks we were there. . . .'[85] Even the populace was sceptical: 'If the Atlantic Wall [coastal defences against the invasion] did not hold, how should these earth walls and ditches?' was one typical comment collected by Ohlendorf's public opinion researchers.[86]

In the cities devastated by air-raids other gangs of concentration camp inmates were employed searching for unexploded bombs, bodies and survivors among the debris. 'We were looking like dead persons, all of us looking very bad,' the same Norwegian recalled after being transferred to this dangerous work. He received no thanks from the pallid people contemplating the ruins of their homes: 'Some of them were hollering to us, "It is your fault that we are bombed."'[87] Perhaps the gang was mistaken for Jews. When 'terror flyers' were shot down and bailed out many were executed on the spot or handed over to the SD for 'special treatment'. In Hungary Eichmann strove to deport the last Jews within his grasp before the Red Army closed all communication to Budapest. Arrow Cross gangs rounded them up for him or herded them together for slaughter in scenes reminiscent of the first *wild* actions in Poland. In Slovakia the SS anti-partisan divisions liquidated the fugitive remains of the rebel army and the many young Jews who had joined to fight, and despatched civilians to labour camps.

Hate and destruction filled almost every corner of Himmler's world; it accorded with the message he had proclaimed since he was a young man; evidently it fulfilled him.

Since September Hitler had been planning a surprise Panzer attack through the Ardennes very similar to that with which he had opened his lightning western campaign in 1940. The aim was to split the bulk of the US armies in the centre and south from the British forces in Belgium and Holland, drive through to Antwerp and so deprive the western allies of their major supply port. He believed that such a blow would gain time for the production and deployment of the V rockets, new U-boats and jet fighter aircraft, but above all 'deprive the enemy of his belief that victory is certain' – so he explained to the commanders who were to take part, so he must have explained to Himmler many times. 'Wars are finally decided by one side or the other recognising that they cannot be won.'

From outside the group delusion at Führer headquarters, it is plain that the operation, which Hitler designated with the deliberately misleading defensive codename 'Wacht am Rhein', had no chance of lasting success: acute fuel shortages, the overwhelming allied air superiority, ultimately the weight of armour the Red Army was massing to hurl against the eastern fronts he had weakened by drawing off troops for the west doomed the plan from the start. Hitler professed to disbelieve the intelligence appreciations of Russian strength and intentions, but at some level below the manic confidence he radiated probably he knew the Ardennes gamble could not be sustained militarily. Consequently he stressed the moral angle and predicted that 'a few more heavy blows' would cause the artificial enemy coalition to collapse. They had to show the enemy that 'whatever he does, he can never reckon on capitulation. Never! Never!'[88]

This was the message Himmler had been carrying to his Volksgrenadier divisions and the Volkssturm, and also to the enemy by means of Prützmann's secret Werwolf organisation. It is perhaps significant that in October Himmler had sent to Kaltenbrunner and Prützmann a London Reuter report of a speech by the British Foreign Secretary, Eden, concerning the demand for unconditional surrender, and it appears he marked one passage for special attention. Translated into English this ran: 'Himmler, the chief and responsible man of the Gestapo, is already making preparations for the continuation of resistance during the allied occupation of Germany. The purpose of this organisation is to lay the foundation for a secret organisation to operate over several years.'[89]

On the eve of the Ardennes gamble on which Hitler and the leading members of the regime, grasping at visions, placed all their hope, Himmler probably reached the height of favour and influence with his Führer. In November after the German Nineteenth Army in Alsace had been isolated in the heights of the Vosges by US and French thrusts to the Rhine, Hitler had confirmed him in the appointment Bormann claimed to have proposed, Supreme Commander Upper Rhine with jurisdiction extending from the Swiss frontier to the Saar. His primary task was to hold the Nineteenth Army bridgehead on the west bank of the Rhine without calling on the reserves Hitler was massing for the thrust into Belgium. He deployed Replacement Army divisions with hastily improvised Volksgrenadier, Volkssturm and anti-aircraft units, but in the event his capacity for command in the field was scarcely tested. Eisenhower chose not to pinch out the Nineteenth Army pocket, instead turning the US Seventh Army northwards to concentrate with the Third Army against the Saar. Another mark of Hitler's favour was the choice of the Waffen-SS Panzer divisions, Leibstandarte, Das Reich, Hohenstaufen and Hitler Jugend, formed into the Sixth Panzer Army under SS-Oberstgruppenführer Sepp Dietrich – the first time an SS officer had commanded an army – to spearhead the main thrust to Antwerp. The Fifth Panzer Army formed of Wehrmacht divisions under General von Manteuffel was assigned the subsidiary target of Brussels.

It seems that Himmler shared Hitler's optimism about 'Wacht am Rhein'. He had moved with his headquarters train to the Black Forest railway line near Triberg at the beginning of December, and there he told Kersten that they would drive the British and Americans into the sea.[90] And Eichmann, visiting the new field headquarters at some time in early December, returned to Budapest apparently inspired with confidence about the outcome of the war. He told the leader of the Jewish community that Germany had passed the low point and was going to win. 'A new weapon is being produced, against which the allies will be powerless.'[91]

In darkness and mist before dawn on 16 December fourteen German infantry divisions moved off from the wooded slopes of the Eifel across a seventy-mile front towards five divisions of the US First Army holding this sector of the Ardennes. Behind them 10,000 assault guns opened on the US positions, and salvoes of V-1 rockets blasted off, targeted on Liège and Antwerp. The higher commanders believed the full aim of the assault unobtainable, but the morale of the troops was high, largely the result of the uncompromising message Goebbels and Himmler had been proclaiming since 20 July. The spirit is captured in a letter written by an Untersturmführer (junior lieutenant) of SS-Panzerdivision Hitler Jugend to his sister as he waited to jump off: 'Some believe in living but life is not everything! It is enough to know that we attack and will throw the enemy from our homeland. It is a holy task.'[92]

Five Panzer divisions started up behind the infantry. Aided by total surprise and thick weather which kept the allied aircraft grounded, sections of the American front were overwhelmed and considerable early gains made, particularly by von Manteuffel's Fifth Panzer Army. Only one SS Panzer unit made significant progress; this was the 1st Battle Group of the Leibstandarte, led by Obersturmbannführer Joachim Peiper, which penetrated nearly thirty miles. During this advance the twenty-nine-year-old Peiper and his subordinates lived up to the savage reputation the Waffen–SS had acquired in the east. A group of about 170 US prisoners who had laid down their arms near Malmédy were taken into a field beside the road on the line of advance and mown down by machine-gun fire from two half-tracks parked to face them. The single US officer who survived later testified: 'When they ceased firing after approximately five minutes, maybe three minutes, they came into the group to those men who were still alive, and of course writhing in agony, and they shot them in the head. . . .'[93]

The investigation found that seventy-one of the Americans were mass-acred. It was far from the only SS atrocity in the campaign, or indeed in the west. The division Das Reich had earned a notorious reputation in anti-partisan operations in the mountains of Auvergne earlier in the year and had added to it in wake of the allied landings in June by burning the village of Oradour-sur-Glane and massacring the entire population in retaliation apparently for the death of an officer shot by a French sniper.

On 21 December Gottlob Berger wrote to Himmler urging him to curtail his activity as Supreme Commander Upper Rhine and return to Führer headquarters. His reason was not only the rumour-mongering from certain quarters – 'Reichsführer-SS is in disgrace, the Wehrmacht-tack' – but because he sensed that 'if the Reichsführer-SS is not at headquarters, our political work, the foundation of everything, suffers tremendously.'[94] Himmler had Brandt thank him for the hint and inform him that his command on the Rhine would not last long.[95]

He paid his customary attention to presents that Christmas for his families, his host of *Paten* or sponsored SS children, his Party colleagues and SS-Führers and families; the file cards for Wölffchen's boy, Thorisman, for instance, show that he received the mischievous clown of German *Volk*-tale, Tyll Eulenspiegel, chocolate and sweets – and for his ninth birthday three weeks later a fretsaw kit and chocolate.[96] Each member of his industrial Freundeskreis received two pounds of coffee and 100 cigarettes, and his generals and divisional commanders a thoughtful hamper containing a bottle of red and one of white wine, cognac, two pounds of coffee, a packet of tea, 100 cigarettes, chocolate, hare- and goose-liver pâté, toothpaste, shaving cream, soap, razor blades and a comb.[97] He took Berger's advice, travelling 150 miles north on Christmas Eve to the Führer headquarters used for the Ardennes offensive, Adlerhorst, or Eagle's Eyrie, by Bad Nauheim near Frankfurt, and inviting General Guderian to dine. As he expressed it in a letter afterwards, 'I spent the festive season at the front since in addition to my other activities I am for the moment commanding an Army Group on the Upper Rhine.'[98]

Fall from Grace

The Soviet winter offensive began before dawn on 12 January 1945 from a salient across the Vistula west of Sandomir between Lublin and Cracow on Marshal Koniev's 1st Ukrainian front in the General Gouvernement. Batteries of heavy and medium guns at a density of 300 to the kilometre unleashed a terrifying barrage along the German line; the storm lasted almost two hours, rocking the ground, hurling earth, concrete, guns, vehicles, men and pieces of men in the air, shaking the nerves of even the strongest survivors. Soviet punishment battalions advancing beneath the arch of noise took the front-line trenches. The armour followed. By evening advanced columns of heavy tanks had broken through to a depth of some twenty-five miles. Two days later Marshal Zhukov, commanding the 1st Belorussian front immediately north of Koniev's, launched equally stunning surprise attacks from two bridgeheads on the west of the Vistula south of Warsaw; by evening his tanks, too, ranged twenty miles behind the German lines. The German intelligence predictions were realised. These two Soviet Army Groups alone had five times the manpower and armour, seven times the artillery and seventeen times the air power of the forces in their path.[1] Immediately north of Zhukov, Marshal Rokossovskii, commanding the 2nd Belorussian front, opened an attack directed north-westerly for the Baltic coast. Hitler had not only refused to heed the intelligence assessments, he had refused permission to establish a main battle line [*Grosskampflinie*] several miles back from the front. Consequently Koniev's and Zhukov's tanks, slicing through headquarters and tactical reserves alike, were able to race on almost at will towards their first objectives on the way to the old Reich border and the Oder, bypassing Warsaw.

In the west, meanwhile, the Ardennes offensive had failed to do much more than drive a deep wedge into the US line. The weather, which had kept the allied air forces grounded, had restricted the German columns to twisting country roads which tended diagonally across the line of advance. Over Christmas the skies had cleared, releasing the allied aircraft, and the jams of tanks and supply vehicles clogging roads and crossings had provided concentrated, sitting targets. The bombers also strafed railways, roads, supply vehicles and depots in the rear, making it impossible to maintain the already insufficient supplies of fuel to the front. Despite renewed pleas by General Guderian, now Chief of the General Staff, to return to the defensive and transfer the weight of forces east, it was not until 8 January that Hitler conceded defeat in his strategy, by then reduced to the aim of keeping the initiative in the west by attack, not until the 14th after Koniev and Zhukov had smashed through the thin defences along the Vistula that he was shocked into accepting Guderian's arguments. He left the Adlerhorst the following evening and established his headquarters at the Chancellery in Berlin on the morning of the 16th. Despite bomb damage to great parts of the building and craters in the garden, now softened under snow, his own rooms and study were unscathed.

He had aged immeasurably over the past year. The defeats and spectres of total disaster haunting him in the sleepless early mornings, the tense and unhealthy life he had been living without remission within close-guarded compounds which, as Speer realised in his own prison cell after the war, differed little from a prisoner's, above all the sustained blows to his self-image as the heaven-sent leader of the *Volk* had left their mark. His hair was grey, his moustache quite white, his face both puffy and drawn, the skin around the eyes giving an impression of total exhaustion; his gait was stooped, his movements so slow and dragging that they suggested premature senility and his left arm and hand shook embarrassingly.[2] Yet it is evident that he had lost none of his aura; his eyes retained a penetrating gleam 'creating a fearsome and wholly unnatural effect' according to one young officer who saw him for the first time, his lips their cruel downward compression. His will was harsh. Most surprisingly he retained and radiated unshakeable confidence. It was what his entourage demanded. They had selected themselves as his adherents happy to surrender everything, conscience, will, reasoning power, to his view of the world and his genius. Now in the all-surrounding gloom it was more than ever necessary to believe in him. His response was no doubt aided by amphetamines. It seems likely that after abandoning the habit briefly after 20 July and then after a bout of jaundice in late September he was taking them again both orally and intravenously.[3]

So group fantasy, which demanded a leader to bring hope, fed on the fantasy of the leader. The spiral is revealed at its most blatant in the relationship between Hitler and his young naval Commander-in-Chief, Grossadmiral Karl Dönitz. Dönitz's overt goal was to resume the offensive against the western powers with the new U-boats designated Types XXI and XXIII about to come into service. It seems evident, however, from his memoranda and the reports of his discussions with Hitler that underlying this ambition was the simple desire to prove himself to his Führer.[4]

For his part, Hitler used Dönitz's arguments to support his own strategy. The offensive power which the new U-boats would unleash in the spring became an article of faith, and with it Dönitz's insistence that the Baltic and particularly Danzig Bay were vital for U-boat training. It was evident to the General Staff that the armies holding East Prussia and Kurland beyond should be brought back to help build the defences before the

Oder, but Hitler would not hear of it. U-boats were more important than land operations, he said; they alone would be able to take the offensive to the western allies.[5]

Dönitz's optimism and the taut, professional manner in which he lent encouragement to outrageous expectation is a well-documented example of how the Führer system worked and continued working almost to the end, feeding on delusion. As always, fear buttressed the system. From 20 July the scarred features of Kaltenbrunner had generally been visible at situation conferences. For the soldiers, especially those like Guderian and von Rundstedt, Supreme Commander in the west, who had toyed with treason earlier, probably even for Keitel and Jodl, Kaltenbrunner could only have been a dread reminder of the disgrace and agony of their fellows, whose judgement seemed to be confirmed with every passing day. They could argue with Hitler about tactical dispositions, but the time for large action had passed. Neither Göring, completely discredited by the failures of the Luftwaffe, nor the new star at Court, Dönitz, would consider lending their services to rebellion. Neither would even support Guderian's strategic arguments, the one because of the weakness of his own position, the other because he was focused exclusively on U-boat training in the Baltic and proofs of his own loyalty and determination. Himmler, the one figure with the power to alter the system, was, in the wake of 20 July, far too dangerous to approach. He had in any case identified himself with the spirit of total war for the Führer.

On 17th January, Warsaw fell to Zhukov's forces; on the 19th Lodz fell, and Koniev's forces took Cracow; on the 20th the advanced formations of Koniev's Fifty-second Army crossed the German border east of Breslau and two days later spearheads of his Fourth Tank and Fifth Guards Armies reached the Oder north of Breslau and established a bridgehead on the western bank. Over some 350 miles between Koniev and Rokossovskii, pressing north-westerly for the Baltic near Danzig, the German forces were split, crushed, bypassed or encircled. Units in towns designated fortresses to be held at every cost dug into the icy ground; others made their way back in more or less confusion towards the Reich alongside Germans and *Volksdeutsche* only recently settled in the region by one or other of Himmler's agencies now fleeing in justified terror of the Red soldiers. Thousands more civilians were being evacuated by sea from the ports of West and East Prussia.

In this near catastrophe with the armies between the Vistula and Oder broken in every joint, Hitler called Field Marshal Schörner from Kurland to take over what remained of the Army Group in the central sector in Silesia, and Himmler from his Rhine command to build up and reform the remnants of the forces in the north as a new Army Group Weichsel or Vistula. Schörner was a dedicated Nazi with a ruthlessness that would have fitted him for the SS. It is evident from the methods both he and Himmler employed that they were appointed because they could be relied on to stamp out what Hitler perceived as the defeatism and treachery behind the collapse. He rejected Guderian's renewed pleas to bring back Army Group North from Kurland, and took the equally perverse decision, in Guderian's eyes, of refusing to reinforce the Oder front with Sepp Dietrich's Sixth SS Panzer Army, then refitting after being pulled out of the Ardennes on 8 January; he had earmarked this 'fire brigade' for Hungary.

Already, before the Soviet offensive from the Vistula, he had sent two elite SS Panzer divisions, Totenkopf and Wiking, from the central front to Hungary to relieve German forces trapped in and around Budapest by two Russian army groups. Since then the Russians had succeeded in clearing the eastern half of the city, Pest, in savage street fighting. The SS Panzerkorps fought its way almost to the suburbs of Buda on the other bank of the Danube still in German possession, but Hitler was determined that the city should be held, consequently no break-out was attempted. Such was the position as he reaffirmed his intention to send the Sixth SS Panzer Army to Hungary. As he explained it at the situation conference on the afternoon of 23 January, the Hungarian oil fields and the Vienna basin were vital since they produced 80 per cent of Germany's oil; without them it would be impossible to continue the war.[6] However, the directive he had sent von Rundstedt three days before to prepare for the immediate transfer of the SS Panzer Army to the east explained the move as not allowing the enemy to call the tune everywhere. He had decided on 'halting the Russians and going over to the offensive'.[7]

Hitler retained enormous faith in the Waffen-SS and may really have expected the Sixth Panzer Army to turn the tide in the south-east; he had always staked much on surprising the enemy. His dispositions may even have been designed for the long term – after the anticipated crack in the enemy coalition when the Anglo-Americans had rallied to his side against Stalin. Already on the 19th he had authorised von Ribbentrop to put out peace feelers to the west via Allen Dulles.[8] It is also possible that he was suffering from amphetamine toxicity and displaying the typical signs of elation with consequent impaired judgement.

'Do you think the English can be really enthusiastic about all the Russian developments?' he asked Göring and Jodl after the situation conference on the 27th, by which time both Zhukov's and Koniev's armies were massed along and in places across the Oder; one bridgehead was less than fifty miles from Berlin. Göring provided the standard answer which he knew Hitler wished to hear, and which he must have heard himself from Hitler's mouth so often: the British had not expected them to hold off the western allies like madmen while the Russians drove deeper and deeper into the country. 'They entered the war to prevent us going into the east, not to have the east come to the Atlantic.' Göring concluded that if the Russian successes continued they could expect a wire – from Churchill – within a few days.[9]

Himmler, who probably had more direct knowledge of western thinking than most through his intelligence services, buoyed himself up on the same hope. It is notable, however, that he had taken no part in the strategic planning which had brought the present situation about. He remained content, as he had always been, for Hitler to dictate grand strategy; he simply carried out the functions assigned to him, and echoed the Führer line. According to Guderian, Himmler was as dismissive as Hitler when he had tried to warn him before Christmas of the Russian build-up and the weakness of the eastern front.[10]

The German people who had to stand in the breach while the miracle matured were more realistic. Ohlendorf's public opinion reports appear to have ceased by this time, but a wired request from SS-Hauptsturmführer Rolf d'Alquen, serving in the so-called 'Propaganda' unit of Himmler's former Army Group Upper Rhine, to his brother, who was chief of the SS-Propaganda Regiment in Berlin and chief editor of the SS paper *Das Schwarzen Korps*, provides a telling vignette. It was dated 20 January:[11]

> The mood in the fighting troops due to the events on the east front becomes more nervous and serious by the day. . . . Should the situation deteriorate further in the next few days it is to be expected that the troops will no longer be able to bear the anxiety and their fighting spirit will be paralysed. . . .
> The mood in the local populace is, apart from the unthinking, similar. . . . In this grave situation I feel myself duty-bound to make the urgent request to the commander to attempt to come up with a word of deliverance for us . . . from Führer headquarters. Perhaps it would be possible as a start to find out from circles close to the Führer whether the Führer has answered the question for his closest entourage 'What is to happen now?', and perhaps he can be stirred to say this openly either in person or through the mouth of his representative. . . .

D'Alquen went on to say that all thinking people in the Army and the population were convinced that a decisive change in the war was no longer possible with conventional means. He suggested that a statement be put out that the front had to be held for a short time, then a weapon would be deployed which would bring the decisive turn in their fortunes. He felt it his duty, D'Alquen concluded, to ask that at least the Führer be made aware of this mood of the front.

It is extremely unlikely that Bormann would have allowed such a message to reach Hitler; Ohlendorf's reports had been judged too strong for a long time. However, Gunter d'Alquen believed it important and, as he wrote, 'typical' enough of the 'psychological condition of the troops' to send it to Dr Brandt at Himmler's new field headquarters at Deutsch Krone in Pomerania to the north of the Soviet breakthrough: he asked him to bring it to Himmler's attention.[12] Himmler replied on 30 January with a letter to be forwarded to Rolf d'Alquen:[13]

> . . . I know the troops have severe anxieties, but I have the impression that you yourself are the most oppressed. I consider your proposal absolutely impossible.

The troops must be told that, bitter as it is, they must do their duty now more than ever, and only if the west is guarded now will the German forces in the east be in the position first to parry the thrusts and then to become active again.

From you yourself I expect also the inner bearing of an SS man. I hope you are aware that one is only at the end if one is beaten in the heart.

A week later he wrote to Heydrich's widow Lina in reply to a letter of hers. He described his task in Pomerania as very difficult, but he had the 'firm conviction' that they would first hold the Russian advance, then throw it back and regain the lost territory: 'as improbable as it might appear at present, during the course of this year, which represents a *fortissimo* of the war, this struggle will end victoriously for us because we cannot be defeated. . . .'[14]

And on 12 February he wrote to an Obergruppenführer Schlessmann consenting to his petition that a certain Fräulein have her baby in a Lebensborn home. 'The situation here was very difficult,' he concluded in reference to his command 'but I have the firm conviction we will master it.'[15]

Guderian and other Army officers have left scathing descriptions of Himmler's command of Army Group Vistula. No doubt their strictures can be accepted: he had no experience of leading troops in the field; he was inclined to immerse himself in sudden enthusiasm and details, and had grown accustomed to issuing orders from his desk to be carried out virtually regardless of the situation or resources on the spot. Nevertheless it was customary after the war, especially for officers of the regular services, to depict Himmler in the most grotesque light and invest him with every shortcoming. This was both a psychological and political necessity. By saddling him with the odium of crime, and in large measure the responsibility for disaster, they presented their own service as honourable, disguised their complicity and provided a scapegoat for the most terrible moral and material defeat suffered by the nation. There was no reason, in any case, for regular Army officers to be sympathetic towards the SS.

In the very short term Himmler's methods were effective. His energy and commitment, above all his capacity – indeed his taste – for absolute ruthlessness succeeded in halting the rout at the Oder. He improvised divisions from the remnants of the beaten armies, naval and Luftwaffe units, anti-aircraft batteries, frontier guards, youths and ageing men of the Volkssturm, and imbued them with his spirit of fanatical determination to beat back the invader. Commanders were instructed to hold positions regardless and, if they felt themselves unable to do so, to hand over to another who had the will. Geheime Feldpolizei and Ordnungspolizei units received instructions to shoot deserters out of hand or to hang them summarily as examples. Many of his divisional commanders and two Korps commanders, the former Police generals, von dem Bach-Zelewski and Reinefarth, had established their reputation in anti-partisan warfare where atrocity was the rule. So too his Chief of Staff, SS-Brigadeführer Heinz Lammerding, who had served as Chief of Staff to Eicke in the Totenkopf division and subsequently to von dem Bach before being appointed to command Das Reich, in which capacity he had brought the horrors of the east to France, most notoriously to the village of Oradour-sur-Glane.

With such executives, it is not surprising that when Goebbels' Press Officer, Wilfred von Oven, visited the Oder front in mid-February his first vivid impression was of bodies of deserters hanging from the girders of broken bridges.[16] The following month Goebbels visited Schörner's Army Group in Silesia and found the same sanction in use: 'professional stragglers', as Schörner described them to him, were hanged on the nearest tree with a placard around their necks: 'I am a deserter and have declined to defend German women and children.'[17]

Inspired on the one hand by passion to defend homeland and women-folk against the Red Army, whose soldiery were avenging SS atrocities in Russia with rape and barbaric cruelties, terrorised on the other hand by the treatment meted out to deserters by their own police, the scratch formations of Army Group Vistula contested every position savagely and bled the Russian forces as Himmler had promised.[18] They were aided by a sudden thaw which hampered operations across the Oder and the movement of tanks and supplies up the over-extended Russian lines. Yet in view of the crushing enemy superiority, it could only be a temporary reprieve. It was Himmler's failure to represent this forcefully to Hitler or to support Guderian's arguments for releasing the armies dissipated along the Baltic coast to concentrate them in defence of the Reich that justifies the scorn of the military. Guderian represented him as terrified of Hitler's rages; Kersten and Schellenberg, too, referred to his constant fear of Hitler. It is evident from what Himmler told his other close confidant, Professor Gebhardt, that he realised Hitler was making strange decisions. Despite it he was unable to break free from the Führer's dominance, unable to break the habit of obedience which he could justify as loyalty.

It is easy to criticise from the outside and despise the moral cowardice which prevented him standing up to Hitler, rather burying his head in the group rationalisations for continuing the war at the expense of his men and the German people as a whole. Viewed from his own world, it is difficult to see what else he could have done. It was not only Hitler who was determined never to give in; every member of the leading circle expressed the same bitter spirit of defiance. In early February Roosevelt, Churchill and their military staffs met Stalin and his military chiefs at Yalta in the Crimea. The joint communiqué issued on the 13th reiterated the allies' resolution after victory to divide Germany between them. It appeared finally to remove the hope of a split in the enemy camp, at the same time giving powerful reinforcement to the will to fight on. Hitler greeted the communiqué with a cry of triumph;

it confirmed his views on the uselessness of negotiating from weakness –
although he had authorised von Ribbentrop to try. 'If we lose the war,
Germany will cease to exist!' he exclaimed. 'What matters now is to keep
our nerve and not give in.'[19] Goebbels had no difficulty in using the terms
of the communiqué to spread this mood to the people.

From a practical point of view also Himmler had no choice but
to follow his Führer. The western allies had not only refused to do
business with him, they had branded him as the leading war criminal
after Hitler and had vowed to hunt down all war criminals and bring
them to justice. On the simple level of survival he had no interest in
surrender. Schellenberg, Kersten and no doubt Ohlendorf, speaking for
the banking and industrial Freundeskreis, were still urging him to make
large concessions to the west by releasing Jews and concentration camp
inmates in order to open negotiations to end the war. Since Hitler would
not countenance this, Schellenberg wanted him to remove Hitler and take
power, otherwise 'one day history would hold him responsible for his lack
of decision' – that at least was Schellenberg's post-war account.[20] Yet to
take power without bringing on a civil war Himmler would have needed
the support of Dönitz, Göring and above all the Party, represented by
Martin Bormann, but even to have broached the subject in that quarter
must have been fatal. Already his long absences from Court were providing
opportunities for his rivals – especially Bormann and it seems Kaltenbrunner
as well now – to undermine his position. It is probable that his fear of Hitler,
which most close observers noted at this period, was an indication of doubt
and confusion underlying his public optimism. On the one hand Kersten
and Schellenberg were engaged – as Schellenberg put it – in an almost
daily struggle for his soul,[21] on the other hand there was the hate-filled,
destructive atmosphere at the Chancellery, his fear of Hitler's rages, his
suspicion of what his rivals were plotting behind his back.

He of course was feared by them. He was the most feared man
in the Reich with the most feared organisation behind him.

By mid-February 1944, Himmler had been forced by further Russian
advances to move his command post to Birkenhain, near Prenzlau, some
thirty miles west of the Oder, fifty miles north of Berlin. A large mansion
purchased for the SS before the war, now extended with the usual timber
barracks, served as Army Group headquarters. A personal headquarters
train, called 'Steiermark', stood on a nearby siding in birch woods. The
cover name was 'Birkenwald'.

Order No. 1 for installations 'Birkenwald'

1. Like all field headquarter sites Birkenwald is to be kept secret. Any
disclosure of its position, use etc. will be punished as high treason.

2. It is to be kept unconditionally secret when the RFSS is in residence . . .[22]

He confessed to Goebbels early in March that his reason told him they had little hope now of winning the war but, he added, his instinct led him to believe that a political opening would emerge sooner or later.[23] Of course he had to say that; he knew it would get straight back to Hitler and Bormann.

He was still seeking that political opening himself. His negotiations with the American Jewish organisations via the Red Cross in Switzerland had more or less foundered because Kaltenbrunner had brought them to Hitler's attention, but a new hope had emerged from Sweden. This was Count Folke Bernadotte, whose uncle was chief of the Swedish Red Cross. Bernadotte arrived in Berlin on 17 February, ostensibly on behalf of a Swedish Red Cross team seeking to repatriate Swedish-born women who had married Germans but since lost touch with them. His real purpose was to bargain with Himmler for the release of prisoners (especially Scandinavian) from the concentration camps.[24] He had no authority to speak on behalf of the allies but he hoped to play on Himmler's desire to establish a relationship with the west. Himmler took care to cover himself by ensuring that Bernadotte saw Kaltenbrunner and von Ribbentrop first, then on 19 February received him at Professor Gebhardt's hospital at Hohenlychen conveniently close to his field headquarters, Birkenwald. He wore field-grey uniform without decorations, and hornrimmed spectacles; Bernadotte's first impression, like that of everyone else who met him, was of 'quite an unimportant official, whom one would hardly have noticed if one had met him in the street'. Nevertheless it is evident from Bernadotte's further description that, whatever his inner doubts, Himmler was well able to maintain his public front:

He seemed strikingly and amazingly obliging. He displayed traces of humour with a hint of grimness, which he used to relieve the tension. Least of all was there anything diabolical in his appearance. Of the cold hardness in his face, of which I heard so much, I saw none. In his talk with me he showed himself to be a very lively individual – quite sentimental in his attitude towards the Führer – and he showed that he was full of enthusiasm as well. It was a highly remarkable experience to listen to the man who had employed the most scandalous means to send millions of people to their death, talking with rapture about the gentlemanly methods of warfare between the Germans and British in France in the summer of 1944, when action was interrupted in the middle so that both sides could collect their wounded. . . .[25]

When Bernadotte asked whether it was not pointless to continue the struggle, Himmler replied that every German would fight like a lion before surrendering. As for his attitude towards Hitler, he used almost exactly the words he had used in arguments with Kersten: as a soldier and a German, he could not go back on his oath. Moreover he owed everything he was to Hitler: 'How can I betray him? I have built the SS on the basis of loyalty. I cannot now abandon that basic principle.'

He said he would not release Scandinavian prisoners without 'compensation', and suggested an undertaking by the Danish and Norwegian underground that they would stop further sabotage. Of course Bernadotte could not agree to this and eventually they reached the compromise that Scandinavian prisoners could be transferred to a single camp where they would be looked after by the Red Cross. The movements would be carried out by a convoy of Red Cross vehicles supplied by Sweden.

Bernadotte, evidently tipped off by Schellenberg, presented him with a work on Swedish rune-stones at the end of the meeting, and could see that he was moved by the present. He came away with the impression that the Reichsführer was one of the most complicated people he had ever met.

Afterwards Himmler charged Schellenberg with seeing that the agreement was carried out despite the difficulties to be expected from Kaltenbrunner and probably von Ribbentrop as well. Schellenberg begged him, according to his own account, to return to Berlin and arrange for peace in the west. Since capitulation could not even be mentioned in Führer headquarters he probably advocated an SS putsch to remove the entire Führer circle before it was too late. Whatever the arguments in what he described as a 'stormy conversation' it seems evident that Himmler, who had formed a favourable impression of Bernadotte, was anxious to keep open this possible line of contact with the west, and may well have authorised Schellenberg to negotiate peace terms which Bernadotte could carry to Eisenhower. Schellenberg stated in his memoirs that Himmler did so, but next day revoked everything.[26]

The talk at Hohenlychen coincided with the end of a thrust by Himmler's Third Panzer Army against Zhukov's right flank. Himmler had been against the attack until more fuel and ammunition could be brought up but Guderian had forced the plan through during an angry meeting with Hitler in the Chancellery. Himmler had had to look on in silence, as Hitler raged and screamed; he finally suffered the indignity of having an officer from Guderian's staff, General Walther Wenck, attached to Army Group Vistula to command the operation.[27] Now, after a promising start, the attack had petered out. As Bormann wrote to his wife, 'Uncle Heinrich's offensive did not succeed. . . .'[28]

The Soviet High Command had been concerned for some time about the gap Guderian had tried to exploit between Zhukov's right and Rokossovskii's left flank in Pomerania, and now sent orders to both marshals for a linked attack north for the Baltic coast at Kolberg. Rokossovskii launched his assault on the morning of 24 February; Zhukov followed on 1 March, achieving complete tactical surprise, for Himmler and the Army staff had expected him to begin the drive for Berlin and had disposed the reserves accordingly. The Soviet tanks sliced through the German defences, forcing another pell-mell retreat of soldiers and civilian refugees alike, and reached Kolberg on the 4th, trapping large forces between the two pincers.[29]

That evening Goebbels found a dismal mood at the Chancellery: 'The generals hang their heads and the Führer alone holds his head high.'[30] Even Hitler was somewhat depressed though, in contrast to the mood in which Goebbels had found him at the beginning of the week, and the shake in his left hand had increased greatly. He launched into a criticism of the General Staff for deploying their forces before Berlin. He (Hitler) had always expected the Soviets to move on Pomerania first, but he had allowed the staff to have their way. Himmler, he complained, had also taken the view that the offensive would be aimed at Berlin.[31]

Himmler, whether broken by the strain of commanding an army group – as his military enemies asserted – worn out by the unending work of the several posts he was filling, and no doubt aware that his star had waned with the Führer, or simply facing reality after his earlier hopes of driving the Russians back, had retired to bed at Hohenlychen. According to Goebbels, who visited him there on 7 March, he had suffered a severe attack of angina, but was recovering. He was unlikely to have been frank about his health with Goebbels. According to his personal secretary, Brandt, he had had too much to do and had tried to keep doing it despite a protracted bout of flu.[32] The explanation may be that he was suffering the crippling headaches and stomach cramps that afflicted him at times of crisis and decision. Kersten described him as in a highly nervous state. According to his account this was because of an order Himmler had received from Hitler to destroy the concentration camps and their inmates rather than allow them to fall into enemy hands.[33]

Kersten had just returned from Stockholm, where he had agreed to negotiate on behalf of the World Jewish Congress for supplying food and medicines to the concentration camps and releasing Jews to Sweden and Switzerland. At first, however, he could not even talk Himmler out of the senseless slaughter decreed in the Führer order: if National Socialist Germany were to be destroyed, Himmler said, their enemies and the criminals now sitting in the concentration camps were not going to be permitted the triumph of emerging as victors. 'They will go under with us! That is the clear and logical order of the Führer, and I will see that it is carried out thoroughly and meticulously.'[34] Kersten persisted, but it took him a week to work Himmler round to the point at which he agreed not to pass on Hitler's order to destroy the camps on the enemy's approach, instead to have them handed over in an orderly manner. Kersten felt sure that Himmler would have been prepared to make much wider concessions had he not been in constant fear of Hitler and his circle, especially Goebbels and Bormann. Despite this over the next days he did manage to wring from him the release of batches of Jews and other prisoners from different camps.[35]

For any analysis of Himmler's character, March was the testing month. The war was lost irrecoverably. In the area of his own command, roads were filled with beaten troops and civilians fleeing west; Zhukov's tanks pressed through when they came upon them, mowing the ragged columns down indiscriminately with gunfire, grinding stragglers into the mire beneath their tracks. In Silesia it was the same. Visiting the front there, Goebbels found frightful evidence of Soviet atrocity visible everywhere along the road. In return he found German troops were beating Soviet prisoners to death with shovels or rifle butts. [36] He found it necessary to tone down the 'indescribable' tales of Red Army rape and savagery in his propaganda lest he terrify the population. In Hungary where the Buda side of the capital had finally fallen to the Red Army in mid-February, accompanied by a similar orgy of rape and insensate slaughter, Sepp Dietrich's counter-offensive with the Sixth SS Panzer Army ground to a halt for want of fuel. By 15 March, with his tanks and assault guns stationary targets, he began an attempt to save what he could; his withdrawal soon turned into rout.

In the west, spearheads of the US First Army had crossed the Rhine at Remagen in the Eifel on 7 March over a bridge whose main charges failed to detonate. Another bridgehead on the eastern bank of the Rhine was established further south by the US Third Army in the night of 22 March, and on the 23rd Anglo-American forces under Montgomery made a major crossing of the lower Rhine south of the Dutch frontier at Wesel. By the 26th twelve bridges had been constructed here to feed the advance, and the way was open to the Ruhr and the Westphalian Plain.

Meanwhile in the skies over the Reich waves of enemy bombers continued to range freely by day and night. Berlin and the industrial cities were being converted into wastelands of rubble and gutted buildings whose numbed survivors, deprived of sleep, lived as best they could in the cellars beneath, like 'wanderers who have discovered a ruined city in a desert', Stephen Spender thought when visiting what had been Cologne immediately after the war, 'camping there, living in the cellars and hunting amongst the ruins for the booty, relics of a dead civilisation'.[37] Firestorms created in residential districts killed thousands; water and electricity supplies were dislocated; transport came to a standstill. Already rations had been reduced to subsistence level. Perhaps worst of all it was plain that the leadership had no answer either to the air terror or to the invasions on several fronts.

'The morale of the German people, both at home and at the front, is sinking ever lower,' Goebbels entered in his diary for 12 March, and he noted that criticism did not now stop short even of the Führer himself.[38]

The following week an SD report on the mood of the workers in Mecklenburg suggested a weary cynicism directed against the leaders and officialdom:[39] and further reports from other areas on 28 March depicted a populace totally alienated from the Party and disbelieving everything it was told, especially it seems announcements in the name of the Führer. 'Do they believe the German *Volk* has completely given up thinking?' was one comment reported from Baden. 'Do they believe they can still jolly the German *Volk* along with phrases and empty promises?' Another comment from Baden suggested that they should not always be told they would inevitably win the war; it should be made clear how their enemies could still lose it. Everywhere refugees had spread stories of chaos during evacuations caused by the failure of responsible leaders and officials. From Hamburg it was reported that Party officers in the street in uniform were made aware of the animosity of the people towards them. Comments recorded at Lüneburg about a Führer proclamation included: 'The Führer is prophesying again!' and 'It is always the old record.'[40]

Apprehension of defeat and worse lurked behind the eyes of women and between the phrases of Party and SS leaders who could not mention it by name. The knowledge was latent at Führer conferences, personified in the racked figure of the Führer himself, now driven by the air assault on Berlin to live in the complex of concrete bunkers beneath the Chancellery, listening to reports of disaster, lack of fuel, lack of reserves, clasping his right hand over his left to try and still the shaking that transmitted to his whole frame. At times he still compared his situation with that of Frederick the Great before the miracle which turned the Seven Years War; he would stare into the stern blue eyes looking out from his portrait of the great man behind his desk, drawing strength from his will. More often he blamed Göring, von Ribbentrop, the generals – he should have purged them instead of Röhm and the SA in 1934 – ministers, the professionals and intellectuals of the old school, and now Himmler for letting him down. He laid the blame for the rout in Pomerania directly on Himmler. In the course of a diatribe against him on 11 March, he told Goebbels that Himmler had fallen prey to the Army General Staff from the beginning of his command. Goebbels entered in his diary: 'The Führer accuses him [Himmler] of flat disobedience and intends to give him a piece of his mind on the next available occasion and make clear that in the event of a repetition of such an instance an irreparable breach would occur between him and Himmler. . . .'[41]

The opportunity occurred when Himmler came to Berlin on the afternoon of the 15th. The day before Brandt had described him as having recovered from the illness which had kept him to his bed: 'Happily he is now almost back to his old self again.'[42] What he was like after his interview in the Chancellery bunker is not recorded nor what Hitler said to him, but in the evening Hitler told Goebbels in a telephone conversation that he had given him 'an extraordinarily severe dressing-down'.[43]

The grotesquely swollen ego that made Hitler lay the blame for catastrophe on everyone but himself provoked the desire, since he had to fall, to bring everything down with him. Lust for the destruction of his enemies, the driving force of his years in power and of the war itself, turned on the German *Volk* who had proved biologically inferior, and failed him. 'The rabble aren't going to have the chance to cover up their cowardice by a so-called revolution this time,' he had told Albert Speer as early as the previous November. 'I guarantee that! No city will be left in the enemy's hands until it is a heap of ruins.'[44] Speer, the friend with whom he had shared his passion for architecture, his monumental building plans for the thousand-year Reich, his devotion to the cause of his *Volk*, had seen the masks drop away to reveal 'nothing but iciness and misanthropy'.[45] Now Hitler was planning to extend the scorched-earth policy in the east to the Reich itself, ostensibly to deny the invaders means of sustaining their assault on the homeland, emotionally to vent his hate and to repay the ultimate insult to the world of his creation in blood and ashes.

Of the top leadership, only Speer was able to remove himself and look into the vortex from the outside. After returning from an inspection tour of the Rhineland industries in mid-March convinced that the war was lost economically, he set about writing a memorandum – on the day Himmler received his dressing-down – to dissuade Hitler from his policy of destruction. His responsibilities brought him into close contact with the industrialists and financiers who had known for a long time that the war was lost, and who were trying to plan for after the war; no doubt Speer was acting for them in part. No doubt he was also starting to work his own post-war passage from the ruins. It required great moral and physical courage, nevertheless, to tell Hitler the war was lost. In four to eight weeks, he wrote, the final collapse of the German economy was to be expected with certainty. After that the war could not even be sustained militarily. To destroy Germany's remaining resources could not, therefore, affect the outcome; it could only deprive the German people of their means of further existence. 'We have no right at this stage to carry out demolitions which might affect the life of the nation.'[46]

Hitler disregarded his plea. On 19 March he issued a decree to Gauleiters, instructing them on the approach of the enemy to destroy everything in their path, all factories and utilities, power stations, water- and gas-works, dams, all transport and communications facilities and rolling stock, fuel depots and food and clothing supplies of all kinds. When Speer remonstrated, he told him that if the war were lost the nation also would perish. That was inevitable. There was no need to consider the basis for even a primitive existence – on the contrary it was better to destroy it themselves.

'The nation has proved itself weak,' he went on – there is no reason to doubt Speer's recollection since it was the basis of the *Weltanschauung* and he said the same thing many times – 'and the future belongs solely to the stronger eastern nation. Besides, those who will remain after the battle are the inferior; for the good will have fallen.'[47]

Speer somehow survived his protest and continued to survive despite dedicating himself to sabotaging the decree wherever and whenever he could. This is the more remarkable since Hitler had established itinerant courts martial to try and summarily execute military commanders who disobeyed orders, failed in their duty or uttered 'defeatist' remarks. The first victims had already been shot.

However Speer escaped, he demonstrated that it was possible for one of the inner circle to break free and actively to rebel. Himmler could never make the break. His roots in the ideology went deeper than Speer's; he was also a politician of subtlety and was still attempting to sell the west the view he had developed of the SS as the instrument of anti-Bolshevik order in an Anglo-American–German western Europe. He had to conceal his attempts at negotiation both from the paranoid group in the Führer bunker and from his own senior officers, who looked to him for the strong lead he had always given. For this was, of course, the very situation for which the Schutzstaffel had been created. They were the Führer's praetorian guard, the final bulwark when all others proved weak to preserve the National Socialist state and prevent its subversion from within.

Torn by irreconcilable conflicts between loyalty and rationality, myth and insupportable reality, between fear of the Führer bunker and fear of humiliation and execution as a war criminal at the hands of the allies, Himmler manoeuvred cautiously, acting the different parts required of him by different groups, picking the brains of von Dohnanyi, Albrecht Haushofer and other prisoners of 20 July, twisting but never making a decided alteration of course one way or the other to stake all on the outcome, hoping somehow to glimpse a way past the rocks and the six-headed monster. This seems to be the explanation of his behaviour from March to the end, and it seems to delineate his character. Whether he renounced National Socialism emotionally, whether he returned to God as he told the Finance Minister, von Krosigk, later, whatever inner turmoil and tearing he experienced were concealed behind his vacillations and his actor's masks. Goebbels wrote of him on 7 March as 'one of our strongest personalities'.[48] Guderian, who had opportunity to study him closely during these last months, described him as 'the most impenetrable of Hitler's disciples'.[49]

On 17 March, two days after Himmler received the dressing-down from Hitler in Berlin, Kersten broached the idea that he (Himmler) should meet representatives of the World Jewish Congress. Himmler was horrified: the Führer would have him shot on the spot.[50] Kersten pointed out that as chief of the frontier service he could keep the entry of the Jews secret and Hitler, Bormann and Goebbels need never hear of it. At length Himmler agreed that Kersten should arrange a meeting at his own country property, Hartzwalde. On the eve of Kersten's departure for Stockholm on this errand, he sent him a personal letter to say he was convinced that, 'notwithstanding the bloody wounds inflicted on all sides, wisdom and reason must prevail, and with these the humane heart and willingness to help.'[51]

By this date, 21 March, Guderian had persuaded Himmler that for the sake of his health, obviously worn down by overwork in his many posts, he should at least give up command of Army Group Vistula. According to his account Himmler, still lurking at Hohenlychen although suffering only from a head cold, did not take the idea amiss; but he could not, he said, suggest it to the Führer. Guderian offered to put it to Hitler for him and he agreed. Three days later Goebbels heard that Himmler wished to give up his command; he thought it a good idea. After all, he entered in his diary, Himmler's task had merely been to plug the hole in the defences. Unfortunately he had been diverted by a quest for military glory – an indication of the gossip in the Führer circle – and had failed completely. If he continued it could only 'tarnish his good political reputation'.[52]

General Gotthard Heinrici was appointed to relieve him in command of Army Group Vistula. He arrived at the Birkenhain headquarters on 22 March. Himmler greeted him standing by his desk, behind which hung a portrait of Frederick the Great. When both were seated, the staff officers laying out maps and a stenographer ready to take down his words, Himmler launched into an interminable report of his stewardship of the front which convinced Heinrici that 'in four months he had failed to grasp the most basic elements of good generalship.'[53] However that may be, at length, after the staff officers had left, Himmler ushered Heinrici to a settee on the far side of the room out of earshot of the stenographer and confided in a low voice that he had taken steps to negotiate peace with the west through a neutral country. There are several possible explanations for this revelation: he may have been seeking to bolster his ego before this taut, serious, greying old military man who was taking over a task in which he realised he had failed conspicuously; or, knowing that the military situation was desperate, he may have been bolstering Heinrici's determination to continue fierce resistance with the hope of a favourable turn of events. It is even possible that the confidence was a move to establish rapport in case he should need him on his side in an SS putsch against Hitler and the Party. Heinrici wondered if it were a devilish provocation to test his loyalty, so he recalled later.[54] Yet he knew the war was lost as surely as any other general. Guderian, who had briefed him on his new post, had tried to persuade Himmler to insist on a discussion with the Führer about surrender terms only the previous afternoon. But 'there was nothing to be done with this man. He was afraid of Hitler.'[55]

Himmler may have mentioned the negotiations to Heinrici because he felt close to success, indeed this may even explain why he was prepared to give up command of the Army Group. The talks he referred to had been opened by Karl Wolff in February using an Italian businessman, Baron Luigi Parrilli, concerned about Hitler's scorched-earth policy in northern Italy, and assisted by officers of the Swiss secret service. With these go-betweens Wolff had secured a secret meeting with Allen Dulles in an OSS safe house in Zurich. It had been made plain to him before the meeting that the allies would not deal with Hitler or Himmler, and he had sworn several times that he came entirely on his own initiative without their knowledge. It was then that he learned for the first time from his Swiss interlocutor of Himmler's systematic murder of millions of Jews in the east. It was a story Dulles had to pretend to believe; Wolff continued to tell the same story to the end of his long life in 1984. As always he made a good military impression and apparently convinced Dulles and his émigré expert on German affairs, Gero von Schulz-Gaevernitz, that he had parted company from his Nazi masters. Dulles had to believe this too, for Roosevelt was looking for an armistice in Italy to release US forces.

The circumstantial evidence is against Wolff's story. He had been in Germany on 6 February, immediately prior to flying back to Italy and opening the drive for negotiations with Dulles,[56] and had spent the best part of the day with Himmler, whose appointments calendar read: '13.45 SS-Obergruf. Wolff; 14.00 Meal with Wolff, Oberg, Seyss-Inquart. . . . 15.00 SS-Obergruf. Wolff.'[57] The same day Wolff and von Ribbentrop had an audience together with Hitler in the Chancellery and received permission to explore contacts with the west. Himmler knew that he and Hitler were unacceptable to the west; it must be assumed that Wolff's brief was to deny his attachment to the regime – for reasons which will appear. In any case, at the end of his meeting with Dulles, during the course of which he had gained in confidence, Wolff assured the Americans that he would be able to talk the Supreme Commander, Kesselring, around to a surrender and concluded, '*Meine Herren*, have a little patience and I will present you Italy on a silver salver.'[58]

Since that first meeting Kesselring had left Italy to take over from von Rundstedt as Supreme Commander, West. He had been replaced by General von Vietinghoff, a Prussian with iron principles of loyalty to his oath, who still had to be talked around when Wolff, on 19 March, made a second, secret journey across the Swiss border to meet Dulles and Gaevernitz, this time joined by the Deputy Chief of Staff of the US Fifth Army, General Lemnitzer, and the British Director of Military Intelligence, Allied Forces Italy, General Airey. Again Wolff made it clear that he had taken it on his own shoulders to arrange for the surrender of Italy and the German Army Group holding the north of the country. In doing so, he appeared to cut across an approach by Kaltenbrunner, also inspired by Hitler or Himmler, probably to exert pressure on the allies to take the carrot he (Wolff) was offering: this was the threat of fanatical resistance in a fortified 'Alpine redoubt' around Berchtesgaden which, because of the nature of the terrain, would take years to subdue. Kaltenbrunner was offering to bargain away this actually mythical Alpine fortress for a guarantee by the west not to allow Austria to be occupied by the Russians or divided into zones, instead to be an area excluded from war crimes trials. Belief in the Alpine fortress was a major reason for the allies to want the surrender of German forces in Italy, which could otherwise be withdrawn into this redoubt. When Dulles raised the question on 19 March, Wolff took advantage of the story: 'Madness!' he replied. 'It would only bring added suffering to the German people. Everything possible must be done to prevent such last-minute resistance.'[59] He brought up another of Himmler's bargaining counters himself, the political prisoners in concentration camps under threat of Hitler's decree that they should be killed rather than allowed to fall into allied hands.

Whether Wolff was actually playing a larger game and hoping to bring about a surrender in the west as well as in Italy – carrying out Himmler's intentions on his own account, for it had been made absolutely clear to him that the only terms on offer were unconditional surrender – whether he was manoeuvring to persuade Himmler that he was still acting for him, whether he *was* still acting for him in a deeper scheme than his simple, soldierly bearing indicated to Dulles and his colleagues, is not discernible through the fog of disinformation put up then and since. He told Dulles that he intended going to Kesselring's headquarters in the west to try and enlist his support in persuading von Vietinghoff to surrender the armies in Italy.[60] Presumably he reported to Himmler that he was going to Kesselring to enlist his support for the general conclusion of peace with the western powers. Such was the position when Himmler confided to Heinrici that he had taken steps to negotiate peace in the west. Perhaps he felt optimistic.

Had he learned of Stalin's reaction he might have felt highly optimistic. The Russians had been informed of the talks by the western allies on 12 March. They had not been invited, indeed their request to attend had been turned down on the ground that the object was merely to arrange for a German plenipotentiary to travel to allied headquarters, Italy, for the real negotiations for an armistice – where Soviet officers would be most welcome. Stalin, suspecting or pretending to suspect that the west was dealing behind his back, had his Foreign Minister, Molotov, fire off a fiercely insulting note on 22 March implying that a separate peace was being struck with Germany which excluded the Soviet Union.[61] This came on top of a bitter wrangle between Stalin and the west on the future of Poland. Probably it was intended as a shot in that dispute. However, it is also very possible that Stalin did believe that – as he put it in a subsequent cable to Roosevelt – the negotiations in Switzerland had ended with an agreement with the Germans whereby Kesselring was to open the western front and permit the Anglo-American forces to advance to the east. Anxious as both Roosevelt and Churchill had become about Stalin's post-war designs and overbearing manner, neither would or probably could have deceived him in this way at this stage of the war. On the other hand it is very likely that the fact of Wolff's journey to Kesselring's headquarters in Bad Nauheim after the conclusion of his talks in Switzerland was planted on Soviet intelligence by Schellenberg to foster the impression that a general peace *was* being concluded in the west. Driving a wedge into the enemy alliance had, after all, been Nazi policy for years, and also the policy of the 20 July conspirators, whose ideas Himmler was still soliciting. If this was the case, the visit Wolff paid to Kesselring on 23 March was a part of the overall scheme. He had not severed his links with Hitler and Himmler; he was merely prepared to do so. This seems a more likely explanation of his visit to Bad Nauheim than his own story to Dulles of using Kesselring to persuade von Vietinghoff to capitulate.

Meanwhile disquiet over Stalin's intentions in eastern Europe had led to a major argument between the western allies over strategy. Churchill wanted an Anglo-American thrust straight for Berlin to secure the Reich capital as a bargaining counter to hold Stalin to the Yalta agreements and balance the prestige the Red Army would acquire shortly when it took Vienna. Roosevelt supported Eisenhower in wanting the main thrust in southern Germany to meet the Red Army on the Danube and seal off the 'Alpine redoubt' before it could be organised for defence. Here it is evident that Kaltenbrunner and Schellenberg had pulled off a coup worthy of Heydrich. Western military intelligence reports on the possibility of Hitler holding out in his impenetrable Alpine fastness, manufacturing armaments and secret weapons in bomb-proof factories hollowed out of the mountains, training elite corps in guerrilla warfare to liberate Germany from the occupying powers read almost as if dictated in the RSHA. Hitler's despatch of elite SS units, especially Sepp Dietrich's Sixth SS Panzer Army to the south-eastern theatre instead of to the Oder, which had so annoyed Guderian, his determination to hold northern Italy, all appeared as confirmation that German strategy was 'directed primarily to the safeguarding of the Alpine zone'.[62]

There were elements of national politicking in the strategic dispute since, if the northern thrust were chosen, the British Field Marshal, Montgomery – anathema to the US generals – would gain the laurels for taking Berlin. With hindsight it is apparent that the way would have been opened for him by German generals in the west, anxious to allow the Anglo-Americans to reach the city before the Red Army. That was not clear at the time. America was by far the senior partner in the western alliance, and on 28 March Eisenhower wired Stalin an outline of his plans which ruled out a direct advance on Berlin. It is not clear whether this message, which drew a sharp protest from Churchill since the strategy had not been endorsed by the combined Chiefs of Staff, was at least partly intended to allay Stalin's suspicions about Dulles' negotiations with Wolff. It appeared to have that effect. Stalin welcomed the plan, and replied that he too was relegating the Reich capital to an objective of secondary importance. On the same day he called a major command conference to finalise plans and preparations for a gigantic assault on Berlin to be launched no later than mid-April.[63]

The sharp disputes and intrigues developing between the three powers and the part played in them by Wolff's manoeuvres in Switzerland might suggest that at five minutes past twelve, as Guderian termed it, Himmler came close to his objective of splitting the enemy coalition. The part played by the 'Alpine redoubt' also poses questions about Hitler's apparently eccentric troop movements, suggesting that he may not have lost that genius for deception which had brought him power and all his successes. However, the lack of restraint shown by the allied leaders in their internal disputes was more a measure of Germany's absolute loss of bargaining power than a last-minute success for the policy of splitting the coalition. With the Reich powerless, it was natural that the allies should squabble over the carcase. That, at least, is the picture that emerges from the documents so far available. Moreover

Himmler's extermination programmes had ruled out all possibility of his acceptance as a negotiating partner by the allies – hence his parallel efforts through Bernadotte, Kersten and the Jewish representatives in Stockholm to indicate his conversion to the dictates of 'wisdom and reason . . . the humane heart and willingness to help'.[64]

Wolff had chosen a bad time to visit Kesselring: spearheads of General Patton's Third US Army had established a bridgehead across the Rhine near Oppenheim the previous night. It is not surprising that the Field Marshal had little time to discuss Wolff's project when he called. However, Wolff sent an optimistic message to Dulles that Kesselring would be ready for further discussion in three days.[65] Was this on his own behalf or intended for Stalin's agents?

From Bad Nauheim Wolff drove on 24 March to Berlin, a tiring journey since he was forced off the autobahn on to side roads by 'deep flying' enemy aircraft strafing anything that moved. He arrived at the Chancellery shortly before noon and was received by Himmler in quarters occupied by his own successor, Hermann Fegelein, outside the damaged and shuttered building; they were joined shortly by Kaltenbrunner. Wolff's story for Dulles, repeated after the war when self-preservation demanded that he keep his American friends and protectors believing he had been acting on his own from the start, was that Himmler reproved him for meeting Dulles without his consent, after which he was subjected to hostile questioning by Kaltenbrunner, who wanted to arrest him on the spot. He talked his way out of the situation by saying that he had succeeded in making direct contact with the west on the pretext of negotiating for the release of a captured SS-Standartenführer. In view of Himmler's methods and multiple sources of information about Wolff's activities this is simply incredible, and makes it virtually certain that, whether he had already decided to repudiate his masters or not, he had returned to Berlin specifically to report on the mission Himmler had ordered him to carry out. Schellenberg's silence on the entire episode supports this interpretation, for, according to Wolff, Kaltenbrunner drove him down to Bavaria the following day to a castle where the SD Berlin offices had been evacuated, and there he was questioned by Schellenberg's experts. Probably he was, but probably it was a debriefing rather than a hostile interrogation.

He returned to Berlin with Kaltenbrunner on the 26th to report to Himmler, who had established his field headquarters at Hohenlychen since leaving Birkenhain. His enemies said that this was because the red crosses painted on the roof of the hospital spared him the danger of enemy air-raids. His two small children by Häschen Potthast were under Professor Gebhardt's protection at the hospital at this time,[66] presumably Häschen as well, and it must be assumed that this was an important factor in his choice of place. Also it was in quiet countryside within convenient distance of Berlin. When Wolff rang him to report that he was back Himmler was annoyed at his late return and said he could not see him; he had been ordered to Hungary to stiffen German resistance there, and was catching the night train to Vienna.[67]

The reason for his journey to Hungary was to administer exemplary punishment to units of Sepp Dietrich's Sixth SS Panzer Army. Reports of Dietrich's withdrawal in defiance of orders to stand fast had reached Hitler; Guderian, who was with Hitler at the time, described him as going almost out of his mind with rage. The outburst was caused not so much by imminent loss of the oil fields, fatal as this must be, rather by the fact that he had been let down by his loyal guard, the Waffen-SS, not simply the Waffen-SS but his own elite Leibstandarte. He had a message sent by radio ordering all four divisions, Leibstandarte, Das Reich, Totenkopf and Hohenstauffen, to be stripped of their armbands – the stripe on the men's lower left sleeve denoting division or regiment. It seems that these had already been removed for security reasons, but Dietrich, bitter at this reward for five years' absolute commitment at the front, cabled back that he would shoot himself rather than carry out the order. Hitler had commissioned Himmler to go and see that the punishment was administered. Goebbels, who recorded in his diary 'a sort of presentiment of doom' among the military around Hitler, noted that the generals were nonetheless rubbing their hands at this disgrace for their rivals.[68]

No doubt Himmler gave Dietrich's officers one of his quiet exhortations to fanatic resistance; no doubt he hinted to Dietrich that he had opened promising lines to the west. He also took the opportunity in Vienna to speak to the Gauleiter, Baldur von Schirach, about the Jews working in industry and on the repair of roads, railways and bridges. He wanted them taken under the best possible conditions and with the best medical care to Linz or Mauthausen; they were, he said, his soundest investment. Von Schirach understood from this that he wanted to 'redeem himself with his good treatment of the Jews'.[69]

Wolff meanwhile, on his way back to Italy, paid a brief call on his family at St Wolfgang on the Wolfgangsee some twenty miles east of Salzburg and Berchtesgaden and arranged for them to move to the South Tyrol. This suggests that by this date, almost the end of March, having seen the mood of mixed fatalism and fantasy around the Führer and the loss of nerve in the populace, he had made up his mind to renege on his oath and save what he could – at the least that he wanted all his options open, for it would be easier if it came to it to spirit his family over the border to Italy from the Tyrol. Himmler evidently drew this inference when he heard the news. On Easter Sunday, 1 April, the day before Wolff was due back in Switzerland to continue his talks with Dulles, Lemnitzer and Airey, Himmler called him by telephone to tell him that his family was to remain at St Wolfgang; he had taken them under his personal protection, so Wolff remembered the conversation. His wife and boys had become hostages for his loyalty.[70]

As recalled by the member of the signals company at Verona, who made the connection for this 'Blitz Reichsführergespräch', the threat was expressed in more subtle terms.[71] After Himmler had announced himself, Wolff wished him Easter greetings.

'Danke schön, Wölffchen, danke schön!' Himmler replied in a weary, resigned voice, then after a short, almost embarrassed pause, 'Tell me, what is this remarkable story about your wife? Yesterday morning, she departed head over heels from St Wolfgang.'

Wolff must have anticipated the question. 'I had news from Salzburg that the mood there was very hostile to Higher SS-Führers, therefore I advised my wife it would be better to take the children into the Reich.'

'Didn't you give any thought to the impression that would make? The Kreisleiter called me up on that account today. I know the position in Salzburg exactly. Affairs have certainly not gone so far as you assume.'

'Of course I will send my wife back to St Wolfgang at once.'

'Do that, Wölffchen, as quickly as possible.'

After some discussion about the prisoner exchange serving as cover for the talks in Switzerland, Wolff asked whether Himmler could tell him anything about the military position.

There was a short pause. 'I still believe as ever, Wölffchen, that all goes well. If not, then we must all just die a heroic death.'

The following day, Easter Monday, Himmler received Count Bernadotte for the second time at Hohenlychen. Bernadotte found him looking 'rather serious and nervous', prepared to admit that the situation was extremely critical – not however without hope. Bernadotte tried to put it to him that if he considered that his country faced disaster his thinking should not be confined to loyalty to Hitler; someone with his immense responsibilities could not simply follow his leader blindly. At this point, apparently, Himmler was called to the telephone, and afterwards the talk was confined to the ostensible purpose of the visit, the Scandinavian prisoners in the camps. After initial refusal to release any, Himmler began to compromise and eventually consented to allow all Danish and Norwegian women and the sick to be taken to Sweden.

Afterwards Bernadotte drove back to Berlin with Schellenberg. During the break in his talk with Himmler he had been asked by Schellenberg once again whether he could not go to Eisenhower and discuss the possibilities for a capitulation on the western front. Impossible, he had replied, the initiative had to come from Himmler. Schellenberg returned to the subject now. Himmler would not hesitate to ask him (Bernadotte) to propose capitulation to Eisenhower were it not for Hitler; the Reichsführer was torn between his desire to save the country from chaos and his vow of loyalty. No doubt Schellenberg was acting on Himmler's instructions when he raised the matter; perhaps that is why he simplified Himmler's extraordinary dilemma: it was not simply that his whole career and organisation had been constructed around loyalty to the Führer, it had also been constructed on absolute hostility to Bolshevism. He could no more consider surrendering to the Russians than Hitler could, and while the western allies insisted on unconditional surrender, east and west simultaneously, he felt himself unable to do any more than Hitler to stop the fighting. All his attempts at negotiating had been for an exclusively western solution.

On the same day in Switzerland, Baron Parrilli arrived alone for the armistice talks with Dulles, Lemnitzer and Airey. Wolff, he told them, was too depressed to come.[72]

On 12 April President Roosevelt died. Central Berlin was shaking beneath one of the nightly air-raids, the Chancellery and nearby blocks blazing when the Reuter's newsflash was intercepted at about 11.00 p.m. Shortly after midnight Goebbels arrived back from a visit to the eastern front at what remained of the Propaganda Ministry, the greater part of which had been gutted and destroyed by fire a month ago almost to the night. He was greeted with the news on the steps. 'I shall never forget the look on his face,' one of those who had rushed out to meet him recalled later.[73] He stood for a moment transfixed, his sharp features lit by the fires of the city. Then ordering champagne, he summoned aides and press representatives into his study and called the Chancellery bunker on his private line.

'*Mein Führer!* I congratulate you! Roosevelt is dead. This is the miracle of the House of Brandenburg. . . .'[74]

In that taut, fantastical world it is not surprising that the US President's death should have been likened to the death of the Czarina Elizabeth which had brought deliverance to Frederick the Great at the eleventh hour. Hitler, who had already heard the news, suggested to Goebbels that the US Army might soon be exchanging artillery fire with the Red Army over the roof of the Reich Chancellery. He had summoned Speer and Dönitz so that he could tell them personally. When they arrived he thrust the Reuter's message at them, 'Read this! Roosevelt is dead!' His words tumbled out in his excitement, 'Who was right! The war is not lost. . . .'[75]

Himmler does not appear to have been called. Perhaps he was too far away; he was establishing a headquarters at Ziethen Castle, Wustrow, on the Baltic coast to the east of Lübeck Bay, to which he could move when Berlin fell. More probably it was because he was out of favour. Sepp Dietrich's 'failure' in Hungary on top of his own failure to halt the Russian thrust into Pomerania had made a bitter impression on Hitler. Goebbels' diary entry for 30 March had recorded Hitler talking of Dietrich's 'guilt before history', and he noted that 'Himmler's standing with the Führer has accordingly sunk noticeably.' Himmler was a punctilious person, Hitler had told him, but no commander. He totally lacked the divine spark.[76]

Schellenberg, who was summoned to Ziethen Castle on the day Dönitz and Speer reported to the Führer bunker to be included in the rejoicing over Roosevelt's death, found Himmler in great distress over the way he had been almost completely abandoned by Hitler.[77] This was on top of his continuing indecision about his own responsibilities. Now there was no escaping that militarily the war was lost. The oil fields of Hungary, the industrial and mining regions of Silesia, the Saar and most of the Ruhr had been overrun. US armies stood on the Elbe, with a bridgehead across less than fifty-three miles from Berlin; Soviet armies lined the Oder–Neisse system with a bridgehead less than forty miles from the capital. The Reich had been squeezed into the shape of a sand-glass with the pinched-in central passage scarcely 100 miles wide. Inside this a teeming refugee population of millions, mostly women and children and the old, were moving westwards with prams and handcarts of possessions, away from the Red soldiery towards the Anglo-Americans. In the other direction columns of starving prisoners were forced from concentration camps threatened by the Anglo-American advance; many had already been evacuated from eastern camps. Those who fell or faltered were shot or clubbed to death by their guards.

Himmler took Schellenberg for a long walk in the woods to try and worry out his response to the situation. The questions were those he had been grappling with for weeks. He was terrified that Kaltenbrunner would inform on him to Hitler when Kersten brought a representative of the World Jewish Congress to meet him in a few days' time. Kaltenbrunner would be in Austria, Schellenberg reminded him; Himmler had appointed him his deputy with plenipotentiary powers for the whole southern region if – more properly when – the Reich were cut into two halves by the junction of US and Soviet forces. Himmler was equally concerned about Hitler's sharply deteriorating health and erratic decisions; underlying everything was anxiety over his personal impasse. Schellenberg urged him again to take power from Hitler and surrender in the west. How could he? Himmler asked; he could not confront Hitler with the position and tell him he must resign – he would fly into one of his rages and shoot him out of hand. Nor could he shoot Hitler or poison or arrest him. The military machine would come to a standstill. Such was Schellenberg's account of his state of mind.[78]

No doubt Himmler was correct in believing that any attempt at a coup would lead to chaos. While there were many generals like his own successor, Heinrici, already sidestepping their orders and trying to create a situation in which more Germans, soldiers and civilians alike, would be able to surrender to the western allies, there were others fanatically loyal to their oath and determined to fight to the last. Himmler had contributed essentially to this spirit with his own calls for fanatic commitment, and the setting up of the Werwolf organisation. Only the previous afternoon he had issued a decree which was broadcast several times over the course of the next few days. It opened with the statement that the enemy was forcing the surrender of towns by threatening bombardment by tanks and artillery; the stratagem would not succeed: 'No German town will be declared an open town. Every village and every town will be defended and held with all means. Every German man responsible for the defence of a town who infringes against this obvious national duty loses his honour and his life.'[79]

Goebbels was sending out similar exhortations in daily Werwolf broadcasts. Dönitz was showing equally fanatic commitment: sending naval personnel to strengthen the forces before Berlin, he issued decrees as savage as Himmler's:

> Our military duty, which we fulfil regardless of what may happen to right or left or around us, causes us to stand bold, hard and loyal as a rock of the resistance. A scoundrel who does not behave so must be hung and have a placard fastened to him. 'Here hangs a traitor who by his low cowardice allows German women and children to die instead of protecting them like a man.'[80]

Above all were those at Court like Bormann and Kaltenbrunner whom Himmler could no longer trust. He told Schellenberg on their walk that he and Rudi Brandt were the only people he could trust completely. In these circumstances it does seem that he was right to question the possibility of an SS putsch that would not be betrayed before it began. Jürgen Stroop's recollections tend to confirm Schellenberg's account of Himmler's mood. Stroop reported to him the following day, 14 April, at his headquarters train, 'Steiermark', at Hohenlychen. Himmler appeared overtired and not well, but his hands and nails were, as always, well cared for, Stroop remembered, and he received him extremely cordially, enquiring after his family as he always did. After listening to Stroop's detailed report of the last weeks in his Rhine–Westmark command – congratulating him on his handling of von Kluge's 'suicide' – Himmler gave him a general review of the military and political situation. It was then that he expressed some of his own worries, and characterised Hitler's behaviour as 'peculiar'. It was possible, he said, that the Führer was ill. He went no further, of course. Finally he asked Stroop to join his personal staff at Ziethen Castle from where he intended moving up to Denmark.[81]

Stroop turned down the offer, the first time in his life he had ventured to disagree with his Reichsführer. He was committed to organising a Werwolf group in the Alps, he said. He could not let his men down.

'Do you believe the Third Reich will win the war?' Himmler asked.

'Certainly! Because it is clear that no one and nothing can conquer the Germanic spirit that has been aroused by Adolf Hitler.'

Apparently the answer convinced Himmler that Stroop was not flying southwards merely to save himself and his family. Tears in his eyes, he embraced him, 'If the thousand-year Reich has such loyal soldiers of Adolf Hitler as you, my dear Stroop, then it cannot perish!'

So Stroop parted from him for the last time. To judge by his talks with Moczarski in the condemned cell he remained firm in his loyalty to 'Adolf Hitler' and 'Heinrich Himmler' to the end. 'Loyalty, only loyalty, unconditional loyalty, that is the most important quality of a true man.'

'You speak so often of loyalty,' Moczarski said to him, 'but to whom should one be loyal? Was it right to remain loyal to people who led your country to catastrophe?'

Stroop became very agitated: they had lost the war only because the intrigues of the reactionary, Anglo-Saxon, Jewish, socialist, communist and masonic Internationale had subverted the *Volk*; they had been too liberal . . .[82]

Shortly before his execution, Stroop was asked by the Polish prison governor whether, as a party to the murder of women and children in the Warsaw ghetto, he had come to terms with his conscience. He felt no remorse that Jews had been murdered, Stroop replied. His arrogant convictions struck all who saw him to the end. He went to the gallows with a calm and soldierly bearing.[83]

On the day he took his last farewell from 'der treue Stroop', Himmler sent a wire in response to queries from the Kommandants of Dachau and Flossenbürg instructing them on no account to surrender their camps to the enemy, but to evacuate them immediately: 'No prisoner may fall into enemy hands alive.'[84] This ran counter to a promise he had given Kersten the previous month that he would not pass on Hitler's destruction order, but instead ensure the camps and inmates were handed over in orderly fashion. The promise had been rendered worthless by both Bormann and Kaltenbrunner, the former by issuing the Führer decree to Gauleiters concerned, the latter by instructing the Kommandants directly. On 7 April it seems Kaltenbrunner had given such an order to the Kommandant of Bergen–Belsen on the British line of advance. The information had reached representatives of the World Jewish Congress in Stockholm who had contacted Kersten, still in Sweden; in a series of night telephone calls to Brandt Kersten had succeeded in getting Himmler to reverse the destruction order.[85] Yet on 14 April Himmler was wavering again with his instructions to Dachau and Flossenbürg to evacuate all prisoners. Presumably this was to cover himself from Kaltenbrunner's and Bormann's machinations and Hitler's rage when he learned that Belsen had been allowed to fall intact into enemy hands.

This happened the next day, 15 April. What was found inside the wire staggered imagination; as recorded in the British Army Report, 'both inside and outside the huts was a carpet of dead bodies, human excreta, rags and filth.' Those inmates still alive tottered or crawled in ragged prison garb, skeletal figures infested with lice, eyes empty of hope or relief or any human feeling.[86]

It was about this date that Himmler ordered Eichmann to report to him. He was planning to negotiate with Eisenhower, he said, and instructed him to go to the Theresienstadt camp immediately and arrange for all the prominent Jews there to be taken to a safe place in the Tyrol so that he could use them as hostages in his negotiations.[87]

Meanwhile he had ordered Wolff back from Italy to Berlin to report; at the same time Schellenberg's chief of intelligence for south-east Europe,

SS-Obersturmbannführer Wilhelm Hoettl, had travelled to Zurich to place the 'Alpine redoubt' squarely on the western bargaining table. Dulles still assumed that the 'redoubt' was an attempt by Himmler and Kaltenbrunner to scotch Wolff's negotiations. Wolff appeared to fear this too. Instead of returning, he sent a report by courier, and when Himmler called him again on the 15th with a peremptory summons to Berlin in person, he left a note for Dulles to say that if he came back he would bring the surrender negotiations to a successful conclusion; if, however, he should be arrested and executed, he asked Dulles to protect his two families and defend his honour by making it known that he had acted not from personal motives but solely 'to save the German *Volk*'.[88] It is evident that on the eve of returning to Berlin to report to Himmler Wolff had to make some such protestations or he could hardly have continued his pretence – if pretence it still was – that he was not acting on his chief's instructions.

At 5.00 a.m. on the 16th the darkness to the east of Berlin was flushed by flames from over 8000 artillery pieces and multiple rocket launchers. Air and earth erupted and merged in thunderous dissolution as Zhukov launched one arm of the final offensive for the Reich capital. Little over an hour later the sky over the Neisse was rent by a similar concentrated bombardment from Koniev's batteries. US forces meanwhile had been halted on the Elbe in keeping with Eisenhower's promise to Stalin. By evening Koniev's tanks had broken through to a depth of some nine miles but Zhukov had met fierce resistance and, spurred by Stalin's displeasure at his relatively poor results, continued to hurl in more armour by night. Such was the position as Wolff flew in to a field strip to the south of Berlin in response to Himmler's summons. He was met by Professor Gebhardt, who drove him to the Adlon Hotel, undamaged parts of which still welcomed important visitors to the capital. Next morning the Professor drove him to Himmler at Hohenlychen.

Again, there is only Wolff's description of his meetings,[89] first cordially with Himmler over lunch, then joined by Kaltenbrunner, who immediately accused him of having negotiated an armistice on the Italian front. He denied it, acting the misunderstood, finally the enraged victim of malevolence while Himmler sat silent and undecided between them. At last, as Himmler appeared unable to settle the dispute, Wolff said they should take it to the Führer. Himmler declined to go himself but agreed to let the Führer decide. So Kaltenbrunner and Wolff drove off together back to Berlin. 'If I am hanged,' Wolff said in an unconcealed threat to reveal Kaltenbrunner's own attempts at negotiations if he accused him before Hitler, 'my place on the gallows will be between you and Himmler.' When they reached the Chancellery Wolff told Hitler that he had succeeded in opening a door to the 'President's Palace' in Washington; apparently he received Hitler's consent to continue his efforts.

'Should you fail,' Hitler told him, 'then I shall have to drop you exactly like Hess.'[90]

So, with a mixture of guile and threat, Wolff, according to his own unverifiable and in part unbelievable account, carried off his second great deception. On the 19th he flew back to Italy to resume his betrayal – on behalf of the *Volk* – of his Führer and the Reichsführer he had been pleased and proud to serve the previous year. It took a further ten days of negotiation and deadly intrigue before he succeeded in bringing about the capitulation of all German forces in Italy, effective from 2 May.

After the war Dulles saved him from being indicted alongside his rival, Kaltenbrunner, and other surviving leaders in the trial of the major war criminals at Nuremberg. At his deNazification process later, Dulles' German expert Gaevernitz spoke up for him and he walked free with Category III, minor accountability, soon reduced to Category IV, fellow-traveller status. Resuming his interrupted career in public relations and assisted by his banking and industrial contacts from the old Freundeskreis, he rode the West German economic miracle, by the 1960s possessing a lakeside country mansion, a higher income and in many respects a more enviable standard of living than he had enjoyed under Himmler. All this was shattered in the wake of Eichmann's capture and trial when he was brought to court himself in Germany on charges of abetting the murder of Jews. Found guilty, he was given the curious sentence of fifteen years in prison, but his American patrons had not forgotten him, nor his friends from the Third Reich, and a way was found of releasing him on grounds of ill-health.[91]

Thereafter he never ceased in public and private to protest the unjustness of his conviction – as his biographer Jochen Lang wrote, a pattern of his generation. As a very young man he had served imperial Germany as an officer in an elite regiment and won the Iron Cross, 1st and 2nd Class, for bravery in the trenches; as Himmler's loyal, thoroughly Aryan right hand he had not flinched at the necessary mass murder to purify the blood of the *Volk*, had won favour with the Führer and, finally entrusted with independent high command, had succeeded in impressing Dulles and Gaevernitz as an honest soldier who had turned against his masters. Afterwards, like the Bundesrepublik itself, he had risen from the ashes of the Reich as a business success. He was the ultimate chameleon. Outwardly he maintained he had nothing on his conscience. Perhaps if he admitted inwardly what he had been party to he might have answered himself defiantly as Stroop answered the prison governor; there is no telling. Before his death full of years in 1984 he had assisted in the preparation of the forged 'Hitler Diaries'.[92]

Since so much of the inner history of the Third Reich in its final convulsions has to be pieced together from the tales of such survivors as Wolff and Schellenberg, it is impossible to know exactly who in April 1945 was plotting against or with whom, or quite how, as the leaders searched desperately for personal escape routes from the ruins. Hitler himself remained true to his convictions. By the time Wolff saw him for the last time it is fairly certain he had decided to stay – and die – in Berlin. On 15 April Eva Braun's bed and dresser had been brought down from her Berlin apartment to the room next to his in the bunker beneath the Chancellery. Although preparations were being made to transfer Führer headquarters to the Obersalzberg there must have been many in Hitler's entourage who felt, as his secretary Gerda Christian did when she saw his mistress take up residence, that now he would never leave.[93]

Goebbels also appears to have decided to stay – and die heroically – in Berlin. As Gauleiter of the city and mastermind of the Werwolf broadcasts he was determined that no white flags should fly. More significantly he was the creator and custodian of the legend of the Führer and his Reich and he had a vision of how the legend was to be perpetuated down history. He saw it in terms of grand cinema – that at least was how he introduced it to his staff on 17 April – a colour epic showing to audiences down the ages the *Götterdämmerung* in Berlin, 1945. 'Hold out now,' he told them, 'so that a hundred years hence the audience does not hoot and whistle when you appear on the screen.' Apparently his aides thought he had gone off his head.[94]

Himmler's tergiversations in these weeks stand in complete contrast to the consistency of Hitler and Goebbels. He appeared to switch violently between fanatic loyalty to the person of the Führer and his recognisably 'peculiar' decisions, and a vision of himself as the Führer's successor negotiating an alliance with the west against the Russians. Even that idea was split between his hope of proving himself acceptable by releasing prisoners and, on the other hand, using his important group of prisoners as 'hostages' to force a bargain.

The dichotomy was very apparent by 19 April, the eve of Hitler's birthday. On the one hand he had arranged to see two men he still hoped might be a bridge to the west, Count Bernadotte again, ostensibly on behalf of Scandinavian prisoners, and a representative of the World Jewish Congress named Norbert Masur on behalf of Jewish prisoners. Masur had taken his courage in his hands and flown with Kersten to Tempelhof airport, Berlin; thence they had driven to Kersten's country house where they were awaiting Himmler. Himmler was in Berlin, locked in private discussion with the Minister of Finance, Schwerin von Krosigk, about the necessity of ending the war quickly with or without Hitler to preserve German capital assets. On the other hand Himmler had ordered the evacuation of Neuengamme concentration camp, and behind the fighting front his writ for fanatic resistance was being imposed by the special 'flying summary court martial' teams headed by 'mostly very young SS officers . . . blindly fanatical'[95] who hunted shirkers and deserters and hanged them on the nearest tree or lamppost. And shortly before midnight after returning to Hohenlychen, Himmler ordered champagne to toast the Führer's birthday on the hour.[96] Next day he was to drive to Berlin to join the other paladins offering good wishes in person at the Chancellery.

Such behaviour and the way he preserved different fronts of normality to deal with such different characters as Bernadotte, Kersten and Schellenberg,

Wolff, Kaltenbrunner and Stroop, and indeed Hitler himself, could suggest a schizoid personality. According to the theory, he was perceiving or dealing not with the real outer world, but with a distorted version of it generated by his destructively divided ego, viewing the outside world with a 'false-self-system' from which the real 'self' had withdrawn. Loyalty to a Führer who was so obviously draining the precious blood from the *Volk* because they had proved too weak for the struggle, or on the other hand continuing attempts at negotiations with a 'west' which was not going to deal with him both seem irrational and impractical. His breakdown and retreat to Hohenlychen, followed by hectic activity, his suspicions that others were plotting his ruin, were symptoms which might have come from a textbook example of schizoid behaviour.

This reinforces the other indications: his adolescent diaries, obsessive work routine and meticulous performance of duty – 'he is a punctilious person' Hitler had told Goebbels that month[97] – his constant intellectualising and moralising – 'like a man from some other planet' Guderian wrote, his imagination 'vivid and even fantastic'[98] – and above all perhaps the strong suggestion from the concentration camps, medical experimentation and factory murder of sado-masochistic drives: in theory the split 'anti-libidinal' ego persecuting its twin 'libidinal' ego, the real 'self' divided against itself in a sado-masochistic relationship. Applying the theory to his whole career, it could illumine those occasions during the war when he appeared to be travelling with the opposition and with Hitler at the same time – in particular the mystery of his ambivalent attitude on 20 July 1944 – as well as those key episodes before the war when he courted his earliest hero and mentor and actual chief, 'the good Captain Röhm', before stabbing him in the back for Hitler, and did the same again for his other mentor and chief, Gregor Strasser. These events are explicable, indeed predictable, if that quality he liked to stress above all others, loyalty, was simply a part of a 'false-self-system' – the 'ego' of everyday living – which his withdrawn and divided inner self had built up to deal with the frightening outside world. There was no reality, no vitality to it; it was an intellectualisation, dissociated, generalised and dead. In crisis it could only mirror the frustration, anxiety and guilt felt by his tortured inner 'self'. He both wanted his Führer and drew back from him in fear; he wanted the approval of the west and drew back in fear.

It is a beguiling explanation. It may not be correct for his whole life. In extreme situations 'normal' people may experience schizoid dissociation or withdrawal into an inner self observing the body as it were outside as it carries on life in automatic mode. Descriptions by survivors of concentration camps abound in the 'unreal' or dreamlike quality of their lives inside the wire.[99] Hitler was perhaps experiencing such an illusion, observing an automatic Führer-figure moving phantom armies on the maps; the generals and adjutants who played along with the fantasy, Keitel and Jodl and a new Chief of the Army Staff, General Hans

Krebs – appointed at the end of March when Guderian had been unable to cope with the situation any longer – perhaps all in the underground bunker shared the disembodied feeling. Goebbels appears to have been looking on at himself as if at a character in an epic. Similarly Himmler, facing the end with all escape routes barred – by his own rhetoric, by the myth of 1918, by the organisation of the SS and its motto, by the allied agreement on unconditional surrender, and by his own status as the most wanted war criminal after Hitler – and now spurned by Hitler, to whom he had dedicated his life and served exhaustively in the most dread tasks (so he might have reasoned), had every pressure to take refuge in schizoid flight from reality.

Alternatively there is the simple explanation. His nerves were not strong enough for the ordeal: inadequacy he had always sought to conceal with extreme conviction and exhortations to hardness had been exposed by this ultimate test. Like a hunted animal, he was twisting frantically in every direction to find escape, using the methods of guile and camouflage and treachery with which he had climbed to and retained his power.

On 20 April spearheads of Zhukov's Second Guards Tank Army reached the north-eastern suburbs of Berlin; at 11.00 a.m. the city itself came under fire from his artillery. To the southwards Koniev's armour raced towards Zossen, some twenty miles from the capital, intent on beating Zhukov to the goal. Overhead massed allied bombers greeted Hitler's birthday with sticks of high explosives and incendiaries. It was a public holiday. The faces of women and girls who emerged after the bombs to queue for food were white and tight with fear, images of Russian soldiers behind their eyes. Youngsters of the Volkssturm, manning makeshift barriers of rubble across the streets, held their jumping nerves. Refugees crowded westwards, wheeling possessions around fallen masonry and craters. There was no public transport to impede, only occasional official cars and lorries as the higher bureaucracy and officers cleared out of the ministries and from the other direction the paladins drove in to pay their birthday respects at the Chancellery.

The façade of the building still stood. SS men of Hitler's personal guard with drilled, impenetrable eyes and machine guns manned the entrances and checkpoints; silver death's heads, silver runes shone against black – their honour was loyalty. The grand halls and marble corridors were abandoned or gutted and blackened and strewn with debris; cracked walls were buttressed with timber, windows boarded or blanked with card; masonry dust danced to the thud of nearby shells in shafts of spring sunlight from the gaps in the roof. But the Court of Honour before the old Chancellery building still stood, and there newsreel cameras had been set up to record the ceremony as Göring, von Ribbentrop, Himmler, Goebbels, Speer and other ministers went through the ritual of congratulating Hitler on his fifty-sixth birthday. 'He looked closer to seventy than fifty-six,' one witness recalled. 'He looked what I would call physically senile.'[100] Afterwards he shuffled out to the cratered devastation of the garden, escorted by Göring, Himmler and Goebbels, to inspect and confer medals on a contingent of Hitler Youth. Did Himmler observe his everyday self performing as it was accustomed in deference to the Führer, smiling encouragement at these – mere boys who had fought the Russians?

From the sun the paladins followed Hitler down the steps, slowly to the artificial light and continuous hum of the air-conditioning in the lower bunker. Hitler received Dönitz, Keitel and Jodl individually in his small conference room, then came out to the corridor which served as main chamber for the daily situation conferences. He looked an old man, Dönitz's adjutant wrote, 'broken, washed-up, stooped, feeble and irritable'.[101] He was urged to leave and establish his headquarters at the Obersalzberg as planned, before the Russians encircled the city and cut off all escape. He was noncommittal, but he agreed the others might leave and that Dönitz should set up a headquarters in the north to take over the defence of that area – a decision he had taken some days previously for the eventuality of the country being divided into two halves by the junction of US and Soviet forces. Himmler was among the many who advised him to leave at once, but what else he said to him, or what manner Hitler adopted towards his long-serving and most loyal Reichsführer, is not recorded. It was the last time they met.

It was also Himmler's last time in Berlin. Probably he conferred with 'Gestapo' Müller and gave instructions about the remaining political prisoners rounded up after the 20 July plot; it would have been unlike him not to leave his desk tidy. Most of the opposition groups had been liquidated, one of the last batches earlier that month after Canaris' diaries had been discovered by accident in a safe in an Abwehr headquarters post. Kaltenbrunner had brought the find to Hitler with some passages marked for his attention. A glance had confirmed Hitler in the belief he had long held: he had been the victim of a gigantic conspiracy to rob him of victory. He ordered the destruction of the whole circle. Müller gave the necessary instructions, and in the early dawn of 9 April at Flossenbürg camp Canaris, Oster, other Abwehr officers and Pastor Dietrich Bonhoeffer had been led out naked to the gallows; von Dohnanyi, paralysed after ill treatment, had been hanged the same morning at Sachsenhausen.

George Elser, the alleged single-handed assassin of the November 1939 bomb plot in the Bürgerbräukeller, had been liquidated at much the same date at Dachau. Again the order was signed by Müller: Eller, as the special prisoner was known in camp records, had to be taken out and killed inconspicuously during the next air-raid on the environs, his death to be recorded as 'mortally wounded in the terror attack'.[102] Whether Müller's instructions originated from Hitler or Himmler is not known, but evidently he had to be silenced in case the allies surprised the camp and freed the inmates – and the execution had to be disguised.

Another twenty-eight political prisoners were executed that day, 20 April. There remained at least three other groups, one, the most fortunate as it turned out, including Schacht, Halder, Frau Goerdeler – whose husband had already been executed – and others arrested on grounds of kinship, were among those important prisoners whose safety had been entrusted to Eichmann; they were eventually released in the Alps. Other groups were held in the damaged remains of the Prinz Albrecht Strasse building, and in the Lehrterstrasse prison, Berlin. Whether Himmler gave instructions to silence these is not known; it is probable. All Gestapo records were being destroyed; the living testimony was as important, and so far as is known none survived. A few of those in the Lehrterstrasse were killed by Russian shells the next day. The rest were taken out in batches on the night following, placed against a wall and shot. Among these was Albrecht Haushofer.[103]

Almost a year later his mother and father committed suicide together by a stream not far from their Bavarian house, leaving instructions that no memorial or means of identification should ever be placed on their grave.[104]

Two victims known to have been arrested and executed on Himmler's direct orders were Dr Sigmund Rascher and his wife.[105]

The End

Himmler drove to Ziethen Castle after leaving Berlin on 20 April. Although he arrived late at night Schellenberg, waiting impatiently to take him to the Jewish representative, Norbert Masur, convinced him that they should go at once. So it was they arrived at Kersten's property, Hartzwalde, at two in the morning of the 21st. Kersten came out to meet them and took Himmler aside before they entered in order to stress the extraordinary significance of this first discussion with a representative of the race the Third Reich had set out to annihilate. It was a chance to show the world and future generations that the harsh policy had been reversed. Kersten knew his patient intimately. The simple way he chose to explain the opportunity before him is as significant for an understanding of Himmler's mind as the response – which Kersten had heard so often before: 'If I had had my own way, many things would have been done differently.'[1]

Inside, Himmler greeted Masur in his friendly manner and the two sat down around a table with coffee with Kersten, Schellenberg and Brandt, who had come with them from Ziethen. Himmler started the substantive discussion, as Schellenberg and Kersten had feared he would, with a historical ramble on predictable lines about the necessity they had been under of solving the Jewish problem in Germany, how he had tried to do so by emigration but none of the countries which pretended to be friendly towards Jews had co-operated. Coming to the war years, he explained the crematoria in the camps in the east as necessary for the thousands of victims of epidemics. After some three-quarters of an hour either Masur – by Schellenberg's account – or Kersten – by his own account – managed to bring him down to concrete proposals for the future. In the end, he agreed that his previous promises that no more Jews would be killed and that the camps would be handed over to the allies intact would be honoured. In the meantime he would release the Jewesses held in Ravensbrück, provided this was kept absolutely secret and as an additional precaution the women were described as Poles. Apparently he had received Hitler's permission to release Polish women from the camp.[2]

It was five o'clock by the time the discussion ended and Himmler said goodbye to Masur. Kersten walked out with him to his car. Before getting in Himmler talked for a while in the self-justificatory manner he always used with his confessor, admitting that the war was lost and that they had made many serious mistakes; they had wanted greatness and security for Germany but were leaving behind a heap of ruins. For himself, he had always wanted what was best, but so often he had had to work against his real convictions.

As a loyal soldier I had to obey, for no state can survive without obedience and discipline. It rests with me alone to decide how long I still have to live since my life has now become meaningless. And what will history say of me? Petty minds, bent on revenge, will hand down a false and perverted account of the great and good things I have accomplished for Germany. . . .[3]

As he climbed into the car, and held out his hand to Kersten, thanking him deeply for the years he had treated him with his 'magic skill', his eyes were moist – whether from self-pity or from the knowledge that he would never see his 'Magic Buddha' again is not revealed.

'My last thoughts are for my poor family,' he said before the car drove off.

Kersten travelled to Stockholm a few days later. There the leader of the Jewish delegation expressed doubt about Himmler's assurances. Kersten told him that, from his knowledge of his former patient's character, he would keep his promises.[4]

From Hartzwalde, Himmler, Schellenberg and Brandt drove to Hohenlychen, where Count Bernadotte was waiting. A smörgåsbord breakfast had been laid on in pre-war abundance. Himmler, looking utterly exhausted, but keyed up, gave Bernadotte the impression of being unable to remain long in one spot and of darting from place to place as an outlet for his anxiety. He tried to press delicacy after delicacy on the Count, who was used to simple toast and coffee. When he sat down himself he ate hungrily, drummed with his fingers on the table or tapped his front teeth with his nails – a sure sign he was nervous, Schellenberg explained quietly. Bernadotte pressed him on the evacuation of the Scandinavian prisoners from Neuengamme, and they discussed taking the Jewish–Polish women from Ravensbrück by means of the Red Cross convoy, but once again Himmler did not tackle the central issue of war or peace; again it was left to Schellenberg afterwards on the way back to Berlin to suggest to Bernadotte that he fly to Eisenhower to set up a conference with Himmler. Again Bernadotte said it was impossible; the initiative had to come from Himmler. As they parted he said, thinking perhaps of the smörgåsbord, 'The Reichsführer no longer understands the realities of his own situation. He should have taken Germany's affairs into his own hands after my first visit.'[5]

Returning to Hohenlychen, Schellenberg was called to Himmler soon after midday; he was in bed, 'the picture of misery', and said he felt ill. Schellenberg told him there was nothing more *he* could do; it was up to him (Himmler) now; he had to take some action. After lunch, they drove north to Ziethen Castle. They were held up in endless jams of troops and refugees and just before Wustrow were attacked by low-flying planes. As they drove on Himmler confided to Schellenberg for the first time that he dreaded the future.[6]

The first test of the agreement reached with Masur came the following day, 22 April. Schellenberg's representative, SS-Obersturmführer Franz Göring, arrived at Ravensbrück and instructed the Kommandant, SS-Sturmbannführer Suhren, to have the women to be evacuated marched to a camp at Malchow, where the Red Cross transports would meet them. Suhren refused, citing the Führer's order passed to him by Kaltenbrunner to liquidate the women on the approach of the enemy. Göring rang Brandt and described the impasse; Brandt contacted Himmler and shortly rang back to the Kommandant with orders to release the women. Suhren, now by Göring's account, completely at a loss, asked about a group of experimental subjects whom he had been ordered explicitly to liquidate – fifty-four Polish and seventeen French women who had been inoculated with disease, then cured by surgery. Again Göring rang Brandt; this time the decision from Himmler took longer, but after two hours Brandt rang back to say that the Reichsführer had ordered the release of the *Versuchskaninchen* (experimental rabbits), as they were known in the camp.[7]

Some 15,000 women were released from Ravensbrück that day and transported to freedom in a fleet of buses of the Swedish, Danish and International Red Cross, leaving about 2000 sick in the women's camp together with some who volunteered to remain behind to look after them.

Meanwhile in the Berlin bunker Hitler had broken down and admitted for the first time that the war was lost. The immediate trigger was the failure of SS-Obergruppenführer Felix Steiner, commanding what had been a reserve army group near Eberswalde rather under thirty miles north-east of the capital. Steiner's forces had been decimated in the fighting over the past weeks and his SS-Panzergrenadier divisions transferred to fill gaps in other sectors; his 'Eleventh Panzer Army' consisted now of little more than a headquarters staff, a police division, naval ratings sent by Dönitz, Luftwaffe ground staff, Hitler Youth armed with hand weapons and fewer than fifty tanks, many without fuel. Whether Hitler realised the extent of the attrition or not, he had ordered Steiner to advance towards Berlin and hurl himself on Zhukov's right flank, then fastened in the northern suburbs of the city. Steiner simply did not obey. Hitler, waiting with rising expectation for news of his attack, sent out repeated requests for information until in the middle of the afternoon situation conference on the 22nd word came that Steiner had not moved. The effect was electric. The blood drained from Hitler's face and he flopped back in his chair trembling. His appearance and manner suggested a stroke or a heart attack. Moments later he ordered all adjutants and aides out. Only Keitel, Jodl, Krebs, General Burgdorf – Hitler's chief military adjutant – Bormann and the stenographer, Gerhard Herrgesell, remained with him, and they witnessed an extraordinary scene as, alternately shouting and sobbing, suffused with colour or blanched, he released the pent-up tensions of months: he had been betrayed, the war was lost, the Third Reich a failure; he would give up the supreme command and merely conduct the battle of Berlin to its end; he would not surrender, but shoot himself; anyone who wanted to leave could do so.[8] There were naturally many versions of this tirade, which lasted hours; according to the stenographer Herrgesell the cause and central theme was not simply betrayal but betrayal by the Waffen-SS; 'he said that he was losing confidence in the Waffen-SS for the first time. He had always counted on the Waffen-SS as elite troops who would never fail him.'[9]

This was the message Fegelein phoned through to Himmler, back again at Hohenlychen after evacuating Ziethen Castle, apparently after news of the extent of the Russian advances: the Führer was raging that the Wehrmacht had deceived him all along, now the SS was leaving him in the lurch. The report had deeper meaning for Himmler than Fegelein could have guessed, for he had at last taken the decision to betray Hitler himself – at least he had despatched Schellenberg that afternoon to Lübeck, where he hoped he would find Bernadotte. He was to tell the Count that he (Himmler) was prepared to ask him officially and in his own name to take a message of surrender to Eisenhower.[10] Now, however, he phoned Hitler and urged him once more to leave the city before it was too late. No doubt he assured him of his loyalty. No doubt he tried to probe Hitler's mood and discover whether he seriously intended abdication and suicide; despite his recent fall from grace he still considered himself the natural heir.

Afterwards he called Fegelein and arranged to meet him at Nauen on the main road into Berlin from the west some twenty miles from the city centre for a fuller discussion of the significance of the outburst. Professor Gebhardt, who wished to go to the capital to be confirmed by Hitler as head of the German Red Cross – a post he hoped would provide useful cover with the allies – accompanied him in another car. Apparently, Fegelein did not appear at the rendezvous, and Himmler, unwilling or fearing to visit the bunker in person, sent Gebhardt on to offer the Führer the 600 men of his escort battalion for the defence of Berlin. By the time Gebhardt arrived and gained audience, Hitler had recovered sufficiently to show him where he wanted Himmler's men stationed. Before leaving, the Professor asked him whether he had any message for the Reichsführer.

'Give him my love,' was the delphic reply.[11]

Schellenberg eventually caught up with Count Bernadotte next day, 23 April, near the Danish border at Flensburg, and persuaded him to see Himmler that night at Lübeck. They met at the Swedish Embassy there at 11.00 p.m. but were immediately forced down to the cellars by an air-raid. The electricity supply was cut off and Bernadotte, surveying Himmler by candle-light, was struck by his appearance of 'indescribable' exhaustion and nervousness. He seemed to be struggling hard to keep up a façade of calm.[12]

It was midnight before they were able to leave the cellar and start the discussion, still by candle-light. Himmler said that on the last three occasions they had met, although the situation of the Reich had been hopeless, he had been unable to break his oath to the Führer and attempt to stop the fighting. Now, however, the position was different. Hitler was in Berlin, determined to die with its inhabitants, indeed it was probable that he was already dead – and if not he would certainly be dead within the next few days. He would have died in the struggle to which he had devoted his existence, the fight against Bolshevism.[13]

In this new situation, he went on, he had a free hand. In order to protect as much of Germany as possible and prevent further bloodshed, he was prepared to capitulate on the western front and allow the Anglo-American forces to advance eastwards. And he asked Bernadotte to transmit this message to the Swedish government so they could convey it to General Eisenhower.[14] 'To capitulate to the Russians, however, is impossible for us Germans and particularly for me. We shall continue fighting them until the front of the western powers has replaced the German front.'[15]

Bernadotte could not accept that the west would consider separate peace talks, but he agreed to take the proposal to his government provided Himmler included Norway and Denmark in the capitulation, and allowed the Scandinavian prisoners concentrated at Neuengamme to be taken to Sweden by the Red Cross transports. Himmler agreed and, after consultation with Schellenberg, wrote a brief note for Bernadotte to hand to the Swedish Foreign Minister. It was absolutely non-committal, referring simply to 'a number of problems which I had the opportunity of discussing with him [Bernadotte] today'.[16] It is by no means impossible that he and Schellenberg were still seeking to precipitate the long-expected break-up of the enemy coalition for both knew probably better than Bernadotte that the western powers would neither consider a separate peace nor negotiate with Himmler. More probably it was sheer desperation. After leaving the meeting at about 1.30 in the morning of the 24th, Himmler, who was driving his heavy armour-protected car himself for some reason, started off so quickly that he went straight into a ditch and barbed-wire entanglement, and all of them, including Bernadotte, struggled for some fifteen minutes to get the vehicle back on the road.[17]

Meanwhile the official heir-apparent, Göring, who had flown south to Berchtesgaden, had drawn the same conclusions from Hitler's outburst of the 22nd. He also believed that the only course of action was capitulation in the west while continuing the fight in the east – indeed this was common currency throughout the government and military leadership – but where Himmler went about it in serpentine secrecy, he wired Hitler direct: '*Mein Führer!* In view of your decision to remain at your post in the fortress of Berlin do you agree that I take over, at once, total leadership of the Reich with full freedom of action at home and abroad . . . ?'[18] He was incautious enough to fix a time limit of ten that night, the 23rd; if by then he had received no reply he would assume Hitler had lost freedom of action and would consider himself, as his official deputy, fully empowered to act.

The early deadline set by Göring, and Himmler's remark to Bernadotte that Hitler was probably already dead, indicate that, under the influence of the reports from the bunker, both expected Hitler to shoot himself sooner rather than later. However, Hitler had relapsed into what was probably amphetamine-induced tranquillity after the storm of the previous day, and resumed direction of his make-believe armies as if nothing had happened. Bormann was able to use Göring's wire to persuade him that the Reichsmarschall was usurping his authority and was guilty of high treason. In view of his earlier services to the Party, Hitler was not willing to order the death penalty, but he did agree that Göring should be stripped of all offices and his title of Deputy Führer. Bormann drafted a suitable message and it was sent off about the time Himmler steered nervously out of Lübeck in the dark.

No one in the top leadership had taken Göring seriously for a long time, least of all Himmler. Dönitz's adjutant, Kapitän zur See Walther Lüdde-Neurath, recorded him making a Reichsmarschall joke at the Admiral's dinner table the previous October. '*Donnerwetter!*' Göring was supposed to have said in the wake of the 20 July attempt. 'If that had succeeded I would have had to handle things.' This had brought shouts of laughter; then Himmler, suddenly serious, had turned to Dönitz, 'However, one thing is certain, Herr Grossadmiral, the Reichsmarschall will in no wise be the successor.'[19] Despite his low standing, Göring's removal left Himmler the obvious choice to succeed. He certainly believed it himself. He constructed a shadow Cabinet in his mind, and discussed its composition with Dönitz, who agreed to serve under him, and with von Krosigk, Ohlendorf and no doubt ministers like Speer, who had come north to Dönitz's new headquarters at Plön, between Lübeck and Kiel. Since it was evident that the allies would not treat with Nazis, he decided on a new name for his administration, the Party of National Concentration (Nationale Sammlungspartei). He even took the chair at a military conference after Keitel and Jodl moved out of Berlin to establish Wehrmacht headquarters in the north at Rheinsberg.[20]

Churchill and the new President of the United States, Truman, predictably dismissed Himmler's offer of capitulation in the west and, suspecting another attempt to split the alliance, informed Stalin. When this news was conveyed to Schellenberg he set about arranging yet another – the fifth – meeting between Himmler and Count Bernadotte. However, before that could take place the secret of the negotiations was out. Churchill's Foreign Secretary, Eden, attending a conference at San Francisco, mentioned it to the British Director of Information Services, Washington, who passed it to a colleague at Reuters and on the 28th it was broadcast around the world.

Bernadotte heard it that afternoon while listening to the British 'black' propaganda station Radio Atlantik. It was also picked up at naval headquarters and Dönitz immediately called Himmler. It would be surprising if he had not learned of the talks long since as he and Himmler had conferred almost daily since the Admiral's move to Plön[21] and they had an identical view of the overall position. Dönitz was still conducting the massive naval evacuation of civilians and troops caught on the Baltic coast behind the Russian advance. According to his account Himmler denied the story, but said he was not going to issue a public statement. What Himmler may have said was that he could not meet Bernadotte again until the fate of the Führer were known. That is speculation but he did not go to the meeting Schellenberg arranged, once more in Lübeck. Schellenberg went alone to meet Bernadotte with Himmler's permission to negotiate on a limited capitulation in Scandinavia.

It was nine that evening before the sensational news of Himmler's earlier negotiation was received in the Führer bunker. It was picked up on Stockholm Radio by one of Goebbels' staff, and handed to Bormann. At the time Hitler was talking to Ritter von Greim, an Air Force general whom he had ordered to Berlin so that he could promote him field marshal and appoint him Commander-in-Chief of the Luftwaffe in succession to the deposed Reichsmarschall. Von Greim, an ardent National Socialist, had flown himself in on the final leg through heavy Russian flak with the rather more ardent aviatrix Hanna Reitsch as passenger – a reckless adventure that had cost him the use of his right foot. Now, three days later, he was still recovering from his wound in the bunker.

When the message was handed to Hitler, the eruption was spectacular. It was the ultimate betrayal – 'der treue Heinrich', longest-serving paladin, chief of his own guard, beside whom all other traitors paled. Hanna Reitsch described him raging like a madman with puce, distorted face and shuffling up and down the corridor of the bunker thrusting the scarcely credible report at everyone he met, all of whom reacted in an equally hysterical or stunned fashion. Finally Hitler retired to discuss the sensation with Bormann and Goebbels.[22]

It seems that the first result of the discussion was the execution of Fegelein. He had been arrested the previous day for two days' absence from the bunker situation conferences. When discovered he was at the flat off the Kurfürstendamm in which he kept his mistress. In the confusion she made her escape, but the arresting officer seized a travelling bag which they had been packing together and this was found to contain a chamois pouch packed with diamonds and other precious stones, jewellery, three gold watches, Reichsmarks, Swiss Francs and false passports. It was not difficult to deduce that he was planning flight. Hitler stripped him of his rank, and he was handed to 'Gestapo' Müller. In his account of the last days in the bunker, James O'Donnell speculates that Fegelein was handed to the Gestapo rather than summarily court-martialled and shot because Hitler and Bormann believed they had at last found the source of leaked intimate information about the personalities around the Führer which had been broadcast for months by the British black propaganda station – namely Fegelein's mistress.[23] However this may be, Fegelein's life was forfeit by the time the news of Himmler's treachery reached the bunker, and he was executed that night – whether because he was a convenient and obvious target for Hitler's wrath at the Reichsführer, whether, as some accounts have it, because under interrogation he admitted to knowledge of Himmler's treachery, or whether it was because he was believed to be the source of the leaked information will probably never be known.

Afterwards Hitler went into the room where von Greim was lying and ordered him to fly out of the capital, first to organise a Luftwaffe attack on the Russian positions now less than a mile from the Chancellery, second to order Himmler's arrest: 'A traitor must never succeed me as Führer,' he said, his voice hoarse and shaking, lips trembling.

There is a manic surrealism about these last hours in the Führer bunker only surpassed by the real horrors outside. Youths of the Volkssturm, veterans of Himmler's escort battalion, smooth-faced sea cadets and midshipmen from Kiel, and SS units raised in Scandinavia, Belgium, France and the east – 'bewildered young men dragooned from half of Europe', as one of the doctors operating in the emergency casualty station in the cellar of the new Reich Chancellery described them[24] – fought with hand weapons against overpowering matériel odds as the Russians blasted their way towards the city centre with artillery and air power, devastating everything in their path, pulverising the already cratered streets and fractured buildings into unrecognisable heaps and smouldering pits; the defenders were torn, smashed, pulped in the demolition. Minor casualties were forbidden to leave their posts – and most did not for fear of the summary court martial teams and the grisly evidence of their presence hanging from lampposts; those dragged or carried into the overflowing hospitals and cellar casualty stations were usually unconscious and in need of major surgery. Doctors, steeped in blood and dazed with lack of sleep and the ever-lengthening queues of mutilation, heard from those able to speak of the now hopeless battle; 'the younger ones, many under sixteen, were terrified and bawling.'[25] Civilian casualties far outnumbered the military, and the prior stark fear of the women survivors found frightful realisation. Primitive and drunken bands of Red soldiery on the search for prey roamed ruins and cellars where the recently dispossessed huddled for shelter in the dark. The lowest estimate for the number of rapes reported was 90,000; the real figure must have been far in excess.[26] The official figure for suicides in April was 6400.[27]

After the new Field Marshal and Luftwaffe Commander-in-Chief had been assisted up the bunker steps on crutches accompanied still by his dauntless *Genossin*, Hanna Reitsch, thence into an armoured car that was to take the pair to an aircraft waiting on the broad avenue leading to the Brandenburg Gate, Hitler married Eva Braun. She wore a short black dress with gold clasps at the shoulder straps, apparently Hitler's favourite outfit, and looked serenely happy. One of Goebbels' *Gau* inspectors, wearing brown Party uniform with a Volkssturm armband, performed the simple ceremony for a 'war couple' in the small conference room with Goebbels and Bormann as witnesses. Afterwards the bridal pair were joined for champagne and sandwiches in the study next door by Goebbels and Bormann, Krebs, Burgdorf, Hitler's secretaries and other bunker residents, including Frau Goebbels, who had come earlier in the week with her six children to live and end their lives there. The talk became nostalgic.

In the middle of the party Hitler disappeared with a secretary; he was more concerned with his plans for suicide and posterity than with the ceremony by which he had rewarded Eva's devotion, so shining beside Göring's and Himmler's hollow protestations, and he began to dictate his testament. It was similar in some ways to Himmler's exculpations: during the more than thirty years since he had volunteered for the First World War, which had been forced upon the Reich, he had been actuated solely by love and loyalty to his people. 'It is untrue that I, or anyone else in Germany, wanted war in 1939. It was desired and instigated solely by international finance conspirators of Jewish blood or working for Jewish interests. . . .'[28]

After lengthy restatement of his political creed, he dealt with the succession:

I expel from the Party the former Reichsmarschall, Hermann Göring. . . . In his place I appoint Grossadmiral Dönitz as Reichspresident and Commander-in-Chief of the armed forces.

Before my death I expel from the Party and from all his offices the former Reichsführer-SS and Reich Interior Minister, Heinrich Himmler. In his place I appoint Gauleiter Karl Hanke as Reichsführer-SS and chief of the German police, and Gauleiter Paul Giesler as Reich Interior Minister. . . .

Bormann's influence is discernible here, although the surprising decision to appoint Dönitz as his successor must have been maturing in Hitler's own mind for some time. It was the Grossadmiral's reward for his fanatical, in the last months blind, devotion, support and optimism that triumphed over every setback. Goebbels was named as Reich Chancellor, Schörner Army Commander-in-Chief, Bormann Party Minister.

Finally Hitler returned to his earliest obsession: 'Above all I enjoin the leadership of the nation and adherents to scrupulous observance of the race laws and merciless resistance to the world-poisoner of all peoples, international Jewry.'

By the time the testament was ready for signing it was four in the morning of the 29th. He also made a private will, in which he paid tribute to Eva Braun, who 'of her own free will entered this city which was already besieged, in order to share my fate. At her own desire she goes to death with me as my wife. . . .'[29]

Later that morning copies of the political testament were entrusted to reliable officers who were instructed to break through the Russian cordons in the city and take them to Dönitz and the new Army Commander-in-Chief, Schörner. In the afternoon Hitler had his Alsatian, Blondi, put down with poison, an unmistakable sign that his own suicide was close, and gave cyanide capsules to his two secretaries; he wished, he told them, that his generals had been as reliable as they.

That evening at the situation conference the Kommandant of Berlin, General Weidling, described a hopeless position with ammunition running out, no air drops, the Russians within the government quarter and only four blocks from the Chancellery; he believed the fighting must come to an end within twenty-four hours and asked permission for his forces to attempt a mass break-out. Hesitant with reluctance, Hitler gave permission for small groups to try – only to withdraw it later. He still retained faint hopes of relieving 'armies' supposed to be closing on the capital. At one the next morning, the 30th, even this was extinguished: a message from Keitel indicated that all these forces were on the defensive or encircled. Evidently Keitel had gone over to the traitors and was holding the generals back deliberately, so it was perceived in the underground imagination. Bormann wired Dönitz with a Führer order to proceed at once, ruthlessly against all traitors. Hitler and Eva Braun committed suicide together that afternoon, 30 April. Afterwards the corpses were carried up to the garden, laid side by side and soaked with petrol; Russian artillery sounded nearby as the petrol was ignited and Bormann, Goebbels and the few other witnesses to the funeral spontaneously stiffened in the Hitler salute.

In his testament Hitler had explained his new appointments as necessary 'to give the German people a government of honourable men to fulfil the duty of continuing the war with all means'. Goebbels and Bormann, the new Chancellor and Party Minister, despatched a message to Dönitz that evening to inform him that he had been appointed Hitler's successor in place of Göring – without telling him that Hitler was already dead – then made contact with the Russians and arranged for General Krebs and an interpreter to pass through the lines to negotiate a cease-fire. The aim, as they told General Weidling that night, was to inform Stalin and only Stalin of Hitler's death, and arrange a local cease-fire in order to allow the new government to assemble in Berlin and capitulate to the Soviets.[30] Krebs set off early the following morning, 1 May, arriving at the forward command post of General Chuikov shortly before four. Directly he told him of Hitler's suicide and read out the testament naming the new government, Chuikov telephoned his chief, Marshal Zhukov, who phoned Moscow and roused Stalin. Stalin forbade discussion with Krebs 'or any other Hitlerites'; Krebs was informed that the only terms were unconditional capitulation to the USSR, USA and England.

Krebs continued to argue doggedly for Soviet recognition of the new German government and an armistice for negotiations, but hours of circular talk returned always to the same block: the Russians would only accept unconditional surrender to all the allied powers. Krebs could not deliver this since Dönitz, the new head of government, knew nothing of the latest events in Berlin.[31]

It was not until that afternoon, after Krebs had returned to report in person on his fruitless talks, that Goebbels and Bormann accepted that their bid to split the enemy coalition had failed and sent Dönitz news of Hitler's death: 'Führer died yesterday 15.30 hours. Testament of 29.4 transfers to you the office of Reichspresident. . . . Reichsleiter Bormann intends coming to you today to clarify the position. . . .'[32]

That evening Frau Goebbels administered poison to her six children, and some time afterwards she and the little club-footed doctor climbed the bunker steps and emerged into the darkness of the garden, where they took poison together. Like Hitler, Goebbels shot himself in the temple as he bit on his capsule.

Such is the story of the last two days in the bunker as it has emerged from the residents who survived and from the Russian records of Krebs' conversation and the messages sent. How much accords with the legend Goebbels wished to foster, how much is hearsay from rumour or even fabrication will remain debatable.

Bormann and the others (apart from Krebs and Burgdorf, who committed suicide) now prepared to break out in small groups through the Russian ring and from the city – at which point Martin Bormann disappeared from the historic record.

Himmler had received the first indications of his banishment on 29 April when von Greim and Hanna Reitsch – having cheated the Russian gunners by taking off *with* the wind over the Brandenburg Gate, just clearing the heroic statuary – flew in to Plön and informed Dönitz that the Führer had ordered the Reichsführer's arrest for treason. There was little Dönitz could do: Himmler had a substantial entourage of high SS officers and a large part of his formidable escort battalion. After the war the adjutant responsible for his security, SS-Sturmbannführer Heinz Macher, himself a much decorated fighter of the dreaded division Das Reich, described these men as 'the most piratical, bravest and experienced warriors to be found in all Germany'.[33] Besides, Dönitz needed all the organs of internal security and intelligence that Himmler still controlled in the northern zone and in occupied Norway, Scandinavia and Holland, and the units he controlled by virtue of his position as Chief of the Replacement Army and the Volkssturm.

It is evident that they were co-operating closely. Macher recalls that Himmler visited Dönitz's headquarters practically every day, driving over with a detachment of his escort in a motorcade from headquarters he had established in the police barracks, Lübeck. He was at Plön again on the 30th, the day after von Greim arrived. Top of the agenda for discussion was the response that should be made to the Gauleiter of Hamburg, who had expressed the determination to spare the city further destruction by surrendering it to Montgomery's troops – if necessary leading his people against any German forces sent to stop him. After the discussion Dönitz sent a message to the Gauleiter stressing the vital importance of holding the line of the Elbe against the western allies. Since the Russians were expected to sweep on westwards beyond the demarcation line of their zone as agreed at Yalta, this suggests that Himmler was still seeking to provoke the break-up of the enemy coalition, and Dönitz was accepting his political judgement.

It was while Himmler was driving back to Lübeck after this meeting, slowed by constant enemy air attacks and the streams of refugees and disheartened troops foot-slogging on all roads, that Dönitz received the astonishing news he had been appointed Hitler's successor. Albert Speer, who was with him when his adjutant, Lüdde-Neurath, brought in Bormann's message, appeared equally stunned and took a moment or two to recover sufficiently to offer his congratulations. That, at least, is the story perpetuated after the war, although Speer more or less admitted that Hitler had probed him on his opinion of Dönitz's suitability during their penultimate conversation in the bunker.[34] Dönitz told Lüdde-Neurath to request Himmler's presence at once, meanwhile to take the necessary precautions. His own precaution, according to his memoirs, was to hide his pistol under papers on his desk, safety catch off.[35] The implication is that, despite the graphic descriptions brought by von Greim and his intrepid mistress of the scenes in the Führer bunker when Himmler's treachery had become known, Himmler was still behaving as the obvious successor, and was still regarded as such in the northern area, as indeed all memoirs agree.

Lüdde-Neurath sought out Korvetten-Kapitän Ali Cremer, who was in command of the U-boat men guarding the headquarters, and told him to be prepared for anything. 'Himmler will not like our chief becoming the Führer's successor.' Cremer stationed his men behind trees around the building.[36]

Directly Himmler saw Dönitz's summons after his return to Lübeck, he called Macher. 'This I don't like. We've just left him. Something must have happened. Please take enough men.'[37]

Macher picked out thirty-six of his most reliable, battle-hardened veterans and they drove back to Plön in a convoy of armoured troop carriers and open Volkswagens. It seems probable that they arrived about midnight. The blacked-out buildings were just visible in the faintest moonlight. Macher sensed that all was not as it should be, and jumped out alone. A single officer walked out to meet him, the glint of the Knight's Cross at his throat; it was Cremer. Half-turning, Macher made out the shapes of the men Cremer had stationed in the trees. 'Oh God, those poor bastards!' he thought. 'We'll blow them away with the greatest of ease.'[38]

It did not come to it. After friendly greetings Macher and Cremer and five large SS men escorted Himmler to the building, where Lüdde-Neurath conducted him to Dönitz's room and left the two together. What was said will never be known. By Dönitz's post-war account he simply handed Himmler Bormann's message and watched as his face paled with surprise and dismay.

He had evidently taken a seat for after a moment's consideration he rose, bowed to congratulate Dönitz and said, 'Allow me to be the second man in your government.' There could be no question of that, Dönitz replied. He had no use for him. Himmler then tried to convince him of the advantages he would gain by having him in his administration. Dönitz was 'amazed by his belief that he had great resonance abroad'.[39]

It is difficult to understand why Himmler should have been surprised by the message since von Greim had left no doubt that he was considered a traitor in Berlin and barred from the succession. The rest of the opening vignette is entirely credible. He must have been shocked that the successor was Dönitz, a political innocent, whom he was advising. Yet he would have accepted it; the habit of obeying Führer orders was ingrained. No doubt he displayed that old-world formality mixed with geniality which gave an impression of aloofness – or, as Speer expressed it, behind which he sheltered from familiarity.[40] And no doubt he offered his services because he had convinced himself, as most memoirs agree, that his intelligence and police functions would be indispensable to any German government accepted by the allies. Whether Dönitz refused him curtly is another matter. It was not a decision he had to make at once. Neither of them knew that Hitler was dead, indeed Bormann's earlier message enjoining Dönitz to proceed at once, ruthlessly, against all traitors, had ended: 'The Führer is alive and conducting the defence of Berlin.' Both thought he was still doing so for at 1.22 in the morning, after they had been talking for an hour or so, Dönitz broke off the discussion to send a reply to the wire from Bormann which had occasioned the meeting:

> '*Mein Führer!* My loyalty to you will be unshakeable. I will therefore undertake further attempts to relieve you in Berlin. If fate nevertheless compels me to lead the German Reich as your appointed successor, I will conduct this war to an end befitting the uniquely heroic battle of the German *Volk*. Grossadmiral Dönitz.[41]

Whatever was discussed at that late-night meeting, it was not the comparatively short affair Dönitz suggested in his memoirs. They resumed talking after this wire was sent while Macher and two other SS officers drank Hennessy brandy with Lüdde-Neurath and Cremer in the canteen, and dawn was up before they broke off for breakfast. Before travelling back to Lübeck the SS party met von Greim and Hanna Reitsch, who took the opportunity to berate Himmler for betraying the Führer. 'That is high treason, Herr Reichsführer,' she said after asking for a private word.

'High treason? No. You'll see, history will evaluate it differently. Hitler wanted to continue the fight. He was mad with his pride and his honour. He wanted to shed more German blood when there was none left to flow. Hitler was insane. It should have been stopped long ago.'

'Hitler died bravely and honourably,' she retorted, 'while you and Göring and the rest must now live branded as traitors and cowards.'

'I did what I could to save German blood and rescue what was left of our country.'[42]

It is not surprising that Schellenberg, who reported back at Lübeck that morning, 1 May, found Himmler 'in the worst possible mood. He was playing with the idea of resigning, and was even talking of suicide.'[43] When Schellenberg tried to discuss his negotiations over Denmark and Norway Himmler was too nervous and distracted to listen; in any case, he said, he could no longer take any action. Instead he took Schellenberg with him to Plön to report on his talks.

It is evident from this account as well as from the record of their subsequent meetings that Dönitz had not told Himmler he had no use for him;[44] had he been sacked, Himmler would not have talked of resigning. He was, of course, indispensable, particularly in the present situation. The people and the majority of the troops in the north were as disaffected by the continuing futile struggle and the daily strafing by allied aircraft as the Gauleiter of Hamburg. To maintain the fight as Dönitz clearly intended – both out of loyalty to his Führer, and so that he could continue his naval rescue of Germans from the east and from undoubted Red Army atrocity, internment and, as he believed, slavery – he needed the fearful sanctions dispensed by Himmler's organisations, SD, Gestapo, Geheime Feldpolizei. He did not shrink from them. His naval police, nicknamed *Kettenhunde* (chain-dogs) from chains of office around their necks, were as notorious as Himmler's flying court martial teams: trees along the plains of Brandenburg and Holstein bore their terrible warnings: 'Here hangs a traitor who by his cowardice allows German women and children to die instead of protecting them like a man.'

Himmler and Schellenberg arrived at Dönitz's headquarters at two in the afternoon of 2 May; Dönitz invited them to lunch. Himmler brought the news that the Gauleiter of Hamburg was still determined to surrender the city,[45] and Albert Speer, who was present, offered to drive over and attempt to dissuade him. His mission was overtaken by events as British tanks were reported in the streets of Lübeck. They had broken out of a bridgehead across the Elbe at Lauenburg, some twenty-five miles south-east of Hamburg, and raced north to the Baltic coast in order to prevent the Russians advancing across the base of the Schleswig-Holstein–Danish peninsula and so reaching the North Sea – the very possibility Himmler had been hoping to exploit to prise the alliance apart.[46]

A hasty evacuation northwards was imperative – Plön was scarcely thirty miles from Lübeck – and Dönitz ordered the transfer of his headquarters to the Navy Cadet School, Mürwik, near Flensburg, hard up against the Danish border and beyond the line of the Kiel Canal, which would provide a defensible tank ditch. Meanwhile it had been decided to send a delegation under Generaladmiral von Friedeberg to Montgomery to offer a local capitulation of German forces in the north. It was a tactic to get around the west's refusal to accept one-sided surrender while still buying time to rescue the German troops and civilians trapped in the east.

Dönitz arranged to meet von Friedeberg to give him his instructions personally at the Levensau Bridge over the Kiel Canal that evening on his way north, and took with him von Krosigk, whom he had decided to appoint Foreign Minister. Himmler told Schellenberg that he had persuaded Dönitz to make this appointment during their all-night discussion. It was his final triumph over von Ribbentrop. The meeting was delayed as Dönitz's car was strafed by low-flying aircraft which forced him and von Krosigk to jump out and dive for the ditch.

The SS headquarters motorcade, also making for Flensburg, was caught in a full-scale air-raid on Kiel. The leader of the Belgian Waffen-SS travelling with the convoy in a Volkswagen driven on potato Schnapps has left a vivid picture of SS generals, police Führers, staff and secretaries throwing themselves over garden walls in blind confusion while Himmler, wearing a leather crash helmet and sitting in the driving seat of his heavy Mercedes at the head of the column, shouted '*Discipline*, gentlemen! *Discipline!*'[47]

Later that night Himmler was joined in his car by Dr Werner Best, one of the intellectuals Heydrich had recruited for the SD in the early days, now Minister Plenipotentiary in Denmark. During their discussion about Schellenberg's negotiations and the policy to be adopted for the occupied Scandinavian countries, Himmler said he was certain that if he had been allowed even half an hour with Eisenhower he could have convinced him of the necessity of joining forces with them to drive the Russians back.[48] Forced by the threat from the air to make a detour, it was three next morning, 3 May, before he finally steered his column into Flensburg. He asked Best to take the SS women staff with him across the border into Denmark so that they could have a wash and something to eat before returning to work.

Best was back across the border later that morning to attend a conference Dönitz had called at his new headquarters in the Cadet School, Mürwik. Berlin had capitulated the previous afternoon; German forces in Italy had surrendered. US and British troops had shaken hands with the Russians in the north and in the centre of the country. The main question on the agenda was whether Dönitz should shift his headquarters to Denmark or Norway – or even Prague – to continue the struggle from outside the Reich. The Reich Commissar for Norway, Josef Terboven – who had begun his Party career in 1927 as the plant of the ultra-reactionary coal baron, Emil Kirdorf – the Commanders-in-Chief of Norway and Denmark and Keitel and Jodl believed that he should. Werner Best, Speer and von Krosigk argued against it. Dönitz deferred any decision until he had heard the result of von Friedeberg's armistice proposals but he sent his trusted right hand from the U-boat war, Admiral Godt, and his son-in-law Günther Hessler on a special mission to spy out the land in Norway.

Von Friedeberg returned late that night with Montgomery's answer:

he was prepared to accept the surrender of all forces on his western and northern flanks – Holland, Friesland, Schleswig-Holstein and Denmark – but not Army Group Vistula fighting the Red Army on the eastern front. Dönitz called a meeting of his Cabinet next morning, 4 May, to discuss the terms. Himmler drove up in his Mercedes and escorting staff cars in the panoply of Reichsführer-SS and chief of the German police and argued that Holland and Denmark should not simply be given up; they and Norway were valuable trump cards which could be used to bargain for concessions. He was supported by Jodl, who was convinced that the enemy coalition must break up now that Germany was about to be partitioned and they should fight on until this happened.[49] Their arguments did not persuade the meeting. On the one hand there were too many indications of disaffection among troops and civilians – threatened uprisings and mutinies; on the other hand Montgomery's conditions seemed to fulfil the twofold aim of saving further bloodshed and destruction in the west while allowing them to carry on the struggle against the Russians in order to bring more Germans from the east into the western zone. Probably it had simply been borne in on Dönitz, now that the Führer's death had had time to sink in, that further struggle was pointless. It is even probable that, like his chief civilian advisers, Speer and von Krosigk long before, he had seen a chink of light in the west and had begun to think of working his passage that way.

At all events he sent von Friedeberg back to Montgomery's headquarters to sign the surrender of German forces in the stipulated areas, and that evening after hearing from him that the cease-fire had been concluded, to take effect at eight o'clock the following morning, 5 May, he sent out the necessary instructions to military and naval commanders. After his fanatic edicts and rhetoric of fighting to the last man, Dönitz's sudden conversion to reason came as such a surprise that some naval officers suspected that the enemy had penetrated the code and sent a fake signal.

For Himmler, the cease-fire in the north marked the end of the road. His life's work was finished; as he had told Kersten, only ruins remained. He had lost his Führer, thus the clear guiding principle – above all he had lost his Führer's trust. The mystical symbol of authority had passed to Dönitz. There is ample testimony to his confusion in the weeks leading up to this moment, but surrounded by his entourage and the realities of title, uniform and power he had played up to the part expected of him. Now that Dönitz had given up the struggle against the west there was no more he could do. Hitler was no longer there to give him the ultimate backing he had always expected in crises. Moreover the oath which all members of the armed forces had pledged to the Führer was now due to Dönitz as his legitimate successor. Dönitz had claimed it in his first address to the armed forces immediately after his accession on 1 May. That was the trump card, and it was the card played by Himmler's enemies, and all those around Dönitz desperate to avoid charges of war crimes by shifting the odium on to the SS and the person of the Reichsführer.

Now Dönitz told Himmler he had to go. How he did it and whether he explained that it was necessary because he had to distance his government and the German armed forces and people from the crimes of the regime will never be known, nor how easy or difficult Himmler made it for him. Perhaps this was the time Himmler tried to convince Dönitz of his great resonance with the west. But he went quietly. In January he had written to his doubting Propaganda officer, d'Alquen, 'one is only at the end if one is beaten in the heart.' This was his position now.

Still he did not let it show. The following evening, 5 May, the day of the cease-fire, he gathered his entourage, including Ohlendorf, Hans Prützmann of Werwolf, Rudi Brandt, his brother Gebhard, many departmental chiefs, police and Waffen-SS leaders, Rudolf Höss, formerly Kommandant of Auschwitz, and gave a final, farewell speech. There is no written record, and the subsequent accounts are contradictory. That given by his first biographer, Frischauer, who probably heard it from Gebhard Himmler, is perhaps the most likely. Himmler hinted that destiny had a great new task for him but did not say what it was. He would have to undertake the task alone, but a few of them might accompany him.[50]

Rudolf Höss described this speech, but only as it affected him. He did not mention any task, certainly not Werwolf. 'There was no more talk of fighting,' Höss wrote. 'Save yourself, who can, was the watchword.'[51] He could scarcely believe his ears or eyes. The world had fallen in, 'our world', yet there was Himmler, beaming and in the best of humour telling them to go into hiding.

> If he had said: '*So, meine Herren*, it is over, you know what you have to do,' that I would have understood – that would have conformed to what he had been preaching for years to the SS: self-sacrifice for the idea. *So* however he gave us our last order: 'submerge in the Wehrmacht!' That was the dismissal from the man, whom I had looked up to so much, in whom I had such firm faith, whose orders, whose remarks were gospel to me. . . .[52]

He and a colleague, Maurer, looked at one another dumbly. Yet each had his family to think of, and they obeyed this last command, Höss wrote. No doubt they were relieved that there was to be no final suicidal stand. They had already been provided with false papers and positions in various arms of the Wehrmacht; the Concentration Camp Inspectorate seems to have 'submerged' *en masse* in the Navy. Höss's chief, Glücks, went to a naval hospital post; Höss became Bosun's Mate Franz Lang in the Navy Signal School on the island of Sylt. Like the others he carried a phial of cyanide with him.[53]

Himmler had provided himself with the papers of a former sergeant in the Geheime Feldpolizei named Heinrich Hitzinger; the real Hitzinger had been executed for defeatism. He carried at least two phials of cyanide and had had a hole drilled in his molars to take one of them. No doubt all these preparations had been made ostensibly for Werwolf. There can be no doubt that he was clear about his fate and those of his chief accomplices should they fall into enemy hands.

Von Krosigk and Ohlendorf claimed afterwards that they told him his duty was to go straight to Montgomery and take the responsibility on his own shoulders for all that the SS and indeed the Nazi regime had done. Von Krosigk, once a Rhodes Scholar at Oriel College, Oxford, from whence he had returned to Germany a convinced Fabian socialist, had served Hitler faithfully from 1933 onwards – until the collapse; Ohlendorf, whom Himmler called the keeper of the Holy Grail of Nazism, had led one of the most infamous Einsatzgruppen in mass murder in Russia. If they did advise Himmler to give himself up it was an impertinence. Apparently he told them that political developments would favour him. He would go into hiding and await them.[54] This sounds likely, and he was, of course, correct about the cold war. One of his female secretaries, Doris Mehner, who had had cause to be grateful for his thoughtfulness in the early morning of 3 May – when he had asked Werner Best to take the secretaries across the border for a bath and breakfast – recalled that when he said farewell and thanked her for her services, he told her to go back to Bavaria and rest. They would soon meet again; then there would be a great deal of work to do.[55] He was still convinced that, after the inevitable split between east and west, he and his organisation would hold the balance for order in central Europe. Whether this was the schizoid flight from reality or whether he was simply preserving face before his followers must remain speculative, but there seems little doubt that he did maintain a most extraordinarily confident public front.[56]

Von Friedeberg meanwhile had been despatched to Eisenhower's headquarters at Rheims to try and arrange a similar local cease-fire with the Americans in the central and southern sectors. He was told that surrender must be unconditional to all the allied powers simultaneously. When he reported this early on 6 May Dönitz sent Jodl to Rheims. He got equally short shrift from General Bedell Smith, acting for Eisenhower. The Americans had liberated Buchenwald concentration camp recently, and were under the influence of the nauseous scenes there. Photographs had been published in the service paper *Stars and Stripes*; von Friedeberg was given copies to take back to Flensburg with him and Jodl was given an hour to obtain authority for unconditional surrender, failing which the talks would be broken off. When this message was received from Jodl, the most obstinate advocate of continuing the fight in the east, Dönitz and his Cabinet finally gave up. At 2.30 in the morning of 7 May, Jodl signed the formal end of the war on all fronts, effective from midnight, 8 May. The allied celebration parties were already under way.

Dönitz and his colleagues had one final task – to distance themselves and the armed services from the crimes of the regime they had served. 'We have nothing to be ashamed of,' Dönitz decreed. 'We stand without a spot on our honour as soldiers and can with justice appear full of pride and honour. . . .'[57] And a few days later – after Keitel had been arrested – Jodl stressed to his staff that their attitude to the enemy powers had to be:

> They [the enemy] have conducted the war for the sake of the [international] law. Therefore we wish to be handled according to the law. We must continually point out international law to the allies. . . . We should stress to the allies the point at which our compliance in matters of the capitulation treaty ceases, that is if our honour should be attacked. . . .[58]

As part of this unsavoury humbug – which was carried on for the next twenty or thirty years, indeed to this day, with such easy success that it must have astounded and perhaps even convinced the perpetrators themselves – the most notorious of Hitler's ministers had to be formally rejected. Thus Dönitz had letters of dismissal typed out for Goebbels, Bormann, Rosenberg, still Minister for the Occupied East, Thierack, Minister for Justice, and Himmler. Whether Himmler received his is doubtful; it was found in Dönitz's desk, unsigned, after he and his 'government' had been unceremoniously rounded up on 23 May and transported to prison cells:

> Dear Herr Reichsminister – In view of the present situation, I have decided to dispense with your further assistance as Reich Interior Minister and member of the Reich government, as Commander-in-Chief of the Replacement Army, and as Chief of Police. I now regard all your offices as abolished. I thank you for the service which you have given to the Reich.[59]

After Hitler, whose death was as yet unknown to the western allies, Himmler was the most wanted Nazi, and there were many rumours that he had been sighted, or was making his way with a picked SS band to the mountains. He was, it seems, lying low in Flensburg with Häschen Potthast, his two children, Ohlendorf and others including Professor Gebhardt, who described him in later testimony as 'so lonely' in this final period during the British occupation.[60] On 10 May, he left Häschen and, accompanied by Brandt, Ohlendorf, Professor Gebhardt, Heinz Macher and his military adjutant, Werner Grothmann, set out by car to make his way to Bavaria,[61] thence, according to Stroop, to join those many other SS-Führers who had gone south-east to establish Werwolf in the Alps. Certainly Hans Prützmann preceded him and, according to Stroop, organised the crossing of the Elbe.

Here they had to leave the cars and continue on foot, mixing in the straggles of refugees and soldiers making their way home, sleeping in the open or in railway stations or farmers' haylofts. Himmler had shaved off his moustache, donned a black patch over his right eye and wore the uniform of a sergeant in the Geheime Feldpolizei; his two adjutants were disguised as privates in the same organisation – a hierarchy that was, perhaps, indicative of his need to be superior. In the event it led to his downfall, for the Geheime Feldpolizei was one of the organisations on the allied black list, and sergeants and above were subject to automatic arrest. Another thing Himmler did not know was that British intelligence had been tipped off by the Danes that he was making his way south to Bavaria, and they were on the lookout.

His disguise, although theatrical, was effective, no doubt because the patch broke up the distinctive dark line of his brows. Nevertheless, on 21 May, he and his two adjutants were arrested as members of the Geheime Feldpolizei at a British control point near Bremervörde, midway between Hamburg and Bremen. They were transported to a camp at Westertimke, near Bremen, searched and interrogated. Himmler was not recognised, but since he and his party had come from Flensburg and possessed notes issued in Flensburg, they were sent to an interrogation centre at Barfeld, near Lüneburg, where those with even remote knowledge of the Nazi leadership were concentrated.[62] He and his two adjutants arrived there at some time after noon on the 23rd.

Himmler had still not been recognised – at least by the British – but he now declared himself. Why he did so remains a mystery. The answer probably lies in the state of his mind rather than any external pressures from fellow prisoners or his adjutants or the fear of discovery.

In schizoid theory it was entirely predictable. The pressures had mounted to such an extent that his real, inner self was attempting as a last, desperate defence not so much suicide as murder of that 'false self' which it was observing.

On a non-analytical, commonsense level it can be imagined that after nearly a fortnight on the run, sleeping rough, then caught and subjected to the humiliations of search and interrogation, bundled into army trucks as a completely undistinguished prisoner, Himmler's sense of his worth and dignity was outraged; perhaps he simply needed to assert his status. He had been under immense nervous strain, with the necessity of keeping up a confident public face for months; he may just have snapped. Or the realities of captivity under enemy occupation may at last have broken into the illusion of his underground 'mission' in the Alps, although not, it seems, his illusion of his 'resonance' with the allies.

It was lunchtime, by the recollection of one of the intelligence officers at Barfeld camp, Chaim Herzog – later President of the State of Israel – when the Sergeant-Major reported to the commanding officer, Captain Selvester, that three of the newly arrived prisoners were insisting on seeing him; one claimed to be Heinrich Himmler. Selvester went to his office and had the men sent in. As he recollected twenty years later, one was small and ill-looking, the other two tall and bearing themselves like soldiers – Grothmann and Macher. Sensing something unusual, he ordered the two large ones taken away and held apart from the other prisoners. The smaller one then removed an eye-patch he was wearing and put on a pair of spectacles. 'His identity was at once obvious,' Selvester recalled, 'and he said, "Heinrich Himmler" in a very quiet voice.'[63] The story as it reached Chaim Herzog was that he stood to attention and said, 'Ich bin der Reichsführer-SS.'[64]

Selvester then sent for an intelligence officer to interrogate him, and called Montgomery's chief of intelligence, Colonel Michael Murphy, at Second Army headquarters, Lüneburg. While waiting for Murphy to drive over, Himmler's signature was tested against a facsimile, and he was stripped and given a full body search. Two small brass cases were found in his clothes, one containing a glass phial which he claimed was medicine for his stomach cramps. Selvester assumed it was poison and guessed the phial from the empty case was in his mouth. Hans Prützmann, who had been captured earlier, had committed suicide by biting on a poison capsule two days before, and no doubt Selvester had heard about it. In any case he ordered thick bread and cheese sandwiches and tea for Himmler and watched him closely as he ate. He noticed nothing.

Murphy had given instructions that Himmler was not to be interrogated before he arrived. Nevertheless, the intelligence officer could not resist showing him pictures of the piled corpses and living skeletons found at Buchenwald and asking for his comments.

Himmler countered with the question, 'Am I responsible for the excesses of my subordinates?'[65]

Since all concentration camp Kommandants, officials and guards captured had pleaded superior orders for their actions, this brought the question of responsibility full circle.

Selvester had a British Army uniform brought in for Himmler in place of the uniform he had been living in for days, but he refused it, apparently worried that he would be photographed wearing it; all he would accept were boots, socks, underpants and a shirt, around which he wrapped an Army blanket.[66] Selvester, watching him keenly over the period of hours he was in his custody, found it 'impossible to believe that he could be the arrogant man portrayed by the press before and during the war'.[67] Himmler showed himself concerned for his two adjutants, asking repeatedly about their whereabouts, and seemed quite prepared to talk, and almost jovial at times. His main object, it appeared, was to gain an interview with Montgomery or even Churchill to offer his organisation to stem the Russian advance threatening western Europe.

Chaim Herzog recalls that Himmler could easily have passed for a small, anonymous clerk but 'his eyes, it was noted at the time, were steely and bereft of all expression.'

Colonel Murphy arrived at about eight that evening and had Himmler taken out unceremoniously in his blanket and bundled into his car. According to Herzog, Murphy was 'using all forms of epithets including "Come on you bastard!" or "We'll teach you!"'[68] Himmler probably did not understand the colloquialisms but the abusive manner must have been unmistakable. He was driven to Second Army headquarters outside Lüneburg, where an interrogation centre had been established in a red-roofed villa, No. 33

Uelznerstrasse, whose windows looked out through limes bordering the street to the pine forests of Lüneburg Heath. There, in a room on the first floor, Sergeant-Major Austin gave him much the same treatment. Austin had been looking after Hans Prützmann in this same room when he had committed suicide, and both he and Murphy were very conscious that Himmler was probably carrying the second poison phial in his mouth. He pointed to a couch and ordered him to strip.[69]

Himmler stared, according to the account Austin gave the press the following day, saying 'He does not know who I am.'

'Oh, yes I do,' Austin replied. 'You're Himmler. *Ausziehen!* Get undressed!' Himmler continued trying to stare him out, then lowered his gaze, sat on the couch and undressed. He was subjected to another thorough body search by a Second Army doctor, C.J.L. Wells, who told him to open his mouth. Wells saw a small black knob protruding between a gap in his teeth on the lower right-hand side.

'Get up and come closer to the light,' he said, indicating the window.

Himmler did as he was told, and opened his mouth again. Wells was about to put his fingers inside over the black knob – the stopper of a glass phial of potassium cyanide – when Himmler jerked his head away to the side, flicked the phial out with his tongue and crushed it between his teeth. Did images of Bavaria flood the timeless moment as the poison stunned his nerve centres . . . *Das Brauneck dort so freundlich schaut, zum Geigerstein als seine Braut* . . . 'What a miserable creature is man. . . . The heart is turbulent until it rests in the ground' . . .

He was jumped by Austin and Colonel Murphy, who up-ended him on the floor and held his feet high while Wells gripped his throat. He had already lost consciousness. Emetics and a stomach pump were tried, but at some time during the undignified struggle over the next fifteen minutes his life left him – the official time of death was 11.04 p.m., 23 May. A naked, awkwardly shaped body lay on the floor surrounded by splashed water, buckets and swabs, the detritus of the fight to save him – and the red-faced officers who had let their prize catch slip away perhaps looked at one another in justified confusion. Himmler was transmuted in his favourite analogy to a link in the eternal chain between ancestors and future generations, a pulse in the German blood – in the bloodstream of Europe and mankind.

Two days later Sergeant Austin baled his corpse in camouflage netting, tied it round with Army telephone wire, dropped it in the back of a lorry and drove off to inter it on Lüneburg Heath. He dug the grave himself. 'Nobody', he reported, 'will ever know where he is buried.'[70]

The few belongings Himmler had had with him on his last journey were distributed among the intelligence staff at headquarters. Niall MacDermot of counter-intelligence had his black eye-patch and glasses. The glasses were thick; it was clear he had been very short-sighted. The case bore a Munich optician's name. MacDermot kept them for several years until, coming across them one day, in a moment of disgust he threw them in the rubbish bin.[71] He presented the eye-patch to the chief of Danish intelligence to thank his service for their assistance. It can be seen in Copenhagen, a reminder of the improbable manner in which Himmler, when all around sought to disclaim any association with him, also chose to deny the Reichsführer-SS.

Reference Notes

Documents are detailed by their box and piece number (Imperial War Museum, London), their reel and frame (Fr.) number (US National Archives microfilm), or class and piece number (Bundesarchiv, Koblenz).

Books are detailed by author (or editor) and page number, or by author, key word or words from title, and page number if an author has more than one book listed in the select bibliography.

The following articles are also detailed by author and page number only:

Angress & Smith   W.T. Angress and B.F. Smith, 'Diaries of Heinrich Himmler's Early Years', *Journal of Modern History*, XXXI, March–December 1959, pp. 206 *ff.*

Hallgarten   G.W.F. Hallgarten, 'Mein Mitschuler Heinrich Himmler', *Germania Judaica, Bulletin der Kölner Bibliothek zur Geschichte des deutschen Judentum*, No. 2, 1960/1, pp. 4–7.

Loewenberg   P. Loewenberg, 'The Unsuccessful Adolescence of Heinrich Himmler', *American Historical Review*, 76(3), 1971, pp. 612 *ff.*

The following abbreviations are used:

BA	Bundesarchiv, Koblenz
DC	Document Centre, Berlin
F/Vorträge	C-in-C Kriegsmarine (Navy) reports and discussions with the Führer (microfilm Nav. Lib.)
G.H.	Gebhard Himmler, H.H.'s brother
Gruf	SS-Gruppenführer
HD	Himmler documents, Hoover Institution on War, Revolution and Peace, Stanford University, Calif., USA
H.H.	Heinrich Himmler
H.H. book list	in BA *Nachlass Himmler/II Leseliste*
H.H. diary	in HD, Hoover Institute, Stanford University
IfZ	*Institut für Zeitgeschichte*, Munich
IMT	International Military Tribunal; evidence and documents presented at the trials of the major war criminals, published Nuremberg, 1948; English language edition (unless otherwise stated)
IWM	Imperial War Museum, London
MGM	*Militärgeschichtliche Mitteilungen* (journal of military history)
NA	US National Archives, Washington DC
Nav. Lib.	Naval Library, Ministry of Defence, London
PRO	Public Record Office, Kew Gardens, London
RFSS	Reichsführer-SS, Heinrich Himmler
Stuf	SS-Sturmbannführer
T–175	Microfilm class at NA (Fr. = frame number)
VJHZ	*Vierteljahreshefte für Zeitgeschichte* (quarterly journal of contemporary history)
Wiener Lib.	Wiener Library, London

Chapter 1: Background

1 H.H. diary, 15.12.1919
2 Kersten diary, 12.9.1944; cited A. Besgen, *Der stille Befehl*, Munich, 1960, p. 35
3 H.H. diary, 15.7.1910
4 Trevor-Roper, *Witch Craze*
5 Ibid., p. 39
6 Ibid., p. 53
7 Kamen, pp. 16 *ff*
8 J. Mitchener, *Spanish Travels and Reflections*, New York, 1968, pp. 190–1
9 Kamen, pp. 126 *ff*
10 Ibid., pp. 162–5
11 M. Reich in *Die Zeitung* (exile paper), London, 25.5.1945 (Wiener Lib.)
12 H.H. diary, 24.11.1921
13 Guntrip, p. 37
14 Laing, p. 73
15 Guntrip, p. 38
16 Laing, p. 82
17 M. Wallace, 'Schizophrenia', *The Times*, London, 20.1.1986
18 Ibid., 3.3.1986
19 Guntrip, p. 21
20 Ibid., p. 63
21 H.H.diary, 1.12.1921
22 Ibid., 11.11.1919
23 Smith, pp. 113–14
24 H.H. diary, 5.2.1922
25 Guntrip, p. 58
26 H.H. diary, 20.10.1919
27 See Guntrip, p. 38
28 See E. Conze, *Buddhist Thought in India*, Allen & Unwin, 1962, p. 87
29 Guntrip, p. 191
30 Andersch, opening sentence (p. 13)
31 Ibid., pp. 16–17
32 Ibid., pp. 116–17
33 Kamen, p. 162
34 Trevor-Roper, *Witch Craze*, p. 38

Chapter 2: Youth

1 Hallgarten, p. 5
2 Andersch, p. 61
3 Hallgarten, p. 5
4 Smith, p. 21
5 Ibid., pp. 24–5
6 Frischauer, p. 17
7 Andersch, pp. 47–52
8 Hallgarten, p. 5
9 Frischauer, p. 16
10 Ibid., p. 15
11 H.H. diary, 13.7.1910
12 Hallgarten, p. 4
13 Ibid., p. 6
14 Ibid.
15 Ibid.
16 Loewenberg, p. 616
17 H.H. diary, 17.7.1912

18 Ibid., 29.7–5.8.1914
19 Ibid., 23.8.1914
20 Ibid., 30.8.1914
21 Ibid., 28.9.1914
22 Ibid., 2.10.1914
23 'Franzosen, Franzosen, O gebt nur recht acht
Für Euch wird no Pardon gemacht.
Uns're Kugeln pfeifen und sausen
Und verbreiten Euch Schrecken und Grauen
Wenn wir da so unheimlich hausen.'
Cited Smith, p. 63
24 Ibid., p. 43
25 H.H. diary, 16.8.1915
26 Smith, p. 51
27 Ibid., p. 52
28 Ibid., p. 53
29 Ibid., pp. 56–7
30 29.11.1918; HD Roll 98, folder 2; cited ibid., p. 59
31 Ibid., p. 60
32 A. de Tocqueville, *Democracy in America*, Schocken Books, New York, 1961 (6th edn 1974), I, p. 515
33 P. Roubiczek, *Existentialism For and Against*, Cambridge University Press, 1964, p. 131
34 *Die Tüchtigkeit unserer Rasse und der Schutz der Schwachen*, Berlin, 1895
35 See Nowak, p. 20
36 Cited A. Dorpalen, *Heinrich von Treitschke*, Yale University Press, 1957, pp. 232, 149
37 See B. Russell, *The History of Western Philosophy*, Allen & Unwin, 1946, p. 795
38 See Pools, p. 8
39 See G. Franz, 'Munich: Birthplace . . . of the National Socialist German Workers' Party', in *Journal of Modern History*, XXIX (4), December 1957, p. 325
40 Prof. Gebhardt testimony in *Doctors' Trial*, Nuremberg, IX, p. 3958 (IWM)
41 See Nowak, p. 22; Ackermann, pp. 196–7
42 Andersch, p. 61
43 H.H. diary, 24.9.1919
44 Ibid., 2.11.1919
45 Ibid., 7.11.1919
46 Ibid., 17.11.1919
47 Ibid., 18.11.1919
48 Ibid., 19.11.1919
49 See Heygate, p. 40
50 H.H. diary, 19.11.1919
51 Ibid., 28.11.1919
52 Ibid., 8.12.1919
53 Ibid., 27.12.1919
54 Ibid., 19.10.1919

55 See Smith, p. 79
56 Thewelweit, p. 61
57 Ibid., p. 434
58 H.H. diary, 4.11.1919
59 Ibid., 1.12.1919
60 Ibid., 21.12.1919
61 Ibid., 24.12.1919
62 Ibid.
63 Ibid.
64 H.H. book list, No. 36
65 Ibid., No. 23; and see Smith, p. 74; Ackermann, p. 25
66 H.H. diary, 15.12.1919
67 Ibid., 26.12.1919
68 3.3.1920; HD Roll 98, folder 2; cited Smith, p. 90
69 H.H., G.H., I. Zahler to Himmler parents, 24.3.1920; ibid.
70 H.H. diary, 24.11.1921
71 H.G. Adler; cited Ackermann, p. 25
72 H.H. book list, No. 47
73 Ibid., No. 51; cited Smith, p. 91
74 By J. Howald; book list, No. 61; see Smith, p. 59
75 By Mayrhofer; book list No. 59; see ibid.
76 Ibsen, p. 20
77 H.H. diary, 27.5.1922
78 Ibsen, pp. 86–7
79 Ibid., p. 222
80 H.H. book list, No. 65
81 H.H. diary, 6.11.1921
82 Lu Zahler to H.H., 22.11.1920; T–175, Roll 99, Frs 2619999 *ff*
83 Kaethe Loritz to H.H., 6.12.1920; ibid., Frs 2619888–91
84 H.H. quotation collection; HD Roll 98, folder 2; cited Smith, p. 107
85 H.H. diary, 1.11.1921
86 Ibid., as dated
87 Ibid., 29.1.1921
88 Loewenberg, p. 635; see also Angress & Smith, p. 210
89 H.H. diary, 26.1.1922
90 Ibid., 11.11.1921; 22.2.1922; 24.2.1922; see Smith, p. 113
91 H.H. diary, 5.2.1922
92 Ibid., 28.11.1921
93 Ibid.
94 Ibid., 3.7.1922
95 Ibid., 27.5.1922
96 H.H. book list, No. 106
97 H.H. diary, 9.6.1922
98 See G. Franz, op. cit. (ref. 39 above), p. 332
99 See Strasser, *Mein Kampf*, p. 35
100 H.H. diary, 24.6.1922
101 Ibid., 26.6.1922
102 Ibid., 29.6.1922
103 Heygate, p. 35
104 Ibid., p. 36
105 H.H. diary, 17.6.1922
106 Ibid.

Chapter 3: Revolutionary
1 See H.H. to SS-Gruf Pohl, 29.11.1941; Heiber, p. 89
2 7.11.1922; cited Smith, p. 130
3 Koehl, p. 13, estimates Nazi Party membership, summer 1923, as *c*.55,000; SA as max. 10,000 (München *c*.2000; Franken *c*.3000; Landshut *c*.1500; others *c*.3000)
4 Smith, p. 134
5 München, 13.4.1922; cited Bullock, p. 86
6 H.H. diary, 29.1.1921
7 Unfinished draft, Schleissheim, 18.4.1923; HD MA Roll 98, Hoover File No. 1
8 Weilheim, 6.7.1923; T–175, Roll 99, Frs 2620195–200
9 Weilheim, 4.3.1924; ibid., Fr. 2620204
10 Weilheim, 4.3.1924; ibid., Frs 2620205–6
11 München, 23.5.1924; ibid., Frs 2619757–9
12 München, 22.5.1924; ibid., Fr. 2619756
13 *The Times*, London, 12.11.1923
14 München, 13.6.1924; T–175, Roll 99, Fr. 2620053
15 Enclosed with above, Fr. 2620049
16 E. Weckerle to G.H., 1.8.1924; *IfZ* microfilm MA 320–234; cited Ackermann, p. 27
17 H.H. to H. Gärtner, 25.1.1924, annex to Gärtner's 2.2.1937 report for the Honour Book of the Old Guard; BA NS 26/1222; cited Ackermann, p. 37
18 H.H. book list, No. 205
19 Ibid., No. 190
20 Ibid., No. 191
21 H.H. diary, 17.2.1924
22 H.H. book list, No. 181
23 Ibid., No. 189
24 Smith, p. 141
25 H. Günther, *Ritter, Tod und Teufel*, Munich, 1920 p. 143; cited Ackermann, p. 111
26 Fermor, p. 104
27 H.H. book list, No. 202
28 Ibid., No. 220
29 Ibid., No. 180
30 Ibid., No. 171
31 Ibid., No. 176
32 Ibid., No. 207
33 Ibid., No. 208
34 Ibid., No. 43
35 Ibid., No. 148
36 Ibid., No. 175

37 Ibid., Nos 193, 196; see Smith, pp. 143–4
38 H.H. diary, 24.2.1924
39 Ibid., 15.2.1924
40 Ibid., 20.2.1924
41 Ludecke, p. 206
42 Ibid., p. 209
43 Bullock, p. 207
44 *The Times*, London, 2.4.1924
45 H.H. book list, No. 276
46 See Stachura, p. 33
47 München, 13.6.1924; T–175, Roll 99, Frs 2620050–3
48 P.C. rec'd 16.7.1924; ibid., Fr. 2619948
49 Andersch, p. 60
50 München, 13.8.1925; T–175, Roll 99, Fr. 2620374
51 München, 7.9.1925; ibid., Fr. 2620377
52 To R. Kistler, 22.8.1924; HD Roll 98, folder 1
53 München, 2.8.1924; T–175, Roll 99, Frs 2620060–1
54 Ibid., Fr. 2620055
55 Ibid., Fr. 2620057
56 Ibid., Fr. 2620058
57 Strasser, *Mein Kampf*, p. 15
58 Ibid.
59 Manvell & Fraenkel, p. 256; Smith, p. 159
60 25.11.1925; cited Stachura, p. 42
61 H.H. book list, No. 220
62 Ibid., No. 216
63 Ludecke, p. 258
64 He did not receive his Party No., 14,303, until 2.8.1925, why this late is not clear; see Aronson, p. 266, note 74
65 Ludecke, p. 259
66 Smith, p. 52
67 Ludecke, p. 268
68 Ibid.
69 Manvell & Fraenkel, p. 256, note 13
70 A. Wykes, *Himmler*, Pan Books, London, 1973; no reference cited, but it sounds in character.
71 H. Heiber (ed.), *The Early Goebbels Diaries*, Weidenfeld & Nicolson, 1962, p. 116; cited Manvell & Fraenkel, p. 17
72 13.4.1926, ibid., p. 78; cited ibid., p. 16
73 Aktenvermerk 16.12.1939; T–175, Roll 88, Fr. 2611405
74 Aktenvermerk, Berlin, 19.12.1939; ibid., Fr. 2611406
75 Allen (ed.), p. 266
76 'Die Lage der Landwirtschaft', *NS Briefe*, 1.4.1926
77 Stachura, p. 69
78 Broszat (ed.), p. 54, note 2

79 See Höhne, *Death's Head*, pp. 23–4; Koehl, p. 22
80 To Forstamtmann Roschatt, 17.7.1926; T–175, Roll 99, Fr. 2620089
81 Ibid., Fr. 2620090
82 Ludecke, p. 93
83 15.2.1926; Lochner (ed.), p. xx
84 6.11.1925; ibid., p. xvi; see also 16.6.1926, ibid., p. xvii
85 6.7.1926; ibid., p. xvii
86 Andersch, p. 60
87 See Smith, pp. 161–2
88 *Befehl* No. 1, 13.9.1927; DC Sch. 425; cited Aronson, p. 48
89 Ibid.
90 Ibid.
91 Strasser, *Mein Kampf*, p. 44
92 H.H. book list, No. 247
93 Ibid., No. 262
94 Strasser, *Mein Kampf*, p. 45
95 H.H. book list, No. 235
96 Ibid., No. 269b
97 Hesse, *Siddhartha*, p. 138
98 Ibid., p. 166
99 Backdated to 6.1.1929; see Koehl, p. 32
100 Allen (ed.), p. 266
101 A. Krebs, *Tendenzen und Gestalten der NSDAP; Erinnerungen*, Deutsche Verlags Anstalt, Stuttgart, 1959, p. 210
102 Ibid.
103 Cited in Höhne, *Death's Head*, p. 50

Chapter 4: Reichsführer-SS

1 See Abraham, p. xviii; D. Geary in Stachura (ed.), pp. 90 *ff*
2 Cited Pools, pp. 151–2
3 Fromm, p. 31
4 Calic, p. 6
5 4.12.1931; cited Stachura, p. 92
6 17.10.1930; cited ibid., p. 55
7 Strasser, *Mein Kampf*, p. 64
8 Ibid., p. 65
9 Berghahn, p. 24
10 St. A Potsdam, Bd 2170, Rep 37, Gutsarchiv v. Arnim-Beitzenburg, B1 36f; cited Gossweiler, p. 244
11 Strasser, *Mein Kampf*, p. 45
12 Ibid.
13 Aronson, p. 51
14 Ibid., p. 53
15 Höhne, *Death's Head*, p. 68
16 Führerbesprechung der SS-Gruppe Ost; DC Sch. 425/3; cited Aronson, p. 53
17 Ibid., pp. 53–4
18 Cited Gossweiler, pp. 263–4
19 Reproduced in Ackermann, pp. 262–3
20 Moczarski, p. 126
21 Ibid., p. 127
22 Cited Aronson, p. 258, note 29

23 Cited Calic, p. 24
24 Aronson, p. 24
25 Cited ibid., pp. 23–4
26 Ibid.
27 Ibid., p. 259
28 See p. 56
29 DC SS-Pers.-Akt. Heydrich; cited Aronson, p. 311
30 Cited Aronson, p. 38
31 Ibid., p. 35
32 See Calic, pp. 58–9
33 v. Lang, p. 65
34 W. Best, Aufzeichnungen, 1.10.1949; BA; cited Calic, p. 85
35 See Koehl, p. 56
36 See Calic, pp. 88 *ff*
37 List in Aronson, pp. 318–19
38 Berghahn, p. 5
39 Koehl, p. 53
40 Gossweiler, p. 288
41 H. Frank, *Im Angesicht des Galgens*, Munich, 1953, p. 108; cited Stachura, p. 106
42 Ibid.
43 See Calic, pp. 101 *ff* citing Hans-Peter von Heydebreck
44 IMT PS–3337; cited Gossweiler, p. 295
45 Ibid., pp. 205–6
46 See Gossweiler, pp. 206 *ff*; Abraham, p. xxxvii; Pools, p. 464
47 Cited Bullock, p. 222
48 Cited ibid., p. 224
49 See Calic, p. 129
50 Aktenvermerk: T–175, Roll 88, Fr. 2611416
51 30.1.1933; Fromm, p. 72
52 Aktenvermerk; T–175, Roll 88, Fr. 2611416
53 2.2.1933; Fromm, p. 72
54 Cited Diels, p. 81
55 Aronson, p. 154
56 Fromm, p. 73
57 *The Times*, London, 28.2.1933
58 Diels, pp. 192 *ff*
59 Cited Diels, p. 194
60 See for instance Fromm, p. 74; Calic, p. 113
61 Fermor, p. 130
62 DC SS-Pers.-Akt. Heydrich; cited Aronson, p. 311
63 Diels, p. 91
64 Cited Berben, opp. p. 1

Chapter 5: Night of the Long Knives
1 Frischauer, p. 46
2 See Aronson, pp. 113–14
3 Eicke to H.H., 10.8.1936; cited Aronson, p. 106
4 Broszat (ed.), p. 67
5 Ibid., p. 58

6 See B. Bettelheim, *The Informed Heart*, Illinois, 1960, p. 225
7 Broszat (ed.), p. 61
8 Ibid., p. 60
9 Diels, p. 135
10 Ibid., p. 136
11 Frischauer, p. 45, states that Himmler's library indicates that he was seeking inspiration from Torquemada and Fouché.
12 File note of Staatsanwalt Stepp, 6.12.1933; cited Aronson, p. 326
13 Aronson, p. 131
14 Berben, p. 62
15 Ibid., p. 4
16 See ibid., pp. 231–4
17 Broszat (ed.)., p. 56
18 Berben, p. 114
19 Ibid., pp. 112–13
20 Cited Aronson, p. 169
21 Strasser, *Mein Kampf*, p. 45
22 OSAF Order 1403/33, 8.9.1933; cited Aronson, p. 326
23 v. Lang, pp. 362–3
24 Heiber, p. 20
25 Moczarski, pp. 103–4
26 Ibid., p. 104
27 Heiber, p. 20
28 Frischauer, p. 62
29 5.4.1939; v. Hassell, p. 55
30 14.3.1934; cited Aronson, p. 326
31 Führertagung SS-Oberabschnitt E, Breslau, 19.1.1935; B NS 19/1092
32 29.12.1933; BA NS 19/271; cited Ackerman, p. 72
33 Diels, p. 92
34 Ibid., p. 408
35 Ibid., pp. 409–12
36 Ibid., p. 379
37 Ibid., p. 385
38 Ibid., p. 386
39 v. Lang, p. 34
40 Lützows' notes; cited Diels, p. 416
41 18.12.1938; v. Hassell, p. 39
42 O.v. Heydebreck to E. Calic; cited Calic, p. 146
43 Ibid., p. 147
44 Stachura, p. 123
45 Overy, p. 30
46 See Gossweiler, p. 433
47 Ibid., p. 276
48 See ibid., p. 270; Vogelsang, p. 154
49 See Vogelsang, pp. 149–50
50 See Aronson, p. 154
51 Führerbesprechung der SS-Gruppe Ost; DC Sch. 425/3; cited Aronson, p. 53
52 See Abraham, pp. 217–18; Gossweiler, p. 464
53 Winterbotham, p. 54

54 Ibid., pp. 82–8
55 See discussion in Padfield, pp. 140–2, 148–50
56 Bülow to v. Neurath, 16.8.1934; cited Gossweiler, pp. 475–6
57 Cited Gossweiler, p. 276
58 v. Lang, p. 31
59 28.11.1933; cited Gossweiler, p. 16
60 Gisevius, *Bitter End*, p. 149
61 Koehl, p. 98
62 A. Boyle, *Montagu Norman*, London, 1967, p. 194
63 Noakes (ed.), p. 208
64 Cited Gossweiler, p. 451
65 *Weissbuch*, p. 52; cited Gossweiler, p. 429
66 Cited Gossweiler, p. 439
67 Cited ibid., pp. 493–4
68 Koehl, p. 99
69 Cited Noakes (ed.), pp. 211–12
70 Ibid., p. 212
71 Diels, p. 423
72 Dr Kloeppel's statement: DZAP R Md I 25 794/3 299F; cited Gossweiler, p. 552
73 v. Lang, p. 34
74 Gisevius, *Nebe*, p. 144
75 Gisevius, *bitteren Ende*, pp. 215–16
76 See Koehl, p. 100; Hohne, *Death's Head*, p. 121
77 Gisevius, *Bitter End*, p. 167
78 See Koehl, pp. 100–1; Gisevius, *Nebe*, p. 146
79 2.7.1934; cited Gossweiler, p. 157
80 v. Lang, p. 40
81 Koehl, p. 317
82 Der Reichsverteidigungsminister, Berlin, 24.9.1934; IWM F2 AL 2704 E313
83 Gisevius, *Nebe*, p. 154
84 To the Gestapo, 11.10.1934; T–175, Roll 89, Frs 1536 *f*; cited Smith, Petersen (eds), pp. 58–60
85 Stachura, p. 124
86 Gisevius, *Bitter End*, p. 146

Chapter 6: Chief of the German Police
1 19.1.1935; T–175, Roll 89, Frs 1507–8; cited Smith, Petersen (eds), pp. 53–4
2 See v. Lang, p. 86
3 19.1.1935; op. cit. (ref. 1 above), Fr. 1502
4 Schellenberg, p. 72
5 Cited Höhne, *Death's Head*, p. 165
6 Moczarski, p. 111
7 See T–175, Roll 88, Frs 2611342 *ff*
8 Ibid., Frs 2611302 *ff*
9 22.5.1936; T–175, Roll 89, Frs 1558 *ff*
10 To SS-Gruf Besprechung, 8.11.1936; BA NS 19/HR 3; cited Ackermann, p. 248

11 Circular to SS officers, SS Leitheft, 8.12.1937; cited Ackermann, p. 72
12 Undated plan of RFSS; BA NS 19/320; cited Ackermann, p. 253
13 To SS-Oberführer Dr Wacker, 23.7.1938; BA NS 19/neu 1705; cited Ackermann, p. 46
14 14.8.1938; IWM H/13/16
15 See v. Lang, p. 46
16 Winterbotham, p. 138
17 8.11.1936; op. cit. (ref. 10 above)
18 Prof. Gebhardt's testimony, *Doctors' Trial*, Nuremberg, IX, p. 3981
19 Roberts, p. 90
20 Transcript of the ceremony, 4.1.1937; v. Lang, pp. 43–4
21 At Reichsbauerntag, Goslav: IMT 1918–PS
22 RFSS, *Die Schutzstaffel als antibolschewistische Kampforganisation*, Zentralverlag der NSDAP, Munich, 1936, p. 9 (Wiener Lib.)
23 See Die Weltwoche, Zurich, 12.12.1947 (Wiener Lib.)
24 19.1.1935; op. cit. (ref. 1 above) Frs 1507–8
25 RFSS, *Schutzstaffel*; op. cit. (ref. 22 above), p. 3
26 Ibid., p. 5
27 Ibid., p. 6
28 Ibid., p. 15
29 Ibid., p. 20
30 Ibid., p. 24
31 Ibid., p. 29
32 Ibid., p. 31
33 Voltaire, *Candide*, Hodder & Stoughton, 1976, pp. 1–2
34 Winterbotham, p. 146
35 See R. Olden, *Hitler the Pawn*, Gollancz, 1936, p. 401
36 Winterbotham, p. 157
37 RFSS to Chef des SSHA, HA Ordnungspolizei, HA Sicherheitspolizei, 27.4.1938; IWM H/6/228
38 10.7.1937; Fromm, pp. 214–15
39 To Akademie für Deutches Recht, 11.10.1936; cited Ackermann, p. 142
40 Vogelsang, p. 88
41 Broszat (ed.), p. 177
42 Ibid.
43 IWM H/13/48
44 28.5.1938; IWM H/13/49
45 IWM H/13/50
46 4.6.1938; IWM H/13/54
47 See Krausnick and others, pp. 158–60
48 *Westdeutscher Beobachter*, 16.1.1937 (Wiener Lib.)
49 18.2.1937; T–175, Roll 89, Frs 1869 *ff*
50 See Diels, pp. 381–2
51 Heygate, p. 72

52 Ibid., p. 74
53 H.H. to Eckhardt, 25.12.1937; cited
   Heiber, pp. 45–6
54 See Ackermann, pp. 68–9
55 H.H. radio broadcast; *Westdeutscher
   Beobachter*, 16.1.1937 (Wiener Lib.)
56 See v. Lang, p. 58
57 See Berben, pp. 35–6
58 6.9.1938; Fromm, p. 243
59 Roberts, pp. 89–90
60 Schielke; cited Moczarski, p. 109
61 27.1.1937; cited Krausnick and others,
   p. 448
62 See Koehl, p. 135
63 14.12.1937; cited Ackermann, p. 143
64 8.11.1937; T–175, Roll 90, Fr. 2399
65 To A. Lehner, 18.5.1937; cited Heiber,
   p. 47
66 Koehl, p. 124
67 See Höhne, *Canaris*, pp. 178, 209
68 Ibid., p. 177
69 v. Lang, Sibyll (eds), p. 22
70 C. Burckhardt, *Meine Danziger Mission 1937–1939*, Munich, 1960, pp. 57–8;
   cited Calic, pp. 236–7
71 See Aronson, pp. 327–8
72 From SS Leitheft 3, 2 Jahrgang,
   22.4.1936; cited Ackermann, p. 159
73 Heydrich to Ch. der Sicherheitspolizei
   (and all State and Criminal Police),
   12.6.1937; IWM AL 2531/2
74 Heydrich order, 4.1.1937;
   BA R 58/990; cited Herbst, p. 105
75 Heydrich to SD-Führer der
   SS-Oberabschnitte, 4.9.1937;
   BA R 58/990; cited Herbst, p. 105
76 v. Lang, Sibyll (eds), p. 46
77 See Calic, p. 243
78 Prof. Dr K. Astel to RFSS, 14.6.1937;
   RFSS to Prof. Dr Astel; BA NS 19/176;
   cited Ackermann, pp. 284–6
79 Correspondence between Dr Gütt and
   H.H., Dr Wagner and H.H., January
   1938; IWM H/6/268–74
80 H.H. to M. Bormann, 26.4.1938; IWM
   H/6/67
81 1.5.1936; see Heiber, p. 44
82 See Heiber, p. 50
83 H.H. to SS-Stuf A. Graf Kottulinsky,
   16.9.1938; cited Heiber, p. 61
84 H.H. to A. Rosenberg, 27.7.1938 and
   15.12.1938; cited Heiber, pp. 58, 62
85 v. Lang, pp. 73–4
86 Cited in G. Lean; *Frank Buchman:
   A Life*, Constable, 1985, pp. 203–4
87 Ibid., p. 236
88 Roberts, pp. 89–90
89 22.5.1936; T–175, Roll 89, Frs 1565–6
90 8.11.1937; T–175, Roll 90, Fr. 2438
91 Frischauer, p. 75

Chapter 7: Expansion
1 'Hossbach' memo., 5.11.1937;
   IMT 386–PS
2 See A.E. Simpson, 'The Struggle
   for Control of the German Economy,
   1936–1937', *Journal of Modern History*,
   XXXI, March–December, 1959,
   pp. 37 *ff*
3 Undated file note; T–175, Roll 88,
   Fr. 2611415
4 See Overy, p. 56; Vogelsang, p. 152
5 W. Treue (ed.), 'Hitlers Denkschrift
   über die Aufgaben eines Vierjahres-
   planes', *VJHZ*, 3 (1955), p. 205; cited
   Herbst, p. 66
6 See Herbst, p. 67
7 Young, p. 30
8 Höhne, *Canaris*, p. 262
9 'Hossbach' memo.; op. cit. (ref. 1
   above)
10 See v. Lang, p. 80
11 Calic, p. 257
12 Gisevius, *Nebe*, pp. 273–4
13 See Höhne, *Canaris*, pp. 254 *ff*
14 Ibid., p. 255
15 See Gisevius, *Nebe*, p. 280
16 Beck, cited Hoffmann, p. 68
17 See Höhne, *Canaris*, p. 222
18 W. Canaris, 'Politik und Weltmacht',
   in R. Donnevert (ed.), *Wehrmacht
   und Partei*, Leipzig, 1938, p. 48; cited
   Höhne, *Canaris*, p. 224
19 See ibid., pp. 253–63
20 Simpson, op. cit. (ref. 2 above), p. 44
21 Jahreslagebericht 1938; Boberach, 2,
   p. 74
22 v. Lang, p. 85
23 Ibid., p. 86
24 Vogelsang, p. 54; Koehl, p. 142
25 Vogelsang, pp. 104–5
26 Overy, p. 113
27 See Höhne, *Canaris*, p. 275
28 Cited v. Lang, p. 86
29 Canaris' lecture, 'Die nationalpolitische
   Stellung des Offiziers . . .', 22.4.1938,
   IfZ F 6/1, p. 1; cited Höhne, *Canaris*,
   p. 283
30 See v. Lang, pp. 89–90
31 Boberach, 2, p. 79
32 M. Reich in *Die Zeitung* (exile paper),
   London, 25.5.1945 (Wiener Lib.)
33 3.7.1938; T–175, Roll 90, Fr. 2346
34 20.4.1938; IWM H/15/250, p. 1
35 Ibid., p. 2
36 Ibid., p. 3e
37 Ibid., p. 4g
38 3.7.1938; op. cit. (ref. 33 above), Frs
   2342–3
39 Henderson, p. 136
40 See Padfield, p. 165

41 See ibid., pp. 166–9
42 See Overy, pp. 85–6
43 Ibid., p. 86
44 Cited G. Schreiber, 'Zur Kontinuität des Gross- und Weltmachtstrebens der deutschen Marineführung', *MGM*, 2/1979, p. 126
45 See Young, pp. 132–3; Overy, p. 87
46 See M. Gilbert, p. 63
47 28.6.1938; Fromm, p. 235
48 E.g. Hitler, pp. 403, 444, 447, etc.
49 See Lifton, p. 50
50 Roberts, p. 265
51 See Olden; op. cit. (ref. 35, ch. 6), p. 393
52 Jahreslagebericht 1938; Boberach, 2, p. 21
53 Roberts, p. 264
54 Boberach, 2, p. 23
55 Einsatz des SD in Falle CSR [Czechoslovakia], Berlin, June 1938, p. 1; IWM AL 2570
56 Ibid., p. 7, 2c
57 See Hoffmann, pp. 112–21
58 Young, pp. 46–57
59 See Hoffmann, pp. 119–21
60 See v. Lang, p. 100
61 Gisevius, *Nebe*, p. 186
62 Moczarski, p. 121
63 Ibid., pp. 119–20
64 R. Byron's diary, 6.9.1938; *Spectator*, 22.8.1987, pp. 22–3
65 Ibid., 8.9.1938; in ibid., 29.8.1987, p. 22
66 Ibid., 11.9.1938; ibid.
67 v. Lang, p. 100
68 Aktenvermerk für Frl. Potthast, 18.2.1938; T–175, Roll 88, Fr. 2611412
69 See v. Lang, p. 185
70 Henderson, pp. 300–1
71 IMT 1780–PS; cited Bullock, p. 430
72 Cited Höhne, *Canaris*, p. 283
73 Goerdeler; cited Young, p. 135
74 Ibid., p. 120
75 Testimony Z. Grynszpan, Eichmann trial, 25.4.1961; cited M. Gilbert, p. 68
76 See instance in July 1942, cited in M. Gilbert, p. 713
77 8.11.1938 before SS-Gruppenführern; T–175, Roll 90, Frs 2585 *ff*
78 See v. Lang, p. 105
79 Berlin, 9.11.1938, 23.55 hours; IWM AL/2531/1
80 München, 10.11.1938, 01.20 hours; ibid.
81 Ogilvie-Forbes despatch No. 2, 16.11.1938; PRO FO 371/21637; cited M. Gilbert, p. 73
82 G. Treuhaft, 'The Darkest Hour', *The Times*, London, 7.11.1988
83 Blitz, Berlin, 1.11.1938, 14.30 hours; IWM AL/2531/1
84 Berlin, 12.12.1938, 20.00 hours; ibid.

85 Cited Calic, p. 285
86 'Die Aktion gegen die Juden am 9/10.11.1938'; Boberach, 2, p. 26
87 See M. Gilbert, p. 69; see G. Treuhaft, op. cit. (ref. 82 above)
88 'Die Aktion . . .', op. cit. (ref. 86 above)
89 27.11.1938; v. Hassell, pp. 31–2
90 Young, p. 152
91 Ibid., p. 234
92 Ibid., p. 236
93 Cited ibid., p. 327
94 20.12.1938; v. Hassell, p. 39
95 Ibid.
96 See v. Lang, p. 106
97 Kersten, pp. 294, 297
98 Frischauer, p. 121
99 Kersten, p. 294
100 Ibid., p. 109
101 Hestons, p. 35
102 Kersten, p. 300
103 Ibid., p. 301
104 Cited v. Lang, p. 193
105 *Daily Mail*, London, 17.4.1945 (Wiener Lib.)
106 Roberts, p. 89
107 Notes on RFSS visit to Wewelsburg, 15–18.1.1939; T–175, Roll 88, Fr. 2611409
108 Ibid.
109 H.H. speech, 2.7.1938, from unnamed German newspaper (Wiener Lib. Press archive PC4)
110 29.1.1939; T–175, Roll 90, Fr. 2492
111 Ibid., Frs 2494–5
112 Cited e.g. Calic, p. 554
113 P. Dukes, *An Epic of the Gestapo*, Cassell, 1940, p. 183
114 v. Lang, p. 117
115 SIS report, 18.3.1939; cited Aster, p. 74
116 Gisevius, *bitteren Ende*, p. 362
117 Stein, p. 26
118 Ibid., p. 14
119 8.11.1938; op. cit. (ref. 77 above)
120 Cited Bullock, p. 469

Chapter 8: War
1 Aster, p. 274
2 R. Byron's diary, 6.9.1938; *Spectator*, 22.8.1987, p. 22
3 Hitler, p. 444
4 Ibid., p. 317
5 Ibid., p. 347
6 Ibid., p. 772
7 Ibid., p. 447
8 Ibid.
9 Aster, p. 307
10 Nowak, pp. 77–8
11 Lifton, p. 62
12 Cited Fleming, p. 20

13　IMT 630–PS
14　Nowak, pp. 80–1; Lifton, p. 69
15　See Klee, pp. 83 *ff*
16　See ibid., pp. 84–5; and E. Klee (ed.);
　　Dokumente zur 'Euthenasie', Fischer
　　Verlag, 1985, pp. 69 *ff*
17　See for instance judgement of District
　　Court Hanover against
　　SS-Sturmbannführer K. Eimann,
　　20.12.1968 (2Ks 2/67) cited in ibid.,
　　pp. 70 *ff*; see Lifton, p. 78
18　Lifton, p. 63
19　IMT 798–PS
20　David Irving suggests that Himmler was
　　close to Hitler at this period and repro-
　　duces a fragment of Himmler's diary,
　　28.8.1939, in *The War Path* (Papermac,
　　1978), pp. 255–6. This fragment sug-
　　gests that Himmler contributed nothing
　　to Hitler's decisions; he seems merely to
　　have deferred to Hitler's genius at close
　　quarters.
21　Canaris' notes, 22.8.1939; cited Höhne,
　　Canaris, p. 387
22　Henderson, p. 337
23　Cited Höhne, *Canaris*, p. 349
24　See e.g. Calic, p. 299
25　Schmidt; cited Bullock, p. 505
26　Henderson, p. 287
27　Shirer, p. 161
28　Aufzeichnung, 3.9.1939, 1 Skl, Teil
　　CVII; PG 32183 (Nav. Lib.)
29　Broszat (ed.), p. 71
30　Schellenberg, p. 72
31　Ibid., p. 73
32　See Kersten, pp. 305–7
33　Ibid., p. 306
34　See v. Lang, p. 138
35　See Schellenberg, p. 75
36　See v. Lang, Sibyll (eds), p. 92
37　Ibid., pp. 92–3
38　Heydrich decrees, 3.9. and 20.9.1939;
　　cited Noakes, p. 136
39　Broszat (ed.), p. 74
40　Höhne, *Canaris*, pp. 363–4
41　Ibid., p. 361
42　Cited ibid., p. 364
43　Lahousen note on conference in Führer
　　train; cited ibid., p. 364
44　Erlass, 7.10.1939; cited Ackermann,
　　p. 204
45　See v. Lang, Sibyll (eds) p. 61
46　Frank's diary, 19.12.1939; IMT
　　USSR–223; cited M. Gilbert, p. 105
47　Information supplied by M. Tregenza
　　(biographer of Christian Wirth) to
　　author, 9.6.1989
48　26.9.1939; Overy, p. 95
49　Herbst, p. 100
50　See Stein, pp. 30, 271

51　From GFP regulations, p. 6; cited
　　Höhne, *Canaris*, p. 365
52　Stein, p. 30
53　Ref. H.H. speech, 8.11.1938; op. cit.
　　(ref. 77, ch. 7); and G. Berger to H.H.,
　　10.2.1940, re decree of 18.5.1939
　　authorising increase of Totenkopf units
　　to 40–50,000 men in the event of war;
　　T–175, Roll 104, Frs 2626613 *f*; cited
　　Stein, p. 33
54　Dienstweisung für das Ergänzungsamt
　　der Waffen-SS, 29.10.1939; T–175, Roll
　　104, Frs 2626776 *ff*; cited Stein, p. 36
　　note.
55　G. Berger historical report to H.H.,
　　5.6.1942; IWM H/15/264
56　SS-Befehl, 28.10.1939; BA NS 19/1791
　　(reproduced as appendix Dok. 4 in
　　Ackermann)
57　To Gauleiters, 22.9.1940; IMT 1918–PS
58　S. Lorentz, *The Destruction of Warsaw
　　Castle*, Warsaw, 1947; cited Woods,
　　pp. 14–15
59　Gisevius, *Nebe*, p. 198
60　Strasser, *Mein Kampf*, p. 146
61　A. Zoller, *Hitler Privat*, Droste,
　　Düsseldorf, 1949, p. 181; cited Bullock,
　　p. 523
62　Bern University, Hist. Inst., reproduced
　　in Calic. p. 326
63　'Innenpolitischen Lage', 10.11.1939;
　　Boberach, 2, pp. 442–3
64　See e.g. Höhne, *Canaris*, pp. 386 *ff*;
　　Ritter, pp. 145 *ff*
65　See Höhne, *Canaris*, p. 392
66　See Ritter, pp. 149–50
67　v. Lang, p. 149
68　See Calic, pp. 325–6
69　See Payne-Best, *The Venlo Incident*,
　　London, 1950, pp. 130–2; Strasser,
　　Mein Kampf, pp. 146–7; Gisevius,
　　Nebe, pp. 211–12
70　A. Haushofer to Frau K. Haushofer,
　　23.12.1939; cited Douglas-Hamilton,
　　p. 106
71　v. Lang, p. 141
72　29.2.1940; T–175, Roll 37, Fr. 238
73　7.9.1940; IMT PS–1918
74　v. Hassell, p. 117
75　v. Lang, p. 141
76　Ibid., p. 143
77　29.2.1940; op. cit. (ref. 72 above)
78　K. Wolff; 'Eichmanns Chef Heinrich
　　Himmler', *Neue Illustrierte*, No. 17,
　　23.4.1961, p. 24
79　See IWM H/28/374
80　See IWM H/28/323 *ff*
81　IWM H/3/367
82　IWM H/3/368
83　19.5.1941; IWM H/3/382

Chapter 9: Racial Warrior

1 H. Johst, *Ruf des Reiches – Echo des Volkes! Eine Ostfahrt*, Munich, 1942, p. 86; cited Ackermann, p. 227
2 See v. Lang, p. 147
3 See H.H. to v. Ribbentrop re the Führerbefehl, 23.4.1940; IWM H/6/217
4 See G. Berger report on recruitment, 5.6.1942; IWM H/15/264
5 See extracts from letters of Nordland recruits; IWM H/6/220
6 Gärtner to H.H., 9.5.1940; T–175, Roll 104, Frs 2626360 *f*; cited Stein, pp. 53–4
7 Berger to H.H., 2.7.1940; ibid., Frs 2626144 *ff*; cited ibid., p. 97
8 Report of Reichskommissar für die Festigung deutschen Volkstums, 25.3.1943, p. 7; IWM H/28/224
9 v. Lang, p. 154
10 See H. Krausnick, 'Denkschrift Himmlers über die Behandlung der Fremdvölkischen im Osten', *VJHZ*, 5, 1957, p. 195
11 Ibid., pp. 196–8
12 Ibid., p. 197
13 v. Lang, Sibyll (eds), p. 68
14 See Lifton, p. 77; Sereny, p. 56; for numbers of victims see Nowak, p. 83
15 Information supplied by M. Tregenza (biographer of Christian Wirth) to author, 9.6.1989
16 Wiesenthal, pp. 271–2
17 See Sereny, p. 56; 'That patients were sent to these Institutions to be gassed was confirmed by Franz Suchomel.' And see ibid., pp. 54 *ff* for discussion of whether the killing centres were designed as training centres for exterminators.
18 W. Koppe to J. Sporrenberg, 18.10.1940; BA Zentrale Stelle für Landesjustizverwaltungen, vol. 9, 806–7; cited Fleming, p. 21
19 See v. Lang, Sibyll (eds), pp. 45–6
20 Cited Calic, p. 433
21 The Joint Distribution Committee; see v. Lang, Sibyll (eds), pp. 63 *ff*
22 See Reitlinger, p. 134
23 Lifton, p. 14
24 H.H. notes written in special train, 28.5.1940; *VJHZ*, op. cit. (ref. 10 above), p. 195
25 See Manvell & Fraenkel, pp. 100, 102
26 Kersten, p. 88
27 6–8.2.1940; Kersten, pp. 334–6
28 Erlass, 22.6.1940; BA R 43 11/311, Bl. 42; cited Herbst, p. 127
29 1 Skl., 3.6.1940; cited Salewski, 3,

pp. 105 *ff*; map, ibid., p. 121
30 See Salewski, 3, pp. 122 *ff*
31 Meldung No. 104, 11.7.1940; Boberach, 5, p. 1362
32 Meldung No. 103, 8.7.1940; ibid., p. 1353
33 Meldung No. 105, 15.7.1940; ibid., p. 1376
34 Meldung No. 107, 22.7.1940; ibid., p. 1402
35 See Koehl, p. 120; Krausnick and others, p. 276
36 Broszat (ed.), p. 96
37 Jahrbuch der AWi der DAF, 1940/41, pp. 61 *f*; cited Herbst, p. 163
38 To officer corps Leibstandarte, 7.9.1940; cited Ackermann, pp. 147, 154
39 Krausnick and others, pp. 270, 461
40 See v. Lang, p. 156; Kersten, pp. 184–5
41 Shirer, p. 356
42 Stein, p. 90
43 Meldung No. 107, 22.7.1940; Boberach, 5, p. 1402
44 Shirer, p. 359
45 To Aunt Bessie, 7.8.1940; cited M. Bloch, *The Duke of Windsor's War*, Weidenfeld & Nicolson, 1982, p. 103
46 31.7.1940; Halder, 2, pp. 49–50
47 10.8.1940; v. Hassell, p. 162
48 22.9.1940; ibid., p. 166
49 See Calic, p. 403
50 See IMT 446–PS; see Whaley, pp. 17–18
51 See Stein, pp. 98 *ff*
52 Berger's report; op. cit. (ref. 4 above)
53 23.12.1940; Kersten, p. 69
54 21.12.1940; ibid., pp. 67–8
55 23.12.1940; ibid., p. 69
56 28.12.1940; ibid., pp. 70–1
57 5.1.1941; ibid., pp. 72–3
58 Vermerk der Reichskanzlei, 6.11.1941; BA R 43 11/278 Bl. 103; cited Herbst, p. 154
59 16.12.1940; BA R 7/2017; cited ibid.
60 15–17.1.1941; Kersten, p. 74
61 Ibid.
62 Ibid., pp. 75–7
63 18–19.1.1941; ibid., pp. 77–9
64 v. Lang, p. 194
65 Manvell & Fraenkel, p. 261, note 20
66 15.5.1940; Heiber, p. 80
67 See Kersten, p. 91
68 Doris Mehner who joined H.H. staff 1943; Manvell & Fraenkel, p. 267, add note
69 Ibid., p. 261, note 20
70 See Bullock, pp. 581–2; Calic, p. 400
71 3.2.1941; Kersten, p. 46
72 7.2.1941; ibid., p. 50
73 Ibid., pp. 48–51

74 See Berben, p. 87
75 Höss November 1940 report to RFSS; Broszat (ed.), p. 178
76 Lifton, p. 187
77 Ibid., p. 156, note
78 Broszat (ed.), p. 179
79 Ibid., p. 178
80 Ibid., p. 180
81 10.3.1941; Kersten, p. 173
82 IMT PS 447; cited Noakes, p. 617; Halder, 2, p. 419
83 Minute of 2.7.1941, Heydrich to four HSSPFs, summarising 'basic instructions'; cited Noakes, pp. 620–1
84 Testimony of Sonderkommando Cdr.; cited Krausnick and others, pp. 62–3
85 IMT EC–126 and ND 2718–PS; cited Bullock, p. 591
86 See evidence of von dem Bach-Zelewski; IMT IV, p. 36; see Koehl, p. 180; Reitlinger, p. 161
87 11.11.1941; Kersten, p. 119
88 Ibid., p. 120
89 See Canaris to Halder, 27.8.1940; Halder, 2, p. 79
90 18.5.1941; v. Hassell, p. 209
91 See Hess, p. 69
92 18.5.1941; v. Hassell, p. 207
93 6.4.1941; Kersten, p. 173
94 16.4.1941; ibid., p. 174
95 17.4.1941; ibid., p. 175
96 Whaley, p. 174
97 Ibid., Appendix A
98 Hess, p. 70
99 18.5.1941; v. Hassell, p. 207
100 Douglas-Hamilton, pp. 165 ff
101 Frau Lina Heydrich, cited Calic, p. 380
102 See PRO INF/1/912; Calic, p. 380
103 F. Mennecke to wife, 24.11.1941; cited Lifton, p. 135
104 Cited Nowak, p. 192, note
105 See Boberach, 6, p. 1812
106 Ibid., 6, pp. 1917–18
107 Moczarski, pp. 151, 436
108 Cited M. Gilbert, p. 152; and see v. Lang, Sibyll (eds), p. 73
109 Schellenberg circular, 10a Js 39/60, p. 239; Landgericht München II; cited Fleming, pp. 44–5
110 See Lifton, p. 274
111 Reichsarzt-SS to RFSS, 29.5.1941; IWM H/28A/ 364
112 See Lifton, pp. 270 ff
113 Broszat (ed.), p. 157; see also Höss's statement in *Bulletin of the Main Commission for the Investigation of Nazi Crimes in Poland*, Wydawnictwo Prawnicze, Warsaw, 1960, XIII, pp. 130 ff, 149, where again he cannot give a more exact date for his summons to

Berlin than 'sometime in the summer of 1941'.
114 Broszat (ed.), p. 157
115 Ibid., p. 181
116 v. Lang, Sibyll (eds), p. 75
117 Broszat (ed.), p. 158
118 Ibid.
119 See Halder, 2, pp. 328, 336, 419; Warlimont, p. 164; Calic, p. 439
120 30.3.1941; Halder, 2, pp. 336–7
121 16.6.1941; v. Hassell, p. 212
122 Meldung No. 179, 17.4.1941; Boberach, 6, p. 2204
123 Meldung No. 190, 29.5.1941; ibid., 7, p. 2354
124 Meldung No. 192, 9.6.1941; ibid., p. 2380
125 Meldung No. 194, 16.6.1941; ibid., p. 2408
126 Meldung No. 195, 19.6.1941; ibid., pp. 2418–19
127 Hinsley and others, I, pp. 467–72, 475–7
128 Whaley, p. 231
129 Ibid., p. 80
130 Ibid., p. 242
131 Meldung No. 196, 23.6.1941; Boberach, 7, p. 2426

Chapter 10: Endlösung
1 IMT, XXII, p. 352; cited Stein, p. 273
2 To Korpsführern in Kharkov, 24.4.1943; IMT 1919–PS
3 Cited v. Lang, Sibyll (eds), p. 80
4 F. Landau's diary, 14.7.1941; cited M. Gilbert, p. 171
5 IMT NO–2456; cited H. Heiber; 'Aus den Akten des Gauleiters Kube', *VJHZ*, 4, 1956, p. 72
6 Hinsley and others, 2, p. 671
7 K. Wolff; op. cit. (ref. 78, ch. 8), p. 22
8 Ibid.
9 Ibid.
10 Witnesses at Wolff's trial, 1964; see v. Lang, p. 172
11 Cited Krausnick and others, p. 68
12 See especially 'Wirtschaft' Meldungen in Boberach, 7
13 See Overy, p. 132
14 See Besprechung in Führer HQ on Generalplan Ost, undated; IWM H/5/85; see also Meldung No. 196, 23.6.1941; Boberach, 7, pp. 2433–4
15 See Broszat (ed.), pp. 158–9; for a more detailed description see *Reminiscences of Pery Broad SS-man in the Auschwitz Concentration Camp*, Panstwowe Museum, Auschwitz, 1965, pp. 54 ff; see also Central Commission for Investigation of German Crimes in

Poland, *German Crimes in Poland*, Warsaw, 1946, I, p. 83

16 Dr S. Klodzinski testimony; cited Lifton, p. 259

17 See M. Gilbert, pp. 76–7; Irving, p. 325

18 4.10.1941; v. Hassell, p. 231

19 15.9.1941; cited Krausnick and others, p. 526

20 See v. Lang, p. 173

21 Moczarski, p. 155

22 Heydrich to Wolff (im Hause), 2.11.1941, re meeting of 4.10.1941, p. 5; IWM H/6/118

23 Ibid., p. 6

24 See Meldungen Nos 195, 19.6.1941, and 210, 11.8.1941; Boberach, 7, pp. 2424 *ff*, 2638 *ff*

25 See M. Gilbert, p. 210

26 NA NO–365; cited Fleming, p. 71

27 Trevor-Roper (ed.), *Table Talk*, p. 162

28 H. Heims, *Adolf Hitler, Monologe im Führerhauptquartier, 1941–1944*, Hamburg, 1980, p. 106; cited Calic, p. 520

29 Schellenberg, p. 359

30 Kersten, p. 112

31 Ibid., p. 116

32 Ibid., pp. 117–18

33 Ibid., p. 119

34 Jeckeln's interrogation, 14.12.1945; Hist. State Archives, Riga; cited Fleming, p. 75

35 To SS-Korpsführern, Kharkov, 24.4.1943; IMT 1919 PS

36 Cited Reitlinger, p. 186, note

37 H.H. to R. Heydrich, 26.11.1941; IWM H/6/120

38 See Riga trial (50) 9/72, verdict, pp. 69–73; cited Fleming, pp. 78–9; observers and brutal laughter heard by Col. W. Bruns; see Fleming, pp. 80–1

39 Jeckeln interrogation, op. cit. (ref. 34 above); cited Fleming, p. 96

40 26.12.1941; T–175, Roll 108, Fr. 2632287; cited Stein, p. 135

41 See Stein, pp. 134, 168

42 v. Lang, Sibyll (eds), p. 89

43 See Fleming, pp. 91–4; and Raul Hillberg, *The Destruction of the European Jews*, Holmes & Meier, London, 1985, pp. 165–6. Dr Lange's is the last name on the list of 14 who attended.

44 Krausnick and others, p. 85

45 v. Lang, Sibyll (eds), p. 91

46 Ibid., pp. 77–8

47 See description of Jewish gravedigger, Y. Grojanowski; cited M. Gilbert, pp. 255 *ff*

48 Foreign monitoring service, Washington DC; cited F. Watts (ed.), *Voices of History*, New York, 1943, p. 121; cited M. Gilbert, p. 285

49 Meldung No. 256, 2.2.1942; Boberach, 9, p. 3235

50 Cited Aronson, pp. 62–3

51 Kersten, pp. 90–1

52 Schellenberg, p. 30

53 Kersten, p. 90

54 Cited Aronson, p. 62

55 Manvell & Fraenkel, p. 262, note 3

56 Heydrich to Wolff, 21.10.1941, re meeting 4.10.1941; IWM H/6/118

57 26.1.1942; Heiber, p. 101

58 31.1.1942; ibid., pp. 101–2

59 Dr Wetzell's opinion, 27.4.1942, in H. Heiber, 'Der Generalplan Ost', *VJHZ*, 6, 1958, p. 297

60 Ibid., p. 294

61 Ibid., p. 296

62 H.H. to Chef RuSHA, Oct, 1940; BA NS 19/neu 604; cited Ackermann, p. 208

63 H.H. to K.H. Frank, Jan. 1941; ibid.

64 Anordnung No. 67/1, p. 9 III 3, 19.2.1942; IWM H/1/236

65 See Henry & Hillel, pp. 153 *ff*

66 Ibid., p. 152

67 K.-H. Huber, *Jugend untern Hakenkreuz*, Ullstein, Berlin, 1982

68 4.3.1942; IWM H/6/156

69 Conference report of govt of G.G., 30.3.1942; cited Ackermann, p. 207

70 Anordnung No. 70/1, 23.3.1942, 'Änderung des Begriffes "artverwandtes Blut" '; IWM H/6/98

71 10.11.1940; Kersten, p. 57

72 RFSS, Berlin, 7.3.1942; IWM H/6/165

73 H.H. to O. Pohl, 8.5.1942; BA NS 19/421; cited Ackermann, p. 133

74 15.5.1942; Heiber, p. 120

75 To Oberabschnittsführern und Hauptamtschefs, 9.6.1942; T–175, Roll 90, Frs 2664 *ff*

76 7.4.1942; IWM H/6/26

77 Ibid.

78 30.4.1942; IWM H/6/29

79 See Stein, pp. 170–2

80 H.P. Kraemer to Leitung der Reichskanzlei, 7.4.1942; IWM H/10/281

81 H.H. to R. Heydrich, 24.4.1942; IWM H/10/283

82 See Sereny, pp. 102–3

83 Ibid., p. 111

84 See K. Smolen, *Auschwitz, 1940–1945*, Panstwowe Museum, Auschwitz, 2nd edn, 1966, pp. 64 *ff*, 69; see Höss's statements in Polish custody;

cited Sehn, p. 114; see also Garlinski, pp. 117–18
85 Broszat (ed.), p. 108
86 Cited Krausnick and others, p. 104
87 V. Brack to H.H., 28.3.1941; cited Lifton, p. 279
88 See ibid., p. 280
89 Alexander, *Prolonged Exposure*, p. 20
90 Ibid.
91 Dated 'B' November, 1942; cited ibid., p. 27
92 Alexander, *Miscellaneous Aviation*, pp. 10–12
93 See ibid., pp. 12–13; also testimony A. Pacholegg; IMT 2428 PS, XXX, p. 351; also Berben, p. 129
94 13.4.1942; exhibit 316 (1986) Dachau Museum, Dachau
95 5.4.1942; cited Berben, p. 128
96 IMT XXX, p. 351
97 See v. Lang, p. 186
98 Alexander, *Prolonged Exposure*, p. 22
99 Dr Lutz to L. Alexander; cited ibid., p. 40
100 Alexander, *Miscellaneous Aviation*, p. 13
101 See Lifton, p. 273
102 Alexander, *Prolonged Exposure*, pp. 44, 41
103 Cited Aronson, p. 266, note

Chapter 11: Factory Murder
1 See C. MacDonald, *The Killing of SS-Obergruppenführer Reinhard Heydrich*, Macmillan, 1989, pp. 118 *ff*, 155 *ff*
2 Ibid., pp. 175–6; Calic, p. 477
3 R. Hildebrandt, *Wir sind die Letzten*, Berlin, 1947, pp. 135–6; cited Reitlinger, p. 215
4 Hoettl, p. 30
5 Schellenberg, pp. 323–4
6 Meldung No. 290, 11.6.1942; Boberach, 10, p. 3805
7 Meldung No. 288, 1.6.1942; ibid., p. 3773
8 L. Heydrich, *Leben mit einem Kriegsverbrecher*, Pfaffenhofen, 1976, p. 119; cited Calic, p. 477
9 See Höhne, *Canaris*, p. 471
10 9.6.1942; T–175, Roll 90, Fr. 2664
11 Ibid., Frs 2664 *ff*
12 30.11.1941; v. Hassell, p. 240
13 22.7.1942; cited v. Lang, p. 182
14 See e.g. Meldung No. 289, 4.6.1942; Boberach, 10, pp. 3787–8
15 See Henry & Hillel, pp. 199–202
16 21.6.1943; Heiber, p. 214
17 Meldung No. 292, 18.6.1942; Boberach, 10, p. 3840
18 See IMT, VI, p. 191

19 H.H. to Greifelt, 12.6.1942; cited Heiber, *Generalplan Ost*, op. cit. (ref. 59, ch. 10), p. 325
20 Ibid.
21 16–17.7.1942; Kersten, pp. 132–5; and see detailed plans for *Wehrdorfen* (defensive villages) and the raising and training of their peasant/farmer militia companies in HSSPF Russland-Mitte to RFSS, 28.1.1944; IWM H/28/282
22 16.7.1942; Kersten, p. 132
23 Brandt memo., 7.7.1942; IMT NO–216; cited M. Gilbert, p. 373
24 Broszat (ed.), p. 182
25 See Garlinski, p. 119
26 Broszat (ed.), p. 161; and see K. Smolen, op. cit. (ref. 84, ch. 10), p. 65
27 Lifton, p. 14
28 Fleming, p. 127
29 Broszat (ed.), p. 171
30 Ibid., p. 182
31 Ibid., p. 171; however Dr O. Wolken stated 'about eight minutes'; cited Lifton, p. 165
32 F. Müller, work-Kommando survivor, speaking in Claude Lanzmann's film *Shoah*
33 Broszat (ed.), p. 169
34 Ibid., p. 183
35 Ibid., pp. 183–4
36 Kersten, p. 304
37 v. Lang, p. 338
38 21–22.7.1942; Kersten, pp. 137–8
39 19.7.1942; Heiber, p. 131
40 Sereny, pp. 151–2
41 Franz Suchomel (Guard) testimony in Claude Lanzmann's film *Shoah*; Samuel Rajzmann's testimony at Nuremberg; cited M. Gilbert, p. 395 *ff*; Gustav Borak's testimony at Demjanjuk trial; *The Times*, London, 5.3.1987
42 US interrogation of K. Gerstein, 4.5.1945; cited H. Rothfels; 'Augenzeugenbericht zu den Massenvergassung', *VJHZ*, 1, 1953, pp. 191–2
43 G. Sereny, 'Displaced Persons in the World's Dock', *The Times*, London, 14.2.1987
44 Broszat (ed.), p. 161
45 Gerstein interrogation, op. cit. (ref. 42 above), p. 192
46 Sereny, op. cit. (ref. 43 above)
47 Gerstein interrogation, op. cit. (ref. 42 above), p. 192
48 19.7.1942; Heiber, p. 132
49 Ibid., p. 133
50 To RSHA, ?.7.1942; IWM H/1/125
51 Kersten, p. 302
52 RFSS Pers, Stab HA, Munich, to

RFSS, 8.7.1942; T–175, Roll 88, Fr. 2611336

53 Dr Brandt to Glasindustrie . . . schule, 28.7.1942; Heiber, p. 134
54 'Die Goten auf der Krim', 14.7.1942; IWM H/1/219
55 Alexander, *Prolonged Exposure*, p. 22
56 H.H. to H. Backe, 30.7.1942; Heiber, p. 135
57 A copy in Wiener Lib.
58 8.8.1942; Kersten, pp. 148–9
59 Ibid., pp. 151–2
60 See R.C. Zaehner, *The Bhagavad-Gita*, Oxford University Press, 1969, p. 20
61 Ibid., ch. 4, v. 8
62 Ibid., ch. 4, v. 7; Kersten, p. 152
63 'Gespräche des RFSS am Mittagessen am 13.9.1942': T–175, Roll 88, Frs 2611398–99
64 H. Krausnick (ed.), 'Himmler über seinen Besuch bei Mussolini vom 11–14 Okt. 1942', *VJHZ*, 4, 1956, pp. 425–6

Chapter 12: The Herrenmensch
1 Overy, p. 159
2 Ibid., p. 193
3 8.11.1943; Milch Docs, vol. 63, 5901–2; cited ibid., p. 177
4 Meldung No. 357, 8.2.1943; Boberach, 12, p. 4770
5 Ibid., p. 4771
6 Ibid., p. 4772
7 See Hestons, pp. 82–3, 87; see Kersten, p. 166, for confirmation of injections
8 Cited Irving, p. 446
9 10.11.1942; Kersten, p. 161
10 Ibid., p. 160
11 See Erickson, p. 1
12 Cited Irving, pp. 455–6
13 21.11.1942; Kersten, p. 127
14 18.12.1942; ibid., p. 261
15 20.12.1942 re 12.12.1942; v. Hassell, p. 290
16 A. Fischer, *Sowjetische Deutschlandspolitik* . . . , Stuttgart, 1975, p. 41; cited Höhne, *Canaris*, p. 479
17 Hestons, p. 59
18 Ibid., p. 57
19 Irving, p. 480
20 Hestons, pp. 88, 139, 159
21 12.12.1942; Kersten, pp. 165–6
22 Ibid., pp. 166–7
23 Hestons, p. 115
24 19.12.1942; Kersten, p. 168
25 Ibid., p. 169
26 H.H. to M. Bormann, 20.1.1943; IWM H/6/252
27 M. Bormann to G. Bormann, 16.1.1943; cited Trevor-Roper (ed.), *Bormann Letters*, p. 1

28 F. Gilbert (ed.), pp. 17–20
29 See Padfield, p. 268
30 See Stein, pp. 203–4
31 To Korpsführern in Kharkov, 24.4.1943; IMT 1919–PS
32 Overy, p. 223
33 18.3.1943; IWM H/6/244
34 See RFSS to Inspekteur für Statistik, 18.1.1943, and RFSS to Chef des RSHA, 18.1.1943; IWM H/5/260 and H/5/259
35 Testimony SS-Unterscharführer Karl Frenzel, SS-Oberscharführer Hubert Gomerski; Sobibor Trial Prosecution Docs, Prosecutor's Office, Frankfurt/ Main; see also File No. 8 Js 5302/60, Prosecutor's Office, Düsseldorf; see also File No. P Ks 3/50: 'The Case against Erich Bauer', Prosecutor's Office, W. Berlin; see also testimony Jewish witnesses in Novitch, pp. 59, 108, 154–5
36 Testimony Moshe Bahir; cited Novitch, pp. 154–5
37 RFSS to Chefs SIPO and SD, 9.4.1943; BA NS 19/neu 1570; cited Fleming, p. 137
38 R. Brandt to Inspekteur für Statistik, 10.4.1943; cited ibid.
39 See v. Lang, Sibyll (eds), p. 112
40 Fleming, p. 139
41 Meldung No. 377, 19.4.1943; Boberach, 13, p. 5145
42 Ibid.
43 Hestons, p. 46
44 Meldung No. 365, 8.3.1943; Boberach, 13, p. 4902
45 Ibid., p. 4903
46 Berichte zu Inlandsfragen (Grüne Serie), 2.8.1943; ibid., 14, pp. 5562–3
47 Ibid., pp. 5561–2
48 See Herbst, p. 185
49 See Kersten, p. 206
50 3.9.1943; Kersten, p. 211
51 7.9.1943; ibid., p. 214
52 22.3.1942; v. Hassell, p. 258
53 Royce (ed.), p. 57
54 Deposition by F.X. Sonderegger, 9.9.1948; *Akten der Lüneberger Staatsanwaltschaft*, IX, p. 250; cited Höhne, *Canaris*, p. 508
55 Ibid., IX, p. 299; cited ibid., pp. 508–9
56 Schellenberg, p. 408
57 See Höhne, *Canaris*, p. 488
58 A. Kraell report on the Schmidhuber case, 25.8.1948; *Akten der Lüneberger Staatsanwaltschaft*, III, p. 166; cited Höhne, *Canaris*, p. 529
59 25.5.1943; v. Hassell, p. 317
60 v. Lang, pp. 196–7
61 See Royce (ed.), p. 36

62 Berichte zu Inlandsfragen (Rote Serie), 19.8.1943; Boberach, 14, p. 5646
63 Ibid., 26.8.1943; ibid., p. 5675
64 Wolff's account, cited v. Lang, p. 200
65 See e.g. *Evening Standard*, London, 25.8.1943; *Die Zeitung* (exile paper), London, 27.8.1943 (Wiener Lib.)
66 25.8.1943; T–175, Roll 88, Fr. 2611390
67 See Dulles, *Underground*, p. 159
68 See Puppi Sarre testimony; ibid., pp. 163–4
69 Cited G. van Roon, *German Resistance to Hitler*, London, 1971, p. 376
70 RFSS to K. Frhr v. Eberstein and H. Müller, Chef Amt IV RSHA, 15.1.1943; cited Heiber, p. 183
71 See Meldungen Nos 356, 4.2.1943, and 357, 8.2.1943; Boberach, 12, pp. 4750, 4760
72 Cited Royce (ed.), pp. 39–40
73 28.3.1943; v. Hassell, p. 307
74 Meldung No. 360, 18.2.1943; Boberach, 12, pp. 4822–3
75 30.9.1941; IMT VI, p. 128
76 P. Roser testimony; IMT VI, p. 291
77 Ibid., p. 296
78 M. Labussière testimony; ibid., p. 172
79 Ibid.
80 Decree, 14.12.1942; cited H. Marsalek, *Die Geschichte des Konzentrationslagers Mauthausen*, Stuttgart, p. 150; cited Speer, *Slave State*, p. 316
81 Speer to RFSS, 5.4.1943; IWM H/13/75
82 O. Pohl to R. Brandt, 19.4.1943; IWM H/13/76
83 Testimony Mme. Vaillant-Couturier; IMT VI, pp. 205–6
84 Ibid., p. 207
85 Ibid., p. 208
86 Testimony M. Lampe; IMT VI, p. 184
87 Ibid., p. 185
88 Ibid., pp. 185–6; and see J.F. Veith's testimony; ibid., pp. 234–5
89 Testimony M. Lampe; ibid., p. 186
90 Ibid., p. 193
91 See Alexander, *Prolonged Exposure*, pp. 21–2
92 E. Holzlöhner, S. Rascher, E. Finke, *Bericht über Abkühlungsversuche am Menschen*, undated, read by H.H., 21.10.1942; cited ibid., p. 50
93 Cited Alexander, *Prolonged Exposure*, p. 23
94 Ibid.
95 24.10.1942; ibid., p. 25
96 Versuchsanordnung B; cited ibid., p. 34
97 Ibid., p. 35
98 Ibid.
99 Ibid., p. 33
100 Ibid., p. 36
101 See Lifton, p. 249
102 Testimony Mme Vaillant-Couturier; IMT VI, p. 212
103 See Lifton, p. 270
104 See RFSS to O. Pohl, 2.8.1943, and O. Pohl to R. Brandt, 2.8.1943; IWM H/28/370
105 Dr Miklos Nyiszli; cited Lifton, p. 359
106 15.12.1942; IWM H/13/70
107 5.3.1943; Heiber, pp. 195–6
108 See Stein, p. 268
109 Erickson, pp. 94–5
110 H.H. speech at Tagung R.P.A.-Leiter, 28.1.1944; T–175, Roll 94, Fr. 2614801, cited Stein, p. 182
111 Heiber, *Generalplan Ost*, op. cit. (ref. 59, ch. 10), p. 292
112 RFSS to HSSPF Russland, Chefs HA Orpo, RSHA etc., 6.1.1943; Heiber, pp. 179–80
113 See Moczarski, pp. 187–8
114 RFSS to Pohl, Krüger, Globocnik, RSHA, Wolff, Gen. QM Wagner, Wehrmacht, 2.10.1942; IWM H/28/380
115 ?.1.1943; IWM H/28/383
116 See M. Gilbert, p. 524
117 16.2.1943; IWM H/21/157; and see Heiber, p. 190
118 5.1.1943; IWM H/1/31
119 18.1.1943; IWM H/1/23
120 ?.1.1943; IWM H/1/33
121 Moczarski, p. 186
122 Ibid., p. 190
123 See Stein, p. 47; Reitlinger, p. 170, Wirth (ed.), p. 10
124 20.4.1943; Wirth (ed.)
125 Moczarski, p. 195
126 Ibid., p. 196
127 20.4.1943; Wirth (ed.)
128 See M. Gilbert, p. 557
129 Moczarski, p. 201
130 22.4.1943; Wirth (ed.)
131 24.4.1943; ibid.
132 Moczarski, p. 213
133 Ibid., p. 230
134 Ibid., p. 210
135 13.5.1943; Wirth (ed.)
136 Moczarski, p. 210
137 16.5.1943; Wirth (ed.)
138 Moczarski, p. 252
139 Ibid., p. 262
140 Ibid., pp. 257–8
141 Sereny, pp. 50, 157
142 Ibid., p. 162
143 Ibid.
144 Frank to RFSS, 13.5.1943; IWM H/15/178
145 See Speer, *Slave State*, p. 135

146 Hansen-Nootbar to author, July 1982
147 Dieselmaat U–333 to F. Lynder, 14/15.11.1978; cited Padfield, p. 322
148 19.5.1943; Heiber, p. 212
149 22.5.1943; ibid., p. 213
150 RFSS to HSSPF Ostland and Chef WVHA, 21.6.1943; Heiber, pp. 214–15
151 RFSS to O. Pohl, 3.12.1943; IWM H/15/183

Chapter 13: Chief of Intelligence
1 Kersten, p. 302
2 A. Greiser to RFSS, 16.3.1943; IWM H/28/84
3 E. Kaltenbrunner to RFSS, 20.7.1943; IWM H/28/39
4 SS-O'stuf Jarrow, Chef Sich. und SD Einwanderer Zentralstelle to O. Globocnik, 10.2.1943; IWM H/28/76
5 RFSS to RuSHA, Volksdeutsche Mittelstelle, Stab. HA RKF, HSSPF Ost . . . etc., 16.2.1943; IWM H/28/77
6 Ibid.
7 R. Brandt to Frau Walter, 14.5.1943; Heiber, p. 211
8 Chef RuSHA to RFSS Pers. Stab, 18.1.1944; IWM H/28/97
9 O'gruf Heissmeyer to R. Brandt, 24.4.1944; IWM H/28/98
10 RFSS Pers. Stab. to RSHA, Berlin, 28.5.1944; IWM H/28/99
11 2.4.1943; IWM H/15/220
12 14.4.1943; IWM H/15/222
13 Aktenvermerk, 5.6.1943; IWM H/15/229
14 Gauleiter Bohle to RFSS, 4.2.1944; IWM H/15/235
15 RFSS to all offices of SS and police, 10.8.1943; IWM H/15/210
16 E. Grawitz to RFSS, 30.9.1943; Heiber, p. 235
17 T–78/R, Roll 466, Frs 644031–45; cited Erickson, p. 135
18 7.9.1943; Heiber, p. 233
19 Vermerk, 7.9.1943, re H.H. remark of 3.9.1943; T–175, Roll 88, Fr. 2611418
20 F/Vorträge, 9–10.8.1943; cited Padfield, p. 315
21 See for instance Dönitz handwritten memo. on Hitler; cited ibid., p. 316
22 Hestons, p. 114
23 Ibid., p. 138
24 9.9.1943; cited Irving, p. 567
25 F/Vorträge, 9.10.1943; cited Padfield, p. 315
26 See Speer, *Slave State*, p. 206
27 Ibid., p. 207
28 4.9.1943; Kersten, p. 211
29 To Reichs- and Gauleiters, Posen,

6.10.1943; T–175, Roll 85, Frs 152 *ff*
30 B. v. Schirach, *Ich glaubte Hitler*, Hamburg, 1967, p. 269
31 A. Speer, 'Antwort an E. Goldhagen', in A. Reif, *Albert Speer*, Munich, 1978, p. 389
32 Schellenberg, pp. 354 *ff*
33 9.12.1943; Kersten, p. 195
34 Schellenberg, p. 423
35 Press cutting (unnamed), 22.5.1948; Wiener Lib. Biog. archive, Reel 24
36 K. Wolff to Frau Wolff, 29.9.1943; cited v. Lang, p. 218
37 22.8.1943; Heiber, pp. 230–1
38 30.10.1943; ibid., p. 231
39 R. Hildebrandt to RFSS, 1.12.1943; ibid., p. 246
40 RFSS to R. Hildebrandt, 17.12.1943; ibid., pp. 246–7
41 R. Brandt to E. Kaltenbrunner, 3.11.1943; IWM H/28/20
42 See Herbst, p. 273
43 Ibid.
44 R. Brandt to SS Pers. HA, 22.10.1943; Heiber, p. 239
45 R. Brandt to M. Sollmann, 9.1.1944; ibid., p. 249
46 See enclosure in HSSPF Russland-Mitte to RFSS, 3.2.1944; IWM H/28/282
47 RFSS to SS-Gruf Taubert, 26.2.1944; T–175, Roll 88, Fr. 2611294
48 RFSS to W. Wüst, W Sievers . . . etc., 31.3.1944; Heiber, p. 256
49 RFSS to W. Keilhaus, 27.4.1944; T–175, Roll 88, Fr. 2611300
50 RFSS to O. Pohl, 26.2.1944; ibid., Fr. 2611298
51 O. Pohl to RFSS. 22.5.1944, and RFSS to O. Pohl, 31.5.1944; ibid. Frs 2611297, 2611296
52 Index 322 (January 1942 = 100); see Herbst, p. 343
53 See ibid., p. 347
54 W. Huppenkothen; 'Canaris und Abwehr', *IfZ*, ZS 249, cited Höhne, *Canaris*, p. 553
55 See Hoffmann
56 IMT (German ed.), XXXVI, p. 532; cited Gossweiler, p. 314
57 Speer to Kammler, 17.12.1943; cited Speer, *Slave State*, p. 219
58 See Broszat (ed.), p. 165; v. Lang, Sibyll (eds.), pp. 202 *ff*
59 v. Lang, Sibyll (eds), p. 207
60 9, 16, 17.6.1944; Kersten, pp. 162–4
61 H. Knatchbull Hugessen to For. Office, No. 794, 24.5.1944, and For. Office minute sheet 2, 26.6.1944; PRO WO 208/685A

62 For. Office to Washington, 3.6. and 1.7.1944; ibid.
63 Gen. Salmuth; cited Irving, p. 614
64 5.5.1944; T–175, Roll 92, Frs 3476 *ff*; cited Smith, Petersen, p. 202
65 NA Tb 242–211, see ibid., p. 203
66 24.5.1944; T–175, Roll 92, Fr. 4639; cited ibid., p. 203
67 21.6.1944; T–175, Roll 93, Frs 3961 *ff*; cited ibid., pp. 203 *ff*
68 Broszat (ed.), p. 139
69 IMT RF–348; and see IMT VI, pp. 330–1
70 See Berichte zu Inlandsfragen (Weisse Serie) Wirtschaft, 8.6.1944; Boberach, 17, p. 6582
71 Dr A. Poschmann; cited Speer, *Slave State*, p. 210
72 Speer, ibid., pp. 210–11
73 IMT VI, pp. 303 *ff*
74 21.6.1944; op. cit. (ref. 67 above), p. 200
75 Anlage, 12.2.1944 Vermerk RF [SS], in R. Brandt to M. Sollmann, 14.2.1944; Heiber, p. 251
76 See Berichte zu Inlandsfragen (Grüne Serie), 4.5.1944, and (Weisse Serie), 18.5.1944; Boberach, 17, pp. 6509, 6544

Chapter 14: The Plot against Hitler
1 Dulles, *Surrender*, pp. 22 *ff*
2 Peter (ed.), pp. 34–5
3 Ibid., pp. 126–7
4 S. v. Krosigk, *Es geschah in Deutschland*, Tübingen, 1952, p. 346; cited Zeller, *Freedom*, p. 274
5 H. Kaiser's diary, 20.2.1943; IWM AL 911
6 Dr W. Naumann to RFSS, 19.1.1944, 3.30 hours; IWM H/16/192
7 Cited Padfield, p. 361
8 War Diary Naval Operations Division, 10.6.1944; Nav. Lib.
9 Meldungen aus den SD-Abschnitten, 8.6.1944; Boberach, 17, pp. 6572–3
10 Ibid., 19.6.1944; ibid., p. 6596
11 Ibid., 28.6.1944; ibid., p. 6613
12 See Gen. H. Speidel, *Invasion 1944*; cited Royce (ed.), p. 92
13 Ibid.
14 Ibid., p. 95
15 Cited Cave-Brown, pp. 740–1
16 See Royce (ed.), p. 95
17 Ibid., p. 96
18 Moczarski, p. 352
19 31.8.1944; cited F. Gilbert, p. 105
20 See e.g. Peter (ed.), 24.7.1944, p. 44 (Hoepner's testimony), and 1.8.944, p. 119 (Stieff's testimony)

21 Ibid., 3.8.1944, p. 130 (Klausing's testimony)
22 H.H. notes for Führer Conferences; BA NS 19/275, 331; cited Hoffmann, p. 454
23 Peter (ed.), 3.8.1944, p. 131 (Klausing's testimony)
24 Ibid.,. 6.8.1944, p. 158
25 Ibid.
26 Ibid., 30.7.1944, p. 101
27 Ibid., 8.8. and 30.7.1944, pp. 175, 111 (v. Trott's testimony)
28 Ibid., 17.8.1944, p. 248
29 Ibid., 1.8.1944, p. 117
30 Ibid., 24.7.1944, p. 21
31 Gisevius, *Bitter End*, p. 515
32 Ibid., p. 516
33 Meldungen über . . . Meinungsbildung, 13.7.1944; Boberach, 17, pp. 6637–8
34 Bericht an die Parteikanzlei, 14.7.1944; ibid., pp. 6641–4
35 See Gen. H. Speidel, 'History of events preceding 20th July 1944'; IWM AL 914, pp. 12–13
36 See Moczarski, p. 350
37 J. Hansen-Nootbar to author, July 1982
38 See Hoffmann, p. 899
39 RSHA 'Sonderkommission 20.7.1944' report, 26.7.1944; Peter (ed.), p. 86; and see Hoffmann, pp. 472–3
40 See Hoffmann, p. 480
41 Ibid., pp. 480–1
42 See Peter (ed.), p. 226; see Hoffmann, p. 485
43 See Hoffmann, p. 823 re probability that Wagner at Zossen got through to Olbricht at 14.00
44 Gisevius, *Nebe*, pp. 38–9; Gisevius, *Bitter End*, pp. 532–3
45 'Sonderkommission' report, op. cit. (ref. 39 above)
46 20.7.1944, 16.45 hours; cited Royce (ed.), p. 124
47 See Hoffmann, p. 512
48 See Zeller, *Freedom*, p. 388
49 See Royce (ed.), p. 157 for 18.45 hours broadcast
50 Hoffmann, p. 587
51 v. Lang, p. 251
52 Zeller, *Freiheit*, p. 335
53 Kersten, p. 201
54 Ibid., p. 202
55 To officers 545 Inf. Div. Volksgrenadier Div., 26.7.1944; cited Smith, Petersen (eds), p. 218
56 Remer's account; cited Royce (ed.), p. 142
57 J. Hansen-Nootbar to author, July 1982
58 Cited Zeller, *Freedom*, p. 437
59 26.7.1944, op. cit. (ref. 55 above)
60 Manvell & Fraenkel, p. 263, note 14

61 Meldungen aus den SD-Abschnittsbereichen, 22.7.1944; Boberach, 17, p. 6651
62 Meldungen über . . . Meinungsbildungen, 28.7.1944; ibid., p. 6684
63 Padfield, p. 373
64 To staff officers and officials, 24.7.1944; cited Royce (ed.), p. 187
65 Rundschreiben No. 4, 20.7.1944, 21.20 hours; ibid., p. 183
66 Wire to all diplomatic missions, 24.7.1944; ibid., p. 188
67 Padfield, p. 373
68 Royce (ed.), p. 180
69 Rundschreiben, op. cit. (ref. 65 above)
70 Wire, op. cit. (ref. 66 above)
71 To Luftwaffe, 21.7.1944; Royce (ed.), p. 180
72 24.7.1944, op. cit. (ref. 64 above)
73 Meldungen über . . . Meinungsbildungen, 28.7.1944; Boberach, 17, pp. 6684–5
74 Rundschreiben No. 7, 21.7.1944, 11.35 hours; Royce (ed.), p. 184
75 See Moczarski, p. 242; Royce (ed.), p. 182
76 See Zeller; *Freedom*, p. 371; Royce (ed.), p. 182
77 21.7.1944; T–175, Roll 93, Frs 3919–20; cited Smith, Petersen (eds), pp. 245–6
78 17.11.1938; T–175, Roll 88, Fr. 2611474
79 26.7.1944, op. cit. (ref. 55 above)
80 Ibid.
81 DNB Presseschreibrundfunk, 24.7.1944; Wiener Lib. Press archive PC 5, Reel 4
82 Voice of the SS, 20.8.1944, 11.30 hours; ibid.
83 See e.g. H. Johst to RFSS, 3.4.1944; Heiber, pp. 256–8; also 'Himmler als Redner', in Smith, Petersen (eds), p. 259, citing collection of reactions to his speeches in T–175, Roll 118, Frs 3393–3556
84 To Wehrkreis Cdrs, 21.9.1944; T–175, Roll 93, Fr. 5402; cited Smith, Petersen (eds), p. 246
85 5.9.1944; Kersten, p. 221

Chapter 15: Most Powerful Man in the Reich
1 See Erickson, p. 259
2 21.9.1944, op. cit. (ref. 84, ch. 14)
3 L. Hahn; cited Deschner, *Warsaw*, p. 17
4 E. Rode's testimony; cited Woods, p. 74; and see Deschner, *Warsaw*, p. 79
5 Archives for the Central Commission for the Investigation of Nazi Crimes in Poland, 1100/Z/VK 1056; cited Woods, p. 76

6 Ibid., 1100/Z/VK 1981; cited ibid., p. 77
7 Erickson, p. 274
8 Cited ibid., p. 285
9 Erickson, pp. 289–90; Deschner, *Warsaw*, p. 157
10 M. Gilbert, p. 714
11 Cited Royce (ed.), pp. 382 *ff*
12 26.7.1944, op. cit. (ref. 55, ch. 14)
13 See E. Kaltenbrunner to M. Bormann, 25.10.1944; BA EAP 105/34; cited Hoffmann, p. 620
14 Peter (ed.), 22.7.1944, p. 7
15 Ibid., 24.7.1944, p. 11
16 Ibid., 25.7.1944, p. 50
17 Schellenberg, p. 410
18 See Höhne, *Canaris*, p. 582
19 Peter (ed.), 5.9.1944, p. 351 (Goerdeler's testimony)
20 Ibid., 16.8.1944, p. 242
21 Ibid., 20.8.1944, p. 279
22 See Howe, p. 247
23 Peter (ed.), 12.10.1944, p. 445 ('Gerüchte um den 20 Juli 1944')
24 P. Vassen (eyewitness); cited Royce (ed.), p. 199
25 Eyewitness to the execution; cited ibid., pp. 210–11
26 Fernschreiben to all Gestapo offices, 17.8.1944, 22.40 hours; IWM AL 2581
27 Fernschreiben to all police stations, 21.8.1944, 17.00 hours; ibid.
28 Blitz, to all Gestapo offices, 22.8.1944, 21.00 hours; ibid.
29 See 'Mordregister' in Royce (ed.), p. 182
30 Hoffmann, pp. 630, 871
31 Moczarski, p. 342
32 Ibid., pp. 345–54
33 RFSS to W. Wüst and W. Sievers, 17.8.1944, concerning J. Meier, *Das Ahnengrab in Kult und Recht*, 1944; Heiber, pp. 281–2
34 Ibid., p. 283
35 Br. Political Warfare Executive Report, 2.10.1944; PRO FO 371/39083; cited R. Lamb, *The Ghosts of Peace*, Salisbury, Wiltshire, 1987, p. 239
36 See Kersten, p. 223
37 12.9.1944; A. Besgen, *Der stille Befehl*, Munich, 1960, p. 35
38 Strik-Strikfeldt, p. 207
39 To Wehrkreis Cdrs, 21.9.1944; BA NS 19/323; cited Ackermann, p. 55
40 Manvell & Fraenkel, p. 263, note 14
41 Cited Trevor-Roper (ed.), *Bormann Letters*, pp. 119–20
42 See *Hamburger Fremdenblatt*, 20.10.1944; Wiener Lib. Press archive
43 Moczarski, pp. 362–3

44 RFSS to K. Gutenberger, 18.10.1944; Heiber, p. 291

45 *Hamburger Fremdenblatt*, 24.10.1944 and 14.11.1944; Wiener Lib. Press archive

46 Rechtsanwalt Greuter. 'Himmler contra Hitler', *Die 7 Tage*, 1, No. 6, 17.12.1948; Wiener Lib. Press archive

47 Dulles, *Surrender*, pp. 43 *ff*

48 See Kersten, pp. 238–9

49 Dulles, *Surrender*, p. 45

50 10.12.1944; Kersten, p. 239

51 See Wheeler-Bennett (Dep. Head Political Warfare) to Eden and Churchill, 25.7.1944; PRO FO 371/39062; cited Lamb, op. cit. (ref. 35 above), pp. 296–7

52 See M. Gilbert, pp. 754 *ff*

53 Broszat (ed.), p. 164

54 K. Becher testimony; IMT II, pp. 369–72; cited Fleming, p. 168

55 See v. Lang, Sibyll (eds), p. 212 and see Irving's suggestion that Hitler wanted to free the Jews for currency; Irving, p. 717

56 v. Lang, Sibyll (eds), p. 235

57 Schellenberg, p. 429

58 2.12. and 8.12.1944; Kersten, pp. 204, 229

59 Trevor-Roper (ed.), *Bormann Letters*, p. 140

60 31.10.1944; cited Manvell & Fraenkel. p. 206

61 Churchill to Eden, ?.12.1944; cited Lamb, op. cit. (ref. 35 above), p. 298

62 IMT VI, p. 228

63 Ibid., p. 245

64 Ibid., p. 247

65 Cited v. Lang, Sibyll (eds), p. 247

66 Ibid., pp. 253–4; M. Gilbert, p. 753

67 Dr Kastner; cited v. Lang, Sibyll (eds), pp. 254–5

68 29.11.1944; Kersten, pp. 203–4

69 Broszat (ed.), p. 143

70 v. Lang, Sibyll (eds), p. 224

71 Broszat (ed.), p. 143

72 R. Weiss, *Journey through Hell*, London, 1961, p. 189; cited M. Gilbert, p. 765

73 A. Oppenheimer testimony, Eichmann Trial, 7.6.1961, sess. 68; cited M. Gilbert, p. 763

74 V. Dupont testimony; IMT VI, pp. 250–1

75 IMT VI, p. 309

76 A. Balochowsky, testimony; ibid., p. 307

77 Ibid., p. 314

78 Ibid., p. 311

79 M. Lampe testimony; ibid., p. 191

80 V. Dupont testimony; ibid., pp. 251–2

81 Broszat (ed.), p. 143

82 24.4.1943; IMT 1919 PS; cited Smith, Petersen (eds), pp. 200–1

83 IMT 682–PS; cited IMT VI, p. 379

84 See Bericht an den Reichsschatz-minister der NSDAP, 28.10.1944; Boberach, 17, pp. 6721, 6722–6

85 H. Cappelen testimony; IMT VI, p. 283

86 Bericht . . . , 28.10.1944, op. cit. (ref. 84 above), p. 6726

87 H. Cappelen testimony; IMT VI, p. 286

88 Fragment Führer Conferences 28, 12.12.1944, cited Wilmot, p. 578

89 R. Brandt to O'gruf Dr Kaltenbrunner, O'gruf Prützmann, 3.10.1944 (this passage scored with two lines in margin); IWM H/15/242

90 2.12.1944; Kersten, p. 204

91 Dr Kastner; cited v. Lang, Sibyll (eds), p. 254

92 Captured, unposted letter; cited Wilmot, p. 582

93 V.T. Lary Jnr testimony at Malmédy Massacre hearings, p. 1033; cited Stein, p. 279; see also IMT 1634–PS, and IMT VI, pp. 375–7

94 G. Berger to RFSS, 21.12.1944; Heiber, p. 299

95 See ibid., note 2

96 H.H. present card index, reproduced in v. Lang, pp. 372–3

97 R. Baumert (Stabsführer Pers. Stab RFSS) to R. Brandt, 27.12.1944, and Anlage; Heiber, pp. 300–1

98 RFSS to M. Ruhland, 11.1.1945; Heiber, p. 302

Chapter 16: Fall from Grace

1 Erickson, p. 447

2 Descriptions by Adml Assmann; cited Irving, p. 750; and G. Boldt; cited Bullock, pp. 703–4

3 Hestons, p. 140

4 See Salewski, 2, p. 522; Padfield, pp. 388–9

5 F/Vorträge, 22–23.1.1945; Nav. Lib.

6 Ibid.

7 Cited Stein, p. 235

8 See Irving, p. 759

9 Fragments of Führer Conferences No. 24, 27.1.1945; cited Wilmot, pp. 626–7

10 Guderian; cited Manvell & Fraenkel, p. 208

11 R. d'Alquen to G. d'Alquen, 26.1.1945; IWM H/13/231

12 SS-Stuf. Kriegbaum (for d'Alquen) to R. Brandt, 28.1.1945; IWM H/13/232

13 RFSS to R. d'Alquen (enclosed in

R. Brandt to Kriegbaum), 30.1.1945; IWM H/13/233

14 RFSS to Frau Lina Heydrich, 7.2.1945; Heiber, p. 306

15 12.2.1945; Heiber, p. 305

16 W. v. Oven, *Mit Goebbels bis zum Ende*, Buenos Aires, 1949, 2, p. 245; cited Reitlinger, p. 404

17 8.3.1945; Trevor-Roper (ed.), *Goebbels Diaries*, p. 80

18 See Erickson, p. 517

19 Cited Irving, p. 769

20 Schellenberg, p. 438

21 Ibid., p. 437

22 4.2.1945; IWM H/1/202

23 7.3.1945; Trevor-Roper (ed.), *Goebbels Diaries*, p. 71

24 See Hewins, pp. 109 *f*

25 Ibid., p. 118

26 Schellenberg, p. 437

27 Col. Eismann narrative in J. Thorwald, *Es begann an der Weichsel*, Stuttgart, 1950, p. 285; cited Reitlinger, pp. 405–6; and H. Guderian, *Panzer Leader*, London, 1952, p. 413; cited Manvell & Fraenkel, p. 212

28 20.2.1945; cited Manvell & Fraenkel, p. 213

29 See Erickson, p. 522; Trevor-Roper (ed.), *Goebbels Diaries*, 4.3.1945, p. 40

30 Ibid., p. 46

31 Ibid., pp. 40–1

32 R. Brandt to H. Johst, 14.3.1945; Heiber, p. 316

33 5–12.3.1945; Kersten, pp. 276–7

34 Ibid., p. 277

35 See ibid., pp. 278–83

36 8.3.1945; Trevor-Roper (ed.), *Goebbels Diaries*, p. 82

37 S. Spender, *European Witness*, Right Book Club, London, 1946, p. 22

38 12.3.1945; Trevor-Roper (ed.), *Goebbels Diaries*, p. 112

39 Bericht an das Reichsministerium für . . . Propaganda, 19.3.1945; Boberach, 17, p. 6732

40 Ibid., 28.3.1945; ibid., pp. 6733–4

41 11.3.1945; Trevor-Roper (ed.), *Goebbels Diaries*, p. 103

42 R. Brandt to H. Johst, 14.3.1945; Heiber, p. 310

43 15.3.1945; Trevor-Roper (ed.), *Goebbels Diaries*, p. 145

44 Speer, *Spandau*, p. 200

45 Ibid.

46 Speer Doc. 027; cited Bullcok, p. 707

47 A. Speer testimony; IMT XVII, p. 35; cited Bullock, p. 707

48 Trevor-Roper (ed.), *Goebbels Diaries*, p. 71

49 Cited Manvell & Fraenkel, p. 215

50 17.3.1945; Kersten, p. 281

51 21.3.1945; Archive Kersten, Stockholm; cited Fleming, pp. 177–8

52 21.3.1945; Trevor-Roper (ed.), *Goebbels Diaires*, p. 191

53 See Ryan, pp. 61 *f*

54 Ibid., p. 71

55 Guderian, op. cit. (ref. 27 above), p. 387; cited Reitlinger, p. 414

56 v. Lang, p. 263, states that on returning to Italy on 8.2.1945 Wolff ordered every indication of contact with the enemy to be reported to him.

57 Himmler papers deposited by Manvell & Fraenkel in Wiener Lib.

58 v. Lang, p. 269

59 Dulles, *Surrender*, p. 116

60 Ibid.

61 Erickson, p. 527; Wilmot, p. 688

62 SHAEF Intelligence survey, 11.3.1945; cited Wilmot, p. 690

63 See Erickson, p. 529

64 To Kersten, 21.3.1945, op. cit. (ref. 51 above)

65 v. Lang, p. 272

66 See Doc. Book I, Case I, Doctors' Trials, W. Grothmann affidavit, p. 70, and *Doctors' Trials*, Nuremberg, IX, Prof. Gebhardt's affidavit, p. 3963; IWM

67 Dulles, *Surrender*, pp. 135–6

68 27.3.1945; Trevor-Roper (ed.), *Goebbels Diaries*, p. 245

69 B. v. Schirach testimony; IMT XIV, p. 374; cited Manvell & Fraenkel, p. 224

70 v. Lang, p. 274

71 See Mittag (undated); Wiener Lib. Press archive 138/1

72 Dulles, *Surrender*, p. 129

73 Frau I. Haberzettel; cited Trevor-Roper, *Last Days*, p. 100

74 Testimony cited ibid.; and O'Donnell, p. 117

75 A. Speer, *Erinnerungen*, Propyläen, Berlin, 1969, p. 467

76 30.3.1945; Trevor-Roper (ed.), *Goebbels Diaries*, p. 281

77 Schellenberg, p. 439; Hewins, p. 131

78 Schellenberg, p. 439

79 DNB Presseschreibrundfunk (Inland), 12.4.1945; 14.15 hours; Wiener Lib. microfilm PC5, Reel 4

80 Geheimerlass Gr. Adml Dönitz, 7.4.1945; SSD MBKO 6611; IWM

81 Moczarski, p. 359

82 Ibid., p. 87

83 Ibid., p. 417

84 Cited Fleming, p. 178; see Berben, p. 184

85 See Fleming, p. 178
86 Br. Army report; cited M. Gilbert, p. 794
87 v. Lang, Sibyll (eds), p. 258
88 See Dulles, *Surrender*, p. 158; v. Lang, pp. 278–9
89 See v. Lang, pp. 279 *ff*
90 Ibid., p. 282
91 See ibid., pp. 322–39
92 Ibid., p. 350
93 O'Donnell, pp. 132–3
94 Trevor-Roper (ed.), *Goebbels Diaries*, intro., p. xxxii, citing R. Semler, *Goebbels The Man Next To Hitler*, 1947, p. 56
95 J. Thorwald, *Die grosse Flucht*, Stuttgart, p. 427; cited Stein, p. 247
96 Schellenberg, p. 442
97 30.3.1945; Trevor-Roper (ed.), *Goebbels Diaries*, p. 281
98 Guderian, op. cit. (ref. 27 above), p. 422; cited Manvell & Fraenkel, p. 215
99 See Laing, p. 78
100 Capt. P. Hartmann; cited O'Donnell, p. 52
101 W. Lüdde-Neurath, *Regierung Dönitz*, Musterschmidt, Göttingen, 1953, p. 27
102 Hoffmann, pp. 305–6
103 See ibid., p. 632; Douglas-Hamilton, p. 236
104 See Douglas-Hamilton, p. 242
105 See Alexander, *Prolonged Exposure*, pp. 19–20

Chapter 17: The End
1 21.4.1945; Kersten, p. 286
2 See Schellenberg, p. 444; Kersten, pp. 286–9
3 21.4.1945; Kersten, p. 292
4 27.4.1945; ibid., p. 293
5 Schellenberg, p. 445
6 Ibid., p. 446
7 F. Göring's declaration, 24.2.1948; Schellenberg Defence Exhibit 36; NA; cited Fleming, pp. 179–81
8 See O'Donnell, p. 138; Trevor-Roper, *Last Days*, p. 118; G. Boldt, *Hitler's Last Days*, Sphere, 1973, p. 118
9 Herrgesell to P. Knauth, *Time*, 21.5.1945; cited Stein, p. 242
10 Schellenberg, p. 448
11 Trevor-Roper, *Last Days*, pp. 125–6
12 Hewins, p. 129
13 See ibid., p. 139; Schellenberg, p. 450
14 See Hewins, p. 139; Fleming, p. 183, citing Report on the Case of W. Schellenberg, 1980, p. 104; NA
15 Ibid.; cited ibid.
16 Cited Fleming, p. 184

17 Schellenberg, pp. 450–1
18 Cited Trevor-Roper, *Last Days*, p. 130
19 Lüdde-Neurath, op. cit. (ref. 101, ch. 16), p. 38
20 See ibid., p. 86
21 H. Macher to F. Lynder; cited Padfield, p. 403
22 Captain Work's Interrogation Summary, 'The Last Days in Hitler's Air Raid Shelter', 8.10.1945; NA; see also Trevor-Roper, *Last Days*, p. 169; O'Donnell, p. 240
23 See O'Donnell, pp. 213 *ff*. But according to Hanna Reitsch in 'Interrogation Summary . . .', op. cit. (ref. 22 above) Hitler simply ordered him shot for desertion
24 Prof. E.-G. Schenck; cited O'Donnell, p. 177
25 Ibid., p. 172
26 Mayor E. Reuter; cited O'Donnell, p. 202
27 Ibid., p. 201
28 Cited e.g. Lüdde-Neurath, op. cit. (ref. 101, ch. 16), pp. 120–1
29 Cited Bullock, pp. 726–7
30 See Erickson, p. 607
31 Ibid., p. 614
32 Cited Padfield, p. 410
33 H. Macher to F. Lynder; cited Padfield, p. 408
34 See Speer, *Erinnerungen*, op. cit. (ref. 75, ch. 16), p. 482
35 K. Dönitz, *10 Jahre und 20 Tage*, Athenäum, Frankfurt, 1958 (1963 edn), p. 346
36 A. Cremer to F. Lynder; cited Padfield, p. 408
37 H. Macher to F. Lynder; cited ibid.
38 Ibid.
39 K. Dönitz, *40 Fragen an Karl Dönitz*, Bernard & Graefe, Munich (4th edn), 1980, p. 164; Lüdde-Neurath, op. cit. (ref. 101, ch. 16), pp. 86–7; Padfield, pp. 408–9; Steinert, pp. 62–3
40 Speer, *Erinnerungen*, op. cit. (ref. 75, ch. 16), p. 489
41 Padfield, p. 410
42 Hanna Reitsch in 'Interrogation Summary . . .', op. cit. (ref. 22 above)
43 Schellenberg, p. 455
44 And see Steinert, pp. 119–20: 'May 4th, the RFSS Heinrich Himmler, has placed himself at the disposal of the Gr. Admiral for the solution of the refugee problem and the maintenance of public order.'
45 Speer, *Erinnerungen*, op. cit. (ref, 75, ch. 16), p. 495

46 Wilmot, pp. 704–5; Padfield, pp. 415–16; Steinert, p. 139

47 Le Degrelle, *Die verlorene Legion*, Stuttgart, 1955, pp. 473 *ff*; cited Reitlinger, p. 443

48 See Dr Best to Fraenkel; Manvell & Fraenkel, p. 241

49 Steinert, pp. 148–9; Reitlinger, pp. 443–4; Speer, *Erinnerungen*, op. cit. (ref. 75, ch 16), p. 497, confirms Himmler's attitude while not mentioning his presence at this conference, no doubt for the same reasons which prompted his manifold other evasions.

50 Frischauer, p. 255

51 Broszat (ed.), p. 148

52 Ibid.

53 See ibid., pp. 148–9

54 See Frischauer, p. 254

55 D. Mehner to Fraenkel; Manvell & Fraenkel, p. 273

56 And see his last speech in Trevor-Roper, *Last Days*, pp. 225–6

57 Order regarding attitude to be adopted to occupying powers; OKW KTB, 11.5.1945; cited Padfield, p. 427

58 OKW KTB, 15.5.1945; cited Padfield, p. 426

59 Cited Trevor-Roper, *Last Days*, p. 226

60 Prof. Gebhardt testimony; *Doctors' Trials*, Nuremberg, IX, p. 3980; IWM

61 J. Kiermaier; cited Manvell & Fraenkel, p. 244

62 President C. Herzog (former Intelligence Officer with 32nd Guards) to author, 2.2.1988

63 Selvester; cited Manvell & Fraenkel, p. 245

64 To author, 2.2.1988

65 Niall MacDermot (formerly Chief Counter Intelligence 21st Army Gp HQ) to author, 9.6.1988

66 Manvell & Fraenkel, p. 247

67 *Manchester Guardian* and *Daily Telegraph* (London), 28.5.1945, state trousers and boots.

68 C. Herzog to author, 2.2.1988; and see H. Harris to *The Times*, London, 31.1.1983

69 Frischauer, p. 10; *Daily Telegraph*, London, 28.5.1945

70 Frischauer, p. 258

71 Niall MacDermot to author, 9.6.1988

Glossary

Abwehr Armed Forces secret- and counter-intelligence service
Anschluss German union with Austria (1938)
Barbarossa codename for the German invasion of Russia (1941)
Eindeutschung the reclamation of German racial stock for the Reich from foreign peoples
Endlösung final solution, a common German notion at this period, here used chiefly in connection with the 'Jewish question'
Gestapo *Geheime Staatspolizei*, Secret State Police
GFP *Geheime Feldpolizei*, Secret Military Police
HSSPF Higher SS and police leader (Führer), Himmler's regional commander
KPD Communist Party
Kripo *Kriminalpolizei*, Criminal Police
Lebensunwertes Lebens beings unworthy of life
Machtergreifung Nazi seizure of power (1933)
Minderwertigen those of inferior value
OKH *Oberkommando des Heeres*, Army High Command
OKW *Oberkommando der Wehrmacht*, Armed Forces High Command
Ordnungspolizei uniformed police
RFSS Reichsführer SS
RSD *Reichs-Sicherheitsdienst*, (SS) Reich Security Service (Führer-protection)
RSHA *Reichs-Sicherheitshauptamt*, (SS) Reich Security Head Office
RuSHA *Rasse und Siedlungshauptamt*, (SS) Race and Settlement Head Office
SA *Sturmabteilung*, Nazi paramilitary arm
Schutzhaft Protective custody
SD *Sicherheitsdienst*, (SS) Security Service
Sipo *Sicherheitspolizei*, (SS) Security Police
Sippenhaft arrest of kin
SPD Social Democratic Party
SS *Schutz Staffeln*, literally Protection Units
SSPF SS and police leader (Führer), Himmler's district commander
Totenkopf Death's Head
Verfügungstruppe the first SS field troops

Volkssturm   the peoples' army or home defence units
Waffen SS   SS field troops
WVHA   Economics and Administration Head Office of the SS

SS Ranks

Untersturmführer   junior lieutenant
Obersturmführer   lieutenant
Hauptsturmführer   captain
Sturmbannführer   major
Obersturmbannführer   lieutenant-colonel
Standartenführer   colonel
Oberführer   brigadier
Brigadeführer   major general
Gruppenführer   lieutenant general
Obergruppenführer   general
Oberstgruppenführer   colonel-general

Select Bibliography

confined to works listed in References and Notes

D. Abraham, *The Collapse of the Weimar Republic*, 2nd edn, Holmes & Meier, New York, 1986.

J. Ackermann, *Heinrich Himmler als Ideologe*, Musterschmidt, Göttingen, 1970.

L. Alexander, *Miscellaneous Aviation Medical Matters*, SHAEF, 1945.

——, *The Treatment of Shock from Prolonged Exposure to Cold*, SHAEF, 1945.

W.S. Allen (ed. and trans.), *The Infancy of Nazism: Memoirs of Ex-Gauleiter Albert Krebs*, Franklin Watts, New York, 1976.

A. Andersch, *Der Vater eines Mörders*, Diogenes, Zurich, 1980.

S. Aronson, *Reinhard Heydrich und die Frühgeschichte von Gestapo und SD*, Deutsche Verlags Anstalt, Stuttgart, 1971.

S. Aster, *1939: The Making of the Second World War*, André Deutsch, London, 1973.

P. Ayçoberry, *The Nazi Question*, Routledge & Kegan Paul, London, 1979.

P. Berben, *Dachau, 1933–1945*, Norfolk Press, London, 1975.

V.R. Berghahn, *The Americanisation of West German Industry, 1945–1973*, Cambridge University Press, Cambridge, 1986.

K.W. Bird, *Weimar, the German Naval Officer Corps and the Rise of National Socialism*, Grüner, Amsterdam, 1977.

P.R. Black, *Kaltenbrunner: Ideological Soldier of the Third Reich*, Princeton University Press, Princeton, 1984.

H. Boberach, *Meldungen aus dem Reich*, Pawlak, Herrsching, 1984.

M. Broszat, *Hitler and the Collapse of Weimar Germany*, Berg, Leamington Spa, 1987.

—— (ed.), *Kommandant in Auschwitz: Autobiographische Aufzeichnungen von Rudolf Höss*, Deutsche Verlags Anstalt, Stuttgart, 1958.

A. Bullock, *Hitler: A Study in Tyranny*, Odhams, London, 1952.

E. Calic, *Reinhard Heydrich: Schlüsselfigur des Dritten Reiches*, Droste, Düsseldorf, 1982.

D. Calleo, *The German Problem Reconsidered*, Cambridge University Press, Cambridge, 1978.

A. Cave-Brown, *Bodyguard of Lies*, Star, London, 1977.

G. Deschner, *Reinhard Heydrich*, Stein & Day, New York, 1981.

——, *Warsaw Rising*, Pan, London, 1972.

R. Diels, *Lucifer ante Portas*, Deutsche Verlags Anstalt, Stuttgart, 1950.

J. Douglas-Hamilton, *Motive for a Mission*, Macmillan, London, 1971.

A. Dulles, *Germany's Underground*, Macmillan, New York, 1947.

——, *The Secret Surrender*, Weidenfeld & Nicolson, London, 1967.

D. Ehlers, *Technik und Moral einer Verschwörung*, Kassel, Bonn, 1964.

J. Erickson, *The Road to Berlin: Stalin's War with Germany* , vol. 2, Weidenfeld & Nicolson, London, 1983.

P.L. Fermor, *A Time of Gifts*, Penguin, London, 1979.

G. Fleming, *Hitler and the Final Solution*, Hamish Hamilton, London, 1985.

M.R.D. Foot, *Resistance: An Analysis of European Resistance to Nazism*, Eyre Methuen, London, 1976.

W. Frischauer, *Himmler: The Evil Genius of the Third Reich*, Odhams, London, 1953.

B. Fromm, *Blood and Banquets*, Bles, Petworth, Sussex, 1942.

J. Garlinski, *Fighting Auschwitz*, Fawcett Crest, Greenwich, Conn., 1975.

F. Gilbert, *Hitler Directs His War*, Oxford University Press, Oxford, 1950.

M. Gilbert, *The Holocaust: The Jewish Tragedy*, Collins, London, 1986.

H.-B. Gisevius, *Bis zum bitteren Ende*, Fretz & Wasmuth, Zurich, 1954; (English trans.) *To the Bitter End*, Jonathan Cape, London, 1948.

——, *Wo ist Nebe?*, Droemersche Verlaganstalt, Zurich, 1966.

K. Gossweiler, *Die Röhm Affäre*, Rugenstein, Cologne, 1983.

H. Guntrip, *Schizoid Phenomena: Object-Relations and the Self*, Hogarth Press, London, 1977.

F. Halder, *Kriegstagebuch*, ed. H.-A. Jacobsen, Kohlhammer, Stuttgart, 1963.

U. von Hassell, *Vom andern Deutschland*, Atlantis, Zurich, 1946.

H. Heiber, *Reichsführer: Briefe an und von Himmler*, Deutsche Verlags Anstalt, Stuttgart, 1968.

N. Henderson, *Failure of a Mission: Berlin 1937–39*, Hodder & Stoughton, London, 1940.

C. Henry and M. Hillel, *Lebensborn: Children of the SS*, Hutchinson, London, 1976.

L. Herbst, *Der totale Krieg und die Ordnung der Wirtschaft*, Deutsche Verlags Anstalt, Stuttgart, 1982.

W.R. Hess, *My Father, Rudolf Hess*, W.H. Allen, London, 1986.

H. Hesse, *Demian* (trans. W.J. Strachan), Panther, London, 1969.

——, *Siddhartha* (trans. H. Rosner), Peter Owen, London, 1954.

L. and R. Heston, *The Medical Casebook of Adolf Hitler*, William Kimber, London, 1979.

R. Hewins, *Count Folke Bernadotte: His Life and Work*, Hutchinson, London, 1949.

J. Heygate, *These Germans*, Hutchinson, London, 1940.

F.H. Hinsley, E.E. Thomas, C.F.G. Ransom and R.C. Knight, *British Intelligence in the Second World War*, HMSO, London, 1979–84.

A. Hitler, *Mein Kampf*, 795th edition, Zentralverlag der NSDAP, Munich, 1943.

W. Hoettl, *The Secret Front*, Praeger, New York, 1954.

P. Hoffmann, *Widerstand, Staatsstreich, Attentat: Der Kampf der Opposition gegen Hitler*, Piper, Munich, 1969.

H. Höhne, *Canaris: Patriot im Zwielicht*, Bertelsmann, Munich, 1976; (English trans.) *Canaris*, Secker & Warburg, London, 1979.

——, *The Order of the Death's Head*, Secker & Warburg, London, 1969.

R. Höss, *see* Broszat (ed.).

E. Howe, *The Black Game*, Michael Joseph, London, 1982.

H. Ibsen, *Brand*, Gyldendalske, Copenhagen, 1922.

D. Irving, *Hitler's War*, Hodder & Stoughton, London, 1977.

H. Kamen, *The Spanish Inquisition*, Weidenfeld & Nicolson, London, 1965.

P. Kennedy, *The Rise of Anglo-German Antagonism, 1860–1914*, George Allen & Unwin, London, 1980.

F. Kersten, *The Kersten Memoirs, 1940–45*, Hutchinson, London, 1956.

E. Klee, *'Euthanasie' im NS-Staat: Die Vernichtung lebensunwerten Lebens*, Fischer Verlag, Frankfurt/M, 1986.

H. Klotz (ed.), *The Berlin Diaries*, Jarrolds, London, 1934.

R.L. Koehl, *The Black Corps: The Structure and Power Struggles of the Nazi SS*, University of Wisconsin Press, Madison, 1983.

H. Krausnick, H. Buchheim, M. Broszat and H.-A. Jacobson, *Anatomy of the SS State*, Collins, London, 1968.

R.D. Laing, *The Divided Self*, Penguin, Harmondsworth, 1966.

J. von Lang, *Der Adjutant: Karl Wolff: Der Mann zwischen Hitler und Himmler*, Herbig, Munich, 1985.

—— and C. Sibyll (eds), *Eichmann Interrogated*, Bodley Head, London, 1982.

W. Laqueur, *The Terrible Secret*, Weidenfeld & Nicolson, London, 1980.

G. Lean, *Frank Buchman: A Life*, Constable, London, 1985.

R.J. Lifton, *The Nazi Doctors*, Macmillan, London, 1986.

L.P. Lochner (ed.), *The Goebbels Diaries*, Hamish Hamilton, London, 1948.

K. Ludecke, *I Knew Hitler*, Jarrolds, London, 1938.

R. Manvell and H. Fraenkel, *Heinrich Himmler*, William Heinemann, London, 1965.

K. Moczarski, *Gespräche mit dem Henker*, Droste, Düsseldorf, 1978.

J. Noakes and G. Pridlam (eds), *Documents on Nazism*, Jonathan Cape, London, 1974.

K. Novak, *Euthanasie und Sterilisierung im Dritten Reich*, Vanderhoech & Ruprecht, Göttingen, 1978.

M. Novitch, *Sobibor: Martyrdom and Revolt*, Holocaust Library, New York, 1980.

J.P. O'Donnell, *The Berlin Bunker*, Pan, London, 1975.

R.J. Overy, *Göring: The Iron Man*, Routledge & Kegan Paul, London, 1984.

P. Padfield, *Dönitz, the Last Führer*, Victor Gollancz, London, 1984.

J. Passmore, *The Perfectibility of Man*, Duckworth, London, 1970.

K.H. Peter (ed.), *Spiegelbild einer Verschwörung*, Seewald, Stuttgart, 1961.

H. Peuschel, *Die Männer um Hitler*, Droste, Düsseldorf, 1982.

J. and S. Pool, *Who Financed Hitler?*, Macdonald & Jane's, London, 1978.

G. Reitlinger, *The SS: Alibi of a Nation*, Arms & Armour Press, London, 1981.

G. Ritter, *The German Resistance*, George Allen & Unwin, London, 1958.

S.H. Roberts, *The House That Jack Built*, Methuen, London, 1939.

H. Royce (ed.), new edn E. Zimmermann and H.-A. Jacobsen (eds), *20 Juli 1944*, Berto-Verlag, Bonn, 1952.

C. Ryan, *The Last Battle*, New English Library, London, 1985.

M. Salewski, *Die deutsche Seekriegsleitung, 1939–45*, Bernard & Graefe, Munich, 1975–84.

W. Schellenberg, *The Schellenberg Memoirs*, André Deutsch, London, 1956.

F. von Schlabrendorf, *The Secret War Against Hitler*, Hodder & Stoughton, London, 1966.

K. Schuschnigg, *Im Kampf gegen Hitler*, Molden, Vienna, 1969.

A. Schweitzer, *Big Business in the Third Reich*, Eyre & Spottiswoode, London, 1964.

J. Sehn, *Oświęcim–Brzezinka (Auschwitz–Birkenau) Concentration Camp*, Wdawnictwo Prawnicze, Warsaw, 1961.

G. Sereny, *Into That Darkness: An Examination of Conscience*, Picador, London, 1977.

W. Shirer, *Berlin Diary*, Hamish Hamilton, London, 1941.

B.F. Smith, *Heinrich Himmler: A Nazi in the Making, 1900–1926*, Hoover Institute Press, Cal., 1971.

B.F. Smith and A.F. Petersen (eds), *Heinrich Himmler: Geheimreden, 1933–1945*, Propyläen, Berlin, 1974.

A. Speer, *Spandau: The Secret Diaries*, Macmillan, New York, 1976.

——, *The Slave State*, Weidenfeld & Nicolson, London, 1981.

S. Spender, *European Witness*, The Right Book Club, London, 1946.

P.D. Stachura, *Gregor Strasser and the Rise of Nazism*, George Allen & Unwin, London, 1983.

—— (ed.), *The Nazi Machtergreifung*, George Allen & Unwin, London, 1983.

G.H. Stein, *The Waffen SS: Hitler's Elite Guard at War, 1939–1945*, Cornell University Press, Ithaca, New York, 1966.

M.S. Steinert, *Capitulation 1945*, Constable, London, 1969.

O. Strasser, *Hitler and I*, Jonathan Cape, London, 1940.

——, *Mein Kampf: Eine politische Autobiographie*, H. Heine, Frankfurt/M, 1969.

W. Strik-Strikfeldt, *Against Stalin and Hitler*, Macmillan, London, 1970.

K. Thewelweit, *Male Fantasies, vol. I: Women, Floods, Bodies, History*, University of Minnesota Press, 1987.

F. Thyssen, *I Paid Hitler*, Hodder & Stoughton, London, 1941.

H.R. Trevor-Roper, *The European Witch Craze of the Sixteenth and Seventeenth Centuries*, Penguin, Harmondsworth, 1967.

——, *The Last Days of Hitler*, Macmillan, New York, 1947.

——, (ed.), *Hitler's Table Talk*, Weidenfeld & Nicolson, London, 1953.

——, (ed.), *The Bormann Letters*, Weidenfeld & Nicolson, London, 1954.

——, (ed.), *The Goebbels Diaries: The Last Days*, Secker & Warburg, London, 1978.

H.A. Turner, *German Big Business and the Rise of Hitler*, Oxford University Press, Oxford, 1985.

R. Vogelsang, *Der Freundeskreis Himmler*, Musterschmidt, Göttingen, 1972.

R.G.L. Waite, *The Psychopathic God: Adolf Hitler*, Signet, New York, 1978.

——, *Vanguard of Nazism: The Freikorps Movement in Post-war Germany*, Harvard University Press, Cambridge, Mass., 1952.

W. Warlimont, *Inside Hitler's Headquarters*, Weidenfeld & Nicolson, London, 1964.

B. Whaley, *Codeword Barbarossa*, MIT, Cambridge, Mass., 1973.

S. Wiesenthal, *The Murderers Among Us*, William Heinemann, London, 1967.

C. Wilmot, *The Struggle for Europe*, Collins, London, 1952.

F.W. Winterbotham, *The Nazi Connection*, Weidenfeld & Nicolson, London, 1978.

A. Wirth (ed.), *Es gibt keinen judischen Wohnbezirk in Warschau mehr*, Luchterhand, Darmstadt, 1960; (English trans.) *The Stroop Report*, Secker & Warburg, London, 1980.

W. Woods, *Poland: Eagle in the East*, André Deutsch, London, 1969.

A.P. Young, *The 'X' Documents*, André Deutsch, London, 1974.

E. Zeller, *Geist der Freiheit*, Müller, Munich, 1953; (English trans.) *The Flame of Freedom*, Wolff, London, 1967.

E. Zimmermann and H.-A. Jacobsen (eds) – see H. Royce (ed.).

Index

Names have been omitted from this index if they occur in a secondary or commentating role, for example, those of authors (with exceptions), witnesses to events and victims who are otherwise unknown and who appear only once.